European Environmental Law

The International Library of Environmental Law and Policy
General Editor: Robert Lee

Titles in the Series

European Environmental Law

Edited by

Ludwig Krämer

European Commission, Belgium

ASHGATE
DARTMOUTH

Published by
Dartmouth Publishing Company
Ashgate Publishing Limited
Gower House
Croft Road
Aldershot
Hants GU11 3HR
England

Ashgate Publishing Company
Suite 420
101 Cherry Street
Burlington, VT 05401-4405
USA

Ashgate website: http://www.ashgate.com

British Library Cataloguing in Publication Data
European environmental law. – (International library of
    environmental law and policy)
    1. Environmental law – European Union countries
    I. Kramer, L. (Ludwig)
    341.7'62'094

Library of Congress Control Number: 2002043977

ISBN 0 7546 2310 6

Printed in Great Britain by The Cromwell Press, Trowbridge, Wiltshire

Contents

PART III   IMPROVING ENVIRONMENTAL STANDARDS IN EUROPE

Acknowledgements

The editor and publishers wish to thank the following for permission to use copyright material.

American Journal of Comparative Law for the essay: Eckard Rehbinder and Richard Stewart (1985), 'Legal Integration in Federal Systems: European Community Environmental Law', *American Journal of Comparative Law*, **33**, pp. 371–446.

Blackwell Publishing Limited for the essay: Philippe Sands (1990), 'European Community Environmental Law: Legislation, the European Court of Justice and Common-Interest Groups', *Modern Law Review*, **53**, pp. 685–98.

EPP Publications for the essay: Derek Osborn (1992), 'The Impact of EC Environmental Policies on UK Public Administration', *Environmental Policy and Practice*, **2**, pp. 199–209.

Frank Cass Publishers for the essay: Ken Collins and David Earnshaw (1992), 'The Implementation and Enforcement of European Community Environment Legislation', *Environmental Politics*, pp. 213–49.

Fordham International Law Journal for the essay: Koen Lenaerts (1994), 'The Principle of Subsidiarity and the Environment in the European Union: Keeping the Balance of Federalism', *Fordham International Law Journal*, **17**, pp. 846–95. Copyright © 1994 Fordham University.

Kluwer Law International for the essays: Gerd Winter (1996), 'On the Effectiveness of the EC Administration: The Case of Environmental Protection', *Common Market Law Review*, **33**, pp. 689–717. Copyright © 1996 Kluwer Law International; Richard Macrory (1992), 'The Enforcement of Community Environmental Laws: Some Critical Issues', *Common Market Law Review*, **29**, pp. 347–69. Copyright © 1992 Kluwer Academic Publishers; Kurt Deketelaere (1997), 'Environmental Planning and Spatial Planning from a European Community Perspective', *European Environmental Law Review*, November, pp. 307–17. With kind permission of Kluwer Law International.

Oxford University Press for the essays: Ludwig Krämer (1991), 'The Implementation of Community Environmental Directives within Member States: Some Implications of the Direct Effect Doctrine', *Journal of Environmental Law*, **3**, pp. 39–56. Copyright © 1991 Oxford University Press; Richard Macrory (1996), 'Environmental Citizenship and the Law: Repairing the European Road', *Journal of Environmental Law*, **8**, pp. 219–35. Copyright © 1996 Oxford University Press; Derrick Wyatt (1998), 'Litigating Community Environmental Law – Thoughts on the Direct Effect Doctrine', *Journal of Environmental Law*, **10**, pp. 9–19. Copyright © 1998 Oxford University Press; Peter Pagh (1999), 'Denmark's Compliance with European Community Environmental Law', *Journal of Environmental Law*, **11**, pp. 301–19. Copyright © 1999 Oxford

University Press; Wouter P.J. Wils (1994), 'The Birds Directive 15 Years Later: A Survey of the Case Law and a Comparison with the Habitats Directive', *Journal of Environmental Law*, **6**, pp. 219–42; Rhiannon Williams (1995), 'The European Commission and the Enforcement of Environmental Law: An Invidious Position', *Yearbook of European Law*, pp. 351–99; Ludwig Krämer (2000), 'Thirty Years of EC Environmental Law: Perspectives and Prospectives', *Yearbook of European Environmental Law*, pp. 155–82. Reprinted by permission of Oxford University Press.

Sweet & Maxwell Publishers for the essays: Dirk Vandermeersch (1987), 'The Single European Act and the Environmental Policy of the European Economic Community', *European Law Review*, pp. 407–29; Nigel Haigh (1987), 'Environmental Assessment – The EC Directive', *Journal of Planning and Environmental Law*, pp. 4–20.

University of California Press for the essay: Jans H. Jans (1993), 'Waste Policy and European Community Law: Does the EEC Treaty Provide a Suitable Framework for Regulating Waste?', *Ecology Law Quarterly*, **20**, pp. 165–76. Copyright © 1993 Ecology Law Quarterly.

Every effort has been made to trace all copyright holders, but if any have been inadvertently overlooked the publishers will be pleased to make any necessary arrangement at the first opportunity.

Series Preface

Environmental protection is an increasingly important issue for legal scholars. This is not simply because of greater concern about the environment, but because the topic has assumed a central significance in debates about regulation. *The International Library of Environmental Law and Policy* is designed to provide the reader with the necessary material to understand the regulatory enterprise in the contexts of different environmental problems and environmental media. Increasingly we witness the adoption of legal and policy mechanisms across different jurisdictions – the spread of ideas of precaution or the growth of trading in permits provide good examples. The Libary pulls together the most significant material from legal and other periodicals to form an essential compendium for those wishing to study the role of law in protecting and conserving the environment.

Environmental law has tended to find its way first into the law curriculum and then into stand-alone programmes in Law Schools in the relatively recent past. Certainly as an area of legal practice the subject has developed initially in the United States of America and then elsewhere in the latter part of the twentieth century. Yet the underpinning ideas of property rights as a means of allocating the use of natural resources together with the protection of those rights from infringement has deep, deep roots in the common law. But it might be argued that through the industrialization of the nineteenth century, the environment was not always well protected and environmental measures on air or water quality began to appear on the statute book, driven initially by human health concerns rather than any wider ecological interest. From this beginning environmental law has wandered far from its private law roots, and in most jurisdictions consists of a plethora of rules based in statutes but also in looser, softer legal instruments such as by-laws, circulars, guidance notes and codes.

For all of this, there is no shortage of environmental damage and certainly environmental litigation abounds. Patterns of regulation change. The early command and control structures of environmental regulation, in which permits are given to pollute in order that polluting activity can be controlled are eroding. In their place comes a variety of economic instruments – taxes, quotas, targets, and tradable capacities – allowing greater economic freedom to decide quite how and when investment in environmental improvement might be made. Driven by ideas of ecological modernization and the hope of a double dividend of environmental protection alongside economic growth, we see these regulatory models spread as concepts developed in one jurisdiction are taken up in another. More than this, much of the regulation becomes tied to globalization, as cross border instruments are developed, or notions of free trade demand harmonized processes lest competition is distorted or the movement of goods and capital inhibited.

So the series is entitled *environmental law and policy* and many of the essays included in the series engage very directly with the policy underpinnings of the legal rules. Some go further and ask questions about the very enterprize of public law in seeking to impose ever more elaborate systems of administration in the hope of generating environmental improvement. Perhaps the move towards economic instruments begins to suggest a reversal of some of this process and a move back towards more private law based processes. Even environmental activists may have lost some faith in the promises of the public law process to deliver transparency and participation in environmental decision-making and the accountability of the polluter. We see the growth of more locally based action arising out of consumer boycotts or the assertion of rights to protection in a movement in opposition to more institution and technocratic forms of regulation.

This is the turbulent world of the environmental lawyer, and many working in it are there not by accident, but in order to further the cause of environmental protection. For all the clarity of purpose, however, the journey to any solutions seems long and hard. Bringing together the best of the jurisprudence in this area is a small step along the way, but a necessary beginning.

Professor Robert Lee
ESRC Centre for Business Relationships, Accountability, Sustainability and Society (BRASS)
Cardiff University, Wales

Introduction

The collection of 19 essays on European environmental law – that is, the environmental law of the European Union – which are assembled in this book spans a period of almost 20 years, during which European environmental policy and law became progressively established. Legal writers in almost all European countries agree that the influence of European environmental law on the 15 member states of the European Union is considerable; estimations are that, at present, between 50 as a minimum and 100 per cent of national environmental law has its origin in European environmental law. Moreover, it seems that the influence of European environmental law will grow further, on the one hand, because of the obligations of ten – and tomorrow perhaps more – states from Central and Eastern Europe which are preparing to accede to the European Union and which will take over the existing European environmental law in full and, on the other hand, because, via this accession and adaptation process, law in other Eastern European countries will progressively become influenced by developments of European Union law. Furthermore, the USA's apparent retreat from a leadership role in global environmental law will inevitably cause non-industrialized states to look more frequently at Europe when they examine how to combine economic growth with an appropriate protection of the environment.

Because European environmental law has developed without an explicit legal basis in the European Treaties there was no time to take extensive consideration of theoretical concepts, legal theories or the interdependency between European and national law. European legislation was made in order to address specific urgent environmental issues. It was only at a later stage that the offspring 'environmental law' was recognized, surrounded by constitutional and institutional frameworks, and that it became the subject of legal scholars' attention.

As the European Union might therefore be called a philosophy in action, it is not really surprising that most contributions to this volume discuss concrete proposals for change, improvement or better quality; this is evidenced in the essay titles ('impact', 'keeping the balance', 'repairing', 'effectiveness', 'implication' and so on). So it more or less follows that many of the concepts of environmental policy and law were first generated by political and institutional developments inside the European Union and that these led to reactions from legal writers, rather than vice versa. For this reason, the selection of essays in this volume was not made with the aim of assembling new legal theories or extravagant considerations on European environmental law. Rather, it attempts to give an idea of the efforts from different sides – academics, practicing lawyers, politicians, administrators – to improve the effectiveness of environmental policy and law, even where an author might be either privately or openly sceptical about, or even opposed to, European political and economic integration.

Europeanization of Environmental Law and Policy

The volume is divided into three Parts which focus on the most relevant features of European environmental law. Part I deals with the progressive transfer of responsibilities for environmental issues from the national to the European level. This process provoked a considerable degree of interest, but also concern, among lawyers. The European standard-setting process which tried simultaneously to balance the legitimate interests of member states and the requirements of the 'regional globalization' – that is, the European Union – was new and is, even today in 2003, innovative and of the highest legal interest.

The opening essay by Eckard Rehbinder and Richard Stewart (Chapter 1) attempts to describe legal integration in Europe under the auspices of federal legal systems. The essay is a concise summary of the authors' renowned book on the same subject[1] which for a long time remained the best publication on European environmental law and policy. In Chapter 2 Dirk Vandermeersch uses the 1987 amendment of the EC Treaty, which inserted, for the first time, a specific chapter on environmental policy into the Treaty, to draw a balance of the past and give a perspective of future European environmental policy. Next, Philippe Sands (Chapter 3) turns his particular attention to the judicial process in the European Union and the possibilities for environmental organizations to influence the development of European environmental law – sometimes, perhaps, with a little too much optimism. By contrast, Derek Osborn (Chapter 4) looks at European development from an entirely different angle: at the time of writing, he was a British government official who held a very prominent position working on environmental issues. In Chapter 5 Koen Lenaerts, who has since become a judge at the European Court of First Instance, retraces the balance between European member states – 'sovereign' states in the classical terminology of public international law – and the common European environmental legislative initiatives which are necessarily the source of many different considerations – particularly since most European lawyers have been trained in a specific national legal culture and, quite naturally, view European law with some conservative national concern. In the next essay (Chapter 6) Richard Macrory, who has worked in both Brussels and London, looks at the European road from the perspective of both capitals and suggests a number of rather practical measures for bringing the European legislative and administrative practice closer to its citizens. Finally, Gerd Winter (Chapter 7) critically examines the emerging European environmental administration and reminds the reader of the need to improve its effectiveness – an exhortation which was, and is, more than justified, but probably applies to each administration, whether it works on environmental matters or not.

Overall, the lawyers' criticism of the process by which decision-making in environmental matters is progressively shifted from the nation-state to the European level has remained relatively limited. Looking back at the 30 years or so of environmental law and policy in Europe, this process can be considered a success, as the European Union, the citizens and the individual national administrations have all accepted the transfer of sovereignty which is inherent in the transfer of responsibilities.

Application and Enforcement of European Environmental Law

Part II deals with the important mechanisms set up by the European Union to monitor the application and enforcement of European environmental law. The European system of application and enforcement of law is based on the rule of law: Article 220 of the EC Treaty lays down the requirement that 'in the interpretation and application of this Treaty the law is observed'. The pre-court control by the European Commission and the final arbitration by the Court of Justice constitutes a system that is unique for monitoring the application of environmental law, at a global as well as a regional level. Indeed, only recently has the international legal community been confronted with the USA's refusal to accept judgments from the International Criminal Court and, more generally, from any court which it did not set up itself.

In the European Union, accepting judgments from a non-national court is a legal reality: to date, in environmental matters alone, the Court of Justice has issued more than 300 judgments against member states for breaching their obligations under European law. And, in 2000, this abandonment of the principle of national sovereignty took a further important step: the Court of Justice applied a recent amendment of the EC Treaty and imposed a penalty payment of 20,000 Euro per day against any member state that had not complied with its obligations under European environmental law.[2] And while member states are often slow to implement European environmental provisions, they accept the Court's judgments as the final arbitration and adapt their laws.

As the world cannot be divided into black and white or good and bad, no dispute settlement system that is based on the prevailing of the economically stronger party's rules can hope to definitely settle disputes. As things currently stand, the regional European system, which is based on the rule of law and which gives an independent non-national court the final word, may well serve as a model for environmental policy approaches and dispute settlement mechanisms in other regions of the world.

As the instinct of lawyers is normally to preserve – I am reluctant to repeat the word 'conservative' – it is hardly surprising that questions of compliance and implementation, of legal standing and of monitoring systems for European environmental law continue to provoke a wealth of legal essays in Europe. From this discussion it is becoming increasingly evident that the application of the numerous environmental provisions and rules is the biggest legal challenge for environmental law, in Europe as well as in any member state, and at local as well as international levels. Adopting new environmental provisions that are unenforceable or not enforced means adopting placebo legislation that may well do more harm than good to the environment. All the essays in Part II of this volume centre on this problem of making (European) environmental law work. At the same time, they also describe a number of loopholes, what these loopholes are, what lessons are to be learnt from past experience and what instruments should be used in order to make application and enforcement more effective.

In Chaper 11 Rhiannon Williams, who worked for some time with the European Commission, looks at the Commission's enforcement role. Because the Commission simultaneously acts as a political body for the development of new environmental policies and as an enforcement body, it is tasked with taking enforcement actions against the member states which it needs for conceiving and shaping a progressive and successful European environmental policy – a truly invidious position.

The Court of Justice was also innovative in developing new enforcement principles, such as that of financial liability of states or the doctrine of the direct effect of European legislation. The application of this doctrine is the subject of essays by Ludwig Krämer (Chapter 8) and Derrick Wyatt (Chapter 12). As these authors have rather different legal backgrounds, their essays, written in 1991 and 1998 respectively, give a good demonstration of the evolving nature of European environmental law.

In Chapter 9 Ken Collins, for almost two decades the very influential chairman of the European Parliament's Environmental Committee, describes, together with David Earnshaw, the problems of implementation and enforcement from a more political angle. Next, Richard Macrory (Chapter 10) tries to look at the European enforcement mechanism as a whole, in particular from the perspective of a common law lawyer. Finally, Peter Pagh (Chapter 13), by describing Denmark's compliance with European environmental law, illustrates the continuing problems of monitoring and enforcing environmental rules. His essay makes it clear that these problems are not limited to the enforcement of European law, but are instead a specific feature of environmental legislation, wherever it is produced.

Improving Environmental Standards in Europe

Part III addresses the issue that the European legislator might proudly claim to have never forgotten: environmental law aims to protect the environment by means of law. Over the last 30 years European environmental law has sincerely tried to change the European environment and progressively effect improvements in administrative planning, in the levels of water and air pollution and in the conservation of natural habitats as well as of species of fauna and flora. And because the Treaty on European Union assigns to European environmental policy the task of improving the quality of the environment, it is natural for lawyers to critically survey the legislative measures adopted in order to assess whether or not this new flood of European environmental rules yields an added value.

Arline Sheehan's essay (Chapter 14) comments on an early example of the effect of European environmental law: Directive 82/501 was drawn up after a very serious environmental accident in Seveso (Italy) and undertook to provide for preventive measures in order to avoid accidents in chemical plants. Although this directive initially met with considerable suspicion, it has since become one of the European Union's major exports, having been appropriated by many states, and even international bodies. In Chapter 15 Nigel Haigh, whose publications have had a very large audience in the UK, discusses another very important piece of European legislation that ensures, for the first time in European law, the participation of the public concerned in environmental impact assessments. His essay, written prior to the effective application of that legislation, anticipates numerous problems and conflicts which later materialized.

Next, Jan Jans (Chapter 16) questions the European framework legislation on waste – a problem which is of continuing concern even today, ten years later. In the same way, Wouter Wils' essay on the application of European legislation on nature conservation (Chapter 17) touches on problems that have not yet found definite solutions in Europe: confronted with the multitude of land uses in the form of urban development, agriculture, transportation systems and economic activities, nature slowly but progressively retreats – and neither politicians nor lawyers have found the instruments to halt this disappearance of nature in (Western) Europe. In Chapter 18 Kurt Deketelaere examines this process from the perspective of planning and planning law and arrives at less worrying conclusions.

Finally, Ludwig Krämer's essay looks back at 30 years of environmental law and policy and tries to project the lines of past development into the future.

All the essays in Part III are marked by the knowledge that legislation alone cannot hope to stop, let alone reverse, environmental degradation, and that it requires continuous, daily efforts on the part of legislators, administrations, economic operators, environmental organizations and academics to monitor the condition and the evolution of the environment and the effect of the measures taken in order to rectify, where necessary, the steps taken. The environment (both in Europe and elsewhere in the world) is now sick, but it is not sufficient to give it some legislative 'medicine' and expect it to recover. Instead, uninterrupted observation and long-term treatment is necessary to strengthen the patient, prevent new negative influences and improve its self-healing capacities. No essay in this collection complacently assumes that enough is being done to protect Europe's environment.

The Limitations of the Discussion

This collection of essays does not reflect one of the most important features of European legal tradition: the diversity of the legal culture. For editorial reasons, the collection had to be limited to essays, leaving aside contributions to books; furthermore, it had to be limited to English-language essays. I undertook some research[3] and estimate that English-language essays comprise about 15 per cent of all publications on European environmental law. It is for this reason that this volume only contains essays from authors of five European member states – France, Italy, Spain, Greece, Sweden and Austria; other EU member states are not represented, nor are countries such as Norway and Switzerland and states in Central and Eastern Europe. The great diversity of legal tradition in Western Europe, which is sometimes seen as a superfluous tradition, but which is in reality a source of continuous inspiration and also of innovation, has therefore not been reproduced here.

Nevertheless, it is hoped that the reader will get an impression of the struggles of legal writers, coming from courts, administrations, universities or private practice, who critically followed the establishment, growth and evolution of European environmental law. These authors are anxious to ensure that this European law evolves in alignment with national legal traditions and that environmental policy guarantees an appropriate protection of the environment that will not unduly hamper the Europeanization, if not globalization, of trade and industry. Despite all its imperfections and weaknesses, European environmental law has become a sort of model that is more than placebo law in that it tries to be effective and repair those parts of the legal system that do not give sufficient protection. Contributions from legal scholars are indispensable to the evolution of European environmental law, as it is only the critical discussion of the law and its effect on the environment that will allow errors to be corrected, gaps to be filled, arbitrary administrative measures to be controlled and too much influence from economic operators on standard-setting to be avoided. Europe is far from having permanently ensured the necessary protection of the environment. However, there is no doubt that, without critical assistance from writers – legal and others – the European environment would be in a much worse state.

Looking Forward

Nobody knows exactly what the future will bring. The accession of ten new states to the European Union, envisaged for 2004, will certainly make the decision-making process more complicated and more difficult. Framework legislation is likely to increase, as diversity within the EU becomes greater. Globalization and the free circulation of goods within Europe will make it more difficult to adopt local, regional or even national progressive environmental protection measures. The implementation and monitoring of legislative and practical applications will be of paramount importance. Considerable efforts will have to be made to prevent the effects of EC-wide environmental standards varying significantly within the European Union. In addition, politicians, as well as lawyers, will have to carefully examine ways of making sure that the three biggest challenges to the environment are contained: the threatening climate change, the continued degradation of the natural environment and the omnipresence of chemicals in the environment.

On a worldwide scale, the biggest threat to the environment, next to climate change, is, of course, poverty. Industrialized countries do not make specific efforts to formulate global rules of law which create justice all over the planet, and the European Union is not yet an exception to this. The French philosopher La Rochefoucauld's statement that, between the strong and the weak, it is legislation that creates freedom and freedom (that is, absence of legislation) that suppresses is more than 300 years old; yet, at a global level, this approach has not led to effective environmental legislation for all. The European Union will have to sharpen its activity in this area over the next few years.

Notes

1   Rehbinder and Stewart (1985). This book was part of a larger research project under the leadership of Mauro Cappelletti (Florence) about 'Integration through Law. Europe and the American Federal Experience'.
2   Court of Justice, case C-387/97, *Commission* v. *Greece*, ECR 2000, p.I-5047. The case concerned the unauthorized discharge of waste on land, which is prohibited under European law.
3   See Kromarek (1989) which lists 478 publications, of which 47 are essays in English; Macrory and Hollins (1995) list 940 titles, of which 116 are essays written in English. Eckard Rehbinder has published 133 essays, of which 31 are in English; Jan Jans has published 110 essays, of which 30 are in English. I myself have published 124 essays, of which 44 are in English.

References

Kromarek, P. (ed.) (1989), *Bibliography of European Environmental Law*, Bonn/London/Paris/Brussels: Institut für Europäische Umweltpolitik.
Macrory, R. and Hollins, S. (1995), *A Source Book of European Community Environmental Law*, Oxford: Clarendon Press.
Rehbinder, E. and Stewart, R. (1985), *Environment Protection Policy*, Berlin/New York: de Gruyter.

Part I
Europeanization of Environmental Law and Policy

[1]

ECKARD REHBINDER
RICHARD STEWART

Legal Integration in Federal Systems: European Community Environmental Law

This article examines the development and implementation of European Community environmental law and policy. Drawing on US as well as Community experience, it first develops hypotheses about the incentives for and pattern of integration of environmental law in federal systems. It then examines the progress of Community environmental law and the institutional factors that have shaped it. The conclusion assesses the initial hypotheses in light of the European experience and offers an evaluation of the current situation of environmental law in the Community.

I. INTEGRATION IN ENVIRONMENTAL LAW

What are the incentives that operate for and against integration in a federal system, and what form of harmonization is likely to result? We examine these questions in the specific context of environmental law.[1]

Integration of environmental law in a federal system occurs through two basic approaches: central determination by a federal/community authority (legislature, executive authority or court), or coordination of law and policy by member states through negotiated agreement, development of common working understandings, conscious parallelism in judge-made law, and so on. The latter approach has been of scant importance in the European Community (EC) and the United States (US). This Article therefore focuses on the first

---

ECKARD REHBINDER is Professor of Law, University of Frankfurt.
RICHARD STEWART is Professor, Harvard Law School.

This article is a product of a larger project on European legal integration in light of the American federal experience under the general editorship of Professor Mauro Cappelletti, of the European University Institute and Stanford Law School, where assistance and encouragement is gratefully acknowledged. An expanded version, with more extensive analysis of the US, as well as Community law, is forthcoming in book form.

1. By "environmental law", we include measures to control air, water and noise pollution, waste disposal practices, hazardous substances, and radioactivity. We also include environmental impact procedures, land use planning, and protection of nature, landscape, flora, and fauna. The latter two categories of environmental law have not been extensively developed at the Community level.

approach. The degree of integration achieved in particular areas reflects institutional arrangements and the following incentives and disincentives to integration:

A. Incentives for Integration

Removal of trade barriers with respect to products and resources. The adoption by different states of different environmental regulations with respect to products impedes free commerce among states, thus reducing producer revenues and economic welfare, and may impose cumulative and potentially inconsistent regulatory burdens on producers seeking to sell their products or services in more than one state. Adoption by a state of stringent controls or taxes on the use of its resources (for example, extraction of energy minerals or use of a site for toxic waste disposal) may also impede commerce and reduce the welfare of persons in other states.

Removal of the "competitive distortions" and relocation incentives caused by differing controls on industrial processes and natural resource development. Different regulatory requirements governing industrial processes do not threaten free trade and consumer welfare as directly as differential product regulations. But adoption by one state of more stringent controls will increase the costs of producers located within that state, creating a competitive advantage for producers in states with less stringent controls.[2] This advantage may cause firms to locate new facilities in states with less stringent controls or even relocate existing facilities to such states. Competition among states to attract or retain industry may encourage laxity in controls everywhere. Those states and interests in favor of more stringent environmental controls will accordingly favor measures to achieve equivalent (and relatively high) levels of control in all states.

Transboundary spillovers. Transboundary spillovers are unlikely to be adequately dealt with by resort to the municipal law of either the originating or receiving state, which may often have a municipal bias. In addition, the receiving state may face serious difficulties in enforcing remedial measures against activities in originating states.

Economies of scale in research, analysis, and decisionmaking. To the extent that environmental regulatory problems in different

---

2. In theory, with perfect information and perfect labor markets, and no interjurisdictional spillovers, industries in a state with strict environmental standards would not be competitively disadvantaged because workers in that state would accept lower wages in return for the environmental benefits produced by regulation; lower wages would offset the higher costs to industy of complying with strict environmental standards. In practice, however, labor markets are imperfect and spillovers exist.

states present common scientific, technological, and analytical issues, there may be economies of scale in acquiring and processing the necessary information once on a centralized basis, rather than many times on a decentralized basis. In addition, adequate resources to perform the necessary work may not be available in some states.

Achievement of more stringent and effective controls through centralized direction. As noted above, "competitive distortions" may hinder the adoption by states of effective environmental controls. Centralized decisions may also favor more stringent environmental controls because central bureaucracies and political actors are less subject to short term political accountability and more attuned to the achievement of longer term objectives.

Need for common front in international negotiation. In order to achieve greater bargaining power in international negotiation, a common environmental policy may be desirable. This has, for example, been a strong incentive for EC regulation of chemical manufacture and sale.

B. Disincentives to Integration

Variations in preferences. Citizens in different states often have different preferences for enhanced environmental quality versus economic and industrial development and higher money incomes. Because of political and administrative factors, integrated environmental policies often tend to be uniform. Uniformity can result in insufficient environmental quality in states with a high preference for environmental quality, and excessive environmental quality in those states with low preferences. These discrepancies will generate opposition to integrated environmental policies.

Differences in geographic, ecological, and industrial conditions. Quite apart from differences in preferences, the uniform environmental standards that often result from integregation may be inappropriate because of geographic and ecological differences that can significantly alter the consequences of a given amount of pollution. For example, welfare losses attributable to reduced visibility are much greater in scenic than industrialized areas. Organic waste discharges that can cause serious damage to a stream or river may have little effect if discharged into deep ocean sites. Uniform environmental quality standards and uniform technology-based source controls fail to deal fully with these variations, resulting in overcontrol in some areas and undercontrol in others.

Resentment of centralized direction. Common environmental policies, particularly if formulated and enforced by central authority, cause resentment of the resulting interference with member state autonomy. This resentment is likely to be especially severe when it infringes on industrial policies and land use and development decisions.

Differences among legal and administrative systems in member states. Considerable reliance must be placed on state and local authorities to implement and enforce common environmental policies, particularly in the case of industrial process regulation and land use and natural resource management. Differences in legal and administrative systems will often translate into differences in implementation and enforcement, hindering effective harmonization.

Diseconomies of scale and information processing. To the extent that decisions about environmental policy are made centrally, information must be gathered and processed centrally. In addition, central authorities will have to monitor state and local implementation and enforcement. This will introduce substantial information processing costs, and tend to introduce multiple and redundant layers of decisionmaking and review.

Functional interconnection between environmental regulation and local functions. Many forms of environmental regulation involve traditional local functions such as zoning and other forms of land use control, water supply, waste disposal and so on. So long as these functions are exercised by local officials in response to local circumstances and pressures, the effective degree of integration in environmental policy is substantially reduced. On the other hand, to centralize the exercise of such functions would create very substantial diseconomies and seriously intrude upon local autonomy.

Industrial and commercial opposition to integrated policies. Particularly in the area of industrial process regulation, integrated environmental policies are more likely to be protective of the environment than decentralized policies, imposing costs upon and restricting development by industry and commercial interests. They will accordingly tend to oppose integration. Transboundary polluters will oppose such measures for similar reasons.

C. *Mechanisms of Integration*

The several underlying incentives and disincentives to integration are accommodated in different ways by the various available legal mechanisms of integration. We first examine mechanisms of complete integration, and then discuss mechanisms of partial integration.

Centralized determination of environmental law and policy. Centralized legislative or executive determination of environmental law is the most direct and obvious method of insuring integrated environmental policies. However, it can also be the most destructive of state autonomy, and may result in uniformities that exhibit various diseconomies. Central adoption of regulatory standards and screening programs (which review particular development projects or new products like chemicals on a case-by-case basis under general criteria like "unreasonable risk") has been the dominant mechanism for integration of environmental laws and policies in the US and the EC. Once established, centrally determined law and policy must be implemented and enforced. The most reliable means of insuring that such implementation and enforcement occurs in an effective and uniform way is through federal/community administrative agencies and courts charged with responsibility for issuing regulations and permits, monitoring, initiating enforcement actions, and adjudicating controversies.

State implementation of federal/community law. An alternative mechanism of integration that encourages greater responsiveness to different conditions and preferences in member states is for central authorities to determine environmental measures and laws, but leave their implementation and enforcement in the first instance to member states while retaining powers of supervision and review. These powers may allow a central authority to: institute litigation against member states, compelling them to undertake implementation/enforcement; impose sanctions for implementation failure, such as cut-offs of funds; directly assume implementation/enforcement responsibilities when member states have failed to do an adequate job; or develop federal/community law that would allow environmental advocates to challenge and remedy deficient implementation/enforcement by member state authorities through litigation in member state or federal/community courts.

Federal/community encouragement of state environmental measures. In lieu of adopting regulatory standards and programs (whether implemented centrally or by member states), central authorities could seek to encourage state adoption of similar environmental measures through research and information programs, subsidies to underwrite the administrative costs of such programs, or waiver of federal law that would otherwise displace such programs. The central authority may impose criteria which state programs must meet in order to qualify for subsidy or waiver. Alternatively, the central authority may urge states to adopt standards to deal with certain environmental problems, with the threat of more intensive central intervention if state action is not forthcoming.

Judicial invalidation of state environmental measures that impede trade. The methods of integration discussed above are positive efforts to obtain a minimum level of environmental protection in all states, as well as to eliminate the barriers to trade created by nonharmonized state measures. In contrast, courts applying the "negative commerce clause" doctrine or its equivalent,[3] may act to invalidate state product standards that are more restrictive than those adopted by neighboring states. In so doing, they eliminate barriers to trade (including the threat posed by multiple and potentially inconsistent state regulations to manufacturers' ability to realize economies of scale) without regard for achieving minimal levels of environmental protection.

Total harmonization is achieved when all states enforce the same standards or measures. There are, however, a variety of institutional strategies other than total harmonization which can mediate the competing claims of integration and local autonomy.[4]

With the technique of *minimum harmonization*, member states are permitted to adopt measures controlling products, processes, or natural resource development that are more stringent than those adopted by central authorities or by agreement among member states. However, they may not adopt less stringent measures. The minimum "floor" provided by this method limits state competition for industrial development through weaker environmental measures, while allowing those states with stronger preferences for environmental quality to give them effect. This approach, however, allows barriers to trade to persist.

Partial harmonization. Under this approach federal/community law governs only interstate product transactions—for example, the sale in state A of automobiles or chemicals manufactured in state B. This technique allows a state to impose stricter or laxer controls on domestic products, but forbids imposition of stricter standards on imports.[5]

---

3. European Court of Justice, case 120/78, Rewe-Zentrale AG v. Bundesmonopolverwaltung für Branntwein (*Cassis de Dijon*), [1979] ECR 649; case 53/80, Officier van Justitie v. Koninklijke Kaasfabriek Eyssen BV (Nisin), [1981] ECR 409; case 272/80, Biologische Productenn BV (Pesticides), [1981] ECR 3277; Commission, OJ No. C 256, 3 Oct. 1980, p.2; Oliver, *Free Movement of Goods in the E.E.C.*, parts VII and VIII (1982); Sandalow & Stein, (eds.), *Courts and Free Markets* Ch. III (1982); Weber, *Schutznormen und Wirtschaftsintegration* 102 et seq., 147 et seq. (1982)

4. For a discussion of harmonization techniques in the EEC see Slot, *Technical and Administrative Obstacles to Trade in the EEC* 80 et seq. (1975); Schmeder, *Die Rechtsangleichung als Integrationsmittel der Europäischen Gemeinschaft* 71 et seq. (1978); Stein, Hay & Waelbroeck, *European Community Law and Institutions in Perspective* 416 et seq. (1976); Europäisches Parlament, Bericht über den Vorschlag der Kommission der Europäischen Gemeinschaften an den Rat für ein Allgemeines Programm zur Beseitigung der technischen Hemmnisse im innergemeinschaftlichen Warenverkehr, die sich aus der Unterschiedlichkeit der einzelstaatlichen Vorschriften ergeben, EP Doc. 15/1968-69; Weinstock, "Nur eine Umwelt? Europäische Umweltpolitik im Spannungsfeld Zwischen Ökologischer Vielfalt und Ökonomischer Einheit," 6 *Zeitschrift für Umweltpolitik* 1, 29, 33, 34 et seq. (1983).

5. In order to illustrate the implications of partial harmonization, consider the example of controls on automobile emissions of air pollutants.

State A, in order to achieve higher environmental quality, could adopt stricter standards for cars manufactured and sold within A, but its manufacturers would be

Optional harmonization. Under this strategy, states may adopt their own standards, but if a state adopts a standard different from the federal, community standard for interstate transactions, a domestic or foreign manufacturer selling products in that state may elect to comply either with the federal community standard or the state standard.[6]

The advantages of partial and optional harmonization in eliminating trade barriers while partially accommodating differences in states' preferences for environmental quality are limited by the fact that manufacturers wishing to export to other states must meet two standards, one for intrastate transactions and another for interstate transactions. Manufacturing different products to meet different standards may increase costs by reducing scale economies and thus provide firms with financial incentives to follow the more stringent standard in order to reach the widest possible market with a standardized product. This undercuts the economic advantage to a state of a less stringent standard for intrastate transactions.

Alternative harmonization. Under this approach, federal/community law establishes two or more alternative standards or means of compliance which a member state may elect. For example, to control water pollution a state may be allowed to choose between an ambient standards approach or an approach based on uniform technology-based source controls. Alternative techniques for measuring ambient standards may be authorized.[7]

Recognition of other states' product certification is a harmonization technique designed to eliminate repetitive licensing or testing procedures. Certification by the state of manufacture that a new chemical has met standardized EC testing protocols is an example. As the example indicates, the recognition technique is most appropriate when the underlying regulatory requirements have been har-

---

vulnerable to import competition from State B manufacturers, who would have the right to sell their cars in A upon compliance with the less stringent and costly federal community standard.

Alternatively, State A could adopt laxer standards for cars manufactured and sold within A, resulting in lower environmental quality and giving A manufacturers a cost advantage over imports. On the other hand, if A manufacturers wished to sell their cars in B, they would have to tool up to meet the more demanding federal community standard.

6. Optional harmonization is similar to partial harmonization, but there are two important differences. First, a state must affirmatively "opt out" of federal community standards. Second, when State A adopts laxer standards, State B manufacturers who sell within State A need only comply with State A's standards rather than the stricter federal community standards, undercutting the competitive advantage that State A manufacturers would otherwise enjoy.

7. The federal/community authorities will ordinarily have a clear preference for one set of standards or means of compliance. Selection of the alternative will ordinarily be allowed only under narrowly defined criteria, and it may be subject to later review.

monized. But even where they are not, the technique could be applied to limit review and testing by the importing state to that necessary to ascertain compliance with those of its requirements that go beyond the manufacturing state's.

Strategies that allow the states considerable discretion in implementing and enforcing centrally determined standards are also mechanisms of partial integration. Still greater decentralization can be achieved under a regime that allows states to set environmental quality standards or product or process controls in the first instance, subject to centralized review under general criteria.

Centralized research, analysis, and recommendation present a still more modest approach towards integration. Economies of scale in research and analysis, reinforced by the tendency of centralized decisionmaking to favor strong environmental protective measures, are realized through central generation of information and dissemination. But basic policy determinations, implementation, and enforcement are left to the member states.

D. *The Logic of Integration in a Federal System*

How are the considerations for and against integration likely to operate in a federal system, and what form of harmonization is likely to result? We here offer some working hypotheses concerning the interplay between integration incentives and integrative mechanisms to be tested by the evidence canvassed in later chapters. We evaluate and refine these hypotheses in the final part of this article.

Let us assume, for purposes of initial analysis, that the only relevant actors are states. All states want both environmental quality and economic growth; there is, however, a tradeoff between these two goals, at least in the short to medium term. Different states, for a variety of reasons, make this tradeoff differently. Some states give greater weight to environmental quality, and therefore favor more stringent environmental controls (environmental states), while other states favor economic development with less stringent environmental controls (polluter states). When products, capital, and labor cross state boundaries, each state's tradeoff between environmental quality and economic performance is affected by other states' environmental policies. This interdependency, explained in greater detail below, creates two dominant incentives for harmonization: the removal of trade barriers and competitive distortions, and the desire to increase the stringency of environmental controls. In order to understand the effects of these incentives, one must distinguish two basic categories of regulation: product regulation and regulation of industrial processes. The relations between these two categories of regulation and the two basic incentives for harmonization are depicted visually by the following matrix:

	Eliminate Trade Barriers and Competitive Distortions	Promote Environmental Quality
Product regulation	[1]	[2]
Process regulation	[3]	[4]

For each element of the matrix one must examine the incentives for harmonization on the part of both polluter states and environmental states.

First, consider the question of trade barriers in connection with product regulation (element 1 of the matrix). If environmental states can exclude heavily polluting or risky products from polluter states, polluter states will be denied access to markets in environmental states. They will accordingly have an interest in harmonization. Assume initially that we are dealing only with total harmonization. In a system requiring unanimous consent of all states, the level of control at which harmonization will occur will depend on how polluter states evaluate the tradeoff between the costs associated with more stringent controls and the benefits of expanded markets. More precisely, the level of control to which polluter states will assent is the lowest level at which the marginal costs and benefits of increased control are equal for any polluter state. However, this incentive for harmonization disappears if polluter states can successfully challenge the exclusion by environmental states of polluter states' products as an undue restraint on trade. Such litigation would have little success in the US under prevailing interpretations of the commerce clause, but might have greater success in the EC in light of *Cassis de Dijon* and its interpretation by the European Commission.[8]

Now consider the incentives for product harmonization from the perspective of states wanting to promote environmental quality (element 2 of the matrix). Such environmental states' manufacturers will be undercut in product competition by polluter states' manufacturers. If a negative commerce clause doctrine prevents them from excluding the products of polluter states, they will suffer this competitive disadvantage in all markets. But even if exclusion is

---

8. For discussion of the *Cassis de Dijon* decision, supra n. 3, and "negative commerce clause" doctrine in the EC, see authors cited supra n. 3. For discussion of Community law prior to *Cassis de Dijon*, see Schermers, "The Role of the European Court of Justice in the Free Movement of Goods," in Sandalow & Stein, supra n. 3 at 222 et seq.

possible, the environmental states will have to compete in polluter state markets, and economies of scale may preclude the development of a less controlled product for those markets. In order to avoid the competitive disadvantages of differential standards, environmental states will support harmonization, preferably at a level close to what they would adopt for themselves in the absence of trade.

Now consider regulation of processes from the perspective of trade barriers (element 3 of the matrix). Here there is no common interest in harmonization. Environmental states can not exclude products from polluting states on the ground that manufacturing processes in those states are less well controlled. Nothing in the US or EC negative commerce clause doctrine would permit this.[9] Accordingly, products from polluter states have free access to markets in environmental states, and polluter states have no interest in harmonization.

From the perspective of promoting environmental quality (element 4 of the matrix), environmental states have a strong incentive to support harmonization in order to avoid the competitive disadvantages that they will suffer by reason of higher process costs. These disadvantages are likely to be greater than in the case of product regulation because there is no hope of excluding products from polluter states. The resulting cost disadvantage can give rise to a flight of capital and labor to polluting states. But polluter states will have no interest in harmonization because they can continue to market their products in other states even though the processes that produces them are less controlled.

Now consider the case of another category of states, those that import products but do not manufacture them. In the absence of transboundary spillovers, they would oppose any process controls at all, since their citizens would bear the cost of controls but enjoy none of the benefits. In this respect, they may be more opposed to integration than polluter states, which would presumably not oppose a community standard at the lowest common denominator level. On the other hand, in the case of product controls, an importer state would not only bear all or most of the costs of control, but would also enjoy the benefits of control. Thus, the control level it would

---

9. In the Community, Art. 36 of the EEC Treaty and the rule of reason test developed in *Cassis de Dijon*, supra n. 3, definitively limit the grounds on which a member state can rely in order to introduce product controls. Compensation for competitive disadvantages incurred by domestic manufacturers due to lenient process requirements abroad applicable to their foreign competitors is not permissible. Nothing in US precedent under the negative commerce clause doctrine would permit such measures.

favor would depend upon its relative preference for environmental quality.

Transboundary spillovers will create support for harmonization on the part of receptor states, but not originating states.

In a federal system requiring unanimous consent, there will, in the case of product regulation, be support from both polluter and environmental states for harmonization through mutual adoption of uniform standards. To the extent that a *Cassis de Dijon* principle restricts the ability of environmental states from excluding polluter state products, the support of environmental states for harmonization will be increased and the support of polluter states will be decreased. In the case of process regulation, it is difficult to see why there would be any harmonization at all above the lowest common denominator level, since it would never be in the interests of polluter or importer states to agree to more stringent controls.

In a federal system allowing harmonization on the basis of some form of majority vote, the incentives are similar in direction, but deleting the requirement of unanimity will mean uniform product regulation at a more stringent level. In addition, some uniform process regulation is likely to occur, depending on the voting power of environmental states and the intensity of their preferences for environmental quality. The implications of transboundary spillovers are more complex, and depend upon the pattern of spillovers and the configuration of net importing and net exporting states.

What is the relevance of the number of states and their size relative to that of the federation? Where states' internal markets are small relative to that of the federation, the support of both environmental and polluter states for harmonization of product regulation is likely to be strengthened. Such a configuration would also increase the support of environmental states for harmonized process regulation, and strengthen the opposition of polluter states to such harmonization.

Given the possibility of less than total harmonization, what form would harmonization likely take? In the case of product regulation, polluter states would want total harmonization at the lowest possible level. Environmental states would, in the case of both product and process regulation, favor either total or minimal harmonization, depending on the level at which the two forms of harmonization would likely occur.

Partial and optional harmonization apply only to product regulation. They allow polluter states access to environmental states, but only at the price of controls more stringent than they would otherwise prefer. Environmental states are protected against competition from polluter states' products in their own domestic markets, but must either suffer a price disadvantage or develop an alternative line of products in order to compete in polluter state markets.

Alternative harmonization is another compromise technique that narrows but does not eliminate the competitive disadvantages suffered by environmental states.

The above analysis would indicate that in the US there would be a very high degree of uniform product regulation through federal legislation, and a considerable but lesser degree of federal process regulation, much of which might take the form of minimum harmonization. In the case of the European Community the analysis would predict for product regulation (before *Cassis de Dijon*) considerable uniform harmonization (at an intermediate level) or optional or partial harmonization. It would predict no harmonization at all in process regulation. Yet there is some harmonization of process regulation in the EC, and perhaps more harmonization of product regulation than might be expected. What might account for this? The following factors might be considered:

> Unanimity on a variety of issues may be achieved through a process of reciprocal concession over time, even though there would not be unanimity on any single issue considered in isolation. Polluter states may go along with proposals for harmonization that are intensely supported by environmental states, in exchange for later concessions on other issues. This process of "logrolling" need not be explicit. Implicit norms of reciprocity may develop, allowing sequential concessions without explicit agreement. In the case of product regulation the ability of an environmental state in the absence of harmonization to adopt and enforce regulations that will restrain trade is also an incentive for polluter states to acquiesce in harmonized initiatives.

> Environmental states tend to be the most industrially developed and economically and politically powerful states. Despite the rule of unanimity, these states may have a disproportionate influence on Community decisionmaking. Process harmonization will be a strong objective for such states, because it will impose costs on less developed states that will restrict economic and political competition from them.

> Multinational firms with manufacturing plants in both polluter and environmental states may find it to their net advantage to have harmonized regulation at levels higher than polluter states would prefer, and will therefore lobby

polluter states in which they have plants to support such harmonization.

Government officials of polluter states, particularly those in environmental ministries, may personally tend to favor higher environmental controls but would face strong local opposition if they attempted to adopt such controls unilaterally. By acquiescing in Commission initiatives, they can secure their objectives through the back door.

Polluter states may believe that the EC as an institution is on balance quite favorable to their interests. Psychologically it may be difficult to oppose otherwise plausible Commission proposals unless the economic disadvantage imposed on industries in polluting states is severe.

These factors, which may explain why significant EC harmonization has occurred, would tend to predict an even greater level of harmonization through federal legislation in the US. Most large industrial enterprises operate in many states and would therefore strongly oppose significant barriers to trade arising from differential standards, particularly given the small size of most domestic state markets. Moreover, the existence of national media and national politics tends to favor the development of a national environmental constituency.

II. THE ENVIRONMENTAL LAW OF THE COMMUNITY

Summary of Community Environmental Law

In the last decade, beginning with the declaration of the Paris summit meeting of October 1972, the Community institutions have developed environmental policy as a quasicommon policy of the Community.[10] There is no express Treaty mandate. Rather, the development of Community environmental policy has been based on the general harmonization provision of Art. 100 and the "last resort" provision of Art. 235 of the EEC Treaty; in some cases, specific powers contained in the Treaty in the framework of the common agricultural and transport policies as well as Arts. 2 (b), 30 and 37 of the Euratom Treaty have been used. Although the legal basis for Community environmental policy is far from secure, this development has not met with much political opposition in the member states. Of course, legal writers have voiced their reservations.[11] However, the European Court of Justice seems to be generally favorable to the

---

10. See Bungarten, *Umweltpolitik in Westeuropa* 150 et seq. (1978).

11. See, e.g., Behrens, *Rechtsgrundlagen der Umweltpolitik der Europäischen Gemeinschaften*, passim (1976); von Moltke, "The Legal Basis for Environmental Policy," 3 *Envt'l Pol. & L.* 136 (1977); Kaiser, "Grenzen der EG-Zuständigkeit," 15 *Europarecht* 97 (1980). Also, the House of Lords has been critical; see House of

384   THE AMERICAN JOURNAL OF COMPARATIVE LAW   [Vol. 33

Community environmental policy. In two infringement actions concerning the product requirements of the directive on detergents and the gas oil directive[12] it could have rested with the argument that different national requirements clearly have a direct effect on the functioning of the Common market as required by the wording of Art. 100 of the EEC Treaty. However, it proceeded in a dictum to approach the general problem, stating that ". . . it is by no means ruled out that provisions on the environment may be based upon Art. 100 of the Treaty. Provisions which are made necessary by considerations relating to the environment and health may be a burden upon the undertakings to which they apply and if there is no harmonization of the national provisions on the matter, competition may be appreciably distorted." The few other environmental cases the Court has as yet decided do not address the issue.

The objectives of Community environmental policy, principles to guide its implementation, priorities for action and implementation are set forth in the environmental programs of the Community. To date, three such programs have been established, the last covering the period until 1986.[13] The first environmental program focusses on the most urgent pollution control problems while the two later programs place more emphasis on the preventive aspect of environmental policy, although in practice traditional pollution control still clearly prevails in the Community environmental policy. The focus of Community environmental policy is on problems related to trade and competition, i.e. industrial pollution and environmental and health problems posed by widely marketed products. Problems such as land use planning, protection of nature and landscape, and protection of flora and fauna are of minor importance. However, within these limits, environmental policy is not a simple appendix of trade policy but clearly a policy in its own right. Pursuant to the environmental programs, the Community has developed a remarkable legislative activity. About 80 regulatory texts, among which about 40 are directives, have been produced.[14]

Water pollution is a priority of Community environmental policy; it is the field of environmental policy in which the Community

Lords, Select Committee on the European Communities, Session 1977-78, Approximation of Laws under Art. 100 of the EEC Treaty, *22nd Report* 131 (1978).

12. Case 91/79, Commission v. Italy, [1980] ECR 1099, 1106; case 92/79, Commission v. Italy, [1980] ECR 1115, 1122.

13. OJ No.C 112, 20 Dec. 1973, p. 1; OJ No.C 139, 13 June 1977, p. 1; OJ No.C 46, 17 Febr. 1983, p. 1.

14. For a detailed description of the Community environmental law, see Johnson, *The Pollution Control Policy of the European Communities* (2nd ed. 1983); Cathala, Roche & Tregouet, *Le Droit Européen de l'Environnement* (1979); Krämer, "Umweltpolitik" in von der Groeben, von Boeckh, Thiesing & Ehlermann (eds.), *Kommentar zum EWG-Vertrag* 1609 et seq. (1982).

has most actively engaged and most comprehensively legislated. The major strategies are water quality standards, effluent standards for hazardous substances and product standards. The Community has established a system of water quality standards for surface water based on the relevant water uses, most important among which are standards for the abstraction of drinking water under the drinking water directive of 1975.[15] The framework directive on the aquatic environment of the Community of 1976 tackles the problem of water pollution by hazardous substances. It provides for the establishment of effluent standards for a list of very hazardous substances. These standards are to be set forth in implementing directives. The process of standard setting has proven quite lengthy. One of the reasons is that, due to disagreement among the member states on the appropriate strategy, the framework directive empowers the member states to use, in lieu of effluent standards, water quality standards; the equivalence of both standards is not easy to establish. To date, only three substances have been regulated by implementing directives. With respect to less hazardous substances, the member states are to reduce pollution by setting forth national water quality standards and implementation plans which ultimately shall be harmonized by the Community. The directive on detergents of 1973 sets standards for the biodegradability of pollutants contained in detergents. With respect to Rhine pollution as well as marine pollution, the Community participates in international conventions.

Air pollution has long been a relatively low priority for the Community. Emissions from motor vehicles have been regulated as early as 1970 and since 1973 the relevant emission standards have gradually been stiffened and expanded to additional substances, marking a shift from mere trade to environmental policy in this field. Nonetheless, the Community standards are far more lenient than the comparable US standards. Presently there is much controversy among the member states about West Germany's demand to stiffen the standards while the introduction of unleaded gasoline in the Community was conceded. With respect to sulfur dioxide and particulate matter, the directive of 1980 on limit values for sulfur dioxide and suspended particulate matter introduces a system of mandatory ambient air quality standards and non-binding guide values which must be implemented by national programs, the ultimate deadline for meeting the mandatory standards being 1993. Likewise, ambient air quality standards for nitrogen oxides have been adopted. Recently, due to widespread forest damage from air pollution suf-

---

15. All Community environmental directives, regulations, recommendations and resolutions are reprinted trilingually in Burhenne, *Environmental Law of the European Communities* (1976 and supplements).

fered by some member states in central Europe, especially West Germany, air pollution has become an action field for Community environmental policy of high importance and much controversy as well. Apart from the proposals in the field of motor vehicle pollution, the Community, under West German pressure, has adopted a directive on major industrial installations that prescribes for the first time use of the state of the art of emission control. The follow-up proposal on major combustion plants even proposes the introduction of uniform Community emission standards.

Community activity concerning noise is primarily limited to traffic noise caused by widely marketed products such as cars, aircraft and construction machinery. The only strategy used is product standards.

Regulation of waste disposal is a Community activity in which the preventive approach plays a more substantial role. There is a framework directive on waste of 1975 which establishes some basic principles of waste disposal, such as the requirement to dispose of waste without causing pollution, to prevent waste, to establish waste disposal plans and subject waste collection and disposal to the requirement of a permit. Implementing directives on toxic and hazardous wastes (1978), on PCB waste (1976) and waste oil (1975) specify these principles. Some recent recommendations or directives aim at the prevention of waste (paper and board, beverage containers). A directive adopted in 1984 regulates the import, export and transit of hazardous wastes in the Community.

In the field of chemicals, the early Community activities focussed mainly on classification, packaging and labelling requirements, i.e. basically on the information provided to users of chemicals. Also, in the framework of the PCB directive of 1976, some chemicals were prohibited or severely restricted. However, the 6th amendment of the framework directive on dangerous substances in 1979 introduced a comprehensive harmonized screening procedure for all new chemicals, imposing on manufacturers and importers notification and testing requirements before the marketing of new substances; two further sets of tests are required when certain production thresholds are exceeded or upon request of the competent agency. National notification and testing is recognized throughout the Community. The directive on major industrial accidents of 1981 attempts to tackle the problem of chemical accidents by introducing strict safety requirements.

In the field of radioactivity, the Community, due to its limited mandate under the Euratom Treaty, has focussed on the establishment of health standards for the exposure of workers and the general public (1959, 1976). With respect to nuclear safety and waste disposal, all attempts of the Commission to introduce binding principles have as yet failed, mainly because some member states want to preserve options for an independent national nuclear policy. The Commission's proposal for a Community consultation procedure for the siting of nuclear power stations in border areas has not been adopted. In the field of nuclear waste, Art. 37 of the Euratom Treaty establishes a Community consultation procedure. However, other binding obligations have not been adopted.

With respect to land-use planning, protection of nature and landscape, and protection of fauna and flora, the Community focusses on financial aids granted in the framework of the common agricultural policy. Apart from that, the Community regulatory activity is only sporadic, mainly covering matters regulated by international conventions to which the Community and/or the member states are parties.

Finally, the Commission in 1980 submitted to the Council a proposal to introduce environmental impact assessment in the Community for major projects liable to adversely affect the environment. The proposal has been very controversial; however, the Council has ultimately been able to agree on the procedure and the directive was adopted in March 1985.

B. *Environmental Problems Addressed and Solutions Chosen*

What are the characteristics of and underlying rationales for the current pattern of Community environmental law?

1. *Lack of Focus, Depth, and Comprehensiveness.* Perhaps the most striking feature of Community environmental law is its lack of focus, depth, and comprehensiveness.[16] Critical problems covered by federal legislation in all developed federal systems are not addressed, while less important problems are often minutely regulated. Water pollution and wastes have received relative priority while air and noise pollution have been neglected. No environmental sector is comprehensively regulated by the Community. Even waste disposal is no exception. Although it is covered by a framework directive, the framework is applied by only a few implementing directives for particular kinds of waste. Widely marketed products such as motor vehicles, detergents, and chemicals are

---

16. Bothe, "The Trends in Both National and International Politics for Achieving a Uniformity of Standards in Pollution Matters," 2 *Zeitschrift für Umweltpolitik* 293, 303 (1979). Contra, Weinstock, supra n.4 at 13, 20, 30 (attesting that the Community has a "surprisingly complete system" of environmental law while simultaneously complaining of lack of priorities and depth of regulation and characterizing Community environmental law as "patchwork").

rather comprehensively regulated. However, the emphasis is on regulating new products, while existing products are relatively ignored.

Compared to the multitude of environmental problems arising in an industrial society and normally addressed by federal environmental law, Community environmental law is no more than a kind of regulatory patchwork, covering at most a fifth of the relevant problem areas. This is primarily due to the pragmatic, *ad hoc* approach taken by the Commission in identifying and developing subjects for harmonization. Community environmental policy does not function by identifying priority areas of environmental protection for Community harmonization and leaving less important areas to member state legislation. Instead, it identifies narrow, politically and administratively manageable problems of varying environmental importance. However, the recently adopted third environmental program represents some departure from this pattern.

2. *Multiplicity of Underlying Rationales.* A second characteristic of Community environmental law is that selection of subjects for harmonization can not be explained by any single factor.

Many authors maintain that the primary rationale for Community environmental policy is the desire to eliminate obstacles to trade and distortions of competition. They argue that Community environmental policy can only be incidental to economic and competition policy.[17] This opinion derives from the economic foundation of Community legislative powers granted by Articles 100 and 235 of the EEC Treaty. But, this argument overlooks the distinction between motivation and constraint.

The limitations of Articles 100 and 235 do indeed constrain environmental policymaking in the Community. Because the Commission must justify new policy proposals in the framework of the existing legal structure, it tends to address environmental problems that have some substantial economic impact. The emphasis of Community environmental law on pollution and the neglect of land use, natural resources, and protection of nature are a clear indication that, although environmental programs are more broadly conceived, Community environmental policy can not dissociate itself from the economic foundation of the legislative powers granted by Articles 100 and 235.

---

17. Bungarten, supra n.10 at 226; Weidner & Knoepfel, "Implementation der EG-Richtlinie zur SO_2-Luftreinhalte Politik, 4 *Zeitschrift für Umweltpolitik* 27, 63 et seq. (1981). Weinstock, supra n.4 at 7 et seq, 13 et seq, 42, 44 (stating that Community environmental policy can only be conceived as competition policy, but on p. 20 saying that the regular foundation of environmental directives on both Arts. 100 and 235 of the EEC Treaty underlines the double function of the policy). See also von Moltke & Haigh, "EC — Major Issues for 1981," 7 *Envt'l Pol'y & L.* 23 (1981).

However, it does not follow that Community environmental policy is motivated by trade and competition considerations. The thesis of the exclusively economic motivation of Community environmental law is wrong because it ignores the fact that environmental priorities for the common environmental policy are set by the Community environmental programs, which are not based on narrow trade-related economic concerns, but seek to promote environmental quality as an important goal in its own right. To be sure, economic considerations of a broader sort play a role in the impulse for harmonization, which often comes from "environmental states" that seek to achieve, by harmonization, a Europeanization of the economic burdens imposed on their industry by progressive environmental policy. The political bargaining within the Council over strategies and tools has often been marked by the attempt of polluter states to retain competitive advantages arising from the absorption capacity of a comparatively clean environment. A more differentiated analysis of the motivations for selection of topics for Community law is accordingly necessary.

Community regulation is strongest in the case of products associated with health or environmental hazards. According to the conventional wisdom, product regulation is the obvious candidate for harmonization on economic grounds, and the strength of Community measures in this area is therefore taken as evidence that economic considerations dictate community policies. But the economic premise of the conventional wisdom is subject to serious question. It may well be that different product requirements distort competition less than different process requirements. Process requirements are limited to national manufacturers; they harm their competitive position in both the national and foreign markets. Product requirements are equal for all producers for a given national market.[18] The degree of distortion depends on the size of the national market in which stricter standards are introduced[19] and on the market share of domestic industry in that market. Moreover, the cost of having different product requirements in different national markets is often overestimated by neglecting their connection with other market factors, such as market phases and product innovation.[20]

Nonetheless, different national requirements for products can not be tolerated in an integrated market because they are a direct threat to the functioning of the Common Market. The desire to eliminate obstacles to trade clearly constituted the rationale for

18. Walter, *International Economics of Pollution* 70, 71 (1975).
19. Gray, "Commercial Policy Implications of Environmental Controls," in Walter (ed.), *Studies in International Environmental Economics* 159 at 172-173 (1976).
20. Gröner, "Umweltschutzbedingte Produktnormen als Nicht-Tarifäre Handelshemmnisse," in Gutzler (ed.), *Umweltschutz und Wettbewerb* 143, 156 et seq. (1981).

early Community action in the environmental field. Indeed, most such action was called for by the general program of 1969 for the elimination of technical obstacles to trade.[21] Another motivation for the Community's legislative action has sometimes been, as in the case of toxic substances, the need to establish a common bargaining position towards third countries. However, even with respect to product regulation, Community environmental policy has gone beyond exclusive emphasis on economic harmonization. The current emphasis is on progressive solutions for health and environmental protection.

Outside the area of product regulation, contrary to what an exclusively economic foundation for Community environmental policy would imply, there is no clear emphasis on pollution from large industrial sources. Some directives, such as those on the aquatic environment, nuclear safety standards, toxic waste, and chemical accidents, and the directive on environmental impact assessment are conceptually or practically relevant only to large projects. Others, such as the SO_2 limit values and PCB waste directives, will be more relevant for large projects than for non-point pollution. However, there are many Community directives, such as those on water quality standards, waste disposal, and use of chemicals, that regulate pollution from small sources. The 1980 progress report of the Commission even stresses the need for a still stronger Community commitment to regulating diffuse pollution from small sources.[22]

In many respects, Community process regulations reflect primarily health and environmental priorities rather than economic considerations. For example, directives such as those on waste disposal, SO_2, chemical accidents, and protection against radiation are clearly motivated by the perceived urgency of the health, safety, and environmental problems addressed. Moreover, empirical evidence does not support the view that industry in environmental states suffers severe competitive injury from progressive national solutions and the lack of harmonization.[23] Some authors maintain that the emphasis of early Community environmental policy on water pollution was motivated by economic considerations. Since different national regulations for control of water and air pollution have a fairly equal cost incidence on the industry concerned, this reasoning can

---

21. Of 28 May 1969, OJ No.C 76, 17 June 1969, p.1, as updated by the Council Resolution of 17 Dec. 1973 on industrial policy, OJ No.C 117, 31 Dec. 1973, p.1.

22. Commission, Progress Made in Connection with the Environment Action Programme and Assessment of the Work Done to Implement It, Communication from the Commission to the Council (Progress Report 1980), DOC COM(80)222 final, Annex I, p. 8.

23. For an empirical research project in this field, see Knödgden & Sprenger, "Umweltschutz und Internationaler Wettbewerb," 1981 *IFO-Schnelldienst* No. 1-2 at 43.

not explain the Community emphasis on control of water rather than air pollution. However, economic considerations did motivate extension of water pollution regulation for hazardous substances to all Community watercourses, and they also play an important role in selecting strategies and tools for addressing the relevant problem. The dearth of Community legislative activity relating to land use, natural resources, and protection of nature is also more easily explained by the lack of economic incentives for harmonization.

Some environmental problems, such as climatic impacts of air pollution, and protection of migratory or endangered species, are by their nature so international that harmonized action at the Community level was considered appropriate, even in the absence of strong trade and competition concerns. The need for Community intervention to remedy serious transboundary pollution problems is also an important motivating factor. The emphasis of post 1973 Community environmental policy on water pollution is clearly motivated by the fact that several member states are riverains of the Rhine and that the heavy pollution of this river is an urgent environmental problem. Marine pollution is another example of a common transboundary interest. Although transboundary pollution has thus at times been a strong argument in favor of Community legislation, it has recently hampered political bargaining on other initiatives because national claims of sovereignty were affected.[24]

There is accordingly no single rationale for Community legislation in the environmental area. The internationality of a problem, transboundary pollution (including marine pollution), the perceived seriousness of the environmental problem in the light of the inadequacy of most or even all national solutions, the greater environmental efficiency of centralized solutions, the objective of eliminating distortions of competition — all may help to explain the identification and development of candidates for harmonization and/or the substantive solutions adopted. It is not easy to identify a primary rationale even for a single directive. Although the economic interest of environmental states in shifting the burden of progressive environmental policy to industry throughout the Community is an important impetus to Community environmental policy, it does not explain the consensus on a particular proposal.

The sequence and timing of legislative initiatives depends on the environmental programs' selection of candidates for harmonization and on unilateral member state initiatives reported to the Commission under the information/standstill agreement. Of course, the fi-

---

24. Examples are the fate of the Rhine Chloride Convention and the protracted negotiations on the major accidents (Seveso) and the environmental impact assessment directives.

nal adoption of Commission proposals is largely determined by the speed of the political bargaining over a proposal. The selection of candidates for harmonization is not simply a function of the urgency of environmental problems. The Community has not always addressed the most serious environmental problems first. The state of existing knowledge, preferences of member states, the prospective political chances of a proposal, and public awareness all play an important role in setting priorities.

For example, Community commitment in the field of radioactivity had long been limited to protecting workers and the general public by setting radiation safety standards. Serious problems such as the location and safe design of nuclear power plants were addressed by the Community only when they had become a political issue in several member states. Community regulation of toxic substances was originally limited to classification, packaging, and labeling requirements. The restructuring of this regulatory system by the sixth amendment to the directive of 1967 and the directive on major accidents were responses to the enactment of toxic substances legislation in the United States and Japan and the Seveso accident in Italy. Even the emphasis on water pollution control can not be explained entirely by the urgency of water pollution in the Community. The aquatic environment, drinking water, and source of drinking water directives are designed to address urgent pollution problems. But, directives such as the fish water, shellfish water, and bathing water directives seem to be more the result of political spillover effects from successful legislation in areas of urgency. Finally, the disequilibrium between water and air pollution control existing in Community environmental policy can hardly be explained by differences in the seriousness of the relevant environmental problems.

3. *Environmental Policy Diversity along National Lines.* The third important characteristic of existing Community environmental law is its strong tendency to take the form of nationally non-uniform standards. The problem of uniformity in environmental law is a sub-issue of the larger problem of federalism or, in the context of the European Community, supranationalism. The question is basically whether the member state or the Community is the optimal level of decisionmaking. An environmental problem may be addressed at the Community level with a uniform ("total harmonization") or a non-uniform solution, including measures which provide for partial, optional, minimal or alternative harmonization.[25]

The Community example shows that supranational environmental legislation need not necessarily involve uniform standards

---

25. See text, supra at 374-78.

and controls. The frequent use of non-uniform standards in the Community may be explained by the still embryonic stage of the Community, and the primary role that the member states, acting either through the Council or outside of Community institutions, play in environmental policymaking. Seen in this perspective, non-uniform standards represent an inferior form of supranational decisionmaking. However, non-uniform standards may also be seen as a necessary response to the diverse environmental and economic conditions, population densities, and values existing in member states. As such they can mitigate many of the shortcomings of supranational decisionmaking and even promote public acceptance of supranational policies.[26]

The balance between uniformity and diversity is quite different in product and in process regulation.

Prior to 1969, harmonization of product regulation had been used by the Community as a vehicle for aggressively promoting integration. Hence, the prevailing harmonization concept was unification of law ("total harmonization"). The new member states insisted upon a more pragmatic approach that encroached as little as possible on the member states and left them the power to legislate for the domestic market. As a result, optional harmonization became the rule, and total harmonization has required special justification.[27] As will be discussed later, the choice between total and non-total harmonization of product requirements is to a certain extent predicated on environmental considerations. However, the choice also reflects the general change in harmonization concepts.

Total harmonization has never played an important role in process regulation. As early as the first environmental program, the Community established the rule that member states in principle are free to set standards stricter than those in a Community directive.

Harmonization strategies in product regulation. Many product directives, especially those regulating detergents and chemicals, set uniform requirements. Some of these directives are relatively old and have merely been adjusted to technical progress in recent years; in these cases, their continued use may reflect the inertial effects of traditional concerns with creation of a truly integrated market. However, this rationale does not explain why some recent and wholly new product directives choose total harmonization while others choose optional harmonization. Some authors[28] believe the

---

26. See Weinstock, supra n. 4 at 6, 25, 26, et seq. (viewing non-uniform standards as transitory).
27. See Dashwood, "Hastening Slow: The Community's Path Towards Harmonisation," in Wallace, Wallace & Webb (eds.), *Policymaking in the European Communities* 273, 288 et seq. (1977).
28. Dashwood, supra n. 27, at 289; Slot, *Technical and Administrative Trade in*

perceived seriousness of the health or environmental hazards presented by a product explains the choice. But this argument is not very convincing if one compares, for example, detergents, which are subject to total harmonization, and motor vehicle emissions, which are subject to optional harmonization. In general, advocates for strong Community environmental policies favor total harmonization.

An alternative to total harmonization with no negative effects on economic integration is optional harmonization. The member states are obliged to grant products meeting the (generally stricter) Community requirements access to their market but may set other (generally laxer) standards for the domestic market. Thus, the motor vehicle, tractor, motorcycle, and construction machinery directives set maximum standards whose observance guarantees the producer access to the whole common market. Each member state may retain or introduce less stringent national requirements, in which case it must allow use of a vehicle or machine that conforms merely with them. Optional harmonization may at first glance appear to confirm the prevalence of economic interests over environmental considerations in regulation of exhaust emissions and noise, because it allows lower national standards and leaves enterprises the choice of complying either with the stricter EEC or the more lenient national standards. For these reasons, the European Parliament has denounced it on various occasions.[29]

However, the negative environmental impact of optional harmonization is tempered by economy of scale considerations. Insofar as an industry is export oriented, different standards for home and export production will normally run counter to the requirements of mass production and economies of scale. Therefore, producers of cars, motorcycles, and tractors normally opt for the stricter EEC standards in order to have the advantages of a European production line. Thus in practice, optional harmonization is often but a means of flexibility in implementation of new Community standards, i.e. it leaves industry time to adjust to such standards.[30]

Optional harmonization also enables member states and industry to experiment with progressive national solutions to the technical problems posed by exhaust emissions and noise. It does so by

---

the EEC 83 (1975); Stein, Hay & Waelbroeck, *European Community Law and Institutions in Perspective* 416 (1976).

29. European Parliament Resolution of 10 Feb 1972, JO No.C 19, 28 Feb. 1972, p.29; EP-Doc. 181/71, at No. 26 and 96.

30. Slot, supra n. 28 at 83; Henssler, "Einige Aspekte des Abbaus Technischer Handelshemmnisse im Verkehr," in Götz, Rauschning & Zieger (eds.), *Umweltschutz und Internationale Wirstschat* 173 at 174 (1975); Röhling, *Überbetriebliche Technische Normen als Nichttarifäre Handelshemmnisse im Gemeinsamen Markt* 142 (1972); Schmeder; supra n. 4 at 72, 268.

permitting a member state to set stricter domestic standards so long as it leaves industry the choice of whether to comply with them. Thus, the German car industry has voluntarily agreed to reduce car emissions considerably below the level established by the relevant Community directive. From an environmental point of view, optional harmonization could also be interpreted as an accommodation to divergent environmental conditions and divergent national policies on regulation.[31] For example, in a member state with low car density and few urban areas, strict controls over automobile emissions may seem unwarranted.

In a few cases the Community has provided for minimum harmonization of product requirements, which allows a member state to set stricter mandatory national standards. Although minimum product harmonization is not forbidden by the prohibition on discrimination by nationality under Art. 7 of the EEC Treaty, it is at variance with the idea of harmonization to create a fully integrated market. Minimum harmonization causes direct competitive disadvantages to the industry of the member state setting stricter standards because scale economy considerations may force the industry to export products meeting the stricter domestic requirements; these requirements are likely to involve higher costs per unit, handicapping such industry in competition in the markets of other states who adhere to the laxer community standards. Manufacturers who seek to compete in the domestic market of the state with stricter standards may suffer similar burdens.

Nonetheless, the 1978 directive on lead content of gasoline adopted a minimum harmonization strategy. It establishes a harmonized minimum level of 0.40 g/l for lead in gasoline, but permits member states to set a stricter lead level as low as 0.15 g/l. This regulation clearly allows existance of technical obstacles to trade, whose elimination is the ultimate goal of harmonization. The lead directive is a compromise necessitated because West Germany considered its standard of 0.15 g/l as vital and was unwilling to sacrifice it to European harmonization, while the other states considered the West German standard as economically unacceptable. The directive illustrates the inherent limitations of Community environmental policy, but at the same time also demonstrates the degree of its emancipation from trade policy. In this case free trade was sacrificed to achieve a political compromise which, environmentally, is at least a second best solution. The example also shows that minimal harmonization is not simply a convenient way of escaping all responsibility since even the Community solution of 0.4 g/l represents progress over the levels previously allowed in member states.

---

31. Slot, supra n. 28. at 84.

396   THE AMERICAN JOURNAL OF COMPARATIVE LAW   [Vol. 33

Moreover, as the recent discussion on stiffening the lead standard shows, the optional stricter standard may ultimately become the Community solution.[32]

Sometimes a technique of partial harmonization can reconcile environmental and political concerns which militate in favor of minimal harmonization of product requirements, with trade considerations which would require total or at least optional harmonization. The potential of this harmonization technique is evidenced by the directive on the quality of water intended for human consumption. Under this directive, member states are empowered to set stricter mandatory national quality standards for water intended for human consumption, especially for that used in the food industry. These stricter requirements may not be applied to foreign products; thus, the erection of technical obstacles to trade is avoided. However, for economic and environmental reasons this harmonization concept is not appropriate where foreign firms have a large share of the domestic market.[33]

Harmonization strategies in process regulation. There may be more latitude for diverse process related requirements in member states because divergent national requirements have only indirect impact on competition within the Community. Therefore, process related directives almost invariably employ minimal harmonization, i.e. the Community sets minimum environmental standards and member states may establish more stringent requirements. Even directives without express powers of this kind are interpreted to intend only minimal harmonization, e.g. the SO_2 limit values directive and the waste directives.

The motivation for minimum harmonization is that in the absence of a Community initiative some member states would not be sufficiently responsive to the common Community interest, such as the need to address an urgent environmental problem, cope with transboundary spillovers, or diminish the attractiveness of "pollution havens". On the other hand, there generally is no strong Community interest in preventing other member states from going beyond the minimum. Normally, only member states with strong environmental preferences, a particularly clean environment, or access to more advanced control technologies are expected to make use of this option. If distortions of competition result from such

---

32. In this respect, the borderline between minimal and alternative harmonization is fluid. See Weinstock, supra n. 4 at 27, 29. See also Krämer, supra n. 14 at No. 41.

33. For criticism of partial harmonization as an integration mechanism, see Röhling, supra n.30 at 140-141; Schmeder, supra n.4 at 72; Seidel, "Beseitigung der technischen Handelshemmnisse," in *Die Aneleichung des Rechts der Wirtschaft in Europa* 733, 740 et seq. (1971).

measures, as would be expected when a member state sets stricter emission or specification standards although not necessarily in the case of stricter ambient quality standards, they will primarily disadvantage the member state concerned and can easily be remedied by it.[34]

Sometimes, diversity in control measures is also achieved by alternative harmonization. For example, the aquatic environment directive establishes a system of uniform effluent standards, but permits a member state to opt for water quality standards if it can prove to the Commission that the water quality standards can be met without applying the effluent standards. These two strategies will result in varying environmental quality. Effluent standards, when used as the sole pollution control strategy, require unnecessary control in clean areas and (perhaps) insufficient control in polluted areas. Ambient standards permit uniformly polluted levels of environmental quality everywhere, allowing states who choose this alternative to take advantage of environmental conditions that permit higher discharge levels. The directive provides that the grant of the option is to be reviewed at a later date. The advantage of this approach over minimal harmonization is that it contains a built-in mechanism that allows for eventual total harmonization.[35] However, in the long run, minimal harmonization in the Community context may be more likely to stimulate total harmonization through stricter standards initially adopted by one or a few states.[36]

Conflicts over industrial location play a prominent role in both minimal and alternative harmonization.[37] The primary interest of polluter states today is preserving competitive advantages for their existing industries rather than attracting new industries. In the 1960s, Belgium was a pollution haven, in the sense that its lax environmental measures attracted new industry, but it has long since become a heavily polluted country and has been compelled to stiffen its environmental controls. Even Greece, a classic flag of convenience state for shipping, is now attempting to regulate its shipping

---

34. Bungarten, supra n.10, at 231. See also Weinstock, supra n. 4 at 26 et seq., 42 et seq.; Krämer, supra n. 14. Contra, Amaducci, "Fresh and Sea Waters of the EEC: Common Solutions?", 1975 *Diritto Communitario e degli scambi Internazionali*" 513, 526 (because of the impact on localization of industry).

35. See Weinstock, supra n. 4 at 26 et seq., 42 et seq. (calling this concept "two-tier harmonization").

36. The option accorded in the SO_2 limit values directive to utilize, in lieu of the common ambient air quality standard and associated measurement methods, a fixed alternative standard and associated measurement methods is not designed to protect national interests in environmental diversity. Rather, it is a concession to established monitoring practices in the member states.

37. See Weinstock, supra n. 4 at 7 et seq., 34 et seq. See also Pritzel, "Die Umweltpolitik in den Intereuropäischen und Innerdeutschen Beziehungen," 13 *Deutschland-Archiv* 834 at 835 (1980).

industry in order to protect the marine environment of the Mediterranean Sea. That the typical pollution haven problem does not exist in Europe seems due to the fact that polluter states have other disadvantages which deter investors.[38]

4. *Conservativism.* It is a widely held opinion that Community environmental law is characterized by lowest common denominator solutions.[39] This view is correct only in a qualified form. "Environmental" states, i.e. member states which have developed a progressive solution for a particular environmental problem, do not sacrifice their solution to Community harmonization.[40] Very often the Council adopts the progressive solution for the whole Community. In these cases, Community environmental policy often represents the highest, although not necessarily optimum, common denominator. In cases of sharp conflicts of interest among member states, the common resort to vague compromise formulae, harmonization of environmental protection principles instead of standard setting, and minimal or alternative harmonization may be considered lowest common denominator harmonization. They are lowest common denominator in the sense that they allow "polluter" states to more or less have their own way or, in the case of minimum harmonization, bind them to a solution low enough that they can agree to it. Such a solution may still represent progress beyond existing law in many member states. At the same time, progressive states are generally permitted to retain their more stringent standards. However, once the Community has adopted an environmental directive progressive changes are very difficult because member states defending the status quo have a stronger bargaining position than states who wish to change it, and arguments based on harmonization are greatly weakened.

Whether its lodestar is the policy of "environmental" or "polluter" states, Community environmental policy is generally more conservative than innovative in terms of the tools and strategies used.[41] The Community's role is to generalize and diffuse solutions

38. For Ireland see Conservation Foundation News Letter, August 1982 at 213. For developing countries, see Knödgen & Sprenger, supra n. 23; Knödgen, "Environment and Industrial Siting," 2 *Zeitschrift für Umweltpolitik* 407 (1979).

39. In this sense see Bungarten, supra n. 10 at 126, 230 (policy of the weakest member state); Behrens, supra n.11 at 254, 258; Weidner & Knoepfel, supra n.17 at 62; Krämer, supra n.14 at No. 48. See also Progress Report 1980, supra n. 22, Annex I at 11. See generally Marx, *Funktion und Grenzen der Rechtsangleichung nach Art. 100 Ewg-Vertrag* 146 et seq. (1976) (because of the structural conservativism of harmonization and the lack of substantive criteria for positive policymaking).

40. Institute for European Environmental Policy, *Annual Report 1981* at 2 (1982).

41. In this sense see Behrens, supra n. 11 at 258; Krämer, supra n. 14 at No. 49. See generally Marx, supra n. 39 at 156. The environmental programs in their

adopted in one or more member states by introducing them throughout the Community. The solutions of these member states normally set the framework for the Community solution. The "outrider" role of environmental states is, therefore, an essential prerequisite to the success of progressive policy proposals.[42] In this sense, national environmental policy always has a European dimension. At the Community level, on the other hand, attempts at new solutions are rarely made. An exception is perhaps the PCB directive, which had no parallel in existing member state regulation.

5. *Conclusion.* The deficiencies of Community environmental policy are obvious. Nevertheless, Community environmental policy may be called a success.[43] This is due not so much to the considerable quantity of directives and other legislative texts produced after adoption of the first environmental program; rather, it is because the Community has been able to adopt a number of quite important directives with major effects or implications. Examples are the sixth amendment to the hazardous substances directive of 1967, which introduces a screening procedure for new chemicals; the major accidents directive which addresses the problem of chemical accidents; the bird protection directive, which amounts to a fundamental departure from long established customs in some member states; the sulfur dioxide limit values directive establishing, on a Community-wide basis, ambient air quality standards, which most member states did not previously use as a control strategy; the aquatic environment directive which addresses the urgent problem of hazardous water pollutants; the major industrial installations directive which mandates the use of state-of-the-art control technology in the field of air pollution; and perhaps even the amendments to the motor vehicles directive which shifted the emphasis from abolition of technical obstacles to trade to protection of health and environment. For the future, the environmental impact directive must be added to this list. On balance, the record is much better than many critics of Community environmental policy assert.

---

programmatic parts sometimes proclaim wholly new solutions, but with respect to concrete actions they do not attempt to free Community policy from its linkage to member state policies.

42. Von Moltke, "Europäische Umweltpolitik," 2 *Zeitschrift für Umweltpolitik* 77 at 82-83, 87 (1979); Weinstock, supra n. 4 at 12; Institute for European Environmental Policy, *Annual Report 1981* at 3 (1982).

43. Von Moltke, supra n.42 at 77, 78; Kupfer, "Einflüsse der EG auf die Deutsche Umweltpolitik," in *IWL-Forum* 1981-II 57, 61-62 (1981); Krämer, supra n. 14 at No. 44.

400   THE AMERICAN JOURNAL OF COMPARATIVE LAW   [Vol. 33

III LEGAL, INSTITUTIONAL, AND OTHER FACTORS SHAPING THE INTEGRATION PROCESS

In this section we examine the legal and institutional constraints, the role played by the Commission, the Council, and member states in the Community policymaking process, and other factors that have shaped the development of Community environmental law and affected the pattern of measures that have emerged.

A. Legal Constraints

1. *Articles 100 and 235 of the EEC Treaty.* Community environmental policy has developed under legal constraints because the Community was designed as an economic institution and environmental protection was not an original objective of the Treaties. Articles 100 and 235 of the EEC Treaty in conjunction with the preamble and Art. 2 of the EEC Treaty do not provide a secure legal basis for the development of environmental policy as a new common policy within the framework of the Treaty. Environmental policy goals can in principle be pursued only as incidental to harmonization measures motivated by trade or competition considerations.

The assessment of many legal writers is that these deficiencies in Community legislative powers have played and will in the future play a significant role in impeding the development and implementation of Community environmental policy.[44] However, in practice these limitations, although not insignificant, have not proven very onerous. Thus, the Commission could state in 1980: "Recourse to Art. 235, either on its own or in conjunction with another Article of the Treaty, has not caused any particular difficulties."[45] The Community institutions have not had to make concessions on the substance of any new proposal in order to meet or still objections to their legislative power. Using a pragmatic, incrementalist approach and concentrating on problems where the benefits of common action were evident, they have step by step established a network of over eighty legislative texts for the protection of the environment, thereby creating a mosaic of precedents[46] as to the legislative competence of the Community which will be hard to overrule. The deficiencies in the legal basis for Community environmental policy were compensated by the political will of the member states.[47] This is all

---

44. Behrens, supra n. 11 passim; von Moltke, supra n.11; House of Lords, Select Committee, *22nd Report*, supra n.11; but see Close, "Harmonisation of Laws: Use or Abuse of the Powers under the EEC Treaty?" 3 *Eur. L. Rev.* 461 (1978).

45. Progress Report 1980, supra n. 22 at 6.

46. Bungarten, supra n. 10 at 159, 175.

47. Von Moltke, supra n. 42 at 79.

the more remarkable as the member states have had quite different views and priorities with respect to environmental issues.

Controversies between France, on one hand, and the other member states and the Commission, on the other, as to the Community powers for the protection of the environment marked the beginning of the common environmental policy in 1972.[48] Their result was that the several environmental programs were adopted only as a joint resolution of the Heads of State and Governments (now called the European Council) and of the Council of the Community. A further result was that the division of labor between the Community and member states was not clearly delineated. The development of a common environmental policy also aroused much criticism among legal writers.[49] However, there was no serious political challenge to Community powers for environmental matters in the early years following adoption of the first environmental program.[50] The German *Bundesrat*, originally very critical, accepted in 1975 that the Community had legislative powers over matters directly related to trade, industry, or economic affairs in general,[51] and that this provided a basis for a Community environmental program.

Due perhaps to the increasing density and scope of Community environmental legislation,[52] the situation has recently changed somewhat. In 1978, the British House of Lords published a report critical of the ever increasing extension of Community environmental law,[53] and other national parliaments have joined in this criticism.[54] In the West German *Bundesrat*, it has been suggested that the *Länder* should have the right to veto a Commission proposal.[55] It also is remarkable that Community officials who had cleared the way for recognition of Community environmental powers by publishing a series of articles in the early 1970s,[56] but from then on had

48. See Pleinevaux, "European Policy of Protection of Rivers and Waters against Pollution," in Ionesco (ed.), *The European Alternatives* at 394 et seq. (1977).

49. See supra n. 44.

50. Bungarten supra n.10 at 228 in 1978 could still state that there was no serious attempt to challenge the legislative competence of the Community in environmental matters.

51. See *Bundesrats-Drucksache* 142/75, 282/76.

52. This is the interpretation of Kapteyn, "Annotation," 16 *C.M.L. Rev.* 703, 706 (1979). See also House of Lords, Select Committee, *22nd Report*, supra n. 77 at No. 22(5), partially reprinted in 4 *Envt'l Pol'y & L.* 193 (1978).

53. House of Lords, Select Committee, *22nd Report*, supra n.11. Cf. von Moltke, supra n.42 at 82, who believe that the House of Lords is the precursor of future political resistance to the expansion of the Community into environmental policy.

54. See Kaiser, supra n.11 at 100, 102 (with further references). See also von Moltke, supra n. 11; Vygen, "Ergänzung des EWG-Vertrages im Hinblick auf eine Europäische Umweltpolitik," 6 *ZRP* 58, 60 (1974).

55. See Kaiser, supra n. 11.

56. See, e.g., Carpentier, "L'action de la Communauté en Matière d'Environnement," 1972 *Rev. Marché Commun* 381; Scheuer, "Aspects Juridiques de

not bothered to discuss the question, have more recently felt compelled to defend once again the legal position of the Community.[57]

The real issue is not so much the superficial controversy over interpretation of legal notions, but rather the realization of politicians outside the governments of member states that every new piece of Community environmental legislation shifts legislative power from member states to the Community and therefore erodes the power of national parliaments.[58] These reservations may cause some governments to be more prudent in agreeing to new directives. Legally, they will remain unimportant as long as private litigation concerning environmental directives does not increase. Member states which have participated in a directive's development will not normally challenge its conformity with the Treaty in infringement proceedings.[59]

The most visible practical result of the limitations inherent in Articles 100 and 235 is the emphasis of Community environmental policy on environmental problems related to trade and industry. The Community has concentrated on regulation of products, control of pollution from stationary sources, and waste disposal. Further substantive expansion into other areas of environmental policy, especially natural resources and land use, is improbable.[60] Denmark pointed out very early that it did not favor expansion of Community environmental policy into protection of nature beyond the directive concerning wild birds, the regulation on whales, and the accession of the Community to some treaties for protection of wild fauna. Denmark sees its traditional links with other Scandinavian countries threatened by the automatic transfer of foreign relations powers to the Community once a directive has been issued and a subject area is occupied by "internal" Community rules.[61] It therefore has gen-

---

la Protection de l'Environnement dans le Marchë Commun," 1975 *Rev. Marché Commun* 441.

57. See, e.g., Béraud, "Fondements Juridiques du Droit de l'Environnement dans le Traité de Rome," 1979 *Rev. Marché Commun* 35; Close, "Harmonisation of Law: Use or Abuse of the Powers under the EEC Treaty?," 3 *Eur. L. Rev.* 461 (1978).

58. House of Lords, Select Committee, *22nd Report*, supra n. 11 at No. 15, 16.

59. See also, e.g., European Court of Justice, case 91/79, Commission v. Italy, [1980] ECR 1099. Weiler, "Supranationalism Revisited — Retrospective and Prospective," EUI Working Paper No. 2, at n. 84 quite correctly speaks of "political estoppel".

60. See also Progress Report 1980, supra n. 22, Annex I at 36, 37.

61. See Progress Report 1980, supra n. 22 at 6; Lachmann, "Some Danish Reflections on the Use of Article 235 of the Rome Treaty," 18 *C.M.L. Rev.* 437-438, 447, 459 (1981). The reason is the jurisprudence of the European Court of Justice to the effect that Europeanization of a particular area amounts to a transfer of foreign relations powers to the Community under Art. 113 of the EEC Treaty. See case 22/70, Re European Road Transport Agreement, [1971] ECR 263; cases 3, 4 and 6/67, Kramer (Biological Resources of the Sea), [1976] ECR 1279; opinion 1/76, Re The Draft Agreement Establishing a European Laying-Up Fund for Inland Waterway Vessels (Rhine case), [1977] ECR 741; opinion 1/78, Re International Rubber Agree-

eral reservations against any further Community expansion. The majority of member states have also objected to any Community regulatory activities regarding land use planning.[62]

The reservation of particular areas of environmental policy to state legislation is a phenomenon that also exists in many federal states which grant the federal government broad legislative powers. Controversies over the exact scope of federal powers are also common and should not be interpreted as a special deficiency of the European Community. Especially in West Germany and Canada, controversies over the legislative power of the federal government are part of the day to day business of environmental politics.

However, it must be noted that the refusal of member states to let the Community legislate in areas such as natural resources and land use has significant practical consequences. Specifically, the shift announced in the second environmental program from pollution control towards rational use of natural resources and from the remedial to the preventive approach can at best be only partially implemented. Any Community involvement in the solution of certain truly international matters, such as international protection of wildlife, is also put into question. This is an indication that there are definite limits to Community power to implement a coordinated concept of environmental policy. These limits are not so much legal as institutional and political. Their primary source is the decisionmaking procedure established by Articles 100 and 235, under which all member states must agree that a particular problem should be addressed at the Community level.[63]

A more interesting question is whether the insecurity of the legal basis for environmental policy has political consequences for proposals within the core area of Community environmental policy. More precisely, the question is whether the alleged absence of Community legislative competence is frequently and in some cases successfully used as an argument against adoption of a particular proposal. This is not the case. Although there are frequent controversies among member states and the Commission as to the Treaty provision on which to base a particular directive, the dispute is not whether the Community has power in a particular matter but rather reflects different and broader considerations.[64]

---

ment, [1979] ECR 2871; Mastellone, "The External Relations of the EEC in the Field of Environmental Protection," 30 *Int'l & Comp. L. Q.* 104 (1981).

62. See 78 *Umwelt* (Informationen des Bundesministers des Inneren) 44 (12 Sept. 1980).

63. Wallace, "National Bulls in the Community China Shop: The Role of National Governments in Community Policy-Making," in Wallace & Webb (eds.), supra n. 27 at 33, 45.

64. See Behrens, supra n.11 at 259, 292-293; Bungarten, supra n. 10 at 181 et seq.;

404   THE AMERICAN JOURNAL OF COMPARATIVE LAW   [Vol. 33

Some member states, such as West Germany and the Netherlands, and also the Commission favor a liberal interpretation of Art.
100, while other member states prefer to rely on Art. 235 whenever
the particular environmental problem is not directly related to trade
or industry. One may interpret these divergencies as an expression
of different approaches to legal integration. Art. 100 stands for a
broad interpretation of Community powers with respect to expansion into new areas, while recourse to Art. 235 is the expression of a
narrow view of the Common Market and the normal powers granted
to the Community. However, a member state may also have internal reasons for preferring a particular Treaty provision as the legal
basis for Community action. For example, West Germany prefers
Art. 100 and accepts Art. 235 as at most an additional basis because
the Federal Government has only limited legislative power.[65]

Although controversies of this kind may cause delay and absorb
time of personnel which could be better devoted to policy formulation, they do not normally impede adoption of a proposal. Member
state objections to Commission proposals normally do not contest
the legislative powers of the Community, but instead are based on
national interests such as different priorities, policies, strategies, or
patterns of implementation in the particular field. Even where the
need for harmonization is at issue, the issue is normally not interpretation of Articles 100 or 235. Normally the relevant member
state merely has different priorities and does not want Community
legislation for political reasons. The fate of the more controversial
recent directives, such as the aquatic environment, SO_2 limit values,
toxic substances and major industrial installations directives, clearly
shows that the issues relate primarily to different policies and
strategies.

When a member state considers its interest as paramount to the
interest in harmonization, it may veto adoption of the directive or
insist on major changes, such as resort to optional or alternative harmonization, national exceptions, or a shift from substantive regulation to mere coordination of member state implementation.[66] The
lack of a secure legal basis for Community environmental legislation
does not play a significant role in the decisionmaking process.
Therefore, contrary to what has often been argued,[67] to the extent
there is any danger of lowest common denominator Community so-

---

Pleinevaux, supra n.48 at 397; Offermann-Clas, "Die Kompetenzen der Europäischen
Gemeinschaften im Umweltschutz," 6 *ZRP* 47, 55 et seq. (1983).

65. See *Bundesrats-Drucksache* 142/75.

66. Von Moltke, supra n.11 at 138, after having stated that the Treaty does not
allow establishment of a comprehensive environmental policy, admits that the existence of a secure legal basis is no guarantee for such policy (e.g. European transport
policy).

67. See authors cited supra n. 39.

lutions for environmental problems,[68] it has nothing to do with the limitations of Community legislative powers. It is instead an institutional and political problem.[69]

Finally, the narrow harmonization concept underlying Art. 100 does not seriously impede, as a legal matter, the Community's power to adopt innovative policies or strategies. It has been argued that the harmonization power under Art. 100 is irreconcilable with a comprehensive, coordinated concept of environmental policy and that it prevents the Community from addressing environmental problems not yet regulated by at least one member state.[70] However, this argument ignores the instrumental function of the legal provisions which grant powers for development of a policy. The environmental programs of the Community clearly show a perspective that goes beyond eliminating obstacles to trade.[71] That they are unlawful has never been asserted. The political practice has largely been emancipated from a narrow concept of harmonization.[72]

It is recognized that harmonization has not only the function of abolishing barriers to trade and distortions of competition but also of implementing substantive policies.[73] And where Art. 100 fails, the member states have easily resorted to Art. 235, either in conjunction with Art. 100 or even as an exclusive basis for legislative power. Also, given the rapid expansion of environmental law in all member states, the problem of finding regulation by at least one member state in order to establish a need for harmonization has lost much of its practical significance,[74] especially since it is sufficient that a particular environmental problem be covered by general regulations. This is demonstrated by the PCB waste directive which establishes a special regime of waste disposal for substances previously covered only by the general waste disposal laws of member states. Further, it has never been suggested that the Community, when harmonization is justified, is legally barred from adopting regulatory techniques that have not previously been used in the relevant national laws. The relative conservativism of harmonization in the field of environmental protection[75] is an institutional and political, rather than a legal, problem.

---

68. See text, supra at 398-99.

69. In this sense see also Behrens, supra n. 11 at 254, 258; Krämer, supra n. 14 at No. 48.

70. Bungarten, supra n. 10 at 125; Behrens, supra n. 11 at 295-296; Marx, supra n.39 at 155-156; von Moltke, supra n.11 at 138.

71. In the same sense see Behrens, supra n. 11 at 295-296. Contra, Marx, supra n. 39 at 156.

72. This is admitted by Bungarten, supra n. 10 at 227.

73. Behrens, supra n.11 at 249/250; Close, supra n.44 at 467; Marx, supra n. 39 at 48.

74. Behrens, supra n. 11 at 258.

75. See text, supra at 398-99.

2. *Legal mechanisms for implementing community environmental policies.* The directive has proven to be a suitable instrument for implementing Community environmental policy.[76] Due to its enormous flexibility — ranging from mere coordination of member state policies to the setting of detailed standards and associated measurement methods — it has been possible, when the political will existed, to devise the kind, depth, and intensity of regulation appropriate to the kind of environmental problem to be addressed and to the particular conditions of the member states that had to incorporate the directive into their system of environmental law and implement it within their administrative organization. The European Court of Justice's recognition of the principles of direct effect and supremacy for directives has also blurred the distinction between regulation and directive and thus removed some of the directive's legal disadvantages.[77] Therefore, the kind, depth, and intensity of regulation via directive today largely depends on the political will of the member states; it is not a function of the availability of legislative instruments.[78] Commission proposals for detailed environmental regulation have sometimes been reduced by the Council to mere harmonization of environmental protection principles or coordination of member state policies. However, this has nothing to do with deficiencies of the directive as a legislative instrument, but was motivated by political considerations, such as the rejection of excessive harmonization.

The lack of direct Community authority to implement and enforce Community programs is, however, a severe legal constraint on Community environmental policymaking. State and local governments have the dominant, if not exclusive, role in implementation and enforcement. This extreme decentralization of authority, reinforced by the control of these governments over land use decisions and, with minor exceptions, regulation of individual activity, imposes significant limitations on the realization of the policy objectives of Community legislation. These factors are less important in the case of product regulation, where the regulated industry normally favors uniformity and where oversight of implementation is easy. But many member states and regulated industries have a history of economic interest in delaying or diluting implementation and enforcement of directives that call for regulation of industrial

---

76. Schmeder, supra n. 4 at 53; Behrens, supra n. 11 at 252, 258; Ipsen, *Europäisches Gemeinschaftsrecht* 695 (1972). Contra, Slot, supra n. 28 at 89 et seq.

77. See Timmerman, "Directives: Their Effect Within the National Legal System," 16 *C.M.L. Rev.* 533 (1979); Usher, *European Community Law and National Law: The Irreversible Transfer?* 19 et seq., 70 et seq. (1981), both with further references.

78. See the authors cited supra n. 76.

processes. Industries in states with a history of lax regulation will be anxious to preserve the cost advantages which they have enjoyed and which may be important to their ability to stay in competition with industries elsewhere. The member states in question wish to pursue regional or local development objectives, and labor market problems. This is normally done without industry threats to locate new or existing plant abroad because the interests of member states and industry largely converge. Other factors influencing implementation and enforcement are the different administrative and judicial systems and the political cultures existing in the Community. There are considerable variations among member states as to participation in administrative proceedings and the role administrative and judicial review play in controlling implementation and enforcement. Access to administrative proceedings and the extent of information and participation rights available are quite varied. There are fundamental differences in the roles played by, say, West German, Dutch, French, and British judges in controlling national implementation and enforcement. These differences reflect differences in access to the court, the number and kind of issues taken to the court, the politicization of review of politically controversial environmental decisions, the powers of the court with regard to the executive branch, and feedback effects to the political process. A gap between what is proclaimed in legislative texts and what happens in practice is a general phenomenon of environmental law, especially in federal states. However, in the Community it gains particular significance because it occurs in a political society in which the features separating its components are still much stronger than those uniting them. This gap threatens the unfinished integration process.

B. Institutional Constraints

Institutional constraints are far more significant impediments to effective environmental regulation at the Community level than are legal constraints.

1. *Lawmaking Procedures.* The rather cumbersome constitutional structure of the Community and in particular of its lawmaking procedure does not work well when there are fundamental conflicts of interests on a proposal, which is often the case in environmental regulation. The frequently long delay, in cases of strong controversy, between an initial proposal and its final adoption as a directive indicates that Community lawmaking procedure is not well suited to the resolution of such conflicts. One reason why political decisionmaking in controversial fields takes so long is the multilevel organization of the political process. It reflects the involvement of multiple levels of government and the existence of complex net-

works of inter-governmental relations at the member state and Community levels.[79] Since there is at most only weak direct representation of national interests other than governmental ones at the Community level, member states must coordinate the various interests at the national level. Moreover, since the Commission has lost much of its political leadership as a driver of European integration and maker of substantive policies, there exists no open and ongoing forum for formulation of the Community interest.[80] Consequently, the struggle among competing interests is more complex than that normally existing in a nation state.

2. *Filtering of Interests.* A second institutional constraint is the systematic filtering of interests in the Community policy process.[81] The environmental programs fix the scope of Community lawmaking only to a limited extent. Other factors are who has the right of initiative, who in fact makes initiatives, and who ultimately has the power of decision. It is certainly not true, as maintained by some authors,[82] that the Commission's monopoly. on proposing initiatives prevents development of policies that reflect and balance all interests concerned. The Commission, at least in the area of environmental policy, is not blindly committed to the idea of integration. It rather actively pursues substantive environmental policies. However, since the Community bureaucracy is insulated from the pressure of concrete social, economic, and environmental problems, its perception of the urgency of such problems does not necessarily reflect the weight of societal preferences.[83] Other factors equally important in filtering expression of environmental interests include the decisionmaking monopoly of the Council,[84] the principle of unanimity established by Articles 100 and 235 and by the Luxembourg compromise, and the virtual absence of open participation by parliaments, the media, and interested organizations.[85] All this has the result of shifting societal conflicts of interest to the level of national interests. Societal interests are thereby systematically filtered and distorted.

Also contributing to the filtering of environmental interests are:

---

79. See Wallace, supra n. 63 at 33-34; Hull & Rhodes, *Intergovernmental Relations in the European Community* 72 (1976); Webb, "Variations on a Theoretical Theme," in Wallace & Webb (eds.), supra n. 27 at 1 et seq.

80. See also Wallace, supra n. 63 at 35 et seq.

81. This thesis was developed by Marx, supra n. 39 at 157, and expanded by Weidner & Knoepfel, supra n. 17 at 61 et seq. See also Wallace, supra n.63 at 43.

82. Marx, supra n. 39 at 157.

83. Id.

84. In the same sense see id.

85. For the role of parliaments see authors cited infra n. 116 and 117. For the role of organizations see Schwaiger & Kirchner, *Die Rolle der Europäischen Interessenverbände* 47 et seq. (1981).

the weakness of the European Parliament, which is not compensated by greater involvement of national parliaments in the process of formulating a national position towards Community environmental policy; the lack of a truly European public opinion; and the almost complete decentralization of implementation and enforcement of directives. These factors retard Community reaction to environmental preferences even more than for other issues, such as economic and energy matters. National governments in particular act to filter out the expression of new environmental preferences, while economic interests find easier access to the policy process. The Environment and Consumer Protection Directurate-General of the Commission acts as an agency with an environmental mission, but it is politically too weak to prevail over the member states.

The initial decision to expand Community activities into the area of environmental protection as well as the first substantive proposals of the Commission occurred when the problems of environmental protection had been "discovered" by the mass media as well as the general public throughout all or most of the member states. The high measure of public awareness and at the same time the lack of experience with the political and economic constraints within which environmental policy has to operate presumably contributed greatly to the initial success of Community expansion into this area. However, the two years following adoption of the first environmental program were marked by the reluctance of many member states to put the programmatic declarations of the environmental program into operation. All kinds of jurisdictional obstacles were erected and the willingness to compromise was small. By the time this learning period was over and Community environmental policy had gotten seriously underway, the initial enthusiasm for environmental protection had been replaced in member states by a more sober assessment of the costs and benefits associated with it. Most of the environmental directives were adopted during this later stage. The Commission, however, did not readily take into account these changes in attitudes and preferences towards the environment in the member states. It thus continued making strong proposals. The member states in turn resisted many Commission proposals in the interest of new economic and energy concerns. The new preference for ambient quality instead of emission standards, the reluctance to further modernize the motor vehicle directives, and the general slowdown in Community legislative activities since 1980 are all expressions of this resistance.

By the same token, the under-staffing and under-budgeting of the Environment and Consumer Protection Directorate-General must be seen as a deliberate effort by the member states to temper environmental initiatives. The budget of the Environment and Consumer Protection Service remained level in real terms over many years. Given the ever increasing responsibility of the Service, this budgetary policy has meant that major programs provided in the environmental program could not be adequately implemented.[86]

This filtering process poses serious problems of political legitimacy because of gaps in the Community legal structure in relation to environmental regulation. Although the harmonization power necessarily includes Community authority to establish substantive policies in the area to be harmonized, neither Art. 100 nor the Treaty as a whole provide any guidance as to the content of these policies. The logic of the Treaty is that harmonization has an essentially "negative" function: the elimination of trade barriers caused by different regulations in member states. But environmental policy is inescapably "positive"; once the Community intervenes, it must determine what kind and level of environmental protection the Community should pursue.[87] In theory, the Treaty must provide some normative direction as to the content of positive Community measures in order to legitimate the transfer of powers from member states to the Community. But the Treaty provides no such direction in the case of environmental policy. In a democratic political system, democratic bargaining processes compensate for such a lack of substantive standards for legislation. However, in the present state of the Community's development, the lack of legitimating substantive standards are not being remedied by democratic decisionmaking.

3. *Consequences of Institutional Constraints.* These structural features of the Community policy process explain many of the deficiencies of environmental policy. The patchwork character of Community environmental law reflects the pragmatic approach of the Commission in making policy proposals. This approach is in turn explained by the unwillingness of member states to agree to comprehensive transfer of sovereignty as well as by technical and personnel problems. The lack of consensus among member states concerning priorities, a characteristic handicap for a new policy not

---

86. The recent increases in the budget of the Service are mainly due to the pressure of the European Parliament. Member states which place higher values on environmental quality will not always resist the tendency to underbudgeting because they can often protect their interests by building sufficient flexibility into a directive to enable them independently to pursue their own national policy goals. An example is the regionalization concept adopted for economic and energy reasons by the gas oil directive. The regionalization is optional so that some member states, such as West Germany, could apply the stricter of the two Community input standards throughout their territory.

87. See Marx, supra n. 39 at 146 et seq.; von der Groeben & Möller, *Möglichkeiten und Grenzen einer Europäischen Union*, Vol. I: *Die Europäische Union Als Prozess* 391 (1980).

explicitly mandated by the Treaty, also contributes to the importance of political expediency in the Commission's selection of proposals. The Commission is often forced to take priority action in response to national initiatives, about which it is informed under the information/standstill agreement, in order to avoid new obstacles to trade and preserve Community options for new environmental legislation.[88]

Because of these structural factors, Community environmental policy has not been as truly innovative as might have been expected from the shifting of decisions to a higher decisionmaking level. The solutions of one or more member states normally set the framework for Community solutions.[89] Because there is no forum for the formulation of a Community interest and because societal interests are transformed — and distorted — into national interests, it is not possible to develop a Community environmental policy completely divorced from member state policies.

These structural factors also help account for the fact that the development of Community environmental policy often comes to a virtual standstill when the national policies are too far apart. Negotiations on a controversial proposal easily take several years. Resolution of the conflict is often possible only by resort to lowest common denominator politics. Such solutions involve a compromise formula vague enough for general agreement by everybody, or expressly leave member states substantial discretion.[90] Examples are the shift from substantive solutions to procedural ones or to simple coordination of member state policies; optional harmonization; minimal harmonization (priority for stricter national law); granting of options between two Community strategies; national exceptions; and use of a recommendation to encourage national measures rather than a binding directive. From the perspective of effective environmental regulation, these "escape" devices are not necessarily bad because they often allow progressive or innovating states to maintain freedom of action.

However, concealing lack of true consensus by resort to vague formulae will almost invariably cause serious problems in the future. A prominent example is Article 6 of the aquatic environment directive which lists criteria for selecting "hazardous" substances and for setting effluent and quality standards for such substances. The directive does not indicate priority among these criteria (toxicity, biodegradability, bioaccumulation, technical and economic feasi-

---

88. Bungarten, supra n. 10 at 174; Weidner & Knoepfel, supra n. 17 at 63 et seq. See generally Wallace, supra n. 63 at 39; Marx, supra n. 39 at 157.

89. See text, supra at 398-99.

90. See authors cited supra n. 39.

bility) nor does it establish qualitative and quantitative guidelines for their application.[91] Moreover, these criteria are not exclusive. It has therefore been extremely difficult to establish the list of most hazardous substances and the associated effluent standards.

Also, compromises which grant member states a choice between two fundamentally different strategies (alternative harmonization) do not necessarily lead to final resolution. The history of implementing directives to be issued under Article 6 of the aquatic environment directive again provide a good example. These directives are to set effluent and water quality standards for the most hazardous pollutants (list I) identified under the directive. The controversy between the United Kingdom, on the one hand, and the Commission and the other member states, on the other, over the best strategy for control of water pollution by dangerous substances was seemingly resolved by allowing the two competing strategies — effluent and water quality standards — to coexist. However, this conflict still dominates the political bargaining over determination of standards for list I substances because each side suspects that the other side, in setting the relevant standards, will gain cost advantages for its industry. This conflict has as yet prevented agreement on more than three particular standards. On the other hand, it presents a chance for ongoing negotiating and eventual convergence.[92] Thus the United Kingdom, which used to stiffly oppose effluent standards, has now accepted the need for effluent standards for new sources of mercury. The need to issue implementing directives can also provide a useful opportunity for reconsideration of an initial compromise that tolerates measures since shown to be unwise. Thus, alternative harmonization may initiate a learning process that ultimately leads to a common and uniform solution.

4. *Reasons for the Relative Success of Community Environental Policy Despite Institutional Constraints.* The relative success of Community environmental policy despite institutional constraints appears to have two reasons.

The most important is that there is often at least some common interest of all member states in harmonized environmental policies. Economic considerations may militate in favor of a common solution, especially in the area of product standards. The institutional

---

91. See Keune, "Kollidierende rechtliche, politische und wirtschaftspsychologische Gesichtspunkte bei der Auswahl der Stoffe für die Liste I der EG-Gewässerschutz-Richtlinie," 17 *ZfW* 193 (1978); Malle, "EG-Gewässerschutz—Vorschriftenflut Droht," 1978 *Umwelt* 422, 424-425; *The Environment in Europe, Bulletin of the Institute for European Environmental Policy,* No. 19, Supplement (September 1982).

92. See von Moltke & Haigh, supra n. 17 at 27-28; Weinstock, supra n. 4 at 29, 32, 45.

mechanisms of the Community afford the member states a forum for exchanging innovations in environmental policy. Harmonization removes the economic disadvantages each member state would incur when introducing environmental controls individually because it imposes equal or at least similar economic burdens on industry throughout the Common Market. Finally, where transboundary pollution is involved, the problem can, as a practical matter, be addressed only by the Community.

The other reason is that harmonization of environmental law is in some respect easier than harmonization of a more traditional body of law. In administrative law the formal, dogmatic, and systematic elements are less important than in private or criminal law. Since environmental law is mostly administrative law, the technical harmonization work is less difficult, and the role of conservative jurists who adhere to traditional solutions is less important.[93] What counts are substantive interests, protection levels, strategies, and implementation systems. Harmonization in the field of environmental law is normally confined to protection levels and strategies. It does not encroach on the traditional body of general administrative law or require administrative reorganization. Although in real terms substantive interests are much more significant than legal technicalities,[94] it appears that negotiation over substantive interests is easier than over legal technicalities or administrative reorganization. The difficulties with the directive for environmental impact assessment are a good example. Finally, environmental law is relatively young in all member states. It has undergone considerable and rather frequent changes in a single decade. Therefore, there are less reservations against changes brought about by new Community environmental legislation, so long as they are not regressive.[95]

C. *The Role of Commission, Council and Member States in the Integration Process*

Although the development of environmental policy may be interpreted as a substantive deepening of European integration, environmental policymaking has not remained unaffected by the developments which have resulted in the destruction of the institutional balance and decline of the supranational decisionmaking procedure established by the Treaty. These developments include the following: the Commission has declined as a force of integration; the Council has emerged as the major political force in the Community;

---

93. Schmeder, supra n. 4 at 26.

94. Id.; but see Wallace, *National Governments and the European Communities* 13 (1973).

95. Contra, Marx, supra n. 39 at 156.

intergovernmental decisionmaking has taken priority over supranational decisionmaking; and institutional sub-systems, such as the Committee of Permanent Representatives and the various technical committees and working groups established at the Council level, have become an integral part of the Community decisionmaking system.[96] However, the Commission exercises more influence on the development of environmental programs than in other areas of Community policymaking.[97]

1. *The Commission, Council, and Member States.* The Commission has retained much of its early role as an institution for initiating policy proposals in the area of environmental protection.[98] The major factor in identifying and developing candidates for harmonization is the Commission bureaucracy. Nonetheless, member states are increasingly influencing both the identification and development of candidates for harmonization. The member states have exerted a much larger influence on the third environmental program than the first two, and made clear their objections to further extension of Community activities regarding natural resources and land use. Several larger member states and the Council have become involved in initiating environmental policy proposals.[99]

Member states have also been able to indirectly set the pace of environmental legislation by taking unilateral national initiatives which established the framework for future action by the Community. Under the information/standstill agreement of 1973[100] such initiatives must be reported to the Commission. The Commission must then decide within the time limit established by the agreement[101]whether it wishes to make a Community proposal. Because the time limit is too short, the member state can generally adopt its measure, which often then serves as the basis for eventual commu-

---

96. See Pryce, *The Politics of the European Community* 63 (1973).

97. See generally Weiler, supra n. 59 at 28 et seq; Henig, *Power and Decision in Europe* (1980); Pryce, supra n. 96 at 61 et seq.

98. Bungarten, supra n. 10 at 168.

99. Normally, such a move does not involve submitting a fully formulated draft directive; rather, the relevant member states will call upon the Commission to make a proposal. Since Commission proposals are not made from scratch but normally lean on national models, it is difficult to determine retrospectively who took the initiative. Institute for European Environmental Policy, *Annual Report 1981* at 3 (1982).

100. Agreement of the Representatives of the Governments of the Member States meeting in Council of 5 March 1973 on information for the Commission and for the Member States with a view to possible harmonization throughout the Communities of urgent measures concerning the protection of the environment, OJ No.C 9, 15 March 1973, p. 1, as amended by the agreement of 15 July 1974, OJ No.C 86, 20 July 1974, p. 2.

101. The Commission is allowed two months to notify to the member state concerned of its intent to make a proposal and another three months to submit the proposal to the Council, which must then decide on the proposal within five months.

nity harmonization measures several years later. Thus, the relevant national government is able to go forward with its initiative. Sometimes after several years the Community makes a proposal for harmonization which is usually based on the national model. National initiatives thus create a *fait accompli* for later harmonization.[102]

The stage of the policy process where national interests of member states are most vigorously asserted is the bargaining within the Council over the contents of a Comission proposal. Here the conflicting interests of the national governments (and sometimes even conflicting interests within national governments) and the views of the Commission undergo a lengthy and complex process of mutual adjustment and accommodation in which both strategies and tactics of the principal players exercise an important influence on the final outcome.

The environment and industry groups within the Committee of Permanent Representatives play a particularly important role in ensuring that the directive which finally emerges is compatible with the national interests affected. Issues that remain controversial within these groups are decided by the Council. There, the acting president and the Commission may act as mediators.[103] The relative slowness in decisionmaking is an expression of the complexity of this political bargaining process which involves multiple levels of government.[104]

It would perhaps be an overstatement to identify the Commission as a pacemaker for progressive environmental policy and the Council as an institution more concerned with moderating the economic and administrative costs of environmental regulation. Sometimes, the Council adopts directives more stringent than the original Commission proposal. The Commission often makes strong proposals (for example, a proposal for total harmonization) to use as bar-

---

102. See von Moltke, supra n. 42 p. 84-85. Bungarten, supra n. 10 at 186. In recent years the number of notifications has fallen substantially. See Commission, Fifteenth General Report of the European Communities (Brussels 1981), No. 363; Third Environment Action Program, OJ No.C 46, 17 Feb. 1983, Annex No. 13. This may be a sign of the general slowdown of environmental policy, but probably also reflects efforts on the part of national authorities to bypass the notification requirement in order to avoid involving the Community in national policy proposals.

103. See Pryce, supra n. 96 at 67.

104. Hull & Rhodes, supra n. 79 at 72. Although the Working Group on the Environment works more extensively than other Council groups, the average time lag between submission of a proposal to the Council and its formal adoption is about two years. However, many noncontroversial directives are adopted within eighteen months, while more controversial directives may require more than four years before their formal adoption. To permit final adoption, proposals have sometimes been entirely restructured; the level of environmental protection afforded by a directive has sometimes been considerably weakened; and on still other occasions the Council has opted for techniques of optional harmonization, minimal harmonization, alternative harmonization, or national exemptions.

gaining chips. Nevertheless, the Council normally does opt for solutions that temper the economic and administrative costs of environmental regulation and are less supranational than the Commission proposals. The Commission's distance from the real problems of implementation may lead to some overproduction of legislative texts as well as inappropriate substantive solutions.[105]

Environmental policymaking is clearly a process of intergovernmental bargaining.[106] However, environment policy is, on the whole, still more supranational in its decisional patterns than other policy areas. This is evidenced by the virtual absence of package deals. Reasons may be the absence of strong politicization, the remoteness of the decisionmaking process from national attention, its bureaucratization, and the lack of sufficient public pressure.[107] Although environmental policy, due to its interrelation with economic and social policy, is an important and controversial field of national politics,[108] a particular environmental directive is seldom a political issue in member states before its adoption by the Council. It may become such an issue after its adoption, but then it is normally too late. Recent exceptions to this pattern are the environmental impact assessment directive, the baby fur seal directive, and the West German proposals for stiffening the automobile emission standards.

Controversies between member states seldom concern the question of whether any common solution should be adopted. In the areas of pollution and product related requirements, the member states have, by adopting the environmental programs, committed themselves to further development of Community environmental policy. There is also agreement that protection of nature and regulation of land use should in principle remain within the competence of member states.

The conflicting national interests that emerge in the Community policymaking process reflect a variety of factors, including different environmental protection philosophies, different priorities, different strategies of coping with environmental problems, different environmental conditions and geographic location, different economic problems and conditions, and different administrative structures or monitoring systems.[109] Short term considerations

---

105. See Institute for European Environmental Policy, *Annual Report 1982* at 9 (1983); Malle, supra n. 91 at 422. See generally Hull & Rhodes, supra n. 79 at 23.

106. See generally Wallace, supra n. 94 at 83 et seq.

107. Hull & Rhodes, supra n. 79 at 7-8; Wallace, supra n. 84 at 13.

108. Bungarten, supra n. 10 at 224; von der Groeben & Möller, supra n. 87 at 383-384, 391.

109. See Progress Report 1980, supra n. 22 at 5-6, Annex I at 7; Pleinevaux, supra n. 48 at 400; von der Groeben & Möller, supra n. 87 at 397-398; Kupfer, supra n. 43 at 60.

often prevail over medium or long term considerations.[110] Member states that place low value on domestic environmental policy (polluter states) object to substantive increases in environmental protection. Conversely, member states with stricter national environmental policies (environmental states) try to achieve Europeanization of the burdens which they have imposed on their industry. Even if they do not achieve this goal, they are unwilling to lower domestic standards. Therefore, the principle that member states may retain and introduce stricter national standards has recently found wide acceptance as a means of achieving at least minimal harmonization, thereby narrowing both the environmental protection and industrial cost gaps existing among member states. With respect to products, optional harmonization may fulfill a similar function.

Divergent opinions on the methods for implementing common policies, especially on strategies and, to a lesser extent, tools, are another source of controversy. Member states are reluctant to give up established national patterns of implementation and enforcement and therefore seek the Community solutions most consistent with their national systems of environmental protection.[111]

There are some member states, such as the Netherlands, which have traditionally favored strong Community environmental measures. West Germany tends to advocate progressive Community solutions for economic reasons. In other member states, such as Italy and Belgium, there is a large implementation gap which allows them to agree to rather strict Community measures because they anticipate that they will not have to be fully implemented. Member states located at the margins of the Community, which have large underdeveloped, relatively clean regions for which expensive environmental controls are too costly in relation to the benefits derived from them, are often more reluctant to agree to a preventive environmental policy than the richer, more densely populated states in the center of the Community.[112] But generalizations are hardly possible. There are no permanent coalitions. Depending on its interests, any member state can be a positive or negative force with respect to a particular proposal. A general classification of all states on the periphery of the Community (United Kindgom, Ireland, Italy, and Greece) as polluter states and of all central states (France, West Germany, Netherlands, Belgium, Luxembourg, and also Denmark) as environmental states is not supported by the past experience of

---

110. See Pleinevaux, supra n. 48 at 400; Pritzel, supra n. 47 at 835.

111. See Institute for European Environmental Policy, supra n. 105; see generally Wallace, supra n.94 at 13.

112. See Rat von Sachverständigen für Umweltfragen, *Umweltgutachten* No. 1667 (1978); Weinstock, supra n.4 at 34 et seq.

Community environmental policy.[113]

Given the predominance of national interests in the Community policy process, the formulation of these interests is of vital importance. It is clear that in all member states the national executive authorities are by far the most important single factor.[114] They all avoid public debate because they prefer bureaucratic bargaining and because public debates would foster interagency conflicts. Thus, only a limited elite participates in the formulation of the national interest.[115] Industry exerts considerable influence using its traditional client relations with the bureaucracy. The impact of national parliaments on the formulation of national policies regarding Community matters has remained weak, although some parliaments, especially in the new member states, have recently tried to play a more active role.[116] Likewise, environmental groups are weak in most member states because they do not have a truly European perspective which would enable them to influence the formulation of national interests regarding Community policy. Rather, they focus on national policy objectives.[117]

D.   *Towards a Theory of Consensus Formation in Community Environmental Policy*

It is rare in Community environmental policy for negotiations to fail. In most cases, a compromise on a particular policy proposal is ultimately reached, although its achievement may require years of negotiations in the sub-groups of the Committee of Permanent Representatives as well as in the Council. The price is often considerable attenuation of the original Commission proposal.[118] In the present state of knowledge, it is difficult to formulate a theory as to

---

113. Von Moltke, supra n. 42 at 83; Institute for European Environmental Policy, *Annual Report 1981* at 6-7 (1982); for argument favoring the classification rejected in the text see Weinstock, supra n.4 at 34 et seq., who, however, admits that an empirical base for it does not exist. In particular, Weinstock concedes that the affinity of the central states is not particularly great.

114. See Sasse, "Governments, Parliaments and the Community of Members," in Sasse, et al., *Decision-making in the European Community* 1, 7 et seq., 68 (1977); Wallace, supra n. 63 at 39 et seq.

115. Wallace, supra n. 63 at 47, 57.

116. See Sasse, supra n.114 at 72; id., "The Control of the National Parliaments of the Nine over European Affairs," in Cassese (ed.), *Parliamentary Control over Foreign Policy* 137 (1980); Wallace, supra n.63 at 47-48; Foyer, "Le Contrôle des Parlements Nationaux sur la Fonction Normative des Institutions Communautaires," 1979 *Rev. Marché Commun* 161; Schweitzer, *Die Nationalen Parlamente in der Gemeinschaft, ihr Schwindender Einfluss in Bonn und Westminster auf die Europagesetzgebung* (1978); Rochère, "Le Parlement Britannique et les Communautés Européenes," 1978 *Rev. Trim. Dr. Eur. 595;* Gulmann & Clauson-Kaas, "Control by the Danish Parliament of Community Legislation," 16 *C.M.L. Rev.* 227 (1979).

117. See Schwaiger & Kirchner, supra n. 85.

118. Bungarten, supra n. 10 at 174.

1985]   EUROPEAN COMMUNITY ENVIRONMENTAL LAW   419

which factors lead to consensus. Of course, general negotiation theories can be applied to the Community decisionmaking process. An important factor seems to be the dynamics of long lasting negotiations, i.e. the "entanglement" of the negotiators which ultimately exerts such pressure on the representatives of dissenters (especially where the dissenter is a single state), that a compromise can be reached.[119] It appears that the new member states, especially the United Kingdom and Denmark, are tougher negotiators and risk blocking ongoing negotiations more often than the old member states. But on the whole, no member state is willing to assume the responsibility for causing the failure of negotiations that have lasted for years and in which mutual trust in the willingness of all negotiators to contribute to an agreement has been built up.

Interesting theories have been advanced by von Moltke[120] and Dashwood[121] to explain the dynamics of the Community negotiation game. Von Moltke, with his "consensus cycle" theory, specifically addresses environmental policymaking, while Dashwood's "radiator effects" theory is a general one also applicable to environmental policymaking. According to von Moltke, the impulse for a Community proposal regularly comes from existing or proposed national legislation. The Commission then makes its proposal which leans on the national model, but the other member states are, at first, unwilling to accept the proposal. In the meantime, one or more other member states consider the proposal as the basis for new or modified national legislation, often without considering its Community source or the national debate. This cycle eventually brings closure to the national debate and the Community proposal is ultimately adopted, at least in modified form. Dashwood's ideas go in the same direction, although he is more cautious in generalizing. Dashwood states that if a member state unilaterally adopts or accepts the substance of a Commission proposal as the basis for national reform, agreement on it at the Community level becomes possible. The Community proposal has a "radiator effect" on the national policy process which in turn "radiates" back to the Community process.

These theories, however interesting they may be, are too simplistic to explain the consensus shaping process within the Community political system. They do not explain what made the other,

---

119. See generally Iklé & Leites, "Verhandlungen-ein Instrument zur Modifikation der Nutzenvorstellungen," in Shubik (ed.), *Spieltheorie und Sozialwissenschaften* 255 et seq. (1965).

120. Von Moltke, "Environmental Impact Assessment Procedures," at 4 et seq., (unpublished) paper given at the International Seminar on "Protection and Rational Management of the Environment and Natural Resources in Europe — The Key Role of Land Use Planning," Strasbourg 17-18 Dec. 1981; expanded in: Institute for European Environmental Policy, *Annual Report 1981* at 4 et seq. (1982).

121. Dashwood, supra n. 27 at 295-296.

"uncommitted" member states ultimately agree to the possibly modified Commission proposal. To overcome this weakness, one could argue that whenever at least two member states favor a Commission proposal, it will be adopted because two out of the ten member states are by necessity represented in the national debate, because they have anticipated the possible arguments for and against a regulation of the kind envisaged by the proposal, and because their endorsement gives it democratic legitimacy. However, given the marked differences among member states with respect to environmental policy priorities, environmental protection levels, economic conditions, strategies and implementation systems, such a hypothesis is implausible as long as the policy process in the "uncommitted" member states is not included in the analysis. It is more probable that the national debate leading to adoption of the substance of a Commission proposal in a particular member state is but a special form of the political process in all member states for formulating a national position on the proposal. In any event, the "uncommitted" member states must also be prepared to·incorporate the proposal into national law after its adoption. Therefore, it would seem that the adoption of a proposal as a national measure is neither a necessary nor a sufficient condition for reaching agreement at the Community level.

Nevertheless, von Moltke and Dashwood may have developed at least the first part of a theory of consensus formation in Community environmental policy. It is clear that there are always member states that have no strong economic interest in the harmonization of environmental policy. With respect to processes, polluter states should normally oppose harmonization because their industry would lose cost advantages it previously enjoyed. With respect to products, the economic interest of polluter states in harmonization depends on the size of their own market and the export orientation of their industry. Indeed, if the *Cassis de Dijon* doctrine were expanded, their industry would in the future be entitled to free access to foreign markets having stricter requirements, reducing the incentive for polluter states to seek harmonization in order to ensure access to foreign markets on more favorable terms.

Accordingly, the explanation why consensus on environmental harmonization is reached within the Community must often lie in factors other than a common economic interest in adoption of a particular directive. Implicit norms of reciprocity seem to be most important. When several member states are strongly interested in a particular policy proposal, the other member states may ultimately acquiesce because they need their support on other issues of harmonization. National officials may also support Community initiatives because they favor progressive environmental measures and believe that they can be more easily introduced domestically through a Commission directive than through the national legislative process. Finally, the Treaty norms calling for establishment of a Common Market and the abolition of barriers to trade seem to promote consensus on harmonization of product regulation. All told, there seems to be a common value system that allows for a fair amount of harmonization even in the presence of conflicting economic interests.

However, reciprocity has its limitations. There are policy proposals that have never been adopted by the Council despite support from some member states. The Commission proposal on environmental impact assessment was close to becoming such an example. Evidently, the reciprocity incentives for "uncommitted" member states to accede to a proposal may be outweighed by other national interests generated by factors ranging from different environmental protection philosophies to administrative structures incompatible with the proposal. In order to have explanatory power, the consensus cycle theory must be able to measure and determine the vector of these various elements in order to determine when member states will ultimately acquiesce in a proposal despite lack of interest in it or even in the presence of a countervailing interest. This task appears to exceed the present state of knowledge. A further qualification of the consensus cycle theory is that it does not explain a policy's content, i.e. the substantive terms upon which an agreement is reached.

E. Dynamic Factors and the Problem of Obsolescence in Community Environmental Law

1. *Changes in Knowledge and Technology.* A sound environmental policy is unthinkable without adequate scientific and technical information concerning environmental problems. It is also necessary to accommodate changes in knowledge and the resulting changes in the perception and definition of environmental problems. The Community is not well equipped for these tasks.

Subject to some qualification for nuclear energy, the Community has no research facilities of its own for developing or acquiring the scientific and technical information needed for sound regulation. It has to rely on information provided by experts from national governments, on the advice of consultants from universities and research institutes selected for the preparation of a particular proposal, and on research results generated through Community financed research programs by scientists from national governments (so-called concerted action programs) or from independent research institutions (so-called indirect action programs).[122] These procedures have several shortcomings: national government experts may be biased; the selection of consultants is not without risk; and it is not easy to ensure that the research results are relevant to regulatory policy choices. Moreover, the usual strategies and tools for implementing Community environmental objectives afford little flexibility for accommodating changes in knowledge. Sometimes Community law invokes broadly defined regulatory principles, such as use of "best practicable means of control", leaving member states the task of making them operable. In theory this approach allows speedy adaptation to new technological knowledge, but in practice it can lead to a lack of real harmonization and the danger of a severe implementation gap. Therefore, most Community environmental directives avoid this approach, but instead establish specific numerical standards (such as emission, specification, input, and ambient standards) or of lists of hazardous substances that must be controlled. Because of member states' interest in controlling policy outcomes, standard setting and listing is not left to the discretion of the Commission. This approach, of course, prolongs the cumbersome decisionmaking procedure for adopting directives. Accordingly, by the time a directive is adopted, its scientific or technological basis is or will soon be outdated. The fate of the aquatic environment directive is a good example. In any event, once directives are adopted, it is very difficult to adjust them in response to new scientific or technical knowledge and resulting changes in the definition of the relevant environmental problem.

2. *Legal Obsolescence.* The problem of legal obsolescence has been aptly analyzed in the general context of Community legislation by Calabresi, Dashwood, and Marx.[123] Marx points out that the Spaak report, which elaborated the essential structures of the EEC Treaty, was based on an erroneous idea of stability and that therefore the

---

122. The sectoral research and development program in the field of the environment, which runs from 1981 to 1985, provides for an appropriaton of 42 million European Account Units (about US $40 million) of which 33 million are appropriated to indirect action in the field of environmental protection. The research topics of the program include: sources, pathways, and effects of selected pollutants, such as heavy metals, organic micro-pollutants, asbestos, selected air and water pollutants, and noise pollution; reduction and prevention of pollution, such as by pollution abatement technologies and clean technologies; protection and management of natural environments, such as ecosystems conservation and bird protection; and environmental information management. Council Decision (76/311/EEC) of 15 March 1976, OJ No. L 74, 20 March 1976, p. 36. There are also special research programs in specific areas, particularly nuclear energy.

123. Calabresi, "Incentives, Regulation and the Problem of Legal Obsolescence," in Cappelletti (ed.), *New Perspectives for a Common Law of Europe* 291 et seq., in particular at 297, 301 (1978); Dashwood, supra n. 27 at 295-296; Marx, supra n. 39 at 144 et seq.

concept underlying Art. 100 of the EEC Treaty is a static one.[124] Since the functioning of the Common Market is affected by differences between national regulations independent of their content, the primary purpose of Art. 100 is harmonization. Article 100 provides no guidance as to the content of a directive harmonizing a particular area. Consequently, amendment of an existing directive can not be justified by the objective of ensuring the functioning of the Common Market. Therefore, strictly speaking, the Community has no legislative competence to modify a directive once issued under Art. 100. Practice and prevailing opinion has ignored this legal nicety,[125] and it is improbable that the European Court of Justice would deny that the Community has legislative powers to amend existing directives. Nonetheless, as has been described by Calabresi and Dashwood,[126] serious institutional problems of obsolescence remain, especially with respect to product regulation.

The initial adoption of a directive for harmonization of product requirements is probably much easier than agreement on its modernization. In the initial stage of Community lawmaking, all member states have some interest in adopting a directive because the differences between national provisions have substantial impacts on trade. This incentive no longer exists once the area has been harmonized. Legal innovations in an area already harmonized can no longer be motivated by trade policy. Instead, they must be based exclusively on environmental policy objectives as to which the economic interests and opinions of the member states concerned may greatly diverge. Even if a member state proposes to amend an existing directive on the ground that it has not achieved its objectives — which is the argument of West Germany in proposing to stiffen the automobile emission standards — other member states may have other priorities, such as protection of the industry affected or of jobs, and therefore may object to any amendment.[127] On the other hand, unilateral innovation by a single member state may no longer be possible. Under the principle of supremacy, the harmonized law is paramount to national law and Art. 36 of the EEC Treaty does not justify a violation of this principle.[128] Logic would seemingly govern

---

124. Marx, supra n. 39 at 144 et seq.

125. See Behrens, supra n. 11 at 50, 253; Marx, supra n.39 at 47-48; Schmeder, supra n.4 at 10; Vignes, in *Le Droit de la Communauté Economique Européene*, vol. 5 at 154, Art. 100 annotation 4, (1973). Contra, House of Lords, Select Committee, *22nd Report*, supra n. 11 at No. 13(4).

126. See authors cited supra n. 123.

127. Here, the description of Community environmental policy as "lowest common denominator" policy certainly has some truth to it. See Dashwood, supra n.27 at 295-296. See also Progress Report 1980, supra n. 22 Annex I, at 11; Kupfer, supra n. 43 at 63 et seq.

128. See European Court of Justice, case 148/78, Pubblico Ministero v. Ratti,

even where a directive has become obsolete because it has failed to achieve its objectives, although this case is not yet covered by the supremacy jurisprudence of the European Court of Justice. In any case, a member state proposing new national legislation inconsistent with an existing directive would find it difficult to push this initiative through its own legislative bodies. Therefore, as a practical matter, it may still have to seek the agreement of the other member states.

The problem of legal obsolescence in Community environmental law is somewhat mitigated by the establishment in most environmental directives of a special decisionmaking procedure for the adaptation of the directive to scientific progress. This procedure is established by the Council resolution of 1975 on the adaptation of environmental directives to technical progress,[129] but is often modified in particular respects in the relevant environmental directives. An environmental directive normally creates a Committee chaired by a representative of the Commission and composed of representatives of the member states. The Commission has the right of initiative. The Committee decides on the Commission's proposal by a qualified majority. If the Committee approves the proposal, it is adopted. If it rejects the proposal or no opinion is adopted, the matter must be brought before the Council, which is also to act by a qualified majority. If the Council has not acted on the proposal within three months after the proposal has been submitted to it, the measures proposed can be adopted by the Commission.

The adaptation procedure is designed to relieve the Council of the technical work involved in adjusting existing directives to technical progress. The procedure has been used to establish stricter standards when warranted by the improvement of scientific knowledge or technical progress.[130] The Commission is not allowed to use the procedure where important political or economic questions are involved.[131] In such a case, the Commission has to submit the proposal directly to the Council. However, the Council also acts on these proposals by a qualified majority rather than by unanimous vote.

[1979] ECR 1629; case 251/78, Firma Denkavit Futtermittel GmbH v. Minister, [1979] ECR 3369; Kupfer, supra n. 43 at 63 et seq.

129. Council Resolution of 15 July 1975 on the adaptation to technical progress of Directives or other Community rules on the protection and improvement of the environment, OJ No.C 168, 25 July 1975, p. 5. See Behrens, supra n.11, 60 et seq., 255-256. See generally Mathijsen, *A Guide to European Community Law* 61-62 (1980).

130. Contra, Slot, supra n. 28 at 107.

131. This would be contrary to Art. 155 of the EEC Treaty. See European Court of Justice, case 25/70, Einfuhr- und Vorratsstelle v. Köster, [1970] ECR 1161, which, in principle, recognized that the adaptation procedure is in conformity with the Treaty provided the relevant committee is given clear direction as to the contents of the measures to be adopted.

The adaptation procedure shows that the Community is aware of the danger of legal obsolescence. The requirement of a qualified majority in an area in which the Community could initially legislate only by unanimous vote lowers the institutional barrier to adjustment of existing environmental directives. The structure of the procedure reflects a sense of need for more supranationalism in areas where the initial decision to establish harmonized policies has already been made.[132] That it does not solve all problems is evidenced by the fate of the German endeavors to stiffen the emission standards for motor vehicle exhaust emissions.

It should be noted that the adaptation procedure is not applicable where a problem is not yet covered by a directive. Thus, broadening the scope of an existing directive in response to new scientific or technical knowledge requires action similar to that for adoption of the original directive. In such cases, however, threatened unilateral action by a member state will exert leverage on the Community.[133] The Community may be compelled to broaden the scope of the directive or issue a new directive; otherwise, the member state can go forward with its national initiative. However, the jurisprudence of the European Court of Justice in *Cassis de Dijon* and in the line of cases following this decision[134] may impose some constraints on member state ability unilaterally to adjust national regulation of products to scientific progress.

IV. CONCLUSION: EXPLAINING AND EVALUATING INTEGRATION OF COMMUNITY ENVIRONMENTAL POLICY

A. *The Complexity of Integration Processes in Federal Systems*

In Part I, we presented a model of regulation in a federal system and generated a number of hypotheses. The history examined in Parts II and III broadly supports these hypotheses, but also shows that the model's assumptions are crude and that important qualifications are required in order to take into account the actual complexities that determine the pace and products of integration.

1. *The Incentives for Integration.* In the EC (as in the US) centralized product regulation is more pervasive and intrusive than process regulation, which in turn is more fully established than regulation

---

132. In the same sense see Slot, supra n. 28 at 107.

133. Dashwood, supra n. 27 at 295-296.

134. See European Court of Justice, case 120/78, Rewe-Zentrale AG v. Bundesmonopolverwaltung für Branntwein (*Cassis de Dijon*), [1979] ECR 649 and the authors cited at n. 3.

of land use and natural resources.[135] As predicted, the degree of centralization in product regulation is comparable, in the two systems (ignoring the lack of direct Community enforcement power), whereas process regulation is substantially more centralized and intrusive in the US than in the EC. Preclusion of more stringent state measures is not uncommon for product regulation, but is quite rare for process regulation.

The model's biggest defect is its failure to predict the patchy but substantial amount of process regulation in the EC. The model predicted that no such regulation would occur in a system requiring unanimous consent of member states, because those states with relatively low process standards (polluter states) would find it against their economic self-interest to agree to higher Community standards. At best, Community standards would be set at the lowest common denominator level of standards in the laxest polluter state and would consist of minimum harmonization.

This variance between prediction and experience is due to the fact that the actual decisionmaking process in the EC is more complex than a model of economically calculating unitary actors allows. Environmental ministers and officials play a substantial role in representing member states in Community decisionmaking, and are likely to emphasize environmental goals even if they conflict with strictly economic calculations. Unless the matter becomes one of "high politics,"[136] their influence may be substantial. Even political leaders of "polluter" states may personally believe that more vigorous environmental policies are socially desirable in the long term, and may therefore acquiesce in Community initiatives. The lack of direct domestic political accountability for Community decisions enlarges their freedom of action in this respect. In addition, the leading role of the Commission's Environmental Directorate-General in formulating and shepherding proposed environmental directives through the policy process can not be ignored. Perhaps most important are the complex norms of reciprocity and consensus that appear to characterize relations among member states in the decisional process. These norms and associated practices may often lead a member state to acquiesce in a proposal that it would not otherwise affirmatively embrace.

On the other hand, the implementation gap that exists in the EC may mean that agreement upon process regulation directives may be more apparent than real. To some degree, polluter states

135. The generalization excludes the special US situation of federal management of the lands and natural resources owned by the federal government.
136. Hoffmann, *Gulliver's Troubles or the Setting of American Foreign Policy* (1969) [cited following the German translation: *Die Zukunft des Internationalen Systems* 376 et seq. (1970)].

may acquiesce in environmental initiatives, giving ritual due to norms of reciprocity and consensus while foreseeing that implementation shortfalls will enable them to follow something like a lowest common denominator approach with relatively minor adverse domestic economic impact.

The evidence in other respects also shows a more complex pattern of motivation and interaction than the model allows. Rivalry among "polluter" and "environmental" states is an important political reality, as the controversy over toxic water pollutants in the EC illustrates. But the distinction between "polluter" and "environmental" states is ambiguous. Consider, for example, West Germany and Ireland. Which is the "polluter" state and which the "environmental" state? As regards importing states, there is some evidence to support the hypothesis that such states, unconstrained by effects on industrial development and employment, will seek to impose strong product regulations in order to protect their consumers. The controls imposed by Denmark on chemicals are an example. On the other hand, in the case of automobiles there is no evidence that importing states such as Ireland or Greece are eager to impose additional controls. This circumstance probably reflects relatively low concern for environmental values and a greater concern for cost effects on consumers in such states.

Perhaps all that can be said in general is that economic differences and rivalries among states are important factors in the evolution of environmental regulation in a federal system, and that their general tendency is to shape regulation in the pattern predicted by our model. But actual outcomes are strongly affected by other factors that were left out of the simplified model and examined in Part III. It does not appear feasible at this point to develop a more complex model that would take these additional factors into account and still yield empirically testable hypotheses with strong predictive and explanatory power.

The integration theories developed by political scientists fail to provide much help in this task. Judged by the experience with environmental regulation, they fail to provide convincing insight into the process of regulation in federal systems, in particular in the European Community.

The neofunctionalist integration theories claim that the increasing entanglement of nation states in a network of international dependencies and institutions impairs their capability to act independently. They also claim that these entanglements — at least under certain further conditions and not necessarily in a continuous process — create a need for further cooperation and, ultimately, for

428   THE AMERICAN JOURNAL OF COMPARATIVE LAW   [Vol. **33**

supranational institutions and supranational decisionmaking.[137] In this perspective, the growth of integration is explained as an endogenous ("spillover") effect of previous steps of integration.

The critics of neofunctionalist theories maintain that the political independence of nation states is unbroken and that international systems such as the Community exercise only a loose coordination function. Integration is, in their view, confined to peripheral policy areas. Areas of "high politics", i.e. those policy areas which are considered by central policymakers as vital to the maintenance and adaptation of the national political system, to the allegiance of its citizens, and to its visibility to other nations, remain in the domain of the nation state.[138]

It has been argued that the Community's development as a whole provides examples to support both theories,[139] and that this is also true of Community environmental policy.[140] From the perspective of the neofunctionalist integration theories, the development of a Community environmental policy could be interpreted as a product of the interrelation between already existing economic integration and the emergence of a new problem closely related to the economy. Since environmental problems arise to a large degree as a side effect of economic activities — if understood in the broad sense of including consumption activities — the existing economic integration required a concomitant integration of environmental policy in order to avoid the establishment of new barriers to trade or new distortions of competition. However, the fact that Community environmental policy, through an incremental process of extending the scope and objectives of directives, has been largely emancipated from constraints of trade and competition policy and has developed as a separate policy in its own right indicates that environmental policies are not simply a function of preexisting integration. They themselves represent a new form of integration, which can not be

---

137. See Haas, *The Uniting of Europe* 291 et seq. (1958); id., "The Study of Regional Integration: Reflections on the Joy and Anguish of Pretheorizing," 24 *Int'l. Org.* 607 (Autumn 1970) (special issue on "Regional Integration: Theory and Research," Lindberg & Scheingold, eds.); Lindberg, *The Political Dynamics of European Economic Integration* (1963); Lindberg & Scheingold, *Europe's Would-Be Polity: Pattern of Change in the European Community* 117 et seq., 141 et seq. (1970); Schmitter, "Three Neofunctional Hypotheses about International Integration," 23 *Int'l. Org.* 161 (1969); id., "A Revised Theory of Regional Integration," 24 *Int'l. Org.* 836 et seq. (1970); Nye, *Comparing Integration Processes* (1969); Etzioni, *Political Unification* 102 (1965).

138. Hoffman, supra n.136; Zellentin, *Intersystemare Beziehungen in Europa* 183 et seq. (1970); Galtung, *The European Community: A Superpower in the Making* (1972).

139. Häckel, "Theoretische Aspekte der Regionalen Verflechtung," in *Regionale Verflechtung der Bundesrepublik Deutschland, Schriften des Forschungsinstituts der Deutschen Gesellschaft für Politik,*" vol. 33 at 15 et seq. (1973).

140. Bungarten, supra n. 10 at 157 et seq.

fully explained by the economic logic of previous integrative steps. Accordingly, neofunctionalist theories, at least in their present form, can not adequately explain the history of Community integration in the environmental area.

Arguing from the perspective of the critics of the neofunctionalist theories and using the distinction between high and low politics, environmental policymaking would normally belong to low rather than high politics. While complete transfer of powers for environmental policymaking from member states to the Community would be considered a severe encroachment on the central policy functions of the national policy system, the transfer of more or less isolated, narrowly defined powers in the field of the environment does not normally meet with much objection, although it is associated with some loss of democratic legitimacy. It is only in rare cases that environmental issues become so highly politicized that supranational decisionmaking, even in the attenuated form practiced within the Community, is not accepted by one or more member states. This politicization may reflect the reservation of a functionally related policy area to national decisionmaking (such as energy policy), a strong sense for the preservation of national sovereignty (such as in the case of transboundary pollution or accidents), or day to day politics (a single issue becoming so controversial that a transfer of decisionmaking competences is unacceptable).[141]

The siting of nuclear power plants and major chemical plants in border areas and the salinity of the Rhine are or were such politicized issues. It is not surprising that these issues have seriously impeded further progress of the integration process in environmental policy. However, these issues are not typical of Community environmental policy and, with the exception of siting nuclear power plants, agreement on them has ultimately been reached.

Moreover, the distinction between high and low politics appears to have little predictive or analytical value. Environmental policy is intimately related to competition, distribution, economic, and labor market policies. Its character as a positive rather than negative intervention[142] moves it into the center of political and societal controversies over fundamental issues of economic and social policy in many member states.[143] Issues such as SO_2 control, toxic water pollution, and automobile emissions are of great economic and political

---

141. Von der Groeben & Möller, supra n. 87 at 392-393.

142. Von der Groeben & Möller, supra n. 87 at 383-384, 391; Bungarten, supra n. 10 at 224; Krämer & Rummel, "Hindernisse und Voraussetzungen für die Europäische Union," 1976 *Aus Politik und Zeitgeschichte* (Supplement B3 to Das Parlament) at 10 et seq.

143. See the authors cited supra n. 141.

significance. But this has not precluded agreement within the Community.

There is a tendency to retrospectively label issues on which Community agreement is not reached as "high politics", and label issues on which there is agreement as "low politics". This approach, of course, robs the distinction of all explanatory power.

2. *Specific Characteristics of Environmental Problems.* The model developed in Part I also neglects certain specific characteristics of environmental problems that have an important impact on the ways in which integration of regulatory law occurs in federal systems such as the EC and the US.

The nature of environmental problems is such as to make court litigation, whether privately or publicly initiated, relatively ineffective and inappropriate as a "front line" response. The limited capacities of courts in dealing with technical issues, the expense of litigation and the fact that environmental quality is a collective good, and the need for ongoing coordination and supervision all dictate that environmental problems must largely be addressed through administrative systems of regulation or resource management. Thus, measures to harmonize private or public tort or nuisance law, and so on have little to contribute to effective integration of environmental policy.

In addition, the type of environmental problem to be controlled, to a large extent, determines the type of regulatory approach that must be employed.

Where products, such as automobiles, are sold in integrated markets, uniform regulation is most feasible, and manufacturers have substantial incentives to favor such regulation. Where the environmental significance of a product, such as automobile air pollution, can be expressed in consistent, quantitative terms (such as emissions per mile of operation), uniform standards are feasible. Where consistent, quantitative measures of environmental significance are not feasible, e.g. hazardous chemicals, case by case screening of products will be necessary, but such screening can be performed centrally for all products.

Uniform regulation is less feasible for industrial processes. Uniform technology-based controls may be economically inappropriate in light of varying natural conditions because they require excessive controls in relation to environmental benefits in some areas, e.g. ocean outfalls, and inadequate controls in others. Uniform environmental standards may be inappropriate because of wide regional variations in the cost of achieving such standards, the desirability of maintaining some areas of exceptionally high environmental quality, and fear of "competitive distortions". On the other hand, it is very difficult to reach agreement on a system of non-uniform environmental quality standards. Some combination of the two approaches is often preferable to either alone.

Uniform measures are least feasible in natural resource management (including land use planning, and protection of wilderness and wildlife) and where it is necessary to regulate the activities of large numbers of individuals. Such regulation involves government functions that are strongly localized in response to variations in local conditions and traditions. Centralized or integrated uniform regulation would involve substantial diseconomies of scale.

3 *The Importance of Institutional and Historical Context.* The only institutional difference between the EC and US recognized in the model developed in Chapter I is that legislation in the Community requires unanimous consent (a premise which, as we have seen, requires qualification), whereas the US employs a form of majority rule. While this difference has been important, experience shows that there are additional basic differences in institutional and historical contexts in the Community and the US which have powerfully shaped the evolution of environmental policy in the two systems.

Federal environmental policies in the US arose after far-reaching economic and political integration had already occurred.[144] Economic integration made central product regulation efficient, and created a demand by environmental states and some industries for central regulation in order to prevent economic rivalry, "competitive distortions", and weak state standards as a result of state by state regulation. Political integration provided the foundation for federal implementation and enforcement of environmental policies through federal administrative agencies and courts. The federal lawmaking structure, which includes a nationally elected President, direct representation in Congress, an expansive legislative authority over commerce, a fully developed federal court system, and a federal bureaucracy with direct enforcement powers, has facilitated centralization of environmental policy in the US. (The principle of state representation in Congress and functional constraints on implementation and enforcement by central authorities have, however, limited centralization.) Because far-reaching economic and political integration had already occurred by the time environmental issues became important, the dominant motivation of federal environmental initiatives has been to correct weak, inadequate state regulation resulting

---

144. For the following section see generally Slot, supra n. 28 at 153; Roth, *Freier Warenverkehr und Staatliche Regelungsgewalt in Einem Gemeinsamen Markt* 337 (1977).

from economic rivalry and inability to realize scale economies rather than to remove barriers to trade or promote integration.

Environmental policy in the US is more extensive than in the EC because the US federal government enjoys important resources and powers which the EC lacks. These include the federal government's ownership of one third of the nation's land and an even larger share of its important natural resources; its formidable taxing and spending powers; and its licensing authority over major industrial facilities. EC authorities do not exercise comparable powers.

In the EC, the development and implementation of a common environmental policy has been constrained by the Community's origin as an economic institution, the differences in language and culture among member states, the politically insecure and limited definition of the Community's legislative powers, the lawmaking structure dominated by the Council and representatives of member states rather than the European interest, the lack of a fully developed Community court system, and the lack of a bureaucracy with direct implementation and enforcement authority. The development of common environmental policy is also constrained by the stagnation and even decline of integration in other areas, and especially by the decline of decisional supranationalism.[145] On the other hand, environmental policy is itself a factor of "substantive integration," influencing the direction and strength of the integration process. It has given European integration a new impulse,[146] although simple expansion of Community policy into a new area such as environmental protection does not fully compensate for the lack of overall substantive and institutional deepening of integration.[147]

These differences between the US and the EC may influence their respective capacities to generate particular types of policy issues. Consider, for example, the issue of environmental diversity. From the viewpoint of aesthetic and cultural values, it may be desirable to balance environmental and economic goals by ensuring exceptionally high environmental quality in pristine or scenic areas and accepting lower quality in other areas. In other instances (for example, when protection of public health is the dominant concern) it may be appropriate to have a uniform level of environmental quality, which implies sharply different levels of source control in different regions, depending on natural factors and the existing degree of economic development. But integration is viewed by many in the EC as synonymous with uniformity in control requirements in

---

145. Contra, Kaiser, supra n. 11 at 97 et seq. (in this connection speaking of expansion and restriction of integration).

146. Bungarten, supra n. 10 at 175.

147. Cf. Kaiser, supra n. 145.

order to eliminate barriers to trade and "competitive distortions". Accordingly, the US may be able to tolerate and achieve greater diversity in environmental standards and controls than the EC because its environmental policy is not linked with the process of political and economic integration.[148]

Due to the enormous differences in language, culture, and attitudes, there may be a greater need for harmonization in Europe.[149] However, harmonization measures tend to be centralist in character, such as the expansion of the "negative commerce clause" doctrine following the *Cassis de Dijon* decision. This tendency may reflect the lack of a federal tradition in most member states. Since the majority of member states are highly centralized, it may well be that Community policymakers coming from these states simply transpose centralist policy concepts to the higher unity and disregard the great potential for diversity existing in developed federal systems for shaping the division of powers between the Community and its member states.[150]

B. The Extent and Role of Community Environmental Law in European Integration

1. *The Degree of Integration Achieved by EC Environmental Policy.* The European Community's environmental policy has been more successful than one would have expected at its beginning in 1973. Since adoption of the first environmental program, the network of Community environmental law has steadily expanded. No fewer than forty-five directives or amendments have been adopted, and about thirty other regulatory texts, including recommendations, resolutions and decisions, have been issued. Many of the directives adopted by the Council, and in some cases by the Commission, cover a very narrow field of environmental protection or are of a technical nature. However, the Community has also adopted a number of quite important directives, e.g. the 1973 amendment to the motor vehicle emissions directive, the framework directive of 1976 on the aquatic environment, the sixth amendment of 1979 to the hazardous substances directive, the SO_2 limit values directive of 1980, the major accidents directive of 1982, the major industrial installations directive of 1984 and the environmental impact assessment directive of 1975.

It is remarkable that the original preoccupation of Community environmental policy with the elimination of barriers to trade and

---

148. Roth, supra n. 144 at 339.
149. Slot, "Handelsbarrières, Nationalrecht en Europeesrecht," 28 *Sociaal-Economische Wetgeving* 233, 262 (1980).
150. This is the interpretation by Slot, supra n. 144 at 261, of *Cassis de Dijon*.

hence with product related requirements has largely been replaced by the development of environmental policy in its own right. The most important reason for addressing environmental problems in a common or harmonized fashion is no longer that differing national regulations compromise the Community policy of eliminating technical obstacles to trade; rather, it is the interest of member states in an environmental problem as such (although this interest is not necessarily directed at the environmentally most serious problems). This does not mean that economic considerations such as the elimination of technical barriers to trade or distortions of competition have become irrelevant. They are an important factor limiting the scope and direction of Community activities. They also determine the acceptance of a proposal by member states, the length of a particular decisionmaking process, and the willingness of member states to implement the directive.

Within these limits, it is now accepted throughout the Community that there is a need for public intervention to protect the environment and that for a number of environmental problems the Community is the most appropriate decisionmaking level. There is no fundamental divergence of opinion as to the basic strategies to be employed in controlling pollution. There is common agreement on the use of regulatory controls rather than litigation or the extensive use of charges or other economic incentives. Furthermore, critics, such as some industrial associations, of particular measures are convinced of the general need for Community environmental policy.[151]

In important respects, however, environmental policy has fallen well short of complete integration. First, the coverage of Community measures is incomplete. Regulation of new products is relatively comprehensive, but major gaps exist in the regulation of existing products. Apart from a framework directive on wastes, which covers the whole area of wastes but whose obligations are rather vague, no single environmental sector is comprehensively regulated by the Community. Substantial steps have been taken to deal with water pollution and toxic substances, but the equally important field of air pollution has been neglected. The pragmatic, piecemeal procedure of the Commission for proposing new legislation has resulted in directives in areas where harmonization is a low priority, while neglecting other areas which need a considerable amount of harmonization. Some water quality measures, especially the bathing, fish, and shellfish water directives, were not really mandated by urgent needs for a harmonized solution, whereas too little work has been done in other areas, especially air pollution.

Second, there is a considerable political and regulatory imple-

---

151. Cf. von Moltke & Haigh, supra n. 17.

mentation gap in Community environmental policy. The deadlines set for compliance in the environmental programs and the deadlines in framework directives for the adoption of new policy proposals have proven totally unrealistic. As a result, the third environmental program to a great extent represents the continuation of work already begun or envisaged by the previous environmental programs.

In 1980, the Commission issued a comprehensive and remarkably frank document on the present state of work on environmental affairs.[152] In this report the Commission admitted that it was much more successful in controlling water pollution than air pollution. It stressed the principle of prevention and defined a number of tools for implementing a preventive policy. The Commission made it clear that, apart from the pre-market testing of new chemicals, the preventive policy was still in its incipiency. It is characteristic of the low degree of public attention given to the development of Community environmental policy that this document received little notice.[153]

Third, with the exception of some directives such as the sixth amendment of the toxic substances directive and the PCB directive, Community environmental policy tends to follow protection levels and strategies already existing in several member states and does not generate innovative approaches for implementing harmonized policy objectives. On the other hand, the common assertion that Community environmental policy is confined to lowest common denominator solutions is not entirely justified. Various techniques that permit compromises in the harmonization effort allow environmental states to retain progressive solutions, while polluter states may have to stiffen their environmental controls, but not necessarily to the degree existing in environmental states.

However, serious problems of rigidity and obsolescence may arise after the Community has issued a directive in a given area. In the absence of a preexisting directive, polluter states have an incentive to agree to harmonized initiatives for product regulation in order to preclude enforcement by environmental states of stiff standards to exclude imports from polluter states. Once a directive is adopted, however, environmental states are barred from unilateral introduction of stiffer controls. Accordingly, polluter states

---

152. Progress Report 1980, supra n. 22.

153. Besides the European Parliament, which has passed a resolution on the progress report (Resolution of 20 Nov. 1981 on the state of the Community's environment, OJ No.C 327, 14 Dec. 1981, p. 83; EP-Doc. 1-276/81), only the subcommittee on environmental affairs of the British House of Lords' Select Committee on the European Community has conducted a general inquiry to evaluate the state of Community environmental policy and contribute to the formulation of a national position on its future direction. See von Moltke & Haigh, supra n. 17 at 27.

have no economic incentive to agree to modernization of the relevant directive, and only when there are paramount environmental reasons are they likely to agree to an amendment. The short-cut procedure for adapting of existing environmental directives to technical progress does not effectively compensate this structural problem.

Fourth, the linkage of environmental policy with other areas of Community policy has as yet been relatively weak.[154] The report of 1980 on the progress made in implementing the environmental program and the third environmental program now identify this as a priority area.[155] The enormous task of ensuring consistency between agricultural and environmental policy, which has proven difficult even at the national level, is still in its incipiency in the Community.[156] There is also little integration between environmental policy and transport policy. The Commission's green paper on transport infrastructure[157] mentions environmental concerns in its programmatic part but ignores the subject entirely when it comes to concrete measures. In both policy areas the Commission's Directorate-General on Environment, Consumer Protection, and Nuclear Safety suffers the further handicap that there is no explicit authority in the Treaties to compel other Directorates-General to consider environmental effects.[158] It is remarkable that the recent directive on environmental impact assessment for national projects does not provide an equivalent procedure for assessing the environmental effects of Community projects and programs. It remains to be seen whether, once the directive is adopted, it will lead to pressure on the Commission to assess the environmental effects of its own programs,[159] at least in areas where Community legislation mandates consideration of environmental effects, such as under the bird directive and the directive on farming in mountainous and other less favored areas.

Finally, Community environmental policy has failed to achieve full integration because of national differences in the effectiveness of implementation of environmental directives and because of the lack of effective Community control over such national implementation.

---

154. See von Moltke & Haigh, supra n. 17 at 29; Institute for European Environmental Policy, *Annual Report 1982*, at 5 et seq. (1983); Kromarek, "New Trends in Community Environmental Policy," *European Parliament*, PE 74.086/Ann. I p. 14 et seq. (1981).

155. Progress Report 1980, supra n. 22 at 8; Third environmental program, OJ No.C 46, 17 Feb. 1983, p. 1.

156. Within the purely national context, a major difficulty stems from the fact that agriculture is the responsibility of a separate, "mission-oriented" administration, and the environmental administration normally has at best a right of consultation.

157. DOC COM(79)550.

158. Von Moltke & Haigh, supra n. 17 at 29.

159. In this sense see id.

An additional disincentive for harmonization may be the European Court of Justice's intervention in national regulation through enforcement of "negative commerce clause" principles. Theoretically, extension of the approach taken in the *Cassis de Dijon* decision[160] could promote integration of environmental product regulation because free access of products from polluter states to the markets of environmental states gives environmental states a strong incentive to urge harmonized solutions. But the *Cassis de Dijon* approach simultaneously removes the incentive of polluter states to agree to such solutions. The political experience of the Community shows that progressive national solutions often set the pace for the Community solution. National diversity can accordingly be a force for integration. Compelling negative uniformity by dismantling national controls may therefore have a counter-productive effect with regard to environmental protection.[161] In evaluating the potential impact of *Cassis de Dijon*, however, it must be considered that the Community had already reached a high degree of harmonization for products before that decision was issued. As a practical matter, therefore, the impact of *Cassis de Dijon* will be limited to existing chemicals, the one area where Community regulation is still rather patchy, and even then member states may be able to justify restrictive national policies on health and safety grounds.

2. *Environmental Policy and Substantive Approfondissement.*[162] The expansion of the Community into environmental protection represents development of a kind of common policy not provided for by the Treaty. Although Community environmental policy can arguably be based on a "dynamic" interpretation of the Preamble and Articles 2, 100, and 235 of the EEC Treaty, it is clear that the framers of the Treaty had a rather narrow vision of a common market as a primarily economic institution and never anticipated that the Community could become involved in environmental protection as such. The Community's initial decision to expand its activities into environmental protection therefore has a constitutional character.

The further development of Community environmental policy following adoption of the first environmental program shows that,

---

160. European Court of Justice, case 120/78 (20 Feb. 1979), Rewe-Zentrale AG v. Bundesmonopolverwaltung für Branntwein *(Cassis de Dijon)*, [1979] ECR 649.

161. In this sense see von Moltke, supra n. 42 at 82 et seq.; Weidner & Knoepfel, supra n. 17 at 64. Roth, supra n.144 at 327 also objects to complete elimination of technical barriers to trade because of the loss of innovative capacity.

162. *Approfondissement* is the French word for deepening. The expression "substantive *approfondissement*" is used by Weiler, "Supranationalism Revisited—Retrospective and Prospective," EUI Working Papers No. 2, at 27, to refer to expansion of Community activity into new areas and to the expansion of supranational decisionmaking.

despite divergences of opinion as to the exact scope of Community powers, there has been no serious challenge to the new common policy. Of course, as compared with agriculture, the degree of Europeanization of environmental policy is still relatively low. Using the scale of one to seven developed by Lindberg and Scheingold to measure the degree of substantive Europeanization of a policy,[163] before adoption of the first environmental program Community environmental policy could be rated at two, meaning the very beginning of Community involvement. At present a three rating would seem appropriate: there is substantial Community involvement, but national regulation still clearly dominates. On the other hand, more progress has been made in environmental policy than in other areas where the Community has a clear Treaty mandate to act, such as transportation or the free movement of capital, or where the Community has for many years been attempting to develop or implement a common policy, such as monetary union, regional policy, and consumer policy.

On the whole, the development of common environmental policy has become an important contribution to the overall integration process.[164] This contribution is mainly one of substantive *approfondissement*. The expansion of the Community into a new policy area not covered by the Treaty and the continuous growth of Community environmental law have given new impulses to the integration process. Development of the Community environmental policy does not fully compensate for the stagnation or even decline in older policy areas for which a clear Treaty mandate exists. However, it evidences the vitality of the Community as a forum for addressing novel problems for which common solutions are needed.

The contribution of Community environmental policy towards strengthening Community institutions and decisional supranationalism is less. Although in the field of environmental policy the Commission has retained much of its original function of initiating new policy proposals, the overall decline of decisional supranationalism and the return to intergovernmental decisionmaking have also left their marks on environmental policymaking. As elsewhere, the Council, as representative of member state interests, is the Community's central decisionmaking body. It offers a forum for member state bureaucracies and also indirectly for some interest groups to

---

163. Lindberg, & Scheingold, supra n. 137 at 71.
164. Bungarten, supra n. 10 at 175; von Moltke & Haigh, supra n. 17 at 23. The statement by von der Groeben & Möller, supra n.87 at 384, that Community environmental policy did not contribute to growth of the system is obviously untenable if one defines, as the authors do (at 345), this notion to encompass both institutional growth and extension of the scope of the Community.

bargain over a particular proposal in order to adjust it to national interests.

It has been suggested that the high degree of legal integration achieved by the jurisprudence of the European Court of Justice through the principles of direct effect, supremacy, and preemption may have dysfunctional effects on decisional supranationalism.[165] Experience with environmental policy does not support this hypothesis. The growing role of the member states in Community decision-making is reflected in the Council, the Committee of Permanent Representatives, and joint Commission/member state committees such as the waste management committee and the various committees for adjusting directives to technical progress. But this development is not primarily a response to the form of directives' legal effect (direct effect/supremacy or simple state obligation). It is rather a response to the economic and political importance and complexity of the substantive policies and strategies at issue. It is not so much legal integration, but rather the substantive integration of highly complex interventionist policies, such as environmental policy, that has brought with it a diminution of decisional supranationalism.[166]

The increasing specificity of many environmental directives has also stimulated a greater national role. To the extent that the margin of discretion normally granted member states in implementing a directive is shrinking towards zero, member states have a vital interest in influencing relevant policy proposals as early as possible. This factor may also explain the dislike of the British House of Lords for Community environmental law.

C. Assessment of Community Institutions and Environmental Policy

1. *Contributions to Environmental Goals.* The establishment of Community environmental policy as a kind of common policy is in itself an important contribution to the European integration process at a time when the Community has experienced a considerable decline in decisional supranationalism and stagnation in securing other common policies. Nevertheless, the contribution of the common environmental policy to European integration must also be evaluated in light of its substantive contribution to environmental protection. Whatever the intrinsic value of integration in its present inchoate state, the price paid for European integration may be too high if it is associated with unsatisfactory substantive solutions.

The tendency of Community environmental policy toward con-

---

165. In this sense see the suggestion of Weiler, supra n. 159 at 44-45.
166. In the same sense see id. at 43.

servative solutions can not be ignored. Another serious problem, at least with respect to product regulation, is the lack of incentives for amending a directive to deal with obsolescence. But the contributions of Community policy to environmental goals are often substantial. The tendency is not to create entirely new solutions, but rather to generalize existing national solutions by expanding their application from one or several to all member states. But this process produces progress in polluter states of a kind that either they would never have achieved by acting independently or would not have achieved as quickly. At the same time, environmental states do not normally sacrifice their solutions to European integration. This approach establishes a moderately progressive Community "floor" while permitting member states with strong environmental preferences, special problems, or innovative solutions to go further.

However, this strategy of minimum harmonization has its limitations. The first environmental program states that environmental progress at the national level must be realized in a form which does not compromise the functioning of the Common Market. Stricter national law for products is inconsistent with this principle. Although sometimes allowed, as in the lead directive, it is contrary to the traditional idea of harmonization underlying Art. 100 of the EEC Treaty. In the case of process requirements, stricter national law does not so clearly endanger the functioning of the Common Market, but the freedom of member states to go beyond Community minimums may be sharply constrained by competitive economic factors. Nonetheless, Community environmental policy has meant at least relative progress in addressing environmental problems.

Since each member state can be a "polluter" or an "environmental" state with respect to a particular environmental problem, involvement in the process of Community environmental policymaking means a continuous cross fertilization of European policymakers with progressive national solutions. Furthermore, Community environmental policy is also a learning process in that solutions either rejected or not seriously considered by a particular member state may cause it to rethink its position when the same solutions are proposed as part of a future directive or an amendment to an existing directive. This process of reconsideration is more pointed when a Community directive uses the alternative harmonization technique because a member state is continually confronted with the experience of other member states under an alternative available strategy, especially under directives that call for a periodic review of the Community and the alternative solutions. In view of these opportunities for mutual learning, the fact that Community environmental policy has not provided novel solutions and often lags behind the expectations of environmental interest groups should not be overemphasized.

Further development of Community environmental policy is desirable. This is especially true for problems which member states, acting individually, cannot hope to adequately address, e.g. acid rain, ozone transport, fluorocarbons, carbon dioxide, migratory species, and toxic substances. For some of these problems even the Community is in some respects too small a decisionmaking unit. Further integration is also appropriate in many other areas of industrial process regulation. Harmonized solutions for industrial process regulation would not only remove considerable distortions of competition within the common market but would also afford polluter states the opportunity and incentive to introduce progressive solutions that they can not realistically be expected to introduce independently.

2. *Institutional Issues.* Community environmental policy suffers from the same institutional deficiencies that characterize the Community political process as a whole. The non-public process of Community decisionmaking is dominated by member state ministers and bureaucrats. Outside access to this process is generally limited to well organized industry interests. This process is deficient in political legitimacy, and fails to generate a European constituency of broad public support for the initiatives that are adopted. To the extent that they attract attention, Community initiatives may be regarded as a circumvention of established democratic decisionmaking procedures in member states. In addition, the "filter" effect of Community decisionmaking processes and the requirement of unanimity hinder the adoption of effective, progressive Community environmental initiatives. Even if such initiatives are adopted, there is little Commission authority or Community law that ensures their effective implementation once they have been incorporated into national law.

By contrast, federal initiatives in the United States must be adopted through the normal processes of representative democracy. Administrative implementation is subject to procedural rules designed to ensure access by environmental and community groups, as well as by industry. Implementation gaps, while persistent, are addressed through administrative monitoring of performance and judicial remedies.

Most of the institutional problems of Community environmental policy are, however, a reflection of historical and political factors that are unlikely to change substantially in the foreseeable future. Therefore, it is highly unrealistic to propose changes in the system focusing solely on environmental policy. This is true of proposals to

442　　　THE AMERICAN JOURNAL OF COMPARATIVE LAW　　　[Vol. 33

grant the European Parliament legislative powers for environmental matters.[167] It would also be unrealistic to expect the member states to agree to an amendment of Articles 100 and 235 of the EEC Treaty substituting majority rule for unanimity in environmental matters.

This does not imply that marginal changes addressed to specific problems of environmental policymaking do not merit attention. For example, the lengthy and cumbersome process for implementing framework directives, such as standard setting under the surface water directive, could be ameliorated by introducing an abbreviated procedure based on the regulatory agency model. Under this approach, which is already followed in adapting environmental directives to technical progress, the Commission, a Council working committee, or a joint body would give detailed content to framework directives. If the framework directive fixes clear general standards, the requirements of Art. 155(4) of the EEC Treaty are arguably met.[168] It is doubtful, however, whether member states would agree to such a waiver of their powers.[169] As a matter of policy, an abbreviated procedure may also be questioned as a further depoliticization of Community decisionmaking.

Another potential marginal change would be to improve the procedure established by the information/standstill agreement of 1973 for the coordination of member state and Community environmental initiatives. This procedure does not function well because the deadlines set by the agreement are too short to allow the Community to prepare legislative proposals. It has been proposed that member states be obliged to report drafts which are still in a preparatory stage so as to afford the Commission more time for formulating its own position on the draft.[170] However, this proposal ignores the realities of national political processes. National parliaments can not be barred from changing tabled legislative drafts.[171] Also, given the slow pace of Community decisionmaking, any extension of the deadline for Community reaction to a national legislative initiative

---

167. But see Faure, *Pour une Politique Européene de l'Environnement* (1977); Behrens, *Rechtsgrundlagen der Umweltpolitik der Europäischen Gemeinschaften* 298 et seq. (1976); Steiger, *Competence of the European Parliament for Environmental Policy* (1977). See also von Moltke, supra n.11 at 138.

168. See Behrens, supra n. 11 at 62; Slot, supra n. 128 at 162; Economic and Social Council, OJ No.C 131, 13 Dec. 1972, p. 29, 30 (Oct. 1972); European Parliament Resolution of 16 Oct. 1981, OJ No.C 287, 9 Sept. 1981, p. 137.

169. For example, it is not realistic to expect member states to leave the task of setting effluent and water quality standards under the framework directive on the aquatic environment to a management committee. This is because the fundamental disagreement over effluent and water quality standards has not been overcome by letting the two strategies coexist see text at 411-12 but, rather, continues to dominate the ongoing bargaining over particular standards.

170. In this sense see Rat von Sachverständigen für Umweltfragen, *Umweltgutachten* No. 1663 (1978).

171. Von Moltke, supra n. 42 at 86.

will undermine the ability of member states to implement innovative environmental policies. All in all, this is probably too high a price to pay for the "intrinsic value" of integration. The marked reluctance of member states in the recent past to report drafts shows that they are not prepared to pay this price.

Procedures to mandate assessment of the environmental impacts of policy proposals made by the "mission oriented" Directorates-General of the Commission in fields such as agriculture and transport[172] could improve Community policymaking by integrating the preventive approach to environmental policy with sectoral economic policies, although the experience in the US under NEPA suggests that the effective degree of integration likely to result would be modest. A necessary requirement for making such an impact assessment effective would be to institutionalize an internal review procedure whereby the Directorate-General for Environment, Consumer Protection, and Nuclear Safety would comment on program proposals made by the other Commission Directorates-General.

Several steps might be taken to ensure better implementation and enforcement. The US Council on Environmental Quality has in the past played a very useful educational and catalytic role in promoting federal environmental initiatives by collecting and disseminating information on the implementation of existing measures and identifying priority areas where new or strengthened measures were needed. Establishment of an EC institution with this responsibility, perhaps as an independent arm of the Commission or Parliament, or by giving the responsibility to a private institute, should be explored.[173] In addition, new law could be created to guarantee environmental and neighborhood groups procedural rights to obtain judicial review of administrative decisions in member states implementing, or failing to implement, Community directives.[174]

3. *The Future Prospect.* During the debate in 1980 on the West

---

172. As has been proposed by the European Parliament Resolution of 18 Feb. 1982, OJ No.C 66, 15 March 1982, p. 87.

173. In the same sense see von Moltke & Haigh, supra n. 17 at 30.

174. It is not very probable that the European Court of Justice will create a Community remedial law allowing litigants, especially environmental organizations, to challenge deficient implementation and enforcement by member states of Community directives. The Court has on various occasions held that judicial review is, in the Community's present state of development, essentially within the responsibility of the member states; see, e.g., case 33/76, Rewe v. Landwirtschaftskammer, [1976] ECR 1989; case 45/76, Comet v. Produktschap voor Siergewassen, [1976] ECR 2043. It would probably be more realistic to create a body of Community administrative law by using the normal harmonization procedure of a directive. The public participation provision contained in the recent directive on environmental impact assessment, however unsatisfactory it may be, is a first step in the direction of creating transnational private rights for controlling the implementation and enforcement of environmental directives.

German toxic substances bill, the government sought to claim political credit for several provisions in a proposed regulation on chemicals without making it clear that it was merely incorporating the sixth amendment of the EC directive on toxic substances into national law. Opponents of the bill called for stiffer controls, which in some respects were clearly inconsistent with the directive, and in other respects were arguably preempted because the directive might be considered to have occupied the field of chemicals regulation.[175] Nothing could show more clearly that Community environmental policy has no true constituency among, and no symbolic value for, the peoples of Europe. This represents a sharp contrast with the US, where national environmental issues often generate strong views among citizens; this phenomenon ultimately reflects a sense of nationhood in that all share a common destiny and choice.

The formulation of the European interest that justifies shifting a regulatory problem from the national to the supranational level is based on utilitarian considerations rather than on any idealistic commitment to an "intrinsic value" of integration. It is only when member state governments and societal groups influencing their decisions consider the Community as the better decisionmaking level—because new barriers to trade or distortions of competition are to be avoided, because a genuine international problem is to be tackled, or because a progressive state solution embodied in a Commission proposal suggests a departure from normal domestic legislative procedures—that the governments agree to a transfer of national competences and accept a supranational solution.[176]

Unless in a particular case a member state has paramount countervailing interests, this approach allows for some further development of Community environmental law—if not an expansion into entirely new areas, then at least a certain *approfondissment* of existing legislation along the lines devised by the environmental program. The marked retardation of Community legislation since 1980 indicates that this progress will be slower than in previous years. As long as the contents of the supranational solutions are on average not greatly superior to national ones and as long as the lack of political participation of the electorate and societal groups concerned about the environment in the Community decisionmaking process perpetuates a "democracy deficit", there is a real danger that fur-

---

175. See Hartkopf, "Chemikaliengesetz vom Deutschen Bundestag Verabschiedet," 78 *Umwelt-Mitteilungen des Bundesministers des Inneren* 10 (12 Sept. 1980); Deutscher Bundestag, 8. Wahlperiode, Unterausschuss "Chemikaliengesetz" des Ausschusses für Jugend, Familie und Gesundheit, Protokoll über die öffentliche Anhörung, 3-4 March 1980 (Protokoll Nr. 4); but see Deutscher Bundestag 8. Wahlperiode, 225. Sitzung (25 June 1980), at 18173, 18175, 18179, 18185 where several speakers stress the limitations originating from Community law.

176. See Bungarten, supra n. 10 at 111 et seq.

ther development of Community environmental law will be regarded as illegitimate. Such illegitimacy will ultimately strengthen disintegrative forces. Such forces already threaten economic integration in areas mandated by clear Treaty provisions, such as elimination of trade barriers.[177]

Environmental policy stands in even greater need of political legitimacy than trade and commercial policies forming the "classic" field of European integration.[178] This is so because environmental policy is not explicitly legitimized by the Treaty and, due to lack of suitable decision criteria, can not ultimately be legitimized by resort to legal rules alone. Further, the contents of environmental policy can not be derived by recourse to the market process.

This assessment shows that European integration can not easily be separated into several independent elements such as decisional (institutional), legal, and substantive integration. Without decisional legitimacy, the process of substantive *approfondissement*, to which Community environmental law has contributed so much, may ultimately be threatened.[179] Without substantive legitimacy based on superiority of solutions to environmental problems, the effects of continuing legal integration in the field of environmental protection may be increasingly resented. If this assessment is correct, we should be cautious in advocating more harmonization in the field of environmental protection as long as the basic process of Community decisionmaking remains unchanged. As stated earlier, there are important areas of environmental policy where further harmonization is desirable in principle. These include international problems that can only be addressed transnationally, although even the Community is sometimes too small a decisionmaking unit. There are other environmental problems where divergent national measures leading to interference with the Common Market or the delay of some member states in addressing these problems justify Community commitment. Further attention to implementation and enforcement of existing directives is needed. But steps to accomplish these objectives must be tempered by an awareness of the fragile legitimacy of existing Community institutions and of the potential negative effects of harmonization on initiatives by member states.[180] In some cases, coordination and encouragement of national measures may be sufficient.[181] In other cases, concentration of pollution control measures

---

177. E.g., unilateral restrictions of trade recently introduced by some member states; see Deringer & Sedemund, "Europäisches Gemeinschaftsrecht," 35 *NJW* 1189-1190 (1981).

178. Weiler, supra n. 159 at 43-44.

179. See Bungarten, supra n. 10 at 157 et seq.

180. Weidner & Knoepfel, supra n. 17 at 63 et seq. See generally Roth, supra n.144 at 327.

181. See Bungarten, "Umweltpolitische Aspekte einer Europäischen Integration,"

on densely populated and highly polluted "action regions"[182] may be worth trying. This form of regionalization of pollution control is preferable to any kind of regionalization along national boundaries because it does not compromise political and economic integration, while taking into account environmental diversity. On the other hand, any concept of a "two tier" environmental policy that separates member states into "environmental" and "polluter" states according to their geographical closeness to the center of the Community[183] should be rejected. Its simplicity conceals that the state of the environment and even environmental values are not congruent with national territories. Besides such reorientation of harmonization policy, efforts to open the existing process of Community decision and to develop a European constituency should not be foreclosed.

---

in von der Groeben & Möller (eds.), *Möglichkeiten und Grenzen einer Europäischen Union*, vol. 2 at 165 et seq. (1976).

182. Kromarek, supra n. 154 at 12.

183. Contra, Weinstock, supra n. 4 at 34 et seq.

[2]

The Single European Act and the Environmental Policy of the European Economic Community

By Dirk Vandermeersch

Attorney, Cleary, Gottlieb, Steen & Hamilton, Brussels

Introduction

On July 1, 1987, the Single European Act (the S.E.A.) entered into force, effecting a series of amendments to the EEC Treaty pursuant to which the European Economic Community was created in 1957.[1] Of these amendments, those dealing with the creation of the "internal market" have aroused great interest and controversy, in particular as concerns their possible effect on the rules concerning the free movement of goods developed by the European Court under Articles 30 and 36 EEC.[2] Less attention has been given so far to the provisions of the S.E.A. that deal with the environmental policy of the Community.[3] Upon analysis, however, they raise as many questions and uncertainties as do the provisions concerning the internal market.

The S.E.A. inserts a title "Environment" into the EEC Treaty which did not before contain any provision concerning the environment and a possible role of the Community in its protection. The S.E.A. thus gives a "constitutional" base to the Community's environmental policy and defines its objectives. However, political manoeuvring among the Member States during the negotiations leading to the S.E.A. has resulted in a compromise text which aims at preserving certain competences with the Member States and keeping the Community's action within certain generally defined boundaries. The problems created by this compromise are the subject of this article.

I shall first briefly describe the statutory bases for the EEC's environmental policy as they existed in the EEC Treaty, prior to its amendment by the S.E.A. In a second section, the new provisions of the Treaty concerning the Community's environmental policy will be described and their impact examined. A

---

[1] O.J. 1987 No. L 169, 1–28.

[2] See N. Forwood and M. Clough, "The Single European Act and Free Movement," (1986) 11 E.L.Rev. 383; for a general comment of the Single Act, see J. De Ruyt, *L'Acte unique européen*, 1987; P. Pescatore, "Observations critiques sur l'Acte Unique européen," paper presented at the Institut d'Etudes européennes, Brussels on March 1, 1986, and "Some critical remarks on the "Single European Act," (1987) 27 C.M.L.Rev. 9; P. VerLoren van Themaat, "De Europese Akte," 1986 S.E.W. 464; J. W. De Zwaan, "The Single European Act: Conclusion of a unique document," (1986) 26 C.M.L.Rev. 747; J.P. Jacqué, "L'Acte unique européen," 1986 R.T.D.E., 575; H. J. Glaesner, "Die Einheitliche Europäische Akte," 1986 EuR 119; C. Gulmann, The Single European Act—some remarks from a Danish perspective, (1987) 27 C.M.L.Rev. 31; D. Edward, "The impact of the Single Act on the institutions," (1987) 27 C.M.L.Rev. 19; R. Bieber, J. Pantalis and J. Schoo, "Implications of the Single Act for the European Parliament," (1987) 27 C.M.L.Rev. 767.

[3] See, M. Zuleeg, "Vorbehalten Kompetenzen der Mitgliedstaten der Europäischen Gemeinschaft auf dem Gebiete des Umweltschutzes," [1987] NVwZ 280, and comment by H.J. Rabe, [1987] EuR 177.

408   THE SINGLE EUROPEAN ACT AND THE ENVIRONMENTAL POLICY OF THE EEC

third section will address the legislative process; finally, in a fourth section I shall examine the so-called "safeguard" clauses.

The EEC environmental policy under the 1957 Treaty of Rome

The treatment of environmental policy in the EEC Treaty prior to its amendment is easy to describe: it is non-existent. The original EEC Treaty did not provide for a Community policy in the field of the environment and, as a matter of fact, did not even contain the word "environment." This state of affairs is not surprising, as the protection of the environment was certainly not on the forefront of peoples' minds in 1957. The obvious question then is: how could a supra-national institution, as is the EEC, evolve towards the adoption of legislation on the environment, which is binding upon its Member States, if those Member States had not, by virtue of express treaty provision, transferred their sovereign powers to that institution?

The objectives of the EEC and the environment

Article 2 EEC states that the Community "has as its task, by establishing a common market and progressively approximating the economic policies of Member States, to promote throughout the Community a harmonious development of economic activities, a continuous and balanced expansion, an increase in stability, an accelerated raising of the standard of living and closer relations between the States belonging to it." The Preamble to the Treaty indicates that the Member States "affirm as an essential objective of their efforts the constant improvement of the living and working conditions of their peoples." Notwithstanding the economic orientation of the language, the motives of the drafters of the EEC Treaty were certainly not exclusively economic. However, for political (and practical) reasons the way chosen for the integration of the countries of the Old Continent was mainly an economic one. This approach towards European unity could have had considerable consequences for the development of an EEC environmental policy; a pragmatic approach was adopted, however, and EEC environmental law over the years developed into a considerable body of legislative instruments. This development was crowned by the recognition by the European Court in 1983 that environmental protection is one of the Community's "essential objectives" which could even justify derogations from such basic legal principles as the freedom of trade and of competition.[4]

If, as further discussed below, the EEC Treaty could be interpreted to provide the legal means to take environmental measures, it did not specify the objectives and the substantive standards that the Community should take for guidance in devising and implementing its policy. As a result, the definition of these objectives and the setting of these standards was left with the Council, which enjoyed almost unlimited liberty in doing so.

The first environmental measures taken by the Community mirrored the economic approach of the EEC Treaty: they were measures that reflected a

---

[4] Case 240/83, *Procureur de la République* v. *Association de défense des brûleurs d'huiles usagées*, [1983] E.C.R. 531, 549.

THE SINGLE EUROPEAN ACT AND THE ENVIRONMENTAL POLICY OF THE EEC   409

desire to unify the market, *i.e.* measures aiming at facilitating the movement of products from one Member State to another or at equalising competitive conditions between companies subject to differing national environmental legislations. In other words, the main purpose of these first environmental measures was to abolish obstacles to trade between the Member States. Only gradually did the environmental actions taken by the Community acquire legitimacy on their own and were they no longer primarily motivated by economic concerns.

In the early seventies, it became clear that the Community wished to develop a Community environmental policy where the protection of the environment and the improvement of the quality of life would be the prime motivators. At their meeting of October 19–20, 1972, the heads of state or of government gave the green light to the development of such policy[5] and the first Community Action Programme on the Environment was approved by the Council of Ministers on November 22, 1973.[6] The Council stated on that occasion that the harmonious development of economic activities referred to in Article 2 EEC could not be imagined "in the absence of an effective campaign to combat pollution and nuisances or of an improvement in the quality of life and the protection of the environment."

The first Action Programme set out the objectives of the Community's environmental policy (including the prevention and control of pollution and nuisances, the maintenance of a satisfactory ecological balance and the sound management of natural resources) from an exclusively environmental point of view; no reference was made to a need for such measures in order to preserve or obtain a unified market. The Programme called for the harmonisation of national policies, which should have as their aim the improvement of the quality of life: economic growth, it was stated, should not be viewed from purely quantitative aspects.[7] A second five-year Action Programme followed in 1977.[8] The third Action Programme, approved in 1983, signalled a growing emphasis on preventive measures and the creation of new policies, even where the subject matters in question were not yet regulated by the Member States.[9] The Council let it be understood in 1983 that the Community environmental policy would have its own priorities, unaffected by "short-term fluctuations in cyclical [economic] conditions" that could put the timing and appropriateness of its implementation into doubt.

The numerous environmental measures taken by the Community (most often in the form of a directive) in implementation of the successive Action Programmes were generally based on Article 100 EEC often in combination with Article 235, and occasionally exclusively on the basis of Article 235.

While at its inception the environmental policy gave rise to animated debate

---

[5] 1972 Bulletin of the European Communities, no. 10, 21.

[6] O.J. 1973 No. C 112, 1–53.

[7] This does not mean that economic considerations will not play a part in devising environmental measures. The First Action Programme states in this respect that the Community environmental policy must "help to bring expansion into the service of man by procuring for him an environment providing the best conditions of life, and reconcile this expansion with the increasingly imperative need to preserve the natural environment." The objective is to reconcile, not to subject.

[8] O.J. 1977, No. C 139, 1–46.

[9] O.J. 1983, No. C 46, 1–16.

410   THE SINGLE EUROPEAN ACT AND THE ENVIRONMENTAL POLICY OF THE EEC

between scholars as to its basis in the Treaty,[10] in practice the Community did not feel hampered by any "constitutional" shortcomings that would restrict the scope of its environmental action. The legal bases that could be found in the EEC Treaty for such action nevertheless each posed their own specific problems and, undeniably, a certain unease persisted as to the propriety of certain of the Community initiatives in the field of the environment. I shall now briefly summarise the problems raised by Articles 100 and 235 as a ground for EEC environmental action.

Article 100

Article 100 EEC provides for the harmonisation of Member States' laws:

> "The Council shall, acting unanimously on a proposal from the Commission, issue directives for the approximation of such provisions laid down by law, regulation or administrative action in Member States as directly affect the establishment or functioning of the common market."

Taken literally and exclusively in its historical context, Article 100 only provides an incomplete base for environmental action. The Article would only permit action by the Community if such is done in reaction to an existing Member State measure that affects the functioning of the common market. This view was generally held within the Commission and the European Parliament at the early stages of the development of the Community environmental policy.[11] Later, legal writers began to hold a more flexible view on the possibilities offered by Article 100 and argued that the Community could take measures even where no Member State had adopted legislation on the subject matter.[12]

In 1980, the European Court held that Article 100 could be a basis for environmental action. The European Court did, however, maintain a link with the need to preserve a unified market:

> "It is by no means ruled out that provisions on the environment may be based on Article 100 of the Treaty. Provisions which are necessary by considerations relating to the environment and health may be a burden upon the undertakings to which they apply and if there is no harmonisation of national provisions on the matter, competition may be appreciably distorted."[13]

---

[10] See J. Touscoz, "L'action des Communautés européennes en matière d'environment," [1973] R.T.D.E. 29; R.C. Beraud "Fondements juridiques du droit de l'environnement dans le Traité de Rome," [1979] R.M.C. 35; A. Gérard, "Les limites et les moyens juridiques de l'intervention des Communautés européennes en matière de protection de l'environnement," [1975] C.D.E. 14; H. Scheuer, "Aspects juridiques de la protection de l'environnment dans le Marché commun," [1975] R.M.C. 441.

[11] M. Carpentier, "L'action de la Communauté en matière d'environnement," [1972] R.M.C. 381, 390 (M. Carpentier was the head of the Commission's environment division at the time) and A. Armengaud, *Rapport fait au nom de la commission juridique sur les possibilités qu'offrent les traités communautaires en matière de lutte contre la pollution du milieu et les modifications qu'il faut éventuellement proposer d'y apporter*, Doc. EP 15/72, April 17, 1972, 16.

[12] See for a general discussion of the application of Article 100, H. C. Taschner, "Angleichung der Rechtsvorschriften," in Groeben et al, Kommentar zum EWG-Vertrag, 1983, 1695, in particular 1713, and E. Rehbinder and R. Stewart, *Environmental Protection Policy*, 1985, 21.

[13] Case 91/79, *Commission* v. *Italy* [1980] E.C.R. 1099, 1106.

THE SINGLE EUROPEAN ACT AND THE ENVIRONMENTAL POLICY OF THE EEC   411

It results from the above that Article 100 cannot be used where the measure bears no relationship at all to the functioning of the common market. Thus, the protection of fauna and flora cannot be assured on the basis of Article 100.

Article 235

Article 235 EEC permits Community action in fields that are not expressly regulated in the Treaty:

> "If action by the Community should prove necessary to attain, in the course of the operation of the common market, one of the objectives of the Community and this Treaty has not provided the necessary powers, the Council shall, acting unanimously on a proposal from the Commission and after consulting the Assembly, take the appropriate measures."

Article 235 is not a catch-all clause, however. Its wording makes clear that a link must exist with the functioning of the common market. However, the different wording in Article 100 ("directly affect the functioning of the common market") and in Article 235 ("in the course of the operation of the common market") permits the conclusion that this link need not be as close as is required for the application of Article 100. It arguably suffices that the measure taken on the basis of Article 235 concerns a subject matter that bears some relationship to economic activities. Article 235 can thus be used to regulate environmental problems which are related to economic activities but whose effect on competitive conditions within the Community cannot be established and hence cannot be addressed on the basis of Article 100.[14]

The relationship between certain environmental measures that have been taken by the Community and economic conditions has been tenuous, however. A case in point is Directive 79/409 of April 2, 1979 on the conservation of wild birds.[15] The Directive mainly concerns the hunting, capture and killing of wild birds; it was issued on the basis of Article 235 and justified as follows:

> "Whereas the conservation of the species of wild birds naturally occurring in the European territory of the Member States is necessary to attain, within the operation of the common market, the Community's objectives regarding the improvement of living conditions, a harmonious development of economic activities throughout the Community and a continuous and balanced expansion but the necessary powers to act have not been provided for in the Treaty."

Needless to say that the above justification simply begs the question and, in fact, reveals the institutional problems facing an economic Community that wishes to legislate in non-economic areas.

A notable difference with Article 100, is that Article 235 does not limit the Community action to the issuance of directives. Article 235 permits action by any of the legal means listed Article 189, including regulations that are directly applicable in all Member States.

---

[14] E. Rehbinder and R. Stewart, *supra*, n. 12, 27.
[15] O.J. 1979 No. L 103, 1–18.

412   THE SINGLE EUROPEAN ACT AND THE ENVIRONMENTAL POLICY OF THE EEC

The combination of Article 100 and Article 235

The Community has in the past adopted a pragmatic approach, and in practice environmental action has often been based on both Article 100 and Article 235. A typical example is Directive 78/659 of July 18, 1978 on the quality of fresh waters needing protection or improvement in order to support fish life.[16] The preamble to the Directive provides the following legal justification for the measures that are taken:

> "Whereas differences between the provisions already in force or in preparation in the various Member States as regards the quality of waters capable of supporting the life of freshwater fish may create unequal conditions of competition and thus directly affect the functioning of the common market; whereas laws in this field should be approximated as provided by Article 100 of the Treaty.
>
> Whereas it is necessary to couple that approximation of laws with Community action aiming to achieve, by means of wider-ranging provisions, one of the Community's objectives in the field of environmental protection and the improvement of the quality of life; whereas certain specific provisions must be laid down in this connection; whereas, since the specific powers of action required to this end have not been provided for in the Treaty, it is necessary to invoke Article 235 thereof."

The EEC environmental policy after the Single European Act

The S.E.A. has inserted a new Title VII, entitled "Environment" in Part Three of the EEC Treaty, the part concerning the "policies" of the Community. Significantly, the S.E.A. has not amended Article 2 EEC, where the "task" of the Community is defined, nor was an addendum made to Article 3, which lists the activities which the Community will develop with a view to bring this task to fruition. Perhaps the drafters of the S.E.A. wished to preserve the notion that the protection of the environment was already within the objectives to be pursued by the Community under the original Treaty.

The new provisions of the EEC Treaty dealing with the environment are numbered 130r through to 130t. Article 130r specifies the objectives of the Community environment policy and sets the substantive standards such policy must observe. It further deals with the realm of environmental regulation that is reserved to the Member States. In a last section, the Article concerns the role of the Community in international matters involving the environment.[17] Article 130s lays down the legislative process for the creation of EEC environmental law. Finally, Article 130t poses the rule that Member States may always impose more stringent protective measures. In addition to inserting a title concerning

---

[16] O.J. 1978 No. L 222, 1–10.

[17] Article 130r(5) will not be discussed in this paper. It provides that "within their respective spheres of competence, the Community and the Member States shall cooperate with third countries and with the relevant international organisations. The arrangements for Community cooperation may be the subject of agreements between the Community and the third parties concerned, which shall be negotiated in accordance with Article 228." It is further provided that this competence of the Community is "without prejudice to Member States' competence to negotiate in international bodies and to conclude international agreements."

THE SINGLE EUROPEAN ACT AND THE ENVIRONMENTAL POLICY OF THE EEC   413

the environment in the EEC Treaty, the S.E.A. has introduced a series of treaty articles concerning the harmonisation of national laws, including environmental laws. They are Articles 100a and 100b.

The objectives of the EEC environmental policy

Article 130r provides that action by the Community relating to the environment shall have the following objectives:

> "— to preserve, protect and improve the quality of the environment;
> — to contribute towards protecting human health;
> — to ensure a prudent and rational utilization of natural resources."

During the negotiations leading to the S.E.A. the Commission had proposed a more extensive description of the elements that would form part of the Community environmental policy.[18] The Commission's proposal listed:

- air protection;
- water protection;
- combating of noise;
- protection of soil and landscapes;
- conservation of fauna, flora and the protection of animals;
- prevention of spilling of natural resources;
- re-use, recycling and destruction of waste;
- incentives to take into account the needs of the protection of the environment;
- prevention and indemnification of damage caused by dangerous industrial activities or by the use or handling of dangerous or toxic substances or products, in particular when more than one Member State is concerned by the risks caused or the need for indemnification; and
- environmental research.

Certain Member States rightfully remarked that a Treaty provision setting forth the objectives of a Community policy need not go into that amount of detail and that such policy would be better served if only certain general goals were set. As a result, the more casuistic approach of the Commission was not followed and the text cited above was adopted.

The preservation, protection and improvement of the environment. The first objective ("to preserve, protect and improve the quality of the environment") seems to encompass the various sectoral and general measures that traditionally have made part of the Community's environmental policy. It covers the measures taken to reduce or eliminate pollution and nuisances (*e.g.* air, water, noise) and to ensure the protection of the ecological balance (*e.g.* the measures controlling biotechnology announced in the Fourth Action Programme). As worded, the first objective seems broad enough to cover also the various measures that relate to the protection of the environmental resources, such as the use and management of land and the protection of flora and fauna.

The protection of human health. The second objective ("to contribute towards protecting human health") at first sight seems superfluous. Indeed, the protec-

---

[18] Jacqué, *supra*, n. 2, at 605.

414   THE SINGLE EUROPEAN ACT AND THE ENVIRONMENTAL POLICY OF THE EEC

tion of human health (as well as animal health, for that matter) should be a prime motivator for any environmental policy and would appear to be already covered by the first objective. However, the mentioning of the protection of human health as a separate and independent objective of EEC environmental law permits measures within the framework of that law whose link with the environment is only subsidiary. A case in point is the EEC's notification system for new chemicals, the so-called Sixth Amendment.[19] The first concern of that system obviously is the protection of users.

Even though the protection of human health is listed as a separate objective, it should always be seen in the broader framework of environmental protection. Since the clause forms part of the Title dealing with the environment, it cannot be used to confer jurisdiction upon the Community in public health matters which up to now generally has been limited to consumer and worker protection issues and, in matters not specifically dealt with in the Treaty, can be regulated on the basis of Article 235 provided a link with the functioning of the common market can be found.

The prudent and rational utilisation of natural resources. The third objective ("the prudent and rational utilisation of natural resources") appears to cover the use of resources that have an economic impact, such as water, timber and minerals. The competence of the Community as regards the use of natural resources is subject to one limitation: in a "declaration" annexed to the S.E.A., the Conference of the Representatives of the Governments of the Member States declared that "the Community's activities in the sphere of the environment may not interfere with national policies regarding the exploitation of energy resources." The impact of this declaration may be limited, however. First, it is significant that the declaration only refers to the exploitation of energy resources. The Community would thus not be subject to restriction as far as the regulation of the utilisation of energy resources is concerned. Secondly, there exists doubt about the legal status of the various multilateral and unilateral declarations that follow the S.E.A. In his provocative analysis of the question, Professor Toth concludes that the declarations have no legal effect: they would in no way restrict, exclude or modify the legal effects of the S.E.A. and would not be subject to the jurisdiction of the European Court.[20] Their status would be that of legally non-binding, judicially non-enforceable statements of intent or declarations of a purely political nature. If Professor Toth's conclusions were to be upheld by the European Court, a Member State would thus not be in a position to challenge the validity of a Community measure on the ground that the measure interferes with its national policy regarding the exploitation of energy resources.

The basic principles of EEC environmental action

As noted above, in the absence of a specific Treaty clause dealing with the environment, the Council of Ministers was virtually at liberty to devise the basic principles that would guide the development of EEC environmental law. As

---

[19] Directive 67/548, as amended by Directive 79/831 of September 18, 1979 O.J. 1979, No. L 259, 10–28.
[20] A. G. Toth, "The legal status of the declarations annexed to the Single European Act," [1986] 26 C.M.L.Rev. 803, 811–812.

THE SINGLE EUROPEAN ACT AND THE ENVIRONMENTAL POLICY OF THE EEC   415

'amended by the S.E.A. the EEC Treaty now provides in its Article 130r(2), as follows:

> "Action by the Community relating to the environment shall be based on the principles that preventive action should be taken, that environmental damage should as a priority be rectified at source, and that the polluter should pay. (. . .)"

A further basic principle that concerns environmental regulation by the EEC is expressed in the framework of the new provisions of the Treaty of Rome dealing with the harmonisation of national laws. New Article 100a(3) provides:

> "The Commission, in its proposals (. . .) concerning (. . .) environmental protection (. . .) will take as a base a high level of protection."

Preventive and remedial action. Article 130r(2) mentions both preventive and remedial action. Interestingly enough, the Article poses no order of preference for these two standards. The fact that preventive action is mentioned first could permit the conclusion that if a choice can be made between preventive and remedial action, priority should be given to preventive action. However, since such priority is not spelled out in the text, both are presumably to be considered as options equally open to the Community.

If remedial action is chosen, priority must be given to "rectification at source," which presumably means that the source of pollution must be eliminated or its impact reduced. Such remedial action obviously comes close to preventive action—a circumstance which perhaps may lend force to the argument that if the Community can make a choice between preventive and remedial action, the preventive action should be preferred.

The polluter pays principle. The principle that the polluter must pay has been professed by the Community as a basic principle of its environmental policy since that policy was first formulated. In the first Action Programme, the principle was formulated as follows:

> "The cost of preventing and eliminating nuisances must in principle be borne by the polluter. However, there may be made certain exceptions and special arrangements, in particular for transitional periods, provided that they cause no significant distortion to international trade and investment. Without prejudice to the application of the provisions of the Treaties, this principle should be stated explicitly and the arrangements for its application including the exceptions thereto should be defined at Community level. Where exceptions are made, the need to progressively eliminate regional imbalances in the Community should also be taken into account."[21]

The above statement was repeated in the successive Action Programmes, including the Fourth Programme, approved by the Council of Ministers on March 20, 1987.

In a Recommendation of March 3, 1975, the Council has set forth specific rules for the application of the "polluter pays" principle and the cases in which an exception to the principle is justified.[22] The principle basically means that the

---

[21] O.J. 1973 No. C 112, 1, 6.
[22] Recommendation 74/436, O.J. 1975 L 194, 1–4.

416   THE SINGLE EUROPEAN ACT AND THE ENVIRONMENTAL POLICY OF THE EEC

entity directly or indirectly responsible for damage to the environment must bear the costs linked to the implementation of anti-pollution measures. In other words, as a rule no state subsidies should be granted to polluters to allow them to comply with their environmental obligations. Member States should only grant subsidies as a transitory measure when the immediate application of "very stringent standards" would lead to "serious economic disturbances"; in addition, Article 92 *et seq.* EEC (the general rules concerning state subsidies, which aim to avoid distortions of competition) must be complied with. The Recommendation further states that Member States may contribute to the financing of public pollution control installations the cost of which cannot be wholly covered in the short term from the charges paid by the polluters using them, or to the financing of research and development. In practice, however, in 1974 the Commission under pressure from the Member States permitted, on a temporary basis, substantial national aid programmes to industry for investments designed to implement new environmental standards.[23] The rationale for the temporary relaxation of the state aid rules in the case of environmental investments was the need to catch up on the substantial backlog that had been incurred in Europe by the time the Community's environmental policy was launched. However, the Commission noted in its Sixteenth Report on Competition Policy (1986), developments since 1974, culminating in the confirmation of the Community environmental policy in the S.E.A., have called into question the concept of a transitional approach to the subsidising of environmental investments as the protection of the environment will remain a major task for an indefinite period. As a result, the Commission has started a review of the application of the "polluter pays" principle. Nevertheless, by decision of December 17, 1986,[24] the Commission has extended the transitional rules on the subsidising of environmental investments until the end of 1992 (subject to withdrawal or modification before that date). Under these rules, environmental aid schemes qualify for exemption from the ban on state subsidies if:

— the aid is intended to facilitate the implementation of new environmental standards;
— the aid does not exceed 15 per cent. net grant equivalent of the value of the investment;
— only companies operating at least two years before the entry into force of the new standards qualify for the aid; and
— the recipient companies must bear operating and replacement costs.

National aid schemes that do not meet the above criteria will be permitted by the Commission only in "special" circumstances, such as the support of research and development.

It should be noted that the "polluter pays" principle applies only to the formulation of Community law. It has never been made mandatory as a general rule for Member States to comply with when they implement their own environmental policy or implement EEC directives. The Member States are bound only by the rules that follow from Article 92 *et seq.* EEC.

New Article 130r(2) poses the rule that the polluter should pay, without, apparently, leaving room for "exceptions or special arrangements." The

---

[23] Commission, Fourth Report on Competition Policy (1974), 175.
[24] Commission, Sixteenth Report on Competition Policy (1986), 259.

absence of a specific proviso allowing exceptions would not, however, seem to have a major impact on EEC environmental policy. Article 130r(2) would not seem to render impossible the granting of subsidies that comply with Article 92 *et seq*. Its provisions indeed concern only "action by the Community" and not action by the Member States. However, the rule would make impossible the issuance of a directive calling for the granting of state subsidies to companies with a view to financing their compliance with environmental obligations under that directive.[25]

A high level of protection. The requirement that EEC measures relating to the environment must "take as a base a high level of protection" is not to be found in the new Title VII on the environment but is part of the new provisions of the EEC Treaty that aim to realise the internal market by December 31, 1992. Consequently, the principle is not an integral part of EEC environmental policy. It only applies to the measures taken to harmonise Member State laws that have as their object the functioning of the internal market. The environmental aspects of these Community measures are therefore only secondary to their main objective, *i.e.* the achievement of the internal market.

In order to achieve the "internal market" (which is defined in new Article 8a as "an area without frontiers in which the free movement of goods, persons, services and capital is ensured"), the S.E.A. introduces a special procedure for the harmonisation of Member States laws that "have as their object the establishment and functioning of the internal market." This special procedure is characterised by the possibility of qualified majority voting in the Council of Ministers (where normally, under Article 100 unanimity is required for the adoption of harmonisation directives) and the possibility for the Council, after December 31, 1992, to "decide that the provisions in force in a Member State must be recognised as being equivalent to those applied by another Member State."

During the negotiations leading to the S.E.A., a number of Member States expressed strong apprehensions about majority voting on harmonisation questions. They feared that majority voting could result in the lowering of standards in a number of sensitive areas such as the protection of the environment. To allay these fears, a series of provisions were inserted in the S.E.A., including the one calling for "taking as a base a high level of protection." If the S.E.A. is a classic example of compromise resulting in open phrases and dubious rules, Article 100a(3) may serve as a good example. What does it mean to "take as a base" and when is a level of protection "high"?

It would appear from the political origin of the clause that what is meant is that the Commission, when formulating a proposal, must take as a starting point of its studies and proposals the rules in effect in the most stringent Member State. The provision cannot be taken to mean that the Community rules ultimately adopted must necessarily reflect or be identical to those most stringent rules. Perhaps, as H. J. Glaësner has suggested, Article 100a(3) simply aims to ensure that the Community standards are such that the burden imposed upon

---

[25] Directive 75/439 of June 16, 1975 on the disposal of waste oils provides that the Member States may grant "indemnities" to disposal companies as a *quid pro quo* for the disposal obligations they assume (O.J. 1978 No. L 42, 43–47). However, the indemnities are to be financed in "accordance with the polluter pays principle," for instance, by a levy on certain oil products.

418   THE SINGLE EUROPEAN ACT AND THE ENVIRONMENTAL POLICY OF THE EEC

less stringent Member States is bearable and that the resulting lowering of the standards in the stringent Member States does not lead to political problems.[26]

The practical impact of the "high level of protection" clause may be further reduced by the fact that Article 100a(4) allows a Member State to derogate from a Community measure that was adopted by qualified majority vote "on grounds of major needs . . . related to the protection of the environment." In other words, if a Community measure fails to reflect the "high level of protection" favoured by the stringent Member State, that State still has a way out and may, under certain conditions, continue to apply the more stringent rules. This possibility may help the other Member States in convincing the stringent Member State to be less adamant in its position that Community law should reflect the "high" level of protection. The recent decision of the Council of Ministers in connection with the car emission dispute between Denmark and the other Member States presents a first example of such calculated use of Article 100a(4). Since 1985, Denmark had been blocking the adoption of the directive proposed by the Commission, arguing for more stringent standards. On July 21, 1987 (barely three weeks after the S.E.A. entered into force), the Council agreed to Denmark's proposal to proceed with the draft directive using Article 100a as a Treaty base. The Council reached a common position on the directive by qualified majority. Denmark voted against the measure and made it clear that it will introduce the more stringent standards, by availing itself of Article 100a(4).

It is not clear how the Articles concerning the internal market (Articles 100a and 100b) relate to those dealing specifically with the environment (Articles 130r through 130t). What criterion is to decide whether a measure concerning the environment must be taken on the basis of Article 100a or on the basis of Article 130s? The question is not without importance as Article 130s requires unanimity within the Council whereas, in principle, a qualified majority suffices under Article 100a. Moreover, if action is taken on the basis of Article 130s, the Community may only act if the objectives sought can be attained better at Community level than at the level of the Member States (the so-called principle of subsidiarity discussed below). Finally, Article 100a measures will be subject to the safeguard clauses in Articles 100a(4) and (5), while in the case of Article 130s measures the more generally worded safeguard clause provided in Article 130t will apply. The S.E.A. does not provide a direct answer to this question, although obviously guidance may be taken from the respective origins and purposes of the two enabling Articles.

One approach would be to limit the application of Article 100a to those harmonisation measures that the Commission had listed or announced in its 1985 White Paper on the completion of the internal market.[27] In that case, the use of Article 100a in environmental questions would be rather limited as the White Paper only mentions the proposals dealing with the regulation of chemical products.[28] We submit, however, that although Article 100a undoubtedly is the offshoot of the White Paper, it is difficult to see on what legal grounds its application could be so restricted. Another approach would be to look at the

---

[26] Glaesner, *supra* n. 2, at 131.
[27] COM (85) 310, June 14, 1985.
[28] The White Paper mentions proposals concern PCB's, asbestos, dangerous substances (Directive 67/548), ammonium nitrate, non-ionic detergents, dangerous preparations and liquid fertilisers.

THE SINGLE EUROPEAN ACT AND THE ENVIRONMENTAL POLICY OF THE EEC   419

nature of the subject matter. While Article 130s deals with a Community policy to protect the environment, Article 100a concerns the harmonisation of Member State measures that have as their "object" the establishment and functioning of the internal market. (In this connection it is useful to note that Article 100a does not concern national measures that merely "affect" the establishment and functioning of the internal market.) Depending on the nature of the subject matter, it should be capable of being brought under one of these two categories of measures. Borderline cases undoubtedly will arise. In case of doubt, we submit that preference should be given to the application of Article 130s, since the provisions of Article 100a *et seq.* are basically of a temporary nature only (that is, they are supposed to have played their role by December 31, 1992). The recent experience with the motor vehicle emissions directive may, however, be an indication that in practice a less-principled approach may be adopted by the Member States and the Community institutions.

The restrictions upon the Community's jurisdiction in environmental matters

While Article 130r(1) spells out the objectives of the Community's environmental policy which is to reflect the principles set forth in Article 130r(2), the third and fourth sections of the same Article introduce a series of restrictions on the Community's jurisdiction so conferred. First, Article 130r(3) sets forth a list of four parameters which the Community must take into account when preparing environmental action. Second, Article 130r(4), first sentence, poses the principle of the subsidiarity of EEC jurisdiction in environmental matters. Finally, the second sentence of Article 130r(4) not only implicitly limits the legal instruments that may be used by the Community to carry out its environmental policy but also provides that in principle the Community has no competence to finance and implement its own measures.

The parameters of EEC environmental action. Article 130r(3) provides:

> "In preparing its action relating to the environment, the Community shall take account of:
> — available scientific and technical data;
> — environmental conditions in the various regions of the Community;
> — the potential benefits and costs of action or of lack of action;
> — the economic and social development of the Community as a whole and the balanced development of its regions."

Article 130r(3) lists a series of substantive parameters that ostensibly are intended to restrict the full realisation by the Community of the stated objectives of EEC environmental policy. It is unclear what exactly is meant by the expression "shall take account of," but it is significant that this expression is chosen instead of, for instance, "shall reflect" and that the requirement refers only to the preparatory stage of environmental action and not to the decisional process. It is submitted that section 3 of Article 130r does not permit derogations from the basic principles set forth in section 2. The parameters contained in section 3 only serve to guide the Community institutions when devising and implementing EEC environmental policy. They constitute restrictions on the freedom of the Community when formulating environmental rules only to the extent that the Community will have to make an assessment of the degree of

420 THE SINGLE EUROPEAN ACT AND THE ENVIRONMENTAL POLICY OF THE EEC

compliance of every proposed measure with each of the four parameters. It is suggested that the role of the parameters is not to go further than the requirement that such an assessment be made and that only when the Council deems it appropriate is the proposed measure adapted to reflect the outcome of the assessment. The expression "shall take account of" cannot mean that if in a given case the parameters are impossible to be complied with without bending one of the basic principles should the subject matter be considered as inappropriate for EEC action, nor does the clause require the Council in each and every case to adapt the proposed measure to reflect the outcome of the assessment.

The role of available scientific and technical data. Article 130r(3) requires the Community, when preparing its action relating to the environment, to take account of available scientific and technical data. The clause could suggest a somewhat unflattering view by the drafters of the S.E.A. (*i.e.* the Member States) of the decision-making process of the Community institutions. It appears to have been inserted at the insistence of the British Government, which reportedly is convinced that the alleged responsibility of the United Kingdom in the acid rain problem is not based on scientific evidence. The practical significance of the clause may be doubted. Its impact might have been more important if it had provided that no measure may be taken unless there is scientific evidence that it will contribute towards alleviating the problem addressed by it. As drafted, the clause would appear to require only *prima facie* scientific evidence that a problem exists and that it may be solved or alleviated by the measure taken. Given the current practices of the Commission when preparing draft environmental legislation, it is submitted that the clause will be complied with without great difficulty by the Community institutions.

The environmental conditions in the various regions of the Community. One of the old (and interminable) quarrels of EEC environmental policy is the dispute between quality objectives and emission limit values, particularly in connection with river pollution. The dispute generally opposes the United Kingdom against the remaining Member States—the first defending quality objectives, the latter emission standards. The United Kingdom favours ambient quality objectives so that its industry can benefit from the high volume of flow in its short watercourses and thus wants its insular situation to be taken into account. The dispute has resulted in the dual approach to water protection, typically reflected in Directive 76/464 of May 4, 1976 on water pollution caused by the discharge of dangerous substances.[29] The quality objectives and limit values dispute is a good example of varying local environmental conditions leading to different approaches to environmental protection.

Article 130r(3), second indent, confirms the general principle that different situations justify different remedies and clearly strengthens the position of those Member States that argue for a differentiated environmental policy taking into account local conditions. The clause may therefore play a significant role in the future development of EEC environmental law.

The cost-benefit analysis. Article 130r(3), third indent, requires the Community to take account of "the potential benefits and costs of action or of lack of

---

[29] O.J. 1976 No. L 129, 23–29; see also Directive 86/280 of June 12, 1986 on limit values and quality objectives for discharges of certain dangerous substances, O.J. 1986 No. L 181, 16–27.

THE SINGLE EUROPEAN ACT AND THE ENVIRONMENTAL POLICY OF THE EEC   421

action." This clause requires a cost-benefit analysis for every environmental action, a feature which may significantly increase the expense of devising and implementing the Community's environmental policy and may cause considerable delay.

It is submitted that Article 130r(3), third indent, only requires the Community institutions to make a judgment about the appropriateness of action in light of its costs and its benefits. The Article does not express any opinion as to the standards that should guide the Community in making that judgment and, it is submitted, would not preclude the Community from taking a certain environmental measure notwithstanding the disproportion between its costs and its beneficial effect on the environment if such effect were deemed absolutely necessary. Such directive could, however, in certain circumstances be subject to challenge under the principle of proportionality as developed by the European Court. Under that principle, the Community must exercise its powers in such a way that no greater burdens are imposed than are required to achieve the aim which it seeks to accomplish.[30] The principle has been described by Professor Schermers as precluding the Community from "requiring large sacrifices to be made by some people in order to obtain a result which is only of small importance to others."[31]

The balanced economic and social development. Pursuant to Article 130r(3), fourth indent, when preparing environmental action the Community must take account of the economic and social development of the Community as a whole and the balanced development of its regions. The clause obviously reflects the fear of some of the less developed Member States that environmental measures will unduly restrict their economic expansion. The development of the economy and the concern for redressing the economic disparities that exist between the various regions have been a basic objective of the Community since its founding. This concern has received additional impetus by the S.E.A. which inserted a new Article 130a in the EEC Treaty, providing that the Community shall aim at reducing disparities between the various regions and the backwardness of the least-favoured regions.

It is argued that Article 130r(3), fourth indent, arguably only requires the Community to have regard to the effects of a proposed measure on the economic and social development of the Community and of its regions and to assess these effects against the advantages of a common measure for the entire Community. Whether the assessment should influence or be reflected by the measure ultimately taken by the Council is up to the Council. Moreover, it is not all clear whether the assessment could even lead to a measure that differentiates between various regions of the Community as concerns its application. Such differentiation could lead to distortions in the competitive position of enterprises as they, temporarily or definitively, would be made subject to different environmental restrictions. Contrary to the differentiations that may result from Article 130r(3), second indent,—the local environmental conditions clause—these differentiations would bear no relationship to the objective environmental factors that may have influenced the decision to make a certain investment; they would only result from the fact that the investment was made in a backward region of the Community.

---

[30] Case 9/73, *Schlüter* v. *Hauptzollamt Lörrach*, [1973] E.C.R. 1135, 1155.
[31] H. G. Schermers, *Judicial protection in the European Communities*, 1983, 65.

422   THE SINGLE EUROPEAN ACT AND THE ENVIRONMENTAL POLICY OF THE EEC

It is submitted that differentiations on economic grounds are not warranted under Article 130r(3), fourth indent. The S.E.A. has specifically provided for the possibility of derogations for certain less-developed regions of the Community with respect to measures that are taken to achieve the internal market. Article 8c provides that the Commission, when proposing such measures shall "take into account" differences in economic developments but adds that if such leads to derogations, "they must be of a temporary nature and must cause the least possible disturbance to the functioning of the common market." It would seem illogical to impose such strict restrictions in connection with the internal market measures and to permit unlimited differentiation in the field of the environment on grounds that do not relate to the environment. If the possibility of differentiation on economic grounds had to be created, it should have been provided for expressly.

The principle of subsidiarity. Of all clauses of the S.E.A. dealing with the environment, Article 130r(4) probably is the most important one. The Article expressly reserves residual jurisdiction to the Member States:

> "The Community shall take action relating to the environment to the extent to which the objectives [of the Community environmental policy] can be attained better at Community level than at the level of the individual Member States."

From a Community perspective, this is clearly a step backwards. As discussed, on the basis of Articles 100 and 235, the Community had virtually unlimited competence to regulate in the field of the environment. Article 100 combined with Article 235 permit all measures that are necessary to attain one of the objectives of the Community, provided a link with the functioning of the common market exists. As noted, the protection of the environment has been recognised by the European Court as one of the basic objectives of the Community and the requirement of a link with the market has been loosely interpreted by the Council without ever having been seriously challenged. It is clear that under Article 235 (and, of course, Article 100) no similar subsidiarity principle exists. It is interesting to note that the abandonment of unlimited jurisdiction of the Community *vis-à-vis* the Member States' jurisdiction has not been compensated by a more flexible decision-making process. As was already the case under Articles 100 and 235, unanimity will be required for environmental action (subject to certain exceptions discussed below).

The obvious question raised by the subsidiarity principle is that of who will judge whether the subject matter is better regulated at Community level than at Member State level. Professor Jacqué has expressed the opinion that it is difficult to imagine that the European Court would review a Community measure on this point, in particular having regard to the fact that in most cases it will have been adopted by unanimous vote in the Council of Ministers.[32] Perhaps the European Court will take guidance from the position that has been adopted in Germany, where the German Constitutional Court has refused to enter into a similar debate. Pursuant to Article 72 of the German constitution, in areas of concurrent jurisdiction of the union and the states, the states are competent to

---

[32] Jacqué, *supra*, n. 2, at 606. See also Jacqué in *Le Traité d'Union européenne*, 1985, 71–74.

THE SINGLE EUROPEAN ACT AND THE ENVIRONMENTAL POLICY OF THE EEC 423

take action to the extent the union has not legislated, which the union may do whenever there is a need for regulation at the federal level. Such need is deemed to exist when the subject matter cannot be effectively dealt with by the individual states. The German Constitutional Court has held that whether such a need is present or not is matter of assessment by the federal legislator, which by its nature is not capable of being reviewed by a court.[33] The Constitutional Court limits itself to checking whether there is no clear evidence that the federal legislator has exceeded the boundaries of the assessment it is required to make.

Similar hesitations to review political and factual assessments can be found in the case law of the European Court. However, if the European Court is willing to accept that in certain circumstances the Community institutions may enjoy a considerable amount of discretion, such discretion cannot be absolute unless it follows clearly from the legal text in question. In the *Racke* case, which involved the setting of monetary compensatory amounts, the European Court held that it could review the legality of the action taken within the following confinements:

> "Since the evaluation of a complex economic situation is involved, [the Community] enjoys [. . .] a wide measure of discretion. In reviewing the legality of the exercise of such discretion, the Court must confine itself to examining whether it contains a manifest error or constitutes a misuse of power or whether the authority did not clearly exceed the bounds of its discretion."[34]

Based on this case law of the European Court, it is not to be ruled out that the European Court will accept certain jurisdiction over the issue of subsidiarity, but only within the strict boundaries that it has imposed upon itself when faced with similar issues of political and factual assessment.

The legal instruments at the disposition of the Community's environmental policy. Of the various EEC legal instruments, the directive and the regulation are of most relevance in environmental matters. A directive is binding upon Member States as to the result to be achieved but leaves the Member States the choice of form and methods. A regulation, however, is binding in its entirety and is directly applicable in the Member States. In the past the Community in implementing its environmental policy has made use of the full array of legal instruments, including directives and regulations, that pursuant to Article 189 are at its disposition. The main vehicle used, however, was that of the directive. The most significant attempt to deal by regulation with an environmental matter of direct relevance to individuals and companies (namely, the draft regulation on the transborder movement of dangerous waste) was transformed by the Council back into a directive (as it had originally been proposed by the Commission).[35]

New Article 130r(4), second sentence, arguably indirectly restricts the tools of the Community environmental policy as follows:

> "Without prejudice to certain measures of a Community nature, the Member States shall finance and *implement* the other measures." (emphasis added).

---

[33] von Münch, *Grundgesetz-Kommentar*, 1978, vol. 3, 26.
[34] Case 136/77, *Racke* v. *Hauptzollamt Mainz*, [1978] E.C.R. 1245, 1256.
[35] O.J. 1983 No. C 186, 3–17.

424   THE SINGLE EUROPEAN ACT AND THE ENVIRONMENTAL POLICY OF THE EEC

The above clause appears to reveal a preference for the use of directives instead of regulations which, as mentioned above, do not need implementation by the Member States. The use of other legal instruments is not excluded, however, since measures of a "Community nature" could still be taken in other forms, such as a regulation or a decision. There can be no doubt that research programs can be considered as measures of a Community nature (especially now that a cost-benefit analysis has become mandatory), but it is unclear when a straightforward regulatory measure will acquire "Community" nature.

While in the field of the environment the S.E.A. appears to push the Community towards the directive as the legal tool of action, as concerns the harmonisation of Member States' laws (which up to now on the basis of Article 100 could only be achieved by way of a directive), all legal instruments may be used in the framework of the achievement of the internal market: Article 100a calls for the adoption of "measures" for the approximation of laws. Consequently, environmental matters that are not of a "Community" nature can still be dealt with by way of a regulation provided they can be fitted within the program to realise the internal market.[36]

The Community is a legislator only. In addition to restricting the legal instruments available to EEC environmental law, Article 130r(4), cited above, also poses the rule that, except for measures of a Community nature, the Community is a legislator only: the implementation (a term appears to encompass enforcement as well) and financing of Community environmental measures is reserved to the Member States.

The above rule generally corresponds with the division of tasks between the Community and the Member States that has been followed so far in EEC environmental law. As a rule, EEC environmental measures have been issued by way of directives, the transposition into national law and the enforcement of which is left to the Member States. This division of tasks has, however, led to a number of practical and legal problems. Member States more than occasionally are late in implementing environmental directives or implement the directives in an incomplete, incorrect or conflicting manner. Sometimes the differences between Member-State implementing laws are a direct result of the directives themselves, as they often are limited to setting general principles or contain open-ended clauses. Cases in point are Directives 78/319 on toxic and dangerous waste and Directive 84/631 on the transborder shipment of dangerous waste.[37] Both directives apply to waste that is contaminated by certain specified substances and is "of such a nature, in such quantities or in such concentrations as to constitute a risk to health or to the environment."[38] The definition of what

---

[36] It should be noted that in a "declaration" annexed to the S.E.A., the Conference of the Representatives of the Governments of the Member States has indicated that, in its proposals pursuant to Article 100a(1), the Commission must give "precedence" to the use of directives if the harmonisation sought involves the amendment of legislative provisions in one or more Member States. Since the declaration only refers to "legislative" provisions, the reservation apparently does not apply to the harmonisation of regulatory or administrative provisions or practices.

[37] Directive 78/319 of March 20, 1978 on toxic and dangerous waste, O.J. 1978 No. L 84, 43–48; Directive 84/631 of December 6, 1984 on the supervision and control within the European Community of the transfrontier shipment of hazardous waste, 1984 O.J. No. L 326, 31–41.

[38] Article 1(b) of Directive 78/319.

THE SINGLE EUROPEAN ACT AND THE ENVIRONMENTAL POLICY OF THE EEC 425

nature, quantity or concentration will trigger the application of both directives is, however, left to the Member States. Needless to say this situation is unfortunate, particularly in a subject matter such as the transborder shipment of waste, which by definition implies the involvement of more than one Member State. A further defect of the traditional division of tasks is that certain subject matters are more efficiently dealt with at Community level. A typical example of such a subject matter is the notification of new chemical substances pursuant to the Sixth Amendment.[39] The role of the Commission under that directive has been more than that of a clearing house; in practice the system has been set up and is closely monitored by the Commission.

The problems caused by the traditional division of tasks between the Community and the Member States have led some, in particular in the European Parliament, to seek a more active role for the Community in the field of administrative implementation and enforcement. The evolution certainly was in the direction of greater involvement of the Community in the daily application of its environmental rules. The drafters of the S.E.A. apparently wished this evolution to be halted and direct Community involvement restricted to measures of a "Community" nature.

The legislative process

It will be recalled that prior to the S.E.A., EEC environmental measures had to be taken on the basis of Articles 100 and/or 235 which require unanimity within the Council of Ministers. The S.E.A. has not significantly altered the legislative process applicable to Community action in the field of the environment except when such action can be taken in the framework of the achievement of the internal market.

Article 130s provides:

> "The Council, acting unanimously on a proposal from the Commission and after consulting the European Parliament and the Economic and Social Committee, shall decide what action is to be taken by the Community."

In order not to rule out entirely the possibility of qualified majority voting at the Council on environmental matters, Article 130s, second paragraph provides:

> "The Council shall, under the conditions laid down in the preceding paragraph, define those matters on which decisions are to be taken by a qualified majority."

It is noteworthy that the environment has not been made subject to qualified majority voting and the cooperation procedure involving the European Parliament—the two basic institutional reforms made by the S.E.A. for most of the Community's policies. Decision-making will remain in principle on a unanimous basis and the role of the European Parliament remains limited to giving an opinion on the proposals by the Commission.

Qualified majority voting and cooperation with the European Parliament will apply when a measure is taken in the framework of the programme to achieve the internal market. Under the cooperation procedure, the European Parliament may reject or propose amendments to a measure as to which the Council

---

[39] See n. 19.

426   THE SINGLE EUROPEAN ACT AND THE ENVIRONMENTAL POLICY OF THE EEC

has reached a "common position" by qualified majority vote. In the case of rejection by the Parliament, unanimity is required for the Council to adopt the measure definitively. In the case of amendments proposed by the Parliament, they must be examined by the Commission, and unanimity is required for the Council to amend the proposal as re-examined by the Commission.

The safeguard clauses

Article 130t confirms a rule which is already to be found in many EEC environmental directives: the norms set forth by the Community are but the minimum requirements that should be complied with. The safeguard clause for stricter regulation by the Member States is worded as follows:

> "The protective measures adopted in common pursuant to Article 130s shall not prevent any Member State from maintaining or introducing more stringent protective measures compatible with this Treaty."

Article 130t raises a number of questions. Why is its application limited to "protective" measures? Is the word protective used in the same meaning as in Article 130r(1) (which concerns the objectives of the Community environmental policy)? In that case measures aiming at preserving or improving the environment would not come within the scope of the safeguard clause. Further, what is the meaning of the expression "adopted in common"? If taken literally, it would mean that the safeguard clause would not apply to measures adopted by qualified majority voting pursuant to Article 130s, second paragraph. Or does "in common" refer to the possibility that differentiated measures may be adopted pursuant to Article 130r(3), second indent? In that case, the safeguard clause would not apply if the directive had already taken into account the local conditions in the more stringent Member State and had not provided for common rules.

The safeguard clause is subject to the general proviso that the more stringent measures that are maintained or introduced by a Member State must otherwise be compatible with the EEC Treaty. The most obvious problem such a measure could encounter is that it may be a violation of Article 30 *et seq.* EEC, which provide for the free movement of goods. As interpreted by the European Court, Article 30 prohibits all measures enacted by Member States which are capable of hindering, directly or indirectly, actually or potentially, intra-Community trade.[40] Such more stringent measures may be justified under Article 36 EEC which permits restrictions on free movement that are justified on grounds of protection of health and life of humans, animals or plants, provided such restriction does not constitute a means of arbitrary discrimination or a disguised restriction on trade between Member States. Recourse to Article 36 is subject to stringent restrictions, however, and it should be noted that since Article 36 does not mention the environment it can only be invoked in respect of environmental measures that concern health or life. Moreover, under the case law of the European Court, the exceptions listed in Article 36 are not reserved to the exclusive jurisdiction of the Member States.[41] The Community may legislate in these areas and, provided the Community measure gives unconditional assurance that

---

[40] Case 8/74, *Procureur du Roi* v. *Dassonville*, [1974] E.C.R. 837, 852.
[41] See, *e.g.* Case 153/78, *EC Commission* v. *Germany*, 1979 E.C.R. 2555, 2564.

its stated objective will in any event be achieved,[42] the Member States' jurisdiction may as a result be pre-empted. Since Article 130t refers to the Treaty as a whole, it must be assumed that these rules, resulting from the interpretation of the Treaty by the European Court will be applicable.

A differently worded safeguard clause will apply when the environmental measure is taken in the framework of achieving the internal market. Article 100a(4) provides:

> "If, after the adoption of a harmonisation measure by the Council acting by a qualified majority, a Member State deems it necessary to apply national provisions on grounds of major needs referred to in Article 36, or relating to protection of the environment (. . .), it shall notify the Commission of these provisions.
>
> The Commission shall confirm the provisions involved after having verified that they are not a means of arbitrary discrimination or a disguised restriction on trade between Member States."

This new clause of the Treaty has given rise to considerable controversy, in particular concerning its possible effect on the case law of the European Court on the free movement of goods.[43] The differences with the safeguard clause contained in Article 130s are notable. Article 100a(4) would appear to go against the preemption theory discussed above and, more significantly, adds the environment to the grounds for exception.

Finally, we note that pursuant to new Article 100a(5), harmonisation measures taken by qualified majority on the basis of Article 100a(1) must, "in appropriate cases," contain an express safeguard clause to the effect that Member States may take "provisional measures" for one of the grounds listed in Article 36, subject to a "Community control" procedure. Since reference is made to Article 36 only, provisional measures on grounds created exclusively to the environment would not be permissible on the basis of Article 100a(5).

Conclusion

The S.E.A. has the merit of having removed any doubt—to the extent such doubt still existed—about the basis in the EEC Treaty for the Community's environmental policy, at least as a matter of principle. It has stressed the importance the Community attaches to the protection of the environment even to the point of providing in new Article 103r(2) EEC that "environmental protection requirements shall be a component of the Community's other policies." In addition, the S.E.A. has spelled out the objectives of the Community's environmental policy and the basic principles it should adhere to. However, in formulating the exceptions and restrictions to the Community's jurisdiction in environmental matters the S.E.A. is less than precise and may give rise to controversy.

An interesting aspect of the new provisions of the EEC Treaty which have been inserted by the S.E.A. is that they may widen the possibilities of challeng-

---

[42] Case 72/83, *Campus Oil Limited et al* v. *the Ministry for Industry and Energy*, [1984] E.C.R. 2727; see D. Vandermeersch, "Restrictions on the movement of oil in and out of the European Community: the Campus Oil and Bulk Oil cases," [1987] J.E.N.R.L. 31.

[43] See in particular Pescatore, *supra*, n. 2.

428   THE SINGLE EUROPEAN ACT AND THE ENVIRONMENTAL POLICY OF THE EEC

ing EEC environmental actions before the European Court. Pursuant to Article 173 EEC, the European Court is empowered to review the legality of the acts of the Council and of the Commission on the grounds of lack of competence, misuse of powers or of infringement of essential procedural requirements, the Treaty or secondary community law. Prior to the S.E.A., such challenge in practice had to involve a claim that the Community lacked competence to act in the field of the environment under Article 100 or 235. However, as a result of the S.E.A., a challenge based on lack of competence can now evolve on the question whether the matter could be better dealt with at Community level instead of at Member State level. Even if the European Court were to limit itself to the kind of marginal review we have described above, the issue of subsidiarity seems more promising to a litigant than the issue of the scope of Articles 100 and 235. In addition, as a result of the S.E.A., a challenge can now also be brought on the grounds that the Community failed to abide by the basic principles set forth in Article 130r(2) or that the Community failed to make the assessments required by Article 130r(3).

EEC environmental actions may be challenged on the above grounds by a Member State, the Council or the Commission. Pursuant to Article 173, second paragraph EEC, private parties could only bring such action if the environmental measure in question is taken in the form of a decision or a decision adopted in the form of a regulation and is "of direct and individual concern" to them. Since the S.E.A. implicitly seems to impose the form of a directive as principal tool of the Community's environmental policy (unless the measure is of a Community nature), private parties seem severely restricted in their possibilities of bringing a claim for annulment before the European Court. They would indeed have to establish that a measure, although adopted in the form of a directive, does not have a general normative or legislative character and convince the European Court that it should as a result ignore the clear wording of Article 173, second paragraph.[44] In addition, the complainant would have to satisfy the "direct and

---

[44] A. G. Toth, *Legal protection of individuals in the European Communities*, 1978, vol. II, p. 61, expresses the current status of the law when he states that a directive can never be challenged by private parties. The wording of Article 173, second paragraph, stands in the way of a holding by the European Court similar to the rule it has adopted in anti-dumping cases, where private parties have been permitted to challenge anti-dumping duties imposed by way of regulations. In the first Allied case, the European Court held:

> "Although it is true that, in the light of the criteria set out in the second paragraph of Article 173, such [anti-dumping] measures are, in fact, as regards their nature and their scope, of a legislative character, inasmuch as they apply to all the traders concerned, taken as a whole, the provisions may nonetheless be of direct and individual concern to those producers and exporters who are charged with practising dumping. (. . .) It is thus clear that measures imposing anti-dumping duties are liable to be of direct and individual concern to those producers and exporters who are able to establish that they were identified in the measures adopted by the Commission or the Council or were concerned by the preliminary investigations." (Joint cases 239 and 275/82, *Allied Corporation* v. *Commission*, [1984] E.C.R. 1005, 1030.)

From the point of view of economic reality, it is difficult to see the difference between companies that were investigated for dumping practices and companies that were investigated for environmental problems. Because the former are made subject to specific rules by way of regulation, and the latter by way of directive, only the former have standing to challenge the Community measure. This is something of a paradox if one realises that non-EEC companies that were allegedly dumping their products on the EEC market have access to the European Court and that, at the same time, such access is denied to EEC-based companies that are suspected of causing environmental problems. In this debate it

The Single European Act and the Environmental Policy of the EEC   429

individual concern" test.[45] That would seem an uphill battle on a very steep hill indeed. Moreover, once the directive has been implemented in the national legal system of the complainant, the only recourse against the measure that could effectively result in the measure being annulled would be the one that may be available under national law.[46]

The S.E.A. has given the EEC environmental policy the recognition and the status befitting its position as one of the Community's fundamental policies. The distrust of some Member States has caused the scope of that environmental policy to be restricted in a way which, before the S.E.A., may have been thought unimaginable. However, the S.E.A. presumably gives expression to certain Member State concerns that heretofore must have played a role in the development of EEC environmental law. The significance of the S.E.A. is that it has not only made these concerns public; it has given them legal status, possibly even to the point of providing grounds for challenging the validity of EEC environmental action.

---

should not be forgotten that certain Member States (for instance, Belgium) have de facto left it to the Community to initiate major new environmental regulations in many areas, and that Community environmental measures, because of their specificity, may in practice only concern a very limited number of "polluters" whose identities are well-known to the Community and whose individual environmental circumstances may have been taken into account (or not taken into account) when the rule was formulated. An example of the latter situation is the application of Directive 78/176 of February 20, 1978 on waste from the titanium dioxide industry (O.J. 1978 No. L 54, 19–24). The validity of this directive and an executory decision taken by the Commission pursuant to it was challenged by BTP Tioxide Limited, a U.K. company (Case 78/79, *BTP Tioxide Limited* v. *Commission*, O.J. 1979 No. C 153, 5). The case was settled, however, and removed from the Register of pending cases on October 3, 1986 (O.J. 1986 No. C 280, 7).

[45] For a discussion of the test, see Schermers, *supra*, n. 31, 205–210.

[46] While Article 173 concerns a direct challenge to the legality of decisions and decisions adopted in the form of regulations, Article 177 gives the European Court jurisdiction to rule, at the request of a national court, on the validity of Community acts, in whatever form they are taken. A private complainant would thus have to convince a national court to submit the legality question to the European Court.

[3]

European Community Environmental Law: Legislation, the European Court of Justice and Common-Interest Groups

*Philippe Sands**

Introduction

European Community (EC) environmental law and policy has come a long way since the Council of the European Communities (Council) approved the first EC Action Programme on the Environment in 1973,[1] following a declaration on the environment by the Heads of State and government of the nine members in October 1972. Since then the EC has adopted three further Action Programmes on the Environment[2] and more than one hundred and fifty acts of secondary environmental legislation.[3] It now seems possible to imagine as an emerging legal reality a Single European Environment, recognising the physical reality that EC Member States share a common environment which transcends national boundaries.

The EC's environmental policies are now keenly followed by the public, corporations and common-interest groups (as defined by the Commission) committed to the protection of the environment. The latter, traditionally hostile to the EC as an engine of economic development, have begun to play a key role in shaping both the legislative programme, through lobbying the Commission of the European Communities (Commission) and the European Parliament as well as Member State governments, and the enforcement of legislation, principally by notifying the Commission of violations by Member States of EC environmental law,[4] but also by using EC law to achieve environmental objectives.[5]

The EC environmental law and policy which is emerging raises a number of questions: how will the EC achieve a balance between the original, and still dominant, objective of economic development and integration, and the new, and still subsidiary, objective

---

*Director, Centre for International Environmental Law (CIEL), School of Law, Kings College London.

1 (For the period 1973–76), OJ 1973 C112/1.
2 Second Programme (1977–81) OJ 1977 C39/1; Third Programme (1982–86) OJ 1983 C46/1; Fourth Programme (1987–92) OJ 1987 C328/1.
3 Secondary EC environmental legislation includes Regulations, Directives and Decisions under the EEC Treaty and Euratom. For a detailed account of the Community's secondary environmental legislation see N. Haigh, *EEC Environmental Policy and Britain* (2nd revised ed, 1989) (excluding relevant legislation on radioactive substances); S. Johnson and G. Corcelle, *The Environmental Policy of the European Communities*, 1989; *Halsbury's Laws of England* (4th ed, 1986) Vols 51 and 52, D. Vaughan (ed) *Law of the European Communities*, at Part 8; E. Rehbinder and R. Stewart, *Environmental Protection Policy* (1985) (Vol 2 of the series *Integration Through Law: Europe and the American Federal Experience*), Cappelletti, Seccombe and Weiler (Gen eds); Haagsma, 'The EC's Environmental Policy: A Case Study in Federalism,' 12 Fordham ILJ 311 (1988).
4 In 1989 the Commission (Directorate General XI) received 460 notifications of alleged violations from individuals or common-interest groups (telephone conversation between the author and L. Kramer, Legal Adviser, DGXI, 7 June, 1990).
5 See for example Case 187/87, *Saarland and Others* v *Ministry of Industry and Others*, [1989] 1 CMLR 529 where environmental protection groups in the Moselle valley, and others, successfully relied on Article 37 Euratom through a preliminary reference to the ECJ to obtain a judgment from a French court in respect of a dispute concerning the disposal of radioactive waste from a nuclear power plant. For an account of the effective use of Article 92 of the EEC Treaty by the Council for the Protection of Rural England to prevent the privatisation of nuclear power in England, see P. Sands, *The Contribution of NGOs to the Progressive Development of International Environmental Law*, paper delivered at the 4th Annual Anglo-Soviet Symposium on International Law, Moscow, May 1990.

of environmental protection? What influence will environmental litigation and advocacy instigated by common-interest groups have in fashioning that balance? And what role will the European Court of Justice (ECJ) play as it is increasingly faced with environmental disputes which have reached Luxembourg through litigation and the enforcement processes available at national and EC level? These will be key questions for the Community over the next decade as it attempts to integrate environmental policies into the whole spectrum of its activities.[6]

This article examines these issues specifically by reference to a number of recent and likely future developments. In the context of EC environmental legislation generally, Part I of the article considers four new acts of EC environmental legislation which mark a new direction in EC law and policy-making. They are also likely to generate significant amounts of environmental litigation. Three of these legislative acts have already been adopted by the EC and will soon become effective: the European Environment Agency Regulation,[7] the Broadcasting Directive,[8] and the Environmental Information Directive.[9] The other act, the draft Waste Liability Directive[10] is still in the legislative process, and is not expected to be adopted before the end of 1990. Together with the existing body of EC secondary legislation, these four acts of secondary legislation will have a significant impact on the enforcement of environmental laws by increasing and standardising the monitoring process, by making more information on the environment available to the public and common-interest groups, and by establishing new causes of action and remedies available under the national laws and before the national courts of the Member States.

Part II of the article considers recent developments in EC environmental litigation and the potential role of the ECJ. Since EC secondary environmental legislation will be the basis of national laws, difficulties of interpretation and application will often fall to be resolved by the ECJ. As will be seen, a number of the provisions in the European Environmental Agency Regulation, the Broadcasting Directive, the draft Waste Liability Directive and the Environmental Information Directive are vague and susceptible to differing interpretations. It is unlikely that the incorporation of the Directive into the national law of the twelve Member States will follow a uniform method or terminology. The ECJ is likely to find itself increasingly called upon to achieve a balance between two of the EC's objectives: economic development and environmental protection. In the context of the ECJ's existing jurisprudence on environmental matters, including in particular the judgment in the 'Danish bottles' case,[11] it is worth considering whether the ECJ is likely to come down in favour of a high standard of environmental protection at the cost of establishing certain barriers to trade and otherwise limiting or altering the direction of the Community's economic development.

Finally, the article concludes by considering some tentative and speculative scenarios that might arise once more information on the environment is available through the work of the European Environment Agency and the Environmental Information Directive, and once the Broadcasting Directive and the draft Waste Liability Directive are in place.

---

6   The Commission has recently stated that '[n]ot only is it no longer possible to maintain the quality of life and sustain economic growth without taking account of the environment; but the success of the other Community policies hinges upon it'; see *Commission Work Programme for 1990*, paragraph 142, in *European Report* No 1558, 27 January, 1990.

7   Council Regulation 1210/90/EEC of 7 May, 1990 on the establishment of the European Environment Agency and the European environment information and observation network, OJ 1990 L120/1.

8   Council Directive 89/552/EEC of 3 October, 1989 on the coordination of certain provisions laid down by law, regulation or administrative action in Member States concerning the pursuit of television broadcasting activities, OJ 1989 L298/23.

9   Council Directive 90/313/EEC of 7 June 1990 on the freedom of access to information on the environment, OJ 1990 L158/56.

10   Commission proposal for a Council Directive on civil liability for damage caused by waste (COM (89) 282 final), 15 September, 1989; OJ 1989 C251/3.

11   Case 302/86, *Commission of the European Communities v Denmark* [1989] 1 CMLR 619.

Part I: EC Environmental Legislation

Background

Community legislation on the environment can be divided into two distinct phases: the first covers the period 1973 to 1986, prior to the amendments made to the Treaty of Rome by the Single European Act (SEA) to provide expressly for environmental protection; and the second, in the period from 1987 onwards, following those amendments.

When it was signed in 1957, the Treaty establishing the European Economic Community (EEC Treaty) had no express provisions relating to environmental protection. However, this did not mean the EC could not legislate on environmental matters. In the absence of a specific Treaty provision for the implementation of a given policy, two Treaty provisions are generally utilised: Article 100, which empowers the Council to issue Directives for the approximation of the laws, regulations or administrative provisions of Member States to remove barriers to trade and distortions of competition, and Article 235 which empowers the Council to take appropriate action to attain one of the objectives of the EC.[12] In this way, Articles 100 and 235 established the legal basis for initial EC environmental legislation, commencing with a 1967 Directive on the classification, packaging and labelling of dangerous substances.[13] By July 1987, when the SEA came into force, the EC had already adopted three Action Programmes on the Environment[14] and established a well-developed body of substantive rules[15] covering the protection of water quality[16] and air quality,[17] the control and management of waste,[18] the control of chemicals,[19] the protection of flora, fauna and countryside,[20] and limitations on permissible noise levels.[21] Moreover, the ECJ had by then expressly endorsed the use of Article 100 to legislate on environmental matters.[22] By 1987 the EC had also become a party to, or had signed, a number of international treaties governing a wide range of environmental matters.[23]

Additionally, by 1987 the EC had also developed an environmental policy which led it to adopt a number of legislative acts more properly characterised as procedural in nature, but which would also have significant substantive impacts. Such acts include four environ-

---

12 See Rehbinder and Stewart, above n 3, 15–42.
13 Council Directive 67/548/EEC on the approximation of the laws, regulations and administrative provisions relating to the classification, packaging and labelling of dangerous substances; OJ 1967 L196. The Directive was originally intended to protect humans, and not the environment, but was amended in 1979, for the sixth time, to provide specifically for a new classification of substances 'dangerous for the environment': Directive 79/831/EEC, OJ 1979 L259.
14 See above n 2.
15 Three types of EC Directive in respect of environmental protection have been identified: Regulation-type Directives, establishing comprehensive substantive Community legislation to eliminate obstacles to free trade and distortion of competition, and to regulate particular environmental problems; Directive setting environmental quality standards, including ambient quality standards and implementation plans and monitoring systems; and Directives establishing environmental protection principles or coordinating Member State policies; see Rehbinder and Stewart, above n 3, 138–142.
16 Commencing in 1973 with Directive 73/404/EEC on detergents; OJ 1973 L347/51.
17 Commencing in 1975 with Directive 75/716/EEC on the approximation of the laws of the Member States relating to the sulphur content of certain liquid fuels; OJ 1975 L307/22.
18 Commencing in 1975 with the framework Directive 75/442/EEC on waste; OJ 1975 L194/39.
19 Commencing in 1967, see above n 13.
20 Commencing initially in 1970 with Regulation 729/70/EEC on countryside protection in agriculturally less favoured areas; OJ 1970 L94/13.
21 Commencing in 1970 with Directive 70/157/EEC relating to the permissible sound levels and the exhaust system of motor vehicles; OJ 1970 L42/16.
22 See Cases 91 and 92/79, *Commission of the European Communities v Italian Republic*, [1980] ECR 1099 and 1115.
23 Commencing in 1975 with Decision 75/437/EEC on the conclusion of the Paris Convention for the Prevention of Marine Pollution from Land-based Sources; OJ 1975 L194/5.

mental research programmes,[24] a number of scientific and technical cooperation agreements between the EC and third countries,[25] a fund for EC environmental action,[26] a Recommendation on the 'Polluter Pays Principle'[27] and, perhaps most important, a Directive establishing mandatory environmental impact assessments in respect of certain public and private projects.[28]

The commencement of the second phase in the legislative development of the EC's environmental policy was marked by the entry into force of the SEA amendments to the EEC Treaty on July 1, 1987, which included the new provisions on environmental protection.[29] Article 18 of the SEA added a new Article 100A to the EEC Treaty. Article 100A(1) grants the Council, acting by qualified majority on a proposal from the Commission in cooperation with the Parliament, the power to adopt measures to approximate national laws to achieve the internal market. Article 100A(3) provides that in respect of proposals concerning, *inter alia*, environmental protection the Commission shall take 'as a base a high level of protection.' Article 100A(4) permits a Member State to apply national provisions on grounds of major needs referred to in Article 36, relating to the protection of the environment.

Article 25 of the SEA added a new Title VII to the EEC Treaty, consisting of Articles 130R, 130S and 130T. Article 130R provides that EC action relating to the environment shall have the following objectives:

  (i) to preserve, protect and improve the quality of the environment;
  (ii) to contribute towards protecting human health;
  (iii) to ensure a prudent and rational utilisation of natural resources.

It further provides that EC action shall be preventive, that environmental damage should as a priority be rectified at source, that the polluter should pay for damage, and that environmental protection shall be a component of other EC policies. It also provides for the principle of subsidiarity[30] and for the EC to participate in international environmental agreements.

Article 130S provides that Title VII action is to be taken by the Council acting unanimously on a proposal from the Commission and after consulting the Parliament, except where the Council, following this procedure, decides otherwise. Finally, Article 130T provides that Member States are entitled to maintain or introduce more stringent protective measures compatible with the Treaty. Shortly after the EEC Treaty changes the Council adopted the fourth Action Programme on the Environment[31] which spelt out in greater detail the EC's commitment to the new Treaty provisions and established the priority areas of pollution prevention, the improvement in the management of resources, international activities and the development of appropriate instruments. With regard to the last-mentioned, the matters specified include effective implementation of the environmental impact assessment Directive,[32] the integration of the environmental dimension in other EC policies, the development of efficient economic instruments (such as taxes, levies, state aids and rebates) to

---

24   First environmental research programme (1973–76), OJ 1973 L175 and OJ 1973 L189; second environmental research programme (1976–80), OJ 1977 L200, OJ 1976 L74 and OJ 1979 L258; third environmental research programme (1980–85), OJ 1980 L72 and OJ 1981 L101; fourth environmental research programme (1986–90), OJ 1984 L3 and OJ 1986 L159.
25   See, for example, scientific and technical cooperation agreement (COST 68 *bis*) on the treatment and utilisation of sewage sludge, OJ 1979 L72.
26   OJ 1984 L176.
27   OJ 1975 L194.
28   Directive 85/337/EEC, OJ 1985 L175/40.
29   On the SEA and the environment see Vandermeersch, 'The Single European Act and the Environment Policy of the EEC,' 12 Eur LR 407 (1987); Kramer, 'The Single European Act and Environmental Protection,' 24 CML Rev 659 (1987); and Haagsma, above n 4.
30   See below n 35.
31   See above n 2.
32   See above n 29.

implement the 'polluter pays' principle, and improved access to information on the environment.

A particularly useful guide to the EC Commission's likely thinking on future legislative instruments is the Report of its own Task Force on the Environment and the Internal Market,[33] which concludes that in the context of the Internal Market new environmental policy mechanisms will need to be developed based on five essential principles:[34]

— the prevention principle;
— the 'Polluter Pays' principle;
— the subsidiarity principle;[35]
— the principle of economic efficiency and cost-effectiveness;[36] and
— the principle of legal efficiency.[37]

The Task Force was convened by the EC Commission in 1988 to identify and consider the implications of the environmental issues arising from the completion of the Internal Market and other developments within the Community, up to 1992 and beyond. The Report expressly recognises that the accelerated economic growth expected as a result of the '1992' programme and the removal of physical, technical and fiscal barriers will have very significant environmental implications. Examples include increases in atmospheric emissions of SO_2 and NO_x of, respectively, 8–9% and 12–14% by 2010,[38] and increases in transfrontier pollution.[39] The Report recognises as a 'central issue ... the linkage between economic growth and environmental impacts.'[40] As EC secondary legislation on environmental protection becomes increasingly geared towards enforcement by common-interest groups as is suggested below, achieving a reconciliation between economic growth and environmental protection will increasingly become an issue faced by national courts and, ultimately, the ECJ.

It is in the context of interpretative and balancing difficulties likely to be faced by the ECJ that I turn now to consider four of the most recent acts of, and proposals for, EC secondary environmental legislation.

EC Environmental Legislation: Emerging Trends

Two of the most important acts of EC environmental legislation may well turn out to be the Regulation establishing the European Environment Agency[41] and the Environmental Information Directive.[42] Together they will have the effect of improving the EC's environmental monitoring system, increasing the quantity and quality of environmental information which is gathered, and making much of that information available to the public. These effects will, in turn, increase public participation in the procedures to control pollution, including the enforcement of environmental laws. The European Environment Agency Regulation, which will enter into force the day after the location of the Agency seat has been decided,[43] is based on Article 130S and is aimed at providing the EC and the

---

33 Task Force Report on the Environment and the Internal Market, EC Commission, December 1989.
34 Task Force Report, above n 33 at p X.
35 '[T]he primary responsibility and decision-making competence should rest with the lowest possible level of authority of the political hierarchy': *ibid.*
36 '[T]he choice of appropriate economic incentives to secure the achievement of existing environmental protection goals with the lowest possible costs for the economy ... and which also offer permanent incentives to further environmental improvements': *ibid.*
37 '[L]egal instruments used should be readily applicable and enforceable': *ibid.*
38 Task Force Report, above n 33 at p V.
39 *ibid*, at p XIII.
40 *ibid*, at p III.
41 See above n 7.
42 Above n 9.
43 Above n 8 at Article 21.

Member States with objective, reliable and comparable information at the European level to enable environmental protection measures to be taken, to assess the results of such measures and to ensure that the public is properly informed.[44] The Agency will be an autonomous entity having separate legal personality, and it will be run by a management board, an Executive Director and a scientific committee.[45]

The Agency's principal task will be to act as a monitoring body, gathering information, establishing the network,[46] providing the EC and Member States with objective information, and recording, collating and assessing data on the state of the environment.[47] Additionally, the Agency will be ensuring that environmental data at European level are comparable, providing European environmental information to appropriate international bodies, ensuring board dissemination of reliable information (and including a report on the state of the environment every three years), and stimulating the development of environmental forecasting techniques and methods for assessing environmental costs.[48] The Agency's assessment functions relate to the pressures on and quality and sensitivity of the environment,[49] and is directed to certain priority areas which are to include 'transfrontier, plurinational and global phenomena' and the socioeconomic dimension.[50] Subject to certain conditions the Agency may publish information and make it available to the public.[51] Significantly, the Agency is open to countries which are not members of the EC and it may turn out to be a model for environmental monitoring arrangements at the international level.[52]

The Environmental Information Directive[53] is also based on Article 130S and is intended to ensure throughout the EC free access to, and dissemination of, environmental information held by public authorities.[54] The draft Directive is also intended to ensure greater environmental protection and the removal of disparities in Member State laws which create unequal conditions of competition. Since the latter objective would tend to increase economic growth and, therefore, as the Commission's Task Force has recognised, environmental damage, the Directive's effects could be considered to have somewhat contradictory tendencies.

Under the Directive any natural or legal person, anywhere in the EC, would be entitled to access to information relating to the environment without having to show an interest,[55]

---

44 *ibid*, at Article 1.
45 *ibid*, at Articles 7, 8, 9 and 10.
46 The European environment information and observation network will comprise the main component elements of national information networks, national focal points and topic centres; *ibid*, at Article 4(1).
47 *ibid*, at Article 2(i)−(iii).
48 *ibid*, at Article 2(iv)−(x).
49 *ibid*, at Article 3(1).
50 *ibid*, at Article 3(2). The priority areas are air and water quality, the state of the soil, of fauna and flora and biotopes, land use and natural resources, waste management, noise emissions, hazardous chemicals and coastal protection.
51 *ibid*, at Article 6.
52 *ibid*, at Article 19. The first ever meeting of Environment Ministers of central, eastern and western European countries meeting in Dublin on June 15, 1990, agreed to compile a register of pollution problems throughout Europe through the new Envrionmental Agency; see *The Observer*, 16 June, 1990, p 3; *The Independent*, 17 June, 1990, p 10.
53 Above n 9.
54 *ibid*, at Article 1.
55 *ibid*, at Article 3. 'Information relating to the environment' is defined as 'any available information in written, visual, aural, or data-base form on the state of water, air, soil, fauna, flora, land and natural sites, and on activities or measures designed to protect these, including administrative measures and environmental management programmes,' *ibid*, at Article 2(a). Possibly with an eye to private enforcement measures, including citizen suit, an earlier draft of the Directive provided that information included 'in particular data relating to emissions and discharges from authorised or declared installations, actual emissions and discharges, measurement, surveillance and monitoring results, particularly where limit values laid down have been exceeded', see Commission proposal (COM(90) 91 final), OJ 1990 C 102/6 at Article 2(a).

at a charge not exceeding a reasonable cost,[56] upon request.[57] The right of free access to environmental information will be subject to certain limitations, including confidentiality of proceedings of public authorities, international relations and national defence; public security; matters which are *sub judice*; commercial and industrial confidentiality, including intellectual property; confidentiality of personal files and data; and requests which are 'manifestly unreasonable' or 'formulated in too general a manner'.[58]

The environmental information which ought to become available to the public and others through the work of the European Environment Agency, and as a result of the Environmental Information Directive, will satisfy one of the necessary prerequisites for common-interest group litigation to ensure compliance with environmental legislation, including ambient quality standards. However, in contrast to the Broadcasting Directive and the draft Waste Liability Directive, the Environment Agency and the Environmental Information Directive will not in themselves provide new substantive environmental causes of action.

The Broadcasting Directive[59] would, on its face, appear to have nothing whatsoever to do with environmental protection. However, in the form in which it was finally adopted in October 1989, it illustrates how EC environmental legislation is turning up in the most unlikely places, and suggests the extent to which the ECJ is likely to find itself facing difficult issues of legislative interpretation and application. The Broadcasting Directive is aimed at establishing the minimum rules needed to ensure freedom of transmission in broadcasting, breaking down national barriers by allowing broadcasters to transmit and retransmit across EC national boundaries and by creating an obligation on Member States to receive such transmissions and retransmissions except in certain limited circumstances set out in the Directive.[60] The Broadcasting Directive establishes minimum standards in respect of, *inter alia*, television programme and television advertising content.[61] In respect of advertisements, as a result of a last-minute amendment inserted by the European Parliament, the Directive now provides in Article 12 that 'television advertising shall not ... (e) encourage behaviour prejudicial to the protection of the environment.'[62] As discussed further below, this establishes the possibility that, following the adoption of the Directive into the national laws of the Member States (to be achieved by October 3, 1991) legal actions could be brought in national courts seeking to prohibit the broadcast of advertising encouraging the public to buy cars or beverages sold in containers which might be considered to be harmful to the environment.[63]

If the Broadcasting Directive causes concern to the advertising industry, the act of EC secondary legislation most likely to generate private litigation against industry, and perhaps even against industry's financiers, is the draft Waste Liability Directive,[64] once it has been adopted into law. This was formally adopted by the Commission on September 15, 1989. While still in the early stages of the EC legislative process, the draft Directive has already generated considerable controversy and is likely to have a complicated and lengthy legislative passage. As proposed by the Commission, the draft Waste Liability Directive

---

56 *ibid*, at Article 4(2).
57 *ibid*, at Article 5(2). The earlier draft of the Directive seemed clearly aimed at increasing public participation in the enforcement of environmental regulations and breaking down national barriers in that process: the Preamble to that draft stated that the Directive 'would help increase public participation in the procedures to control pollution and prevent damage to the environment' and recognised that 'isolated action by Member States cannot adequately guarantee the elimination of obstacles to access to data on the environment held by public authorities, particularly in the case of cross-frontier pollution', see note 55 above.
58 *ibid*, at Article 3(2), (3) and (4).
59 See above n 8.
60 *ibid*, at Article 2.
61 *ibid*, at Articles 10–21.
62 *ibid*.
63 See further below at *Conclusions.*
64 See above n 10.

is based on Article 100A of the Treaty of Rome and not on Article 130S; it is therefore aimed principally at approximating the laws of the Member States by removing existing disparities which could lead to artificial patterns of investment and waste, distort competition, affect the free movement of goods and entail differences in the level of protection of health, property and the environment.[65] It will not have been lost on the Commission that as an Article 100A proposal the draft is subject to the qualified majority voting rule, removing any possibility of a single Member State veto.

The draft Waste Liability Directive provides that

> [t]he producer of waste shall be liable under civil law for the damage and injury to the environment caused by the waste, irrespective of fault on his part.[66]

The draft Directive establishes a standard of strict liability,[67] with provision for joint and several liability in the event of two producers causing the damage or injury.[68] It proposes to establish no ceiling or financial limits on liability, and to impose no mandatory insurance or security requirement. However, the draft does provide for mandatory time limitations for bringing legal proceedings.[69]

One of the most significant aspects of the draft Directive is that it marks the first time, in the environmental field, that the Commission has proposed EC legislation which would not only establish new causes of action in certain Member States, but it would also provide for new remedies to be made available to potential plaintiffs. The key provision in this context is Article 4 of the draft. By Article 4(1), a plaintiff will be entitled to take legal action to obtain:

    (a) the prohibition or cessation of the act causing the damage or injury to the environment;

    (b) the reimbursement of expenditure arising from measures to prevent the damage or injury to the environment;

    (c) the reimbursement of expenditure arising from measures to compensate for damage within the meaning of subparagraph (c)(ii) of Article 2(1);

    (d) the restoration of the environment to its state immediately prior to the occurrence of injury to the environment or the reimbursement of expenditure incurred in connection with measures taken to this end;

    (e) indemnification for the damage.

Draft Article 4 also provides a formula for limiting the extent of expenditures on the restoration of the environment,[70] the right of public authorities to take certain legal actions,[71] and the recognition of certain existing rights of citizen suit (but not the creation

---

65   *ibid*, at Preamble. But see the Opinion of the Economic and Social Committee on the proposal, which calls on the Commission to revise the draft to base its approach on Articles 130R and 130S and not on Article 100A; OJ 1990 C112/23. See above at n 29.

66   *ibid*, at Article 3. The draft Directive excludes certain wastes, including nuclear (Article 1(2)). It distinguishes between 'damage' (defined as 'damage resulting from death or physical injury' and 'damage to property': Article 2(1)(c)) and a new concept of 'injury to the environment' (defined as 'a significant and persistent interference in the environment caused by a modification of the physical, chemical or biological conditions of water, soil and/or air in so far as these are not considered to be damage within the meaning of subparagraph (c)(ii)': Article 2(1)(d)). The 'producer of waste' is defined in Article 2(1)(a) and 2(2).

67   Liability is excluded in the event of '*force majeure* as defined in Community law' (Article 6(1)) and may be reduced or disallowed where 'the damage is caused both by the waste and the fault of the injured party or of any person for whom the injured party is responsible' (Article 7(2)).

68   *ibid*, at Article 5.

69   *ibid*, at Articles 9 and 10.

70   *ibid*, at Article 4(2).

71   In respect of Article 4(1)(a), (b) and (d): *ibid*, at Article 4(3).

of new rights of citizen suit).[72] Finally, draft Article 4 provides that the Directive is to be 'without prejudice to national provisions relating to non-material damage'[73] and sets out the requisite burden of proof in respect of the causal relationship between the producer's waste and the damage or injury to the environment.[74]

The effect of the draft Waste Liability Directive, if adopted in its present form, would be to create in many of the Member States new causes of action, new remedies and, potentially, many new plaintiffs (and defendants). Ultimately it would be for the ECJ to determine who is a 'producer of waste,' what constitutes an 'injury to the environment,' and the extent to which, in respect of restoration of the environment, the costs could be said to 'substantially exceed the benefit arising for the environment from such restoration.' A European Environment Agency and a new regime of free access to information on the environment will provide significantly increased quantities of information on the production, movement and disposal of waste for potential plaintiffs. This in turn is likely to lead to more litigation and private enforcement, particularly if the rules of standing are harmonised to provide common-interest groups with access to national courts to protect the environment in the manner set out in Article 4(4) of the draft Waste Liability Directive. Some of these cases will end up at the ECJ, with that Court having to provide authoritative interpretations of EC law.

Part II: Environmental Litigation Before the ECJ[75]

Background

The Commission's Task Force on the Environment identified 'legal efficiency' (the application and enforcement of EC environmental law) as one of the five key issues which should influence new environmental policy mechanisms in the context of the internal market.[76] It is therefore not unreasonable to expect that the Commission's new environmental policy mechanisms will be translated into legislation of a type which will lead environmental litigation in the EC to increase.

The implementation and enforcement of EC environmental law is primarily a matter for the Member States, monitored and supervised by the Commission, with only a subsidiary role for the public, common-interest groups and corporations. The ultimate arbiter of compliance with, and interpretation of, EC environmental rules is the ECJ, which could receive environmental cases in a number of ways, either directly or on references from national courts. To date, the ECJ has dealt with only a relatively small number of environmental matters, although the number is increasing and is likely to increase further, as

---

72   'Where the law in Member States gives common-interest groups the right to bring an action as plaintiff, they may seek only the prohibition or cessation of the act giving rise to the injury to the environment. If, however, they have taken the measures provided for in paragraph 1(b) and (d), they may seek reimbursement of the expenditure resulting from such measures': *ibid*, at Article 4(4). On standing in national law, see Rehbinder and Stewart, above n 3, 166–171. The logic of the Single Market dictates that eventually the Commission will have to move to establish common rules on the standing of, *inter alia*, common-interest groups to bring proceedings in national courts under EC law to protect the environment. At a Symposium on 'Participation rights of environmental associations and their possibilities of taking legal action in Europe' (OKO Institut, Frankfurt, 15–16 June, 1990), the Legal Adviser to DGXI, Ludwig Kramer, agreed to the creation of a Commission funded Working Committee to formulate proposals for a new EC Directive to harmonise rules relating to legal standing in national courts for individuals and common-interest groups in respect of environmental protection.

73   *ibid*, at Article 4(5).

74   *ibid*, at Article 4(6). The standard in the draft, 'the overwhelming probability,' is a high one.

75   On implementation and enforcement of EC environmental law, see generally Rehbinder and Stewart, above n 3, 137–175.

76   See above nn 33 and 37.

has been suggested above. Nevertheless, from the limited jurisprudence it is possible to discern certain tendencies of the ECJ's practice, as it struggles to set limits to economic integration, and growth, in the name of environmental protection.

Environmental cases can make their way directly to the ECJ in a number of ways. First, the Commission (under Article 169) or a Member State (under Article 170) may bring infringement proceedings against Member States for a failure to fulfil an environmental obligation under the EEC Treaty or secondary legislation. Second, the Member States, the Council, the Commission and, in limited circumstances, private parties may bring proceedings before the ECJ under Article 173 to review the legality of acts of the Community institutions on the grounds set out in that Article.[77] If those grounds are met, the ECJ may declare the act void under Article 174. Third, as a complement to Article 173, the ECJ has jurisdiction under Article 175 to establish that an EC institution has 'failed to act' and order any necessary measures of compliance under Article 176. Article 175 proceedings may be brought by Member States, EC institutions and, in very limited circumstances, private parties. Fourth, under Articles 178 and 215(2) the ECJ has jurisdiction over actions for damages in respect of non-contractual liability of the Community, which essentially covers liability for acts of maladministration and in tort.

Environmental cases also reach the ECJ indirectly through preliminary references from the courts of Member States under Article 177 of the EEC Treaty. This gives the ECJ jurisdiction to give authoritative guidance on the interpretation and validity of provisions of EC law, including acts of environmental legislation. It is this route which is likely to prove most fruitful for common-interest groups.

The vast majority of environmental cases which have so far reached the ECJ are those brought under Article 169 by the Commission against Member States for a failure to implement Directives. These have been useful to determine that environmental Directives may be adopted under Article 100 of the EEC Treaty,[78] that Member States may not plead provisions, practices or circumstances existing in their internal legal system to justify a failure to comply with an environmental obligation,[79] that mere administrative practices which may be altered at the whim of the administration do not constitute the proper fulfilment of an environmental obligation under a Directive,[80] and that the legal obligations imposed on a Member State by an environmental Directive are limited to those dangerous substances specifically listed in that Directive and not to other unlisted dangerous substances as well.[81]

Whilst very few cases have been brought under the Article 177 procedure,[82] it has been

---

77   The ECJ has recently held admissible proceedings brought by the European Parliament under Article 173: see Case 70/88, *European Parliament v Council of the European Communities*, judgment of 22 May, 1990, not yet reported, concerning the legal basis of Regulation 3954/87/Euratom, fixing admissible levels of radioactivity in foodstuffs.

78   See, for example, Cases 91 and 92/79, *Commission of the European Communities v Italian Republic*, [1980] ECR 1099 and 1115.

79   See, for example, Cases 30 to 34/81, *Commission of the European Communities v Italian Republic*, [1981] ECR 3379; Cases 68, 69, 70 and 71/81, *Commission of the European Communities v Belgium*, [1982] ECR 153; Case 134/86, *Commission of the European Communities v Belgium*, [1987] ECR 2415.

80   See, for example, Cases 96 and 97/81, *Commission of the European Communities v Netherlands*, [1982] ECR 1791 and 1819. See also the recent judgment of the ECJ in *Commission of the European Communities v Netherlands*, 14 March, 1990, not yet reported, concerning the failure to comply with Directive 79/409/EEC on the conservation of wild birds.

81   *Commission of the European Communities v Netherlands*, [1989] 1 CMLR 479 (concerning the failure to implement into national law Directive 80/68/EEC on the protection of groundwater against pollution by certain dangerous substances).

82   See, for example, Case 148/78, *Pubblico Ministero v Ratti*, [1979] ECR 1629 (concerning the direct effect of Directive 73/173/EEC on the classification, packaging and labelling of solvents and the compatibility of Italian national law imposing requirements derogating from the Directive); Case 272/80, *Biologische Producten*, [1981] ECR 3277 (concerning the recognition by importing states of tests carried out under the pesticide law of the state of origin); Case 172/82, *Syndicat national des fabricants d'huile*

'anticipated that the preliminary ruling procedure will in the future gain greater importance in environmental matters.'[83] Even before the Single European Act had been signed, under an Article 177 reference the ECJ had held that the protection of the environment was 'one of the Community's essential objectives' which may as such justify certain limitations on the principle of free movement of goods provided that they do not 'go beyond the inevitable restrictions which are justified by the pursuit of the objective of environmental protection.'[84] Perhaps the most significant 177 ECJ case for the future of environmental litigation in the EC is one brought under the 1968 Brussels Convention on Jurisdiction and Enforcement of Judgments in Civil and Commercial Matters (Brussels Convention)[85] and the 1971 Protocol governing its interpretation by the ECJ.[86] Article 5(3) of the Brussels Convention confers jurisdiction in matters 'relating to tort, delict or quasi-delict' on the courts of the place 'where the harmful event occurred.' In *Handelskwekerij GJ Bier* v *Mines de Potasses d'Alsace*[87] the ECJ was asked for the first time to interpret the meaning of the words 'where the harmful event occurred' in a case in which the defendant was alleged to have discharged over 10,000 tonnes of chloride every twenty-four hours into the Rhine river. On a preliminary reference request from the Appeal Court of the Hague, on appeal against a judgment denying Dutch jurisdiction, the ECJ held that Article 5(3) must be interpreted

> in such a way as to acknowledge that the plaintiff has an option to commence proceedings either at the place where the damage occurred or the place of the event giving rise to it.[88]

The decision of the ECJ opens the way for victims of transboundary pollution to choose the jurisdiction in which they wish to bring tort, delict and quasi-delict claims. Whether they decide on the jurisdiction in which they actually suffered the damage or the jurisdiction in which the event giving rise to the damage occurred will depend on a number of factors, including the right of standing, available remedies, legal costs and time delays. In the context of the draft Waste Liability Directive, the *Handelskwekerij* decision could allow the possibility of forum shopping for common-interest groups wishing to bring proceedings against polluters,[89] including perhaps injunctive proceedings.[90]

The ECJ as an Environmental Tribunal

Two recent decisions of the ECJ suggest that court may well provide fruitful opportunities

---

de graissage v *Groupement d'intérêt économique 'Inter-Huiles'*, [1983] ECR 555 (concerning the conformity of national legislation of France with the rules on free movement of goods and Directive 75/439/EEC on the disposal of waste oils); and Case 14/86, *Pretore di Salo* v *X*, [1987] ECR 2545 (concerning the effect of unimplemented Directive 78/659/EEC on the quality of fresh waters on criminal liability under national law).

83 Rehbinder and Stewart, above n 3, 163.
84 Case 240/83, *Procureur de la République* v *Association de Défense des Brûleurs d'Huiles Usagées*, [1985] ECR 531.
85 OJ 1972 L299/32.
86 Protocol of June 3, 1971, Directive 75/464/EEC, OJ 1975 L204/28.
87 Case 21/76, [1976] ECR 1735.
88 *ibid.*
89 The ECJ has recently held that long-arm jurisdiction is only available to victims of direct harm, holding that Article 5(3) 'cannot be construed as permitting a plaintiff pleading damage which he claims to be the consequence of the harm suffered by other persons who were the immediate victims of the harmful act to bring proceedings against the perpetrator of that act in the courts of the place in which he himself discovered the damage to his assets': Case 220/88, *Dumez France SA and Tracoba Sarl* v *Hessische Landesbank, Salvatorplatz-Grundstücksgesellschaft and Lubecker Hypothekebank*, 11 January, 1990, not yet reported.
90 Rehbinder and Stewart take the view that '[l]ong arm jurisdiction probably also applies to injunctive relief': above n 3, 171, citing Jessurun d'Oliveira, 'La pollution du Rhin et le droit international privé,' in *Rhine Pollution* 81, 114 *et seq* (Tjeenk Willink, Zwolle, 1978).

for common-interest groups seeking an 'environmentalist' interpretation and application of EC law.

The first is the decision of the ECJ in the 'Danish bottles' case, brought by the Commission under Article 169 against Denmark for a declaration that a Danish law requiring all beer and soft drinks containers to be returnable was in breach of Article 30 of the EEC Treaty.[91] In 1978 Danish legislation was introduced to allow the relevant Minister to adopt rules limiting, prohibiting or requiring the use of certain materials and types of container for drinks. The legislation was expressed to be an anti-pollution measure, and empowered the National Agency for the Protection of the Environment (NAPE) to administer the law. In 1981 further legislation was adopted pursuant to the 1978 legislation requiring first, that containers for gaseous mineral waters, lemonade, soft drinks and beer to be subject to a compulsory deposit-and-return system, and second, that such containers be approved by NAPE. Following protests from producers of beverages and containers in other Member States and trade associations the Commission called on the Danish Government to change its 1981 law. As a result of the Commission intervention, in 1984 the Danish Government amended the 1981 legislation to allow beverages covered by the 1981 legislation to be sold in non-approved containers, provided that the quantity sold did not exceed 3,000 hl a year per producer or that the beverage was being sold in a container normally used for that product in the country of production in order to test market in Denmark. Additionally, the 1984 amendment required that no metal containers be used, that a return and recycling system be set up, that the deposit per container be equal to that normally charged on a similar approved container, and that the person marketing the product keep the NAPE fully informed to show compliance.

The Commission was not satisfied with the 1984 amendment and in 1986 brought Article 169 proceedings to have the compulsory deposit-and-return system and the Agency approval system declared incompatible with Article 30 of the EEC Treaty. The United Kingdom intervened in support of the Commission. In his Opinion Advocate General Slynn supported the Commission's argument and found both the compulsory deposit-and-return system and the compulsory NAPE approval system to be in breach of Article 30. The ECJ did not follow the Advocate General's Opinion, holding the deposit-and-return system to be compatible with Article 30, but the NAPE approval system to be incompatible with Article 30. In its first judgment after the SEA to deal squarely with the environmental limitations on the establishment of a single market, the ECJ stated that

> the protection of the environment is a mandatory requirement which may limit the application of Art 30 of the Treaty.[92]

The ECJ expressly endorsed its earlier statement in Case 240/83[93] concerning a proportionality test between the environmental objectives to be achieved and the inevitable restrictions on the free movement of goods. The Court found that the deposit-and-return system was

> an indispensable element of a system intended to ensure the re-use of containers and therefore . . . necessary to achieve the aims pursued by the contested rules. That being so, the restrictions which it imposes on the free movement of goods cannot be regarded as disproportionate.[94]

However, as regards the NAPE approval system, the ECJ found that by restricting the quantity of beer and soft drinks which could be marketed by a single producer in non-approved containers to 3,000 hl a year Denmark was in breach of Article 30. This followed

---

91   See above n 11, Case 302/86, [1989] 1 CMLR 619. For a more detailed case note see P. Kromarek, 'Environmental Protection and the Free Movement of Goods: the Danish Bottles Case' (1990), 2 Jo Env L 89.
92   *ibid*, at 631.
93   See above n 84.
94   *ibid*, at 631.

from the fact that

> the system for returning non-approved containers is capable of protecting the environment and, as far as imports are concerned, affects only limited quantities of beverage compared with the quantity of beverages consumed in Denmark owing to the restrictive effect which the requirement that containers should be returnable has on imports. In those circumstances, a restriction of the quantity of products which may be marketed by importers is disproportionate to the objective pursued.[95]

The ECJ evidently considered the result to be a balanced one, and ordered the parties and the intervener to pay their own costs. Insofar as the ECJ upheld the Danish return-and-deposit system, overriding the Opinion of the Advocate-General, the Court has laid down a clear marker that, in the absence of specific EC legislation establishing a rule of environmental protection, it will permit national rules which have a significant effect on trade between Member States, provided that the rules are genuinely intended to protect the environment, and the effect on trade is not disproportionate to the objective pursued.

Since the 'Danish bottles' case the ECJ has had an opportunity to apply its powers of interpretation to the definition of waste in two of the waste Directives.[96] On an Article 177 reference from an Italian Magistrates Court the ECJ held that the concept of waste within the meaning of Article 1 of Directive 75/442 'is not to be understood as excluding substances and objects which are capable of economic re-utilisation.'[97] The effect of the decision, which should be welcomed by environmental common-interest groups, is to widen the definition of wastes subject to EC regulation to include salvaged materials which are capable of reutilization, regardless of the holder's intention or purpose in disposing of the materials. An immediate consequence is that the draft Waste Liability Directive will probably now apply to a range of substances and objects which would previously have been considered to be outside its scope.[98]

There has been too little case law so far to be able to get a clear sense of how the ECJ will draw the line between the EC's objectives of economic development and integration on the one hand, and environmental protection on the other. However, the 'Danish bottles' and Zanetti cases suggest at a minimum that when environmental disputes reach the ECJ it will consider very seriously arguments which are pushing for a strong line on environmental protection. The 'Danish bottles' case, rightly considered to be a 'landmark' decision, may turn out to be the thin end of a large environmental wedge. And the Zanetti case indicates that the ECJ will not shirk from taking a wide and purposive approach to the interpretation of EC environmental legislation, the implications of which are significant in the context of phrases such as 'behaviour prejudicial to the environment' in the Broadcasting Directive and 'injury to the environment' in the draft Waste Liability Directive.

Conclusions

EC environmental law is a fast-developing area, and it is impossible to predict with any certainty the stage it will have reached a decade from now. Bringing together the various strands considered in this article, it is however possible to make some tentative speculations about possible scenarios.

As a result of the European Environment Agency and the Environmental Information Directive, in a few years common-interest groups will have available to them large amounts

---

95   *ibid*, at para 632.
96   Directive 75/442/EEC on waste, above n 18, and Directive 78/319/EEC on toxic and dangerous waste, OJ 1978 L84/43.
97   Joined Cases 206 and 207/88, *Vessosso and Zanetti*, 28 March, 1990, not yet reported, OJ 1990 C110/4; and Case 359/88, *Zanetti and Others*, not yet reported, OJ 1990 C110/4.
98   See above n 10 at Articles 1 and 2.

of environmental information to which they do not have access today. A Dutch environmental group should, in principle, be able to obtain upon request detailed information from a public authority in the United Kingdom on dumping into the North Sea of sewage and other sludge by a particular UK company. If it cannot get the information from the public authority it should be able to get it from the European Environment Agency. Relying on that information, on Article 4(1)(a) of the draft Waste Liability Directive, and on the *Handelskwekerij* interpretation of Article 5(3) of the Brussels Convention, the Dutch group might be able to bring legal proceedings against the UK company in the Dutch courts for an injunction to stop sludge dumping it considered to be harmful to the environment. The Dutch group would have to prove that the plant was causing an 'injury to the environment,' and ultimately this could be a matter of interpretation for the ECJ.

Moreover, if English law had by then been changed to give standing to common-interest groups in respect of environmental damage, that same Dutch group might prefer to bring its case to an English court, again relying on the *Handelskwekerij* case. And then the ECJ would probably have to decide whether Article 5(3) and a Waste Liability Directive gave the English courts jurisdiction to hear an action brought by a Dutch common-interest group against an English power plant for causing 'injury to the environment.' And in so doing the ECJ would no doubt have to decide whether, for the purpose of the law, the EC's environment was shared or whether it was divisible, with legally distinct English and Dutch environments.

Alternatively, it is possible also to imagine a Danish environmental group bringing proceedings in the Danish courts to prevent the transmission from the Federal Republic of Germany into Denmark of television advertisements encouraging the Danish public to buy German beer in metal cans, or containers otherwise deemed environmentally unsound by NAPE. On an Article 177 reference, the ECJ might have to determine whether, under EC law, such German advertisements 'encourage behaviour prejudicial to the environment' within the meaning of the Broadcasting Directive.

In the context of recent developments in EC environmental law, including judgments of the ECJ, neither of these scenarios seem as wild as they might have done before the SEA. One thing is certain: common-interest groups are watching these developments very carefully.

[4]

The Impact of EC Environmental Policies on UK Public Administration

— *Derek Osborn* —

F A (Derek) Osborn is a Deputy Secretary at the
Department of the Environment and Director-General of
the Environmental Protection command. As such he is
responsible for most aspects of the Department's work
on environmental protection, including international and
European Community work, domestic policy on
pollution control and waste management, supervision of
the Majesty's Inspectorate of Pollution and the Energy
Efficiency Office, and the Government's environmental
strategy.

*This paper was delivered at the Royal Institute of
Public Administration Conference, 21 September 1990.*

Most people are now aware that the European Community has developed into
something more than just a common market. Indeed that phrase, once so widely
used, is now rarely heard. In a relatively brief period of time the nature of the
Community has evolved and expanded, so that its many strands are now woven into
most areas of public policy. This is certainly true of environmental policy, where in
the last 20 years the European Community has rapidly become a major factor, or
even the dominant one. In this paper, I shall endeavour to show how and why this has
happened, and the impact it has had on our own policies and practices, before
looking ahead to some possible future developments.

EVOLUTION OF UK ENVIRONMENTAL POLICY

In order to appreciate the impact that the European Community has had it is
necessary to look first at British policy in this area and how it has evolved in response
to British concerns and traditions.

Pollution control has a long history in the United Kingdom. In fact, this was the first
country in the world to introduce systematic controls over air pollution and waste
disposal. This is not altogether surprising – we were after all the first country to
undergo an industrial revolution and widespread urbanization.

Water pollution

The first major legislation was enacted in 1848 in response to public health problems
caused by water pollution, notably an outbreak of cholera. Later in the Victorian era,
the Rivers Pollution Prevention Act 1876 made it a criminal offence to pollute any
British river. The Act introduced the concept of 'best practicable and available

ENVIRONMENTAL POLICY AND PRACTICE / VOLUME 2 / NUMBER 2 / 1992

means' with respect to sewage discharges and also brought the first controls on industrial effluents. It was to remain in force until 1951. In the meantime the Public Health Acts of 1936 and 1937 established a regulatory framework for discharges to public sewers, based on a system of conditional consents for individual discharges. A similar regime was introduced for discharges to rivers by a series of Acts between 1951 and 1974. The 1951 Act also placed a general duty on River Boards and their successors to maintain or restore the wholesomeness of rivers.

No guidance was given as to how this duty was to be defined or achieved, nor on how the conditions attached to discharge consents were to be derived. Discretion was left very much in the hands of the River Board with its local knowledge. Normal practice was to relate consent conditions to the volume, nature and use of the receiving waters. This pragmatic approach meant that stricter controls would be imposed, for example, where a river was used as a source of drinking water than where it was used only for industrial purposes. It recognised water as a valuable resource, including as an acceptable means of water disposal, and made use of its assimilative capacities.

This practice evolved into the philosophy of quality objectives, which were to become the basis for all pollution control and river management. But interestingly the concept was not formalised in legislation until 1989. No national water quality objectives were produced until the mid-1980s – and then only in response to European Community requirements. As far back as 1912 the Royal Commission on Sewage Disposal had recommended a 'normal standard' which a well designed sewage treatment works would be expected to achieve. Although widely regarded as definitive, this standard was never enshrined in legislation and was applied with whatever variation the controlling authorities thought appropriate in any particular case. The 1951 Act included a provision which effectively enabled River Boards to set down standard discharge limits for a whole river or stretch of river, but this was virtually unused and was repealed a decade later.

Similar flexibility was built into the system for controlling drinking water standards. The Water Act 1945 placed on water undertakers a duty to supply 'wholesome' water. This term was undefined by specific standards until well into the 1980s although central guidance was given on what was necessary to protect public health.

Air pollution

The development of legislation on air pollution followed a similar timescale, and not dissimilar principles. The Victorians first saw the need to do something about the uncontrolled emissions from the 'dark satanic mills' of the industrial revolution. Four successive Alkali Acts, consolidated in the 1906 Act, established the basis on which industrial air pollution was to be controlled for the best part of a century. Indeed, the 1906 Act is still on the statute book, though it is finally to be repealed, Parliament willing, by the Environmental Protection Act 1990.

The system was founded upon the principle of best practicable means, or BPM. The duty to use BPM is applied by an Inspectorate, who determine for each individual plant what is necessary to comply. The Inspectorate's determination might take into account economic factors and local environmental conditions. There is no requirement for a discharge consent, as for water, but again central guidance is issued, on a purely administrative basis, as to how BPM is to be interpreted. This guidance might contain 'presumptive' emission standards, but they carry no legal or mandatory force. I should add that this system will change somewhat under the new 1990 Act.

Air pollution from other sources has been dealt with by a range of controls, mainly devolved to local authorities, under the Public Health Act 1936 and the Clean Air Acts of 1956 and 1968. The latter were largely a response to the smogs which threatened the health of those in many British towns and cities, which were largely eradicated by the imposition of smoke control areas: an unusual example of rigid centrally-imposed requirements to deal with a problem of particular severity.

Waste disposal

The regulation of waste disposal also had its beginnings in the last century, although the first truly preventive legislation was the Town and Country Planning Act of 1947. The current system involving comprehensive controls over waste disposal, site licensing and waste disposal plans was only set up under the Control of Pollution Act 1974. Again, control is exercised predominantly at the local level, with central government exercising a largely advisory role, although once again the 1990 Act will bring important changes here.

Planning

Finally it is worth mentioning the development of our planning system, which has evolved since the 1947 Town and Country Planning Act into an effective and widely admired system for protecting both the rural environment and urban amenity – of cardinal importance in this crowded island. Once again the emphasis is on local decision-making, assessing each case on its merits, while taking account of such guidance as central government may issue from time to time (such guidance being given weight of course, here as elsewhere, by central government's appellate function).

This brief sketch of Britain's environmental legislation shows that it has evolved piecemeal over the last century and a half, chiefly in response to particular problems. It has not, in the main, needed to take account of developments or problems in other countries – our island location above all has ensured that by and large both the causes and solutions of pollution problems have lain in our own hands. The hallmarks of this legislation have been flexibility, pragmatism and local decision-making.

ENVIRONMENTAL POLICY AND PRACTICE / VOLUME 2 / NUMBER 2 / 1992

EVOLUTION OF EUROPEAN COMMUNITY ENVIRONMENTAL POLICY

Much of continental Europe has come more recently to tackling issues of pollution control. It has done so often on a quite different basis for a variety of political, geographical and historical reasons. Thus, the advent of environmental issues on the European Community stage, and the resulting attempt to integrate the different national systems, was bound to lead to certain conflicts, the resolution of which would require some adaptation on all sides.

It was in 1972, just before Britain's entry, that the heads of government of the European Community first resolved to establish an environmental action programme. There was no specific basis for doing so in the Treaty of Rome which established the Community; they were responding to the growing tide of environmental awareness which led to the seminal 1972 Stockholm Conference on the Human Environment. At first the pace of legislation was modest. In 1976, for example, eight items of environmental legislation were adopted. In 1980 there were just 13. Recently the figure is running at up to 30 per year. There are now some 280 separate Community regulations, directives and decisions on environmental protection, and there are many more in the pipeline.

They may be split into three broad categories – each reflecting a different reason or justification for Community action in this area. The categories are not self-contained, and there is considerable overlap. The first and simplest, is product standards. This covers everything from the composition of detergents to lawn-mower noise, from vehicle emission standards to the labelling of pesticides. The objective is to ensure that the free circulation of goods within the common market is not hampered by different national restrictions or 'technical barriers to trade'. The environmental dimension of Community policy, finally enshrined in the Single European Act of 1986, is intended to ensure that such harmonisation takes place 'at a high level of environmental protection' – in other words that high standards become the norm.

The second category of legislation, not unrelated to the first, seeks to ensure fair competition between producers by equalising the environmental costs of production – the mythical 'level playing-field'. The argument is that wide disparities in pollution control standards across the Community will penalise those who seek to protect the environment, and could force standards down to the lowest common denominator. In order to secure equal conditions of competition and high standards, controls on industrial emissions in particular should be harmonised.

A third category of legislation is more purely environmental in character: it seeks for example to protect the quality of bathing waters or wildlife and its habitats, to prevent improper disposal of hazardous waste or depletion of the ozone layer. The problems of transboundary pollution provide one justification for community action of this type. But, increasingly the concept of a European Community environmental policy for its own sake has become widely accepted, and this was formally sanctioned with the insertion by the Single European Act of a new environmental chapter in the Treaty of Rome. Recently a new purpose to Community action has been given by the growing attention being given throughout the world to environmental problems of a global nature. In the burgeoning field of environmental diplomacy, the twelve Member States acting in concert, with a united Community position, can exert much greater influence and help develop the global solutions that are needed. This objective was given particular emphasis in a declaration on 'the Environmental Imperative' signed by the twelve heads of government of the Community in Dublin earlier this year.

IMPACT OF EUROPEAN COMMUNITY POLICIES ON THE UK

What, then, has been the impact of this substantial body of new, and of course fully binding, legislation on the long-established pollution control practices in the United Kingdom? An interesting comparison can be made between the last major comprehensive piece of environmental legislation in this country, the Control of Pollution Act 1974, and the Environmental Protection Bill currently before Parliament. Both introduced some radical new ideas and reforms across several different areas of pollution control. But the former was driven entirely by British concerns and priorities. It perpetuated, as we have already seen, some characteristically British approaches to pollution control. It took no account, nor did it need to, of any supra-national issues or requirements.

By contrast the Environmental Protection Bill is heavily influenced, in some parts driven, by European legislation. Several sections are designed specifically to implement Community directives. It has had to be scrutinised at every stage by lawyers to ensure full compatibility with our European obligations. It contains numerous powers for modification or further subsidiary legislation to be made as necessary to take account of future Community requirements. The new Integrated Pollution Control procedures in Part I of the Bill had to take full and detailed account of a number of directives, including those on air pollution from industrial sources, water pollution by dangerous substances, pollution from large combustion plants and public access to environmental information. The new arrangements for local authority air pollution controls and Part II of the Bill on waste have current or proposed EC legislation very much in mind. Part VI implements EC directives on genetically modified organisms, and other clauses deal with Community rules on chemicals.

I am not seeking to suggest that the Bill is merely a British chassis concealing a powerful European engine. The Bill contains important new proposals in their own right, developed here in the UK. Integrated Pollution Control is one of these and one which we hope will prove a popular model in Europe, with good prospects for

ENVIRONMENTAL POLICY AND PRACTICE / VOLUME 2 / NUMBER 2 / 1992

export. But the contrast with the 1974 Act illustrates, I think, the extent to which the European Community has become pervasive in most areas of environmental legislation over the last 15 years. The Community's influence has been particularly felt in the fields of water and air pollution; somewhat less so, up to now, in the areas of waste management, conservation or town and country planning – although in each of these areas some important directives exist and new proposals are coming forward. I should like to look at a few examples from air and water to illustrate this influence.

Let us consider one of the best-known examples of EC environmental law – the bathing waters Directive. Adopted in 1975, this set mandatory standards for a whole range of parameters, to be met at all waters used by large numbers of bathers. Nothing like these standards had previously existed here: as we have already seen, the protection of waters according to their particular use was very much left to the discretion and professional expertise of the relevant local bodies. In implementing the Directive, the UK initially took a very narrow view of its applicability, identifying just 27 waters as coming under the scope of the Directive. But the existence of the Directive enhanced public awareness and expectations. Eventually it was public pressure as much as pressure from the European Commission which led the Government to broaden its application of the Directive.

Now it is applied to all major bathing waters – over 400 at the last count. These waters are all regularly monitored, and the results published. New improvement schemes costing almost £3 billion in total have been set in hand to ensure full compliance with the Directive's standards. Administrative, that is non-legislative, implementation of the standards will soon be replaced by regulations making them statutory.

A related, but more recent example, of Community legislation having an impact on domestic policy is the disposal of sewage to coastal waters through long sea outfalls. For many years governments and the water industry have pursued a policy of improving the quality of inshore coastal waters by extending the length of outfall pipes to take the sewage away from the shoreline. This policy had the blessing of several expert groups, including the Royal Commission on Environmental Pollution. It has, however, become increasingly unpopular with the public: the question of discharging untreated sewage into the sea became almost a philosophical rather than a scientific issue. This itself brought pressure for a re-evaluation of policy in this area. But the impending publication of a proposed Community directive which would require the treatment of all major sewage discharges certainly hastened that review, which led to the change in policy announced earlier this year. The Government has now endorsed the principle that all major sewage discharges should be pre-treated, and a substantial programme of works to implement this is being drawn up. This is an example of the European Community giving a push, possibly a

THE IMPACT OF EC ENVIRONMENTAL POLICIES ON UK PUBLIC ADMINISTRATION

decisive push, to existing pressures for change – in this case even before a directive has been agreed.

I have already described how the notion of quality objectives evolved out of the case-by-case approach to water pollution control in this country. But that approach has come under serious challenge from attempts to introduce through the Community a regime based on uniform emission standards. Such a regime, setting fixed discharge standards from all sources of a given type, is common in some continental countries; it also sits more easily with concerns about equalising conditions of competition and is easier to apply for cross-boundary watercourses.

The UK has resisted for many years attempts from Europe to overturn our flexible, quality objective-based approach. It remains valid as a basis for achieving and maintaining a given standard of water quality, which a uniform emission approach cannot necessarily deliver, as others are coming to realise. Nevertheless, we have been prepared to acknowledge the strengths of an alternative, more precautionary approach for discharges of dangerous substances which have the potential to cause long-term environmental damage. This led to the announcement last year of a new approach to controlling inputs of dangerous substances to water, which seeks to draw together the strongest elements of both the UK and continental approaches. Discharges of these substances need both to use the Best Available Technology Not Entailing Excessive Cost (BATNEEC) and to ensure that tough quality standards are met in the receiving water. This is another idea that we hope will be taken up more widely in Europe.

In the meantime, the need to comply with the relevant EC directives led to the production for the first time of nationally applicable quality standards for a whole range of dangerous substances in water. Many of these standards, previously issued by administrative circular, were made statutory under the Water Act 1989 in order to satisfy European requirements. Indeed, the need to be able to implement EC legislation satisfactorily was a major influence in shaping the new regulatory system which was introduced under the Water Act in conjunction with the privatisation of the water industry.

The impact of European Community legislation on air has been equally significant. The Large Combustion Plants Directive has set firm and ambitious targets for the progressive reduction of emissions from the electricity generating industry, involving multi-billion pound improvements. Air quality standards, which had not previously existed in the UK, have been set for sulphur dioxide, smoke, lead and nitrogen dioxide, and others are in the pipeline. The so-called 'Air Framework' Directive, which requires industrial emissions to be specifically consented, has led directly to the introduction of a formal system of authorisations through the Environmental Protection Bill. At the heart of the integrated pollution control

ENVIRONMENTAL POLICY AND PRACTICE / VOLUME 2 / NUMBER 2 / 1992

provisions of the Bill lies the concept of BATNEEC – a modification of the traditional BPM philosophy and itself drawn from the Air Framework Directive.

What conclusions can be drawn then about the influence of European Community legislation? I think a number of general tendencies can be deduced.

First, the need to modify and adapt often long-established policies is an inevitable part of integration into a pan-European approach. The last 15 years have seen a steady convergence of principles and practices hand in hand with the emergence of a Community environmental policy. The desire to ensure comparability of effort and fair competition tends to encourage not only uniformity of approach, but also uniform standards, harmonised monitoring arrangements and common abatement practices. This has tended to override the case-by-case approach which had been characteristic of previous UK practice in most areas.

Second, Community legislation has brought with it the greater codification which is inherent in most continental law, and which is regarded by the European Commission as essential if it is to carry out its duty of ensuring full and equitable implementation across all member states. This tends to imply fixed, numerical standards and targets, together with strict legal definitions which leave no room for interpretation. It also requires national implementing measures to be in statutory form with the rules and standards clearly set out. This is something the Commission has increasingly insisted upon, with the backing of the European Court of Justice. The traditional UK approach of issuing administrative guidance to the relevant 'competent' authority to back up broad generalised duties or objectives is, for the most part, no longer permissible.

Third, the need to demonstrate compliance with directives has undoubtedly led to a great increase in monitoring and in information about the state of the environment. The Commission relies heavily on such information to enable it to assess whether directives are being implemented to the letter, and most legislation carries with it detailed rules about monitoring, analysis, and the supply of data. Where pollution control authorities might once have tended to monitor only when they suspected a problem, with the occasional check sample, comprehensive – and often very expensive – sampling programmes are now having to be put in place.

Fourthly, Community policy has undoubtedly had an impact in increasing public awareness. The Commission has at times deliberately set out to cultivate and use public opinion against what it sees as foot-dragging by Member States. The existence of a 'higher authority' to which they can appeal or air their grievances, has undoubtedly caught the public's imagination, especially – for reasons which are not entirely clear – in the United Kingdom. The increased levels of monitoring which I have already noted, the 'transparency' which comes with fixed targets and statutory rules, have helped to ensure that the public is better supplied with information about the state of the environment.

206

THE IMPACT OF EC ENVIRONMENTAL POLICIES ON UK PUBLIC ADMINISTRATION

Finally, it is almost certainly the case that Community legislation has brought about higher standards than would otherwise have been the case. This is true of all countries, not just our own. The Commission's proposals have for the most part been 'forcing' legislation, pushing sometimes reluctant Member States, who of course have to bear the costs, into ever tougher commitments and higher standards. It has tended to take the highest level of practice, the strictest standards, the cleanest technologies from around the Community and seek to make these the norm. This, as we have seen, is the way in which the Commission seeks to equalise cost burdens across the Community. And of course the pressure for new legislation comes not just from the Commission, but also from the Member States themselves. Pressure is brought to bear on fellow members of the Environment Council to raise their standards for a variety of reasons, environmental, economic and political. The revolving Presidency of the Council also has an effect, drawing each Member State in turn, as it assumes the mantle of pushing forward Council business, into more 'communautaire' positions. Inevitably, all three factors will sometimes mean in some cases stricter controls than a particular Member State would wish, or deem necessary. But most judges would agree that the overall impact of this body of legislation has been both positive and substantial.

FUTURE DEVELOPMENTS

I should like to conclude with a little crystal ball gazing – brief predictions about the way in which the Community's environmental policy will continue to develop, and its likely further impact.

The growth of public and political interest in environmental issues seems likely to continue unabated, at least for the immediate future. This interest will be fuelled by the growing appreciation of the global environmental problems which confront us. Consequently, the Community will need increasingly to turn its attention outwards, seeking to bring its united influence to bear on the solution of regional and world problems. The resurrection of the natural environment of Eastern Europe, the preservation of the Mediterranean, the conservation of tropical forests and, of course, problems of the greenhouse effect will all be major preoccupations.

Within the Community attention may focus on a number of internal 'structural' issues in the next few years: improved and faster decision-making; better policing and enforcement of existing environmental legislation; new mechanisms for reviewing and up-dating standards; a greater role for the European Parliament.These are all issues which will undoubtedly be addressed in the forthcoming further review of the EC Treaty, due to begin in December of this year.

Environmentalists will hope to see a progressive 'greening' of other areas of Community policy. Environmental costs and environmental thinking should become a factor in Community energy policy and transport policy, in agriculture and

ENVIRONMENTAL POLICY AND PRACTICE / VOLUME 2 / NUMBER 2 / 1992

regional development. It will no longer be acceptable for these separate elements of Community policy to be pursued in isolation from, or even in direct conflict with, one another.

We may also see a number of new strategies emerging to tackle environmental problems. In addition to the traditional regulatory mechanisms, we will see a growing emphasis on economic instruments – tariffs, levies, tax differentials, incentives as a means of effecting environmental aims. Measures to improve consumer awareness and promote sustainable growth strategies will augment the more straightforward 'command and control' instruments of pollution control.

CONCLUSION

I have described at some length the impact which European Community policies have had on the British approach to environmental protection. But I am conscious of having given what might be the very misleading impression of a one-way street. The impact has not all been in one direction. Despite our late arrival on the scene, the United Kingdom's contribution to the emergent Community policy has been substantial. We were starting from a position of considerable strength in terms of our past achievements, our well-established systems of controls, our scientific and administrative expertise. And it is I think generally acknowledged that we have played a valuable and substantial role in helping to shape the form and direction of Community legislation in many areas. Perhaps at times we have been reluctant to embrace fully the fact that we are now firmly 'in Europe', and to accept some of the consequences of this. But at the present time we are fully engaged in all the main environmental debates within the Community and are playing a leading and constructive part. It is undoubtedly the case that the impact of the Community, and perhaps some degree of competition and emulation between the Member States on the development of their environmental policies, has led to significant environmental improvements throughout the Community over the past 15 years. One may reasonably hope to see further improvements in the next 15 years.

POSTSCRIPT

Nearly two years have passed since this paper was delivered. A great deal has happened in the field of environmental policy in this time. At home, the Environment Protection Bill has become an Act; a comprehensive White Paper on the environment 'This Common Inheritance' was published in September 1990, followed up by a well received report on progress a year later; Her Majesty's Inspectorate of Pollution began to implement the new Integrated Pollution Control arrangements, and proposals for a new unified environmental protection agency emerged. The pace of new legislation from the European Community has continued unabated, with important measures passed on water pollution from agriculture and

THE IMPACT OF EC ENVIRONMENTAL POLICIES ON UK PUBLIC ADMINISTRATION

from sewage, on the protection of natural habitats, on environmental labelling of products, and on vehicle emissions, among many others. At the global level, intensive efforts have been made towards international action on climate change, on preserving biodiversity and tropical forests, on protecting the ozone layer and the Antarctic. The recent United Nations Conference on Environment and Development in Rio, the 'Earth Summit' was undoubtedly the most significant single environmental event of the last two decades.

Rereading the paper, its central theses about the relationship between environmental policy-making at national and at Community level still hold true. And many of the predicted future developments in the Community's policy are already beginning to take shape. The Community's response to global problems has, rightly, become a major preoccupation. Attempts have been made to identify new, non-regulatory mechanisms for effecting environmental improvements. The proposal for a harmonised carbon/energy tax exemplifies both those trends.

Structural issues have been tackled in the Maastricht Treaty which, subject to ratification, would give a greater role to the European Parliament, give powers of sanction to the European Court of Justice, and, perhaps most significantly, introduce majority voting as the norm within the Environment Council. The Treaty also incorporates the concepts of sustainable growth and respect for the environment within the fundamental objectives of the Community, and sees a strengthening of the provisions which govern environmental policy. The importance of integrating environmental concerns into other areas of the Community's policy has received recognition, both in the new Treaty and more generally – though much remains to be done to put the principle into practice. The anticipated new emphasis on better implementation and enforcement has also been evident, bringing forward new ideas for a network of national enforcement agencies and (a UK initiative) for a Community inspectorate to 'audit' the performance of national enforcement bodies. Many of these themes are reflected in the Community's new Fifth Environment Action Programme, which is intended to guide the development of EC environmental policy up to the end of the century. The Treaty defines the important principle of subsidiarity, and it is likely that there will be important applications of this principle in the environment field so that action can be taken at the most appropriate level.

I am pleased to be able to say that the UK has taken an active and constructive role in the development of many of these new policies and themes. Our commitment to a progressive and forward-looking Community environment policy has been demonstrated in practice. This bodes well as we prepare to meet the challenge of assuming the Presidency of the Council in the second half of this year.

Derek Osborn
June 1992

[5]

THE PRINCIPLE OF SUBSIDIARITY AND THE ENVIRONMENT IN THE EUROPEAN UNION: KEEPING THE BALANCE OF FEDERALISM

Koen Lenaerts*

CONTENTS

INTRODUCTION

The significant amendments to the Treaty Establishing the European Economic Community ("Treaty of Rome"),[1] most recently codified in the Treaty on European Union ("TEU"),[2] sig-

---

* Judge of the Court of First Instance of the European Communities; Professor of European Law, University of Leuven.

1. Treaty Establishing the European Economic Community, Mar. 25, 1957, 1973 Gr. Brit. T.S. No. 1 (Cmd.5179-II), 298 U.N.T.S. 3 (1958), *as amended by* Single European Act, O.J. L 169/1 (1987), [1987] 2 C.M.L.R. 741 [hereinafter SEA], *in* Treaties Establishing the European Communities (EC Off'l Pub. Office, 1987) [hereinafter EEC Treaty].

2. Treaty on European Union, Feb. 7, 1992, O.J. C 224/01 (1992), [1992] 1 C.M.L.R. 719, *reprinted in* 31 I.L.M. 247 (1992) [hereinafter TEU]. The changes to the

nify "a new stage in the process of creating an ever closer union among the peoples of Europe, in which decisions are taken as closely as possible to the citizen."[3] This statement, in the second paragraph of Article A, reflects the delicate balancing act performed by the drafters of the TEU. On the one hand, *integration* was to be deepened, in particular, through an unprecedented extension of the powers conferred upon the European Community (or "Union").[4] On the other hand, the confidence of the Member States, as well as of their subnational authorities and citizens, was to be maintained through the solemn guarantee of

---

EEC Treaty, *supra* note 1, made by the TEU, *supra*, were incorporated into the Treaty Establishing the European Community, Feb. 7, 1992, [1992] 1 C.M.L.R. 573 [hereinafter EC Treaty].

3. TEU, *supra* note 2, art. A, ¶ 2.

4. Besides introducing a "common foreign and security policy," *id.* art. J, and provisions on "[c]o-operation in the fields of justice and home affairs," *id.* art. K, the TEU extended the powers of the "European Community" (the word "Economic" was understandably deleted from the original EEC Treaty title, *see* EC Treaty, *supra* note 2) to aspects of the following fields:

1) citizenship of the Union, *id.* arts. 8-8e;
2) a common visa policy, *id.* art. 100c;
3) economic and monetary policy (leading to introduction of single currency), *id.* arts. 2, 3a, 102a-109m;
4) education, *id.* art. 126;
5) culture, *id.* art. 128;
6) public health, *id.* art. 129;
7) consumer protection, *id.* art. 129a;
8) trans-European networks (in areas of transport, telecommunications, and energy infrastructures), *id.* arts. 129b-129d;
9) industry, *id.* art. 130;
10) development cooperation, *id.* arts. 130u-130y;
11) social policy matters covered by the Protocol on Social Policy, TEU, *supra* note 2, Protocol on Social Policy. The Protocol, annexed by the TEU to the EC Treaty, forms, in accordance with Article 239 of the EC Treaty, "an integral part [of the EC Treaty]." EC Treaty, *supra* note 2, art. 239. The same applies to an agreement within the protocol. *See* TEU, *supra* note 2, Agreement on Social Policy Concluded between the Member States of the European Community with the Exception of the United Kingdom of Great Britain and Northern Ireland.

In addition, the scope of some pre-existing Community powers has been widened through the TEU, *inter alia*, in the areas of: a) vocational training, EEC Treaty, *supra* note 1, art. 128, *as replaced by* EC Treaty, *supra* note 2, art. 127; b) economic and social cohesion, SEA, *supra* note 1, arts. 130a-130e, *amending* EEC Treaty, *supra* note 1, *as replaced by* EC Treaty, *supra* note 2; c) research and technological development, SEA, *supra* note 1, arts. 130f-130p, *amending* EEC Treaty, *supra* note 1, *as replaced by* EC Treaty, *supra* note 2; and d) the environment, SEA, *supra* note 1, arts. 130r-130t, *amending* EEC Treaty, *supra* note 1, *as replaced by* EC Treaty, *supra* note 2.

the *proximity* of government. In other words, integration was not to lead to undue centralization.

The question then became whether, and to what extent, centralization was necessary for integration to work, without threatening the proximity of government. Article B[5] of the TEU, refers, in this respect, to a precise test. It subjects the pursuit of all of the objectives of the Union - i.e., the objectives to be pursued through the European Communities (the "main pillar" of the Union), the common foreign and security policy (the "second pillar"), and the cooperation in the fields of justice and home affairs (the "third pillar") - to the duty of "respecting" the principle of subsidiarity, as defined in Article 3b of the EC Treaty. Thus, Article 3b is called upon to arbitrate the tension between integration and proximity in all matters dealt with by the Union and its Member States, although only justiciable in the European Court of Justice, within the scope of application of the EC Treaty, and in relation to the powers of the European Community.[6] The relevant part of Article 3b, contained in paragraph 2, reads as follows:

> In areas which do not fall within its exclusive competence, the Community shall take action, in accordance with the principle of subsidiarity, only if and in so far as the objectives of the proposed action cannot be sufficiently achieved by the Member States and can therefore, by reason of the scale or effects of the proposed action, be better achieved by the Community.[7]

The first paragraph of Article 3b states that "[t]he Community shall act within the limits of the powers conferred upon it by this Treaty and of the objectives assigned to it therein"[8] (the *legal basis* requirement). The third paragraph declares that "[a]ny action by the Community shall not go beyond what is necessary to achieve the objectives of this Treaty"[9] (the *proportionality* requirement). As can be seen, all three paragraphs of Article 3b aim at containing the actions of the Community. The first paragraph refers to the division of powers between the Community and the Member States, in which the latter remain the ordinary bearers

---

5. TEU, *supra* note 2, art. B.
6. *See id.* art. L.
7. EC Treaty, *supra* note 2, art. 3b, ¶ 2.
8. *Id.* ¶ 1.
9. *Id.* ¶ 3.

of sovereignty, and hence of public authority, while the Community has only the powers entrusted to it in the Treaty.[10] The two other paragraphs place limitations on the exercise of the powers held by the Community, meaning that the Community cannot fully exercise the powers conferred upon it (i.e., as long as it does not act *ultra vires*). The principles of subsidiarity and proportionality operate as limits to be observed *intra vires* when the Community undertakes an action authorized under one of the enumerated powers.

Because the second and third paragraphs of Article 3b have similar functions, both setting limits *intra vires* on the exercise of Community powers, it is difficult to sharply distinguish between subsidiarity and proportionality. This difficulty is aggravated by the fact that the second paragraph, which applies to the non-exclusive powers of the Community,[11] determines not only the

---

10. A reference to this basic rule is found in Article 4(1) of the EC Treaty: "[t]he tasks entrusted to the Community shall be carried out by the following institutions: a European Parliament, a Council, a Commission, a Court of Justice, a Court of Auditors. Each institution shall act within the limits of the powers conferred upon it by this Treaty." *Id.* art. 4(1).

11. The introductory words of the second paragraph of Article 3b limit the application of the principle of subsidiarity to the "areas which do not fall within [the] exclusive competence" of the Community. *Id.* art. 3b, ¶ 2. The application of the principle of subsidiarity to areas which fall within the "exclusive competence" of the Community would be meaningless, because "the existence of such competence arising from a Treaty provision excludes any competence on the part of Member States which is concurrent with that of the Community." *See* Opinion 2/91, [1993] E.C.R. I-1061, I-1076, ¶ 8, [1993] 3 C.M.L.R. 800, 815. In other words, the Community should not respect the principle of subsidiarity as a limit *intra vires* set to the exercise of its powers in order to leave unaffected the residual powers of the Member States on the basis of possibly achieving the objectives of the proposed Community action in a sufficient manner, since such residual powers no longer exist as a result of the Treaty provision stating the Community's competence. The latter has been affirmed by the Court of Justice with respect to Article 113 of the EC Treaty. *See* Opinion 1/75, [1975] E.C.R. 1355, [1976] 1 C.M.L.R. 85; Donckerwolcke v. Procureur de la République (Preliminary Ruling), Case 41/76, [1976] E.C.R. 1921, 1937, ¶ 32, [1977] 2 C.M.L.R. 535, 552. It has also been affirmed with respect to Article 102 of the Act of Accession of 1972. *See* Commission v. United Kingdom, Case 804/79, [1981] E.C.R. 1045, 1072-73, ¶¶ 17, 18, [1982] 1 C.M.L.R. 543, 570. However, when the exclusive nature of the Community's competence does not flow from the provisions of the Treaty but depends "on the scope of the measures which have been adopted by the Community institutions for the application of those provisions and which are of such a kind as to deprive the Member States of an area of competence which they were able to exercise previously on a transitional basis," the principle of subsidiarity applies to determine "the scope of the measures [to be] adopted by the Community institutions." Opinion 2/91, [1993] E.C.R. at I-1077, ¶ 9, [1993] 3 C.M.L.R. at 816. The principle will then be able to perform its function of shielding the Member States' residual powers against preemption by Community ac-

conditions that must be met "in accordance with the principle of subsidiarity" for the Community to be able to take *some* action under one of its powers ("only if"), but also indicates the permissible *extent* of such action ("and in so far as"). This latter aspect of the second paragraph obviously covers an element of proportionality whose proper object it is, according to the third paragraph, to keep the exercise of *all* Community powers (exclusive and non-exclusive powers) within reasonable bounds. Further analysis will show how this aspect of proportionality, incorporated into the principle of subsidiarity, is to be related to the general principle of proportionality, stated in the third paragraph of Article 3b.

At this stage, it is sufficient to emphasize that the principle of subsidiarity does not reorganize the division of powers between the Community and the Member States. The status of these relations continues to flow solely from the several Treaty articles conferring specific or non-specific powers[12] upon the Community (the first paragraph of Article 3b merely confirms the *acquis communautaire* on this point). Compliance with the principle of subsidiarity was, nevertheless, intended to have some lateral impact on the dividing line between the actual Community powers and the residual powers of the Member States.[13] This is why "subsidiarity" has been developed as a "prin-

---

tion. It is indeed only when the exclusive nature of the Community's competence flows from the constitution itself that Member States lose their residual powers, and thus, any interest in defending such powers, either through the operation of the principle of subsidiarity or otherwise.

12. The specific powers of the Community are referred to in the first paragraph of Article 3b as "the powers conferred upon [the Community] by this Treaty" and cover the various subject-matters dealt with throughout the EC Treaty. *See* EC Treaty, *supra* note 2, art. 3b. The non-specific powers of the Community must be related to "the objectives assigned to [the Community]" and are governed by the conditions set forth in Article 235 of the EC Treaty. *Id.*; *see id.* art. 235.

13. This is due to the non-exclusive nature of almost all Community powers, as derived from several Treaty provisions. Such powers can become "exclusive" to the extent they are exercised. *See* Opinion 2/91, [1993] E.C.R. at I-1077, ¶ 9, [1993] 3 C.M.L.R. at 816. This is nothing else than preemption of the residual powers of the Member States by Community action. *See* M. Waelbroeck, *The Emergent Doctrine of Community Pre-emption-Consent and Re-delegation, in* II COURTS AND FREE MARKETS: PERSPECTIVES FROM THE UNITED STATES AND EUROPE 548, 570 (Terrance Sandalow & Eric Stein, eds. 1982); E.D. Cross, *Pre-emption of Member State Law in the European Economic Community: A Framework for Analysis,* 29 C.M.L. REV. 447 (1992).

1994]   *SUBSIDIARITY AND THE ENVIRONMENT*   851

ciple"[14] of the European Community, with a pace (and a visibility), parallel to the recognition of the new, non-exclusive Community powers (through successive Treaty amendments), especially when the exercise of these powers is to take place on the basis of a qualified majority vote within the Council combined with an increased co-legislative role for the European Parliament.[15]

Consequently, Member States lose the right to veto Community action under the new powers and feel the need to insert an expressly protective clause into the European Community Treaty ("EC Treaty").[16] The principle of subsidiarity constitutes, for them, a judicially enforceable mechanism of self-defense against what they perceive as the risk of excessive use of non-exclusive Community powers, preempting their own residual powers in ar-

---

14. Article 3b belongs to "Part One" of the EC Treaty, entitled "Principles." *See* EC Treaty, *supra* note 2, arts. 1-7c.

15. The SEA introduced an article that addressed cooperation between the Council and the Parliament. SEA, *supra* note 1, art. 149, *amending* EEC Treaty, *supra* note 1, *as replaced by* EC Treaty, *supra* note 2, art. 189c. This gave the Parliament the right to a real dialogue with the Commission and the Council, which included the possibility to weigh on the outcome of the decision-making through the proposal of amendments to the Council's draft decision ("common position"). After acceptance by the Commission, the amendments could be enacted into law by the Council, acting by a qualified majority. The TEU strengthened the role of the Parliament even further through the introduction of the so-called "co-decision" between the Council and the Parliament. This provides for extensive concertation between these two institutions through a "Conciliation Committee." The Parliament has the right, in case of persistent disagreement, to reject the proposed act "by an absolute majority of its component members." EC Treaty, *supra* note 2, art. 189b(2), ¶ 3(c). After the TEU, Article 189c of the EC Treaty ("cooperation") applies, *inter alia*, to: transport, *id.* art. 75; several aspects of the economic and monetary policy, *id.* arts. 102a-109m; vocational training, *id.* art. 127(4); some aspects of the establishment and development of trans-European networks, *id.* art. 129d, ¶ 3; implementing decisions relating to the European Regional Development Fund, *id.* art. 130e; some aspects of the policy on research and technological development, *id.* art. 130o, ¶ 2; the environment (in general), *id.* art. 130s(1); and development cooperation, *id.* art. 130w(1). Whereas, Article 189b of the EC Treaty ("co-decision") applies, *inter alia*, to: freedom of establishment, *id.* art. 54(2); the mutual recognition of diplomas, certificates, and other evidence of formal qualifications, *id.* art. 57(1)-(2); the internal market, *id.* art. 100a(1); education, *id.* art. 126(4), para. 1; public health, *id.* art. 129(4), para. 1; consumer protection, art. 129a(2); some aspects of the establishment and development of trans-European networks, *id.* art. 129d, ¶ 1; and "general action programmes setting out priority objectives to be attained" in the area of the environment, *id.* art. 130s(3).

16. *See* Koen Lenaerts & Patrick van Ypersele, *Le principe de subsidiarité et son contexte: étude de l'article 3B du traité CE*, 30 CAHIERS DE DROIT EUROPÉEN 3, 3-7 (1994); George A. Bermann, *Taking Subsidiarity Seriously: Federalism in the European Community and the United States*, 94 COLUM. L. REV. 332 (1994) (focusing on Part I).

eas covered by Community action.[17] In this sense, the principle of subsidiarity serves as a substitute for the political safeguards protecting the Member States' residual powers, which have largely become obsolete.

Part I of this Article traces the emergence of the principle of subsidiarity in the Community legal order, with some special reference to the environment. Part II analyzes the three paragraphs of Article 3b, again with particular emphasis on the environment. This Article concludes that "subsidiarity" will not stand in the way of the further development of Community environmental policy along the lines that it has been following so far.

I. THE EMERGENCE OF THE PRINCIPLE OF SUBSIDIARITY: FROM A SOUND MANAGEMENT RULE TO AN EXPRESS GUARANTEE OF THE PROXIMITY OF GOVERNMENT

The expression, "principle of subsidiarity," was introduced for the first time into the EC Treaty by the TEU. This does not mean, however, that the plain "common-sense"[18] idea that government should be no more centralized than is strictly necessary for it to achieve the objectives assigned to its powers did not exist at earlier stages.[19] Indeed, the Treaty of Rome, in its 1957 original version, incorporated this idea when shaping the legislative, executive, and judicial powers of the Community.

First, the "directive" must be used in several cases where the

---

17. *Cf.* John A. Usher, *Maastricht and English Law*, 14 STATUTE L. REV. 28, 38-40 (1993).

18. *See* Communication on the principle of subsidiarity, adopted by the Commission on 27 October 1992, for transmission to the Council and Parliament. 25 E.C. BULL., no. 10, at 116 (1992).

> The subsidiarity principle as applied in the institutional context is based on a simple concept: the powers that a State or a federation of States wields in the common interest are only those which individuals, families, companies and local or regional authorities cannot exercise in isolation. This common-sense principle therefore dictates that decisions should be taken at the level closest to the ordinary citizen and that action taken by the upper echelons of the body politic should be limited.

Id. at 118.

19. *See* J. Mertens de Wilmars, *Du bon usage de la subsidiarité*, 2 REVUE DU MARCHÉ UNIQUE EUROPÉEN 193 (1992); P.J.G. Kapteyn, *Community Law and the Principle of Subsidiarity*, 2 REVUE DES AFFAIRES EUROPÉENNES 35, at 38-39 (1991). *But see* A.G. Toth, *The Principle of Subsidiarity in the Maastricht Treaty*, 29 COMMON MKT. L. REV., 1079, 1080-86 (1992).

impact of Community *legislation* on sensitive aspects of national law (resting, at times, on a long standing tradition) is potentially great. Such cases include the harmonization of national laws that "directly affect the establishment or functioning of the common market"[20] or "the mutual recognition of diplomas, certificates and other evidence of formal qualifications."[21] As is well known, "a directive shall be binding, as to the result to be achieved, upon each Member State to which it is addressed, but shall leave to the national authorities the choice of form and methods."[22] It is also well known, however, that Member States often did not play the game of the directive, especially in a setting of unanimous voting within the Council, when they used their veto right in order to obtain a perfectly detailed text.[23] As a result, the objective of the Community legislation, drafted in general terms, to be complemented by further policy choices made at the national (or sub-national) level to achieve the outcome stated in that legislation, has repeatedly been frustrated. At the heart of this phenomenon lies the distrust of Member States, *vis-à-vis* one another, due to the fact that they may not implement the directive with the same faithfulness. Consequently, some Member States will bear the costs of implementation (political, economic, social, environmental, etc.), to a far greater extent than others.[24]

In contrast, some directives were deliberately kept rather vague, making it extremely difficult to monitor their correct implementation. Thus, according to some commentators, many of the pre-SEA directives on the environment, based on Articles 100 or 235 of the EEC Treaty, both of which require unanimous voting within the Council, have passed the obstacle of the veto

---

20. EC Treaty, *supra* note 2, art. 100.

21. *Id.* art. 57(1).

22. *Id.* art. 189, ¶ 3.

23. In its 1992 Communication, *supra* note 18, the Commission noted:

In practice, of course, the distinction between directive and regulation has become blurred . . . . Be that as it may, the directive no longer enjoys any preference over the regulation and, when it is used, it is generally as detailed as a regulation and leaves hardly any margin of manoeuvre for transposal.

25 E.C. BULL., *supra* note 18, at 116, 123(2)(3).

24. The Commission referred to "the risk of encountering resistance from national administrations which, because of a mutual lack of confidence, are anxious to obtain the most detailed regulations possible." Commission Report to the European Council on the Adaptation of Community Legislation to the Subsidiarity Principle, COM (93) 545, at 7 (Nov. 1993) [hereinafter Commission Report to the European Council].

right held by each Member State because of the "important implementation gaps."[25] Although all of this may leave the impression that directives run the risk of regulating either too much or too little, the fact remains that, conceptually, the directive is a legislative instrument intended to avoid unnecessary regulatory density at the Community level.

Second, the *execution* of Community law is, to an important extent, entrusted to the Member States. The first sentence of the first paragraph of Article 5 of the Treaty of Rome states as one of the "principles" of the European Community that "Member States shall take all appropriate measures, whether general or particular, to ensure fulfillment of the obligations arising out of this Treaty or resulting from action taken by the institutions of the Community."[26] In accordance with this provision, the system of *administration communautaire indirecte* has been generally applied in the most diverse fields of legislation, where the Community leaves it to the national administrations to implement and enforce its regulatory schemes.[27] From the beginning, the environment has been one of these fields.

Third, there is the decentralization of the judiciary, with Article 177 of the Treaty of Rome organizing the procedure of requests from national courts to the Court of Justice for preliminary rulings on the interpretation of Community law or on the validity of acts of Community institutions. The mainstream judicial enforcement of Community law, if need be, against Member State authorities,[28] thus takes place in the national courts, while the role of the Court of Justice is limited to what is necessary to guarantee the effectiveness and uniform application of that law.[29] The system essentially relies on the initiative of private parties and the authority of national courts. The Court of Justice

25. Richard B. Stewart, *Environmental Law in the United States and the European Community: Spillovers, Cooperation, Rivalry, Institutions,* U. CHI. LEGAL F. 41, 48-49 (1992).

26. EC Treaty, *supra* note 2, art. 5, ¶ 1 (substantially unchanged from EEC Treaty, *supra* note 1). *See generally* John T. Lang, *Community Constitutional Law: Article 5 of the EEC Treaty,* 27 COMMON MKT. L. REV. 645 (1990).

27. For more details, see Koen Lenaerts, *Regulating the Regulatory Process: 'Delegation of Powers' in the European Community,* 18 EUR. L. REV. 23, 27-33 (1993).

28. EC Treaty, *supra* note 2, art. 177 (substantially unchanged from EEC Treaty, *supra* note 1); *see* René Joliet, *L'article 177 du traité CEE et le renvoi préjudiciel,* 31 RIVISTA DI DIRITTO EUROPEO 591, at 597 (1991).

29. *See* Koen Lenaerts, *Form and Substance of the Preliminary Rulings Procedure, in* LIBER AMICORUM H.G. SCHERMERS 355-80 (Deirdre Curtin & Ton Heukels eds., forthcoming 1994).

has consistently developed that system since it held in its 1963 judgment of *Van Gend en Loos v. Nederlandse Administratie der Belastingen*[30] that "the vigilance of individuals concerned to protect their rights amounts to an effective supervision in addition to the supervision entrusted by Articles 169 and 170 to the diligence of the Commission and of the Member States."[31]

The Court advanced this approach most forcefully in 1991, in *Francovich v. Italy*,[32] where it determined that each Member State must create an action for damages against itself when the Member State does not fulfill its obligation to implement a directive correctly, thereby harming the interests of private parties who would have drawn rights from the directive had it been correctly implemented.[33] In fact, the ruling contains a general principle of Member States' liability for harm caused by their infringement of Community law (that is, other than the non-implementation or incorrect implementation of directives) under conditions to be specified in future Court decisions.[34] It seems likely that future actions for damages in the environmental field will help significantly in elaborating these conditions. This is es-

---

30. Van Gend en Loos v. Nederlandse Administratie der Belastingen, Case 26/62, [1963] E.C.R. 1, [1963] C.M.L.R. 105.

31. *Id.* at 13, [1963] C.M.L.R. at 130.

32. Francovich v. Italy, Joined Cases C-6/90 and C-9/90, [1991] E.C.R. I-5357, [1993] 2 C.M.L.R. 66.

33. *Id.*

34. Cases now pending before the Court are:

(a) Regina v. Secretary of State for Transport *ex parte* Factortame and others, Case C-48/93 [hereinafter Factortame III]. In this case, the High Court of England and Wales asks the Court of Justice whether the United Kingdom is liable, under Community law, for the harm caused to private parties as a result of the infringement of Articles 5, 7, 52, and 221 of the EEC Treaty. *See* Regina v. Secretary of State for Transport *ex parte* Factortame, Ltd. (No. 2), Case C-221/89, [1991] E.C.R. I-3905, [1991] 3 C.M.L.R. 589, [hereinafter Factortame II]; Commission v. United Kingdom, Case C-246/89, [1991] E.C.R. I-4585, [1991] 3 C.M.L.R. 706; and

(b) Brasserie du Pêcheur S.A. v. Federal Republic of Germany represented by the Minister of Health, Case C-46/93. In this case, a German court asked the Court of Justice whether the Federal Republic of Germany is liable, under Community law, for the harm caused to a French brewery, prevented for years from selling beer in Germany as a consequence of the "Reinheitsgebot," which the Court held to be contrary to Article 30 of the Treaty of Rome in its judgment. *See* Commission v. Germany, Case 178/84, [1987] E.C.R. 1227, [1988] 1 C.M.L.R. 780. In both of these cases, the "fault" of the Member State consists of a breach of directly effective provisions of the Treaty. The Court of Justice will have to indicate to what extent the conditions applying to State liability, under Community law, in case of non-implementation or incorrect implementation of a directive, can be transposed to this less specific kind of infringement of Community law by Member States.

pecially so because, as Part II illustrates, liability actions may be a proportional means of monitoring and enforcing the implementation of European environmental law without having to create an overcentralized, Community-wide bureaucracy.

Substantive Community policies were also affected by the principle of subsidiarity before the principle was expressly incorporated in the EC Treaty. Subsidiarity then operated as a mediating concept between integration and proximity. It could require more integration, when that appeared necessary for efficiency, or more proximity, when increased centralized regulation would not help achieve objectives more efficiently. Examples include: (a) the so-called "new approach" to harmonization of national laws, and (b) Community environmental policy.

A. The "New Approach" to Harmonization of National Laws

Regarding harmonization of national laws, the Community, through its political processes, sought for almost three decades to create uniform legislation based on Article 100 of the Rome Treaty. It exhausted itself, however, by considering the smallest details of the subjects at issue. The output was wholly unsatisfactory, with the greatest obstacles to the common market remaining because some Member States were unhappy with the necessary compromises.

In 1979, in *Rewe-Zentral AG v. Bundesmonopolverwaltung für Branntwein* ("*Cassis de Dijon*"),[35] the Court of Justice paved the way to a more realistic approach. It launched the concept of mutual recognition by Member States of each other's laws, even where their content differs. Member States are thus, in principle, required to authorize, in their territory, the marketing of goods and services lawfully introduced into the market of another Member State.[36] An exception is granted where a Member State's own national provisions, containing specific marketing conditions for such goods and services (conditions which apply equally to domestic and out-of-state goods and services), "may be

---

35. Rewe-Zentral AG v. Bundesmonopolverwaltung für Branntwein, Case 120/78, [1979] E.C.R. 649, [1979] 3 C.M.L.R. 494 [hereinafter *Cassis de Dijon*].

36. The basic parallel between goods and services rests on another judgment of the Court. *See* Criminal Proceeding against Alfred John Webb, Case 279/80, [1981] E.C.R. 3305, [1982] 1 C.M.L.R. 719.

recognized as being necessary in order to satisfy mandatory requirements."[37] The protection of the environment is such a mandatory requirement.[38] Thus, the Court accepted as compatible with the free movement of goods Denmark's deposit-and-return system for empty beer and soft drink containers, because this obligation "is an indispensable element of a system intended to ensure the re-use of containers and therefore appears necessary to achieve the [mandatory requirement of environmental protection]."[39] Therefore, the restrictions that it imposes on the free movement of goods could not be regarded as disproportionate.[40]

Building upon the Court's jurisprudence, the Commission's 1985 White Paper[41] on the internal market advocated a new approach to harmonization through Community legislation. Harmonization concerns only the base-level requirements for goods and services to be marketable everywhere in the Community. Beyond that, Member States are obliged to accept differences among their national laws and to consider these laws equivalent, if not in their actual substance, at the very least, in their actual

---

37. *Cassis de Dijon*, [1979] E.C.R. at 662, ¶ 8, [1979] 3 C.M.L.R. at 508-09. Such "mandatory requirements" relate "in particular to the effectiveness of fiscal supervision, the protection of public health, the fairness of commercial transactions and the defence of the consumer." *Id.* In the field of the freedom to provide services, the application of professional rules could be added to the list. *See* Ministère Public v. Van Wesemael and Follachio, Joined Cases 110/78 and 111/78, [1979] E.C.R. 35, [1979] 3 C.M.L.R. 87. In addition, the elimination of possible abuse in the provision of manpower. *Webb*, [1981] E.C.R. at 3325, ¶¶ 17-19, [1982] 1 C.M.L.R. at 719.

38. Commission v. Denmark, Case 302/86, [1988] E.C.R. 4607, 4630, ¶ 9, [1989] 1 C.M.L.R. 619, 631.

39. *Id.* at 4630, ¶ 13, [1989] 1 C.M.L.R. at 631. However, the Danish legislation distinguished between "approved containers" that can be returned to any retailer of beverages and "non-approved containers" that can be returned only to the retailer who sold the beverages. The first category of returnable containers could be used without any limitation. The quantity of beer and soft drinks marketed by a single producer in the second category of containers was, however, limited to 3,000 hectoliters a year. The Court found that this latter aspect of the Danish legislation was not necessary to achieve the mandatory requirement of protection of the environment. *See id.* at 4631-32, ¶¶ 18-22; [1989] 1 C.M.L.R. at 631-32; Ludwig Krämer, *Environmental Protection and Article 30 EEC Treaty*, 30 COMMON MKT. L. REV., 111, 120-27 (1993).

40. *Denmark*, [1988] E.C.R. at 4630, ¶ 13, [1988] 1 C.M.L.R. at 631. For a similar outcome in another context, see Commission v. France, Case 188/84, [1986] E.C.R. 419, Common Mkt. Rep. (CCH) [1985-86] 14,285 (relating to French technical and safety standards for woodworking machines).

41. Commission of the European Communities, Completing the Internal Market: White Paper from the Commission to the European Council, COM (85) 310 (June 1985).

outcome.[42]

As a result, the density of legislation at the Community level is bound to decrease, which in turn will diminish the impact of such legislation on the Member States' laws.[43] But the "survival" of these laws will no longer threaten the Community's main objective—the establishment of the internal market. This is achieved through interaction between the mutual recognition of national laws and *some* central legislation. Legislation in the fields of "health, safety, environmental protection and consumer protection, will take as a base a high level of protection"[44] and will be adopted by the Council acting by a qualified majority on a proposal from the Commission in "co-decision" with the European Parliament.[45]

B. *The Environmental Policy of the Community*

It is in the area of the environment that the principle of subsidiarity (without being named as such) has found its first expression in the Treaty, but in terms rather different from those

---

42. *See* A. Mattera, *Subsidiarité, reconnaissance mutuelle et hiérarchie des normes européennes,* 1 Revue du Marché Unique Européen 7, 7-11 (1991).

43. This result is a converse consequence of the preemption mechanism. *See supra* note 15.

44. EC Treaty, *supra* note 2, art. 100a(3).

45. *Id.* art. 100a(1).

[In addition, i]f, after the adoption of a harmonisation measure by the Council acting by a qualified majority, a Member State deems it necessary to apply national provisions on grounds of major needs referred to in Article 36, or relating to protection of *the environment* or the working environment, it shall notify the Commission of these provisions.

The Commission shall confirm the provisions involved after having verified that they are not a means of arbitrary discrimination or a disguised restriction on trade between Member States.

Id. art. 100a(4) (emphasis added). In case of conflict about the application of this provision, the Commission or a Member State may bring the matter directly before the Court of Justice. *See* James Flynn, *How Will Article 100a(4) Work? A Comparison with Article 93,* 24 Common Mkt. L. Rev. 689 (1987). For the first time, Article 100a(4) has been used to authorize German legislation banning the use of pentachlorophenol. *Agence Europe,* No. 5748, June 12, 1992, at 13. The decision by which the Commission "confirmed" the more stringent German provisions, on the basis of Article 100a(4), was challenged in the Court of Justice by France in an action for annulment brought against the Commission pursuant to Article 173 of the EC Treaty. France v. Commission, Case C-41/93 (Eur. Ct. J. May 17, 1994) (not yet reported). On January 26, 1994, Advocate-General Giuseppe Tesauro delivered his opinion in the case and proposed to the Court to annul the contested decision for lack of statement of reasons in breach of Article 190 of the EC Treaty. The Court followed this opinion and, consequently, quashed the decision in a still unreported judgment. *Id.*

in the second paragraph of Article 3b. Article 130r(4) of the EEC Treaty (inserted by the SEA) reads as follows:

> The Community shall take action relating to the environment to the extent to which the objectives referred to in paragraph 1 [(i) to preserve, protect and improve the quality of the environment; (ii) to contribute towards protecting human health; (iii) to ensure a prudent and rational utilization of natural resources] can be attained better at Community level than at the level of the individual Member States. Without prejudice to certain measures of a Community nature, the Member States shall finance and implement the other measures.[46]

This provision was repealed by the TEU because of the general applicability of the second paragraph of the new Article 3b to all non-exclusive powers of the Community.

The "subsidiarity" test of Article 130r(4) prescribes a comparative enquiry into the efficiency of the Community and the individual Member States in attaining the objectives of European environmental policy (which the Member States must attempt to achieve in accordance with their general duty of loyalty towards the Community, as it flows from Article 5 of the Treaty of Rome). This test does not appear to be particularly protective of the prerogatives of the Member States (or of their subnational authorities); rather, it ensures that the one best placed to act, will act.[47] In that sense, the test can be seen as a more elaborate version of the criterion that, before the adoption of the SEA, Community environmental legislation had to meet under Article 235.[48] The "necessary" character of Community action was judged by the Council acting unanimously on a Commission proposal and after consulting the European Parliament, a decision-making procedure that left each Member State with a veto. Even though the Treaty had "not provided the necessary powers"

---

46. EEC Treaty, *supra* note 1, art. 130r(4).

47. *See* L.J. Brinkhorst, *Subsidiarity and European Community Environmental Policy*, EUR. ENVTL. L. REV. 16, 17-18 (1993). *Cf.* Wolfgang Kahl, *Möglichkeiten und Grenzen des Subsidiaritätsprinzips nach Art. 3B EG-Vertrag*, 118 ARCHIV DES ÖFFENTLICHEN RECHTS 414, 422-23 (1993).

48. EC Treaty, *supra* note 2, art. 235 ("action by the Community should prove *necessary* to attain") (emphasis added). The Court of Justice ruled that "Article 235 . . . does not create an obligation, but confers on the Council an option." Commission v. Council, Case 22/'70, [1971] E.C.R. 263, 283, ¶ 95, [1971] C.M.L.R. 335, 362 [hereinafter *AETR* case]. This statement confirms the responsibility of the political process in determining the necessary character of Community action based on Article 235.

(the word "environment" appeared nowhere in the Treaty), the potential exercise of a Member State's veto right did not stand in the way of the enactment of an extensive range of water and air quality directives.[49] These directives rested on the political judgment, shared by all the Member States, that action by the Community was "necessary" to take care of environmental issues that could not be efficiently addressed by the individual Member States. Furthermore, the directive was chosen as the appropriate normative instrument, which underscored the executive powers of the Member States.[50] Thus, to a political judgment (relating to the "necessity" of Community action) corresponded political safeguards (unanimity in the Council and implementation by the Member States).

The SEA did not really upset this balance by inserting a title relating to the environment in the part of the Treaty enumerating the several specific Community powers. The political safeguards were indeed confirmed in the new Articles 130r and 130s of the EEC Treaty. First, the requirement of Council unanimity (coupled with a mere consultation of the European Parliament) continued to apply.[51] However, the Council could, by unanimous vote, "define those matters on which decisions are to be taken by a qualified majority."[52]

Second, the principle of Member State implementation of Community environmental legislation was expressly stipulated in the last sentence of Article 130r(4). Member States received no special protective clause, but rather, a sound management rule which entrusted a policy matter to that level of government best positioned to achieve recognized common objectives. It has therefore been contended that the subsidiarity provision, despite its insertion in a Treaty containing justiciable provisions, is not judicially enforceable because the criterion of "better" is too indefinite.[53] At the very least, it can be argued that the Court would extend to the political judgment inherent in the operation of the first sentence of Article 130r(4), the deferential attitude that it has always adopted towards the appraisal by the

---

49. For an overview of this legislation, see Rolf Wägenbaur, *Regulating the European Environment: The EC Experience*, U. CHI. LEGAL F. 17, 27-28 (1992).

50. *Id.* at 20.

51. EEC Treaty, *supra* note 1, art. 130s, ¶ 1.

52. *Id.* art. 130s, ¶ 2.

53. LUDWIG KRÄMER, EEC TREATY AND ENVIRONMENTAL PROTECTION 71-77 (1990).

Council of the "necessary" character of Community action based on Article 235.[54]

In short, one can say that Articles 130r to 130t in their SEA version did not upset the constitutional balance of powers laid down in Article 235. They simply expressed a clear commitment to environmental policy and provided the Community and the Member States with some substantive guidance as to the principles which should guide such policy. Although the TEU functions similarly, but in a much more elaborate manner, this is the first time that the constitutional balance of powers has also been altered. These elements will now be examined.

The TEU gives prominence to environmental considerations. Already in the seventh recital of its preamble, Member States affirm that they are "determined to promote economic and social progress for their peoples, within the context of the accomplishment of the internal market and of reinforced cohesion and environmental protection."[55] Thereafter, the TEU amends Article 2 of the EC Treaty to state that the general "task" of the Community is "to promote throughout the Community a harmonious and balanced development of economic activities, sustainable and non-inflationary growth respecting the environment."[56] Furthermore, it adds to the list of "activities of the Community" enumerated in Article 3: "(k) a policy in the sphere of the environment."[57] Finally, Articles 130r to 130t have been amended in several respects relevant to our analysis.

An attempt is made throughout Articles 130r to 130t to reconcile the tension between separate forces. On the one hand, there is a need for a uniform and global approach at the central level in order to effectively protect the environment, especially in view of the many kinds of interstate spillovers. On the other hand, there is the desire of Member States and their subnational authorities ("regions") to preserve their residual power to react to local situations which must be dealt with in a specific way. The balance was established as follows.

---

54. *See* Hauptzollamt Bremerhaven v. Massey-Ferguson, Case 8/73, [1973] E.C.R. 897.

55. TEU, *supra* note 2, pmbl., para. 7.

56. *Id.* art. G.

57. *Id.*

First, Article 130r(1) introduces a new formula[58] which leaves room for the responsibility of the Member States (and their subnational authorities) for the achievement of the environmental objectives listed in the Treaty. It reads: "Community policy on the environment shall contribute to pursuit of the following objectives: "[the first three objectives quoted are the same as in the SEA version of the Article, the fourth one is new] - promoting measures at international level to deal with regional or worldwide environmental problems."[59]

Second, when the Community acts, it is obliged not only to "aim at a high level of protection,"[60] but also to "[take] into account the diversity of situations in the various regions of the Community."[61] To that effect, "harmonisation measures . . . shall include, where appropriate, a safeguard clause allowing Member States to take provisional measures, for non-economic environmental reasons, subject to a Community inspection procedure."[62] Furthermore, Article 130t still provides that "the protective measures adopted in common pursuant to Article 130s shall not prevent any Member State from maintaining or introducing more stringent protective measures," but it now adds that "[s]uch measures must be compatible with this Treaty [and] shall be notified to the Commission."[63] It thus appears that there is no preemption of the Member States' power to increase the environmental protection achieved by Community law, provided that this power is not being used in a protectionist fashion, i.e.,

---

58. *See* EC Treaty, *supra* note 2, art. 130r(1) ("Community policy on the environment shall contribute to pursuit of the following objectives: . . .").

59. *Id.*

60. The TEU extended to the "[c]ommunity policy on the environment" a requirement which, through the SEA, has already been introduced in relation to internal market legislation having an impact on environmental protection, EC Treaty, *supra* note 2, art. 100a, but was lacking in the SEA version of Articles 130r to 130t. *See* Dirk Vandermeersch, *The Single European Act and the Environmental Policy of the European Community*, 12 EUR. L. REV. 407 (1987); Christian Zacker, *Environmental Law of the European Economic Community: New Powers Under the Single European Act*, 14 B.C. INT'L & COMP. L. REV. 249 (1991).

61. EC Treaty, *supra* note 2, art. 130r(2).

62. *Id.*

63. *Id.* art. 130t. This requirement is parallel to that stated in the second paragraph of Article 100a(4). After the adoption of a harmonization measure relating to the internal market, a Member State may apply national provisions to protect the environment. Although this latter provision appears to be more limited than the last sentence of Article 130t, the more stringent national protective measures must in all cases be compatible with the Treaty as a whole, and not just with a specific aspect of it.

to obtain a competitive advantage over other Member States, through a closing off of the national market or otherwise. It is up to the Commission to supervise the action of the Member States in this respect.[64]

Third, "without prejudice to certain measures of a Community nature, the Member States shall finance and implement the environment policy."[65] This means that implementation of Community environmental legislation by the Member States or their subnational authorities remains the rule, and direct administration by the Community itself (e.g., through the "European Environmental Agency"),[66] the exception.

Fourth, the balance of powers characterizing the decision-making process has been altered through the generalization of qualified majority voting in the Council,[67] with the exception ("by way of derogation") of the adoption of "provisions primarily of a fiscal nature; measures concerning town and country planning, land use with the exception of waste management and measures of a general nature [the exception to the exception thus reinstates the principle of qualified majority voting for these matters], and management of water resources; [and] measures significantly affecting a Member State's choice between different energy sources and the general structure of its energy supply."[68] However, the Council may, acting unanimously, define those matters belonging to these categories on which decisions will nevertheless be taken by a qualified majority.[69] The Member States thus keep their veto right for politically sensitive matters (i.e., fiscal provisions, management of water or energy re-

---

64. An important procedural difference, as to the supervision by the Commission, between Article 100a(4) and Article 130t is that the first of these provisions contains a fast-track procedure which authorizes "[b]y way of derogation from the procedure laid down in Articles 169 and 170, the Commission or any [M]ember-State [to] bring the matter directly before the Court of Justice if it considers that another [M]ember-State is making improper use of the powers provided for in [that] Article," EC Treaty, *supra* note 2, art. 100a(4), whereas the policing by the Commission or the other Member States of the reliance by a Member State on Article 130t can only take place in accordance with Articles 169 and 170 of the EC Treaty.

65. EC Treaty, *supra* note 2, art. 130r(4) (confirming same article in EEC Treaty).

66. Council Regulation No. 1210/90 of 7 May 1990, O.J. L 120/1 (1990) (establishing European Environment Agency and European environment information and observation network).

67. EC Treaty, *supra* note 2, arts. 130s(1), (3).

68. *Id.* art. 130s(2).

69. *Id.*

sources) or matters tending to be of great local significance (i.e., town and country planning, land use). In these matters, the European Parliament has only the right to be consulted.

In all other matters relating to the Community policy on the environment, the procedure of cooperation with the European Parliament applies,[70] or even the procedure of co-decision between the Council and the European Parliament as to "general action programmes setting out priority objectives to be attained."[71] The Economic and Social Committee is consulted in all cases, but the newly established Committee of the Regions does not intervene at all. However, in many Member States, subnational authorities bear significant responsibilities in shaping and implementing environmental policy.

The risk of being outvoted in the Council was only offset by some wavering political safeguards (far less effective than the previous veto right). Some examples include: the guarantee that the diversity of situations in the various regions of the Community will be taken into account, the absence of Community preemption of the Member State power to enact more protective legislation (albeit under the supervision of the Commission), or the possibility for the Council to lay down appropriate provisions in the form of temporary derogations and/or financial support from the Cohesion Fund, if a measure based on the provisions of paragraph 1 of Article 130s (that is a measure adopted by the Council acting by a qualified majority in cooperation with the European Parliament) involves costs deemed disproportionate for the public authorities of a Member State.[72] All of these political safeguards, whose judicial enforceability appears rather uncertain in practice, have therefore been supplemented with the general protective clause of the second paragraph of Article 3b. This paragraph is applicable to the environment, in addition to any other non-exclusive power of the Community. In accordance with the principle of subsidiarity, the Community shall take action *only if* and *in so far as* the *objectives of the proposed action* (covered by the Treaty article which serves as the legal basis to the action, *in casu* Articles 130r and 130s) *cannot* be *sufficiently* achieved by the Member States *and* can *therefore*, by reason of the

---

70. *Id.* arts. 130s, 189c.
71. *Id.* arts. 130s(3), 189b.
72. *Id.* art. 130s(5).

scale or effects of the proposed action, be better achieved by the Community. This is to be a judicially enforceable limit *intra vires* of the exercise of the Community powers relating to the environment.[73] As can be seen, the present formulation of the principle of subsidiarity has shifted considerably from the previous one, contained in the first sentence of Article 130r(4) of the EEC Treaty.[74]

It starts out from the responsibility of the Member States to achieve the objectives of a proposed Community action (the new wording of the introductory sentence of Article 130r(1) lends support to this reading of Article 3b, second paragraph). Only *if* Member States, acting on an individual basis, are incapable for whatever reason (i.e., political, legal, economic, technical, etc.) to achieve "sufficiently"[75] the objectives of the proposed action, will Community action be possible, but only to the extent of the incapacity of the Member States.[76] The main object of the clause is to protect the Member States against all forms of preemption, by the Community, of their own residual powers, when they are able to achieve the objectives of the proposed action in a sufficient manner. The principle of subsidiarity thus aims at protecting the proximity of government.

II. *THE BALANCE OF POWER: LEGAL BASIS, SUBSIDIARITY AND PROPORTIONALITY*

A. *Legal Basis: Definition of the Community Power to Act*

The first paragraph of Article 3b codifies the principle that the Community government is one of enumerated powers. Each legislative act must indicate in its preamble the Treaty provision

---

73. For a skeptical view about the actual judicial enforceability of this provision, see Renaud Dehousse, *The Legacy of Maastricht: Emerging Institutional Issues, in* III COLLECTED COURSES OF THE ACADEMY OF EUROPEAN LAW 187, 209-16 (1992).

74. *See supra* note 46.

75. A judgment to be exercised by the Community political process, operating under its normal rules, i.e., in the field of the environment. *See* EC Treaty, *supra* note 2, arts. 130s(1)-(3).

76. Compare the conclusions of the Edinburgh European Council of 11 and 12 December 1992, which state *inter alia* that "the reasons for concluding that a Community objective cannot be sufficiently achieved by the Member States but can be better achieved by the Community must be substantiated by qualitative or, wherever possible, quantitative indicators." 25 E.C. BULL., no. 12, at 15, ¶ 4 (1992).

that serves as its "legal basis."[77] The Court of Justice requires that an explicit reference to a specific Treaty provision be made "where, in its absence, the parties concerned and the Court are left uncertain as to the precise legal basis."[78] This requirement is merely a specific application of the more general requirement under the Treaty to give reasons for all acts.[79] The Treaty provision serving as the legal basis determines the balance of power between the Community and the Member States in at least three ways.

There is first the *substantive* aspect—whether the content of the legislative enactment is within the material scope of powers conferred on the Community in the Treaty provision at hand. If it is not, the Community may have trespassed upon the residual powers of the Member States, unless another Treaty provision could have supplied the necessary powers enabling the Community to act.[80] In short, the main question addressed by the legal basis concept is whether the Community possesses the powers that it seeks to exercise. There are, however, two other aspects to this concept, namely the institutional and the instrumental aspects.

The *institutional* aspect relates to the terms of the decision-making process, which differ from one Treaty provision (and thus, Community substantive power) to another. The explanation of the Community decision-making process under Articles 100a and 130s(1), (2), and (3) may serve as an illustration.[81]

Finally, there is the *instrumental* aspect that a treaty provision serving as the legal basis for a Community legislative act sometimes states the instrument through which the act is to be adopted.[82] This should be seen as one more expression of the

---

77. Commission v. Council, Case 45/86, [1987] E.C.R. 1493, 1518-20, ¶¶ 4-9, [1988] 2 C.M.L.R. 131, 152-53.

78. *Id.* at 1520, ¶ 9, [1988] 2 C.M.L.R. at 152-53; *see* France v. Commission, Case C-325/91, [1993] E.C.R. I-3283, I-3311, ¶ 26.

79. EC Treaty, *supra* note 2, art. 190. For an analysis, see Martin Shapiro, *The Giving Reasons Requirement*, U. Chi. Legal F. 179 (1992).

80. Article 235 of the EC Treaty plays a subsidiary role in this respect. The Court remarked in Commission v. Council that "[i]t follows from the very wording of Article 235 that its use as the legal basis for a measure is justified only where no other provision of the Treaty gives the Community institutions the necessary power to adopt the measure in question." Case 45/86, [1987] E.C.R. at 1520, ¶ 13, [1988] 2 C.M.L.R. at 153.

81. *See supra* notes 70-74 and accompanying text.

82. Articles 54(2), 57, and 100 of the EC Treaty each state the mandatory use of directives. *See* EC Treaty, *supra* note 2, arts. 54(2), 57, 100.

compromise of divided sovereignty between the Community and the Member States. The several types of instruments defined in Article 189 of the EC Treaty (i.e., regulations, directives, and decisions) were not meant to have the same effect in the national legal order. When the relevant Treaty provision mandates the use of a specific instrument for the adoption of Community acts, the legality of such acts depends on the respect of that obligation. However, in many cases, the choice of the instrument to be used for the adoption of Community acts is left open by the Treaty,[83] in which case it will be considered when a decision about the content and the intensity of the proposed action is to be reached. The instruments to be used for Community action in the field of the environment have not been determined in the Treaty, under either Article 100a[84] or Article 130s.[85] They will therefore be the object of political bargaining in the decision-making process.

Since the legal basis determines the existence and the extent of Community powers, as well as the way in which they are to be exercised, the political process cannot choose it as it sees fit. The Court of Justice has indeed characterized the choice of the correct legal basis as a justiciable issue that must be solved in conformity with the Community constitution. The choice, the Court said, "must be based on objective factors which are amena-

---

83. *See id.* arts. 43(2), ¶ 3, 51, 126(4), 128(5), 129(4). Articles 126(4) (education), 128(5) (culture), and 129(4) (public health) deal with "new" powers.

84. *Id.* art. 100a(1). Article 100a(1) simply refers to "the measures" to be adopted with a view to the establishment and functioning of the internal market. But, in spite of the constitutional freedom thus left to the legislative process as to the appropriate normative instrument to choose for each "measure" to be adopted, the drafters of the SEA (which inserted Article 100a into the EEC Treaty) indicated their clear preference for the directive. "In its proposals pursuant to Article 100a(1) the Commission shall give precedence to the use of the instrument of a directive if harmonization involves the amendment of legislative provisions in one or more Member States." SEA, *supra* note 1, Declaration on Article 100a of the EEC Treaty.

85. EC Treaty, *supra* note 2, art. 130s(1). Article 130s(1) states that the political process "shall decide what action is to be taken by the Community." *Id.* The first paragraph of Article 130s(2) refers to "provisions" and "measures" to be adopted, whereas the second paragraph speaks of "matters . . . on which decisions are to be taken by a qualified majority." *Id.* art. 130s(2). However, from the context it appears clearly that these "decisions" are not meant to be "decisions" within the strict meaning of Article 189 of the EC Treaty, but rather the outcome of the process of decision-making. Article 130s(3) requires the adoption of "general action programmes," and "the measures necessary for the implementation of these programmes." *Id.* art. 130s(3).

ble to judicial review."[86] But even if based on "objective factors," the task of judicial review is a sensitive, and at times, unpredictable exercise.[87] And yet, because of its institutional and instrumental aspects, the choice of legal basis is the pivot on which the balance of "federalism" (that is, the balance of power between the Community and the Member States) turns.

The stakes involved in European environmental policy may be important enough to trigger some fierce litigation on the legal basis of the action to be taken, especially when the Council disagrees with the Commission in an effort to preserve the requirement of unanimity for the adoption of Community action. The case-law obviously deals with the EC Treaty provisions in their SEA version. On June 11, 1991,[88] the Court of Justice delimitated the reach of two Treaty provisions, Article 100a and Article 130s. These Articles were relied upon respectively by the Commission and the Council to serve as the legal basis for the 1989 Council Directive on procedures for harmonizing the programmes for the reduction and eventual elimination of pollution caused by waste from the titanium dioxide industry.[89]

The Commission had based its proposal for the Directive on Article 100a, arguing that the act was to harmonize national laws on manufacturing conditions. This would eliminate a factor of distortion of competition in the internal market, even if the actual substance of the Directive related to environmental concerns. Since Article 100a grants the power to the Community to

---

86. *See* Commission v. Council, Case 45/86, [1987] E.C.R. 1493, at 1520, ¶ 11, [1988] 2 C.M.L.R. 131, 153.

87. The Court, however, does not say what "objective factors" are, but simply contrasts this criterion for choosing the correct legal basis of an act with "an institution's conviction as to the objective pursued" by the act. For a critique, see Martin Nettesheim, *Horizontale Kompetenzkonflikte in der EG*, 28 EuR. 243 (1993). This article explains that the conflict between two EC Treaty provisions, which could serve as the legal basis of an act, is especially complicated when both provisions define powers of the Community, not in terms of a subject-matter to be dealt with, but in terms of an (open-ended) objective to be pursued (which is the case for most Community powers). In this latter situation, the conviction as to the objective pursued by the act inevitably plays an essential role in choosing the correct legal basis. If not the conviction of the political institution that takes the decision, then at the very least, the conviction of the Court of Justice when deciding litigation concerning the political institution's conviction. Meanwhile it remains doubtful whether anything is to be gained in labelling the Court's conviction, objective factors, which are amenable to judicial review.

88. Commission v. Council, Case C-300/89, [1991] E.C.R. I-2867, [1993] 3 C.M.L.R. 359 [hereinafter *Titanium Dioxide*].

89. No. 89/428/EEC of 21 June 1989, O.J. L 201/56 (1989).

enact measures necessary "for the achievement of the objectives set out in Article 8a [that is, the 'internal market']," it was argued that it should be the correct legal basis for the proposed directive. The Council disputed this line of argument and altered, through a unanimous vote,[90] the proposed legal basis to Article 130s, which confers on the Community the power to take actions in the field of the environment.

The institutional aspect of these two articles is very different. Article 100a allows the Council to act by a qualified majority and requires the cooperation of the European Parliament.[91] Article 130s requires the Council to act unanimously and allows the European Parliament only the right to be consulted. Thus, the substantive characterization of the proposed directive as a matter relating to the "internal market" or to the "environment" led to a very different process of decision-making to be followed.

The Commission, supported by the European Parliament, asked the Court to annul the Directive, on the ground that the Council had based it incorrectly on Article 130s, rendering the Directive unconstitutional. The Council defended the Directive as being consistent with the EC Treaty. The Court ruled in favor of the Commission, but admitted that the aim and content of the Directive revealed aspects of both internal market and environmental legislation, and therefore, should in principle have been based simultaneously on both EC Treaty articles.[92] This solution, however, could not work in practice, because the procedures of decision-making introduced by these two articles con-

---

90. EEC Treaty, *supra* note 1, art. 149(1), *as replaced by* EC Treaty, *supra* note 2, art. 189a(1) ("Where in pursuance of this Treaty, the Council acts on a proposal from the Commission, unanimity shall be required for an act constituting an amendment to that proposal . . . .").

91. After the TEU, "co-decision" between the Council and the European Parliament applies.

92. The Court specified that the "objective factors" on which the choice of the legal basis for a measure is to be based "include in particular the aim and content of the measure." *Titanium Dioxide*, [1991] E.C.R. at I-2898, ¶ 10, [1993] 3 C.M.L.R. at 383. The Court analyzed "the aim and content" of the contested directive. *Id.* at I-2898-99, ¶¶ 11-15, [1993] 3 C.M.L.R. at 383-84. Finally, the Court concluded that, in principle, a double legal basis was required. *Id.* at I-2900, ¶¶ 16-17, [1993] 3 C.M.L.R. at 384. This means that the Court considered that the Directive equally concerned action relating to the environment, EC Treaty, *supra* note 2, art. 130s, and the establishment and functioning of the internal market, *id.* art. 100a, without it being possible to indicate a hierarchy between these two aspects.

tradicted one another.[93] The Court then explained that in such a case preference had to be given to the legal basis that provides the European Parliament the right to cooperate in the decision-making. The object of the cooperation procedure, according to the Court, was to strengthen the part played by the European Parliament in the legislative process of the Community. This "reflects at Community level the fundamental democratic principle that the people should take part in the exercise of power through the intermediary of a representative assembly."[94] The Court then went on to explain that, from a substantive perspective, Article 100a by itself could be a sufficient legal basis for the Directive, as it obliges the Commission to take as a base, a high level of protection "in its proposals for legislative acts concerning health, safety, environmental protection, and consumer protection."[95] The drafters of Article 100a had indeed envisaged the situation in which "internal market" legislation would require harmonizing the laws of the Member States on some aspects of environmental policy.[96]

---

93. *Titanium Dioxide*, [1991] E.C.R. at 2900, ¶ 17-19, [1993] 3 C.M.L.R. 384.

94. *Id.* at 2900, ¶ 20, [1993] 3 C.M.L.R. 384-85. This language was first used in two judgments. *See* Roquette Frères v. Council, Case 138/79, [1980] E.C.R. 3333, at 3360, ¶ 34; Maizena v. Council, Case 139/79, [1980] E.C.R. 3393, at 3424, ¶ 34.

95. EC Treaty, *supra* note 2, art. 100a(3).

96. Thus, after having stated that the procedures of decision-making laid down in Articles 100a and 130s are incompatible, while the procedure of decision-making laid down in Article 100a is more democratic, the Court returned to the substantive aspect of the legal basis debate, which in the initial stage of its reasoning had led to the conclusion stated in paragraph 16. This second move on substance was introduced with the consideration "that in the present case recourse to the dual legal basis of Articles 100a and 130s is excluded and that it is necessary to determine which of those two provisions is the appropriate legal basis." *Titanium Dioxide*, [1991] E.C.R. at I-2901, ¶ 21, [1993] 3 C.M.L.R. at 385. The Court used the language of what, hereinafter, will be defined as "competitive spillovers." This language was intended to connect the Directive at issue, predominantly (and thus exclusively, given the practical impossibility of a dual legal basis) to the establishment and functioning of the internal market. *Id.* at I-2901, ¶ 23, [1993] 3 C.M.L.R. at 385.

> [P]rovisions which are made necessary by considerations relating to the environment and health may be a burden upon the undertakings to which they apply and, if there is no harmonization of national provisions on the matter, competition may be appreciably distorted. It follows that action intended to approximate national rules concerning production conditions in a given industrial sector with the aim of eliminating distortions of competition in that sector is conducive to the attainment of the internal market and thus falls within the scope of Article 100a . . . .

Id. For an assessment, see René Barents, *The Internal Market Unlimited: Some Observations on the Legal Basis of Community Legislation*, 30 COMMON MKT. L. REV. 85 (1993).

The Court's approach to the substantive aspect of the legal basis litigation has undoubtedly been triggered to a large extent by its frank commitment to "the fundamental democratic principle" of parliamentary representation in the legislative process. This approach could not really be controversial in "a Community based on the rule of law,"[97] even though some Member States might have been surprised to learn that they had surrendered their veto right as to the necessary degree of environmental protection.

However, in its judgment of 17 March 1993,[98] the Court reached the opposite outcome, when it dismissed the action for annulment of the 1991 Council Directive on waste[99] brought by the Commission (again with the support of the European Parliament). The Court accepted Article 130s as the correct legal basis for the Directive (instead of Article 100a), in spite of its ancillary effect on the functioning of the internal market, caused, *inter alia*, by the uniform definition of waste (which might be relevant for the free movement of goods as it relates to waste) and the partial harmonization of conditions of competition (putting an end to the advantages enjoyed by industries established in Member States with a more permissive legislation). For the Court, the free movement of waste and the conditions of competition were not the "object" of the Directive.[100] Its aim

---

97. Les Verts v. European Parliament, Case 294/83, [1986] E.C.R. 1339, at 1365, ¶ 23, [1987] 2 C.M.L.R. 343.

98. Commission v. Council, Case C-155/91, [1993] E.C.R. I-939 [hereinafter *Waste*].

99. Council Directive No. 91/156/EEC of 18 March 1991, O.J. L 78/32 (1991).

100. *Waste*, [1993] E.C.R. at I-968-69, ¶¶ 19-20. In paragraph 20 of the judgment, the Court expressly distinguished its *Titanium Dioxide* ruling, in which the directive at issue was aimed at the approximation of laws relating to the conditions of manufacturing in one precise sector of industry with the purpose of eliminating distortions of competition. According to the Court in the *Waste* case, however, the contested directive had only a lateral impact on competitive conditions. That was not sufficient to require Article 100a. For the Court, recourse to Article 100a is not justified when the draft legislation has only an incidental effect on the harmonization of market conditions within the Community. Parliament v. Council, Case C-70/88, [1991] E.C.R. I-4529, at I-4566, ¶ 17 (restated in ¶ 19 of the *Waste* case). The Court reasoned in terms of "pollution spillovers" in spite of the possible significance on the functioning of the internal market. However, the principal, EC Treaty, *supra* note 2, art. 130s(2), must then prevail over the accessory, *id.* art. 100a, except if in a given case the internal market aspect really appears to be too heavy to still be capable of being regarded as the accessory. It is for such a case that the introductory sentence of Article 130s(2) contains the expression "without prejudice to Article 100a," which will lead to Article 100a serving as the sole legal basis for Community action. *See Titanium Dioxide*, [1991] E.C.R. I-2867, [1993] 3 C.M.L.R. 359.

and content were rather to ensure the management of waste, whether industrial or domestic, in conformity with the requirements of the protection of the environment. In particular, the Directive aimed at implementing the principle of correction by priority at source (stated in Article 130r(2)). The Court's analysis appears to be confirmed by the TEU version of Article 130s(2), which mentions "waste management" as an aspect of the Community policy on the environment to be acted upon in accordance with the general rule of "cooperation" of the Council (acting by a qualified majority) with the European Parliament after consultation of the Economic and Social Committee (i.e., the procedure of decision-making laid down in Article 130s(1)).

Reading the two judgments together leads to the conclusion that it is all a matter of the principal and the accessory:[101] when

---

101. This conclusion may come as a surprise to those who read the *Titanium Dioxide* judgment to hold that any effect of Community environmental legislation on the functioning of the internal market leads to the requirement that Article 100a serve as the legal basis for that legislation. In reality, the Court already qualified that possible impression raised by its *Titanium Dioxide* judgment, when four months later it adopted a *lex specialis derogat legi generali* attitude in order to accept Article 31 of the Treaty Establishing the European Atomic Energy Community as the correct legal basis for Community legislation on maximum permitted levels of radioactive contamination of foodstuffs and of feedingstuffs following a nuclear accident or any other case of radiological emergency, Council Regulation (Euratom) No. 3954/87, O.J. L 371/11 (1987), notwithstanding the incidental effect of that legislation on the functioning of the internal market. *See supra* note 100 (discussing *Waste,* [1993] E.C.R. I-939). Applied to environmental legislation, that attitude forced the Court to weigh the impact of such legislation on the internal market against its significance for the pursuit of the objectives of the Community policy on the environment. That is hardly a predictable exercise, as can be seen through the situation of "waste management:" although the Court assimilates waste to a "good," it has considered, in *Commission v. Belgium,* Case C-2/90, [1992] E.C.R. I-4431, [1993] 1 C.M.L.R. 365 [hereinafter *Walloon Waste*], that the principle of free movement could not as such be upheld. The Court even accepted to apply its *Cassis de Dijon* case law to the discriminatory *Walloon Waste* legislation. *See* P. Demaret, *Trade Related Environmental Measures (TREMS) in the External Relations of the European Community, in* THE EUROPEAN COMMUNITY'S COMMERCIAL POLICY AFTER 1992: THE LEGAL DIMENSION 305, 316, 341 (Marc Maresceau ed., 1992). It is against this background of an awareness that waste is a "good," but then a good containing special risks for the environment and, as a consequence, being of special significance for the pursuit of the objectives of the Community policy on the environment, that the Court must determine, for each aspect of "waste management," the principal and the accessory. In these circumstances it should not really be astonishing that the outcome of the Court's assessment does not always meet with general approval. *See* A. Wachsmann, *Comments, Case C-155/91,* 30 COMMON MKT. L. REV. 1051, 1064-65 (1993). Compare the doubts expressed by Jules Stuyck, on Article 130s serving as the legal basis for Council Regulation (EEC) No. 259/93 of 1 February 1993 on the supervision and control of shipments of waste within, into and out of the European Community, O.J. L 30/1 (1993) [hereinafter Council Regulation

the "object" of Community action, according to its "aim" and "content," is mainly related to the objectives and principles stated in Article 130r, then it must be based on Article 130s, notwithstanding some lateral impact of that action on the internal market (e.g., the elimination of an element of distortion of competitive conditions); when the reverse is true, Article 100a will obviously be the correct legal basis; finally, when the "object" of Community action (always according to its "aim" and "content") relates similarly to the objectives and principles stated in Article 130r and in Article 100a(1), there should, in principle, be a double legal basis. But in view of the incompatibility of the decision-making procedures laid down in Article 100a(1) (after the TEU, "co-decision" between the Council and the European Parliament) and Article 130s(1) (after the TEU, "cooperation" of the Council with the European Parliament) the Court will probably still be inclined to favor the more democratic decision-making procedure, i.e., that which maximizes the co-legislative prerogatives of the European Parliament, namely Article 100a(1). In this respect it is worth noting that the TEU has amended Article 173 of the EC Treaty, giving the European Parliament - in line with the Court's case-law[102] - the right to bring an action for annulment of acts of the Council or the Commission "for the purpose of protecting [its] prerogatives."[103] It may be expected that the European Parliament will continue to watch closely the choice between Article 100a and Article 130s as the legal basis for acts relating to the Community policy on the environment, as it is now the institution whose prerogatives are most directly affected by that choice. For the European Parliament, the difference between the procedures of "co-decision" or "cooperation" is indeed substantial,[104] even though in both procedures the Council acts by a qualified majority.

(EEC) No. 259/93], on the grounds that when Community legislation directly regulates the transportation of waste across Member State borders, it is so centrally concerned with the free movement of goods that in any event Article 100a should be used as legal basis. Jules Stuyck, *Le traitement des déchets dans la (non-)réalisation du marché intérieur*, JOURNAL DES TRIBUNAUX DROIT EUROPÉEN No. 7, at 10, 11 (1994). The Court of Justice, however, upheld Article 130s as the correct legal basis for the Regulation. Parliament v. Council, Case C-187/93 (Eur. Ct. J. June 28, 1994) (not yet reported).

    102. Parliament v. Council, Case C-70/88, [1991] E.C.R. I-2041, [1992] 1 C.M.L.R. 91.

    103. EC Treaty, *supra* note 2, art. 173.

    104. *See supra* note 15.

874   *FORDHAM INTERNATIONAL LAW JOURNAL*   [Vol. 17:846

The only situation in which this legal basis debate seems to be without object is when the Council adopts "general action programmes setting out priority objectives to be attained."[105] Under Article 130s(3), first paragraph, the same procedure of decision-making applies as under Article 100a(1).[106]

On the contrary, the legal basis debate will be intense when the Council acts pursuant to Article 130s(2) - that is, unanimously on a proposal from the Commission and after consulting the European Parliament and the Economic and Social Committee. As already indicated, this procedure of decision-making applies "by way of derogation" to a limited list of politically sensitive matters, and this, according to the text of Article 130s(2), occurs "without prejudice to Article 100a."[107] Thus, in borderline cases of the *Titanium Dioxide* type, i.e. when substantively both articles are equally relevant, the temptation will remain, for both the Commission and the European Parliament, to argue in favor of Article 100a as the correct legal basis. Indeed, in such cases Article 100a(1) contains a radically more democratic decision-making procedure (co-decision between the Council and the European Parliament instead of the mere consultation of the latter institution). Moreover, the Commission should be happy to see the Council act by a qualified majority (Article 100a(1)), since it greatly increases the chances of successfully fulfilling its role of mediation in the several organs of the Council with minimal pressure from the Member States on the content of its original proposal.[108]

Finally, it should be added that legal basis litigation may also arise within Article 130s when the Council, the Commission, and the European Parliament do not distinguish between sections (1), (2), and (3) of Article 130s in an identical way. The prerog-

---

105. EC Treaty, *supra* note 2, art. 130s(3).

106. *See* Commission v. Council, Case 165/87, [1988] E.C.R. 5545, 5562, ¶¶ 19-20, [1990] C.M.L.R. 457.

107. EC Treaty, *supra* note 2, art. 130s(2).

108. When unanimity is needed for the Council to adopt a proposal from the Commission, it may be used to amend the proposal against the Commission's will. *See id.* art. 189a(1). On the contrary, when the Council is authorized to act by a qualified majority on a proposal from the Commission, the proposal enjoys the advantage of a head start, because it will only take a qualified majority to accept it (and the Commission may alter the proposal during the Council's deliberations, per Article 189a(2), in order to have it reach such a majority), while all the Member States must agree (or, at least, abstain during the vote) to amend the proposal.

atives of the European Parliament differ strongly from one section to another (from cooperation through mere consultation to
co-decision), whereas the Commission may see the effectiveness
of its participation in the decision-making affected by the requirement of unanimity stated in section (2). The Council, on
the other hand, could be inclined to give a somewhat larger interpretation to section (2) as it is the only route which continues
to guarantee a veto right to the Member States (which they enjoyed for all Community actions in the field of the environment
prior to the TEU). These divergent interests, held by the institutions in the several procedures of decision-making laid down in
Article 130s, increase the likelihood that they will not always consider the "object" of a Community environmental act (taking
into account its "aim" and "content") to be part of one and the
same section ((1), (2), or (3)) of Article 130s.

B. *Subsidiarity: Assessment of the Need for Community Action*

When the Community finds in the Treaty a sufficient legal
basis to act (and thus has the power to act), further questions
arise as to whether it should act and, if so, to what extent. As we
have seen, both of these questions are addressed in the second
paragraph of Article 3b ("if and in so far as"). The principle of
subsidiarity *sensu stricto* involves the assessment of the need for
Community action (the *if* question). In the case of a positive
assessment, the nature and intensity of Community action will
have to be determined in the light of the several aspects of the
principle of proportionality including the goal mentioned in the
second paragraph of Article 3b that belongs to the principle of
subsidiarity *sensu lato* (the *in-so-far-as* question). As this latter
question is closely linked to the more general principle of proportionality, stated in the third paragraph of Article 3b, the two
will be analyzed together.

According to the second paragraph of Article 3b, the need
for Community action depends on the finding that "the objectives of the proposed action cannot be sufficiently achieved by
the Member States."[109] This finding seems to make the *effectiveness* of the means at the disposal of the Member States the crucial criterion in the following respect: when the means at the
disposal of at least one Member State prove to be ineffective to

---

109. *Id.* art. 3b.

sufficiently achieve the objectives of the proposed action, the need for some Community action[110] will be established, as these objectives will then indeed be "better achieved by the Community."[111]

As it is drafted, the second paragraph of Article 3b sounds rather restrictive as to the need for Community action: "only if" there is a shortcoming in the possibilities of action of some or all Member States, can the Community ("therefore") better achieve the objectives of the proposed action.[112] The greater *efficiency* of the Community is not, as such, presented as an alternative criterion, standing on a par with the criterion of the effectiveness of the means available to the Member States. In other words, if the means available to *all* Member States are perfectly *effective* in order to sufficiently achieve the objectives of the proposed action, but the Community is more *efficient* in achieving these objectives, a literal reading of the Treaty text should prevent the Community from acting. It goes without saying that such a literal reading leads to an unsatisfactory result, because the Community could apparently be forced to abandon actions which are to benefit from economies of scale when undertaken at the European level of government.

The truth of the matter is that two logics were mixed in the final version of the second paragraph of Article 3b.[113] On the one hand, this provision was worded as a direct guarantee of the proximity of government, which requires that the Community abstain from acting if the Member States can sufficiently achieve the objectives of the proposed action (criterion of effectiveness). Only the outcome counts: when the Member States are producing it (whatever the means they have to use), the Community should not take their place. On the contrary, the Community

---

110. In case of discrepancies in the capacity of Member States to achieve the objectives of a proposed action in a sufficient manner, the Community may have to differentiate its action, in accordance with the principle of subsidiarity, in order to take into account these discrepancies. Such a differentiation of action by the Community does not infringe upon the principle of equality between Member States, but might in fact even be necessary to meet the requirements of that principle. *See* Italy v. Commission, Case 13/63, [1963] E.C.R. 165, [1963] C.M.L.R. 289.

111. EC Treaty, *supra* note 2, art. 3b.

112. The final part of the second paragraph of Article 3b rests on the assumption that the Community will necessarily be in a position to fill the gap left by the Member States. *Id.*

113. *See* Dehousse, *supra* note 73, at 207-08.

must take the place of the Member States when they do not produce the required outcome and "therefore" the latter can "be better achieved by the Community." On the other hand, the Treaty authors have shown some sensitivity to *efficiency* concerns as well through the reference to "the scale or effects of the proposed action." However, this element can in principle come into play "only if" the Member States cannot sufficiently achieve the objectives of the proposed action and "therefore" the Community is authorized to act (in which case, it is so authorized irrespective of the "efficiency" of its action).

The criteria of *effectiveness* and *efficiency* would have coexisted more smoothly if the assessment of the need for action by the Community had been made dependent *either* on the ineffectiveness of the means at the disposal of at least one Member State *or* on the greater efficiency of action by the Community (when both the Community and the Member States are in a position to produce the required outcome, but the latter at a considerably higher cost than the Community). The words "and . . . therefore" linking the two parts of the sentence, might, at first sight, appear to constitute a real obstacle to this common-sense interpretation of the test to be applied to assess the need for Community action. However, in actual practice, it should be rather easy for the Community to overcome that obstacle. It is indeed up to the Community's political process (operating according to the rules laid down in the Treaty article serving as the legal basis for the proposed action) to define "the objectives of the proposed action," and nothing prevents that process from including considerations relating to the *efficiency* of the proposed action in the definition of its objectives. It may even be argued that the second paragraph of Article 3b encourages the Community to do so, as it refers to "the scale or effects of the proposed action," a part of the sentence which does not play a direct role in the assessment of the need for Community action, but which takes its full significance in the larger context of the definition of the objectives of *any* proposed Community action. The question whether the objectives of the proposed action can be "sufficiently" achieved by the Member States will then necessarily include an enquiry into the efficiency of the means at the disposal of the Member States to reach the required outcome. Thus, the criteria of effectiveness and efficiency will to a large extent become interchangeable.

In its Communication to the Council and the European Parliament of 27 October 1992, the Commission has made no particular effort to connect its understanding of the principle of subsidiarity to the precise wording of the second paragraph of Article 3b, a provision which is said to contain *in globo* a "test of comparative efficiency between Community action and that of Member States."[114] The test "implies that we have to examine if there are other methods available for Member States, for example legislation, administrative instructions or codes of conduct, in order to achieve the objectives in a sufficient manner."[115] Other factors to be examined are "the effect of the scale of the operation (transfrontier problems, critical mass, etc.), the cost of inaction, the necessity to maintain a reasonable coherence, the possible limits on action at national level (including cases of potential distortion where some Member States were able to act and others were not able to do so) and the necessity to ensure that competition is not distorted within the common market."[116]

The ineffectiveness of the means available to the Member States and the greater efficiency of action at Community level are also stated as *alternative* criteria for the assessment of the need for Community action in the "guidelines" to be used by the Council (adopted by the European Council at its Edinburgh meeting of 11 and 12 December 1992). They are as follows:

— the issue under consideration has transnational aspects which cannot be satisfactorily regulated by action by Member States; and/or

— actions by Member States alone or lack of Community action would conflict with the requirements of the Treaty (such as the need to correct distortion of competition or avoid disguised restrictions on trade or strengthen economic and social cohesion) or would otherwise significantly damage Member States' interests; and/or

— the Council must be satisfied that action at Community level would produce clear benefits by reason of its scale or effects compared with action at the level of the Member States.[117]

For the European Council, the need for Community action

---

114. 25 E.C. BULL., *supra* note 18, at 116.
115. *Id.*
116. *Id.*
117. 25 E.C. BULL., *supra* note 76, at 14-16.

exists when the Council ascertains that one or more of the criteria set in these guidelines are met. This is why the three guidelines are linked to one another with the words "and/or."

The first two guidelines refer to cases in which only the Community is in a position to act *effectively*, mainly in view of inter-State spillovers that cannot really be apprehended "at the level of the individual Member States" (see Article 130r(4) - SEA version).

The third guideline refers to cases in which the Community is more *efficient* than the individual Member States in achieving the objectives of the proposed action in a sufficient manner, even though the latter may also be capable of producing the required outcome (but at a much higher cost). The European Council thus turns the comparative efficiency test into a fully-fledged alternative criterion for the assessment of the need for Community action, which by itself is capable of leading to the recognition of the need for such action "by reason of its scale or effects" (the third guideline takes over these words from the second paragraph of Article 3b, but - contrary to that provision - it interprets the words "and . . . therefore" as "and/or").

It may be concluded that both the Commission and the European Council continue to read the Treaty text as if it were in essence equal to the former Article 130r(4), which prescribes a comparative efficiency test to assess the need for Community action ("the objectives . . . can be attained better at Community level than at the level of the individual Member States").[118]

The guidelines reflect the more fundamental approach of the European Council to "subsidiarity," which it sees as "a dynamic concept" that "allows Community action to be expanded where circumstances so require, and conversely, to be restricted or discontinued where it is no longer justified."[119]

In the field of the environment, it can safely be said that the

---

118. EEC Treaty, *supra* note 1, art. 130r(4). It should be noted that this interpretation of the second paragraph of Article 3b is consistent with the initial draft of that Treaty provision, proposed by the Luxembourg Presidency in April 1991. It introduced as the sole criterion for the operation of the principle of subsidiarity, that the objectives of the proposed action could be "better achieved by the Community than by the Member States acting separately." *Projet de Traité Sur L'Union*, EUROPE DOCUMENTS, July 5, 1991, No. 1722/1723, at 4. Clearly, this is a comparative efficiency test, the only basic ingredient of which is the sheer effectiveness of Member States in reaching the required outcome.

119. 25 E.C. BULL., *supra* note 76, at 13-14.

three guidelines contain an extremely low threshold with regard to the assessment of the need for Community action. From the moment that there is any kind of inter-State spillover there will undoubtedly be transnational aspects which cannot be satisfactorily regulated by action by Member States (first guideline) or risks of distortion of competition or disguised restrictions on trade between Member States or - even more generally - damage to Member States' interests (second guideline). As a result, individual Member States will be ineffective in their efforts to sufficiently achieve the objectives of proposed Community action relating to the inter-State spillover. In addition, the Community will obviously be more efficient than the individual Member States in dealing with such spillover (and this precisely by reason of the scale or effects of its proposed action - see the third guideline). In environmental matters, therefore, the three guidelines will most often combine to support the need for Community action, if relevant spillovers can be traced. The real problem then will be to know what kinds of spillovers are relevant.

I propose to follow the classification of the several types of environmental spillovers elaborated by Professor Richard B. Stewart:[120] product spillovers, pollution spillovers, competitive spillovers, and preservation spillovers.

Product spillovers are created when Member States "seek to exclude products from other [Member] States on the ground that they are environmentally deficient, creating trade barriers" or when the "imposition of different product regulations by [Member] States . . . prevent[s] realization of scale economies in manufacturing and marketing."[121] Article 100a provides the appropriate legal basis for the Community to intervene in such cases and the need for action will flow from the second guideline ("avoid disguised restrictions on trade").[122]

Pollution spillovers occur "when pollutants or wastes generated by industry, transport, or agriculture cross [Member] State boundaries. The polluter [Member] State will have little or no incentive to take the interests of the receiving [Member] State into account in deciding on the extent of environmentally pro-

---

120. Stewart, *supra* note 25, at 45-46.

121. *Id.* at 45.

122. For a recent example, see Council Directive 93/12/EEC of 23 March 1993 relating to the sulphur content of certain liquid fuels, O.J. L 74/81 (1993) (based on Article 100a).

tective measures."[123] Article 130s(1), (2) and (3) contain, in principle,[124] the required legal basis for Community action. The need for such action will be justified under the first guideline ("transnational aspects" which the individual Member States cannot regulate in a satisfactory way, in particular in view of the absence of a serious incentive to do so).

Competitive spillovers result from "the effects of [Member S]tate environmental regulatory decisions on competition and industrial location."[125] Member States might fear that the imposition of strict environmental standards (and the enforcement thereof) could scare away industry and thus put the national economy at a competitive disadvantage relative to that of other Member States. Action at Community level would avoid that risk (and is therefore warranted under the second guideline - "the need to correct distortion of competition").[126] Articles 100a and 130s are both likely to come into play as the legal basis for some aspects of Community action.[127]

Finally, there are the so-called *preservation spillovers*, described as follows: "An especially scenic or ecologically significant natural resource located in one [Member S]tate will be admired by citizens in other [Member S]tates, who will wish to visit it or simply know that it is being preserved. The [Member S]tate in which the resource is located, however, is likely to disregard out-of-state interests."[128] The distinctive feature of this type of "spillover" is that it is not physical or economic, as the natural resource at stake is confined to the territory of one Member State. But the inhabitants of all Member States draw some benefits from that natural resource when they come to view and enjoy it, and in some settings pay a fee for its maintenance. Even when they do not "use" it, inhabitants of Member States may derive benefits through the mere fact of knowing that it exists and is being preserved.[129] The Community undoubtedly finds in Arti-

---

123. Stewart, *supra* note 25, at 45.

124. *See supra* notes 100-03 and accompanying text.

125. Stewart, *supra* note 25, at 45.

126. 25 E.C. BULL., *supra* note 76, at 14.

127. *See supra* notes 96 and accompanying text (discussing *Titanium Dioxide* case and whether Article 100a or 130s was the proper legal basis for environmental directives).

128. Stewart, *supra* note 25, at 45-46.

129. For a convincing argument that "psychic spillovers" should be relevant in order to overcome the apparent obstacle formed by the principle of subsidiarity to deal at

cle 130s a sufficient legal basis to act with a view to preserving such a natural resource. It may even give financial support to the Member State on whose territory the resource is located, if the costs of preservation are deemed to be disproportionate for the public authorities of that Member State (Article 130s(5)). As to the need for Community action, it may be argued that the first guideline applies because there are "transnational aspects" of a particular kind, namely potential users living in other Member States as well as the "existence value" of the natural resource shared by people everywhere. But this is obviously a borderline case, in which the Community must establish that the Member State in question just *cannot* achieve the required level of preservation in a sufficient manner, although the issue looks in all material respects like a local one. Any action by the Community will thus have to be preceded by a statement of the reasons for such action, revealing that the principle of subsidiarity *sensu stricto* will be observed.[130]

C. *Proportionality: Determination of the Nature and Intensity of Community Action*

As indicated earlier, Article 3b contains two expressions of the principle of proportionality: a general one, stating that "any action by the Community shall not go beyond what is necessary to achieve the objectives of this Treaty" (third paragraph of Article 3b); and a more specific one, which takes part of the principle of subsidiarity *sensu lato* directing the Community to take action "only in so far as the objectives of the proposed action cannot be sufficiently achieved by the Member States" (second paragraph of Article 3b). In spite of the difference in wording between "objectives of this Treaty" and "objectives of the proposed action" it seems that the intention of the Treaty authors has in reality been to guarantee that the means chosen do not go beyond what is necessary to achieve the *objectives of the proposed action.* Indeed, any actions by the Community which were to go beyond what is necessary to achieve the "objectives of this Treaty" would by the same token be without legal basis - and thus

---

Community level with issues that are local in a physical or economic sense, see W.P.J. Wils, *Subsidiarity and EC Environmental Policy: Taking People's Concerns Seriously*, 6 J. OF ENVTL L. 83-89 (1994).

130. *See, e.g.,* Communication from the Commission to the Council and the European Parliament on the protection of animals, COM (93) 384 (July 1993).

run afoul of the first paragraph of Article 3b - since all Community powers are strictly defined in order to make possible the achievement of one or more objectives of the Treaty. Going beyond these objectives therefore amounts to acting *ultra vires*. But when the Community assigns some specific objectives to a proposed action, which objectives remain within the limits of the Treaty article serving as the legal basis for the action, it remains meaningful to enquire whether the nature and intensity of the proposed action are not out of proportion with what is necessary to achieve the objectives of that action. On this score there is convergence between the second and the third paragraphs of Article 3b.

That leaves us with the question of why there are two expressions of the principle of proportionality in Article 3b. It certainly is in part an *accident de parcours* in the drafting process of a complex Treaty text, but, this being the case, there are also some differences. First, the principle of proportionality stated in the third paragraph applies to all Community powers whether they are exclusive or not, whereas the proportionality aspect inherent in the principle of subsidiarity *sensu lato* applies, just as the latter principle, to non-exclusive Community powers only. Second, the proportionality of Community action performs a precise function within the operation of the principle of subsidiarity *sensu lato*: the measure of Community action should be limited to what is necessary to fill the policy gap left by the Member States as a consequence of their partial or total incapacity to achieve the objectives of the proposed action in a sufficient manner (the *in-so-far-as* question). In other words, the competing value to be protected by this expression of the principle of proportionality is the sovereignty of the Member States and their subnational authorities. The residual powers of the Member States should not be affected more than is needed in order for the Community and the Member States, or their subnational authorities, to be able to act effectively, in a spirit of loyal cooperation,[131] towards the achievement of the objectives of the proposed action. On the contrary, the competing values to be protected through the general principle of proportionality (third

---

131. EC Treaty, *supra* note 2, art. 5; *see id.* art. 130r(1).

paragraph of Article 3b) are not at all identified.[132] They must therefore be all the values protected under superior Community law, i.e., the "values" stated in the Treaties, or protected as unwritten general principles of law including fundamental rights, or else enumerated in the preamble to the TEU or in the common provisions of that Treaty, where the proximity of government certainly occupies a prominent place.[133] In this latter respect the actual impact of the third paragraph of Article 3b on the nature and intensity of Community action may to some extent coincide with that of the answer given to the *in-so-far-as* question raised in the second paragraph.

It is not astonishing then that the Edinburgh European Council has amalgamated the two expressions of the principle of proportionality, when it declared that "any burdens, whether financial or administrative, falling upon the Community, national governments, local authorities, economic operators and citizens, should be proportionate to the objective to be achieved."[134] It continued that "Community measures should leave *as much scope for national decision as possible*, consistent with securing the aim of the measure and observing the requirements of the Treaty" and that "where appropriate and *subject to the need for proper enforcement*, Community measures should provide Member States with alternative ways to achieve the objectives of the measures."[135]

These sentences indicate the terms of the debate about the proportionality of Community action in the field of the environment: on the one hand, the Community should leave "as much scope for national decision as possible," yet on the other hand, this must happen "subject to the need for proper enforcement."[136] The question is how these two goals can be reconciled. The relevant Treaty provisions (Article 100a and Articles 130r to 130t) endeavor to strike the balance.

First, Article 100a(3), although calling for "a high level of protection," leaves open the possibility of *bona fide* higher national standards of protection of the environment, i.e., if "they are not a means of arbitrary discrimination or a disguised restric-

---

132. *See* Lenaerts & van Ypersele, *supra* note 16, at 52-54, 67-70; J.H. Jans, *Evenredigheiu: ja, maar waartussen?*, 40 SOCIAAL-ECONOMISCHE WETGEVING 751 (1992).

133. TEU, *supra* note 2, pmbl., arts. A, B, F(1).

134. 25 E.C. BULL., *supra* note 76, at 15.

135. *Id.* (emphasis added).

136. *Id.*

tion on trade between Member States."[137] The same applies when Article 130s is to be the legal basis for Community action.[138] Community action leads to "minimum standards," but an important burden of proof weighs on a Member State setting higher national standards: it must establish that it is not in fact distorting competition within the internal market.[139]

Second, Articles 100a and 130s do not specify the normative instruments to be used by the Community, which means that the political process must choose the normative instrument in each case.[140] The Edinburgh European Council has streamlined that choice on the basis of its interpretation of the principle of proportionality. It considered the following: "The form of action should be as simple as possible consistent with satisfactory achievement of the objective of the measure and the need for effective enforcement. The Community should legislate only to the extent necessary. Other things being equal, directives should be preferred to regulations and framework directives to detailed measures. Non-binding measures such as recommendations should be preferred where appropriate. Consideration should also be given where appropriate to the use of voluntary codes of conduct."[141] This statement favors the directive as the most "proportional" normative instrument, on the assumption that it will be used as it was envisaged in Article 189 of the EC Treaty, that is, "[leaving] to the national authorities the choice of form and methods."[142] In its Communication of 1992, the Commission launches a vigorous plea in favor of "systematically reverting to the original concept of the directive as a framework of

---

137. EC Treaty, *supra* note 2, art. 100a(4).

138. *Id.* art. 130t.

139. *See* D. Geradin, *Free Trade and Environmental Protection in an Integrated Market: A Survey of the Case Law of the United States Supreme Court and the European Court of Justice*, 2 FLA. ST. U. J. TRANSNAT'L L. & POL'Y 141 (1993).

140. The directive has always served as the main normative instrument for Community environmental policy. *See* ECKARD REHBINDER & RICHARD STEWART, ENVIRONMENTAL PROTECTION POLICY 33-34 (1985). This does not mean that regulations have not been enacted. *See, e.g.,* Council Regulation (EEC) No. 594/91 of 4 March 1991, O.J. L 67/1 (1991) (relating to substances that deplete the ozone layer); Council Regulation (EEC) No. 259/93, *supra* note 101.

141. 25 E.C. BULL., *supra* note 76, at 15. It must be observed that recommendations, although without "binding force," *see* E.C. Treaty, *supra* note 2, art. 189, are not deprived of any legal effect. *See Grimaldi*, Case C-322/88, [1989] E.C.R. 4407, at 4420-21, ¶¶ 16-18, [1991] 2 C.M.L.R. 265, 276-77 (recommendations to play role in interpretation of national law and in delineating national policy).

142. EC Treaty, *supra* note 2, art. 189.

general rules, or even simply of objectives, for the attainment of which the Member States have sole responsibility."[143] To reach that outcome, the Commission must overcome resistance due to "a mutual lack of confidence."[144]

Already at the Edinburgh meeting of the European Council (December 1992), the Commission had made it known that it would "be tougher about rejecting amendments proposed by the Council and Parliament that run counter to the proportionality rule or would unnecessarily complicate directives or recommendations."[145] Under the Interinstitutional Agreement of 29 October 1993, the Council and Parliament must justify all such amendments in view of the principle of subsidiarity, including its proportionality aspect.[146]

At the Edinburgh meeting of the European Council, the Commission also translated into a concrete undertaking its intention to alleviate the regulatory density of directives in the area of the environment. The Commission promised to make an effort "to simplify, consolidate and update existing texts, particularly those on air and water, to take new knowledge and technical progress into account."[147] In its 1993 Report, it announced that it will make the necessary legislative proposals to replace six

---

143. 25 E.C. BULL., *supra* note 76, at 123. Rehbinder and Stewart distinguish "three types of directives in terms of specificity and legal effect on Member States:"

1. *Typical directives* which closely follow the 'result' model of Article 189 of the E[E]C Treaty.

2. *Regulation-type directives*: The directive itself or an annex to it (which forms an integral part of the directive but can normally be amended by a simplified procedure) contains detailed substantive provisions, such as prohibitions, standards and tolerances, and provisions for implementation, such as testing and measurement methods.

3. *Framework directives*: The framework directive sets out the objectives and basic principles applicable to a broad area of environmental protection. . . . One or more special directives, which may be 'typical' or regulation-type and contain more detailed substantive rules, may fill out the framework directive.

REHBINDER & STEWART, *supra* note 140, at 35.

It goes without saying that, in this latter respect, more responsibilities may be left to the Member States in order to fill out the framework directive. This appears to be what is envisaged by the Commission in relation to several aspects of Community water quality legislation.

144. *See supra* note 18 (discussing Communication on the principle of subsidiarity).

145. 25 E.C. BULL., *supra* note 76, at 18.

146. 26 E.C. BULL., no. 10, at 129-30 (1993).

147. 25 E.C. BULL., *supra* note 76, at 17.

named directives on water quality by so-called "framework directives," reoriented "towards compliance with essential quality and health parameters, leaving Member States free to add secondary parameters if they see fit."[148] These "framework directives" should comprise: (1) a *drinking water quality directive* that "would define general parameters, some of which would be fixed in technical terms at Community level and others at national level"; (2) a *directive on the ecological quality of surface water* "setting general objectives to be fleshed out by national or regional authorities as the case may be"; (3) a *directive on the quality of bathing water*, whose parameters "need to be simplified and adapted to new scientific knowledge" and easily adaptable "in the light of Community criteria and local realities, by a procedure that offers more flexibility than a Council decision requiring unanimity";[149] and (4) a *directive on freshwater management and groundwater protection* defining "guiding principles for the qualitative and quantitative protection of groundwater, integrating it into a general freshwater management policy."[150]

Besides these newly proposed "framework directives," the Commission mentioned two directives adopted in 1991 to control pollution at the source, namely the *Directive concerning urban waste water treatment*[151] and the *Directive concerning the protection of waters against pollution by nitrates from agricultural sources.*[152] The Commission noted that these two directives "comply with the subsidiarity principle in that they simply define an objective leaving Member States free to achieve it in their own way."[153] The Commission adds that the new proposal for a *Directive on the integrated prevention and reduction of industrial pollution* is designed "to supplement existing directives by requiring Member States to adapt minimum discharge standards to best practice. In line with the subsidiarity principle this adaptation will be a matter for the appropriate national authorities and will cover industries dis-

---

148. Commission Report to the European Council, *supra* note 24, at 15.

149. The latter is an early call for application of the second paragraph of Article 130s(2), authorizing the Council, through a unanimous vote, to substitute a qualified majority vote for the requirement of unanimity as far as future revisions of the parameters laid down in the proposed directive are concerned. *See* EC Treaty, *supra* note 2, art. 130s(2).

150. Commission Report to the European Council, *supra* note 24, at 15-16, No. (i).

151. Directive No. 91/271/EEC of 21 May 1991, O.J. L 135/40 (1991).

152. Directive No. 91/676/EEC of 12 December 1991, O.J. L 375/1 (1991).

153. Commission Report to the European Council, *supra* note 24, at 16, No. (ii).

charging the substances appearing on Lists I and II of the 1976 framework directive."[154]

As to air quality, the Commission intends to propose a "definition of objectives or of harmonized monitoring criteria" for Community standards.[155] These standards could streamline and simplify present legislation.[156] At the same time, however, the Commission made it clear that it will not allow the application of the subsidiarity principle to lower or compromise the high level of existing Community environmental standards.[157] The Commission's approach is only meant to enlist, as much as possible, the help of the Member States or their subnational authorities in reaching these standards. That approach is perfectly consistent with Articles 130r to 130t, as they were revised (in part) by the TEU. As mentioned previously, the introductory sentence of Article 130r was drafted in such a way as to emphasize the concurrent responsibility of the Member States to pursue the objectives of the Community policy on the environment.[158] Furthermore, Article 130s(4) states, as a general rule, that the Member States shall finance and implement the environmental policy.[159]

All of this indicates that in the environmental field major efforts are indeed made to "leave as much scope for national decision as possible."[160] Does this not happen, however, at the expense of "the need for proper enforcement?"[161] That question is all the more pressing as it has been argued that the early successes of passing Community environmental legislation, under a regime of unanimous voting in the Council (in accordance with Articles 100 or 235 of the EC Treaty), were precisely due to the fact that Member States did not use their right of veto against legislation whose implementation would in any event be weak and lightly monitored.[162] As a remedy to the perceived implementation gap, proposals were made to legislate more often

---

154. *Id.*
155. *Id.* at 17.
156. *Id.*
157. *Id.*
158. *See* EC Treaty, *supra* note 2, art. 130r.
159. *Id.* art. 130s(4).
160. 25 E.C. BULL., *supra* note 76, at 15.
161. *Id.*
162. *See supra* note 17 (discussing voting procedure in the Council); *see also* Rolf Wägenbaur, *The European Community's Policy on Implementation of Environmental Directives*, 14 FORDHAM INT'L L.J. 455, 465-66 (1990-91).

through regulations (which do not in principle need further implementation) and to establish an enforcement authority at Community level empowered to impose sanctions against offenders of the directly applicable legislation. This authority would resemble the American "EPA" (Environmental Protection Agency), which operates at the federal level.[163]

Such proposals, however, lead to a system that would definitely suffer from the "overload" of centralization, as it is being criticized in the United States,[164] and at the same time would conflict with the tradition of decentralized enforcement of Community law, expounded by the Court's case-law, of which the *Van Gend & Loos* and *Francovich* judgments[165] are the milestones. In addition, in the area of the environment, the tendency towards decentralization has precisely been strengthened through the latest drafting of Articles 130r to 130t of the EC Treaty (by the TEU).[166]

Implementation of Community environmental legislation is therefore largely left to the Member States and their subnational authorities. The proposed elaboration of "framework directives" will confirm that option. The European Environment Agency has been established with the sole objective "to provide the Community and the Member States with:

— objective, reliable and comparable information at European level enabling them to take the requisite measures to protect the environment, to assess the results of such measures and to ensure that the public is properly informed about the state of the environment,

— to that end, the necessary technical and scientific support.[167]

The Agency will thus assist the Member States when they implement Community environmental legislation, but it will not take over their responsibilities.[168]

---

163. Wägenbaur, *supra* note 162, at 468-73.

164. *See* Stewart, *supra* note 25, at 43.

165. *See supra* notes 30-32 and accompanying text (discussing the *Van Gend & Loos* and *Francovich* judgments).

166. *See* Astrid Epiney & Andreas Furrer, *Umweltschutz nach Maastricht*, 27 EuR. 369 (1992).

167. Council Regulation No. 1210/90, *supra* note 66, art. 1(2).

168. This remains so even in view of the "dynamic clause" contained in Article 20 of the European Environment Agency Regulation, Council Regulation No. 1210/90, *supra* note 66, which reads as follows:

The difficulties of implementing Community environmental legislation are often associated with the use of the directive as the normative instrument for such legislation. It is therefore important to point out that the Court of Justice has already gone a long way to diminish the effectiveness-handicap of the directive. First, national courts are obliged, as a consequence of the supremacy of Community law, to "interpret" national law in such a way as to make it conform to a directive for which the time-limit for implementation has expired (whether implementation has taken place or not).[169] This obligation applies in relation to *all* directives even if their content does not as such create enforceable rights and obligations due to a lack of clarity, precision, or unconditionality (i.e., the conditions for it to be capable to produce "direct effect").[170] In particular in the area of the environment, directives (especially "framework directives") will often not meet, at least for several of their provisions, the conditions necessary for them to have "direct effect."[171] However,

---

No later than two years after the entry into force of this Regulation, and after having consulted the European Parliament, the Council shall, on the same basis as this Regulation and on the basis of a report from the Commission with appropriate proposals, decide on further tasks for the Agency in particular in the following areas: - associating in the monitoring of the implementation of Community environmental legislation, in cooperation with the Commission and existing competent bodies in the Member States . . . .

Id. The Agency is only to be "associated" in the "monitoring" of the implementation of Community environmental legislation, and not to be itself charged with such implementation. The Regulation entered into force, in accordance with Article 21, "on the day following that on which the competent authorities have decided the seat of the Agency," i.e., on 30 October 1993, after the Governments of the Member States had determined, on 29 October 1993, "by common accord," EC Treaty, *supra* note 2, art. 216, the seat of the Agency, which will be in Copenhagen. The management board of the Agency met for the first time in Brussels on 17 December 1993. *Agence Europe*, No. 6135 of 23 December 1993. All of this means that the Council must act pursuant to Article 20 of the Regulation no later than 30 October 1995.

169. *See* Marleasing SA v. La Comercial Internacional de Alimentacion SA, Case C-106/89, [1990] E.C.R. I-4135, [1992] 1 C.M.L.R. 305 (most complete statement of this doctrine); J. Stuyck & P. Wytinck, 28 COMMON MKT. L. REV. 205 (1991) (discussing *Marleasing*).

170. *See, e.g.*, Van Duyn v. Home Office, Case 41/74, [1974] E.C.R. 1337 [1975] 1 C.M.L.R. 1; Pubblico Ministerio v. Ratti, Case 148/78, [1979] E.C.R. 1629, [1980] 1 C.M.L.R. 96; Becker v. Finanzamt Münster-Innenstad, Case 8/81, [1982] E.C.R. 53, [1982] 1 C.M.L.R. 499 (discussion of doctrine of direct effect).

171. This was confirmed by the Court of Justice. Comitato di Coordinamento per la Difesa della Cava and Others v. Regione Lombardia and Others, Case C-236/92 (Eur. Ct. J. Feb. 23, 1994) (not yet reported).

[T]he provision at issue must be regarded as defining the framework for the action to be taken by the Member States regarding the treatment of waste and

even if the provisions of the framework directives do not have direct effect, they may serve as a useful reference for the interpretation of national law. They will thus be "invocable" before any national court to that effect.[172]

Second, as it was already mentioned, in case of non-implementation or incorrect implementation of a directive, a liability action will lie, directly under Community law, against the Member State in question. The injured party must establish: (1) that the result prescribed by the directive entails the grant of rights to individuals; (2) that it is possible to identify the content of those rights on the basis of the provisions of the directive; and (3) that there is a causal link between the breach of the State's obligation to correctly implement the directive and the loss and damage suffered by the injured party.[173] Admittedly, it might be difficult for an injured party to succeed at establishing all three elements in relation to environmental directives given the vague (and abstract) substance of many of them, but this should not necessarily discourage the injured party from bringing liability actions against public authorities or even private parties when they appear to infringe upon non-implemented or incorrectly implemented directives. Indeed, the just stated general requirement for Member State courts to interpret domestic law in a way consistent with all Community directives applies also in the context of the operation of national liability law. It may thus occur that a court is in a position of finding a "fault" within the meaning of national liability law when the defendant has knowingly disregarded the content of a non-implemented or incorrectly implemented directive,[174] even if the *Francovich* conditions for State

---

not as requiring, in itself, the adoption of specific measures or a particular method of waste disposal. It is therefore neither unconditional nor sufficiently precise and thus is not capable of conferring rights on which individuals may rely as against the State.

Id. § 14.

172. *See* Ph. Manin, *L'invocabilité des directives: Quelques interrogations*, 28 REVUE TRIMESTRIELLE DE DROIT EUROPÉEN 669, 675-78 (1990).

173. *See* Francovich v. Italy, Joined Cases C-6/90 and C-9/90, [1991] E.C.R. I-5357, I-5415, ¶ 40, [1993] 2 C.M.L.R. 66, 114-15. *See also* John Temple Lang, *New Legal Effects Resulting from the Failure of States to Fulfill Obligations under European Community Law: the Francovich Judgment*, 16 FORDHAM INT'L L. J. 1 (1992-93); J. Steiner, *From Direct Effects to Francovich: Shifting Means of Enforcement of Community Law*, 18 EUR. L. REV. 3 (1993).

174. Since the entry into force of the TEU, it will be almost impossible for private parties to hide behind their lack of knowledge of directives that have not been incorporated into the national legal order. Article 191 of the EC Treaty now prescribes that

liability based on Community law are not entirely met.

Future developments in the case law will have to clarify this matter, but it seems certain, in any event, that just as in the United States, liability actions are bound to play an increasing role as a means of pressing for faithful implementation of Community environmental legislation. Liability actions are thus likely to serve as an efficient alternative to a bureaucratic machinery of centralized supervision.[175] In this sense also, the Court's statement in *Van Gend & Loos* that "the vigilance of individuals concerned to protect their rights amounts to an effective supervision in addition to the supervision entrusted . . . to the diligence of the Commission"[176] remains good law.

The decentralized enforcement of the implementation by Member States and their subnational authorities of Community environmental legislation rests on the idea that interested private parties possess a natural incentive to take the supervision of compliance with that legislation seriously. This may be seen as evidence of the larger function that could be assigned to economic and/or fiscal incentives to make environmental regulation work properly and to increase its chances of producing the

---

directives which are addressed to all Member States shall be published (just as regulations) in the Official Journal of the Community. Directives thus receive the same publicity as regulations, which everyone is deemed to know after their publication in the Official Journal of the Community. Environmental directives are all of the type covered by Article 191. Furthermore, the identical status of directives and regulations as to their publication in the Official Journal of the Community could well become one of the decisive arguments for the Court of Justice to recognize full "horizontal effects" to directives after the expiry of the time left to the Member States for their implementation into national law. The rationale is that Member States will get a first chance to insert directives as smoothly as possible into that law, but when they fail to seize that chance, the directives will operate as do regulations — that is, also between private parties. *See* Walter van Gerven, *The Horizontal Effect of Directive Provisions Revisited, in* LIBER AMICORUM H.G. SCHERMERS 335-53 (Deirdre Curtin & Ton Heukels eds., 1994).

175. *See* Communication from the Commission to the Council and Parliament and the Economic and Social Committee: Green Paper on Remedying Environmental Damage, of 14 May 1993, COM (93) 47 final [hereinafter Green Paper]. "This Green Paper considers . . . the usefulness of civil liability as a means for allocating responsibility for the costs of environmental restoration. Civil liability is a legal and financial tool used to make those responsible for causing damage pay compensation for the costs of remedying that damage. By requiring those responsible to pay the costs of the damage they cause, civil liability also has the important secondary function of enforcing standards of behaviour and preventing people from causing damage in the future." *Id.* at 4; *see* Amended proposal from the Commission for a Council Directive on civil liability for damage caused by waste, O.J. C 192/15 (1991).

176. *See supra* note 31.

envisaged outcome more effectively and more efficiently. In this perspective, so-called "command and control" legislation might possibly be replaced by or supplemented with mechanisms that leave it to the market to determine ways in which the tolerated level of pollution will be allocated among the several pollution sources. The government then has only to set the tolerated level of pollution, to organize a system of tradable emission permits, and to ensure that emissions do not exceed the amount authorized by the permits that every polluter holds. Industry will thus be pressured into choosing between buying emission permits or investing in research and development to prevent pollution altogether. This again is an expression of "subsidiarity," focused this time on the relationship between government regulation and private decision-making as alternative means of reaching a given outcome. Fiscal tools can have a similar finality, but given the sensitivity that is linked for the Member States to any kind of taxation power conferred upon the Community, unanimity is still being required in the Council when it adopts environmental provisions "primarily of a fiscal nature."[177]   This is regrettable because fiscal tools may have as their main purpose and effect to create the appropriate economic incentives for private parties to adapt their behaviour to what is needed for government policy to work, without the government having to "command and control" as such.

CONCLUSION

The foregoing analysis confirms the view held by the Commission on the scope of "subsidiarity," that it "is first and foremost a political principle, a sort of rule of reason. Its function is not to distribute powers. That is a matter for . . . the authors of the Treaty. The aim of the subsidiarity principle is, rather, to regulate the exercise of powers and to justify their use in a particular case."[178]

The European Council had earlier remarked that "the principle of subsidiarity does not relate to and cannot call into question the powers conferred on the European Community by the Treaty as interpreted by the Court."[179] The *acquis communautaire*

177. EC Treaty, *supra* note 2, art. 130s(2).
178. *See* Commission Report to the European Council, *supra* note 24, at 1.
179. 25 E.C. BULL., *supra* note 76, at 13.

as well as the balance between the Community institutions do not therefore come under pressure as a consequence of the statement of the principle of subsidiarity in the Treaty. There is no separate decision on subsidiarity preceding the decision on the substance of Community action. Subsidiarity and substance are necessarily and inextricably intertwined and thus must be part of a single decision-making process.[180]

When taking action, the Community is obliged to state reasons pursuant to Article 190 of the EC Treaty, including those which reveal that the political institutions consider that the action is consistent with the principles of subsidiarity and proportionality. The Court of Justice is likely to enforce that obligation strictly,[181] which means that it will control whether the reasons stated set out the steps that led to the recognition of the need for Community action and further explain why the nature and intensity of the action were necessary to achieve its objectives. It should be borne in mind that judicial scrutiny of the appropriateness of the reasons stated for Community action is about the only practical route for the Court of Justice to supervise the respect by the political institutions of the principles of subsidiarity and proportionality flowing from Article 3b. The idea behind that kind of supervision is that the political institutions ought to be forced to express their reasoning with regard to the operation of subsidiarity and proportionality as limits *intra vires* to Community action. In this manner these institutions will think thoroughly before acting and will be more directly subject to the "political" control of the Member States, their subnational authorities and interested citizens.[182]

---

180. *See* Interinstitutional Agreement between the European Parliament, the Council and the Commission on the procedures of implementation of the principle of subsidiarity, of 29 October 1993, *supra* note 146 and accompanying text.

181. *See* Hauptzollamt München Mitte v. Technische Universität München, Case C-269/90, [1991] E.C.R. I-5469, I-5501-02, ¶¶ 26 & 27.

182. Compare, in relation to U.S. federalism, the statement by Justice Blackmun, writing for the majority of the Supreme Court in *Garcia v. San Antonio Metropolitan Transit Authority*, 469 U.S. 528, at 554 (1985): "[We] are convinced that the fundamental limitation that the constitutional scheme imposes on the Commerce Clause to protect the 'States as States' is one of process rather than one of result." *Id.* The States are therefore to rely on the "effectiveness of the federal political process" to protect their interests rather than on the judiciary, which would enforce a precise substantive "result" mandated by the constitution. It is interesting to note that the stakes involved in the *Garcia* case are not without resemblance to those dominating the present-day subsidiarity debate in Europe. The dissenting opinion by Justice Powell states: "[T]he

As we have seen, in the area of the environment, it should be easy to substantiate the reasons for Community action. As far as the need for such action is concerned, reference will be made to the several types of environmental spillovers. As to the nature and intensity of Community action, it will be sufficient to justify the division of responsibilities between the Community and the Member States for regulation, implementation, and monitoring by reference to their respective capabilities.

---

members of the immense federal bureaucracy are not elected, know less about the services traditionally rendered by States and localities, and are inevitably less responsive to recipients of such services, than are State legislatures, city councils . . . and [local] agencies. It is at these State and local levels - not in Washington, as the Court so mistakenly thinks - that 'democratic self-government' is best exemplified." *Id.* at 575.

[6]

ENVIRONMENTAL CITIZENSHIP AND THE LAW: REPAIRING THE EUROPEAN ROAD*

Richard Macrory**

The English are incurious as to theory, take fundamental principles for granted and are more interested in the state of the roads than their place on the map.

R. H. Tawney

The European Council invites the Conference which should finalize its work in about one year, to adopt a general and consistent vision throughout its work: its aim is to meet the needs and expectations of our citizens while advancing the process of Europe's construction and preparing the Union for its future enlargement.

Presidency Conclusions, Turin European Council, 29 March 1996

1. Introduction

On 1 January 1993, as a result of the Maastricht amendments to the European Treaties, all nationals of Member States acquired under the Treaty something called citizenship of the European Union.[1] This new citizenship may not be uppermost in the civic consciousness of many, and my starting point will be to consider to what extent it can be said to incorporate an environmental dimension. The second half of the title is derived from R. H. Tawney's well-known observation about the English, and to pursue his analogy, there already exist a number of pretty substantial potholes. As someone who in his approach to environmental law has attempted to combine both an academic and a practitioner's perspective I will be suggesting some practical repair jobs. But I will also argue that there are some deeper issues concerning the way that the Treaty is currently structured and has been characterized in law. However effective the

* This article is a revised text of the inaugural Nathan Environment Lecture, sponsored by Denton Hall, Solicitors, and delivered by the author at the Royal Society of Arts on 25 April 1996.

** Barrister, Professor of Environmental Law, Imperial College, London.

[1] Treaty Establishing the European Community, Article 8: '(1) Citizenship of the Union is hereby established. Every person holding the nationality of a member-state shall be a citizen of the Union. (2) Citizens of the Union shall enjoy the rights conferred by this Treaty and shall be subject to the duties imposed thereby.' The Maastricht Treaty established both a European Union and a European Community. The Union is essentially a forum for political cooperation, and only the Community possesses legal entity, and it is within the Community structure that legislation is made. My paper will, therefore, for the most part refer to the European Community.

repairs, these also need to be addressed if the route on which we are embarked is to lead to a more environmental sound destination.

Citizenship is of course both a political and legal concept. Yet I will make no excuse for concentrating on legal conception and principle. The law and legal analysis permeates the structure and operation of the European Community. Some years ago, also at the Royal Society of Arts, Lord Dahrendolf observed that, *'In fact almost every- thing is wrong about the European Community except that it exists as a community of law which united developed democracies in Europe'.*[2] Certainly for my part, I subscribe to the immense significance of the unifying and legitimizing concept of the rule of law. In taking this argument further, I am not going to describe or analyse in detail the substantive content of European environmental policy since my concern will be more with institu- tional and legal structure. But as a matter of general background, and whatever the precise content of future environmental policies, I start from the assumption that the European Community and Union will remain a reality. The role of law in that struc- ture will retain its pervasive significance, and the task of reconciling environmental and economic interests, encapsulated in the notion of sustainable development, will continue to provide a major political and intellectual challenge. At the same time, we have nine applicant countries from Central and Eastern Europe together with Malta and Cyprus. We may be many years away from accession but with negotiations due to formally commence after the end of the Intergovernmental Conference, the institu- tional implications of this prospective enlargement must be addressed.

The concept of citizenship is clearly stated in the Treaty to involve both rights and obligations. The Treaty itself goes on to express a number of individual rights, includ- ing the right to move and reside freely,[3] and the right to vote or stand as a candidate in municipal countries in the country in which he or she is residing.[4] Important procedural rights are provided in the rights to petition the European Parliament and to apply to the newly established Ombudsman.[5] The Treaty in its present form does not, however, provide any legally expressed rights to a healthy environment or indeed quality of life.

The Declaration of the first major international conference on the environment, the UN Conference on the Human Environment held in Stockholm in 1972, clearly emphasised a link between human rights and the environment: Principle 1 declares that, *'Man has a fundamental right to freedom, equality and adequate conditions of life, in an environment of quality that permits a life of dignity and well-being, and he bears a solemn responsib- ility to protect and improve the environment for present and future generations'.* Similarly, the Declaration following the UN Conference on Environment and Development held in Rio de Janeiro in 1992, though giving greater emphasis to the concept sustainable development, made a reference to rights and the environment.[6] Neither Declaration is a legally binding instrument as such, and neither attempt to establish specific environmental rights. Now, however, in the present preparations for the IGC Confer- ence, both the European Commission and a number of Nordic countries are beginning

---

[2] Lord Dahrendorf, 'Education for a European Britain', Royal Society of Arts, 9 June 1991.
[3] Article 8a.
[4] Article 8b.
[5] Article 8d.
[6] Principle 1 states that, 'Human beings are at the centre of concerns for sustainable development. They are entitled to a healthy and productive life in harmony with nature'.

to promote the idea that the Treaty should contain an express inclusion of a right to a healthy environment or some similarly worded phraseology.[7]

Many would argue that there are conceptual impossibilities to formulating an individual right to the environment in general terms which has any legally meaningful sense. The experience of those European countries and of certain States in America, whose constitutions do contain some expression of environmental rights, tends to confirm this.[8] They may end up influencing the interpretation and operation of other legal principles and rules, but are near impossible to invoke in themselves.[9] It is an issue to which I will return to later.

2. Environmental Rights in Community Law

Yet when it comes to specific items of Community environmental legislation concerning environmental quality, the European Court of Justice has been prepared to characterize certain provisions as giving individual environmental rights. Thus in 1991, in a case brought by the Commission against Germany, the Court held that the 1980 Directive prescribing air quality standards for sulphur dioxide and smoke in effect gave individuals the right to air meeting those standards.[10] One characteristic mark of the Directive as a legal instrument is that while Member States are obliged to achieve its goals, it gives Member States a degree of discretion as to how to implement it within their national systems of law and administration.[11] But by characterizing the SO2 Directive as creating individual rights, the Court felt justified in insisting that the Member State no longer had complete discretion as to the means of transposing the obligations within its own legal and administrative system. Instead it held that individuals *'must be in a position to rely upon mandatory rules in order to be able to assert their rights'*.

This firm nexus between the concept of a right and its expression in legally binding national law can be traced back to the mid 1980's in case law concerning rights of free movement of professionals within the Community. Here the Court held that the legal position for individuals must be *'sufficiently clear and precise and the persons concerned*

---

[7] The 1994 Report of the European Parliament's Committee on Institutional Affairs proposed a model constitution for the European Union which included a Title on Human Rights Guaranteed by the Union. These rights included, inter alia, 'Everyone shall have the right to the protection and preservation of his natural environment'. Doc EN/RR/244/244403 27 January 1994.

[8] Article 66 of the Portuguese Constitution contains the most explicit expression of environmental right in European Constitutions by providing that 'everyone shall have the right to a healthy and ecologically balanced environment and a duty to defend it'. Neverethless, only where the state has determined what makes up such an environment are these rights enforceable. For a valuable comparative study which demonstrates the problem of constructing enforceable environmental rights: see, E. Brandl and H. Bungert, 'Constitutional Entrenchment of Environmental Protection: A Comparative Analysis of Experiences Abroad', 1992 *Harvard Environmental Law Review* Vol 16 No 1.

[9] Nevertheless, the UN Sub-Commission on Prevention of Discrimination and Protection of Minorities recently produced an elaborate Draft Declaration of Principles on Human Rights and the Environment: see *Environmental Law Network International Newsletter* 2/1994 at 120, and *RECIEL* 1994 Vol 3 No 5 261. See also, Aguilar and Popovic 'Law-Making in the United Nations: The UN Study on Human Rights and the Environment', 1994 *RECIEL* Vol 3 No 5 197–205.

[10] *EC Commission v Germany* [1991] 1 ECR 2567.

[11] Article 189 EC Treaty. 'A directive shall be binding ,as to the result to be achieved, upon each Member State to which it is addressed but shall leave to the national authorities the choice of form and methods.'

are made fully aware of their rights and where appropriate afforded an opportunity of relying upon them before the national courts'.[12]

Yet it is significant that the SO₂ Directive was to a large degree concerned with the protection of human health.[13] Other environmental Directives have granted what might be termed procedural rights, such as those concerning Access to Information[14] or rights to be consulted during Environmental Assessment procedures.[15] Again, the same justification for insisting that such rights appear in formal national law must apply. But many Directives are concerned purely with the protection of the environment per se rather than the direct protection of individuals. Here, the position in Community law remains less clear, and exposes one of the constant dilemmas of the use of the language of rights in relation to the environment—to what extent can they only be conceived of only in anthropogenic terms and thus largely confined to human health and welfare contexts, or can they extend to all areas of the environment whether or not individuals are affected—in which case who should entitled to ensure their protection?

Yet, the case-law of the European Court remains rather ambiguous. Another case brought by the Commission against Germany in 1991 concerned the Groundwater Directive.[16] This directive is clearly aimed at the protection of the environment rather than human health as such, yet the Court stated that the Directive, in order to guarantee effective protection of groundwater, laid down precise and detailed rules which are intended to create rights and obligations for individuals. Having so characterized the Directive, it justified the Court in again insisting that it had to be incorporated into national law with the precision and clarity necessary to fully satisfy the requirements of legal certainty. Unfortunately the Court did not spell out precisely the rights and obligations it found in the Directive, but it appeared to have been referring to the various prohibitions and requirements for authorizations under the Directive. Industry and other consumers of the environment who may have obligations imposed upon them under Community law are entitled to know precisely what these entail.[17] But we are still left with some degree of uncertainty over the question of rights where provisions are solely aimed at environmental protection.[18]

---

[12] *European Commission v Germany* [1986] 3 CMLR 579. There is another line of authority within the European Court of Justice where the Court has required the formal transposition of Directives into national law but concerned with Directives based on Article 100 or 100A (harmonization in relation to functioning of the common market). Here the justification for formal transposition is distinct and based on the concept of harmonization rather than individual rights. See R. B. Macrory, 'EC Directives and UK Control Policy and Practice', *55th Conference Proceedings National Society of Clean Air*, 1988.

[13] Article 2 of the Directive provides that the specified limit values must not be exceeded 'in order to protect human health in particular'.

[14] Directive 90/313 on Freedom of Access to Information on the Environment OJ 1990 L 158/56.

[15] Directive 85/337 on the Assessment of the Effects of Certain Public and Private Projects on the Environment OJ 1985 L 175/40.

[16] *EC Commission v Germany* [1991] 1 ECR 825.

[17] A similar argument is found in Case C-13/90 *Commission v France* [1991] ECR 1-4327 which again concerned the air quality Directives. In insisting upon formal transposition into national law, the Court in part justified their argument by suggesting that these Directives imposed obligations on potential polluters.

[18] It has been suggested that the Court will in practice be liberal in interpreting that Environment Directives create or imply rights, as the case law quoted above suggest: I. Pernice, 'Kriterien der normativen Umsetzung von Umweltrichtlinien der EG Lichte der Rechtsprechung des EuGH', 1994 *Europarecht* 325. For a lengthier discussion on various forms of transposition see, J. Jans, 1995 *European Environmental Law* at 119 seq (Kluwer: London).

Despite the ambiguities, these principles concerning the transposition of Community obligations into formal national law have had immense significance not least for the structure of UK environmental law. They are entirely the creation of the Court and if anything goes against the apparent wording of the Treaty. And they form what could be described as a family of doctrines developed by the court designed to ensure that Community law has genuine bite within national systems. They include the direct effect doctrine,[19] the doctrine of sympathetic interpretation,[20] and the more recent emergence of principles concerning the right to damages where a Member State has failed in its Community obligations,[21] Each of these doctrines raise difficult issues, but at their root, they can be seen as attempts by the Court to ensure that Community law is fully applied. And they are in effect an implied criticism of the institutional mechanisms already built into the Treaty and specifically designed to ensure compliance with Community obligations. If they were working fully and effectively, the Court would not have had to develop these doctrines in the way they have.

3. Improving Community Enforcement Mechanisms

Persuading countries to comply with supra-national obligations is not, of course, a problem confined to Community law. The last twenty-five years has seen a rapid expansion and growth of international environmental treaties between sovereign states, but ensuring implementation of international treaties has long been the familiar achilles heel of public international law. Earlier environmental Treaties made little or no reference to the question of implementation but left it entirely to the goodwill of the parties concerned.[22] Modern practice is commendably different. In many of the more recent environmental treaties, far more attention has been paid to the issue of implementation and enforcement, and Treaties such as the Ozone Convention and the Climate Change Convention provide for the establishment of implementation committees composed on signatory states with the express task of reviewing the effect-

---

[19] Under this doctrine, even where a Member State has not implemented a Directive properly into national law, certain provisions of Directives provided they are precise and certain may be invoked before national courts but only against Government or other 'emanations of the State' and not other individuals; see, Case-91/92 *Dori v Recreb Srl* [1994] ECR 1-3325 which confirmed that the doctrine could not be invoked against private parties. See generally, S. Prechal, *Directives in European Community Law*, 1995 (Oxford University Press: Oxford). In the environmental field, see especially, L. Kramer, 'The Implementation of Community Environmental Directives: Some Implications of the Direct Effect Doctrine', 1991 *Journal of Environmental Law* Vol 3 No 1 39. In practice, both in the United Kingdom and before the European Court of Justice (but not in countries such as the Netherlands), it has proved difficult to date to convince the courts that environmental directives have direct effect: see, J. Holder, 'A Dead-End for Direct Effect?', 1996 *Journal of Environmental Law* Vol 8 No 2.

[20] Case C-106/89 *Marleasing SA v La Commercial International de Alimantiacion SA* [1990] ECR 1-4135 where the European Court of Justice held that national law whether or not introduced to implement Community obligations must be interpreted in such a way as to ensure conformity with Community directives 'in so far as possible'. The limits of the doctrine are still being worked out.

[21] Cases C-6/90 and C-9/90 *Frankovitch v Italian State* [1991] 1-ECR 5357. For the most recent judgment concerning the principles see, Cases C-46/93 and C 48/93 *Brasserie du Pecheur SA v Germany*; *R v Secretary of State for Transport ex parte Factortame and others* ('Factortame III'), [1996] 75 CMLR 889.

[22] See generally, P. Birnie and A. Boyle, *International Law and the Environment* 1993 (Oxford University Press: Oxford), esp 160 seq; P. Sand, *The Effectiveness of International Environmental Agreements* 1992 (Grotius: Cambridge); D. Freestone, 'The Road from Rio: International Law after the Earth Summit', 1994 *Journal of Environmental Law* Vol 6 No 2 193.

iveness of implementation.[23] Ultimately, however, the pressure that can be brought to bear on recalcitrant states is largely one of peer or political pressure, though the Montreal Protocol has taken steps somewhat further by providing an elaborate procedure for allegations of non-compliance and an express list of measures that might be brought on respect of non-compliance, including both inducements in the form of financial and technical assistance, and sanctions in the form of the suspension of rights and privileges under the Protocol.[24]

Yet in its formal institutional mechanisms for ensuring the Member States implement their obligations under Community law, the European Community has clearly established a far deeper and potentially more effective structure than anything yet devised under other international arrangements. And I would argue that one mark of citizenship within the Community and Union should be an effective legal structure which can guarantee that both national governments and Community institutions will bona fide implement those Community obligations to which they are a party. The Treaty imposes an obligation on the European Commission to ensure that Member States fulfil their duties under Community law,[25] and quasi-legal procedures are provided allowing eventually the Commission to take Member States before the European Court for failure to implement.[26] And since Maastricht, the Court now has power to fine member states that do not comply with its judgments—amendments to the Treaty that were promoted by the UK Government, and giving the Court a direct sanction power that is unique among international courts.[27]

Much could be done to improve the effectiveness of current procedures, especially in the light of prospective enlargement of the Community. This-is not to belittle efforts that have been made in recent years: greater consistency in the reporting requirements by member states concerning various aspects of environmental quality;[28] improved mechanisms for contact between those working within national regulatory bodies though at present this is largely confined to pollution control bodies,[29] and does not involve, for example, those in nature conservation; the acknowledgement by the Council of Ministers of the importance of implementation; and the establishment of the new Environment Agency[30] which may bring a more rigorous approach towards the comparative analysis of the state of environmental quality within different Member States.

It could be argued that many of these developments were in a sense making up for lost time. One of my main concerns is to improve the procedures for ensuring the

[23] Annex IV, Montreal Prototcol on Substances that Deplete the Ozone Layer, 1987; Article 10, Framework Convention on Climate Change, 1992.

[24] Annex V, Montreal Protocol. Freestone, op cit, describes the enforcement regime as 'one of the strictest devised for a global treaty of this kind'.

[25] One of the four defined functions of the Commission under the Treaty is to 'ensure that the provisions of this Treaty and the measures taken by the institutions pursuant thereto are applied'. The existing case-law on standing, however, means that it is not a duty which could be enforced in law by third parties.

[26] In the environmental field see, R. Macrory, 'The Enforcement of Community Environmental Laws: Some Critical Issues', 1992 *Common Market Law Review* 347.

[27] Article 171. The Court has yet to fine a Member State under these procedures.

[28] Council Directive 91/692/EEC, Standardizing and Rationalizing Reports on the Implementation of certain Directives relating to the Environment.

[29] Originally known as the 'Chester Network' after the place of its first meeting and established in 1992, now called IMPEL.

[30] Established under EC Regulation 1210/90. Despite pressure from the European Parliament, the powers and duties of the Agency were at the time deliberately restricted to avoid it becoming directly involved in issues of implementation and enforcement, but its terms of reference are to be reviewed.

national transposition of Community obligations. If Community obligations were faithfully reflected in national law, both in substance and within the time-limits specified, we would be a long way down the path of more effective implementation. Not the whole way by any means, since much would then depend on the effectiveness of national procedures, including such questions as ease of access to the courts or other administrative bodies, but at least there would be a common starting position. The current practice is that the Community obligation under Directives requires the Member State to send texts of their national measures to the Commission within the time-limit specified in each Directive, normally two years, of its being agreed.[31] In practice, this often happens at the last moment, and generally no guidance is given by the Member State to the Commission to relate the national measures to the provisions of the Directive. Indeed, some Member States seem to take an almost perverse pleasure in leaving it to Commission officials to puzzle out the intricacies of what are often complex national laws themselves and relate them to the Directive in question.

For a start, then, I would like to see a requirement for Member States to provide the Commission with a systematic explanation of the relationship between the national measures and the provisions of the Directive—an article by article guide if you like. And, as a acknowledgement of citizen interest in this issues, these should be documents that are publicly available.[32]

Secondly, it needs to be recognized that the reluctance to lose face is a general feature of institutional behaviour. Once national laws have been made, whether in primary legislation or regulations, Member States are likely to resist change or at least will give an exaggerated defence of them against differing interpretations. So I would like to see a general requirement that *draft* legislation proposed to implement a Directive is sent to the Commission at least 6 months before the date for compliance. This may require longer time-limits for compliance—perhaps a general move from two years to three—but is, I believe a price worth paying if the result is a greater opportunity to ensure a truer reflection in national law of Community obligations. The 1994 Packaging Directive does provide something of a model in this respect in that it contains a provisions concerning the requirement of Member States to notify draft measures, though no time limits are provided.[33] Of course, the Commission cannot give a final legal interpretation of Community law which remains the responsibility of the European Court of Justice, and there will remain instances where both Member States and the Commission refuse to compromise on their respective interpretations—but at least there will be greater advance notice of trouble ahead. In practice discussions are sometimes held between Member States and the Commission over draft legislation[34] but it appears to be done in an ad hoc manner. I accept that these discussions will not always be plain sailing or conducted in the spirit of perfect rationality, but my complaint is that there is little consistency in the current approach nor is there apparent acknowledgment by Member States that it is important.

[31] Sometimes three years as in the Environmental Assessment Directive.
[32] It may be that under the Access to Environment Information Directive there would be a legal right to obtain such documentation.
[33] European Parliament and Council Directive 94/62/EC on Packaging and Packaging Waste, Article 16. Reproduced in *JEL* Vol 7 No 2.
[34] Considerable discussions were held between the UK Government and the European Commission over the enforcement provisions in the Water Bill 1989 leading to amendments to the text of the Bill.

226   RICHARD MACRORY

The drafting of Community legislation still often leads to ambiguities and in-consistencies, though the blame cannot always be laid at the Commission; late night negotiations at the Council of Ministers can lead to oddly drafted provisions. But certainly there seems to me to be the need for greater attention to drafting, including the use of interpretation sections, together with the greater use of advisory material, akin to Circulars, issued by the Commission and explaining their understanding of the new Community legislation and containing, for instance, worked examples of its application. And there are times when the Commission could play a more proactive role in assisting national institutions. Art 5 of the Treaty imposes a general duty on Member States to facilitate the achievement of the Community's tasks. Although the provision refers only to Member States, the duty has been interpreted by the European Court to impose a reciprocal duty upon the Commission to cooperate with national authorities.[35] In the field of competition policy and state aids , the Commission in 1993 and 1995 respectively, issued Notices of Cooperation providing guidance on when it would provide assistance to national courts in the provision of relevant information, including information on points of law.[36] I recognize that developing a more proactive approach is not without difficulties. One reason for the Commission's reluctance to over-commit itself in advance of its view of the law is a fear that this will inhibit it from bringing enforcement procedures against a Member State should its opinion later change, akin to a principal of estoppel. My own view is that it should not.[37] But if a Member State were sued for damages under the Frankovitch principles in respect of non-implementation under the principles now being developed by the ECJ, reliance on prior legal interpretation and advice given by the Commission could well provide a justifiable defence. This is acknowledged by the European Court in the latest decision on this issue, Factortame III.[38]

In accordance with one of the Declarations attached to the Maastricht Treaty, one of the tasks during the forthcoming intergovernmental conference will be to reconsider the whole question of the hierarchy of Community legislation.[39] As happened before Maastricht, no doubt it may again be argued that Community Directives, one of the major forms of Community legislation which have existed since the foundation of the Community and are really quite distinct to the Community, are now at outmoded legal instrument. By leaving so much room for manoeuvre for Member States, their form has given rise to the sorts of implementation problem I have already outlined. We do of course have another key form of Community instrument, the Regulation,

[35] Case C-2/88 *Zwartweld* [1990] ECR 1–3365.

[36] Notice of Cooperation between National Courts and the Commission in Applying Articles 85 and 86 of the Treaty, OJ 1993 C39/6; Notice of Cooperation between National Courts and the Commission in the State Aid Field, OJ 1995 C312/8.

[37] Once enforcement proceedings are commenced, however, the Commission may find itself inhibited from redefining issues or raising new points as stated in the Reasoned Opinion.

[38] Joined Cases C-46 and C-48/93 *Brasserie du Pecheur SA v Germany R v Secretary of State for Transport ex parte Factortame* [1996] 75 CMLR 889. According to the Court of Justice, one of the factors to be taken in account when determining whether a Member State should be liable was 'the fact that the position taken by a Community institution may have contributed towards the omission', (para 56).

[39] 'The Conference agrees that the Intergovernmental Conference to be convened in 1996 will examine to what extent it might be possible to review the classification of Community Acts with a view to establishing an appropriate hierarchy between the differing categories of Act.' This Declaration followed unsuccessful proposals made at the time, notably by the European Parliament to reclassify Community acts, which included the abolition of Directives and the creation of a new form of general legal instrument, a 'Loi': see, Resolution of the European Parliament on the Nature of Community Acts, OJ 1991C/129/136.

which generally requires no national implementation measures but has immediate effect within national legal systems. Directives have dominated the environmental field, but there are examples of Regulations being used. But it surprised both Lord Nathan and his colleagues when he chaired a House of Lords subcommittee investigating the implementation of Community environmental law[40] to hear how little in the way of principle developed by either the Council of Minister, or the European Commission, in determining in what circumstances one or other of the instruments is most appropriate. Nor is it an issue that the European Court of Justice has yet been called upon to consider. In 1992 the Sutherland Report called for the transformation of all Directives into Regulations after a period for harmonization, but my own view is that Directives should continue to play a significant role.[41] They acknowledge and attempt to accommodate the diverse legal and administrative cultures which exist within Member States, and may be all the more appropriate should further expansion of the Community take place. But as I have indicated they place considerable demands on the institutional machinery if effective and consistent implementation is to be achieved.

4. Applying the Rule of Law to the Commission

The Community system is as the Court of Justice has consistently argued based upon the rule of law. The procedures I have just mentioned concern Member States' obligations. Yet there remain serious problems when it comes to ensure that the Commission itself complies with the rule of law. A central problem is the question of standing before the courts. All jurisdictions develop rules concerning who may or may not bring cases before the courts, especially where issues of public law are concerned. Standing, especially in the field of the environment where private interests in the conventional sense may not be at risk, has long proved a problem. For the most part in the field of public law the UK courts have shown an increasingly liberal approach in their interpretation of the basic test that the person or organization bringing the case must have 'sufficient interest' in the matter concerned[42] and I do not believe it now presents a major inhibition.

The Treaty provides for challenges of the legality of acts by the Commission directly before the European Court. Member States and the Council of Ministers basically have unrestricted access, and the European Parliament may bring action to protect their own prerogatives. Individual applicants may take action in respect of decisions actually addressed to them personally, but this will be unusual in the environmental field. In those cases where the decision is directed to another person (say the grant of financial assistance to a member state) a third parties may still bring action but

---

[40] House of Lords, 9th Report Session, *The Implementation and Enforcement of Environmental Legislation* 1991–92 (HMSO: London).

[41] See also, G. Winter (ed), 'The Directive: Problems of Construction and Directions for Reform' in *Sources and Categories of European Union Law* 1996 (Nomos Verlagsgesellschaft: Baden-Baden).

[42] For a recent and firmly argued liberal approach see the judgment of Otton J in *R v Her Majesty's Inspectorate of Pollution and the Minister of Agriculture Fisheries and Food ex parte Greenpeace Ltd* 1994 *Journal of Environmental Law* Vol 6 No 2, and case analysis by Purdue, ibid.

must, according to Article 173 of the Treaty, show that the decision or regulation[43] is '*of direct and individual concern*' to them. Early case-law of the European Court, going back over thirty years, has held that this phrase, 'direct and individual concern', implies that the individual is affected by reason of certain attributes which are peculiar to them or by reason of circumstances in which they are differentiated from all other persons, and the European Court has consistently adopted that interpretation in subsequent case-law.[44] The result of this restrictive approach was confirmed last year in the environmental field where environmental groups and local residents attempted to challenge the legality of the Commission grant of structural funds in respect of the construction of power stations in the Canary Islands.[45] The complaint was essentially that the award of the aid had not been in compliance with environmental requirements contained in the relevant structural fund regulations especially those concerning environmental assessment. But whatever the merits of the case, the Court never considered these issues, ruling that the applicants had no standing. It could find no evidence that the applicants, or the members of the association, were affected in some way different from other residents in the area.[46] A similar approach was adopted in the case concerning the challenge to the legality of the Commission not intervening in the French nuclear testing in the Pacific.[47]

Of course, it could be argued that another Member State could have made the challenge and would not have be inhibited by the standing rules. But the political reality is that this is most unlikely, especially in the case of structural funds, if only because most Member States benefit from such funds to a degree.[48] The result seems to be a lacuna in ensuring compliance with law. And I am reminded of the position some years ago when there was no express legal base for Community environment legislation under the Treaty. Other legal bases under the Treaty were sought to justify the legislation, and in certain cases, they were extremely dubious had they been subject to proper legal scrutiny. But, as I remember the late Lord Diplock eloquently espoused at a conference at Imperial College, the problem then was that all Member States had agreed to the legislation in question, with the result that effectively there was no one with standing who could or would challenge the legality of the laws in question.[49] Political expedience and priorities in effect subsumed the rule of law.

It should also be said that the Court of Justice itself has not been consistent in its approach towards standing, at least, in the non-environmental field. A slightly less restrictive approach is apparent in the fields of competition law and anti-dumping.

---

[43] The Court has also recently confirmed that there is no provision in the Treaty for third parties to challenge the legality of Directives, as opposed to Regulations or Decisions: *Asocarne v Council* Case T-99/94, quoted in M. Beloff, supra.

[44] Case 25/62 *Plaumann v Commission* [1963] ECR 95. It would seem that the Court would prefer such issues to be brought to their attention by a reference from the national courts under Article 177, but this will not necessarily deal with the legal control of the Commission's activities.

[45] *Stichting Greenpeace Council and others v EC Commission*, Case T-585/93 12.2.94, 1996 *Journal of Environmental Law* Vol 8 No 1.

[46] For a similar result see, Case T-117/94 *Associazione agricoltori della provinca di Rivigo et all v EC Commission*, concerning a challenge to a decision of the Commission to grant financial assistance for conservation measures under the LIFE fund.

[47] Case T-219/95R *Danielsson and others v Commission of the European Communities*, 22 December 1995.

[48] See, L. Kramer, 'Public Interest litigation in Environmental Matters before the European Courts' 1996 *Journal of Environmental Law* Vol 8 No 1.

[49] R. Macrory (ed), (1982) *Britain, Europe and the Environment* (Imperial College Centre for Environmental Technology: London).

And a rather more liberal approach appears to have been adopted in a recent decision in 1994 falling within the sphere of the Common Agricultural Policy.[50] In that case, a sparkling wine producer in Spain challenged a regulation stipulating that a particular term concerning sparking wine could only be used in respect of wines from France or Luxembourg. Although there were other sparkling wine producers in Spain in the same position, the European Court was prepared to accept that the Regulation in question was of individual and direct concern to the complainant producers, and that they had standing.[51] They had a protected economic interest at stake, a registered trade-mark, and were by far the largest producer of the wine in question, and these factors were sufficient to give them a position distinguished from other producers.

The economic factors clearly in play may permit the Court to develop a rather more liberal test of standing in these sorts of cases as opposed to those concerned with the environment, and maybe we will just have to wait for developing jurisprudence. But the present position is hardly satisfactory, and does not meet my test of citizenship. One political response, at least over the question of structural funds, has been the recent flexing of muscle by the European Parliament using its budgetary powers to impose a greater commitment on the Commission to ensure that the environmental implications of the use of structural funds are more effectively considered. This in fact may have the effect desired in that field,[52] but in many ways represents a failure of the legal system to come to grips with the issue.

Although the Court does not say so explicitly, its restrictive approach towards the definition of standing must to a large degree be due to the familiar floodgates arguments. Time delays before the Court at present are sufficient to raise alarms at the prospect of a whole new tranche of litigation. There will be arguments for amending the provisions of the Treaty to provide for a total liberalization to allow any individual or organization to have standing,[53] but I am not convinced that this would be practicable or necessarily the correct response. One approach might be to relax the standing rules, and develop a more vigorous filtering process for applications, akin to the procedure for leave of application to judicial review in this country — this would help to ensure that cases with little merit would not reach the court. Or perhaps, rather than broadening the standing tests, we need a new independent body with power to bring such cases in the public interest against the Commission and other Community institutions. The Maastricht Treaty did establish a new Community post, the Ombudsman , with the duties to investigate complaints concerning maladministration within Community institutions.[54] The Ombudsman, however, is very much the creature of the European Parliament reporting to the European Parliament. As yet the jury is still out on the effectiveness of this new position, and it is very unlikely that the Ombuds-

---

[50] Case C-309/89 *Cordorniu v EC Council* [1995] CMLR 561.

[51] In other cases, the Court appears to have adopted the view that if the challenged act was truly a Regulation which by its nature had general application, third parties would not the right to challenge it: see, T-472/93 *Campo Ebro v EU Council* [1996] CMLR 1038. In *Cordorniu* the Court appeared to have accepted that an act could both be a true Regulation and of individual and direct concern at the same time.

[52] See in particular, European Parliament Committee on Budgets, Report on the 1996 Draft Budget as modified by the Council A4–0305/95 11.12.95, and Final Adoption of the General Budget of the European Union for the financial year 1996 OJ L 22 29.1.96. I am grateful to David Wilkinson of the Institute for European Environmental Policy for information on these political developments.

[53] See e.g., 'Green ing the Treaty II: Sustainable Development in a Democratic Union', Climate Action Network et al, 1995.

[54] EC Treaty Article 138e.

man would have independent standing before the Court.[55] Nor am I satisfied that a body concerned with maladministration can be an effective substitute for one responsible for ensuring legality.

5. Environmental and Economic Rights: The Uneven Hierarchy

It is perhaps no coincidence that the Court's rather more liberal approach towards standing has appeared in more purely economic areas of the Community interest rather than the environment. And similarly, it is telling that in relation to enforcement some of the Commission's more recent procedural initiatives concerning enforcement appeared in economic fields. In my final theme, then, I want to consider some deeper structural features of the Community as a legal system in its treatment of economic and environmental interests. Whatever precisely the meaning of sustainable development, it clearly implies a far deeper integration of economic, social and environmental concerns that has hitherto been the case. Sustainable development, albeit in rather garbled form, was inserted at Maastricht as one of the tasks of the Community.[56] The Treaty also contains an obligation to integrate environmental protection requirements into other areas of Community policy,[57] again one of the necessary implications of sustainable development.

The Community may have had its origins as a functionalist economic institution, but clearly has developed beyond those boundaries. The acknowledgment by the Court of Justice of the significance of human rights as an element of the Community legal order which is now reflected in the Maastricht Treaty,[58] and even the change of name of the European Economic Community to the European Community and Union under the Maastricht Treaty underlines those developments. As Advocate General, Francis Jacobs put it in a recent lecture,[59] *'This has among other things put an end to the idea that the Community is a purely economic entity and that it is only as a factor of production that an individual has to be considered under Community. That mercantalist approach is simply no longer tenable'.*

But when one looks closer at the current legal structures there is still a long way to go. All systems of law and legal principle are ultimately based on a hierarchical structure —some principles overriding or qualifying others, some mandatory, others merely giving power, some enforceable before the courts, others existing merely as what might be described as gravitational rules. The European Treaty contains no explicit hierarchy as such —indeed the fundamental principle that in case of conflict

---

[55] Other than to protect the interests of the position.

[56] Among the general tasks of the Community defined in Article 2 of the Treaty as amended are the promotion of 'sustainable and non-inflationary growth respecting the environment'. See generally, R. Macrory and M. Hession M, 'Maastricht and the Environmental Policy of the Community: Legal Issues of a New Environment Policy' in *Legal Issues of the Masstricht Treaty*, O'Keefe and Twomey (eds), 1993 (Chancery Publications: London).

[57] Article 130r EC Treaty. 'Environmental protection requirements must be integrated into the definition and implementation of other Community policies.' Although the sentiment is clear, the precise legal meaning of this requirement, let alone its institutional implementation, remain unclear.

[58] Article F2. 'The Union shall respect fundamental rights as guaranteed by the European Convention for the Protection of Human Rights and Fundamental Freedoms signed in Rome on 4 November 1950 and as they result from the constitutional traditions common to the member States as general principles of Community law.' But under Article L this provision is excluded from the jurisdiction of the European Court of Justice.

[59] F. Jacobs, 'Human Rights in the European Union', 1994, Durham European Law Institute.

with national law Community law is supreme is not expressed as such in the Treaty but is entirely a creation of the judiciary. Nor within its own confines does the Treaty explicitly create a structured hierarchy. Yet when one examines its format and the way that it has been interpreted and approached by legal practitioners and the Court of Justice, one can construct a set of interlocking principles and rules, some of which clearly take precedence over others. Understanding the nature and rationale for this approach is of key importance if we are to ever to see a more balanced integration of economic and environmental interests.[60]

At the pinnacle of this pyramid are statements of what can be described as pre-emptive norms given the highest value by the Court. These are binding, have direct effect, and are invocable against Member States, Community institutions, and in many instances by and in some cases against individuals before their national courts. The most obvious are the provisions in Art 30 guaranteeing free movement of goods, and those principles in Articles 85 and 86 relating to competition. We can identify further categories of principles, including a duty on the Community to act in favour of particular goals which may include the environmental integration requirement,[61] down to what may described as statements of interests which provide a legal justification for action by the Community or Member States but do not require any such action to be taken.

If we just contrast two sets of important provisions the dilemma is clear. The Treaty now contains a set of environmental principles, but these do not have any pre-emptive effect; rather, they guide and influence Community action where it is taken. Similarly, the environmental integration requirement is a principle that binds the Community where it takes action, but as the cases on standing illustrate is unlikely to be enforceable other than by another Member State or perhaps the European Parliament. In contrast, Article 30 concerning the free movement of goods has been held to have direct effect, and in essence can be described as a constitutional right. Indeed the freedom of trade has been described by the European Court as a fundamental right of those living within the Community.[62] It can be invoked by individuals and companies before the national courts. It exists quite independently from any measures or policies initiated by the Community or Member States. Any national legislation and any other equivalent measures taken by national governments, whether concerned with Community policy or not, which conflict with the principle can be challenged as illegal.[63] Even Community legislation is in theory subject to the principle.[64] It is true that under both express provisions of the Treaty[65] and principles developed by the European Court[66] Member States in certain circumstances and for certain reasons are

---

[60] See generally, R. Macrory and M. Hession 'Balancing Trade Freedom with the Requirements of Sustainable Development' in *The European Union and World Trade Law*, Emilou and O'Keefe (eds) 1996 (Wiley: Chichester).

[61] Article 130r.

[62] ADBHU [1985] ECR 531. 'The principle of free movement of goods and freedom of competition together with freedom of trade as a fundamental right are general principles of law which the Court ensures observances.'

[63] Since 1969 the Court of Justice has recognized that Community Institutions must comply with basic human rights, and that these doctrines may also apply to Member States when applying Community law. But under Community law they do not apply to national legislation per se, and in this respect can be contrasted with the economic rights granted under the Treaty; see Jacobs, op cit.

[64] Confirmed in ADBHU supra, though in practice the Court is more likely to find other Community policy objectives justify action despite its conflict with Article 30.

[65] Article 36.

[66] The sole called 'rule of reason'.

permitted to retain measures which conflict with the general principle in Article 30, and environmental protection is one such ground.[67] But the burden is very much on the Member State to justify an incursion into the general principle, and does not detract from its general pre-emptive quality.

The whole issue of trade and environment is, of course, high on the international agenda, in the context of General Agreement on Trade and Tariffs and the World Trade Organization and the forthcoming Singapore meeting. Much of the language in the Treaty concerning free movement and the exemptions that are permissible is very similar to GATT. Yet in terms of their internal legal significance, and one might describe as the constitutionalization of economic rights, it is clear that the Treaty has gone further than anything yet attempted internationally.

The rationale for the priority given to these principles and others such as competition law principles is not hard to find. In part it lies in the historical origins of the Community, where following the failure of the proposed European Political Community in 1954, the central thrust was given to the establishment of economic integration, based on a liberal economic order, as a prelude to further political integration.[68] But there are further reasons why from a legal perspective economic rights are likely to be conceptualized and invocable as legally protected interests more readily than environmental concerns. Lawyers traditionally characterize trade freedom as a classical individual right, which should be equivalent to familiar rights of property, and capable of legal protection as such. In contrast, environmental concerns are viewed in law not so much as an aspect of individual freedom or entitlement but rather as an interest which restricts the freedom of what people may or may not do. As such it is an area appropriate for intervention by government but cannot readily be conceived of as a right directly enforceable before the courts in the same way as the freedom to trade.

There are further important underlying differences in the way that trade and environment interests are conceived which inevitably compound the difficulties of giving them equal or equivalent legal status. The economic market in which the freedom to trade or to enjoy other economic rights is a purely human construction, and demands a certain unity of conditions for its effective operation; this reinforces the attraction of a legally and universally applicable right. In contrast, the environment is not of course an artificial concept, but a physical and heterogeneous reality. Effective and efficient environmental management frequently has to be sensitive to very differing natural conditions in the receiving environment, demanding different responses and hardly consistent with the legal concept of universally invocable rights. Furthermore, the apparent absence of any truly objective standard of environmental protection means that it is all the more difficult to construct an enforceable right. It may be within the capacity of the judiciary to judge what is or is not trade restrictive since this can be legally viewed as an objective test, but the courts should not be burdened with the more political task of determining what level of environmental protection is appropriate,[69] especially when in many areas the nature of environmental science

---

[67] In Case 302/86 *Commission v Denmark* [1988] ECR 4607 (Danish bottles), the European Court explicitly recognized that environmental protection, though not mentioned as such in Article 36, was such a ground.

[68] See, the Spaak Report, Brussels 1956.

[69] The contrast between the objective examination of trade restrictive measures and the more political evaluation of environmental appears plausible. But it has to be said that when one examines the cases concerning alleged trade restrictive measures, it is clear the court is often equally faced with many ambiguities, and is often engaged in complex social and political choices.

cannot provide hard and fast answers. The dilemma for the courts can already be seen in case-law of the European Court of Justice concerning the legality of measures taken by Member States which infringe the right of free movement of goods. As I have already mentioned, Member States may invoke environmental reasons for so doing but do they have right to determine the level of environmental protection desired, or should the Court's apply some objective test? In the Danish Bottles case[70] Advocate General Slynn, as he then was, did indeed call for an objective test — 'The level of protection sought must be a reasonable one' — but despite requests from the Court, the European Commission refused to provide guidance on what than reasonable level might be in that case, and the Court decided that they would not interfere or question the Danish Government's determination of the standard of environmental protection they desired to be achieved by the proposed measures.[71] Danish Bottles concerned economic rights of free movement of goods being pitched against government action on the environment, and since such an action implies that a choice as to an appropriate level of environment protection has already been made by a government, it is hardly surprising that the Court felt it did not need to reconsider the question. But if an environmental right was to be invocable to the same extent as an economic right, we would be faced with situations where, unlike Danish Bottles, there was no necessary explicit decision taken by a government on the environmental issue at hand. Courts would be constantly faced with determining the standards themselves. The reluctance to develop environmental rights is understandable.

My argument then is that despite the views of Advocate General Jacobs, the Treaty and its legal interpretation has granted us as citizens general individual economic rights but, in the absence of Community legislation no equivalent environmental rights. Giving greater predominance to the notion of sustainable development within the overall aims of the Treaty, or increasing qualified majority voting for Community environmental measures may be the preoccupation of many environmental interests at present during the Inter-Governmental Conference. But these changes will not in themselves alter that fundamental legal construction and bias contained in the current structure.

6. A New Goal for the Market?

There are no easy solutions, but it is an intellectual challenge that needs to be faced if we are serious about the greater integration of economic and environmental interests implied by sustainable development. One way forward might be to include within the Treaty an individual right to environmental quality, as already been proposed by some quarters.[72] But as I have indicated, there are very real difficulties whether such a right could be expressed in genuinely enforceable or legally meaningful terms, certainly where it concerned environmental quality. This is not to argue that the incorporation of such an statement of rights would be without any legal or political effect, and

---

[70] Op cit.

[71] Alternative approach might be that the role of the court should be determine whether an activity harmed the environment but to leave it to the national authority to dermine what level of harm should be permitted, subject to proportionality.

[72] See supra 7. Some Nordic countries are thought to support the inclusion of such a right during the current Inter-Governmental Conference.

certainly the more that such rights are concerned with procedural requirements (such as the right to information) rather than rights to a particular quality of the environment, the more are they likely to be genuinely enforceable before the Courts. Even statements expressed in general terms may guide the legal interpretation of other rules and principles in a more environmentally sensitive manner. But it needs to be appreciated why such rights are unlikely ever to achieve equal legal status with economic rights. Certainly, the juxtaposition of such an environmental right within the Treaty alongside the existing norms and principles of necessity would create difficult and continuing tensions.

Another response — and in essence what has been taking place for the last twenty years — is to simply carry on with the development of explicit Community environmental legislation as a sort of counterbalance where existing fundamental principles are considered to run counter to environmental interests. This is likely to happen in certain fields, but, although it is too early to determine a definite trend, the pace of Community environmental legislation appears to have slowed in recent years, reflecting in part a greater sensitivity to the subsidiarity principle that now appears in the Treaty. In 1993 and 1994, for example, nearly fifty items of environmental legislation were adopted, dropping to 19 in 1995.[73] Even if qualified majority voting in the Council of Ministers were extended to all environmental matters, the accession of new member states could be expected to make the agreement of new environmental legislation more rather than less difficult.

In any event, such an approach is perhaps over dirigist. Another method, which is more fundamental and long lasting, is to reconsider the purposes of the market whose goals are not defined with precision in the Treaty. Under this model, which I and a colleague have recently suggested,[74] one would take as a starting point the concept of the *'rational and prudent use of natural resources'*, which is now one of the express principles of Community environmental policy, and could be said to be one of the underpinning goals of sustainable development. It is also a goal with which one would hope an economist would have little to disagree with as a general preferred outcome of market principles. If this were expressed explicitly in the Treaty as one of the goals of the market, the basic legal structure and hierarchy of principles would be transformed. Legislation and policies both at national and Community level which conflicted with these goals would in accordance with the existing principles be susceptible to legal review. Policy-makers at both national and Community level would develop an increased sensitivity in the design and development of measures which might conflict with those principles, as they do at present in respect of free movement of goods.[75] Activities of the State which caused or permitted environmental damage would prima facie be contrary to the Treaty as are activities which distort free trade.[76] A true legal integration between market and environmental concerns would lie at the heart of the legal structure, and in essence one would be bringing to bear the full weight of the

---

[73] N. Haigh, *Manual of Environmental Policy: the EC and Britain*, (Longmans: London).

[74] Supra 60.

[75] N. Neuwahl, 'Individuals and Gatt: Direct Effect and Indirect Effects of the General Agreement on Tariffs and Trade in The European Union and World Trade Law', 1996, op.cit.

[76] No doubt the courts would have to develop thresholds since so many activities are environmental damagings but the same developments and drawing back can be seen in the case-law on restrictions of trade and measures of equivalent effect. But the purpose of the proposal is to permit the development of principle rather than lay down over-prescriptive rules in advance.

ENVIRONMENTAL CITIZENSHIP AND THE LAW 235

power of market law and principles developed within the Community behind at least some of the goals of sustainable development.

It takes some imagination to consider the likely outcome of such a change. Indeed far from being a top-down prescriptive solution, it deliberately leaves open the detailed future development of policy and law but against a new, and more balanced legal framework which might be more appropriate for the next century. But in suggesting such a proposal, it will be argued that far from carrying out repairs, I am now pulling up the whole road. My response would be —perhaps echoing the 18th Report of the Royal Commission on Environmental Pollution[77] —that over-obsession with one form of propulsion may end up eventually restricting rather than increasing freedom of choice. Or, in the words of Father Brown '*It isn't that they can't see the solution. It is that they can't see the problem*'.[78]

---

[77] Transport and the Environment, 1994 (HMSO: London).
[78] G. K. Chesterton, *The Scandal of Father Brown*, 'Point of the Pin', 1935.

[7]

ON THE EFFECTIVENESS OF THE EC ADMINISTRATION: THE CASE OF ENVIRONMENTAL PROTECTION

GERD WINTER*

1. Introduction

The implementation of EC administrative law is fundamentally a matter for the Member States.[1] The administrative role of the EC institutions (and the Commission in particular) is in principle limited to supervising the Member States' duties. Nevertheless, a large and steadily growing number of instances of implementational competence have been transferred to the EC institutions, implementation of law deriving both from the Treaties ("primary law") and from secondary legal acts. The wide range of administrative tasks of the EC institutions raises the question of whether and how one could reduce or restructure the workload in order to find an indispensable minimum which meets the demands of both effectiveness and subsidiarity.

An answer to this question must distinguish between the following types of administration through Community institutions:

- tertiary rule-making (section 2);
- direct implementation of EC primary or secondary law in individual cases (section 3);
- supervision of implementation by Member State agencies in individual cases (section 4).

---

* Professor of Law, University of Bremen. This paper is a revised version of an article in Lübbe-Wolff (Ed.) *Der Vollzug des Europäischen Umweltrechts* (Berlin 1996). It was translated by John Blazek.
1. Arts. 3B and 4(1) 2nd sentence EC.

2. Tertiary rule-making

Under the category of "tertiary ruke-making", one can situate law which is promulgated on the basis of secondary legal acts, which in their turn are based on competences in the Treaties. Such tertiary law is most often found in annexes and appendices to regulations and directives (thus forming an integral part of them[2]), but it can also take the form of free-standing regulations and directives.[3] Compared to secondary law, tertiary law is characterized by simplified rule-making procedures. Most of the relevant secondary law acts assign the rule-making competence to the Commission,[4] although it is also sometimes reserved for the Council.[5] The admissibility of such assignment of competence derives from Article 145 3rd indent EC.

In environmental law, it is in the framework of tertiary rule-making that the technical standards disseminated in this sector are set. It can therefore be compared with standard-setting in regulations or administrative guidelines at the national level. However, Community law does not provide any special type of legal act for this area. Instead, regulations and directives are used, and it is not immediately apparent whether they are more statutory or executive in character. It would foster greater legal clarity if a special type were introduced for executive legal acts, for instance a Community Decree.[6] This could also be coupled with a clearer arrangement of the institutions responsible and the rule-making procedures.The European Parliament (EP) and the Council could then be left out of this procedure, thereby being left free to concentrate on

2. See e.g. the particularly extensive annexes to the Chemicals Directive 67/548/EEC.

3. Thus the "subsidiary Directives" issued on the basis of the Water Directive 76/464/EEC concerning limits for waste water discharges from various industrial sectors, Nos. 82/176/EEC, 83/513/EEC, 84/156/EEC, 84/491/EEC, 86/280/EEC.

4. This applies e.g. for the annexes mentioned *supra* note 2.

5. See e.g. Art. 18(1) of the Pesticide Directive 91/414/EEC, on the basis of which the Council through Directive 94/43/EC adopted principles for the assessment of pesticides as appendix VI of the Pesticide Directive.

6. For a more elaborate discussion of this suggestion see Winter, "Summary", in Winter (Ed.), *Sources and categories of European Union Law*, (Baden-Baden 1996), pp. 38 et seq.

working out the more essential orientations in the form of fundamental legal acts, which then might be termed Community Laws. For example, continuing to require that the Water Directive's "daughter" directives (which are meant to specify, for an enormous number of individual substances, emission limits that are even varied depending on the technical processes involved) be decided by the Council and, by way of consultation, the EP makes very little sense – and serves to drag out the covering of the outstanding substances interminably.

A further problem of tertiary rule-making is connected with "comitology". With respect to setting standards in environmental law (but also in other policy areas, particularly agricultural law[7]), the Commission, to the extent that it has been assigned executory competences, is obliged to work together with committees formed by representatives of the Member States. Some of these committees have only a consulting function. In the environmental field, however, most of them are so-called regulatory committees, veritable mini-Councils which can effectively frustrate the intent of the Commission by refusing to give its proposal the necessary qualified-majority approval. In such cases the Council can take up the matter and – with a qualified majority – reach a different decision. However, if the Council fails to do so before certain time periods have passed, the matter falls back into the hands of the Commission ("filet"). In rare exceptions, the relevant legal act allows the Council to prevent – with a simple majority – this falling back ("contre-filet").[8]

Although the Commission understandably regards this procedure as a considerable restriction on its role as the EC's primary executive body, the participation of Member State representatives in the tertiary

---

7. A quantified look at the distribution of the various committee types across the different policy areas is offered in the contribution by Falke and Winter, "'Comitology' in executive rule-making", in Winter (Ed.) op. cit.

8. On the various committee procedures, see the Decision of the Council 87/373/EEC, O.J. 1987, L 197/33. The power of the Council to bind the Commission through such "modalities" is derived from Art. 145 3rd indent EC. In my opinion, however, procedure type IIIb ("contre filet"), which makes it possible for a Commission proposal to fail with a simple negative majority of the Council, is incompatible with this provision.

rule-making process does offer a chance to iron out national divergences in risk assessment, and interests which could not be reconciled earlier at the level of the fundamental legal acts. Moreover, experience acquired at the level of implementation in individual cases and on the national level can provide input into the EC standardization process; this has proven remarkably useful at the national level, for example, in the participation of the German *Bundesrat* in the regulation-setting procedure.[9] Furthermore, the participation of the national administrations usefully increases both their knowledge of, and their willingness to follow, the European rules.

There is still not enough empirical evidence to say with any certainty whether this potential is really fully exploited in practice. From conversations with practitioners, this author has the impression that the technical issues are often overshadowed by official national instructions when the regulatory committees as such influence the substance of a decision; most often it is ministerial officials who sit on these committees, and they see themselves more as representatives of their own countries than as strictly technical experts. In contrast, technical problem-solving appears to gain ground when solutions are first prepared by working groups composed of people from the national specialized administrations (e.g. in Germany the Federal Environmental Protection Agency [*Umweltbundesamt*]). The official committees can then restrict themselves to accepting the compromise reached or, in case of conflict, confirming the lack of agreement, which indicates that the matter cannot be resolved purely technically, but will require a political solution. This way, the regulatory committees would have a sort of double function, either to find technical compromises or to identify "political" problems, which are then sent on to the Council (or, alternatively, to the Commission).[10]

9. Cf. Art. 80 Para. 2 *Grundgesetz.*
10. On a type of European semi-professionalism in standard-setting which is beginning to develop at this level, see Roethe, "Management von Gefahrstoffrisiken in EG-Regelungsausschüssen", in Winter (Ed.), *Risikoanalyse und Risikoabwehr im Gefahrstoffrecht* (Düsseldorf 1995), pp. 115 et seq. See also the empirical estimates in Falke and Winter op. cit.

EC administration 693

Given the technical orientation of the working groups active in the background of the committees, it is logical for them not to meet as closed bodies, but rather to remain open for technical contributions from the social groups affected. With respect to the control of hazardous substances, for example, the practice has developed of representatives from the European Federation of the Chemical Industry participating in meetings. Union representatives and (sometimes) environmental associations are invited, as well (although, due to a lack of personpower, the latter rarely participate). One can see this as offering a potential for more comprehensive problem-resolution, although it carries with it the danger of a lopsided impact of interests until methods are found to improve the opportunities for opposing views to be expressed.

However, even if "comitology" was reformed in this way it would not be the most appropriate procedure for *all* types of standard-setting. Apart from the Council's mistrust of an over-powerful EC executive, the committee procedure dominates so heavily at the EC level as a result of the hurdles which the ECJ erected in its *Meroni* decision for the establishment of EC regulatory agencies. Nevertheless, in the future such agencies will be unavoidable. Such an authority – for instance, the environmental agency equipped with corresponding competences – could take over responsibility for the multitude of more routine rule-making (and individual case decisions), e.g. the classification of new hazardous substances under the Chemicals Directive 67/548. This should still be reconcilable with the *Meroni* criteria, in particular that an independent EC authority may not be granted any room for applying its own discretion, since the activity would consist in the application of material standards and widely-accepted knowledge. Furthermore, it is not impossible that the ECJ might somewhat loosen its *Meroni* criteria – which were established as far back as 1958 – if given a suitable occasion to address the issue.

The third variant to consider – along with the committee procedure and the establishment of EC authorities – would be to draw on the European standardization organizations. Originally, and even today, still acting primarily with respect to economic regulation, with the "New

694 *Winter*   *CML Rev. 1996*

Approach"[11] they have nevertheless begun assuming tasks of consumer protection, e.g. public-interest assignments. The fact that EC environmental law has until now failed to discover them is presumably due to the subject's comparatively high conflict potential, which in the conventional understanding would suggest political-administrative rather than corporatist structures. In keeping with more recent trends at the national level, however, it should be considered whether self-organized standardization organizations with pluralistic structures couldn't also contribute at the European level to public interest-oriented standardization. At the EC level, of course, such a pluralistic approach is made a good deal more difficult by the fact that the standardization boards, if they hope to remain functional, can scarcely take on more than a single representative from the national standardization organizations. This individual will generally come from the major industry which sets the tone at the national level, while smaller companies, consumers and environmental associations would go unrepresented. [12] Other organizational possibilities, which attempt to achieve a specifically European pluralization through participation of the European organizations, are conceivable, but remain to be developed.[13] However they are ultimately structured, though, under Community constitutional law it will scarcely be possible to give binding effect to the decisions of these organizations, nor is such an effect recognized even within the framework of the "New Approach".[14] To this extent, the "Commission plus Comitology" structure, which enjoys indirect national and direct Community

11. On this see Reich, *Europäisches Verbraucherschutzrecht* (Baden-Baden 1993), pp. 345 et seq.
12. This is in fact the practice of the *Centre Européen de Normalisation* (CEN), see Falke, "Standardization by Professional Organizations: the New Conception", in Winter (op. cit. note 6).
13. Proposals have been worked out by Führ, "Reform der europäischen Normungsverfahren", (Typoscript 1995) and Falke and Joerges, "Rechtliche Möglichkeiten und Probleme bei der Verfolgung und Sicherung nationaler und EG-weiter Umweltschutzziele im Rahmen der europäischen Normung", (Typoscript 1995) under a contract from the Büro für Technikfolgenabschätzung des Deutschen Bundestages.
14. Winkel, *EG-Richtlinien und der Europäische Binnenmarkt*, DIN Mitteilungen 1993, p. 389, according to which the CEN standards establish an evidentiary pre-

legitimation, remains indispensable for the aspects of standardization relevant to the public interest.

3. Direct implementation in individual cases

On the whole, only a few individual case-related implementational competences have been assigned to the Commission through primary law,[15] and none at all in the environmental field. Secondary law is substantially more generous in this regard. The legal acts which entrust direct implementation tasks to the Commission have now grown so numerous, and the terms of such assignment vary so widely, that a classification scheme would appear useful.

The Commission can be assigned a directly implementing, a dispute-resolving and a concerting function. Some participation by the Member States is frequently joined to these functions, which can consist of submitting proposals, consultation or agreement, and in its strongest form such participation justifies speaking of an equally-ranked mixed administration.

3.1. *Directly implementing administration*

The Commission acts in a directly implementing manner, e.g. in the framework of the Regulation (EC) No. 1164/94 concerning the cohesion fund, to the extent that it is responsible for authorizing resources from the fund. This concerns benefit-providing administration, while an example of regulatory administration can be found in Regulation (EEC) No. 594/91 on protection of the ozone layer, under which the Commission may authorize manufacturers of certain hazardous substances to exceed the admissible level of production when this is paired with a corresponding reduction of production by a foreign manufactur-

sumption that the product corresponding to them agree with the relevant EC legal act.

15. E.g. Art. 89(2) EC (supervision of competition), Art. 124(1) EC (administration of the social fund).

er. [16] For such authorization, it is necessary to consult with the Member States involved and secure their agreement.

Another example of directly implementing activity of the regulatory type is the role the Commission plays in procuring data within the framework of the Regulation of Existing Chemical Substances (EEC) No. 793/93. Under Articel 10 of the Regulation, the Commission is responsible for demanding certain additional substance tests from manufacturers. The national authorities which respectively act as "rapporteurs" for a specific substance examine the existing data and submit proposals to the Commission for its decision-making. Here the function of the national authority lies in preparing the decision, not (as above) in consultation.

3.2. *Dispute-resolving administration*

An example of the dispute-resolving function of the Commission is when it acts within the framework of the Gene Technology Directive 90/220/EEC.[17] If one Member State objects to the fact that another Member State wishes to authorize the marketing of a genetically-modified organism, and the national authorities responsible cannot reach an agreement, then according to Article 13 the Commission must decide the matter. However, the Commission's decision has legal effect only for the national authorities involved. The national authority remains responsible *vis-á-vis* the company that has applied for the authorization.[18] Depending on the decision of the Commission, the national authority will thus either grant or refuse the authorization. Here, only the activity in the procedural phase of the cross-border coordination of the national authorities can be characterized as "direct implementation".

16. O.J. 1992, L 405/41, Art. 10(8).
17. O.J. 1990, L 117/15.
18. Compare Art. 13(4) of the Directive mentioned. The Regulation mentions only the grant of authorization in case of a positive decision from the Commission, but must also be applied correspondingly to the refusal of authorization in case of a negative decision.

3.3. Concerting administration

An example of this type of concerting administration can be found in the Habitat Directive 92/43/EEC.[19] In the course of drawing up the list of areas of Community significance ("Natura 2000"), each Member State notifies suitable areas to the Commission, which then drafts a list in accordance with Article 4(2), in agreement with the Member States. The draft is then decided on in the Regulatory Committee procedure by the Commission. If a Member State has failed to designate areas which the Commission deems suitable, a "bilateral concertation procedure" is provided under Article 5 which, in the event of continuing disagreement, leads to a decision by the Council. (This decision may be regarded as another case of the dispute-resolving type of direct implementation).

3.4. Assessment

If we look at these structures, the dispute-resolving and concerting functions appear to have a sufficiently justifiable basis, the first because virtually no other authority is available besides the Commission or the Council; and the second because, given the highly sensitive problems at issue (the withdrawal of whole land areas from more intensive exploitation), concertation offers the best chance of success. It is also appropriate to involve administrative or regulatory committees in the dispute resolution,[20] although the type of procedure chosen should match the significance of the issue at hand.[21]

By contrast, where the Commission is involved in administering directly, this give greater occasion for considerations on reform. The

---

19. O.J. 1992, L 206/7.

20. In the case of the Gene Technology Directive 90/220, a regulatory committee is provided for which decides using the procedure IIIa (filet, compare *supra* note 8) (Art. 13(3)).

21. Thus it appears excessive to go through a regulatory committee in procedure IIIb (contre filet), when in the framework of the Chemicals Directive 67/548 the Commission has to resolve a dispute between two national authorities about the substance data to be demanded (compare Art. 18(2) with Art. 30(4)(b) of the named Directive).

first question is whether some tasks couldn't be left to the Member States. However, the relevant decisions are probably all of such a nature that, were a Member State as such made responsible, the specifically *European* aspect of the decision would be given short shrift. For example, if recipient countries could decide about the authorization of resources from the cohesion fund, the interests of the donor countries, which until now have felt themselves to be represented within the Commission, would quite possibly be ignored. In the example of the Existing Chemicals Regulation, if the national authority which is the so-called rapporteur for a given substance could make a binding decision about the demand for additional data, and if the manufacturer were domiciled in another Member State, this would be tantamount to the exercise of sovereignty by an alien authority within a foreign state, which would violate the international law principle of territoriality.

And yet it is precisely the last-mentioned example which offers a possible starting point for reforms. After all, under the currently applicable law, the authority acting as rapporteur enters into a sovereign relationship with the foreign manufacturer, even if until now this has only involved the receipt of data which the manufacturer must provide under Community law. If one wanted to expand this relationship so that the rapporteur was also empowered to order the provision of *additional* data, two possible paths could be imagined:

The first runs along the lines of "horizontal administrative assistance" (*Amtshilfe*), where the authority responsible for a trans-border order calls upon the assistance of the other Member State.[22] The second leads to a concept of deconcentrated and mandated EC administration, which involves an "acting" utilization of a Member State's national administration for the purposes of, and representing, EC administration. In such an acting capacity, the responsible (national) authority would be exercising the sovereign power of the EC, *not* national sovereign

---

22. On examples in the field of direct and indirect taxes, see Meier, "Europäische Amtshilfe – Ein Stützpfeiler des Europäischen Binnenmarktes", (1989) EuR, 237 et seq.

EC administration 699

power.[23] It must then be possible to seek legal protection against its decision from the Court of First Instance. [24]

To the extent that tasks should remain at the EC level, it must be examined (as already referred to with respect to tertiary rule-making) which of them are important enough to be performed by the Commission, and which, due to their routine character, could be transferred to separate EC agencies. Among the latter are the tasks mentioned within the framework of the Existing Chemicals Regulation, to the extent that they cannot be integrated into the above-sketched deconcentrated mandatory administration.

Since sovereign competences are involved, and the doctrinal concept of endowing private actors with sovereign powers (in German law: *Beleihung*) is not provided under Community law, a transfer to private persons or organizations is excluded.

3.5. *Digression: Administration and the integration principle*

To the extent that the Commission or the Council are responsible for direct implementation of law not directly aimed at environmental protection, the question arises of the so-called integration clause, e.g. the provision that environmental protection requirements must be included when setting and implementing other Community policies.[25] This provision is of great potential significance, because it is precisely the "other Community policies" which are generating dramatic levels of additional environmental pollution.

23. The concept would bear a certain similarity to the new legal type of mutual recognition of national regulations for consumer protection (so-called regulative competition), as it is practiced e.g. in EC insurance law. Here again, sovereign power has effects across the border. However, a corresponding amendment of the EC Treaty (for example of Art. 4(1) 2nd sentence, Art. 145 or Art. 155) would probably be required to support the mentioned type of deconcentrated and mandated administration.

24. One example for the fact that legal protection against decisions of subordinate authorities has also otherwise already been opened up by secondary law is contained in Regulation No. 40/94 on the Community trademark (O.J. 1994, L 11/1), Art. 63.

25. Art. 130R(2) 3rd sentence EC.

The prevailing opinion is that the integration clause is not just a general programmatic statement but rather binding law, although it is significantly weakened by the fact that the Community institutions have broad discretion when it comes to application, and only in extreme cases does a violation lead to anullment of a measure.[26] Substantively, therefore, what is involved is a principle, not a rule, if by "principle" one understands a requirement which in application may be balanced against other requirements. A procedural version of the principle can, however, be summarized more rigorously: to the extent that the environmental consequences of a measure compel it, these consequences *must* be taken into consideration. If this is not done, then the measure is already unlawful on that account.

A further question is whether the principle applies only for rule-making, or additionally and independently for administration of individual cases as well. Since Article 130R(2) Sentence 3 – as distinct, for example, from paragraph 3 – covers not only the establishment, but also the implementation of policies, the second option seems correct. However, in administration, the principle mentioned can only influence the exercise of margins of discretion. It does not entail an expansion of intervention beyond the specific primary or secondary law authorization. Thus, the Commission can tolerate an anti-competitive agreement, if at the same time it enhances environmental protection;[27] but it cannot regard an agreement which is *not* intrinsically anti-competitive as unlawful merely because it also has environmentally harmful effects.

A further problem with the integration clause is the question whether a policy (and therefore also its administration) can be *so* far removed from environmental aspects that, despite having de facto environmental effects, it may be fashioned in an "environment-blind" manner, at least as long as the environmental protection interest can still be established as an independent, parallel or subsequent countervailing check. For

26. Hailbronner, "EG-Verkehrspolitik und Umweltschutz", in Rengeling (Ed.), *Umweltschutz und andere Politiken der Europäischen Gemeinschaft* (Cologne 1993), pp. 160 et seq.; Krämer, *E.C. Treaty and Environmental Law*, 2nd ed., (London 1995), p. 58.
27. See on this Krämer, "Die Integrierung umweltpolitischer Erfordernisse in die gemeinschaftliche Wettbewerbspolitik", in Rengeling op. cit. pp. 55 et seq.

example, should an invention's potential environmental effects already be examined at the patent-granting stage, or should this be left (as it has until now) to the structure of administrative-law protective standards (e.g. production plant approval or product licensing)? With respect to the approval of the free transfer of profits from one country to another, should it be examined whether this results in a withdrawal of resources for environmental protection investments, or should this be a matter for production plant-related environmental laws? I wish to limit myself here to posing the question. It would require a more thorough examination to clarify precisely where the lines should be drawn in this area.

4. Supervision of implementation by Member State agencies in individual cases

A distinction can be made between infringements by national authorities of directly applicable Community law and infringements of national law which has incorporated Community law . In the first case it is possible that the authority applied national law which, however, is superseded due to infringement of the directly applicable Community law; most of the time, however, it will be the case that no relevant national law exists which would have to be superseded. While in both variants of this case the illegality consists only in the violation of Community law, in the second case there is first of all a violation of national law, which at the same time, however, also contains an infringement of the Community law behind it.

4.1. *Treaty violation procedure*

As mentioned above, Community law provides only for supervisory action by the Commission as a sanction for its infringement. This applies not only for failure to incorporate EC law into national law, but also for non-compliance in the case of implementation in individual cases.

According to Articles 169, 171 EC, the procedure consists of the following formal steps:
- hearing of the Member State (which is offered in the form of a warning letter setting a time limit for relief);
- an opinion stating the grounds on which it is based (which is likewise linked to the setting of a time limit for relief);
- complaint;
- judgment;
- and in case the judgment is ignored: renewed hearing, opinion and complaint, this time with application for the imposition of a lump sum or administrative fine.

Informal interactions precede and follow these formal actions. These include the flow of information on cases of Community law violation. The Commission does not deploy many systematic monitoring activities; instead, its attention is generally drawn to violations from "outside", primarily by the public, e.g. private individuals, associations, members of Parliament and others, and only rarely by authorities (e.g. of other Member States). By publishing a simple complaint form[28] the Commission has established a sort of semi-official complaint procedure, which includes a self-imposed obligation to check and communicate the result.[29]

Another informal structure which has developed in practice consists of the so-called Package sessions.[30] In such sessions, representatives from both the Commission and the responsible Member State ministries (in Germany, in exceptional cases, from the ministries of the *Länder* as well) meet in order to discuss the complaints relating to the State involved, sort out the unsubstantiated ones, decide how to remedy the substantiated ones and establish the facts for those still in dispute. The Commission, whose bargaining power is based on little more than the possibility of bringing an infringement action, is generally willing to keep quiet if the Member State promises concrete relief measures.

28. O.J. 1989, C 26/8. In 1992, 515 complaints were filed, of which the Commission regarded 121 as presumably grounded. See Krämer, *European Environmental Law. Casebook* (London 1993), p. 394.
29. Compare O.J. 1989 C 26/6. On this, see Krämer, op. cit. p. 394.
30. On this, see the article by Krämer in Lübbe-Wolff op. cit.

Finally, one should mention the consultation which the Commission provides, with respect to the implementation of the judgment, for Member States which have been condemned in the Treaty violation procedure. Here, Commission representatives in the field sometimes negotiate about relief measures, and indeed with a view to and supported by a possible subsequent procedure under Article 171 EC.[31]

A whole series of doctrinal problems arise in connection with the Treaty violation procedure: how long does the period set in the warning letter and the opinion with reasons have to be? How far can the complaint go beyond the criticisms communicated in the preliminary procedure, and the formal opinion beyond the criticisms in the warning letter ("*ne ultra monita*")? Under what conditions does relief before the action is brought or during the course of the judicial procedure remove the legal protection interest of the Commission? To what extent is the Commission's discretion with respect to bringing an action judicially reviewable? and so on.[32] These questions, interesting as they may be in the juridical context, do not grasp the more fundamental problem of the Treaty violation procedure, i.e. the hopeless overload of the Commission were it really to be prepared to prosecute any Treaty violation.

Besides the more informal means mentioned above, a number of alternatives shall be discussed, some of which may be more far-reaching.

4.2. *Direct effect of directives*

To the extent that the Treaty violation by national administrative agencies is due to non-transposition of an EC directive into national law, the individuals concerned may invoke the directive when complaining before a national court about administrative action or inaction. The

31. E.g. following the *Santoña* decision of the ECJ of 2 Aug. 1993, (Case C-355/90), in which certain development measures undertaken in protected areas were condemned, a committee was formed at the local level whose members also included a representative of DG XI (information from the Diputacion Regional de Cantabria of 30.5.1995. I thank Mr. Eulogio Cigaran Bidebieta for the correspondence).

32. See on this Krück in von der Groeben et al., *Kommentar zum EWGV*, as well as von Karpenstein in Grabitz and Hilf, *EGV, Kommentar*, both on Art. 169.

directive may either be invoked as a reference for a new interpretation of the national law, or – should the framing of this law leave no room for such reinterpretation – the directive may even be invoked *contra legem nationalem*, i.e. setting the national law aside.

As is well known, in the context of direct effect, the ECJ has followed the principle of estoppel and subjected this second possibility to the qualification that the directive provision in question not only be precise and unconditional, but also have been intended to bestow a right on the party invoking it.

If the directive provision is disadvantageous in comparison to valid national law, direct effect is accordingly to be denied. At any rate, this applies for two-sided legal relationships between individuals and the State[33] (for in the logic of estoppel, the party burdened by the directive will not invoke the directive against his delinquent State, but will prefer application of the national law) – so-called "vertical" relations – as well as for legal relationships between private parties[34] – so-called "horizontal" relations.

What is still undecided is the case (especially frequent in environmental law) of three-sided legal relationships in the vertical dimension, i.e. when a directive requires that a duty (e.g. a stricter emission value) be created for a "second party", which at the same time represents a legal advantage for a "third party", and when the duty and the right exist not directly between the two participants, but rather *vis-á-vis* the State, in other words when they are not of a private law nature, but rather of an administrative-law nature.

Based on the construction of the ECJ,[35] direct effect could be justified

---

33. Case 80/86, *Kolpinghuis*, [1987] ECR 3982 at 3985.

34. Case C-91/92, *Dori*, (1994) ECR I-3325 at 3356.

35. In my opinion, the following construction is preferable: a Member State which has failed to respect the incorporation deadline acts in bad faith *vis-á-vis* the EC and the other Member States when it continues to apply its own national law. It is a matter of indifference whether the Directive creates rights or duties. Precisely in the case of duties, the inhabitants of the delinquent Member States would obtain unjustified advantages over individuals in the other Member States. The counter-argument (which is also used by the ECJ) that the definition of the Directive, compared to the definition of the Regulation, excludes direct effect, would apply in like manner for direct effect

EC administration 705

for this case if one focuses on the relationship between the favoured third party and the State: the State would be estopped from invoking its own failure to fulfil its obligation under the directive *vis-á-vis* this party. Thus, if the third party complains, the court must apply the directive directly. That this imposes a burden on the "second party" is an unintended side effect in which, in the terms of the *Dori* judgment, no "extension" of the direct effect jurisdiction "to the field of relationships between citizens" should be seen, since no relationship of rights and duties exists between citizens.[36] That the ECJ is ready to accept such burden-imposing unintended legal side effects can also be seen from the *Costanzo* decision, which is once again cited in the *Dori* decision. There, too, a right of the complainant, namely to be fairly considered in the tendering procedure, was the counterpart of a duty of the other competitor, namely to accept that the competitor be awarded the contract. ·

To refer the complainant along the lines of the *Francovich* decision to a damages compensation claim against the delinquent Member State[37] would frequently be unhelpful in the vertical constellation, because the disadvantages generated by abortive legal relationships of an administrative-law nature are expressed more rarely in monetary damages than they are in cases of private-law relationships. Administrative law more frequently intervenes preventively, to stop damages

---

in the case of the concession of a right. Those who stray from the literal wording in one case can not simply return to it when they find it convenient. The other counter-argument, that a duty cannot be imposed on all parties to read the EC Official Journal, is just as inconsistent since, after all, precisely such reading is required in the case of regulations (which indisputably have a direct effect) and imposed on all. Finally, if it is objected that direct effect in cases where the directive has a burdening effect contradicts the principle of *nulla poena sine lege*, this can be taken into account by excluding criminal law measures from direct effect. For a more extended discussion, see Winter, *Directive or framework law?* in op. cit. *supra* note 6. Following A.G. Van Gerven and A.G. Jacobs in earlier cases, A.G. Lenz has also (although equally unsuccessfullfy) called for extending direct effect to cases imposing obligations; see his concluding arguments in case C-91/92, *Dori*, [1994] ECR, I-3328.

36. Jans, *European Environmental Law* (The Hague 1995), p. 173.

37. Joined Cases C-6 & 9/90, [1991] ECR, I-5357. The ECJ also points to this path in the *Dori* decision, see loc. cit. para 28.

from arising in the first place. The example of the unincorporated emissions limit illustrates this: the third party suffers under the higher emission, without this however necessarily giving immediate rise to financial expenditures.

The problems of interpretation described here could be resolved through a clarification undertaken as part of the forthcoming Treaty revision. In this author's opinion, the best solution would be a provision which, in case of failure to incorporate clear and unconditional directive provisions, would guarantee direct effect in both favourable and burdensome cases, with an exception for provisions which trigger criminal sanctions. [38] The same could apply for regulations and decisions which impose an obligation to create national law.

4.3. *No review of individual cases?*

Given the heavy workload of the Commission, one should consider whether legal supervision with subsequent infringement actions should be limited to the creation of national legal norms in the implementation of directives (or in the execution of regulations and incorporation of decisions).[39] Control of the application of Community law in individual cases would then be left to the courts of the Member States.

However, such a proposal should be rejected. The more profound divergences in the implementation of Community law, which necessitate an opinion *ex cathedra europea*, frequently only become apparent as a result of concrete cases. This is precisely the reason why those procedures only involving review by the ECJ of the transposition of

---

38. The Sutherland Report (*The Internal Market After 1992* (1992)) also goes in this direction. However, its proposal, that each Directive be converted after a certain time into a Regulation, goes too far, because it may be reasonable to allow the Member States room for manoevre even after the first transposition.

39. Compare along these lines Ehlermann, "Ein Plädoyer für die dezentrale Kontrolle der Anwendung des Gemeinschaftsrechts durch die Mitgliedstaaten", in *Liber Amicorum Pierre Pescatore* (Baden-Baden 1992), pp. 205 et seq., 209: "for example, the Treaty violation procedure is hardly suited for ensuring that the rules on public tender invitations, so indispensable for the Single Market, are respected on a day-to-day basis by literally tens of thousands of Member State authorities."

legal norms, frequently appear somewhat anaemic. This has sometimes (and not altogether without reason) provided an occasion to reproach the Commission for formalism.[40] In addition, the ECJ's potential for development of the law and the stimulation of legal policy would be largely eliminated if it had to confine itself to this anaemic exercise. While it is true that the preliminary ruling path under Article 177 EC would remain open, in many cases this does not result in procedures in which the national courts decide about Community law violations in administration. For it is precisely in the field of environmental law that disputes are focused on the threat to collective goods, which however – due to the more or less pronounced individualization of the locus standi concepts in the Member States – cannot be brought to court.[41] The "objective" Treaty violation procedure is not dependent on such prerequisites.

It has been considered whether legal supervision, if extended beyond rule-making to administrative practice, should at least confine itself to "inspecting the inspectors".[42] This would mean that individual cases would not be reviewed, but only organizational structures (e.g. the frequency and quality of emission measurements). But such a limitation would also leave unexploited the significance attached to individual cases which are representative of specific problems. For example, under such restrictive conditions we would never have obtained such path-

40. Compare Siedentopf and Hauschild, "Europäische Integration und die öffentlichen Verwaltungen der Mitgliedstaaten", in *Die öffentliche Verwaltung* (1990), 445 at 454, who explain this situation on the basis that the Commission, chiefly limited to contact with the ministerial administration, is largely cut off from administrative reality.

41. A different path would be the association complaint. On its admissibility in the Member States and on an approach for strengthening it through Community law, see the contributions in Führ and Roller (Eds.), *Participation and litigation rights of environmental associations in Europe* (Frankfurt 1991), and Führ, Ormond, Gebers and Roller, *Access to Justice* (Öko-Institut, 1994)

42. House of Lords, Select Committee on the European Communities, Implementation and enforcement of environmental legislation, vol. 1- Report, London 1992.

breaking decisions as *Leybucht* and *Santoña-Delta*, both of which have had a major impact on EC nature protection law.[43]

Instead of excluding individual cases from the start, we should attempt to find a rational way of selecting them. A selection is already being made, if only through the backlog of uncompleted procedures. Criteria could be found by borrowing from those for constitutional complaints under §§93a and 93c of the German law on the procedure of the *Bundesverfassungsgericht* which require e.g. the fundamental significance of the subject matter, a serious disadvantage arising for those affected, or a still-undecided legal issue.

4.4. *Binding supervisory decision of the Commission?*

In order to restrict the infringement action to a few especially important matters, one might consider granting the Commission for the other matters the power formally to establish the existence of a violation of the law, and possibly also to order relief measures. The Commission possesses such a competence in the areas of state aid supervision[44] and supervision over companies with sole and exclusive rights.[45] Under Article 88 ECSC, the Commission is competent to establish Treaty violations, but not to order relief measures.[46]

The decisional competences mentioned have the consequence that the burden of introducing the legal protection procedure is transferred

43. See Wils, "The birds directive 15 years later: a survey of the case law and a comparison with the Habitats Directive", in (1994) *Journal of Environmental Law*, pp. 218 et seq.

44. Art. 93(2)(1) EC.

45. Art. 90(3) EC. Against the view that the provision only admits preventive measures, while repressive measures are reserved for the procedure under Art. 169 EC (as A.G. Tesauro argued in his concluding arguments in case C-202/88, [1991] ECR I-1239 para 30), one can adduce both the very wording and the fact that the often subtle questions of competition control of public companies could be clarified more flexibly by Commission decision than through the more cumbersome Treaty violation procedure. See Pernice in Grabitz and Hilf (op. cit.) Art. 90(73) et seq. See there also on the competence to go beyond the establishment of the violation and prescribe relief measures.

46. See however the possible sanctions under Art. 88(3) ECSC.

EC administration 709

to the affected Member State. If this Member State fails to file the complaint within the time limits provided under Article 173(5) EC, the decision can no longer be attacked. If the Member State does not comply with the decision, the Commission can apply to the European Court of Justice under Article 169 EC, which no longer has to examine the substance of the matter, however, once the decision has become unattackable.[47]

Certainly the affected Member State must be heard before the legal-supervisory decision is issued. Beyond this, it would contribute to securing the factual and legal basis of the decision if it were preceded by a formal procedure in which (particularly for decisions in individual cases) the private party and affected third parties are also heard. However, since the effort this would entail would far outstrip the workload capacities of the Commission, one should consider entrusting the hearing (following the model of the British inquiry) to an independent individual who would give the Commission a recommendation for its decision.

Due to the shifting of the complaint burden to the disadvantage of the Member States, one might suppose that the proposal mentioned could only be realized through a revision of the Treaty. However, to the extent that the legal standards of the relevant substantive law are sufficiently exact and/or a clarification of the legal questions is presupposed by the Community courts, the decision-making competence can also be regarded as an implementing authority, which in accordance with Article 145 3rd indent can be transferred to the Commission. Of course, this would require an express authorization by legal acts relating to specific individual areas[48] or by a general legal act which covers the legal supervision competences in one policy sector or all of them. In so doing, the competence could also be limited to certain areas of obligation or to certain types of measures, which indeed would be particularly logical for a trial phase.

47. See on this in the context of Art. 90(3) Pernice, op. cit.
48. Art. 3(2) of the Directive of the Council 665/89, O.J. 1989, L 395/33 contains an example, according to which the Commission may demand that a Member State and the national contract-awarding authority remedy violations of Community regulations concerning public contracts.

4.5. *Investigating powers relating to legal supervision*

If legal supervision were to encompass not only rule-making, but also administration, factual situations would have to be investigated, for which corresponding powers would be necessary. Article 169 EC does not contain anything of the kind: in its context, it involves the granting of a legal hearing prior to commencing an action, thus from the perspective of the Member States not an obligation, but rather a right. By contrast, active obligations on the Member States to provide information derive from Article 5(1) Sentence 2 EC[49] as well as from a plethora of secondary-law provisions.[50]

   For the Commission, however, what is more interesting than the often dilatory submission of information from Member State governments is the power to undertake its own factual investigations, in particular through on-site examinations, gathering of information and inspection of documents from authorities and private parties, entering property, questioning of witnesses, requests for expert opinions, etc. It is true that the documents presented to the Commission generally suffice for commencing the action, so that the use of special investigative powers need not become virulent. In some complicated cases, which at the same time are significant for development of the law, however, more probing investigation can be useful.

   Under Article 213 EC, it seems as though the Commission requires its own specific secondary-law basis for investigations in each and every case. However, this provision should be interpreted to mean that a special legal basis is needed only for establishing information-related *obligations* (duties to provide information, to permit inspection of documents and to tolerate entry onto property and premises). The power to collect information which is voluntarily given, by contrast, exists as a general primary-law competence, in connection with the legal supervision based on Article 155, 1st indent.[51]

---

49. Grunwald in von der Groeben et al., op. cit. Art. 213, para 3.
50. See the examples in Grunwald in von der Groeben et al., op. cit., Art. 213 paras. 26 et seq.
51. Same result Grunwald in von der Groeben et al., Art. 213 para 23.

The question is whether, beyond this, one can also derive from Article 5(1) Sentence 2 a general duty on the part of Member State authorities to give the Commission information directly via administrative assistance and not just indirectly, via the representative of the Member State. Such direct inter-agency relationships are provided for in a series of Regulations, but also by directives which have (to this extent) direct effect. [52] For the environmental field, one should especially highlight the relationships between the European Environmental Agency and the "domestic contact point" on the basis of Regulation (EEC) No. 1210/90.[53] Although direct contacts of an informal nature presumably go far beyond the scope of such explicit arrangements, a general administrative assistance duty would nevertheless appear to be going too far, in view of the enormous variety of duty relationships and newly-opened information flows that would thus be constituted.[54]

4.6. *Bolstering the Commission's preventive resources?*

As means for helping prevent violations altogether, one could consider either administrative guidelines issued by the Commission to interpret or concretize standards, or Commission participation in the national decision-making process.

---

52. Examples in Pipkorn in Beutler, Bieber, Pipkorn and Streil, *Die Europäische Union*, 4th ed. (Baden-Baden 1993) p. 404.

53. O.J. 1990 L 120/1. The data collection serves not only purposes of statistics, policy advising and informing the public, but can also be used for legal supervision, see the 8th consideration of the Regulation. For an example for direct contacts with national authorities from the sectoral environmental law, see Regulation (EEC) No. 594/91 on protection of the ozone layer, which in Art. 12(1) authorizes the Commission "to collect all necessary information from the governments and the responsible authorities of the Member States" and in para 3 obliges the authorities responsible to conduct investigations which the Commission regards as necessary.

54. Going further, Segond, "Untersuchungsbefugnisse der EG-Kommission", in Ladeur and Winter (Eds.) *Verfassungsprobleme der Europäischen Gemeinschaft*, ZERP-DP 1/1991 p. 104.

4.6.1. *Quasi-administrative guidelines*

As far as administrative guidelines are concerned, the Commission certainly has the inherent power to issue administrative guidelines to its subordinate agencies, guidelines which are internally binding and, by creating legitimate expectations, could be indirectly binding externally as well. Unlike the German federal government *vis-á-vis* the *Länder*[55], however, the Commission cannot issue any binding administrative guidelines to the Member States. Article 155, 1st indent, which might be considered as justifying this,[56] is not explicit enough for such a far-reaching competence.[57]

Nevertheless, the Commission has developed a wealth of informational instruments which, although not legally binding, undoubtedly de facto establish certain ties, whether of such a nature that a Member State who ignores them risks being disadvantaged (e.g. introduction of the procedure under Article 169 EC, or withholding of development funds), or conversely of such a nature that the Commission can be appealed to under confidence protection aspects if discrepancies arise. Such instruments bear labels like "communications", "Community frameworks", "vade mecum", "information notices", "good practice rules", etc., and contain information on the interpretations presented by the European Courts or the Commission of primary and secondary law, or on just how the Commission plans to use the margins of discretion it possesses.[58]

The admissibility of such non-binding instruments is not free of doubt, but can be derived *a maiore ad minus* from the procedural powers of Article 169, Artilce 155, 1st indent EC, as well as from the secondary-law substantive intervention powers.

It appears that this possibility of persuasive "soft law" is used less frequently in the field of environmental policy than in other policy

55. In accordance with Art. 84(2) and Art. 85(2) GG.

56. Thus however Bleckmann, "Zur Verbindlichkeit von Rechtsauskünften der EG-Kommission", (1988) RIW, 936 et seq.

57. Adam and Winter, "Commission guidance addressed to Member States", in Winter, op. cit. *supra* note 6.

58. Adam and Winter, op. cit.; Scherer, "Das Rechnungsabschlußverfahren – Ein Instrument zur Durchsetzung europäischen Verwaltungsrechts?", (1986) *Europarecht*, 52 et seq.

sectors.[59] It might be wise to modify this practice. The detailed documentary materials supporting the complaints should provide a rich source for questions which could form the subject of clarificatory communications.

4.6.2. *Participating in decisions at the national level*

As far as participation of the Commission in the decision-making processes of the Member States is concerned, there are already a few examples of this in the applicable law. Most of the time, it involves cases in which the Member States wish to, and also may, deviate from a rule established in the legal act at issue, provided however that the Commission plays a role. Thus if, in exceptional cases, a Member State wants a project to be exempted from the obligation to perform an Environmental Impact Assessment, it must first notify the Commission.[60] Similarly, a Member State which wishes to take the EC water quality targets as its criterion instead of the EC emission limits for waste water, must demonstrate to the Commission that it can and will meet these targets.[61] Finally: if, for the release of genetically modified organisms, a Member State wishes to shift over to simplified monitoring procedures, it must first obtain authorization from the Commission.[62]

These examples show that preventive participation of the Commission can relate to both decisions in individual cases and the establishment of norms by the Member States.

From a legal policy perspective, however, it is not advisable to extend such participation all too freely, since this would place an unacceptably heavy burden on the Commission. Of course, this does not rule out retaining the procedure for carefully selected, important cases. One should also consider entrusting the Environmental Agency with the preventive control function.

59. An example is the "Community framework" for the admissibility of state assistance for environmental protection, see Krämer, *supra* note 28, p. 48.
60. Art. 2(3)(c) of the EIA-Directive (Directive of the Council 85/337/EEC, O.J. 1985, L 175/40).
61. Art. 6(3) of the Water Directive (Directive of the Council 76/464/EEC, O.J. 1976, L 129/23.
62. Art. 6(5) of the Release Directive (Directive of the Council 90/220/EEC, O.J. 1990, L 117/15).

4.7. *EC environmental inspectorate?*

However appealing decentralized implementation monitoring may sound at first, central control remains indispensable at least where environmental hazards with border-crossing effects are involved, because in these cases the possibility remains that the judgment of decentralized monitoring authorities will be too strongly influenced by a regional or national perspective. In the final analysis, no one argues for far-reaching decentralized aid supervision under Article 93 EC or competition supervision under Article 87. Furthermore, local administrations and courts are sometimes politically or socially involved in local projects, especially the larger-scale ones, whereas the distant monitoring offered by European legal supervision makes necessary corrections possible.

Since the Commission has not got the staff which would be necessary for an effective legal supervision (and they are not supposed to handle routine matters anyway), it would be advisable to set up an environmental inspectorate. The inspectorate should also have a limited number of field offices in selected regions, so that it is accessible for the affected parties and can more readily conduct investigations.

It is a delicate question whether the inspectorate function should be transferred to the environmental agency. Arguing in its favour is the fact that the environmental agency is already engaged in collecting environmental information, plus the fact that the functional expansion of an already-created authority, even under the aspect of an experimental procedure, is easier than establishing a wholly new authority. However, it is problematic to link the task of collecting general information too closely with the tasks of legal supervision and the sanctioning of violations of the law. On the one hand, such a linkage means that information will no longer be made so readily available; on the other, the data collection and presentation could be distorted by political considerations in the sanction context. This was precisely the reason why the German *Umweltbundesamt* was originally conceived solely to procure information, not to regulate (even though this distinction has sometimes been blurred in the meantime).[63]

4.8. *Improvement of sanctions?*

In its decisions in the Treaty violation procedure, the ECJ only establishes that an infringement of Community law exists. Under Article 169 EC, it is not authorized to order concrete relief measures. What the Member State must do or refrain from doing after the decision, it must deduce from the Court's findings. Frequently, however, the operative provisions of the judgment are quite generally formulated, so that what has to be done in a particular case must be derived from the grounds of the decision. For example, the decision of 2 August 1993[64] concerned the construction of a dam and a road through the delta area of several rivers near Santoña in northern Spain. In grounds 35 and 41, the ECJ found these construction measures to be incompatible with the Bird Protection Directive. In the operative provisions of the judgment, however, it only stated generally that Spain, in violation of the Treaty, had failed to implement the measures necessary to prevent harm to the natural areas in the region at issue. At the same time, this example shows that the grounds of the decision do not always give clear indications. Thus, it is not compellingly clear whether the road and dam have to be removed or not.[65]

It would therefore be advisable, within the framework of the forthcoming Treaty revision, to give the Court of Justice the authority to prescribe certain relief measures upon motion of the Commission.[66]

63. See v. Lersner, "Zur Funktion einer wissenschaftlich-technischen Umweltbehörde in Europa", in Callies and Wegner (Eds.), *Europäisches Umweltrecht als Chance* (Taunusstein 1992), pp. 87 et seq.

64. Case C-355/90.

65. In fact, the dam is supposed to be dismantled. The road was given a reprieve, but compensating measures are planned. (For the source, see note 31 *supra*).

66. The ECJ itself once proposed exactly this, see Bulletin of the EC, Supp. 9/75, p. 18. Going further, Karpenstein in Grabitz and Hilf, op. cit. Art. 171, para 4 sees this competence already grounded in the applicable Art. 169.

The frequently difficult question as to the form and jurisdiction in which the required measure must be taken could be circumvented by only naming the measure itself.

A particular problem for operative holdings and further for passive legitimation in the Treaty violation procedure arises as a result of the fact that the decision is directed against the defendant Member State and not against the public body or authority which was responsible for the contested action or omission. That reduces the effectiveness of the decision in those cases in which the Member State possesses absolutely no power to order and sanction the responsible corporate body or authority, e.g. Belgium *vis-á-vis* its regions and the German Federal Republic *vis-á-vis* the *Länder* with respect to subjects under a *Land*'s own administration. To remedy this, it has been proposed that it be possible to direct the supervision against the corporate body or authority.[67] For federal States, whose sub-states after all do possess a partial sovereignty *vis-á-vis* the rest of the world, this should certainly be considered, however only with respect to the sub-states, not any other public bodies.[68]

Authorizing the Court of Justice to make not just findings but also orders in its decisions could also help resolve the problem of failure to respect ECJ decisions and the often equally fruitless subsequent procedure,[69] for it is generally easier to conceal a failure to respect a finding than outright disobedience of an order.

Nevertheless, and despite the sanction possibility which has now been introduced under Article 171(2)(3) EC, the problem of an adequate sanction for non-observance of decisions remains firmly on the agenda. The lump sum and the administrative fine which the ECJ can impose bear little relation to the particular type of Treaty violation, and are to this extent conceived more as a monetary fine or coercive measure. It would be preferable if the sanction could be adapted to

67. Macrory, The enforcement of Community environmental laws: some critical issues, 29 CML Rev., 347 at 357.

68. Thus the German Commission of Inquiry on Constitutional Reform in its Final Report, Part II: Federal Government and Länder, Zur Sache 2/77 pp. 86 et seq., at 93.

69. On this, see covering all policy areas Ehlermann (*supra* note 39) p. 213, and for environmental policy specifically Krämer (*supra* note 28) pp. 430–433.

the specific nature of the given case. Thus, in the agricultural area, the Commission has shifted over to reducing grants from the agricultural fund in the case of unjustified expenditures by the authorities of the Member States.[70] For Treaty violations in the area of allocation of own resources, it demands compensation for the loss of revenues.[71] In aid cases, it generally calls on the Member State to demand that the recipient return the aid received.[72] In the area of the structural fund, in cases of failure to observe the environmental laws, it can delay or reject the financing.[73] A more open authorization in Article 171(2)(2) and (3) would permit the ECJ a more pragmatic sanctioning practice in this respect.

5. Final remarks

Decentralized forms certainly stand in the front line of control over observance of Community law in administration. They deserve increased attention and can be further developed in a number of respects. Nevertheless, central control will remain indispensable, first of all simply because there is considerable direct administration by EC institutions, and secondly because a backup line is necessary where the regional horizon obstructs a more distanced and border-transcending vision. The problem is to find *appropriate* forms, ones which select the relevant cases and ensure the quality and effectiveness of the decisions.

70. On this, see Scherer, *supra* note 58 at 52 et seq.
71. See e.g. Case 303/84, *Commission* v. *Germany* [1986] ECR, 1192.
72. Art. 93(2) EC. Examples in Ehlermann (*supra* note 39), p. 215.
73. Art. 7 Council Reg. No. 2052/88/EEC, O.J. 1988, p. 9. See Krämer (*supra* note 69).

Part II
Application and Enforcement of European Environmental Law

[8]

THE IMPLEMENTATION OF COMMUNITY ENVIRONMENTAL DIRECTIVES WITHIN MEMBER STATES: SOME IMPLICATIONS OF THE DIRECT EFFECT DOCTRINE†

Ludwig Krämer*

The Effect of Community Environment Directives on the Member States

According to established case law of the European Court of Justice, European Community directives can have an effect on national laws when Member States, contrary to the provisions of Article 189, third paragraph, have taken no or insufficient measures to transpose the directive's provisions into national law.[1] The Court applies this theory to all areas of Community activity.[2] As Community directives on the environment go back only as far as 1975, it is not surprising that there have been few Court rulings on the direct effect of environment directives. Literature in the field also contains few examinations of the theory of the direct effect of directives in environment law.[3] This article does not aim to make good the deficit but to outline the basic principles of direct effect (I), the individual provisions of environment directives which have a direct effect (II) and some conclusions which can be reached concerning the field of national law (III).

I. The Direct Effect of Directives

1. The Case Law of the Court of Justice

Unlike Community regulations, which are directly applicable, a directive is binding on the Member State to which it is addressed with respect to the objective to be achieved

---

†The basic ideas of this paper formed the subject of a lecture given on 16 September 1989 at a workshop organized at Imperial College, London by R. Macrory and P. Kromarek on 'The direct effect of EEC environmental directives'. The views expressed are those of the author alone.

*Head, Application of Community Law, Directorate General XI (Environment, Nuclear Safety and Civil Protection), European Commission, Brussels.

[1] Case 41/71 *van Duyn* (1974) ECR 1337; Case 148/78 *Ratti* (1979) ECR 1629; Case 8/81 *Becker* (1982) ECR 53; Case 103/84 *Costanzo* (1988) ECR 339.

[2] The first environmental protection directive was adopted on 16 June 1975 and concerns waste oil disposal (Directive 75/439) OJ L 194/75, 23. Even before this however, directives with environmental content were adopted under Community programmes to dismantle technical trade barriers, eg the directives on pollutant and noise emissions of vehicles, on detergents and chemicals.

[3] B. Jadot, 'Le justiciable et l'inexécution, en droit belge, des directives européenes en matière d'environne-

but leaves the national authorities free to choose how and in what form to implement it (Article 189, third paragraph, EEC Treaty). It often happens that an individual citizen, company or environmental protection group is affected only by the implementing measure adopted by the Member State, whereby rights or obligations are defined.

In considering whether there are rights, in the broadest sense, accruing to the individual from a directive if a Member State has failed to transpose, or transpose correctly, the provisions of a directive into national law, the Court argues that directives contain obligations for the Member States to take or refrain from certain actions. A Member State cannot avoid this obligation by failing to adopt the necessary implementing measures by the relevant deadline or in a correct manner. The core philosophy of the Court's case law is hence a *venire contra factum proprium* of the Member State.[4]

The obligation to act arises from Community law, in particular from the relevant directive. Hence the primary obligation is towards the Community and it is a logical consequence that, in the event of any irregularity relating to measures for implementing a directive, Article 169 of the EEC Treaty provides for the initiation of infringement proceedings by the Commission against the offending Member State.

A directive can also, however, protect an individual, or confer advantages or rights upon him. Article 13 of Directive 77/388,[5] on which Case 8/81 was based,[6] provided for a zero tax rating for the granting and negotiation of credit. After Germany had failed to transpose the directive into national law by the stated deadline, the legal dispute arose as to whether a person granting or negotiating credit could rely on Article 13 of Directive 77/388 and thereby demand exemption from value added tax, or whether the German finance authorities were correct in continuing to apply the differently worded existing German tax rules. Case 103/88 involved a similar situation:[7] Community law required that a public contract be awarded on principle to the least costly bid tendered. Italy had not transposed the relevant directive into national law. An Italian law made it possible to pass over the least costly bid in certain cases which were not provided for by the directive and hence award the contract to the second lowest bidder.

In the preliminary proceedings in both cases, the Court supported the possibility, in accordance with Article 177 of the EEC Treaty, of the individual's relying on the content of the directive. The key sentences of its statement of reasons are as follows:[8]

It follows from well-established case-law of the Court . . . (that) wherever the provisions of a directive appear, as far as their subject-matter is concerned, to be unconditional and sufficiently precise, those provisions may, in the absence of implementing measures adopted within the prescribed period, be relied upon . . . in so far as the provisions define rights which individuals are able to assert against the State.

The Court stated that any other interpretation would mean that the Member State could rid a directive of its binding effect simply by failing to implement it, or

---

ment', *Aménagement* (Belgium) 1987, 34ff. G. Winter: 'Die Vereinbarkeit des Gesetzentwurfs der Bundesregierung über die Umweltverträglichkeitsprüfung vom 29.6.1988 mit der EG-Richtlinie 85/337 und die Direktwirkung dieser Richtlinie,' *Natur und Recht* 1989, 197ff.

[4] Implicitly in Case 148/78 (FN 1), 1642.
[5] Directive 77/388 on a common system of value added tax, OJ L 145/77, 1.
[6] Case 8/81, (FN 1) *Becker.*
[7] Case 103/88 (FN 1) *Costanzo.*
[8] Case 152/84 (FN 1) *Marshall*, 748; Case 8/81 (FN 1) *Becker*, 71.

implement it correctly. That could not be reconciled, however, with the wording of the third paragraph of Article 189.

The Court's view of the effect of directives within national law, even where correct implementing measures are lacking, has gained wide acceptance: almost all national courts act in accordance with it. After the German Federal Fiscal Court abandoned its divergent legal stance under the influence of the Federal Constitutional Court's decision,[9] the French Council of State now appears to be alone in refusing to accept the direct effect of directives in national law; even this stance has recently shown signs of changing as the Council of State is altering its attitude towards the effect of international agreements in French law.

2. *Conditions for Direct Effect*

The terms used by the Court vary even though it usually talks of the 'direct effect' of individual provisions of Community law.[10] For such effects to be felt, the directive's provisions must be precise and unconditional. It should, however, be remembered that the issue is not whether a directive as a whole is precise and unambiguous. Each individual article, and possibly each subparagraph or single sentence, must be looked at separately in relation to the issue of immediate effect.

(a) In deciding whether a provision in a directive is sufficiently precise or clear, consideration has to be given to whether it formulates a sufficiently clear legal position, ie makes conditions and consequences of the facts of the matter clear. A provision *may* confer rights or positions protected in law, but as the directive is addressed to the Member State, this is not necessarily the case. Article 13 of Directive 77/388 quoted above expressly required the Member States to exempt certain transactions from taxation. The Court considered the provisions to be sufficiently precise, however, to ascribe direct effect to them. In Case 380/87[11] the Court took into account the objective of the directive—approximation of laws and protection of the environment from waste—and concluded that no single provision of the directive entitled the individual to use or place on the market plastic bags which were not biodegradable.

In Case 14/83[12] the Court considered the ban on discriminating against women at work as being sufficiently precise. As regards the provision that all persons who considered themselves wronged by sex discrimination had to be able to pursue their claims by judicial process, however, the Court did not consider it to be sufficiently precise for deciding whether specific sanctions could necessarily be inferred from the provision, because, although claims for compensation, fines or similar sanctions might come into consideration in addition to a job offer as a sanction for discrimination in an interview, the directive did not prescribe a specific sanction here.

Thus although it can be inferred from the decision that a Member State contravenes the directive's provisions if it fails to provide for sanctions or for effective sanctions, a claim to a specific sanction cannot be inferred from the directive itself. Advocate General Reischl expressed a similar view in Case 148/78[13] when he declared that a

---

[9] Federal Constitutional Court 75 223 (Credit brokers).
[10] See regarding terminological difficulties R. Kovar, 'Das Verhältnis des Gemeinschaftsrechts zum nationalen Recht,' in: *Kommission (Hrsg): Dreissig Jahre Gemeinschaftsrecht*, Bruxelles-Luxembourg, 119ff (152).
[11] Case 380/87 *Enichem*, judgment of 13 July 1989 as yet unpublished.
[12] Case 14/83 *Colson* (1984) ECR 1907.
[13] Advocate General Reischl, Case 148/78 (FN 1), 1650, *Ratti*.

42   LUDWIG KRAMER

provision of a directive had direct effect if it left the Member States no margin of discretion in the performance of their obligations.

(b) In order to have direct effect, a Community provision must also be unconditional. It must not require additional rulings or measures to be adopted by the Member States in its field of application in order to be effective. This, too, may be explained by the provision on which Case 8/81[14] is based. According to the relevant provision of Directive 77/388 'Member States shall exempt (specific transactions from value added tax) under conditions which they shall lay down for the purpose of ensuring the correct and straightforward application of the exemptions and of preventing any possible evasion, avoidance or abuse'. The Court based its argument definitively on the fact of taxability. If a taxable person could show that he was entitled to exemption within the terms of the directive, the State could not argue in return that it had not yet adopted the provisions for simplifying their application and preventing abuse. The rules laid down by the directive were thus sufficiently unconditional.

It is clear that not all the provisions of the 170 or so Community directives on environmental protection have direct effects. Environment law is a classic area where there are 'instructions' to the authorities to draw up rehabilitation plans, take measurements, establish conditions for the application of modern technologies for environmental protection, etc. The role of the individual in Community environment law, it would appear, has barely been examined; the best this paper can do is cast further light on the area. From a general viewpoint, however, it seems reasonable to say that Community legislation makes environmental protection largely the authorities' responsibility. Nevertheless it would not be out of place, as I hope to show below, to examine the environment directives to find which of their provisions have direct effect.

II. Environment Directives with Direct Effect

1. Maximum Values, Maximum Concentrations and Limit Values

A first group of provisions with direct effect in the light of Court rulings concerns provisions that lay down maximum values for permissible discharges, ie limit values, emission values, etc.

(a) An example of this in the field of protection of the aquatic environment is Directive 76/464[15] and its derived directives, of which Directive 83/513 on cadmium discharges[16] is presented by way of illustration. This Directive lays down limit values and quality objectives for cadmium discharges to the aquatic environment. Limit values are values that may not be exceeded by the emission standards for the individual plants. Since 1 January 1989 a limit value of 0.2 milligrams of cadmium per litre of water discharged has been in force for plants manufacturing cadmium compounds; a maximum of 0.5 grams of cadmium may be discharged per kilogram of cadmium handled.

These values are precise, unconditional and not dependent on any further action by the Council or the Member States. Consequently, they have been applicable since the

---

[14] Case 8/81 (FN 1) *Becker.*

[15] Directive 76/464 on pollution caused by certain dangerous substances discharged into the aquatic environment of the Community, OJ L 129/76, 23.

[16] Directive 83/513 on cadmium discharges, OJ L 291/83, 1.

THE IMPLEMENTATION OF COMMUNITY ENVIRONMENTAL DIRECTIVES   43

beginning of 1989 in the Community even where a Member State has not taken corresponding implementing measures.

Article 6(3) of Directive 76/464, permits Member States in exceptional cases to establish quality objectives in place of the limit values. Quality objectives contain values that may not be exceeded in the air, water or soil. Directive 83/513 specifies a number of quality objectives in Annex II, No 1.1–1.3, from among which the Member States' competent authority selects the appropriate objective. The differences do not relate to the values to be selected, but to the environment medium water, ie inland surface waters (No 1.1), estuary waters (No 1.2) and territorial waters and internal coastal waters (No 1.3). If several quality objectives are applicable to the waters of an area, the quality of the water must conform to each of these objectives (Annex II, No 4). Thus in practice the competent authority does not have discretion to select, but must establish one or several of the specified quality objectives for the waters concerned. These quality objectives are also precise and unconditional: 'The concentration of dissolved cadmium in estuary waters . . . must not exceed 5 µg/l' (Annex II, No 1.2). The quality objectives are therefore also directly applicable.

The Community legislation on discharges of mercury, HCH, carbon tetrachloride, DDT, pentachlorophenol, aldrin, dieldrin, endrin, isodrin, hexachlorobenzene, hexachlorobutadiene and chloroform,[17] like the provisions on cadmium discharges, also have direct effect.

Directive 80/778 on the quality of water intended for human consumption[18]—drinking water and water used in food preparation—does not contain limit values, but maximum admissible concentrations for certain undesirable substances in water. These concentrations may not be exceeded. The provisions of the Directive are precise and unconditional. There can therefore be no reasonable doubt that they also apply directly. This is not in any way diminished by the fact that Article 9 permits derogations from the Directive in order to take account of situations arising from the nature and structure of the ground in the area or situations arising from exceptional meteorological conditions, and that Article 10 permits the maximum admissible concentrations to be exceeded in emergencies. Both cases concern instances of *force majeure* or natural phenomena outside the scope of human (pollutant) activity which do not affect the fundamental requirement to observe the maximum admissible concentrations.[19]

(b) The Community has also established limit values for air pollution, concerning sulphur dioxide, suspended particulates,[20] lead[21] and nitrogen dioxide.[22] The Directives in question specify explicitly that these limit values may not be exceeded in the whole of Member States' territory. Establishment of the limit values is not subject to

[17] Directive 82/176 on mercury discharges from the chlor-alkali electrolysis industry, OJ L 81/82, 29; Directive 84/156 on other mercury discharges, OJ L 74/84, 49; Directive 84/491 on HCH discharges, OJ L 274/84, 11; Directive 86/280 on discharges of carbon tetrachloride, DDT and pentachloraphenol, OJ L 181/86, 16; Directive 88/347 on discharges of aldrin, dieldrin, endrin, isodrin, hexachlorobenzene, hexachlorobutadiene and chloroform, OJ L 158/88, 35.

[18] Directive 80/778 on the quality of water for human consumption, OJ L 229/80, 11.

[19] Article 20 of Directive 80/778 is not mentioned here, as it concerns only cases of a longer compliance period than Article 19, and after expiry on 17 July 1985 of the Article 19 deadline the term 'longer period' is no longer applicable.

[20] Directive 80/779 on air quality limit values and guide values for sulphur dioxide and suspended particulates, OJ L 229/80, 23.

[21] Directive 82/884 on a limit value for lead in the air, OJ L 378/82, 15.

[22] Directive 85/203 on air quality standards for nitrogen dioxide, OJ L 87/85, 1.

conditions, and the Member States have no discretionary scope. Consequently the air quality limit values are directly applicable.

Directive 87/217[23] requires Member States to take the necessary measures to ensure that the concentration of asbestos emitted through discharge ducts into the air does not exceed a limit value of 0.1 mg/m^3. Here, too, the provision is precise, unconditional and complete.[24]

It should be noted that, while the limit values for air pollution apply directly as such, Member States have freedom to decide how they intend to comply. It remains for them to decide whether they prohibit the location of new industrial plant in certain areas, set up a district heating system, require the installation of filters to reduce emissions, restrict motor vehicle traffic, etc.[25] Hence the obligation to comply with the limit values does not, as a rule, imply the obligation to take a specific measure. This will be the case only if a specific measure results, or threatens in the light of practical experience to result, in the limit values being exceeded. This then gives rise to obligations on the Member State to take or desist from, certain action.

2. *Prohibitions*

(a) Another group of environment directives prohibit using certain substances or discharging them to the environment. Such prohibitions are generally couched in absolute terms and thus meet the requirements of direct effect. Examples are the prohibition on the marketing of certain substances and preparations,[26] and the prohibition of the use of benzene in toys[27] or of PBB.[28]

(b) Such prohibitions also include the provisions on the disposal of waste and hazardous waste.[29] Article 5 of Directive 78/319 on toxic and dangerous waste[30] shall be discussed here as an example. It reads:

Member States shall take the necessary measures to ensure that toxic and dangerous waste is disposed of without endangering human health and without harming the environment, and in particular:
—without risk to water, air, soil, plants or animals;
—without causing a nuisance through noise or odours;
—without adversely affecting the countryside or places of special interest.

Hazardous wastes must therefore be disposed of without risk to man or the environment. Uncontrolled discharge, dumping and transport of waste is not permissible. The provisions are unambiguous, both with regard to the wording and their spirit and purpose. They do not allow Member States a discretionary margin eg to permit a

---

[23] Directive 87/217 on the prevention and reduction of environmental pollution by asbestos, OJ L 85/87, 40.

[24] In support of a direct effect also I. Pernice, 'Auswirkungen des europäischen Binnermarktes auf das Umweltrecht', presentation for the 13th annual meeting of the German Environmental Issues Society on 23 November 1989 in Berlin (publication in preparation) MS 52.

[25] Directive 79/117 on the prohibition of plant protection products containing certain active ingredients, OJ L 33/79, 36.

[26] Directive 85/467, OJ L 269/85, 56.

[27] Directive 82/806, OJ L 339/82, 85.

[28] Directive 83/264, OJ L 147/83, 9.

[29] Directive 75/442 on waste, OJ L 194/75, 47; Directive 76/403 on the disposal of PCTs and PCPs, OJ L 108/76, 41; Directive 78/319 on toxic and dangerous waste, OJ L 84/78, 43; Directive 84/631 on transfrontier movements of hazardous waste, OJ L 324/84, 31.

[30] See FN 29; it is remarkable that Article 2 of Directive 75/439 on waste oil disposal as amended by Directive 87/101 refers only to 'avoidable damage to man and the environment', see OJ L 194/75, 23 and OJ L 42/87, 43.

method of waste disposal that poses a risk to human health. They are sufficiently precise and clear, and hence have direct effect.

(c) Pursuant to Directive 80/68,[31] Member States shall prohibit 'all direct discharge of substances in List I' into ground water. This unqualified prohibition leaves no scope for any decision on the part of Member States. However, the situation is different for indirect discharges of List I substances ie introduction into ground water of substances after percolation through the ground or subsoil. In this case, Member States must take 'all appropriate measures they deem necessary to prevent any indirect discharge of substances in List I' into ground water.[32] This provision does not have direct effect to the extent that Member States clearly have a certain latitude.

It is clear that provisions which merely enable Member States to prohibit certain products or activities do not have direct effect, because Member States retain their latitude. This includes Directive 87/416,[33] which permits Member States to prohibit regular leaded petrol.

(d) The view is increasingly taken in the German literature in particular on Article 100a of the EEC Treaty that a Member State, even after the adoption of Community environmental protection legislation based on Article 100a, may take more stringent measures should it deem them to be necessary.[34] I consider this view to be incorrect; this controversy cannot be discussed in depth here.[35] In the final analysis, it will be for the Court to decide on the scope of Article 100a. However, even if the opposite view were to be accepted, this interpretation of Article 100a would not lend support to a negation of the direct effect of clear and unconditional Community provisions. Member States' right to apply stricter measures to protect the environment pursuant to Article 100a(4) of the EEC Treaty (that is the dissenting opinion—in my view, this provision gives Member States the right only to continue applying existing protective measures) does not affect the exact and unconditional character of product-related provisions to protect the environment. Consequently, Article 100a(4) of the EEC Treaty does not influence whether a Community provision has direct effect.

(e) Directive 83/129[36] requires Member States to ensure that fur skins and other products derived from pups of harp seals and hooded seals are not commercially imported into their territory. The prohibition is unconditional and sufficiently precise. It therefore has direct effect.

Pursuant to Article 5 of Directive 79/409 on the conservation of wild birds,[37] Member States are required to take the necessary steps to prohibit the following measures to protect bird species:

—deliberate killing or capture by any method;
—deliberate destruction of, or damage to, their nests and eggs;
—taking their eggs in the wild and keeping these eggs even if empty;
—keeping birds of species the hunting and capture of which is prohibited.

[31] Directive 80/68 on the protection of ground water, OJ L 20/80, 43.
[32] Directive 80/68 (FN 31) Article 4.
[33] Directive 87/416, OJ L 225/87, 33.
[34] See instead Scheuing, 'Umweltschutz auf der Grundlage der Einheitlichen Europäischen', *Akte, Europarecht* 1989, S. 152ff. with further refs.
[35] See instead Langeheine, 'Le rapprochement des législations nationales selon l'article 100A du Traité CEE: l'harmonisation communautaire face aux exigences nationales', *Revue du Marché Commun* 1989, 347ff with further refs.
[36] Directive 83/129 on imports of seal skins, OJ L 91/83, 30.
[37] Directive 79/409 on the conservation of wild birds, OJ L 103/79, 1.

46   LUDWIG KRAMER

Article 6 of Directive 79/409 prohibits the sale and offering for sale of live or dead birds, except for the birds listed in Annex III to the Directive. Article 7 prohibits the hunting of birds other than those referred to in Annex II. Article 8 prohibits means of hunting and methods of capture used 'for the large-scale or non-selective capture or killing of birds', in particular the means, arrangements or methods listed in Annex IV.

All these provisions are clear and unambiguous and not dependent on the implementation of any other condition.[38] The full scope of Article 4(4) of Directive 79/409 has not yet been determined. It states: 'In respect of the protection areas referred to in paragraphs 1 and 2 above, Member States shall take appropriate steps to avoid pollution or deterioration of habitats or any disturbances affecting the birds, insofar as these would be significant having regard to the objectives of this Article. Outside these protection areas, Member States shall also strive to avoid pollution or deterioration of habitats'. Member States are therefore required to avoid pollution and deterioration of habitats and significant disturbances of the birds in the protection areas coming within the scope of paragraphs 1 and 2 of Article 4. This provision, too, is clear and unconditional. The Member States' obligation is not contingent on any discretionary margin. In particular, a balancing of ecological and economic considerations is not permitted. Article 2 of the Directive, it is true, does refer in general terms to the requisite measures to be taken by Member States to conserve birds and mentions that account is to be taken of 'economic and recreational requirements'. However, Article 2 is specifically not referred to again in Article 4, while it is mentioned in Article 3. Consequently, the Court rightly did not regard the economic considerations of Article 2 as a general principle restricting the scope of the various Articles of the Birds Directive.[39] On this interpretation, the requirement to prevent pollution or deterioration of habitats or significant disturbance of the birds also has direct effect. The situation is different, of course, for measures outside protection areas.

In this case, sentence 2 of Article 4(4) requires Member States in general terms to take action to protect birds. Sentence 2 therefore does not have direct effect in view of the margin of discretion it leaves in the performance of obligations.

3. *Obligations to Act*

A number of directives require Member States or the competent authorities to perform certain acts.

(a) These concern primarily the obligation to draw up and carry out rehabilitation programmes or plans. Such provisions are found in Directive 75/440 on surface waters,[40] Directive 76/464 on pollution of the aquatic environment,[41] and the Directives on air quality limit values,[42] although here, too, the rehabilitation programmes need only be drawn up for certain areas particularly at risk. In addition, pursuant to Directive 84/360,[43] Member States must draw up programmes for the introduction of the best available technology to combat air pollution. Directives 75/442 on waste[44] and

---

[38] See European Parliament Resolution of 13 October 1988, OJ C 290/88, 1.
[39] Case 247/85 *Commission* v *Belgium* (1987) ECR 3029.
[40] Directive 75/440 on surface water quality, OJ L 194/75, 35, Article 4.
[41] Directive 76/464 (FN 15), Article 7.
[42] Directive 80/779 (FN 20), Article 3; Directive 82/882 (FN 21), Article 3; Directive 85/203 (FN 22), Article 3.
[43] Directive 84/360 on the combatting of air pollution from industrial plants, OJ L 188/84, 20, Article 13.
[44] Directive 75/442 (FN 29), Article 6.

78/319 on toxic and dangerous waste[45] require Member States to draw up waste disposal plans and programmes, and Directive 85/339[46] requires them to draw up programmes to reduce waste arising from drinks packaging. These provisions in the various directives are sufficiently precise; as a rule, the obligation to draw up and implement the programmes does not depend on any further condition.[47] Nevertheless, the provisions are not directly applicable in accordance with Community legislation. It is obvious that the content of a national rehabilitation plan will depend on the political objectives of the respective Member State. It will depend on the circumstances in an individual Member State whether a national programme to reduce waste arisings from drinks packaging prohibits a certain type of packaging, introduces a deposit system for bottles, imposes an environment tax or levy on certain packages, eg plastic containers, promotes or specifies separate collection of certain types of packaging or relies on legislative or voluntary measures. All of these measures are equally valid so long as they achieve the objective set by Directive 85/339 which, from the environment standpoint, is modest enough. It is therefore impossible, in the absence of such national rehabilitation programmes, to ascribe a direct effect to the provision is a question capable of having consequences in the respective Member State. Consequently, at most the Commission can initiate the Article 169 procedure against a Member State whose competent authorities, in contravention of the Directive, have failed to draw up such plans or programmes.[48]

(b) By contrast, other obligations to act have direct effect. Article 3 of Directive 85/337[49] specifies, for example, that an environmental impact assessment must be carried out for certain public or private projects. At least as far as the projects of Annex I to the Directive are concerned, this obligation is not subject to any preconditions. The clear obligation incumbent on the authorities to carry out an environmental impact assessment before approving to project that falls within the scope of Annex I to the Directive, and to take account of the results in making its decision (Article 8) does not necessarily mean that the impact assessment will be carried out. However, the question concerns the legal consequences arising from the direct applicability of a provision. As will be shown below, failure to comply with directly applicable Community provisions has consequences (sanctions) in that the administrative decision on carrying out the project can be contested or declared invalid, or can lead to criminal, disciplinary to administrative consequences including liability for damages owing to breach of duty.

Directive 85/337 on environmental impact assessment also provides that the public concerned is to be consulted when an impact study is carried out.[50] The Directive does not contain any proviso. Involvement of the public is therefore obligatory in the case of such projects. If consultation is omitted in a case where it is obligatory under Community law, the comments above apply.

---

[45] Directive 78/319 (FN 29), Article 12.

[46] Directive 85/339 on packaging for liquids for human consumption, OJ L 176/85, 18, Article 3.

[47] The situation is different in the directives referred to in n42, which establish limit values for air pollution. Here there is a duty to draw up rehabilitation programmes only for those areas in which Member States consider it necessary. However, the directives also specify that, if the limit values are exceeded, Member States must take measures to prevent a repetition.

[48] See the first annual report of the Commission for Directive 80/779 (FN 20).

[49] Directive 85/337 on environmental impact assessment, OJ L 195/85, 40.

[50] Directive 85/337 (FN 49), Article 6.

48   LUDWIG KRAMER

(c) Article 9 of Directive 84/360[51] establishes comparable conditions, specifying that the public is to be informed of applications for authorization of certain plant likely to cause air pollution, and of the authorizations granted. Article 8 of Directive 82/501 on major-accident hazards[52] specifies that the employees and population in the vicinity must be informed in an appropriate manner of safety measures, correct behaviour in the event of an accident, etc. This provision is also exact, precise and clear. It states in detail the information that is to be supplied and therefore has direct effect.

III. Consequences of Direct Applicability

1. The Case Law of the Court of Justice

The Court has in consistent rulings set out the legal consequences of direct applicability of the provisions of a directive: all national authorities are required to take steps to implement the Community provision.[53] If a measure incorporating the Community provision into national law is lacking, the Community provision is to be applied as if it had been so incorporated. Where necessary, national provisions that contradict Community legislation are to be set aside and not applied. The same applies in cases in which the Community provision has not been incorporated correctly or in full. In this case, too, it follows from well-established case law that Member States have the duty to give the Community provision legal force.

Most of the Court judgments concerned decisions in which individuals cited provisions of Community law in national courts to contest the validity of national provisions. It was deduced directly or indirectly that the direct effect of directives in national law was particularly relevant in legal proceedings. However, this interpretation is too narrow.

The public authorities have a prominent role in environmental law. Member States have to a large extent invested the authorities with the task of protecting the environment; they attempt to carry out this task with authorizations, permits, prohibitions and other measures. Laws frequently do no more than specify a framework, which has to be filled out with individual decisions. In many Member States, environmental protection through the courts has a subordinate role, because pollution of rivers or ground water, lakes and oceans or the air, the disappearance of species or the destruction of habitats do not normally infringe any rights of the individual *vis-à-vis* the authorities, and the law does not normally allow civil action serving as a test case or action in the public interest. A legal system created by and for human beings can scarcely grant that nature has its own rights, at least in so far as a just balancing of conflicting interests is concerned.

The duty derived from Community law, of all authorities in all Member States, to apply those provisions of Community law that have direct effect in the sense described above, is all the more significant. The Court has taken this view for years, but possibly not always expressed it with the requisite clarity. It only recently had the opportunity to make its position clear.

Case 103/88[54], referred to above, concerned—in simplified terms—Article 29(5) of

---

[51] Directive 84/360 (FN 43), Article 7.
[52] Directive 82/501 on major accident hazards of certain industrial activities, OJ L 230/82, 1, Article 8.
[53] See the Court decisions referred to in FN 1.
[54] Case 103/88 (FN 1) *Costanzo*.

Directive 71/305,[55] which required Member States to take account of the most favourable offer in contract award procedures. However, an Italian specification provided in certain cases for the least costly offer to be disregarded and the second-best offer to be chosen.

The Milan local authority cited this Italian provision in a tendering procedure and awarded the contract to the second most favourable bidder. The least costly bidder who had not been chosen, appealed. The matter was submitted to the Court for a preliminary ruling pursuant to Article 177 of the EEC Treaty.

The Court decided that Article 29(5) was sufficiently precise and unconditional to have direct effect. The individual could therefore, so the Court, cite this provision against the State. This applied initially in actions before the national courts. However, it also applied with regard to all other state bodies, ie the authorities including local authorities. Conversely, all public authorities were required to apply Article 29(5) of the Directive on their own initiative. It would be contradictory to grant the individual only the right to cite the direct effect of a provision in legal proceedings designed to give legal protection against administrative acts, but not to require the authorities for their part to observe the provision of Community law. The Court stated in its judgment:

An authority, including a local authority, has the same duty as a national court to apply Article 29(5) of Council Directive 71/305 and not to apply those provisions of national law that are incompatible with it.

2. *Consequences for Environmental Protection*

Applied to the environment sector, this means that all national administrative authorities and the national courts have the duty to give legal force to those Community provisions that have direct effect. National laws, regulations or administrative provisions incompatible with Community environment provisions that are directly applicable have to be set aside.

The consequences of this interpretation of Community law are extremely far reaching. They can only be indicated briefly here for a few sectors:

— The authorities must conduct environmental impact assessments pursuant to Directive 85/337[56] even if there is no national legislation in place. The public concerned has to be consulted in the consent procedure. The considerations submitted must be taken into account in the decision.
— The authorities act unlawfully if they allow households to be supplied with drinking water that exceeds the maximum admissible concentrations for undesirable substances pursuant to Directive 80/778.[57] Decisions by local or regional councils permitting such deviations in contravention of the Community rules are to be disregarded.
— The authorities have to ensure that waste, and in particular hazardous waste, is disposed of without risk to man and the environment, in particular without damage to fauna and flora, odour or noise nuisance, etc.
— The authorities must ensure that applications from plants covered by Directive 84/360[58] for consents and the decisions of the competent authorities in respect of emissions to the air are notified to the public concerned.

[55] Directive 71/305 on award procedures for public construction projects, OJ L 185/71, 5.
[56] Directive 85/337 (FN 49).   [57] Directive 80/778 (FN 18).   [58] Directive 84/360 (FN 43), Article 6.

Problems may arise when the authority's duty to apply Community provisions and refrain from applying incompatible national regulations results in stricter requirements being imposed on individuals. A developer has to provide certain documentation pursuant to Directive 85/337,[59] which would not be required in a consent procedure without environmental impact assessment. In Case 103/88[60] the second most favourable bidder had the right under Italian law to the contract from the Milan authority. If the local authority disregards Italian law owing to the precedence of Community law, it is to this extent acting to the detriment of the second most favourable bidder. However, this action only appears to be to his detriment. The second most favourable bidder is not, in objective terms, being disadvantaged as a result of application by the Milan authority of established law—which of course also includes Community law— and a decision in accordance with proper legal principles.

Similarly, an authority is not imposing a burden on an individual when, for the purposes of a consent procedure, it calls for the requisite documentation pursuant to Article 5(1) of Directive 85/337[61] in order to carry out an environmental impact assessment. It has been obligatory to supply such documentation for projects subject to environmental impact assessment since the entry into force of Directive 85/337 on 3 July 1988. It is not, therefore, the demand from the authorities that imposes a burden on the developer, but the burden follows from the direct applicability of Directive 85/337.

The Court has ruled on several occasions that directives do not have direct effects that impose a burden on individuals.[62] However, these decisions concerned only cases revolving round the question of whether individuals are acting unlawfully by failing to comply with the provisions of a directive that has not, or not properly, been incorporated in national law,[63] or whether directives also create rights—and obligations—on the part of private individuals.[64] The question of the application of Community law by authorities in these cases has still to be decided. However, the conclusion to be inferred from Case 103/88[65] is that an authority must apply the provisions of Community law, even if this imposes additional burdens on individuals. Consequently, the directly applicable provision of a directive is equivalent in its effect to a regulation.

When such cases damage—in the broadest sense—the interests of individuals, eg, loss of privileges, they must be settled in accordance with the principles of state liability, breach of official duty, etc.[66] The Court will doubtless have the opportunity to expand and clarify its case law in this sector.

The obligation to ensure that Community environment provisions with direct effect can be implemented in full is incumbent on all state bodies, the legislator, judiciary and executive. There can be no distinction according to whether the public authority is acting in a sovereign capacity. The UK Government raised such an objection in a lawsuit regarding equal rights for women.[67] The UK Government argued that, when the state acts in the role of employer rather than of sovereign power, it should not be

---

[59] Directive 85/337 (FN 49), Article 6.
[60] Case 103/88 (FN 1) *Costanzo*.
[61] Directive 85/337 (FN 49).
[62] Case 148/78 (FN 1) *Ratti*; Case 152/84 (FN 1) *Marshall*; Case 80/86 (FN 1) *Kolpinghuis*.
[63] Case 148/78 (FN 1) *Ratti*; Case 80/86 (FN 1) *Kolpinghuis*.
[64] Case 1152/84 (FN 1) *Marshall*.
[65] Case 103/88 (FN 1) *Costanzo*.
[66] No case law on this issue.
[67] Case 152/84 (FN 1) *Marshall*.

bound by the direct applicability of directives, as it would otherwise be at a disadvantage compared with private employers.

The Court rejected this argument. The very principle of direct applicability of a Community provision was that the provision had not, or not properly, been incorporated in national law. This was the sole cause of the discriminatory treatment of private and public employers objected to by the UK Government. The defaulting Member State therefore had the means itself to eliminate any discrimination within its territory by applying the Directive correctly.

Applied to the environment sector, this means that it is not only the local and regional authorities, ministries and government departments that have the duty to enforce directly applicable Community environment provisions, but equally it is incumbent on municipal undertakings, public corporations and institutions, schools, universities, hospitals, public utilities, etc.

3. Obligations of the Authorities

Erich Kästner's saying that 'Es gibt nichts Gutes—ausser man tut es', which translates roughly as action speaks louder than words, means that environment legislation is effective (only) where it is applied in day to day environment issues. The concept of 'soft law' developed in the Anglo-American system characterizes many provisions of environment law. Declarations and resolutions, international agreements and national, constitutional or legal provisions on protecting the environment are frequently no more than legal declamations, 'greenspeak', a piece of windowdressing that does nothing to stop the ongoing environmental degradation.

The provisions of Community directives on environmental protection constitute legal norms even where they do not have direct effect. It follows that they have to be applied in the Member States. Member States are accordingly required to provide for legal consequences to ensure that the provisions are applied 'in the field'. It is left to the individual Member State to decide on the form of these sanctions under civil, criminal or public law. The only requirement is that the consequences should be sufficiently severe to ensure that the law is in fact obeyed.[68] The legal consequences (sanctions) in national law for comparable offences can serve as a yardstick. If, for example, national law provides for fines or imprisonment for the unlawful marketing of certain products, a similar penalty will also be appropriate for violations of Community prohibitions. If national law normally considers a decision based on a faulty authorization procedure to be null and void, the same principle must be applied where a consent procedure was carried out without the obligatory environmental impact assessment. The detailed provisions of legal sanctions are also influenced by the equivalence of Community and national provisions: if the national authorization procedure does not have its own provisions on legal consequences but refers to a framework law on administrative procedure or to other administrative principles, such reference is also sufficient with regard to the legal consequences of infringement of Community law. If, however, national law contains specific provisions on the legal consequences, such provisions must also be provided for to deal with infringement of Community law.

It has already been explained that the direct effects of Community provisions apply to all branches of state authority. The administrative authority is therefore required to

---

[68] Case 14/83 (FN 12) *von Colson*; Case 79/83, *Harz* (1984) ECR 1921.

52   LUDWIG KRAMER

apply the provisions of Community law and, if need be, disregard conflicting national provisions. Failure to comply with directly applicable provisions makes the administrative act unlawful (faulty).

It is interesting to note in this context that an unlawful administrative measure in Belgium, Greece, Spain, France and Italy constitutes a breach of official duty, regardless of fault. By contrast, negligence of an official has to be proved in Germany, Ireland, Luxembourg, the Netherlands, Portugal and the United Kingdom. Furthermore, it must also be shown in Germany, Greece, Ireland, Italy, Portugal and the Netherlands that the infringed provision was adopted specifically in the interests of an injured party; such proof is not required in the other Member States.

It appears that, so far, the consequences resulting from the faulty nature of the authority's decision and the objective breach of legal and official duty have not been turned to the advantage of the environment in any Member State. Likewise, the principles of administrative and professional supervision, the powers of superior authorities to give instructions or the rights of monitoring bodies to enter complaints have so far scarcely been used to effect. Because provisions of directly applicable Community law form part of the system of established law that all branches of State authority are required to uphold, the executive authority, as Pernice explained in respect of Federal German law, 'also has the constitutional duty to ignore national legislation incompatible with Community law. Valid Community provisions—supersede contradictory federal and regional environment law, they virtually have constitutional status *vis-à-vis* national law'.[69]

For this reason, administrative provisions, general and specific instructions to lower authorities and other internal administrative measures are both appropriate and necessary wherever it has been established that directly applicable Community environment law has not been respected. Failure to apply provisions of directly applicable directives can probably be seen as breach of official duty.

4. *Right of action of individuals*

(a) The question of whether individuals or associations can initiate an administrative procedure or court action to enforce compliance with environmental provisions, does not solely depend on the content of the provision in question. For example, a ban on hunting certain birds can also be enforced by the authority invested with monitoring and supervisory powers, licensing rights and rights to issue instructions. If the authority fails in its obligation to enforce established law, options such as filing of complaints, petitions for administrative review, etc are available to have the law enforced depending on the gravity of the case. It is therefore not possible to say that right of action of individuals is the only way of having the prohibition deriving from Community law implemented.

If, however, the content of a Community legal norm is designed to protect individuals or associations or their rights, it would be a contradiction of the meaning and purpose of the legal norm if the beneficiaries were unable to enforce this protection by way of administrative procedure or through the courts.

These principles follow from Court rulings. In case 158/80[70] the plaintiffs had demanded before the national court that the authorities ensure observance of Com-

---

[69] Pernice, all other refs above (FN 24) Argument 3.
[70] Case 158/80 *Rewe v Hauptzollamt Kiel* (1981) ECR 1805; Case 68/79 Taxation of spirits (1980) ECR 501.

munity law. Advocate General Capotorti[71] stated that the distinction between civil action serving as a test case and other actions raised particular problems in all Member States. It could not be admissible to grant citizens the right to take action to enforce compliance with directly applicable Community provisions, because this would entail allowing such civil action in respect of Community law. The Court followed this interpretation and ruled that the admissibility of an action should be judged on the basis of national law. However, the Court made two specifications: firstly, a course of action must be possible under the same conditions as apply where respect of national law is concerned. Secondly, enjoyment of the rights and legal status granted by Community law may not be made impossible in practice. The guiding principle of the case law is therefore that the provisions of Community law should not *de facto* be left in a vacuum. At least where the intention is to protect the health and life of individuals, the parties concerned must have the scope to ensure that Community provisions are observed.

(b) The maximum admissible concentrations of undesirable substances in drinking water, as regulated by Directive 80/778,[72] may serve as an example. The Directive is intended to protect human health, ie protect the life and health of individuals. As maximum concentrations have been set that may not be exceeded, the Community legislator in adopting Directive 80/778[73] has established Community-wide standards for protection of the health of individuals. However, provisions intended to protect individuals—including where preventive health protection is concerned—are to a great extent rendered ineffective if the individual cannot on his own initiative enforce this protection *vis-à-vis* the authorities and in the courts. The protection of life and health is after all one of the most elementary human rights in all Member States.

It follows from this that individuals may also enforce their right to obtain supplies of drinking water that conform to Community rules in the courts. This right of action derives from Community law and therefore cannot be undermined or set aside by national provisions.[74] Consequently, the provision of the 1989 UK Water Act depriving individuals of the right to take court action against infringements of the provisions of the drinking water Directive or the corresponding UK implementing regulations is at variance with Community law.[75] It will therefore be interesting to see the outcome of the proceedings in the British courts initiated by British environmental protection groups.

The limit values for air quality, as for drinking water quality, were established with a view to protecting human health. Directive 80/779[76] states: 'in order to protect human health in particular, it is necessary to set for these two pollutants' (sulphur dioxide and suspended particulates) 'limit values which must not be exceeded in the territory of the Member States during specified periods; ... these values should be based on the findings reached in the framework of the WHO, particularly with regard to the dose/effect relationships ...'. Directive 82/884[77] also gives the 'protection of human health' as

---

[71] Advocate General Capotorti Case 158/80 (FN 70), 185.

[72] Directive 80/778 (FN 18).

[73] Directive 80/778 (FN 18); see also the wording of Article 36 EEC Treaty, which mentions the protection of human life and health, not public health.

[74] See page 40.

[75] Water Act 1989, c 15, in particular Article 20; Water Supply (Water Quality) Regulations 1989, SI 1989, No 1147, in particular Article 28, No 4.

[76] Directive 80/779 (FN 20). 4th consideration. [77] Directive 82/884 (FN 21) 3rd and 4th consideration.

the reason for introducing a limit value for lead. The limit value for nitrogen dioxide is justified in a wording similar to Directive 80/779.[78] It is clear on this basis that there are also rights of action against failure to observe air quality limit values.

Individuals also have a right of action in respect of Directive 85/337 on environmental impact assessment,[79] which gives the public concerned by a project covered by the Directive the right to have an environmental impact assessment carried out and a right to be consulted in this procedure. The purpose of this right is to ensure that the interests of the parties concerned are discussed and taken into account in the consent procedure. Were it not possible to assert this consultation right through the courts, the competent authority would be able to frustrate the interested parties' right simply by failing to carry out consultation, without having to fear consequences for the consent procedure.

Other rights that can be asserted by the parties concerned include the right of information pursuant to Article 8 of Directive 82/501,[80] and pursuant to Article 9 of Directive 84/360.[81] Finally, there is the obligation to dispose of waste without damaging the environment, in particular without putting human health at risk and without 'noise or odour nuisance'. The wording, meaning and purpose of these provisions of Directives 75/442[82] and 78/319[83] are clearly also aimed at protecting people living in the neighbourhood of waste disposal plants. Consequently, they have the right to enforce compliance with these provisions through the courts.

(c) Community law still has an impact even where the directly applicable provision of Community environment law does not grant the individual a personal right that he can assert through the courts. An example of this would be the *Becker* case[84] already mentioned, in which the credit broker stopped paying taxes, then contested the notice of assessment from her tax authorities and made the point in the court proceedings that the legal rule taken as justification by the tax authorities had become invalid on the entry into force of Directive 77/388. It is hard to imagine similar circumstances in the environment sector. At most it is conceivable that an individual supplied with drinking water that does not meet Community standards might reduce payment and claim that he had a right to supplies of drinking water that complied with existing legal provisions, to which the provisions of Directive 80/778 also belong.

(d) Finally, there are many provisions of Community environment law that have direct effect, but where individuals or environmental protection associations do not have a status permitting them to take action in national courts. An example of this is Directive 76/464 and the derived directives,[85] which regulate pollutant discharges to the aquatic environment and establish maximum permissible concentrations. A right of action on behalf of seals or fish in the event of the maximum concentrations being exceeded cannot be derived from Community law. Of course, there would be nothing to prevent the national or Community legislator from bringing in a capacity to sue or be sued of agents not directly involved in the subject matter of the action, to permit applications for injunctions or to introduce procedural rules enabling the courts to examine whether a certain conduct—of the administrative authorities, economic operators or polluters—objectively violates established environment law.

---

[78] Directive 85/203 (FN 22) 5th consideration. [79] Directive 85/337 (FN 49).
[80] Directive 85/501 (FN 52). [81] Directive 84/360 (FN 43).
[82] Directive 75/442 (FN 29). [83] Directive 78/319 (FN 29).
[84] Case 8/81 (FN 1) *Becker*. [85] Directive 76/464 (FN 15) and the derived directives referred to in FN 17.

5. Complaints to the EEC Commission

The complaints procedure in the framework of Article 169 of the EEC Treaty operates without any restriction to directly applicable provisions, personal rights and procedural questions. This enables any citizen to lodge a complaint with the Commission on the grounds that Community provisions to protect the environment are not, or not properly, applied. The complaint must be submitted in writing and be properly substantiated. Personal rights do not have to be impaired, it is sufficient to show that Community law is objectively being infringed. The Commission has undertaken to examine all such complaints. It made a declaration that is to appear on the back of a form designed to assist citizens assert their right of complaint:

The following administrative safeguards exist for the complainant's benefit:
— An acknowledgement of receipt will be sent to the complainant as soon as the complaint is registered;
— The complainant will be informed of the action taken in response to his complaint, including representations made to the national authorities, Community bodies or undertakings concerned;
— The complainant will be informed of any infringement proceedings that the Commission intends to institute against a Member State as a result of the complaint and of any legal action it intends to take against an undertaking. Where appropriate, the complainant will be informed of proceedings that have already been instituted in relation to the subject-matter of the complaint.[86]

The Commission therefore assumes the role of European environment ombudsman.[87] Where necessary, it initiates Treaty infringement proceedings pursuant to Article 169 of the EEC Treaty against a Member State which it finds to be violating Community provisions. The citizens of Europe are apparently making increasing use of the complaints procedure, as the following figures show:[88]

Year	1983	1984	1985	1986	1987	1988	1989
Number of complaints	8	11	36	150	138	190	465
Number of Article 169 proceedings	36	100	118	155	186	175	147

However important, useful and effective this procedure is, Community action cannot take the place of application of environment law at the local and regional level, as protecting the environment is basically something that has to be done 'on the spot'. Consequently, securing the direct effect of environment directives and their application in the legal procedures of Member States remains an important task.

IV. Conclusions

(1) Provisions of Community environment directives that are precise and unconditional have direct effect. They are valid in the legal system of Member States even if the

---

[86] Commission, OJ C 26/89, 6.
[87] Also Scheuing (FN 34), 192.
[88] See Commission, 7th annual report to Parliament on monitoring the application of Community law, OJ C 232/89, p. 35 and 59.

56   LUDWIG KRAMER

Member States have not, or not correctly, incorporated the Community provisions in national law.

(2) All state agencies have to respect provisions of directly applicable Community environment legislation. If necessary, they must set aside and not apply incompatible national law.

(3) Provisions of Community environment directives which have direct effect are in particular those which:

(a) lay down limit values, maximum levels or concentrations of substances in an environment medium or in another substance or product;

(b) prohibit certain activities or the use of certain substances;

(c) specify that the individuals or sections of the population concerned are to be informed or consulted.

It must be established in every individual case whether a provision has direct effect.

(4) Member States have the duty to incorporate provisions of Community environment legislation into national law in such a way that their application is effectively ensured. This includes providing for legal consequences (sanctions) in the event of the provision not being respected. These sanctions must be effective and appropriate and be equivalent to the legal consequences applying to contraventions of comparable national provisions.

(5) It depends on the content of the legal rule whether and to what extent individuals can enforce the direct effect of a provision of Community law in the courts. It is always possible to invoke the legislation as a defence. The enforcement of rights deriving from a provision of Community law depends on whether a right of action can be deduced from the overall context of the provision in Community environment legislation.

(6) The Commission investigates violations of Community environment legislation in response to complaints or on its own initiative, and initiates infringement proceedings pursuant to Article 169 of the EEC Treaty where necessary. The admissibility of environment complaints does not depend on infringement of directly protected rights or rights of the individual in relation to actions of the public authorities. In this respect the direct effect doctrine can never wholly replace the enforcement role of the Commission. Nevertheless, the doctrine can clearly be of immense significance in ensuring effective compliance of Community obligations within Member States, though its potential impact in the environmental field has scarcely yet been fully explored or appreciated.

[9]

The Implementation and Enforcement of European Community Environment Legislation

KEN COLLINS and DAVID EARNSHAW

The credibility and acceptability of European Community environment legislation depends to a large extent on its implementation 'on the ground'. This paper considers the problems facing member states when they come to implement Community environment legislation. In recent years greater attention has focused on this aspect of the EC environmental policy process.

The first and second sections of the study consider respectively the state of implementation in the member states and those characteristics of the Community legislative process which have an impact on implementation. The final two sections assess Community enforcement mechanisms and the means through which implementation may be improved. It is suggested that a centralised Community inspectorate, though probably desirable, is at present politically unrealistic if not possibly inappropriate. The development of the alternative 'inspection of inspectors' concept is outlined.

Policy implementation, like policy formulation, is a fundamentally political process on which the success or failure of individual policies depends. Nevertheless, decision-makers and public authorities in general tend to neglect policy implementation and policy delivery as they inevitably become absorbed in the legislative process itself. At European Community (EC) level this problem is particularly acute. On the one hand it is essential for the Commission to maintain the impetus of new legislation; on the other hand the relationship between the member states and the Community implies limitations on the role of Community institutions in policy implementation. Implementation is conducted at arm's length from the legislative process, with many decision points [*Pressman and Wildavsky, 1973*] existing between agreement of legislation and its implementation on the ground. EC environment policy is also relatively young and until the introduction of the Single European Act in 1987 lacked an explicit legal basis. This may have contributed to a climate in which Community policy makers concentrated on the creation of legislation at the expense of implementation [*Macrory, 1992:350*]. While the

214   A GREEN DIMENSION FOR THE EUROPEAN COMMUNITY

processes of initiation, scrutiny, amendment and agreement of EC environment legislation are important, Community legislation will not be worth the paper it is printed on if policies break down or obligations are not fulfilled at the implementation stage.

It is only in recent years that attention has started to focus on the implementation of EC environment legislation. In the Fourth Environmental Action Programme (1987–92) the Commission declared that henceforth it would place greater emphasis on the problem of implementation (and in its resolution on the Fourth Programme the Council of Ministers asked the Commission to send to it and Parliament regular reports on implementation); in the Fifth Environmental Action Programme a full chapter is devoted to implementation and enforcement. A number of well-publicised infringement proceedings commenced by the Commission against member states has also turned the spotlight on the implementation of environment legislation, as has the increasing number of complaints which are now made to the Commission about the poor implementation of EC environment legislation. Since 1988 the European Parliament has adopted no less than ten resolutions (seven on the basis of detailed reports) on the implementation of environment legislation. The European Summit in Dublin in June 1990 declared that 'Community environmental legislation will only be effective if it is fully implemented and enforced by member states', while in October 1991 an informal meeting of the environment Council of Ministers was devoted to implementation, at the instigation of the Dutch Presidency. The Maastricht treaty on European Union includes a declaration stating that 'each Member State should fully and accurately transpose into national law the Community directives addressed to it within the deadlines laid down therein', and in May 1992 the House of Lords Select Committee on the European Communities published a major report on the implementation and enforcement of EC environment legislation.

The implementation of EC environment legislation proved particularly controversial in the debate over the concept of subsidiarity that resulted from rejection of the Maastricht treaty in the Danish referendum in spring 1992. Given prominence in the Maastricht treaty, the principle of subsidiarity refers to the Community taking action 'only if and insofar as the objectives of the proposed action cannot be sufficiently achieved by the Member States and can therefore, by reason of the scale or effects of proposed action, be better achieved by the Community' (Treaty on European Union, article 3b). Some Community governments have been reported as interpreting subsidiarity in a way that could place relatively strict limits on the role of Community institutions, in particular the Commission, in monitoring and enforcing the implementation of Community law. As we shall see, however, the record of member states in implementing EC environment legislation might actually point to the need for rather greater Community intervention in its monitoring and enforcement.

The aims of this study are threefold: first, to examine why the implementation of EC environment legislation has taken on greater importance in recent years; second, to outline the reasons for inadequate implementation, where this occurs, of EC environment legislation by member states; and third, to assess possible mechanisms to improve the implementation of EC environment legislation. Many practitioners and commentators (see, for example, EP [*1990b*]; Clinton-Davis [*1992:201*]) have argued that improving member states' implementation of EC environment legislation is dependent on the creation of an EC environment inspectorate. However, it is suggested here that better implementation is not exclusively, as often portrayed, a matter of creating forthwith a centralised EC environment inspectorate in the strictest sense. No matter how desirable it is to monitor implementation and extend at EC level the mechanisms available for enforcement, such a proposal is probably politically unrealistic in the short to medium term.

The reasons for poor implementation of EC environment legislation are complex and diverse. Not least, the current structure of decision-making within the Community and the characteristics of public administration in the member states can have an important impact on the potential for successful implementation. The difficulties member states face in implementing environment legislation might only be partly ameliorated through increasing the Community's oversight of their activities. It will be seen, rather, that while Community involvement in implementation is necessary, an EC inspection function can be expected only to develop gradually and will need to work in cooperation with member states' own enforcement and inspection bodies.

The paper is divided into four sections. In the first section the state of implementation in the member states in set out. In the second those characteristics of the EC's legislative process that have an impact on the implementation of EC environment legislation are examined. The third section assesses Community enforcement mechanisms. Finally, this contribution examines ways in which the implementation of EC environment legislation might be improved.

The State of Implementation in the Member States

The implementation of EC environment legislation may be said to comprise three components. First, it entails the transposition into

216   A GREEN DIMENSION FOR THE EUROPEAN COMMUNITY

national law of Community directives by means of introducing and adapting national policies, legislation and administrative mechanisms to conform with EC law. Second, this formal legal transposition should lead to practical results and measurable impact. Hence, implementation entails more than merely the adoption of national legislation, even where it reflects perfectly the obligations contained in a directive [*Haigh, 1986a: 4*]. Finally, enforcement and monitoring mechanisms should exist to ensure that implementation is accurate and complete.

The 1980s have witnessed a dramatic increase in the volume of infringement proceedings brought by the Commission for member states' non-implementation of EC environment legislation. Table 1 reports infringement proceedings commenced against member states in the environment

TABLE 1
INFRINGEMENT PROCEEDINGS 1982–90

Year	Partial compliance	Non-notification	Poor Application	TOTAL
1982	1	15	–	16
1983	10	23	2	35
1984	15	48	2	65
1985	10	58	1	69
1986	32	84	9	125
1987	30	68	58	156
1988	24	36	30	90
1989	17	46	37	100
1990	24	131	62	217
TOTAL	163	509	201	873

Source: Eighth annual report to the European Parliament on Commission monitoring of the application of Community law, Dec. 1991.

sector. The table distinguishes between different kinds of failings in implementation: partial compliance indicates that the measures introduced at national level do not fully incorporate Community law; non-notification refers to those cases where member states have failed to notify the Commission of their national measures; while poor application refers to shortcomings in implementation in practice.

There has been a steep rise in infringement proceedings commenced due to non-notification. This reflects the increasing frequency with which member states have delayed implementing EC legislation. The directive

EC ENVIRONMENT LEGISLATION 217

on environmental impact assessment (85/337/EEC), for example, was required to be incorporated in national law by July 1988 but was only implemented during 1990 by Greece, Portugal and Germany and during 1991 by Luxembourg [*CEC, 1991a: 206*]. Of the nine environment directives which entered into force in 1990 the UK incorporated only one into national law by the appropriate date [*HL 53-I, 1992: 12*]. In practice few of the infringement proceedings commenced due to non-notification are pursued further as member states usually adopt national measures and forward them to the Commission.

Several factors may lead to national legislation failing to comply with EC measures. First, the range and complexity of existing national laws can lead to considerable difficulty when it is necessary for them to be adapted to the requirements of Community law. In the case of the UK over 20 items of legislation were required to implement the directive on environmental impact assessment (and in the Commission's view implementation still remained incomplete). As Macrory comments [*1992: 355*], some environment directives also 'cut across conventional boundaries of administrative and legal responsibility', which may lead to the need for national legislation to be adopted in different sectoral and jurisdictional areas. Second, concepts contained in many directives are 'bound to result in different definitions when given effect in each member state' [*HL 53-I, 1992: 14*].

Third, there is a variety of national and subnational administrative structures within the Community through which Community law must be implemented. Differences between member states are bound to result when their legislative and administrative processes are required to fulfil objectives set elsewhere. Fourth, member states' 'legislative culture' may also prevent early compliance with Community legislation. Member states may have a tradition of lengthy consultation aimed at building consensus; a concern for constitutional rectitude requiring time-consuming review of legislative proposals; or an emphasis on legal certainty encouraging highly detailed legislation [*IEEP, 1992a: 168*]. Finally, member states may also on occasion judge that non-compliance is politically expedient. The UK government's delay in both formally and practically implementing the drinking water directive is a prime example. In this case UK government policy was designed to create a more favourable climate for the privatisation of the water industry in England and Wales.

Federal and quasi-federal systems of government within member states can lead to particular difficulties in implementation. Two of the 12 member states (Germany and Belgium) are federations; in two others (Italy and Spain) the regions enjoy a substantial measure of autonomy.

218 A GREEN DIMENSION FOR THE EUROPEAN COMMUNITY

Implementation of EC legislation may be a source of tension between central government, responsible for negotiating legislation at EC level, and regional government, which often possesses competence for its formal and practical implementation. Local and regional authorities may be suspicious that EC legislation could centralise into a government's hands some powers that had previously been devolved to them [*Haigh, 1986b*]. In Germany, for example, environment policy is a policy area where some competition has tended to exist between Bonn and the Länder. The latter are conscious that EC legislation could reinforce the power of Bonn at the expense of their own [*Boehmer-Christiansen, 1992: 194*].

The gradual devolution of power in Belgium means that it is now the three regional governments – Flanders, Wallonia and Brussels – that are primarily responsible for transposing EC environment directives into law. Central government provides only national coordination of the implementation process. In some cases it seems that Belgian central government is even unaware of implementing measures adopted by the regions. In a case brought by the Commission against it for failure to notify measures implementing directive 76/403/EEC (on polychlorinated biphenyls and polychlorinated terphenyls), for example, Belgium did not mention in its defence regional rules known by the Commission to have been adopted but not officially notified [*CEC, 1991a: 209*]. Indeed, an added complication in Belgium is that some national measures remain in force in addition to regional legislation [*CEC, 1991a: 209*]. Sometimes central government has even annulled regulations established at regional level on the grounds that they impinge on its competences but then omitted to put national legislation in its place.

Infringement proceedings brought by the Commission demonstrate the existence of major differences between member states in their compliance with EC environment legislation. Table 2 reports the degree of infringement of Community environment legislation by member state. The table shows the procedures decided upon and current at the end of 1989. From the table it is clear that Greece, for example. has one of the best records for conformity of its national legislation with the require-ments of Community directives. This is due to the incorporation of the text of directives usually word for word into national law (a practice also followed by Ireland and Luxembourg). Nevertheless, Greece also records the second highest score for poor application and the highest score overall for non-notification. Measures are put in place slowly (though relatively accurately) and often fail 'on the ground', due to shortcomings in the application of legislation by regional and local administrations which lack qualified staff, equipment and other resources

EC ENVIRONMENT LEGISLATION 219

[*CEC, 1991a: 211*]. Similarly, the practical application of law is particularly poor in Spain and Italy; in the case of the latter the Commission [*CEC, 1991a: 213*] has stated rather bluntly that 'regional or local authorities often find it difficult to organise or monitor the effective application of the rules'. Though Portugal faces similar problems in the organisation of administration it seems nevertheless to have been relatively successful (see Table 2) in implementing Community directives.

TABLE 2

INFRINGEMENT PROCEEDINGS DECIDED UPON UP TO 31
DECEMBER 1989, BY MEMBER STATE

Country	Partial Compliance	Non-notification	Incorrect application	TOTAL
FRG	14	4	11	29
Belgium	10	11	26	47
Denmark	-	1	4	5
Spain	15	4	38	57
France	15	1	28	41
Greece	2	12	31	45
Ireland	4	5	9	21
Italy	7	8	25	40
Luxembourg	4	3	5	12
Netherlands	14	4	6	24
Portugal	2	3	9	14
UK	6	4	21	31
TOTAL	90	60	213	362

Source: Commission report on implementation of EC environment legislation, Commission of the European Communities, Feb. 1990.

The best performance overall in implementation is achieved by Denmark. In all three stages of implementation referred to in Table 2 Denmark has a better record than other member states. This is a similar picture to that of Denmark's record on implementation in other areas of policy [*CEC, 1991a: 57–61*]. The reasons for Denmark's exemplary record lie in its high level of environmental awareness at both public and official levels; highly effective implementation and monitoring systems; and the close involvement of the Danish parliament, through the Danish delegation in the Council of Ministers, in the negotiation and adoption of new environment legislation. Where discrepancies do exist between Danish and Community environment law it is almost entirely as a result of a deliberate choice made by the Danish government based on a determination to protect the environment.

Germany and the Netherlands are often regarded as possessing a level of awareness about, and a national predisposition towards, environmen-

220   A GREEN DIMENSION FOR THE EUROPEAN COMMUNITY

tal issues similar to that existing in Denmark. However, their record on
implementation is less satisfactory. In both countries a well developed
and sophisticated system of legislation and administration relating to
environmental protection results in a lack of motivation to adapt existing
national measures fully to new Community requirements. The Commission has suggested that the view may also often exist in the Netherlands
that its own measures already conform with Community legislation even
where this is not the case [*CEC, 1991a: 214*]. At the end of 1991 the
Netherlands had still not implemented the 1980 directive on the protection of groundwater against pollution (80/68/EEC) despite a judgement of the Court of Justice against it in 1988. Similarly in Germany, the
main concern could be to amend existing environment legislation as little
as possible when Community directives are transposed. In areas of policy
where the Länder implement EC environment legislation variations can
also exist in the speed with which measures are adopted as well as in
content. Some Länder, for example, lag seriously behind others in
designating special protection areas for the conservation of wild birds
under directive 79/409/EEC [*CEC, 1991a: 211*].

France, like Denmark, has a very good record on notifying the
Commission of measures adopted to implement Community directives.
The conformity and correct application of these measures is less satisfactory. An important issue in relation to implementation by France, which
also impinges on other member states – most notably the UK, the
Netherlands and Germany – is the tendency to transpose EC directives by
means of administrative circulars. Such circulars tend to be subjective,
grant excessive discretion in interpretation, and often lack transparency.
The Commission (and the European Parliament) has long contested the
use of circulars, guidance notes and similar instruments of administrative
law to transpose Community legislation (see, for example, EP [*1988a*];
CEC [*1991a*]). It is argued that administrative circulars interpret legislation but do not implement it. This view has been supported by the Court
of Justice. In recent years France has moved towards the Commission's
position and started transposing EC legislation by statute [*CEC, 1991a:
212*]. Other member states have generally followed suit [*HL 53–I, 1992:
13*].

Table 2 demonstrates vividly that the effective practical implementation of obligations arising from Community environment directives undoubtedly gives greatest cause for concern. Nearly two-thirds of infringement proceedings relate to unsatisfactory application in practice of
Community law. It is not surprising that the practical implementation of
Community environment legislation should be regarded by the Commission [*CEC, 1991a: 221*] as the 'most pressing problem' in the process of

implementation. In some cases the borderline between incomplete legal transposition and a member state's failure to implement EC legislation in practice can, however, be blurred, with failure to introduce the necessary implementing legislation resulting in specific, practical and often localised infringements of Community law. The implementation of the environmental impact assessment directive in the UK is a case in point.

In the Commission's interpretation the UK's implementing legislation contained several omissions and inaccuracies [*CEC, 1991c*]. The main problems concerned the application of the directive to projects for which application for development had been made but consent not granted before the entry into force of the directive; omission from the implementing legislation of the obligation to ensure that an appropriate impact assessment is conducted for several kinds of development project; and the granting of excessive discretion to UK authorities to decide projects subject to the directive.

The incorrect formal transposition of the directive gave rise to doubts about the practical application of the directive in the case of a number of specific development projects, including a salmon farm in Arran, a liquid petroleum gas installation at Grangemouth, a hospital incinerator in South Warwick, the London–Channel Tunnel rail link, the M11 link road in East London and, most notably, the proposed M3 motorway across Twyford Down. In the case of the Commission's action [*CEC, 1991b*] against the UK over implementation of the drinking water directive, the UK government's long-term partial legal transposition of the directive has resulted in a situation where some 4,536 individual practical infringements of the standards set out in the directive are officially acknowledged to exist in local drinking water supplies. In such cases it is the underlying failure of member states to introduce national implementing legislation which gives rise to failure to implement EC legislation in practice.

The distinction between infringement proceedings brought for poor practical application as opposed to incomplete legal transposition can be important. General proceedings taken against a member state for incomplete transposition are one thing but, as Macrory comments [*1992: 356*], 'action initiated in respect of a particular project may have considerable local political impact, possibly even bringing pressure to suspend or bring to the halt construction of the project in question'.

There has been a significant increase in infringement proceedings brought for incorrect practical application of Community environment legislation. Table 1 shows that up to the end of 1985 just five proceedings had been commenced for problems related to practical implementation (no such proceedings were commenced prior to 1983). In 1990 no less than 62 infringement proceedings were commenced for poor practical application of environment directives. Of those proceedings in hand at the end of 1989 213 out of 362 were in respect of failure to apply legislation effectively (Table 2). At the end of 1990 it was 218 out of 371 [*HL 53–I, 1992: 17*]. There is no doubt that the practical application of EC environment legislation, as opposed to its formal legal transposition, has taken on greater importance during the 1980s. This trend was marked in 1988 by the European Parliament producing its first reports which considered in some detail the practical implementation of EC environment legislation [*EP, 1988a; EP, 1988b*]. As stated in one of the Parliament's reports [*EP 1988a: 19*] 'there is some evidence that the Commission is itself also turning its attention to the practical implementation of environment legislation'. The record of infringement proceedings from the early 1980s to date demonstrates that although practical implementation may once have taken second place to formal, legal compliance [*EP, 1988a; Hanf, 1991*], the focus has now shifted towards the former.

The European Community's Legislative Process and Implementation

It has been argued that there ought to be a link between policy implementation, policy delivery and the formulation of policies if those policies are to be successful [*Richardson and Jordan, 1979: 153*]. In the words of Pressman and Wildavsky [*1973: 143*] implementation should not 'be conceived of as a process that takes place after and independent of, the design of policy'. Similar sentiments have also been expressed by participants in Community environmental policy-making. In a 1988 resolution on the implementation of EC legislation relating to water the European Parliament (OJ C94, 11.4.88, p.157) emphasised the need 'for implementation to be considered at a much earlier stage in legislative drafting'. The House of Lords Select Committee on the European Communities [*HL 53-I, 1992: 47*] expressed a similar view when it stated that 'Too much environmental legislation is formulated and drafted with insufficient attention to its eventual implementation'. A number of aspects of the Community's legislative process have an impact on the successful implementation of measures agreed by it.

The Preparation of Proposals

The Commission is of course the principal actor in the initiation and preparation of proposals for Community environment legislation. Within

EC ENVIRONMENT LEGISLATION 223

the Commission its Directorate-General for Environment, Nuclear Safety and Civil Protection, DG XI, is primarily responsible for drafting most proposals in the environment field. In some policy areas DG XI officials will work closely with other directorates general also involved: with DG III (Internal Market and Industrial Policy) for example, in the case of motor vehicle exhaust emissions. Responsibility for initial drafting of most proposals for Community environment legislation rests with some 350 (mostly temporary) DG XI officials. This is clearly a very small, albeit highly productive, bureaucratic resource, particularly if considered in relation to the size of national environment ministries, other directorates general and the corpus of EC environment legislation which has been produced since the mid-1970s. However, DG XI is considered to require additional staff; to be less influential within the Commission than other directorates general; and its priorities sometimes confused [*IEEP, 1992b: 26–30; EP, 1992a*].

The scientific and technical basis of draft legislation has often been questioned. Indeed, considerable agreement exists among environmental pressure groups, scientists and environmental agencies that the Commission needs to improve considerably its consultative procedures so as to have access to a wider and more satisfactory range of environmental data and advice on the basis of which proposals can be formulated [*EP, 1988a: 39; HL 53-I, 1992: 10*]. There is likely, after all, to be a clear relationship between the potential for policy implementation and a well drafted directive which commands the support of specialists. Nevertheless, consultative procedures employed by the Commission are at best *ad hoc* (see, for example, Mazey and Richardson in this volume). As a consequence they tend also to be opaque. Only very rarely does the Commission formally list organisations and individuals consulted during the drafting of legislative proposals or even publish scientific data and technical information on which proposals are based. The quality of legislative drafting by DG XI has also sometimes been criticised. No equivalent exists in the Commission to, say, UK parliamentary draftsmen. The House of Lords Select Committee on the European Communities [*HL 53-I, 1992: 9*] reported critically that within DG XI just ten officials provide general advice on legislative drafting as well as being responsible both for ongoing legal work in connection with the preparation of new legislation and for monitoring implementation in 12 member states, comprising 15 or 16 different legal systems, in nine languages.

Criticisms are also frequently made that the Commission's scientific advisory committees, though a relatively formal component of pre-legislative consultation, are poorly organised and allowed insufficient time to deliberate fully [*EP, 1988a: 40*]. Some members of the Commis-

224   A GREEN DIMENSION FOR THE EUROPEAN COMMUNITY

sion's scientific committees have suggested that the Commission often
seems incapable or unwilling to employ its advisory committees effectively [*HL 227, 1985: 56–7*]. Similarly, little information is available
about the agendas, deliberations and conclusions of advisory committees. It is also relatively rare for authorities likely to be responsible for
practical implementation to be involved in discussions with the Commission during its preparation of proposals. Nor is it probable that those
organisations and individuals most likely to be affected by the implementation of EC environment legislation will be aware of the Commission's
intentions during the early stages of legislative drafting. This tends to
prevent the creation of a favourable climate for swift practical implementation once legislation is agreed.

The Process of Negotiation in the Council of Ministers

Decision-making within the Community brings together the member
states in 'an intensity and size of organised cooperation that are unparel-
leled in other international organisations' [*Wallace, 1982: 113*]. Bargaining between member states is often remarkably complicated, the interactions between national elites complex, and agreement often difficult.
Member states' policy articulation in the Council of Ministers usually has
its roots in their domestic political environment. Council negotiations
therefore usually aim at decisions which are acceptable to relevant groups
in member states' domestic policy community and consistent with
national traditions and practices [*Bulmer, 1983*]. For some member states
this will entail influencing the policy process in such a way as to increase
the stringency of proposed environment legislation. For others it could
mean the opposite.

   One example that shows these processes at work is the Commission's
1986 proposal for a Council directive relating to discharges of aldrin,
dieldrin, endrin and isodrin ('drins') into the aquatic environment (COM
(86) 534). Drins are toxic, persistent and bioaccumulative organochloride
pesticides. Following a Commission-sponsored study of the environmental effects of drins, a proposal was submitted which envisaged a 5ng/l
quality objective for drins and a 0.15mg/kg standard for drins in fish flesh.
A report produced by the European Parliament marshalled considerable
evidence to demonstrate that one member state – the UK – sought to
influence Council discussion on the basis of 'levels of drins currently
found', rather than on the basis of scientific or environmental criteria
[*EP, 1988a: 42–6*]. Its objective was to avoid having to introduce in the
UK a quality objective for drins which would have entailed the introduction of new measures to comply with it. The UK sought 'a standard which
could be met in the majority of UK waters' [*Department of the Environ-*

ment, 1987]. It could of course be argued that UK officials were in fact taking likely future problems of implementation into account, a laudable objective indeed, if it were true. However, by proposing a total drins concentration of 50ng/l and deletion altogether of the fish flesh standard, the UK government differed in opinion not only from its own authoritative Water Research Centre but also from the House of Lords Select Committee on the European Communities which concluded that 'the dangers posed by drins to the United Kingdom environment lead us to consider that there is no safe limit value for the drins, and their use should, in the foreseeable future, be eliminated altogether' [*HL 6, 1987: 25*].

Despite member states' articulation in Council of often deeply entrenched preferences based on national circumstance and practice, negotiation in Council remains best characterised as a search for consensus. Even with the entry into force of the Single European Act in 1987 (which introduced qualified majority voting in Council on proposals for environment legislation related to the completion of the internal market) most environment legislation has up to now been adopted unanimously. In cases where qualified majority voting is available the tendency persists for Council to seek overall consensus. This search for unanimity among the Twelve increases the possibility that EC environment legislation will be vague, ambiguous and sometimes superficial. Scientific credibility and precision are likely to be sacrificed in order to achieve consensus. This may also on occasion result in the incorporation of irreconcilable views into Community law. Directive 76/464/EEC, on pollution caused by dangerous substances, is a case in point. The Council's agreement on this directive, rather than representing a compromise, has been viewed as 'a last ditch expedient included in the Directive to gain the unanimous agreement required for its approval' [*Taylor et al., 1986: 227*]. All member states except one preferred to set specific uniform emission standards for discharges of dangerous substances to the aquatic environment, whereas the UK preference was for environmental quality objectives permitting a range of emission standards [*Haigh, 1984: 96–104*]. Agreement between these opposing viewpoints was not possible and accordingly both approaches were included in the directive, allowing member states to disregard one approach for the other. Hence the dispute was left unresolved but settled temporarily.

Without exception negotiation within the Council of Ministers, whether in its working groups, COREPER or in formal Council meetings, takes place outside the public domain. This has a direct effect on the implementation of legislation it adopts. In the first place it encourages policy-making which emphasises intergovernmental bargaining, often

over unrelated issues. This kind of bargaining is hardly likely to contribute to the certainty or coherence of Community environment legislation (see, for example, EP [*1988a*]; EP [*1992b*]. Second, it provides the
opportunity for Council to adopt declarations and statements to its
minutes interpreting if not qualifying legislation. These usually remain
confidential between governments and the Commission. Such 'secret'
legislation can have serious implications for satisfactory implementation
(see, for example, Haigh [*1984: 53–4*]). The Commission acknowledged
the difficulty in its 1991 report to the European Parliament on the
application of Community law where it stated [*CEC, 1991a: 217*], for
example, that several member states derogate from the requirements of
the directive on the quality of surface water (75/440/EEC) on the basis of
a declaration to the minutes made when the bathing water directive
(76/160/EEC) was adopted. Hence it is possible for member states and, in
particular, their enforcement agencies, local authorities and other
bodies, to embark on the implementation of legislation which has been
agreed through considerable horsetrading and which is only clarified in
intent by reference to generally inaccessible interpretations.

The Form of Community Legislation

Over 90 per cent of Community environment legislation is in the form of
directives. Though very few regulations have been adopted in the environment field it is possible to discern in recent years a trend towards
their greater use. Community legislation on the production and importation of ozone depleting chlorofluorocarbons (1988 onwards), the export
and import of dangerous chemicals (1988), the evaluation and control of
environmental risks of existing chemicals (1992), the EC eco-labelling
scheme (1991), and the establishment of the European Environment
Agency (1990) have, among others been adopted as regulations. Although 'superficially attractive' [*HL 53-I, 1992: 16*] the greater use of
regulations as part of the solution to difficulties faced in implementing
directives is not widely supported. Member states would be reluctant to
sanction the creation of a body of law at EC level which may conflict with
extant national legislation. Similarly, the flexibility and respect for local
legal and administrative traditions and procedures implicit in the use of
directives are probably highly desirable in a political sense at present. The
use of directives can be viewed as an expression of the principle of
subsidiarity in the Community's legislative processes. The House of
Lords Select Committee on the European Communities [*HL 53-I, 1992:
47*] considered, however, that there may be 'scope for some increase in
the use of regulations'. In addition, the possibility could be raised of
greater use of regulations, albeit in a more closely delineated range of

policy areas, should Community competences be more tightly drawn in future through a more resticted application of the concept of subsidiarity.

It is a basic principle of Community law that when directives are adopted they are to be implemented uniformly by the member states (though in some directives different timescales have been specified). For the first time in the Maastricht treaty on European Union a provision is formally incorporated in Community procedure. allowing for temporary derogations from environmental legislation where a member state considers the costs of particular measures to be prohibitive. The Maastricht treaty also allows for financial assistance from the new Cohesion Fund to be made available to compensate the member state(s) concerned. Under the terms of the Maastricht treaty any member state may seek such a temporary derogation so long as the legislation to which it will apply is based on Article 130s(1) of the treaty (that is, under the treaty, passed by a qualified majority in Council and adopted in cooperation with the European Parliament but excluding the large number of environmental measures based on Article 100A); and costs which are deemed disproportionate to the member states' public authorities will have to be incurred to implement the measure. Where these two criteria are met the Council may grant a derogation from the legislation. This provision is a radical departure for Community environment policy, the full impact of which it is at present impossible to assess. It may, however, open the door to Community environment legislation which explicitly accepts different national standards of environmental protection [*Wilkinson, 1992: 12*].

It might also lead to the Council negotiating not only the content of legislation but also, for some member states, its speed of implementation. If the provision is applied widely it could make for considerably greater differentiation in the application of EC environment legislation, making enforcement much more difficult. In support of the provision it can be argued that it will encourage Community institutions to take greater account of economic costs during the formulation of environmental policy. It might also expedite decision making by allowing a member state otherwise likely to oppose a particular measure instead to support it though with a derogation.

The Enforcement of EC Environment Legislation

Responsibility for the implementation of EC legislation rests primarily with member states. Nevertheless, it is clear that wide variations exist in their implementation of EC environment legislation. The Commission can have recourse to formal legal procedures under the treaties, supplemented by a complaints procedure, to ensure member states' com-

228   A GREEN DIMENSION FOR THE EUROPEAN COMMUNITY

pliance. It has also pursued the idea of 'osmosis' between it and national authorities as a way of encouraging implementation. In addition, the European Parliament has also played an important role in monitoring implementation.

Formal Procedures

Each directive agreed by the Council of Ministers specifies a time limit (occasionally several time limits) by when its provisions are required to be incorporated in national law. Member states are also required by directives to notify the Commission of the measures taken. Twice before the implementation date the Commission reminds member states of the requirement to adopt and notify national measures. Monitoring of the communication of national measures by the Commission's directorates general is reasonably routine and involves little political oversight from the college of Commissioners itself. The process can be complicated where individual directives require many separate items of national legislation to implement them. For this reason the Commission now requests member states to specify the provisions of national law in which each article and clause of a directive is implemented. The Commission has had little success in encouraging member states to produce for it synoptic tables cross-referencing national provisions with EC directives [*CEC, 1991a: 221*].

The Commission has recourse to Article 169 of the EEC Treaty where it considers that a member state has failed to comply fully with the provisions of Community legislation. This entails a three-stage procedure: first, the Commission informs the member state (by means of a '169-letter') that it believes an obligation under the treaties has not been fulfilled and requests its observations; second, if the Commission remains dissatisfied a reasoned opinion is forwarded to the member state; finally, proceedings may be commenced before the Court of Justice.

These formal stages set out in the treaty do not do justice to the extent and scope of correspondence and negotiation which is likely to occur prior to the Commission embarking upon each step. For its part, the Commission regards Article 169 proceedings as available only 'when all other means have failed' [*CEC, 1991a: 205*]. Even before starting out on the first stage of the Article 169 procedure the Commission will have extensive bilateral exchanges with national authorities. In September 1991, for example, the Commission forwarded to the UK government a 169-letter relating to the UK's failure to comply with the drinking water directive (80/778/EEC). The despatch of this 169-letter was preceded by no less than ten exchanges of correspondence between the Commission and the UK government and three meetings between Commission and

EC ENVIRONMENT LEGISLATION 229

UK officials [*CEC, 1991b*]. Similarly in the case of the Commission's action against the UK government over the environmental impact asessment directive, some 12 exchanges of correspondence took place and at least one meeting of officials [*CEC, 1991c*]. The charge that is sometimes made that the Commission sails headlong into infringement proceedings would therefore appear not to be justified. On the contrary, the Commission's decision to pursue infringement proceedings is made only after considerable discussion with national authorities. Moreover, in all cases other than the non-notification of national measures each formal stage of the process requires a specific Commission decision to proceed [*CEC, 1991a: 206*].

Relatively few infringement proceedings progress further than the 169-letter stage. In many cases the receipt of a 169-letter is sufficient to encourage a member state to bring its national measures into line with Community legislation. Reasoned opinions and referrals to the Court of Justice 1982–90 in the environment sector are reported in Table 3; and in Table 4 169-letters, reasoned opinions and referrals initiated during 1990 are broken down by member states.

One issue that has been of concern, particularly to the European Parliament (see, for example, EP [*1988a*]; OJ C326, 16.12.91, p.189), is the transparency of Commission enforcement procedures. Until 1989 the Commission was reluctant to acknowledge infringement proceedings against member states prior to the reasoned opinion stage. Commission annual reports to Parliament on the application of Community law, for example, reported only those 169-letters relating to member states' failure to notify national measures, as well as reasoned opinions and referrals to the Court. Letters of formal notice to member states concerning omissions in implementation were not identified, on the grounds that the purpose of the first stage of the Article 169 procedure, rather than bringing a member state to account, is intended to afford it an opportunity to regularise its position [*EP, 1990a: 31*].

In recent years, prompted no doubt by increased emphasis on the implementation of directives required to complete the internal market, as well as by the European Parliament's criticism that many infringement proceedings are kept away from public view, the Commission has increased the information made available to the public about the opening of infringement proceedings. In a resolution adopted in November 1991, following the political furore which surrounded the Commission's 169-letter to the UK government on environmental impact assessment, the European Parliament requested that the Commission 'institute forthwith a procedure whereby Article 169 letters forwarded to Member States are henceforth sent also, for information, to Parliament' (OJ C326, 16.12.91,

230   A GREEN DIMENSION FOR THE EUROPEAN COMMUNITY

TABLE 3

REASONED OPINIONS AND REFERRALS EXECUTED IN 1990, ENVIRONMENT
SECTOR

Country	Reasoned Opinions	Referrals
Belgium	6	2
Germany	2	2
Denmark	--	--
Greece	4	--
Spain	7	2
France	1	4
Ireland	3	1
Italy	7	1
Netherlands	5	1
Luxembourg	1	--
Portugal	1	--
United Kingdom	2	1
TOTALS	39	14

Source: *Eighth annual report to the European Parliament on Commission monitoring of the*
application of Community law, Dec. 1991.

TABLE 4

NUMBER OF PROCEEDINGS INITIED, BY STAGE OF PROCEEDINGS,
ENVIRONMENT SECTOR

Year	Letters of Formal Notice	Reasoned Opinions	Referrals to Court
1982	16	7	--
1983	35	1	--
1984	65	33	2
1985	69	26	23
1986	134	11	10
1987	159	24	3
1988	93	71	11
1989	101	26	21
1990	167	39	14

Source: *Eighth annual report to the European Parliament on Commission monitoring of the*
application of Community law, Dec. 1991.

EC ENVIRONMENT LEGISLATION   231

p.189). By summer 1992 the Commission had not responded to this proposal. It is, nevertheless, recognised as having some force, particularly as there are unlikely to be commercial or similar interests affected by disclosure. The House of Lords Select Committee on the European Communities [HL 53-I, 1992: 46] agreed with the European Parliament's approach. It stated:

> The simple solution ... is to make public all formal correspondence between the Commission and Member States concerning the investigation of complaints – that is Article 169 letters, Reasoned Opinions, and the responses to both. These documents have a formal legal charcter and like other legal documents should be publicly accessible.

The Complaints Procedure

In its investigation of the implementation of Community environment legislation the House of Lords Select Committee on the European Communities stated [HL 53-I, 1992: 17] that 'Without information it is impossible to assess whether compliance takes place, the effectiveness of legislation, or to gauge what further action may be called for'. Yet the Commission has no systematic means to collect information itself. This presents less difficulty in the case of formal transposition (as member states are required to communicate national implementing measures) than it does with practical implementation. Whilst many environment directives specifically require member states to forward reports on implementation to the Commission at regular intervals few do so promptly. When such reports are submitted they have tended to present only a very partial record of practical implementation [CEC, 1991a; HL 53-I, 1992]. As a result the Commission is almost entirely dependent on EC citizens bringing to its attention the alleged failure of member states to implement in practice Community environment legislation.

In recent years there has been a dramatic increase in the number of complaints received by the Commission. The Commission has received complaints about poor implementation of environment legislation from non-governmental organisations, local authorities, embassies and even national authorities, as well as private individuals [CEC, 1991a]. The Commission's intention, announced in the Fourth Environmental Action Programme (COM (86) 485, p.10), to encourage 'private persons, non-governmental organisations or local authorities to bring instances of non-compliance to the attention of the Commission' appears to have been successful.

The tendency of citizens to use the Community as an avenue of complaint has apparently kept pace with the Community's growing

232 A GREEN DIMENSION FOR THE EUROPEAN COMMUNITY

TABLE 5

NUMBER OF COMPLAINTS AND CASES DETECTED BY THE COMMISSION'S OWN INQUIRIES

Year	Environment Complaints	Environment Cases detected	Total Complaints	Total Cases Detected
1982	10	--	352	112
1983	8	--	399	192
1984	9	2	476	145
1985	37	10	585	244
1986	165	32	791	293
1987	150	38	850	260
1988	216	33	1137	307
1989	465	60	1195	352
1990	480	42	1252	283

Source: Eighth annual report to the European Parliament on Commission monitoring of the application of Community law, Dec. 1991.

TABLE 6

COMPLAINTS REGISTERED IN THE ENVIRONMENT SECTOR, 1990

Belgium	17
Denmark	3
France	47
Germany	56
Greece	40
Ireland	19
Italy	33
Luxembourg	3
Netherlands	7
Portugal	19
Spain	111
United Kingdom	125

Source: Richard Macrory, 'The Enforcement of Community Environmental Laws: Some Critical Issues', Common Market Law Review, Vol. 29 (1992), p.364.

involvement in national political life. EC environment policy, which records high levels of public support (see, for example, *Eurobarometer* [*1991: 28–31*]), has been an important part of this process. The number of complaints registered by the Commission in the environment and other sectors 1982–90 is reported in Table 5. The table also demonstrates that the Commission's own monitoring and enforcement mechanisms have not, it seems, evolved at a similar pace to public activism. When broken down by member state (Table 6) it is also clear that the number of complaints received is related to a member state's tradition of environ-mental activism and political protest [*Macrory, 1992: 364*] as well as a readiness to use national legal remedies [*HL 53-I, 1992: 29*].

The timescale for action to be taken by the Commission on the basis of complaints or of its own inquiries is very long. Over three years may elapse between a decision to commence proceedings pursuant to Article 169 and a judgement by the Court of Justice. Even once decisions have been taken to progress through the stages of the Article 169 procedure, many months can pass before execution of the decision. In the case of the 169-letter to the UK government on environmental impact assessment, the Commission decided in March 1991 (nearly three years after the deadline for implementation) to commence proceedings; it was not until October 1991 that the letter was despatched. Such delays can be impor-tant when infringement proceedings concern specific projects as environ-mental damage may occur during the course of investigations. The long timescales involved also provide an opportunity for national authorities to claim (possibly in the face of public opinion) that national rules are actually in order and that reports of Commission investigation are inaccurate.

'Osmosis' with National Authorities

In its Fourth Environmental Action Programme the Commission an-nounced (COM (86) 485, p. 9) its intention to intensify its dialogue with national and regional administrations 'so as to promote a more fully harmonised understanding of and approach to both legal and practical questions concerning implementation'. The Commission's Director General for Environment has since spoken [*HL 135, 1987: 55*] of 'osmosis between national and Community institutions' to achieve this objective. Several meetings, both bilateral and multilateral, take place each year between the Commission's services and national authorities to discuss implementation of environment directives. Occasionally these have in-volved local and regional authorities as well as national authorities. There is a danger that the Commission could pursue close informal relationships with national administrations when recourse to legal procedures for

234   A GREEN DIMENSION FOR THE EUROPEAN COMMUNITY

ensuring compliance might be more appropriate. This concern has certainly been expressed by the European Parliament (OJ C94, 11.4.88, p.156). On the other hand it is important that the Commission should not appear to act peremptorily. Closer dialogue with national authorities and enforcement agencies is one of a number of mechanisms than can contribute to better implementation of Community environment legislation.

The European Parliament and Implementation

The European Parliament began to take an interest in implementation shortly after being first directly elected in 1979. In a resolution adopted in 1983 Parliament requested the Commission to submit annual reports on the failure of member states to fully implement Community legislation (OJ C68, 14.3.83, p.32). The Commission acceded to this request and submitted its first Annual Report on the monitoring of the application of Community law in 1984. Similar reports have been submitted annually. These are referred by the Parliament to its Committee on Legal Affairs and its specialised committees for their opinions. The Legal Affairs Committee produces an annual report on the basis of that submitted by the Commission and the opinions received from the other committees. In September 1990 this procedure was formally incorporated in the Parliament's Rules of Procedure (rule 29c) alongside provisions relating to Parliament's consideration of the Commission's Annual Legislative Programme and its Annual General Report (OJ C260, 15.10.90, p.85). The Commission's decision to prepare Annual Reports made an important contribution to improving the Community's oversight of implementation. Parliament was an important catalyst in this. However, Parliament's monitoring of implementation on the basis of the Commission's Annual Reports tends to emphasise formal legal transposition rather than practical implementation. The sheer range and often complexity of Community legislation makes it difficult for Parliament to exercise detailed or effective supervision over the implementation of Community legislation in its entirety.

The European Parliament's Committee on Environment, Public Health and Consumer Protection therefore took a further step in January 1987 when it decided to produce two major reports on the implementation of environment legislation. Submitted to plenary and adopted by Parliament in 1988, each of these reports dealt with a single environmental medium (air and water) and concentrated on practical implementation (OJ C94, 11.4.88, pp. 151-8). The major part of the report on the implementation of EC legislation relating to water comprised three case studies which considered the practical implementation of the directives on aquatic pollution caused by dangerous substances (76/464/EEC), drinking water (80/778/EEC), and bathing water (76/160/EEC). These were landmark reports which signalled a motivation on the part of the Environment Committee not only to uncover disparities and omissions in the implementation of EC environment law but also to oversee the Commission's exercise of its enforcement function in the environment field. Since 1987 seven reports on implementation have emanated from the Environment Committee. In addition to these reports three resolutions on implementation have been submitted by the Committee and adopted by Parliament's plenary (see also Judge in this volume). The Commission has co-operated closely with the Committee, for example, by responding specifically and point by point to its reports on implementation [see EP, 1990a]. On implementation as on other issues Parliament and Commission have formed a combined front when necessary against Council and member states.

On occasion it has been proposed that Parliament establish a specialised committee devoted to monitoring the implementation of EC environment legislation, either as a sub-committee of the Environment Committee [*HL 53-I, 1992: 43*], an entirely separate committee on implementation, including environment legislation among its competences (OJ C 94, 11.4.88, p.154), or as a temporary committee of inquiry on the implementation of environment legislation. None of these proposals has received significant support among Members of the European Parliament, within the Environment Committee, or from the major political groups in the Parliament. The Environment Committee's record on implementation suggests that a special committee is unnecessary, at least so long as the Committee continues to give priority to this aspect of its work and to produce reports on implementation at regular intervals. In addition, the Parliament is conscious of the administrative and resource implications of such a proposal [*HL 53-I, 1992: 25*]. Finally, the principle that implementation is related intrinsically to policy development has been a major theme of much of the Committee's monitoring of implementation (see, for example, EP [*1988a*]; EP [*1992b*]). It is recognised within the Environment Committee that the creation of a separate parliamentary body intended to monitor the implementation of environment legislation would run counter to its interest in considering implementation as part of the environmental policy-making process.

Improving Implementation and Enforcement

A number of measures can be envisaged that might improve the implementation of EC environment legislation. As noted at the outset,

236   A GREEN DIMENSION FOR THE EUROPEAN COMMUNITY

central to discussion of improving implementation is the idea of granting to the Commission powers of environmental inspection. The problem is that such a proposition is probably unrealistic at this stage in the development of the Community. As we shall see, a possibly more appropriate refinement of the inspection concept, involving a Community inspection audit mechanism (in other words the 'inspection of inspectors') has gained ground. Improving member states' reporting requirements, the setting up of the European Environment Agency, enhancing citizens' access to national courts, and some of the innovations introduced by the Maastricht treaty might also contribute to better implementation.

National Reporting Requirements

Information is one of the most important keys to the full and practical implementation of Community environment legislation. Monitoring the practical implementation of environment directives is particularly dependent on the systematic availability of reliable information on the environment. However, it is clear that the information available to the Commission (and often member states) is inadequate. The House of Lords Select Committee on the European Communities, in its report on implementation, noted [*HL 53-I, 1992: 17*] that 'The lack of information was perhaps the most pervasive theme of the evidence presented to us'. The Commission is entirely dependent for information on occasional studies on aspects of implementation contracted to consultants and environmental institutes, reports submitted by national authorities under specific directives, and complaints. Studies produced by consultants are useful but usually only provide a 'situation report on the implementation of a specific directive at a particular moment' [*IEEP, 1992a: 170*]. They are hardly a satisfactory substitute for long term data compiled systematically on the basis of comparable criteria in each member state. Complaints also possess limitations, in that they arrive randomly, their transmission is related to national traditions of political protest, they often focus on national environmental interests [*Macrory, 1992: 365*], and they are themselves dependent on the availability of information -- both of environmental conditions and standards and of procedures for complaint. The receipt and processing of complaints may also detract Community officials from systematic cross-national monitoring and enforcement of implementation, particularly when resources are limited.

Neither is the requirement, incorporated in many directives, that member states submit regular reports on the measures taken to implement specific directives satisfactory. In the Commission's view [*CEC, 1991a: 208*], national reports have tended 'mainly (to) contain summary descriptions of the administrative and technical measures already in place

EC ENVIRONMENT LEGISLATION 237

or recently adopted. Consequently, they provide little useful information on the practical application of Community environment measures'. From the point of view of an environmental non-governmental organisation which assessed one member state's reports under an environment directive, national submissions 'have been late, incomplete, to a degree disingenuous and not widely canvassed in draft form with non-departmental sources of expertise' [*RSPB, 1992: 145*]. They are also dependent on the monitoring and reporting capabilities of national authorities. In some directives the requirement to submit reports to the Commission is completely absent (such as in the drinking water directive (80/778/EEC)); in others the requirement is formulated very loosely. In the environmental impact assessment directive, for example, it is stated simply (in article 11) that 'Member States and the Commission shall exchange information on the experience gained in applying this Directive'. Finally, some directives limit the Commission's right to publish information submitted by member states, others require publication of a Commission report.

In 1990 the Commission submitted a proposal (COM(90)287) intended to improve the consistency, content and frequency of the reports submitted to it under environment directives. Adopted in December 1991 this directive ('standardising and rationalising reports on the implementation of certain Community Directives relating to the environment' (91/692/EEC)) fixes at three years the interval between national reports under 30 directives, staggering the three year period for different environmental media. The Commission is required to publish a Community report on the implementation of each directive within nine months of receiving reports from member states. In the case of the bathing water directive (76/160/EEC) the 1991 directive provides for a consolidated Community report to be produced within four months of receipt ot the member state reports. This is intended to result in the Commission's report on bathing water quality (produced annually since 1988) becoming more timely.

Probably the most significant aspect of the 1991 directive is that in future national reports submitted under the directives affected by it will be drawn up on the basis of a questionnaire produced by the Commission. Hence the Commission will be in a position to design and set out its information requirements itself. It could therefore be less dependent on information member states deign to submit. On the other hand, a 'commitology' procedure is established for member states to approve the Commission's proposed questionnaire. Commitology refers to the subordination of Commission executive decisions to committees of national civil servants (see Jacobs and Corbett [*1990: 207–12*]). Through this mechanism member states can be expected to keep a close eye on what

238   A GREEN DIMENSION FOR THE EUROPEAN COMMUNITY

information the Commission proposes to extract from them. Nevertheless, the framework for systematic reporting created by this directive is
important in improving the availability at Community level of information on practical implementation during each three year reference
period.

The submission of reports by the Commission, compiled on the basis of
national reports, also requires improvement. Many Commission reports
are produced late, if at all. In a resolution adopted in 1991, the European
Parliament (OJ C326, 16.12.91, p.189) stressed the importance it attaches to the prompt presentation of such reports. A rolling calendar
listing deadlines for the submission of Commission reports to Parliament
in the environment (and public health and consumer protection) field is
now produced for its Environment Committee, enabling it to take action
when Commission reports on implementation become overdue.

*The European Environment Agency: Towards Inspecting the
Inspectors?*

In May 1990 the Council of Ministers agreed to the creation of a
European Environment Agency (EEA) and an associated European
environment information and observation network (regulation 1210/90).
The idea of a EEA was first raised formally by Commission President
Delors in his programme statement to the European Parliament in
January 1989. The role which it was intended the EEA could play in
improving implementation through gathering and processing environmental information was clear. Delors stated [*CEC, 1989: 14*] that 'The
object of the exercise will be ... to give us a network responsible for
measurement, verification, certification, information and sounding the
alert'. The Council regulation establishing the EEA sets out (in article
1(2)) its basic objectives as being 'to provide the Community and the
Member States with objective, reliable and comparable information at
European level enabling them to take the requisite measures to protect
the environment, to assess the results of such measures and to ensure that
the public is properly informed about the state of the environment'.
Although the basic mission of the EEA is restricted to the collection,
collation and analysis of environmental information, particular priority
among its principal areas of activity is given to the collection of 'information which can be directly used in the implementation of Community
environmental policy' (article 3(2)).

The EEA is not (at least yet) a nascent European environment
inspectorate. The reluctance of member states' governments to support
the idea of an environment inspectorate established at EC level is almost
universal. It would entail investing Community institutions with a degree

EC ENVIRONMENT LEGISLATION 239

of involvement in national environmental monitoring and policy which at present member states would not countenance. The need to respect the principle of subsidiarity also implies that it is probably appropriate for the Community first to explore other approaches to better enforcement of EC law before embarking on the creation of a European environment inspectorate. The principle of subsidiarity has figured as a formal basis for Community environment policy (in Article 130R) since the introduction of the Single European Act; in the Maastricht Treaty its application is made explicit across the entire range of Community activity. It is also likely that in future greater attention will be paid to subsidiarity. The idea of an EC environment inspectorate is therefore probably still premature.

In its Opinion on the establishment of the EEA the European Parliament (OJ C96, 17.4.90, p. 114) demonstrated that it had considerable expectations about the role which the EEA should assume. Parliament saw the EEA taking a central place in the development of EC environment policy. For the time being these expectations are certain to be frustrated. On the other hand Parliament was successful in forcing the inclusion, among the tasks of the EEA, of the development of 'uniform assessment criteria for environmental data to be applied in all member states' (article 2(iii)). The Council's agreement was also won to a review of the EEA's tasks two years after its creation (article 20).

The development of 'uniform assessment criteria' is important as it provides a basis for the EEA to become involved gradually in the design, organisation and improvement of environmental monitoring by the member states. It suggests that the EEA could evolve from its current status as a relatively passive recipient of information towards having an increasing involvement in the coordination of environmental measurement and inspection in the member states. In essence the idea can be expressed as 'inspecting the inspectors': it does not envisage the EEA itself taking on an inspectorate role but does encompass the EEA performing an oversight or 'audit' function in relation to the methodologies employed by regulatory authorities in the member states. The review of the tasks of the EEA two years after its creation underlines the dynamic interpretation which can be made of its future role in monitoring implementation. Indeed, the EEA regulation (article 20) states that 'associating (the Agency) in the monitoring of the implementation of Community environmental legislation' will be among those areas where further tasks will in future be decided upon.

The Commission might only give qualified support to the idea of the EEA taking on an audit inspectorate function. During the negotiations over the creation of the EEA the Commission was reluctant to assign monitoring or inspection functions to the EEA. Apart from the difficulty

240   A GREEN DIMENSION FOR THE EUROPEAN COMMUNITY

that it would have faced winning support in Council for such a development, the Commission also sought to defend its own role. It wanted to
ensure that functions envisaged for the EEA were clearly distinct from,
even if complementary to, its own role. The Commission emphasised that
the treaties give it specific responsibilities and prerogatives for the
implementation and enforcement of EC environment legislation. In view
of this it is also doubtful that the Commission was in a position in any case
to sanction what could amount to a transfer of power to a new body.

The Commission's view is that the role of the EEA is to generate
environmental data and to improve its quality and comparability. It
prefers to regard the question of the EEA's role in monitoring implementation postponed until the review of its operation two years after its
creation [*CEC, 1992: 77*]. In addition, it can also be objected that the
Commission is accountable to the European Parliament and as such
exercises its responsibilities subject to its oversight and scrutiny. Notwithstanding the European Parliament's nomination to the EEA
management board of two scientific personalities, the EEA will be much
less amenable to democratic control. Although it could be the case that
the EEA will prove to be an ally of the European Parliament and
responsive to its concerns [*HL 53–I, 1992: 41*], the introduction of
functional agencies such as the EEA raises important questions about
accountablity, control and oversight, particularly where agencies may
acquire powers of inspection or regulation (as in the case of the proposed
European Medicines Agency), however restricted.

The idea of developing a Community audit inspectorate is now quite
widely supported. Some member states, for example, have explicitly
taken up and promoted the concept of an inspectorate or audit agency
overseeing the work of national environment inspectors. In the view of
the UK government such an inspectorate should operate under the
responsibility of the Commission. Former UK Environment Minister
Michael Heseltine stated [*HL 53–II, 1992: 183*]:

> We see the inspectorate and the Agency as separate. The inspec-
> torate would report to the Commission. The powers of enforcement
> lie with the Commission ... We see it as an inspectorate inspecting
> the national inspectors that are responsible for monitoring and
> reporting on the Directives of the Community already in existence.
> The work of the Environment Agency will be ... to collect and
> compare statistics and to make reports.

In contrast the House of Lords Select Committee on the European
Communities has argued strongly [*HL 53–I, 1992: 41*] that the functions
and powers of a EC audit inspectorate should be clearly distinguished

EC ENVIRONMENT LEGISLATION 241

from the Commission's own enforcement functions and that 'the logical home for an environmental inspectorate on the lines indicated is the European Environment Agency'. The Select Committee considered that inspectorate functions would dovetail neatly with the EEA's functions while institutional separation of an inspectorate from the Commission would enable it also to scrutinise more effectively the Commission's own role, in particular in respect of the environmental impact of other Community policies.

Rather than enter directly the discussion over the functions, role and location of an EC audit inspectorate, the Commission (in its Fifth Environmental Action Programme [*CEC, 1992: 75*]) refers instead to its intention to establish an 'implementation network' coordinated by the Commission. The creation of a network of member states' enforcement agencies is an idea which is obviously closely related to that of an audit inspectorate. The concept of an inspection network was first raised at the October 1991 informal environment Council and broadly agreed in principle. In the Commission's view (though based heavily on the conclusions of the informal Council) it would be intended primarily to exchange information and experience and aim at 'the development of common approaches at practical level under the supervision of the Commission'. Despite referring to this network rather loosely as an '*ad hoc* dialogue group' the Commission acknowledges that its central priority would be to promote consistency in the practical application of EC environment legislation.

Both the Commission's idea of an implementation network and the audit inspectorate concept aim at standardising, coordinating and improving the consistency of environmental inspection in the member states. Both would also provide at Community level information about the national inspection and monitoring regimes currently in operation. This would increase the visibility of national environmental regulatory regimes and possibly prompt the improvement of national inspection systems where there are shortcomings. The House of Lords Select Committee on the European Communities considered that an EC audit inspectorate would act as a 'watchdog' over the policies and performance of national regulatory authorities in the member states, particularly in the implementation of EC environment legislation. This goes further than the Commission's implementation network concept. Indeed, it has also been argued [*HL 53–I, 1992: 41*] that the audit inspectorate should have powers to verify the practical implementation of EC environment legislation and the data collected by national authorities.

Inspections and spot checks by Commission officials have in the past caused some controversy [*HL 135, 1987: 76–8*]. The objective of an audit

242   A GREEN DIMENSION FOR THE EUROPEAN COMMUNITY

inspectorate, however, particularly if located within the EEA, would be to co-operate with and assist national inspectorates. The Commission would retain its responsibility for enforcement, possibly acting on the advice of the EEA. While any attempt to improve and monitor the quality of member states' national environmental inspection regimes is likely to run up against the difficulty that member states will be jealous of their own functions, it might be possible to avoid the kind of conflicts between the Community and member states which have resulted from Commission enforcement activities in the past should the basic rationale of an audit inspectorate be to work closely with member states' own agencies and contribute positively, though pro-actively, to their inspection activities.

The Decision-Making Process

Attention was drawn earlier to the impact on implementation of the Community's legislative process. It was argued that some features of the way legislation is designed, drafted and agreed contribute to problems when it comes to be implemented. There is some evidence that the Commission has recognised that it is necessary to consider implementation as part of the process of drafting legislation. Indeed, the Commission acknowledges in its Fifth Environmental Action Programme [*CEC, 1992: 75–7*] that among the reasons for poor implementation are the need for unanimous agreement in the Council of Ministers; a lack of overall policy coherence due to the development of legislation in an *ad hoc* manner; and a too narrow range of legislative instruments available to it. Along with the implementation network mentioned above the Commission therefore proposes the creation of two bodies which are intended to lead to improved implementation of EC environment legislation. The first is a consultative forum comprising representatives of industrial and business sectors, regional and local authorities, trade unions and environmental non-governmental organisations. Through this body the Commission intends to improve the preparation of legislation by increasing the exchange of information between these groups and the Commission. Secondly, the Commission proposes to constitute an environmental policy review group (modelled on the Committee of Directors-General of Industry) comprising representatives of the Commission and the member states at Director-General level, to examine environmental policies and measures. The Commission sees this body as filling the gap which results from exchanges between member states and the Commission usually only occurring over specific proposals and infringement proceedings. The consultative forum could lead to an increase in the visibility of Commission policy development. It might go some way to preparing the ground

EC ENVIRONMENT LEGISLATION   243

for the implementation of legislation which, as discussed earlier, rarely happens at present. The forum might also result in a more open and less *ad hoc* aproach to consultation. Similarly, the policy review group extends the idea of 'osmosis' with national authorities. In a similar vein the Commission also apparently intends to promote practical follow-up on all new environment legislation through training programmes, seminars and workshops involving member states' officials [*CEC, 1992: 76*].

The most serious difficulty associated with Community decision-making is the procedures used by Council to agree legislation. The need for unanimous agreement often leads to legislation based on political compromises and bargains which is difficult to put into practical operation. The Maastricht treaty extends the scope for using qualified majority voting in Council though it also complicates both the choice of legal base and the decision-making procedures which apply. There is considerable agreement that the changes introduced to the EC's legislative process by the Maastricht treaty are bound to cause confusion and delay [*EP, 1992c; Wilkinson, 1992*]. For environment legislation the co-operation procedure (see Judge in this volume) becomes the standard legislative procedure (though with some important exceptions). The new co-decision procedure will apply to environment legislation related to the internal market and environmental action programmes. Co-decision in particular is likely to result in much greater public discussion about proposed environment legislation. More information will come available about the positions adopted by individual member states and their bargaining strategies. By boosting the legislative powers of the European Parliament the Maastricht treaty also goes some way to redressing the Community's democratic deficit. Removing the ability of member states to block agreement on Commission proposals indefinitely will speed up agreement (as it has in other areas of Community policy) and prevent the gradual dilution of standards through lengthy negotiations in the Council of Ministers.

On the other hand, extension of qualified majority voting could mean that member states are more frequently obliged to adopt and implement policies to which they are opposed. As Wilkinson notes [*1992: 14*], this could lead to non-implementation becoming 'a problem even more serious than it already is'. Nevertheless, the extent of this should not be overestimated. The Single European Act has already reduced the range of legislation to which unanimous decision-making applies. Between 1989 and 1992, for example, a majority of Commission proposals in the environment sector were subject to the co-operation procedure (and therefore qualified majority voting) as they were related to the completion of the internal market and therefore based on Article 100a of the treaty. The gradual redress of the imbalance in the legislative powers of the Council and Parliament, especially through the co-decision procedure, will also root Community measures in future in a firmer democratic base.

The Council of Ministers could make a further contribution to improving implementation by itself demonstrating an interest in uniform implementation of environment legislation. The House of Lords Select Committee on the European Communities has proposed [*HL 53–I, 1992: 42*] that the Council regularly review compliance with environment legislation. The Select Committee suggests that consideration of implementation should routinely be placed on the Council agenda and considered on the basis of reports from the Commission and the EEA. In a sense the Council has already made progress in this direction by devoting its October 1991 informal environment Council to the question of implementation. The idea presupposes a willingness among the Twelve to discuss their own failings. It might be that the inter-governmental nature of discussions in Council would deter member states from undertaking future reviews of implementation in that forum.

Enforcement Through National Courts

In several member states access to the courts, particularly in respect of the practical implementation of environment legislation, is fraught with difficulties. Litigation can be expensive, the possibility of judicial review restricted and rules relating to locus standi a major hurdle. Some member states, such as the Netherlands, Germany and Denmark, possess well established procedures for individuals to seek remedies before administrative tribunals and courts for public bodies' non-implementation of environment legislation. In the United States virtually every statute relating to the environment enables 'citizens suits' to be brought under it. The possibility of bringing cases before national courts in environmental matters is important as it raises the possibility of enforcing Community legislation through local, regional and national processes. It would also encourage public participation in environmental protection. Furthermore, an important reason for the growth in the number of complaints to the Commission is the difficulty often of pursuing cases for infringement of EC environment legislation in national courts.

A Community measure enabling environmental non-governmental organisations and private individuals to bring cases for practical infringements of EC environment legislation in national courts would be an important measure which the Commission might usefully consider. This could be achieved through, for example, establishing a general right for Community citizens to take action in national courts over decisions of public bodies in environmental matters. In addition, decentralisation of the complaints procedure might also be envisaged, to allow individuals to lodge complaints over non-implementation with a body in the member state concerned [*CEC, 1991a: 222*]. Complaints would be referred from it to the Commission only if national authorities failed to comply with Community law. Whilst this would have the advantage of reducing the concentration of complaints at Community level it could also have the less desirable effect of erecting a barrier between the citizen and Community institutions.

As in the case of other measures which could lead to improved implementation, the possibility of improving access to national courts is highly dependent on the availability of information about the environment. The difference is that for the use of legal procedures at national level to be effective it is particularly important for private citizens and environmental organisations, as well as public authorities, to have ready access to environmental data. Better information and easier access to it will come about through implementation of the directive on freedom of access to environmental information (90/313/EEC). This directive will be particularly important in those member states which have had the least easy access to information about the environment and the pressures it faces. Lastly, it is not just information about environmental quality that is important but also the ready availability of information about standards set in EC legislation and Community and national environmental policy making processes [*EP, 1988a: 47*]. This points to the need for better diffusion of information about Community legislation and policy making.

The Treaty on European Union

It was noted above that the Maastricht treaty has introduced into Community environment policy the possibility of temporary derogations from legislation where member states are likely to incur substantial costs due to implementation. This could lead to greater variability in the environmental standards applied by member states and, put another way, sanction some member states not to implement Community legislation while others do. The treaty also established a 'cohesion fund' through which those member states with a per capita GNP of less than 90 per cent of the EC average (Greece, Ireland, Portugal and Spain) may apply for Community financial assistance for projects in the environment and transport fields. The fund could be important in helping to meet the costs of Community environment legislation in poorer member states, where implementation may be constrained by lack of resources. However, the fear has been expressed [*RSPB/WWF, 1992*] that there is an inherent tension between the financing by the fund of major infrastructure pro-

246   A GREEN DIMENSION FOR THE EUROPEAN COMMUNITY

jects which might put the environment at risk and its support for projects intended to improve the environment. Certainly, environmental criteria should be built into the operation of the cohesion fund to ensure that the environmental impact of infrastructure projects is fully assessed.

The Maastricht treaty also amended Article 171 of the EEC treaty relating to judgements of the European Court of Justice. Under the Maastricht treaty the Commission may seek imposition of a fine on a member state which persists in flouting Community law after a first judgement of the Court against it. The possibility of instituting economic or financial penalties against member states for non-compliance, possibly by suspending Community subventions, has often been raised. The disadvantage of this idea is that its impact would fall unfairly on the Community's least prosperous member states and regions. While hardly likely to result in substantial financial penalties, the possibility of fining member states for failure to comply with Court judgements increases the range of action available to the Commission to bring moral pressure to bear on member states. After all, it is highly unlikely that fines imposed by the Court would have a major impact on national exchequers. Put differently, 'Fines would probably have to be set at astronomical levels in order to produce results' [*HL 53–1, 1992: 46*].

As well as seeking fines the Commission might also make greater use in future of Article 186 of the EEC treaty which allows the Court of Justice to order interim measures pending its final decision. As noted above, Commission investigations can take years and in the meantime environmental damage might occur. In the 'Leybrucht case' (case 57R/89) the Commission in July 1989, for the first time in a case involving the implementation of environment legislation, applied for interim measures to halt work on a development project underway in Germany which threatened environmental damage. The Commission argued that the project contravened directive 79/409 on the conservation of wild birds and should be halted forthwith pending a final judgement. On that occasion the application failed as the Court considered that the time elapsed (three years) between the Commission's receipt of a complaint about the project and its application to the Court for urgent measures suspending work pending the Court's final decision could not justify it granting interim measures. This adverse judgement could lead the Commission to be more cautious about future applications to the Court for interim measures.

EC ENVIRONMENT LEGISLATION 247

Conclusion

There is no doubt that Community environment legislation raises problems for member states when they come to implement it. These problems result partly from the policy process through which Community legislation is formulated and partly from difficulties encountered within member states' own policy processes when faced with the need to implement legislation agreed at Community level. Since the mid-1980s more attention has been devoted to the implementation of EC environment legislation and to the consideration of ways through which implementation can be improved. Part of the reason for this is that the Community's role in environmental policy-making is now much more central. It is no longer possible to consider national and Community environmental policy as separate and distinct entities. Community policy now largely provides the framework and impetus for environment legislation in the member states. The problem of implementation has taken on greater importance as Community legislation has become a more vital component of member states' environmental protection policies.

In the environment field it is clear that the development of Community monitoring and enforcement mechanisms has not kept pace with the expansion of its legislative role. Such mechanisms are necessary at Community level to ensure that legislation is uniformly applied and that it achieves its objectives. As shown above, however, it may not necessarily be the case that Community enforcement mechanisms have to take the form of a centralised force of Community environment inspectors. The development of EC environment legislation is strongly supported by individuals, amenity groups, environment organisations and local and regional authorities, which look to the Community to set high standards of environmental protection. Poor implementation runs the risk of reducing the credibility and acceptability of Community environment policy. Although greater attention is now being devoted to improving implementation, the fundamental difficulty remains the reluctance of member states to acknowledge the need for the Community to possess a more significant role in monitoring and enforcing policy as well as in developing policy.

REFERENCES

Boehmer-Christiansen, Sonja (1992), Evidence submitted to House of Lords Select Committee on the European Communities, Session 1991–92, 9th Report, *Implementation and Enforcement of Environmental Legislation* (HL 53–II), pp.193–6.
Bulmer, Simon (1983), 'Domestic Politics and European Community Policy Making', *Journal of Common Market Studies*, Vol.XXI, No.4, pp.349–63.

248   A GREEN DIMENSION FOR THE EUROPEAN COMMUNITY

CEC (1989), Statement on the broad lines of Commission policy, presented by the president of the Commission to the European Parliament, Strasbourg 17 Jan. 1989, *Bulletin of the European Communities*, Supplement 1/89.

CEC (1991a), 'Monitoring of the application by Member States of environment directives', Annex C to Commission of the European Communities, Eighth Annual Report to the European Parliament on the application of Community law – 1990, *Official Journal of the European Communities*, C338, 31 Dec. 1991.

CEC (1991b), Article 169 letter from the Commission of the European Communites to the Secretary of State for Foreigh and Commonwealth Affairs, 26 Sept. 1991: directive 80/778/EEC.

CEC (1991c), Article 169 letter from the Commission of the European Communities to the Secretary of State for Foreign and Commonwealth Affairs, 17 Oct. 1991: directive 85/337/EEC.

CEC (1992), *Towards Sustainability: A European Community Programme of Action in Relation to the Environment and Sustainable Development (Fifth Environmental Action Programme)*, COM(92)23 final, 27 March 1992, Vol.II.

Clinton-Davis, Stanley (1992), Evidence submitted to House of Lords Select Committee on the European Communities, Session 1991–92, 9th Report, *Implementation and Enforcement of Environmental Legislation* (HL 53–II), pp.200–201.

Department of the Environment (1987), Minutes of meeting of UK Environment Consultative Group, 28 Jan. 1987.

EP (1988a), Report of the Committee on Environment, Public Health and Consumer Protection on the implementation of European Community legislation relating to water, Doc. A2–298/87, PE 116.085, 14 Feb. 1988. Rapporteur: Ken Collins

EP (1988b), report of the Committee on Environment, Public Health and Consumer Protection on the incorporation into national law of Community directives on the improvement of the quality of the air, Doc. A2–315/87, PE 119.132, 26 Feb. 1988. Rapporteur: Siegbert Alber.

EP (1990a), Notice to Members, Committee on Environment, Public Health and Consumer Protection, Implementation of Environmental Legislation, PE 137.207, 15 Jan. 1990.

EP (1990b), Report of the Committee on Environment, Public Health and Consumer Protection on the proposal from the Commission for a Council Regulation (EEC) on the establishment of the European Environment Agency and the European Environment Monitoring and Information Network, Doc. A3–27/90, PE 133.757, 5 Feb. 1990. Rapporteur: Beate Weber.

EP (1992a), Working Document of Committee on Environment, Public Health and Consumer Protection concerning the staff situation at the Commission's Directorate General for Environment, Public Health and Consumer Protection and the Commission's Consumer Policy Service in 1992 and 1993, PE 156.269, 11 March 1992. Draftsman: Hemmo Muntingh.

EP (1992b), report of the Committee on Environment, Public Health and Consumer Protection on the implementation of environmental legislation, Doc. A3–0001/92, PE 152.144, 6 Jan. 1992. Rapporteur: Jacques Vernier.

EP (1992c), Opinion of the Committee on Environment, Public Health and Consumer Protection on the results of the intergovernmental conferences, PE 155.239, March 1992. Draftsman: Ken Collins

Eurobarometer (1991), No.36, Dec. 1991; Brussels: Commission of the European Communities.

Haigh, Nigel (1984), *EEC Environmental Policy and Britain*, London: Environmental Data Services.

Haigh, Nigel (1986a), 'Keynote Speech: Overview – Problems and Perspectives', *EEB Seminar: The Implementation and Enforcement of EC Environment Legislation*, 27–28 Oct. 1986.

Haigh, Nigel (1986b), 'Devolved Responsibility and Centralization: Effects of EEC Environmental Policy', *Public Administration*, Vol.64, No.2.

Hanf, Kenneth (1991), 'The impact of European policies on domestic institutions and

EC ENVIRONMENT LEGISLATION 249

politics: observations on the implementation of Community environmental directives', paper prepared for presentation at ECPR Workshop on National Political Systems and the European community, University of Essex, 22–27 March 1991.

House of Lords Select Committee on the European Communities, Session 1987–88, HL 6 (1987), 1st Report, *Correspondence with Ministers*.

House of Lords Select Committee on the European Communities, Session 1984–85, HL 227 (1985), 15th Report, *Dangerous Substances*.

House of Lords Select Committee on the European Communities, Session 1986–87, HL 135 (1987), 8th Report, *Fourth Environmental Action Programme*.

House of Lords Select Committee on the European Communities, Session 1991–92, HL 53 (1992), 9th Report, *Implementation and Enforcement of Environmental Legislation*, March 1992; Volume I: Report (HL 53–I); Vol.II: Evidence (HL 53–II).

IEEP (1992a), Evidence submitted by the Institute for European Environmental Policy to House of Lords Select Committee on the European Communites, Session 1991–92, 9th Report, *Implementation and Enforcement of Environmental Legislation*, (HL 53–II), pp.168–173.

IEEP (1992b), Institute for European Environmental Policy, *Assessment of the Fourth and Fifth Environmental Action Programmes*, study produced for European Parliament Committee on Environment, Public Health and Consumer Protection, April 1992.

Jacobs, Francis and Richard Corbett (1990), *The European Parliament*, London: Longman.

Macrory, Richard (1992), 'The Enforcement of Community Environmental Laws: Some Critical Issues', *Common Market Law Review*, Vol.29, pp.347–69.

Pressman J.L. and A. Wildavsky (1973), *Implementation*, Berkeley CA: University of California Press.

Richardson, Jeremy and Grant Jordan (1979), *Governing under Pressure: The Policy Process in a Post-Parliamentary Democracy*, Oxford: Martin Robertson.

RSPB (1992), evidence submitted by the Royal Society for the Protection of Birds to House of Lords Select Committee on the European Communities, Session 1991–92, 9th report, *Implementation and Enforcement of Environmental Legislation*, (HL 53–II), pp.138–149.

RSPB/WWF (1992), *The Cohesion Fund and the Environment*, note by the Royal Society for the Protection of Birds and World Wide Fund for Nature International, March 1992.

Taylor, D., Diprose, G. and M. Duffy (1986), 'EC Environmental Policy and the Control of Water Pollution: The Implementation of Directive 76/464 in Perspective', *Journal of Common Market Studies*, Vol.XXIV, No.3, pp.225–46.

Wallace, Helen (1982) 'National Politics and Supranational Integration', D.Cameron (ed), *Regionalism and Supranationalism*, London: PSI, pp.111–126.

Wilkinson, D. (1992), *Maastricht and the Environment*, London: Institute for European Environmental Policy.

[10]

THE ENFORCEMENT OF COMMUNITY ENVIRONMENTAL LAWS: SOME CRITICAL ISSUES

RICHARD MACRORY*

1. Introduction

> "Community environmental legislation will only be effective if it is fully implemented and enforced by Member States"[1]

In recent years both the European Parliament[2] and the Council of Ministers have stressed the importance of ensuring that Community law is fully implemented within Member States.[3] New mechanisms and procedures are under discussion at a political level, while traditional tools are employed in the meantime. Yet it is a sensitive area. Member States may subscribe to the concept of the supremacy of Community law and the need for better implementation, but are reluctant to accept interference with national administrative arrangements for enforcement.

The field of environmental policy is particularly striking in this context. Since the Community began development of Community environmental policies in 1972 a large body of directives, regulations, and decisions has been agreed, and in terms of the sheer amount of legislation

---

* Denton Hall Professor of Environmental Law, Imperial College, London.
1. Statement of European Council, Bull. EC 6-1990, 18–21, note 4.
2. See European Parliament Resolutions of 11 Apr. 1984, O.J. 1984, C 127/67; of 19 March 1990, O.J. 1990, C 68/172; and most recently of 7 Nov. 1991.
3. At an informal meeting of the Council of Ministers on 11–13 Oct. 1991, it was agreed that there is a need both for the "further development and enforcement of environmental legislation" within the Community and to "improve the compliance and enforcement structures concerning environmental legislation and the implementation within the Member States".

that now exists the programme must be considered one of the success stories of the Community.[4] The aim of this article is to consider the mechanisms associated with the implementation and enforcement of Community environmental legislation, with "implementation" denoting the process by which legal obligations under Community law are fulfilled, while "enforcement" implies the methods available to ensure that implementation takes place. The vast majority of Community environmental laws have been in the form of directives, with the consequence that attention to date has been largely with ensuring that Member States rather than private interests comply with their obligations under these laws. In that context, my particular concern will be with the use of the Article 169 enforcement procedures by the European Commission. I make no excuse for this focus. Although the process has been subject to criticism for reasons that will become apparent, and while new methods of ensuring improved compliance are being considered,[5] the Article 169 procedure will remain a central and critical *legal* tool for enforcement at Community level, whatever the nature of other initiatives agreed upon.

One of the underlying difficulties associated with the implementation and enforcement of Community environmental law is the differing structural character of the legislation that has been agreed. Some directives prescribe explicit and precise goals that must be achieved in a given sector which in theory should be reasonably straightforward to monitor and enforce.[6] Another class contains similarly precise goals within specified sectors or areas but leaves a large element of discretion to Member States in determining where they are to apply.[7] Examples of

---

4. Around 200 regulations, directives, and decisions have been agreed in the environmental field.

5. E.g. at an informal meeting of the Council of Ministers in Oct. 1991, it was agreed that Member States should establish an informal network of national enforcement officers concerned with environmental law.

6. E.g. Directive 80/779 on air quality limit values and guide values for sulphur dioxide and suspended particulates O.J. 1980, L 229/30, Directive 80/778 relating to the quality of water intended for human consumption O.J. 1980, L 229/11.

7. E.g. Directive 78/659 on the quality of fresh waters needing protection or improvement in order to support fish life O.J. 1978, L 229/11; Directive 76/160 concerning the quality of bathing water O.J. 1976, L 229/11; Directive 79/409 on the conservation of wild birds O.J. 1979, L 79/409.

Environmental laws 349

more recent legislation cut across conventional administrative boundaries and sectors, and impose obligations that reach deep into national
decision-màking at many levels. This type of "horizontal" directive,
exemplified by the 1985 Environmental Assessment Directive,[8] raises
acute difficulties for both Member States and the Community institutions when it comes to ensuring full implementation.

2. The role of the Commission

A key function of the European Commission under the Treaty of Rome
is to ensure the effective application of Community law.[9] The Commission's role in enforcement is therefore one of its institutional duties,
yet it was not until the early 1980s, a decade after the initiation of explicit Community environmental policies, that it began to take its role
seriously in this field. The European Parliament played an important
part in the process of galvanizing concern. The disappearance of toxic
waste being transported from Seveso in 1983 revealed the extent of
defective implementation of existing environmental directives governing toxic and dangerous wastes, and the Parliament's subsequent inquiry and Resolution criticized both the Commission and Member
States over their failure to ensure effective implementation of Community environmental legislation.[10] Since that date, the Commission,
largely through its legal unit within Directorate-General XI, has concentrated on improving its enforcement efforts, using both conventional legal processes available under Community law, and less formal methods. Before examining the machinery that is employed, it is
worth asking whether there are particular features of the Community's
programme of environmental legislation which have fostered problems
of poor implementation by Member States.

8. Directive 85/337 on the assessment of the effects of certain public and private
projects on the environment, O.J. 1985, L 175/40. Another notable example of such
a horizontal directive is Directive 90/313 on access to environmental information, O.J.
1990, L 158/56.
9. Art. 155 EEC provides that the Commission shall, " ... ensure that the provisions of this Treaty and the measures taken by the institutions pursuant thereof are applied; ... "
10. European Parliament Resolution of 11 April 1984 O.J. 1984, C 127/67.

Dr. Ludwig Krämer, head of the legal unit within D.G. XI, has argued that a fundamental characteristic of environmental law, both at Community and national level, is the lack of readily identifiable vested interests willing and able to secure enforcement.[11] The same is not true of, say, Competition, Employment or Agricultural Law where the failure by Member States to implement Community law can directly effect economic interests. There is undoubtedly considerable truth in this assertion. Many aspects of the environment are not susceptible to conventional concepts of legal property rights which are capable of enforcement by private interests. Amenity and environmental groups who *would* lay claim to having an interest in general environmental protection may lack the necessary *locus* to commence legal proceedings, or prefer to devote limited resources to creating political rather than legal pressure on defaulting administrations.

There are other aspects, though, of the Community's environmental policies which have contributed to the problems of implementation. The programme is comparatively young, and before the passing of the Single European Act 1987 lacked explicit legal basis under the Treaty.[12] In that climate, the attraction for policy-makers initiating Community activity in this field to concentrate on the creation of an ambitious body of environmental laws, even if this implied legislation at the expense of implementation, would have been understandable. Directorate-General XI still remains comparatively small in staff numbers compared to the rest of the Commission, but its purchase power and influence is considerable given the scope of the legislation now in place.

A further reason relates to the form of legislation adopted. The vast majority of Community laws have taken the form of directives, and many of those now giving rise to serious tensions over interpretation and implementation were passed during the 1970s and early 1980s. The drafting and precise meaning of many of the requirements are open to differing interpretations, and were agreed by Member States at a time

11. Krämer, *EEC Treaty and Environmental Protection* (1990), p. 26.
12. See Art. 130r–t and Art. 100a EEC. Before the amendments to the Treaty, environmental legislation was generally based on either Art. 100 or Art. 235 or both.

when they probably failed to appreciate the extent to which the directives represented more than a commitment of policy intention but a genuine legal obligation. Since that period, the developing jurisprudence of the European Court of Justice, both in relation to the direct effect doctrine[13] the so-called doctrine of sympathetic interpretation,[14] and its strict approach towards the transposition of directives into national laws and procedures, has transformed the legal nature of directives.[15] One can only speculate whether Member States would have readily agreed the terms of some the earlier environmental directives had they appreciated their full legal significance, or had the development in the European Court's jurisprudence occurred at earlier date. Certainly, it might have been predicted that these legal developments, coupled with the Commission's own more intensive efforts at enforcement, would have made Member States more reluctant to agree new directives in the environmental field.[16] This does not appear to have happened – or if it did, has been more than counterbalanced by a growing political imperative given to environmental issues within Europe. Environmental directives with significant resource, legal, and administrative implications have continued to be proposed and agreed.

3. Formal enforcement procedures

The formal legal procedures available to the Commission in persuading a Member State to comply with Community obligations, derive from

13. See, e.g. Case 41/74, *van Duyn* v. *Home Office*, [1974] ECR 1337; Case 8/81, *Becker* v. *Finanzamt Munster-Innenstadt*, [1982] ECR 53; Case 148/78, *Pubblico Ministero* v. *Tullio Ratti*, [1979] ECR 1629. There is as yet no decision of the Court of Justice dealing with the direct effect of environmental directives as such, although the *Ratti* case was concerned with the packaging and labelling of solvents and toxic substances.
14. Case 14/83, *von Colson and Kamann* v. *Land Nordrhein-Westfalen*, [1984] ECR 1891. Again there is no decision of the Court of Justice applying this doctrine to environmental Directives.
15. See, e.g. Case 300/81, *Commission* v. *Italy*, [1983] ECR 449; Case 102/79, *Commission* v. *Belgium*, [1980] ECR 1473, and Case 361/88 and 59/89, *Commission* v. *Germany* 30 May 1991, n.y.r.
16. Rehbinder and Stewart, *Integration through Law: Environmental Protection Policy* (1985) argue to this effect: pp. 316 et seq.

Article 169 EEC, and as such are common to all areas of Community policy. The terms of Article 169 are interpreted to divide into three separate stages; (i) the sending of a formal Article 169 letter to the Member State (ii) the sending of a reasoned opinion and finally (iii) referral to the European Court. The first two stages may, and often do, end in a settlement in that either the Member State complies with the Commission's requirements, or a mutually acceptable agreement is reached without the need for intervention by the Court. As might be expected of any complex process of legal enforcement, these formal stages, and particularly the service of an Article 169 letter are not normally initiated without some considerable forewarning and correspondence between the Member State and the Commission.

The Commission's concern is with a Member State's failure to implement Community agreed obligations, but what is actually implied by the concept of "implementation" is by no means cut and dried. For administrative purposes, the Commission itself has broken down the subject into three main areas: (i) a failure by a Member State to communicate to the Commission national laws and other national measures implementing the Community instruments in question; (ii) incomplete or incorrect transposition of Community obligations into national law and (iii) the failure to apply the Community obligations in practice, whatever the state of the national law.

4. Black letter implementation

The first two categories are, by their nature, confined to the implementation of directives, and are concerned with what might be described as the formal aspect of implementation, ensuring at the very least that the "black letter" national law is in place. Monitoring the failure to communicate national measures within the time-scale specified in the directive is a reasonably straightforward, and quasi-mechanical process; either communication has been made by the specified date or it has not.

In the early 1980s, the Commission standardized the enforcement machinery relating to non-communication across all sectors of Commu-

Environmental laws 353

Table 1. Art. 169 Infringement Proceedings 1982–1990

	Non-communication	Non-conformity	Poor application
Environment			
1982	15	1	–
1983	23	10	2
1984	48	15	2
1985	58	10	1
1986	84	32	9
1987	68	30	58
1988	36	24	30
1989	46	17	37
1990	131	24	62
All sectors			
1982	206	10	37
1983	140	19	27
1984	222	46	17
1985	257	30	14
1986	268	51	54
1987	260	42	125
1988	282	33	117
1989	327	25	169
1990	616	37	162

Source: 8th Report of the Commission to the European Parliament on the enforcement of Community law, 1991.

nity law.[17] Member States are notified within two months of the directive being adopted, that they are required to notify the Commission of the texts of national implementing measures, with a further reminder letter generally sent six months before the deadline specified in the directive. If no notification has been made by the date required, the Commission will generally move straight into Article 169 proceedings without further warning, starting with a formal letter and moving to a reasoned opinion without referring back to Commissioners for approval.

The rise in the volume of legal proceedings for non-communication has been dramatic, with in 1982 just 15 proceedings begun for non-communication in the environmental sector rising to 131 in 1990 (see Table 1). Indeed in 1990, proceedings for non-communication repre-

17. See, e.g. Commission *Manual of Procedures* Fifth Updating, March 1982.

sented almost 60% of the total commenced in the environmental sector, a figure matched on the overall picture. This represents a higher proportion of the three classes of actions than for the previous three years, and could in part simply be attributable to a higher volume of legislation agreed in previous years. At the same time, the Commission has become more confident on legal grounds that the transposition of directives in most cases is required to be in the form of national legislation rather than administrative means, and in this respect has been bolstered by recent decisions of the European Court of Justice.[18] More disturbingly, though, it could suggest that Member States are more complacent on the issue, especially as they must be aware that the European Court of Justice has in its decisions on non-communication showed little sympathy for any excuses made by Member States on internal political or constitutional grounds.[19] In this respect, the Commission's policy of a more aggressive and regularized approach in respect of non-communication may have diluted the shock value of Article 169 proceedings, though in the absence of more effective legal sanctions their tactics are understandable if only to bring to the light the current state of non-compliance with the most basic of obligations.

Determining an infringement of the second type, incomplete or incorrect transposition, is a task that is intellectually much more demanding. Communication of national laws has taken place with the required time-limits but it is argued that they fail to reflect the obligations under the directive in question. This requires both an understanding of the legal meaning of the provisions of the directive, itself not always an easy matter, together with the ability to interpret the meaning of national legislation in the light of the Member State's own legal and administrative practice. The position is made more complex because Member States may have relied upon pre-existing legislation to meet the aims of the directive, in which case its detailed terminology is unlikely to be closely aligned with that of the directive.[20]

18. See especially Cases 361/88 and 59/89, cited note 15 *supra*, concerning implementation of Directive 80/779 on air quality limits values and guide values for sulphur dioxide and suspended particulates O.J. 1980, L 222/30, and Directive 82/884 on limit values for lead in air O.J. 1982, L 378/15.

19. E.g. Case 77/69, *Commission* v. *Belgium*, [1970] ECR 237; Case 79/72, *Commission* v. *Italy*, [1973] ECR 667; Case 52/75, *Commission* v. *Italy*, [1986] ECR 1359.

20. For recent examples where a Member State relied upon pre-existing national law

Furthermore, some of the more recent environmental directives, which cut across conventionally drawn boundaries of administrative and legal responsibility, may as a result prevent the Member State from relying upon a single item of legislation as its means of implementation. The Environmental Assessment Directive[21] offers the prime example, with some countries needing to pass twenty or so individual laws in different sectoral and jurisdictional areas;[22] in communicating the text of these measures to the Commission, only the most selfless of Member States is likely to draw attention to detailed deficiencies that may exist.

Examples have existed where Member States have discussed the draft text of environmental legislation with the Commission well before the implementation date, and common sense suggests that at this stage a Member State faced with criticism may be more ready to modify the final version. In contrast, once national law has been passed, whether by way of primary or secondary legislation, there must be an understandable tendency on the part of the Member State to defend the status quo. Despite this, there appears to be no regular procedure, either as a legal requirement or as a matter of administrative practice, by which Member States and the Commission discuss draft texts of national laws during the period following agreement of a directive and the state for its implementation.[23]

5. Implementation in practice – conceptual and practical difficulties

The third category, non-implementation in practice, is perhaps the most difficult area of enforcement for the Commission, and certainly one

to implement environmental Directives see Case 360/87, *Commission* v. *Italy*, judgment of the Court of Justice 28 Feb. 1991, n.y.r. and Case 131/88, *Commission* v. *Germany*, judgment 29 Feb. 1991, n.y.r. Both cases involved Directive 80/68 on the protection of groundwater against pollution by certain dangerous substances O.J. 1980, L 103/1, and in both the Commission was successful in claiming that the Member State had failed to transpose adequately the Directive into national law.

21. Note 8 *supra*.

22. This has been the case for the United Kingdom and for Germany.

23. During oral proceedings in Case 252/89, *Commission* v. *Luxembourg* and Case 330/89, *Commission* v. *Belgium* on 7 Nov. 1990, both concerning the failure to implement the Environmental Assessment Directive, the Court expressed concern that the Commission had failed to give any response when Luxembourg had sent to the Commission the text of a proposed new law implementing the Directive.

that can touch a raw nerve of the sensibilities of Member States. Examples of this category include the failure of local drinking water supplies or particular stretches of bathing waters to meet prescribed Community standards, the failure of a waste disposal licence to meet the prohibitions contained in the Groundwater Directive, failure to carry out an environmental assessment for a project falling within mandatory classes of the Environmental Assessment, and, in the future, no doubt the failure by public authorities to provide members of the public with information as required under the Access to Environmental Information Directive.[24]

The need to ensure effective implementation in practice has been endorsed by Member States, yet clearly there exist tensions and controversy when the Commission takes steps to pursue this task. To start with, it is not always clear whether a particular example of apparent breaches of Community law should be classified as incomplete or incorrect transposition of the directive or a failure to implement in practice. One can again take the case of the Environmental Assessment Directive where a Member State has failed to introduce the necessary implementing legislation covering all the project classes specified in the directive. A particular project in that Member State is proposed and no environmental assessment is undertaken. Is that a failure to implement the directive in practice, or simply an example of the results of failing to correctly transpose the directive into national law?

At first sight, the distinction seems unimportant. The Article 169 legal procedures are the same whatever category of breach is alleged by the Commission. Yet compared with more general proceedings taken against a Member State for incomplete transposition, action initiated in respect of a particular project may have considerable local political impact, possibly even bringing pressure to suspend or bring to the halt construction of the project in question.[25] Furthermore, injunctive

24. Directive 90/313 O.J. 1990, L 158/56.
25. It is interesting to note the application of the Environmental Assessment Directive in a procedure in the Netherlands, *Texaco* v. *Minister van Economische Zaken*, where the president of the Court suspended, in summary proceedings, the approval of a plan involving construction of a conventional power station. See annotation by H. Sevenster, (1991) *Utilities Law Review*, 65–66.

Environmental laws   357

remedies from the European Court may be available to stop continuing work on an individual project, though the Commission's only experience to date with such proceedings in the environmental sector was unsuccessful.[26] Yet in reality in such cases it is the underlying failure of the Member State to introduce appropriate legislation which has given rise to the problem – indeed the national authorities dealing with such a project may themselves possess no power to require environmental assessment procedures.

The above illustrates a further difficulty with this type of infringement proceedings. Assuming that the national legislation is in place, failure to implement in practice may well be due to the action or inaction of a local or regional public authority, or even a local court. All such bodies fall within the overarching concept of the "Member State", yet in practice it is the central Governments of Member State who assume the responsibility for being at the receiving end of infringement proceedings. It is they who will be expected to take appropriate remedial steps against internal authorities who fail to implement Community obligations, be it by the use of default powers or the promotion of new legislation. In an era of greater regionalization and where federalism is explained by its proponents to imply a real devolvement of powers as much as their centralization, it must be questioned whether the current focus of infringement proceedings against Member States through the medium of central governments is still appropriate. There may well be a case for adopting a practice of permitting proceedings to be taken directly against the particular authority responsible for the failure in practice, at whatever level of government it is placed. Where a local authority makes an illegal planning decision in the United Kingdom, we expect to see judicial review proceedings taken against that body, not against the Secretary of State for the Environment even though he may have overall political responsibility for the planning system. The same should be true of infringement procedures if one is to view Community environmental law as a mature legal system integral to the national systems within Member States, and a stage removed from more straight-

26. Case 57/89 *Commission* v. *Germany*, [1989] ECR 2849.

forward international agreements between individual States represented by their central Governments.

We can identify further areas of tension that arise from dealing with the failure to apply directives in practice. The economic cost of complying with the requirements of directives may often be the root cause of the failure to implement, and while some environmental directives expressly incorporate an economic criterion such as "best available technology not entailing excessive costs",[27] others do not.

An important case before the European Court of Justice in 1990 concerned the failure to implement the standards contained in the Drinking Water Directive[28] in local supplies, and suggests that in such cases the Court will take a strict attitude. Although the directive contained provisions allowing Member States to obtain derogations in exceptional cases, mainly due to particular geographical problems, financial and technical difficulties were not expressly mentioned. The Belgian Government had argued that the costs and complexities of constructing suitable treatment works in the localities specified had caused the delay in compliance. The Court rejected this as an excuse:

> " . . . il y a lieu de rappeler que, selon la jurisprudence de la Cour, un État membre ne saurait exciper des difficultés pratiques ou administratives pour justifier le non-respect des obligations et délais prescrits par les directives communautaires. *Il en va de même pour les difficultés financières qu'il appartient aux États membres de surmonter en prenant les mesures appropriées.*"
>
> (para 24) (author's emphasis)[29]

Many provisions in environmental directives involve various types of discretionary powers to be exercised by Member States or competent

27. See Directive 84/360 on combatting of air pollution from large industrial plants, O.J. 1984, L 336/1.

28. Directive 80/778 relating to the quality of water intended for human consumption.

29. Case 42/89, *Commission* v. *Belgium*, judgment of the Court of Justice 5 July 1990, n.y.r. " . . . according to the Court's case law, a Member State may not rely on practical or administrative difficulties for the justification of failure to respect the obligations and time limits laid down by Community directives. The same holds for financial difficulties, which it is for Member States to overcome by taking appropriate measures." (Editors' translation).

bodies, and the issue here concerns the principles on which the exercise of such discretionary powers should amount to a failure to implement a directive in practice, giving rise to infringement proceedings. There is some emerging case law, though little in the way of developed principle.

A common provision of a number of environmental directives, particularly those concerning water pollution, is a power given to Member State to designate areas falling within the requirements of the directive. In the Bathing Water Directive, for example, Member States must designate areas of water to be subject to the standards contained in the directive, but the definition of bathing water is expressed in quasi-objective terms: all fresh water or sea water in which "bathing is either explicitly authorized by the Member States, or is not prohibited and is traditionally practised by a large number of bathers" (Art. 1.2). This has given the Commission clear leverage to question the determinations made by Member State on the basis that water falling outside the definition had not be designated. Other directives, though, contain no such objective definitions, but are expressed in a way that appears to given a clear discretion to Member States. But the failure by a Member State even to address the question of designation may render the aims of the directive ineffective, and here the European Court has held that in such cases there may be an infringement by the Member State.[30]

A similar issue has arisen in the case of the Environmental Assessment Directive which requires assessment procedures to be carried out in respect of proposals for projects falling within classes specified in the directive. For those falling within Annex I, assessment is mandatory, while for those falling within the much larger list in Annex II, assessment is required only where such projects may give rise to significant environmental effects; Member States are given discretion to determine appropriate criteria and thresholds to decide which particular projects falling within Annex II should be subject to assessment. Some Member States, initially at any rate, considered that this was an unfettered discretion giving them the right to exclude totally whole classes of

---

30. Case 322/86, *Commission* v. *Italy*, [1988] ECR 3995 concerning the failure by Italy to designate waters under Directive 78/659 on the quality of fresh waters needing protection or improvement in order to support fish life O.J. 1978, L 222/1 and under Directive 79/923 on the quality required for shellfish waters O.J. 1979, L 281/47.

projects from their national provisions on assessment. It is an interpretation that the Commission has firmly resisted; in order to achieve the aims of the Directive, Member States are obliged to address the problem of criteria and thresholds for *all* classes of projects specified within the Directive.

The European Court is likely to support this approach. That the failure by a Member State to address the exercise of a discretionary power may amount to an infringement of the directive is hardly contentious. A more difficult question, though, arises when it is sought to question the actual judgments made by Member States in the exercise of such powers. On what principles should both the Commission and the European Court approach to the issue? The Environmental Assessment Directive again provides good examples of the type of issue that increasingly is likely to arise. To what extent is the determination of specific thresholds for Annex II projects by a Member State a reviewable decision? Is the actual scope and content of assessment information provided in a particular case grounds for infringement proceedings? Should the decision by a local authority to grant permission for the proposed project to proceed, in the face of overwhelming evidence of adverse environmental effects, be questionable as a matter of Community law?

Leaving aside the particular wording of provisions of the Directive in question, one can assume that the exercise of discretionary power would be subject to such general principles as proportionality and non-discrimination. Thresholds for Annex II classes of projects, for example, which made a distinction between projects involving national interests and those of other Member States would therefore be contrary to Community law. Beyond that, principles of review are underdeveloped. But some suggestion of an appropriate approach is found in the 1990 decision of the European Court in *Commission* v. *France*[31] concerning Council Regulation 3626/82 of 3 December 1982 on the implementation in the Community of the Convention on international trade in endangered species (the CITES convention). Under the Regulation, Member States are required to issue permits for the importation

---

31. Case 182/89, judgment of the Court of Justice 29 Nov. 1990 n.y.r.

from third countries of certain specified animals or plants, and Art 10(b) provides that the import permit may only be issued where, *inter alia*, " ... it is clear or where the applicant presents trustworthy evidence, that the capture or collection of the specimen in the wild will not have a harmful effect on the conservation of species or on the extent of the territory occupied by the population in question of the species."

The proceedings arose out of the decision by the French authorities in 1986 to grant permits for the importation of some 6000 wild cat skins from Bolivia. It was this decision that the Commission questioned. The decision of the French authorities had been taken against a background of international concern over illicit trade in wild animals from Bolivia, with a meeting of the contracting parties to the CITES Convention calling for a suspension of imports from the country until the Bolivian Government had demonstrated that it had adopted all practical measures to implement the Convention. The Commission had notified Member States of the terms of this Resolution, and in effect argued that in the light of these concerns, the French decision to grant import permits must have been contrary to the terms of Article 10(b) of the Council Regulation. The French argued that the CITES Resolution had no legal effect, and that the decision whether or not to grant import permits was one for national authorities; indeed Article 9 specifically states that Member States shall recognize the decisions of competent authorities of other Member States, and that import permits granted by one country should be valid throughout the Community. The European Court held that there had been a breach of the Directive. In the light of the factual background and the terms of Article 10(b) the French authorities, according to A.G. Mischo,

> " ... n'ont pas raisonnablement pu aboutir a la constation qu'il etait evident que la capture des chats sauvages en question n'aurait pas d'influence notive sur leur conservation ni sur l'entension de l'aire de leur distribution."
> (Opinion, 18 October 1990, para 13)[32]

32. " ... could not reasonably have come to the conclusion that it was obvious that the capture of the wild cats in question would not have a harmful effect on their conservation or on the extent of the territory occupied by their population." (Editors' translation).

This appears to be very close to *Wednesbury* principles of judicial review of administrative decisions, familiar to British courts.[33] Certainly the very particular nature of the decisions that were the subject of the proceedings illustrates just how deep into the decision-making of national authorities the process of enforcement of Community environmental law has reached. British courts have long subscribed to the principle that it is not for them to substitute their own judgment for those in administration entrusted with the task of decision-making. Yet the Bolivian import case comes perilously close to just that. How far the European Court and the Commission will elaborate principles of review which forbear from second judging administrative decisions is likely to prove a challenging area of law over the next decade, especially when set against the political pressures that emphasize the importance of ensuring implementation of Community law in practice.

6. Information gaps and the Complaint Procedure

In the environmental sector, the Commission has no express powers to assist its investigations of the kind it has been granted in the competition field.[34] There are as yet no Community environmental inspectors, working alongside national enforcement officers, although the idea has been mooted in the past, and may yet surface again.[35] In 1990, the

---

33. *Wednesbury Corporation* v. *Ministry of Housing and Local Government*, [1965] 1 WLR 261. In Case 42/84, *Remia BV* v. *Commission*, [1985] ECR 2545 the Court of Justice reviewed the discretion of the Commission to determine the permitted duration of a non-competition clause under Art. 85(3) of the EEC Treaty. The Court recognized that the Commission's decision was based on a complex economic appraisal, and that its grounds for review should be limited, "to verifying whether the relevant procedural rules had been complied with, whether the statement of the reasons for the decision is adequate, whether the facts have been accurately stated, and whether there had been any manifest error of appraisal or misuse of powers". These principles were concerned with the Commission's decision-making functions, but it is suggested they might be usefully adapted to those of national authorities in the sorts of examples given in the text.

34. See Council Regulation No. 17 of 6 Feb. 1962, O.J. Special Edition 1959–62, 87.

35. In Nov. 1991 the UK Government called for the creation of a small Community "Audit Inspectorate" to work alongside national enforcement bodies to monitor and report on compliance with EEC environmental legislation. *Department of the Environment Press Release* 25 Nov. 1991.

Environmental laws   363

Council of Ministers adopted a Regulation establishing a European Environmental Agency, though as yet no location for the Agency has been agreed.[36] In any event, the title of the body is rather misleading, since its terms of reference are clearly restricted to data collection and analysis, largely in cooperation with national authorities. During discussions of the draft proposal, the European Parliament pressed hard for the Agency to have more explicit enforcement functions, but in the event managed only to secure a commitment in the Regulation to review the role of the Agency in this respect two years after it comes into existence.

Against this background, the Commission has been peculiarly dependent on its own complaint system to enable it to be alerted to possible infringements in practice. The procedures, governed by the Commission's internal rules of administration,[37] permit any member of the public, including environmental groups and industries, to notify the Commission of alleged infringements. The system is common to all areas of Community law, and was first developed in the 1960s in the context of the internal market. But it is environmental issues that have given rise to a spectacular growth in the numbers of complaints received, and they now represent almost half of all total number received annually by the Commission (Table 2).

A number of criticisms can be made about the current system. It means that the Commission is, initially at any rate, playing a largely reactive role to the type of issues and subject matter raised; its stated commitment to investigate every complaint received, while a laudable goal of an administration exercising enforcement powers, leaves little room for strategic decision-making, especially given the current limited

36. Regulation 1210/90 O.J. 1990, L 120/1. Despite pressure from the European Parliament to give the agency a more explicit inspection and enforcement function, the Regulation restricts its activities broadly to the gathering and assessment of environmental data, though even this limited role is likely to assist the Commission in its enforcement activities. Art. 20, however, provides that two years after the entry into force of the Regulation (which takes place when its location has been agreed) the Council, having consulted the Parliament and on the basis of a report from the Commission, must decide on further tasks for the Agency including, " . . . associating in the monitoring of the implementation of Community environmental legislation, in cooperation with the Commission and existing competent bodies in the Member States."

37. See note 17 *supra*.

Table 2. Complaints registered by Commission 1982–90

	Environment	All sectors
1982	10	352
1983	8	399
1984	9	476
1985	37	585
1986	165	791
1987	150	850
1988	216	1137
1989	465	1195
1990	480	1252

Source: Table 1 op.cit.

Table 3. Complaints registered in environmental sector 1990

Belgium	17
Denmark	3
France	47
Germany	56
Greece	40
Ireland	19
Italy	33
Luxembourg	3
Netherlands	7
Portugal	19
Spain	111
United Kingdom	125

Source: Commission

man-power involved.[38] When the numbers of complaints are broken down on a country by country basis, it is clear that there are considerable disparities, which reveal as much about a country's tradition of environmental activism and political protest as they do about the state of implementation of Community law (see Table 3).

In the Commission's favour it should be stressed that these realities are recognized, and in the end there is a more balanced approach towards Member States than might be apparent at first glance. Complaints on a particular issue from one Member State may sometimes

38. According to Dr. Ludwig Krämer, the unit in October 1991 had a staff of 10 lawyers, six of whom were on secondment; evidence taken before House of Lords Select Committee on the European Communities (Sub-Committee F) 13 Oct. 1991.

Environmental laws   365

Table 4. Reasoned opinions and referrals to Court of Justice in environmental sector 1989

	Reasoned opinion	Referral to ECJ
Belgium	8	11
Denmark	0	0
France	6	7
Germany	8	8
Greece	5	3
Ireland	5	0
Italy	16	7
Luxembourg	2	1
Netherlands	5	2
Portugal	4	0
Spain	9	3
United Kingdom	8	5

Source: Commission Report on Enforcement of Community Environmental Law 8/2/1990.

lead to an investigation of the state of compliance within all Member States, and the figures on the number of reasoned opinions and referrals to the Court indicate that action against Member States is not eventually dictated by the number of complaints received from each (Table 4).

In 1990, the Commission took the bold step of releasing publicly figures on a country by country basis of the numbers of Article 169 letters that had been issued in the environmental sector, a deliberate political move to highlight the issue of implementation and one that caused considerable disquiet among some Member States at the time. One of the benefits of this unprecedented exercise in public administration was that, as with the reasoned opinions and Court referrals, it confirmed that enforcement action against Member States was not driven by complaint numbers, but probably reflected a reasonable approximation of the relative levels of compliance (Table 5). Nevertheless, when broken down on a sector by sector basis, the figures suggest that the current procedures are vulnerable to the focus of attention of national environmental interests (Table 6). The high number of infringements in the field of water pollution in the United Kingdom, for example, has been largely driven by highly directed campaigns by amenity bodies, while equivalent groups in France appear to have paid particular attention to hunting activities and the protection of wild animals.

Table 5. Article 169 formal letters in environmental sector 1989

Belgium	27
Denmark	5
France	28
Germany	13
Greece	37
Ireland	16
Italy	17
Luxembourg	9
Netherlands	18
Portugal	10
Spain	45
United Kingdom	18

Source: Commission Report on Enforcement of Community environmental law 8/21/90.

Note a number of Member States disputed the accuracy of these figures when they were released, though any errors appeared to have been marginal.

Table 6. Infringement proceedings sector by sector at 31.12.89

	Water	Air	Waste	Chemicals	Noise	Nature*
Belgium	11	3	18	5	2	7
Denmark	2	–	–	–	1	–
France	15	3	2	1	–	20
Germany	9	4	2	3	–	11
Greece	10	4	6	2	3	20
Ireland	7	2	3	2	–	7
Italy	9	4	10	2	3	12
Luxembourg	5	2	2	–	1	2
Netherlands	6	2	2	3	3	8
Portugal	2	1	4	–	–	7
Spain	12	2	10	4	–	29
U.K.	16	5	3	3	–	4

* includes environmental assessment

Source: Table 5 op.cit.

A further concern of present procedures is the extent to which the Commission may be dependent on a Member State's cooperation in complying with the Commission's initial requests for information following the lodging of a complaint. An absolute refusal to respond may result in the Member State being threatened with infringement proceedings for failure to comply with its duty to assist the Commission in its tasks under Article 5 of the EEC Treaty.[39] But the provision of poor or incomplete information by Member States poses peculiar difficulties for the Commission, and while in some cases site-visits have been undertaken or consultants' reports commissioned, the current system is hardly geared to this type of intensive investigatory work, although it may be required.

Defective implementation in practice is likely to be a continuing focus of attention, and while in formal terms the dispute is between the Member State and the Commission it is clear that in practice private parties may find themselves heavily involved in the process. The complainant himself may dispute a decision of the Commission not to initiate infringement proceedings, particularly where his own private interests are being threatened by alleged illegal action, and given the limitations of the direct effect doctrine it may not be possible to raise such issues before national courts. But parties, other than the complainant, may also find their interests at stake. For example, the legality of an authorization given under national law to a private project may be thrown into doubt should the Commission decided to commence proceedings against the Member State for failure to apply the Environmental Assessment Directive; similarly, a permit given to a private operator of a waste disposal facility may be questioned because of its incompatibility with the Groundwater Directive.

Current principles of Community law need development to recognize the reality of these relationships. Private interests which are indirectly involved in this way currently have no rights *vis-à-vis* the Commission to ensure that their point of view is heard during the investigatory procedures. The Court of Justice has continued to confirm that the decision to commence Article 169 procedures is a matter of discretion for the Commission, and that a third party, whether a complainant or, one must presume, another party directly effected by this decision, has no

---

39. "Member States shall take all appropriate measures, whether general or particular, to ensure fulfilment of the obligations arising out of the Treaty or resulting from action taken by the institutions of the Community. They shall facilitate the achievement of the Community's tasks." See also the annotation of Case C-374/89, *Commission* v. *Belgium* in this issue by Prechal.

locus before the Court in such cases to question the legality of its action.[40]

The initiation of infringement proceedings concerning failure to implement in practice, is subject to no period of limitation of the type familiar to national systems of administrative law, and designed to provide legal certainty to private and public interests. The extent to which these types of issues are currently addressed is largely left to the discretion and sense of propriety of the Commission; if the enforcement process is to be strengthened and extended in future, the time may now have come to develop more considered legal principles governing the procedures.

7. Some concluding remarks

The Commission's own achievements to date in revealing the extent to which deficiencies of implementation exist within most Member States underlines the continuing importance of the issue. New institutional arrangements such as the European Environment Agency,[41] the proposed network of national environmental bodies,[42] and the proposed environmental audit inspectorate[43] should all assist in improving the information flow on implementation gaps. But for the foreseeable future the Commission's enforcement role as legal guardian of the Treaty is likely to remain of central importance, and this article has identified a number of areas where current procedures and principles appear to require reassessment to improve both their efficacy and their acceptability. Full implementation of Community law, though, may always be an impossible goal, and in any event is unlikely ever to be achieved solely by the "top-down" mechanisms implicit in the Article 169 procedure.[44] In the long run, it requires a genuine *internal* political will by

40. Case 246/81, *Bethell* v. *Commission*, [1982] ECR 2277; Case 87/89, *Société Nationale Interprofessionelle de la Tomate (SONITO)* v. *Commission*, [1991] 3 CMLR 439.
41. See note 35 *supra*.
42. See note 5 *supra*.
43. See note 34 *supra*.
44. Notwithstanding the proposed provisions giving power to the European Court to impose financial penalties on Member States which failed to comply with its judgments; see new Art. 171(2) of Draft Treaty on European Union, following the 1991 Maastricht Summit.

Environmental laws 369

Member States of the need to implement Community environmental policies, and this in turn demands both the dynamic participation of citizens and amenity groups, and an active recognition by national courts and authorities of their own role in giving effect to Community obligations. Until this occurs, the gap between the law in theory and in practice can be expected to remain intact.

[11]

The European Commission and the Enforcement of Environmental Law: an Invidious Position*

RHIANNON WILLIAMS

I. Introduction

'In a treatise upon photography ... one may assume the existence of the sun. In remarks upon the mischiefs of bureaucracy one may assume the excellence of the civil service.'[1]

The Commission is charged both with enforcement and with overtly political functions. Such duties may not make easy bedfellows. The possible effects of this juxtaposition of responsibilities on the application and enforcement of Community[2] environmental law is of concern in the context of an ostensibly democratic political structure. Few would disagree with the basic principles of democracy, but it is in the mundane practices of daily life that they must be realized, and it is with such practices that this article is concerned.

II. The Constitution of the Commission

There is limited constitutional provision in the EC Treaty. With regard to the Commission, the relevant Articles are 155 to 163. Article 162.2 provides that the Commission shall adopt its rules of procedure so as to ensure that both it and its departments operate in accordance with the provisions of the Treaty. Those rules must be published.

The Rules of Procedure of the Commission which entered into force on 11 September 1993[3] replaced the provisional Rules of Procedure of 1967. There are just over three pages of rules, very much a bare framework, covering points such as the conduct of meetings of the Commission, other decision-making procedures, the preparation and implementation of Commission decisions, and deputizing.

---

* © Rhiannon Williams, 1995. Formerly DG XI European Commission.

[1] Rt. Hon. Lord Hewart of Bury, *The New Despotism* (Ernst Benn Ltd, 1929) 13.

[2] The environmental policy of the European Community is often wrongly referred to as that of the European Union. In accordance with the provisions of the Environment Title of the EC Treaty, environmental law and policy at EC level is here referred to as 'Community' law and policy. The EU is referred to where appropriate, in accordance with Part Two of the EC Treaty.

[3] OJ 1993 L 230/15.

352   *Rhiannon Williams*

Five of the Articles in those Rules of Procedure are of particular relevance here. Article 12 provides that Members of the Commission may be assigned areas in which they have special responsibility. Articles 17 and 18 provide that a number of departments forming a single administrative service shall assist the Commission in the performance of its official functions, and that that administrative service shall consist of Directorates General and equivalent departments, both of which will normally be divided into Directorates, and Directorates into units. Article 20 requires the Legal Service to be consulted on all drafts of or proposals for legal instruments and on all documents which may have legal implications. Article 24 provides that the Commission shall determine, as necessary, rules to give effect to these rules of procedure.

These Articles have led to the creation of a pyramidal structure. At the top of the pyramid are the Commissioners. They each have one or more portfolios of responsibility. Since environmental protection was hived off from consumer protection and became a Directorate General in its own right in 1981, the Commissioner charged with the environment portfolio has been able to focus on that alone.[4]

Generally speaking, for each portfolio of responsibility, there is a Directorate General (DG). As there are currently around thirty DGs and horizontal services (the latter include, for example, the Legal Service, Secretariat-General, and the statistical office, EUROSTAT) and twenty Commissioners, some Commissioners have more than one portfolio. Each DG is headed up by a Director General chosen by the Commissioners, who is accountable to the relevant Commissioner, and, as a representative of the Commission, to the European Parliament.

The pyramidal form of each DG, with the Director General at the top is determined by its divisions into Directorates and units in accordance with the Rules of Procedure. These bare bones will be fleshed out below with regard to DG XI. For the moment it suffices to note that the enormous gaps in the written constitution and rules of procedure of the Commission are filled in to a small extent by the jurisprudence of the European Court of Justice, but mostly by largely secret internal rules and unwritten political and diplomatic practice.

It is interesting to note in this context that the provisional Rules of Procedure of 6 July 1967[5] were never published. This was contrary to Article 16 of the Merger Treaty, which provided that the Commission was to adopt its rules of procedure and ensure their publication. It is arguable that the severely limited nature of the published rules of procedure is inherently unable to ensure the operation of the Commission and its departments in accordance with Article 162.2 of the EC Treaty. Nowhere

---

[4] Except for the latter half of 1992, when Carlo Ripa di Meana resigned the post and it was held temporarily by Karel Van Miert who juggled it with his transport portfolio until Ioannis Paleokrassas was appointed Commissioner with responsibility for the environment in 1993.

[5] Repealed by Art 25 of the current Rules of Procedure.

is there any provision for the openness or accountability or the separation of powers which are vital to ensure that the Commission is able to perform and to be perceived to perform satisfactorily its enforcement functions under Article 155.

All decisions on whether to commence, continue, or close infringement proceedings are taken by the Commissioners. These are the same men and women who, sitting in the same forum, take a host of overtly political decisions, for example: whether to make certain proposals, and if so in what form; who is to be appointed to certain posts; what view to take on certain opinions of the European Parliament; and whether to revise proposals, and, if so, how. In the political arena, it is taken for granted that, in the play off of certain proposals against others, compromises will be made. This is entirely proper. In the enforcement arena, however, it would be entirely improper were such compromises to be made in order to achieve political benefit. Enforcement would cease to be impartial, and the Commission would be unable to ensure its compliance with the first indent of Article 155 of the EC Treaty.

As the functions of legislative proposal and those of enforcement under Article 169 are unique to the Commission among the institutions of the Community, and given the proximity in the exercise of these two functions, one would expect to see safeguards in the system designed to ensure that infringement cases could never be closed for political as opposed to legal reasons. However, there are none. Platitudes in the EC Treaty about the need for independence[6] are of little value unless supported by concrete measures enabling and requiring such independence.

Quite apart from the dangers posed to just and effective law enforcement, it is unfair for each Commissioner to be placed in a situation where the temptation may continually arise (whether as a result of pressure from Member States or otherwise) to compromise enforcement in order to gain the support of a recalcitrant Member State for the adoption or issue of a legal measure, particularly one brought forward within his or her portfolio. It is similarly unfair to the Commissioners if such an improper compromise can be publicly perceived to have been made in circumstances where a difficult decision not to commence infringement proceedings has been taken independently of irrelevant political factors.

Thus, with regard to the application of the principle of the separation of powers to the dual legislative proposal and enforcement functions of the Commission as they may be carried out in accordance with the published Rules of Procedure, three questions arise: whether there is scope for improper political influence upon the outcome of legal procedures, whether it may appear to the public that such behaviour is taking place, and whether it is.

---

[6] See Art 157.

The last is impossible to prove, one way or the other, given the current lack of transparency. With regard to the first, it is submitted that there are no procedural safeguards in place which could effectively minimize the scope for improper political influence of deliberations on matters of enforcement. It would appear that there is a public perception of interaction between the two functions. For example, *The Independent* of 3 August 1992 reported that:

The Home Secretary has told colleagues that Mr Bangemann gave him a private assurance that Britain will not be taken to the European Court of Justice for maintaining its border controls when they are abolished in the rest of Europe next January ... Ministers regard the deal as further evidence of the leverage they are achieving during the British presidency. John MacGregor, the Secretary of State for Transport, also secured a deal, during an informal gathering of ministers, for the Commission to drop its threat to intervene in the Twyford Down M3 controversy, although it would continue to challenge the legality of a road through Oxleas Wood in south-east London.

The perception alone that inappropriate considerations appear to influence the outcome of legal proceedings (whether or not they do so) brings the system into disrepute and distrust. All legal enforcement systems should contain safeguards against the likelihood of such a perception arising. The absence of any such constitutional safeguards at Commission level is echoed within Directorate General XI.

III. The Construction of DG XI

The internal structure of each DG varies, both as between DGs and from time to time. No structural history of the Commission has been written, but it appears that a small environment and consumer-protection service was set up in DG III in 1972, responsible for industrial policy and the internal market. It then became a separate service, and, in 1981, a Directorate General. Consumer protection became an independent service in 1990, and civil protection was then transferred to DG XI from DG V.[7] DG XI's official title is now 'Environment, Nuclear Safety and Civil Protection'.

In February 1990, the Commission's Directory shows that DG XI was structured as follows. The Director General was at the top, together with his choice of advisors and assistants. Directly accountable to him were four small 'units'. These dealt with finance and contracts, relations with the other institutions and environmental information and education, international affairs, and legal affairs and the application of Community

---

[7] See *Management Structures for Environmental Administrations in the European Community*, a summary prepared by Environment Policy Europe for a meeting of Directors General of the Ministries of Environment of the EC under the Presidency of the Portuguese Republic, May 1992, 174.

Enforcement of Environmental Law 355

law. The last is of particular importance in the context of this article, and was then known as DG XI.I.

In addition, there were two large 'directorates'. These were known as 'Directorate A', which covered nuclear safety, the impact of industry of the environment and waste management, and 'Directorate B', which covered water and air protection, nature conservation, and civil protection. Each of these was headed by a Director, and was sub-divided into units (eg. protection and management of water; control of atmospheric pollution and radioprotection).

By the end of 1990 the DG had been restructured 'to respond to the significantly increased workload from the ever-growing body of Community environmental legislation, as well as the call to develop new instruments and integrated systems for environmental protection.'[8] That restructuring included the addition of a third directorate and a task force created in order to deal with matters relating to the European Environment Agency until its establishment. DG XI. I remained a unit outside the directorates, 'directly attached' to the Director General.

Although those in charge of the Units within the Directorates are 'Heads of Unit', of the same status as the heads of directly attached units, the latter are directly accountable to, and have the direct ear of the Director General because of their units' situation. The Heads of Unit within Directorates are answerable to their Directors, who are in turn accountable to the Director General. Heads of Units within Directorates are, therefore, less able to act independently than the Heads of directly-attached units. Not only would they normally gain formal access to the Director General only through and with the consent of their Directors, but that Director will be weighing up their proposed action (whether in proposal, opinion, recommendation, or any other form) in the light of political requirements and the various policy and technical issues which he is juggling.

The directorates perform a variety of functions, including the provision of technical assessment and advice, monitoring the application of directives (eg. with regard to the provision by the Member States of reports), policy development, conceiving and drafting proposals for legislation, and liaison with national implementing authorities and others, as appropriate, to discuss those ideas, drafts, and problems arising in the implementation of the resultant measures. Those functions are overridingly political, and often performed, necessarily, by means of consultation and compromise.

One of the strengths of DG XI. I, the Legal Affairs Unit, was that it was constitutionally separate from the working atmosphere of the directorates. In assessing complaints and infringement files, DG XI. I was required to liaise as appropriate with the units within the directorates, but its Head of

---

[8] Ibid.

Unit was able to make proposals concerning the processing of complaints without having to seek approval for those proposals. There might be strong opposition to a proposal by another unit or directorate, but in any resulting debate, the Head of Unit of DG XI. I had considerable independence in arguing his case before the ultimate arbiter within the DG, the Director General.

In 1994 there was a further reconstitution of DG XI. It took place during an interregnum, when there was a power vacuum. From the end of 1993, information started to circulate unofficially with regard to a proposal, apparently initiated while Laurens Jan Brinkhorst was Director General, for restructuring DG XI. Mr Brinkhorst left the Commission in March 1994 to prepare to fight in the Dutch European elections for his current position as an MEP. The proposal was published by the Assistant Director General, then acting Director General, Tom Garvey, in June 1994. The new Director General, Marius Enthoven, was due to take up his appointment on 5 September 1994.

The proposals included the shunting down of the Legal Affairs Unit to Directorate B. They had not been discussed or circulated either publicly or even among the Heads of Unit in DG XI. The author wrote to the Commission in February 1995 requesting, under Commission Decision 90/ 94, information on the extent to which internal or external consultation on any proposed changes to the structural constitution of DG XI should or must take place. Although the letter was answered in March, the question was not. The Commission did, however, explain that,

As for your last request regarding how any changes to the structural constitution of DG XI may be affected, please note that these matters come under the competence of the Commission, which decides on the proposal presented by the Commissioner responsible for DG XI, in agreement with the Commissioner responsible for personnel and administration, and the President. However, individual mobility and other changes to the structure of the Directorate-General that do not increase the total number of management functions can be decided by the Director-General after agreement from the Commissioner responsible for DG XI, the Commissioner responsible for personnel and administration, and the President.

In short, Commissioner Paleokrassas, who was to cease to be environment Commissioner at the end of the year, proposed, in the absence of a Director General, the modification of the structure of the DG, a step sufficiently serious to warrant the approval of the entire Commission.

The deemed refusal to answer the question about consultation was appealed by the author in April. In May, the Secretary General, D.F. Williamson, replied that:

Proposals to modify the structure of a Directorate General are examined by the Directorate General for Personnel and Administration and the Secretariat General before the decision procedure is launched. No external consultation is

Enforcement of Environmental Law 357

stipulated, as the organisation of its services is the sole responsibility of the Commission.

It therefore appears that, even when major structural alterations to a Directorate General (other than that for Personnel and Administration) are being considered, there is no requirement to consult anyone in the particular DG about them, even its Director General.

The Commission initially refused to approve the proposals put forward by Commissioner Paleokrassas, possibly because they had been submitted at short notice just before the Commissioners' August vacation. The proposals were, however, approved by the Commission on 29 September 1994.

An examination of the current 'directory' of DG XI reveals that Directorate B, to which the Legal Affairs Unit formerly known as XI. I was moved, now covers environmental instruments. The Legal Affairs Unit sits less easily in a Directorate than it did as a directly-attached unit. From now on, decisions regarding the processing of complaints may only go before the Director General once they have been approved by the Director of Directorate B. And that Director is charged with a certain number of political functions. For example, he will be embroiled in the political, compromise culture should DG XI be required to bring forward any new proposals for legislation relating to financial instruments or environmental impact assessment. If he wishes those proposals to be adopted by the Commission, let alone the Council of Ministers, he, and his staff, have to ensure good relations with the Member States. Proceeding with infringements may not in all cases further the cultivation of the relations necessary for policy development purposes. In this regard, the enforcement of Community law on environmental impact assessment has already led to apparent hijacking of the legal process for political aims, as discussed below. Examples of potential conflicts likely to arise out of the new situation of the Legal Affairs Unit are complaints concerning projects financed by LIFE or the Cohesion Fund, or by DG XVI (Regional Policy) administering Structural Funds with DG XI approval.[9]

The previous constitutional situation of the Legal Affairs Unit left much to be desired with regard to the application of the principle of the separation of powers. In particular, the Director General had the difficult job of having to perform the same mental gymnastics as the Commissioners if he was to ensure that political considerations were not to influence his decisions with regard to proposals concerning infringement procedures.

The new situation gives yet another party the same invidious task, and moves the Unit a further step away from a constitutional structure which

---

[9] There have already been at least two challenges to the application of structural funds: Case T-461/ 93 *An Taisce* v *Commission* [1994] ECR-II 733, now being appealed as C-325/94 P and a similar challenge by Greenpeace—Case T-585/93 *Stichting, Greenpeace, Council, and others* v *Commission*, which should be considered by the Court in 1995.

358   *Rhiannon Williams*

would promote and be seen to promote impartial enforcement of environmental law. Again, it is arguable that it is unfair on the Director for him to have to counter pressure from any source to compromise a genuine case for proceeding with an infringement, and then be unable to argue convincingly that there was no possibility of improper or inappropriate compromises being made.

His position is mirrored at a wider level by the Director General of DG XI, and again at a wider level still by the Commissioners themselves. Nowhere is there any guarantee or transparency which could go towards dispelling any suspicion that good infringement cases[10] may be sacrificed to political causes.

IV. The Complaints Investigation Procedure

One of the tasks of the DG XI Legal Affairs Unit is to monitor the implementation and enforcement of Community environmental law (with the exception of radiation protection). This means that it investigates all formal complaints about the application of that law, and is responsible for the day to day handling of the infringement files for those of the complaints which proceed to or beyond Letters of Formal Notice (or Article 169 Letters).[11] In this regard, the unit is contributing to the Commission's compliance with Article 169 of the EC Treaty.

Anyone may make a formal complaint about alleged infringement of Community environmental law to the European Commission. All such complaints are registered by the Secretariat-General, which allocates them a file number, acknowledges their receipt, and informs complainants of the file number in a standard form letter. This explains that the complainant will be 'informed of the outcome' of the Commission's consideration of the complaint, and of 'the action it decides to take'. That outcome might be years away, and there is no undertaking by the Commission to keep complainants informed of the progress of the consideration of their complaints in the meantime. The identity of complainants will, they are informed, be kept confidential.

There is an annex to the letter which sets out the 'aims and general characteristics of the infringement procedure under Article 169 of the [EC] Treaty.' Almost half the annex treats legal proceedings before the Court of Justice, a stage which the vast majority of complaints never reach, and the annex is limited to consideration of the infringement procedure. On

---

[10] Or good men—it has been suggested that the decision to transfer Ludwig Krämer from his position as Head of the Legal Affairs Unit in late 1994 was made because of the political difficulties and embarrassment caused to the Commission by his refusal to compromise on issues of legal principle in enforcement investigations and infringement proceedings—6 Feb 1995, European Report—104 (AVG).

[11] The Unit is also responsible for providing advice on Community environmental law, and for advising other units on draft environmental legislation.

Enforcement of Environmental Law 359

average, however, the files for at least half of all suspected infringements are closed without infringement proceedings beginning.[12] This annex may, therefore, raise false hopes about what complainants can expect, as no mention is made of the time-consuming enquiries which must be undertaken by the Commission prior to the administrative stage of the infringement procedure.

It is the Commission's job to ensure compliance, and in making their investigations they are acting on behalf of the Community, not—directly—on behalf of the complainants. This accounts in theory for the few rights accorded to those complainants: anonymity; being told the outcome of the Commission's consideration of the complaint and the action it decides to take; and indemnity for the cost of the procedure.

However, it is submitted that this approach is flawed. Although it cannot be deduced from the annual reports exactly how many infringement procedures result from formal complaints, those reports repeatedly stress the importance of complaints in the Commission's enforcement procedures. If complainants are repeatedly denied much information about the development of their cases, then not only may abuses occur, which would be less likely in a more open system, but such a system creates distrust and disillusionment, and may in the long term lead to a drop in the number of complaints and concurrent Commission knowledge of genuine infringements.

This point is particularly important with regard to complainants such as some of the non-governmental organizations who often put much work into preparing well-researched and detailed complaints. As complainants' identities are confidential, only those who 'go public' can be questioned about their assessment of the complaints investigation process. Many non-governmental organizations do so. As part of the research for this article, the author therefore prepared a questionnaire which was distributed to a number of major non-governmental organizations in the Community. The results are referred to as appropriate below. Those who responded had between them a history of thirty-one formal complaints, some relating to transposition, some to implementation, and some to both.

The lawyers of the Legal Affairs Unit of DG XI not only investigate all formal complaints about environmental law, but may themselves open files about possible infringements which are brought to their attention from any source—'[In detecting infringements] Commission staff make use of all the sources of information available (meetings with national experts or in Council bodies, Member States' official journals, national or specialized press)'.[13] For all practical purposes, such files are treated exactly the same way as complaint files.

---

[12] See the Eleventh Annual Report by the Commission on the monitoring of the application of Community law (1993) 102.

[13] Ninth Annual Report on Commission Monitoring of the Application of Community Law (1991) IV.

360 *Rhiannon Williams*

The complaint files are initially read by the Legal Affairs Unit lawyers who will decide whether there is clearly no infringement and a recommendation should be made that the file be closed, or whether further information is required from the complainant, or whether there is enough information to suggest that there may be an infringement, such that an informal letter of inquiry (sometimes called a 'pre-Article 169 letter') should be addressed to the Permanent Representative in Brussels of the Member State in question. (The Permanent Representation is a diplomatic presence, and its use at this and later stages in complaint investigations highlights the inappropriately diplomatic nature of the current process).[14]

Whether further information is requested from the complainant or an informal letter of inquiry is to be sent to the Member State, an appropriate letter will be written by those lawyers. Such letters are, in accordance with internal DG XI practice, passed to the appropriate technical or policy unit(s) within the DG for comment and approval.

In the Commission's Manual of Operational Procedures,[15] there is no section specifically on informal investigations. It is explained that complainants are to be kept informed by the services (ie. DG XI.B.3 for environmental complaints) with regard to each complaint by sending to them a letter concerning the results of the steps undertaken with regard to the national authorities at the latest within four months of the registration of the complaint. They are also to receive a letter indicating 'the outcome of the complaint in accordance with the rules regarding publicity: commencement of an infringement procedure, [an outcome not applicable to environmental complaints], or closure.'[16]

The rules regarding publicity are set out in section 15.5.5. They mention the publication of 'brief reports' of the sending of reasoned opinions, applications to the European Court of Justice, and closure of cases in the monthly bulletin and annual reports. Article 169 letters are only to be the subject of such publicity in cases of non-transposition of directives, where Member States have failed to communicate transposing legislation, or for non-execution of a judgment of the Court of Justice (Article 171 EC Treaty). The commencement of infringement proceedings may also be

---

[14] See below 382, and also Macrory in 29 *CML Rev* 347–69 (1992), where he questions whether it is still appropriate for infringement proceedings to be conducted through the medium of central governments.

[15] Sept 1994. This is not a public document, but a copy of that part of it relating to complaints was obtained by the author in March 1995 as a result of an application to the Commission under Decision 94/90. According to the Secretariat General at that time, it was only the second or third time that the information had been formally released by the Commission. Until recently the Manual has only been available in French, so all references to it in this article are based on the author's translations of its provisions. The letter which accompanied the extract pointed out that the Manual 'is not a legal text but contains internal rules of procedure for the Commission Services, which are based on several arrangements and rules established by the Commission. It is therefore an instrument for the staff in their day-to-day work, which has to be adopted and interpreted according to the context.'

[16] Manual of Operational Procedures, section 15.4.1.3.

publicized if there has been a formal request, particularly by an MEP. Such publicity, and its mode, must be authorized by the Commission at the same time as it decides on the case.

Where the complainant is to be asked for further information, this must be done speedily so as to obtain the information as soon as possible and avoid unfounded approaches to Member States.[17] If further information is requested from the complainant, the file will be reassessed when it is received, or a recommendation for closure will be made if it (or an appropriate explanation) is not received by the date specified in the letter.

Informal letters of inquiry to Member States usually request a reply within two months of receipt. When the reply is received, the file is reassessed to see whether a proposal should be made to close it, to send an Article 169 Letter or to request further information or clarification from the Member State. It is not unknown for Member States to fail to reply to informal inquiries within the period requested. In the Manual of Operational Procedures ('the Manual'), it is stated that the Commission has adopted a new procedure in order to deal with this problem: when a request for information addressed to national authorities is not 'satisfied' within two months, a standard-form letter of reminder is to be sent. If there is no reply to this reminder within one month, a standard form telex of reminder referring to the provisions of Article 5 of the EC Treaty is to be sent.[18]

The reason why this new procedure was adopted is not specified, and statistics on Member State replies are not formally available. However, officials within DG XI have stated that an informal survey was carried out by the DG XI Legal Unit in July 1994. The survey was limited, addressing only requests for information addressed to ten of the Member States by the unit from July 1993 to July 1994. One third of the 111 letters in question had not received any reply, only two had been replied to within the two-month deadline, and the average period taken to respond was more than six months. (The longest period taken to respond was more than three years). There is therefore a serious problem.

The provisions of the Manual raise several questions, for example, the meaning of 'satisfied'. It would appear that it would cover not only failures to reply, but also replies where some or all of the information requested was withheld. The reference to Article 5 of the EC Treaty is interesting. The Manual does not go on to say that infringement proceedings against the Member States will be commenced if the information is still not forthcoming. DG XI officials interviewed for this article believe that the Commission will not commence infringement proceedings against Member States for breach of Article 5 of the EC Treaty for failure to supply requested information because of the potential political problems such a step would entail. Article 169 does not appear to warrant such a restrictive

[17] Ibid.
[18] Section 15.4.1.4.

362   *Rhiannon Williams*

interpretation, as it refers to failure to fulfil obligations under the Treaty. It will be interesting to see the extent to which the Commission is now committed to obtaining withheld information, given the extent to which Member State reticence appears to hamper the enforcement function of the Commission in environmental law.

Slightly oddly situated in the same section of the Manual is the comment that the Commission is convinced of the utility of periodic 'packet' meetings with the Member States with a view to the gathering, as quickly as possible, and at the latest six months after the registration of a complaint, the necessary explanations from the Member State concerned. The Legal Service must participate in such consultations.

Packet meetings may be used at any stage of an investigation or infringement proceeding. During them, a number of cases—often those posing particular difficulties—are discussed in an attempt to move forward—either in infringement proceedings or towards closure. The DG XI Legal Affairs Unit aims to have one packet meeting with each Member State every calendar year, though this aim is by no means always achieved. Overall, these are apparently a most helpful way of gathering information, ironing out misunderstandings, and developing relationships between the members of the Unit and the Member States. However, they have allowed the Legal Affairs Unit lawyers to ascertain that some at least of the Member States appear systematically to be receiving copies of the confidential 'fiches' on which proposals in respect of cases are made. One Commission official described how, at such a meeting, a file had been brought out without any attempt to hide its contents, which were copies of all the current fiches for the Member State in question, and it was referred to and worked from throughout the meeting. Such leaking puts Member States at a tactical advantage in the processing of complaints.

When the Legal Affairs Unit has received sufficient information from the complainant and from the Member State by way of reply to informal letters of inquiry, it will decide whether to propose Article 169 Letter or closure.

If the Commission agrees to the sending of an Article 169 Letter, the Member State is usually asked to reply within two months of receipt. (Though it usually takes much longer—often more than six months). If the reply to an Article 169 Letter is unsatisfactory or unforthcoming, then the Commission may decide, again on a proposal from DG XI, to proceed to Reasoned Opinion. If it is desired to bring in further points after the issue of an Article 169 Letter, then a 'complementary' Article 169 Letter must be sent before a Reasoned Opinion can include those points.

At any stage of the investigation of a complaint file it may be decided to close the file or request further information from the complainant or Member State. If the reply to a Reasoned Opinion is unsatisfactory, or none is made, the Commission may decide to commence infringement proceedings.

Enforcement of Environmental Law 363

DG XI has the power only to make proposals as to the development of a complaint or infringement file. All cases are considered by the Commissioners at least twice a year, as no formal step in their development, even their closure, can take place without Commission approval. The meetings at which the biannual consideration of each file takes place are held in early autumn and in early spring. It is also possible that a case will be considered at a 'reunion balai' or 'sweeping up meeting' at Christmas or at the end of the summer session—before the Commissioners' August vacation—if the DG so requests. The cases heard in the sweeping up meetings are limited to those perceived as urgent.

In advance of the meetings of the Commission at which the cases are considered, a 'fiche' for each case is produced by the Secretariat-General. It is a piece of paper, an off-print of the database which records the history and basic substance of each file. The fiches are updated as appropriate by the lawyers of the Legal Affairs Unit, who then include a draft proposal to process the file, for example, 'closure', 'Article 169 Letter', 'no action pending reply to letter to Member State', etc. Reasons must be given for each proposal. The draft proposals are encoded, and the fiches are then circulated to any technical or policy unit within the DG with an interest in the matter. If there is agreement, the proposal will go before the Director General, and is unlikely to be modified by him. If, however, there is disagreement, then the matter is discussed at a round-table meeting chaired by the Director General or his Assistant. A compromise may be reached, or the Director General or his Assistant may decide what the DG's proposal is to be.

That proposal is then submitted, again in fiche form, to the lawyers of the Commission's horizontal Legal Service, which is directly accountable to the President of the Commission. They will notify the lawyers of DG XI's Legal Affairs Unit of any proposals which they disagree with, either because of absence of information or a substantive legal point. At another round table meeting, the Legal Service and DG XI lawyers will attempt to resolve their differences. In so far as they can do so, the proposal is more likely to be rubber stamped by the Heads of Cabinet, and ultimately the Commissioners, who alone can authorize the commencement and development of infringement procedures.

At meetings of the Heads of Cabinet, representatives of the lawyers from the Legal Service will be present. One or more DG XI lawyers may also be present (by invitation). If there is any challenge to a DG XI proposal, the Head of Cabinet of the environment Commissioner or his representative would usually defend it, calling upon the lawyers present for further information as appropriate. If different from the DG XI proposal, the Legal Service representative would state their case, and their arguments will be considered by the Heads of Cabinet. It is the Heads of Cabinet who formally make proposals for processing cases to the Commission. In all cases where the Heads of Cabinet cannot agree on what development is appropriate for a given case, the Commissioners will discuss its merits and decide the future of the file in a meeting to which the lawyers are not allowed access. They may also discuss a case on which there is unanimous agreement at the level of Heads of Cabinet, but it is understood that this rarely occurs.

If the Commission makes a decision different to that proposed by DG XI, whether or not that proposal is acceptable to the Legal Service or agreed by the Heads of Cabinet, there is no requirement for reasons to be given for the decision, and, indeed, none are. At best, this unaccountability is unfortunate, at worst it frustrates Commission lawyers and complainants alike, and brings the impartiality of the infringement control system into question, doing nothing to allay fears that political considerations may be taken into account in deciding the outcome of complaint files.

The sum effect of these procedures is that it is possible for political factors to influence the case at a variety of stages:

— at the level of the making of the proposal, if the head of the legal affairs unit is concerned for his career within the Commission;
— when the technical or policy units of DG XI comment on the proposal, if, for example, any personnel there have an eye upon advancement in national administrations when they return, or upon the advancement of relationships with Member States so as not to jeopardize a project for a new directive for which they are responsible;[19]
— when the Legal Service comments on the proposal if it is an area where the President, for example, is known not to favour the legislation; and
— when it is considered by the Heads of Cabinet and the Commissioners, who are all very much embroiled in political negotiations regarding new legislation, intergovernmental conferences, etc.

Greater transparency in the system would help alleviate any suspicions of such potential for the influence of political factors (whose existence militate against public confidence, even if no improper activity ever occurs), and a formal division of functions would be a step even further in the right direction, as discussed in the conclusion below.

Of the six non-governmental organizations who responded to the relevant question in the questionnaire prepared and circulated by the author, all believed that external political pressure may have played a part

---

[19] In this context it is relevant that there are about 56 DG XI personnel in the technical and policy units who are on secondment from Member State administrations. They may work within the Commission for a maximum of three years before returning to the administration from which they were seconded, and with which their long-term interests lie. Of a total of about 400 personnel in DG XI, there are about 200 Commission civil servants. The rest are made up of those seconded from the Member States, independent 'contractors' and other specialists with limited period contracts of varying sorts. The 56 or so seconded from Member States are therefore not an insignificant proportion of the personnel.

Enforcement of Environmental Law 365

in the outcome or development of their complaints,[20] (most of them believed that such pressure *had* indeed played a part, citing complaints made with regard to, among others, the Cardiff Bay Barrage, the abandoned Wheal Jane tin mine, the disposal in the United Kingdom of organo-phosphate residues, THORP, and a dam on the Irati River in Navarra, Spain). Three of those six non-governmental organizations believed that internal Commission policy factors may have played a part in the outcome or development of their complaints,[21] and two suggested that resourcing/manpower may also have played a part. The last point was not included in the questionnaire, and is examined below. This situation is of concern, particularly with regard to the prevailing belief in the influence of external political pressure on the outcome of complaints.

Although Article 169 Letters are not mentioned in Article 169 of the Treaty, they are now a firmly entrenched part of the formal infringement procedure. They refer to the directive(s) in question, the history of informal correspondence which has been exchanged about the matters at issue between the Commission and the Member State, explain why it is believed that there has been an infringement, request the Member State's comments on the points made in the Article 169 Letter, and explain that no reply, or an inadequate reply may result in the Commission sending a Reasoned Opinion.

Article 169 refers only to bringing matters before the European Court of Justice, the sending of reasoned opinions, and the Commission's duty to give the State concerned the opportunity to submit its observations. According to Commission officials, when the Commission first started investigating apparent infringements, it would enter into correspondence along the lines of today's informal letters of inquiry. If a reply was unsatisfactory, a reasoned opinion would immediately be sent. The Member States, however, began to object, on the grounds that this afforded them insufficient opportunity to reply fully to the Commission's concerns before they were almost at Court. So, as a result of a consensus in the late 1960s or early 1970s, Article 169 Letters became a formal stage in the proceedings. Apparently, there is nothing in writing recording the agreement, and it was not a step formally taken at diplomatic level.

Cases where there is an urgent need to send an Article 169 Letter may, according to the Manual, be included in the Commission's agenda at the request of the responsible Member, with the agreement of the President, (the 'urgent' procedure). During Commission holidays, such a decision may be made by written procedure. The Manual then explains that once the Commission has decided to send an Article 169 Letter, the draft, once drawn up within the relevant DG, and having been approved by the Legal

[20] Including Greenpeace International, the Council for the Protection of Rural England (CPRE) and the South West Environmental Protection Agency.

[21] Greenpeace International and CPRE on the record.

Service, is sent to the Secretariat General by the competent service. The Secretariat General will submit the letter to the competent Member of the Commission for signature after having obtained the opinion of his Cabinet. Once signed, the letter is sent to the Minister for foreign affairs and notified to the relevant permanent representation. Most letters will request a reply within two months, but this period may be reduced at the agreement of the Commission in cases following the 'accelerated procedure'. For all such letters sent during long vacations, an extra month for reply ought automatically to be accepted.

Prior to 1993, the Commission would decide on the need for an Article 169 Letter as appropriate, and it would then be up to the relevant service to draft it and obtain the approval, by amendment of the draft if necessary, of the relevant technical services and the Legal Service prior to its submission to the Commissioner. This sometimes led to long delays between the decision being taken and the letter being sent. So a new procedure was introduced, as explained in the Manual: for the files examined during the 'periodical reports' (those twice yearly meetings to assess each case) the draft Article 169 Letter must be drawn up by the responsible service and transmitted to the Legal Service in time for the preparatory interservice meeting. The rule is less rigid with regard to urgent proposals for Article 169 Letters, which must, however, in any event be executed within four weeks of the authorizing decision of the Commission. A completed text is then submitted to the relevant Commissioner. If he is not able to sign it within two weeks, he must explain himself to the College.

The disadvantage of the current procedure is that it places huge strains on the comparatively tiny number of lawyers within DG XI. Quite apart from writing the drafts, they must all be passed through the relevant technical and policy units in DG XI, and by the Legal Service for approval. That often involves many phone calls, faxes and meetings, not to mention the re-writing. Under current policy, each fiche is increasingly likely to be composed of a number of different complaints. Whilst these will be associated in some way, preparing a draft Article 169 Letter in respect of such a fiche is a much greater undertaking than so doing in respect of just one matter. Under the current procedure, if a proposal is refused, all that work is wasted. And, if a draft cannot be prepared in time, a case where an Article 169 Letter may be justified cannot benefit from the appropriate decision. This may mean that a decision is then arbitrarily taken to close the case under the one year rule.

If the reply to an Article 169 Letter does not satisfy the Commission, then it may, under a similar procedure, send a Reasoned Opinion. These are similarly structured, except that they require the Member State to conform within the period stated, and the consequence of failure to reply, or an inadequate response, may be referral of the matter to the European Court of Justice.

As explained in the Manual,[22] the procedure for authorization of a Reasoned Opinion is basically the same as that for an Article 169 Letter. With regard to Article 169 Letters, the Manual had provided for urgent procedures in urgent cases. For Reasoned Opinions, the Manual states that those procedures may be used in cases where a file is 'urgent and politically important'. The question arises as to the situation where a file is urgent on environmental grounds, but not necessarily politically.

Another major difference is that when a Reasoned Opinion is decided upon, the Legal Service has three months to prepare the draft, agree it with the DG XI Legal Affairs Unit, and send it to the Member State. In contrast with the preparation of Article 169 Letters, therefore, it is the Legal Service which is responsible for the drafting of Reasoned Opinions, (other then in cases of non-communication of national transposing measures, when the responsibility rests with the Legal Affairs Unit). The same provisions apply as for Article 169 Letters with regard to the signature of the letter within two weeks by the Commissioner, and the delays within which replies are requested. Similar procedures apply with regard to the reference of cases to the European Court.[23]

Two final points emerge from the Manual: the possibility of sending complementary Article 169 Letters and Reasoned Opinions if necessary,[24] and an interesting little paragraph on the deadlines for the treatment of files.[25]

With regard to complementary Article 169 Letters and Reasoned Opinions, the Court of Justice has ruled that it is vital that the issues to be addressed by the Court are included in Reasoned Opinions, and that the Member States have had prior notice of those issues. See, for example, the judgment of the Court and the Opinion of the Advocate General in the United Kingdom drinking-water case,[26] and Krämer's commentary on them, in which he concludes, 'Article 169 is therefore a due process provision which aims at avoiding surprise reasoned opinions and surprise applications.'[27] Complementary letters can be vital where an important issue has been omitted, or arises during the proceedings. Prior notice of the contents of Reasoned Opinions usually takes the form of an Article 169 Letter, though it need not—a meeting at which a Member State is given the opportunity to make its case may replace the Article 169 Letter. Commission officials mentioned, for example, an Italian case concerning possible barriers to the import of cars, in which DG III officials called a meeting with the national authorities. The matter was not resolved at that meeting, and a Reasoned Opinion was immediately sent.

---

[22] Section 15.5.2.3.
[23] Section 15.5.2.5 of the Manual.
[24] Section 15.5.2.4.
[25] Section 15.4.1.5.
[26] Case C-337/89 *EC Commission* v *United Kingdom* [1992] ECR-I 6103.
[27] L. Krämer *European Environmental Law Casebook* (Sweet & Maxwell, 1993) 257–9.

Similarly, under Directive 83/189,[28] which provides for the notification of draft legislation by the Member States, the Commission can send the Member State a 'detailed opinion' on the draft. As explained in the Manual, such an opinion is taken to be equivalent to an Article 169 Letter.[29]

One of the frustrations of complainants and DG XI lawyers alike in the field of environmental law is the difficulty associated with processing complaints quickly when there is a danger of imminent damage being caused to the environment contrary to Community law. In total, there is usually four and a half to five years between the sending of an Article 169 Letter, and the Court's judgment. And there may have been many months of informal inquiries in addition. Of the eighteen judgments on environmental law by the Court of Justice from 1992 to 1994, there was, on average, fifty-seven months between the sending of Article 169 Letters and judgment: that is, on average, sixteen months between the Article 169 Letter and the Reasoned Opinion, nineteen months between the Reasoned Opinion and application to the Court, and twenty-two months between that appeal and judgment. The shortest took three years.[30]

It appears, therefore, that the Commission has the ability to move more quickly with regard to interim and other measures in environmental enforcement proceedings than it currently does. For example, in urgent cases a meeting or meetings could be called with the national authorities, in order to enable the Commission to move directly to Reasoned Opinion, with a brief delay for response. No such provision is made in the Manual, but there would appear to be no reason not to proceed in such a way in appropriately serious circumstances. In such cases, there should either be scope for application to the European Court for interim measures, or a speeding up of the normal procedures.

In the paragraph in the Manual on the deadlines for the treatment of files, it is provided that:

A complaint file must be closed or have given rise to the commencement of formal infringement proceedings at the latest one year after the registration of the complaint by the Secretariat-General. Any exception to this rule must be duly reasoned. In the absence of factual data or precise information from the complainant on the behaviour complained of, the file will automatically be closed after one year, after the complainant has been so informed.[31]

This is known as 'the one year rule'.

In the Tenth Annual Report of the Commission to the European Parliament on the monitoring of the application of Community law, it is stated that 'The Commission endeavours to abide by the one-year time

---

[28] Council Directive of 28 March 1983 laying down a procedure for the provision of information in the field of technical standards and regulations, OJ 1983 L 109/8.
[29] At section 15.5.2.2., second para.
[30] All the above figures in this paragraph taken from Ludwig Krämer's article in *EUGRZ* (1995) 46.
[31] Section 15.4.1.5.

limit but this has proved impossible in many cases because of the complexity of the dossier.'[32] This would seem to imply that the rule is not rigid. However, DG XI officials have expressed grave concern about the arbitrary use of the rule. One official referred to it as a 'cynical exercise to cut down on complaints.' It was apparently ostensibly introduced to reduce the number of current case files, and increase the satisfaction of complainants. However, a combination of factors means that it favours unco-operative Member States. Some DG XI officials claim that it has been systematically applied regardless of whether a Member State has replied within the period requested. In such circumstances, no proposal to commence infringement proceedings can be made because of lack of information, and closure of such cases has resulted. It was also claimed that there have been cases where a complaint has been registered, but misattributed, and no account has been taken of the resulting 'loss' of one or two months of DG XI's time in the calculation of one year.

In this connection, it should be remembered that within the year following registration, the Legal Affairs Unit must have written to the Member State and sent two reminders if no response has been forthcoming. If there is still no response, the lawyer in charge of the file must propose its closure or an Article 169 Letter. If it is a really serious situation in the view of the Legal Service, then it may be conceded that the time should run. Or, if there is a petition on the point before the European Parliament, it is apparently more likely that the case will be kept open because of the embarrassment of having to explain arbitrary closure to the Parliament. Thus, complainants would be well advised to send simultaneous petitions and complaints in order to avoid arbitrary closure of their case files.

Even where a Member State is silent, the burden of proof in making the case is taken to rest with the Commission, even though there is no judgment of the European Court on the point. But silence damages the environment. Either Commission practice as to the processing of complaints on which there is no information from the Member States, or its practice on obtaining that information must be changed if Community environmental law is to be enforced and the environment protected. The use of the Commission's resources must be justified, but the one-year rule appears to be reducing the environmental case-load of the Commission at the expense of both environmental protection and law enforcement.

Another administrative rule regarding the conduct of the enforcement procedures is the application of the *de minimis* rule. Information about this was requested by the author in February 1995 from the Secretariat General under Commission Decision 94/90. The reply given in March was that the point was treated in the last sentence of section 15.4.1.5 of the

---

[32] Tenth Annual Report of the Commission to the European Parliament, 9.

370   *Rhiannon Williams*

Manual. This, however, does not refer to a *de minimis* principle concerning established infringements deemed not to be worth pursuing, but to the one-year rule. DG XI officials are concerned about the application to cases of a *de minimis* rule, which started about two years ago, apparently on the initiative of the President's Cabinet, after input from several Cabinets with regard to complaint handling in general.

Under the rule, a judgment is apparently made with regard to each case as to whether it is 'opportune' to proceed. In deciding this, the following factors are taken into account—whether it is a *cas précis*, or specific situation, and the extent of its relevance beyond the particular complaint. In this regard, one problem with environmental complaints is that they often concern specific situations. So if a project is carried out without environmental impact assessment, for example, under the *de minimis* rule, the Commission could take the view that it may be difficult to argue that there is still sufficient interest under the above criteria in pursuing the case if the damage has already been done. At the very least it would appear that there is an interest in ensuring that such a case would not recur, for example by obtaining an appropriate commitment from the Member State in question. Indeed, there are good grounds for arguing that an application to the Court of Justice should still be made in appropriate circumstances.

In *Commission* v *Germany*,[33] it was held that the object of an application to the Court was specified in the Reasoned Opinion, and that even if that object was eliminated after the specified delay, the action maintained an interest with a view to the establishment of the basis of responsibility which a Member State might incur, as a result of its infringement, with regard to other Member States, the Community or individuals. Although this only strictly refers to cases where the situation changes after the issue of a Reasoned Opinion, the underlying logic is arguably wider.

With regard to relevance beyond the particular complaint, if the complainant can prove an infringement, he, or the DG XI Legal Affairs Unit, must still be able to prove that it is a case worth pursuing. This is inherently difficult because most complainants are only aware of what is happening in their immediate neighbourhood. They tend not to be aware of the wider situation. It can therefore be more difficult to construct a general case showing a wider problem unless appropriate complaints are made by others at the same time. Ironically, the Council for the Protection of Rural England's impression of the process, in its response to the author's questionnaire, was that there is 'undue focus by the Commission in pursuing project-specific or individual cases rather than generic complaints' associated with transposition or general implementation.

No announcement has been made by the Commission that the Manual is now publicly available. Nor is there a high level of awareness amongst

---

[33] Case C-361/88 [1991] ECR I-2567.

Enforcement of Environmental Law 371

the non-governmental organizations of either its contents or of the other administrative procedures and principles which can so greatly influence the outcome of a case. None of the non-governmental organizations who responded to the relevant questions in the questionnaire were aware of the content of these rules, for example, and almost all had never heard of them.

Further problems for complainants with regard to access to information arise in relation to their knowledge as to whether a decision has been taken about the future of the case, and, if closure is decided upon, of the reasons for that decision. There is no binding requirement that complainants must be informed of the reason why 'their' file has been closed or been processed in any other way. There is also no requirement to inform them of the taking of any decision in respect of it other than the final one. In most cases, further information is provided, but this is very much on a case by case basis. In a letter to the author of May 1995, D.F. Williamson, the Secretary General, writes:

the services themselves keep complainants informed of action taken on complaints, by sending them communications on the representations made by the national authorities and the follow-up to the complaint (whether proceedings have been initiated, an Article 93(2) EC proceeding has been commenced, or it has been decided to close the case), including a summary of the reasons for the decisions taken. The dates of expedition of correspondence between the Commission and Member States could be communicated.

Those non-governmental organizations who responded to the relevant questionnaire questions were, almost universally, not in general satisfied with the reasons given by the Commission when a case was closed. The Royal Society for the Protection of Birds (RSPB) commented, 'In a recent case we felt closure to have been premature, but also felt handicapped by not being given access to the full reasoning behind the decision.' The Council for the Protection of Rural England (CPRE) commented; '[there] clearly must be political reasons for not pursuing some complaints . . .'. In some, but not all of its cases, Greenpeace International were 'extremely concerned about the type of reasoning given by the Commission for closing the file.' The World Wide Fund for Nature (WWF UK) had an even more basic complaint: that even though they were original complainants with regard to Cardiff Bay, as of April 1995 they had still not been notified of the Commission's decision to close the file, whilst another non-governmental organization had been informed of its closure in November 1994.

In theory, a summary of the reasons for the decision taken by the Commission in regard to a particular case should not take too long to draft as they should be encoded on the fiche to justify the proposal to process or close the case. It might be helpful in this regard if the Commissioners were to be required to explain in writing decisions differing from proposals, and all such explanations, together with approved proposals and the reasoning behind them were to be made public in order to safeguard against improper political influence in the Commission's enforcement functions. Indeed, such a step would appear to be entirely in keeping with Mr Williamson's letter to the author of May 1995 referred to above.

Despite the fact that there have always been provisions regarding the period within which letters are to be written, all those who replied to the questionnaire were very dissatisfied with the time it takes the Commission to process complaints. CPRE referred to a case closed after over three years, and Greenpeace International lamented their experience that:

the Commission can take anything up to two years before it begins to take an active role in investigating the dossier. In the case of THORP ... by the time the Commission came to its final decision in 1994 not to pursue the UK for failure to apply Directive 85/337, the UK Government had already taken its decision to authorise the operations at the plant, and the plant had effectively been given the go-ahead to commence operations. We are concerned that the Commission uses its slow processing of complaints to avoid taking timely, but politically controversial decisions.

The RSPB commented that it was not just a question of length of time:

One problem is the sheer unpredictability and variability in processing time. Also, the cycle of [Heads of Cabinet] meetings is obviously more fixed and infrequent than the occurrence of complainable problems! No sensible system of prioritisation by urgency or seriousness appears to operate ... It is often hard to know in a period of silence whether any 'processing' is taking place at all.

The question of lack of understanding of any prioritisation process was also raised by Council for the Protection of Rural England, who commented that it would be useful to have an indication of the Commission's priorities as to which types of complaints it sees as important to pursue.

Many of the above problems are exacerbated by the persistent understaffing of the DG XI Legal Affairs Unit. At the end of 1994 it comprised thirteen lawyers: that is, a head of unit and one lawyer for each Member State. That would be a fair average of the situation over the past few years. It is simply not enough to cope with the hundreds of cases and infringements, the copious mail, the written and oral questions from the Parliament, the appearances before Parliamentary committees, the assessment of all transposing legislation communicated by the Member States, the provision of legal advice to other units, for example on draft proposals, etc. In addition to the inadequate number of staff, their turnover is rapid. In the past eighteen months, seven of the fourteen lawyers in the unit at the beginning of that period have left. It has been the pattern for years that many of the unit's lawyers leave within twelve to eighteen months, and it takes about six months to get 'into' the job.

Enforcement of Environmental Law 373

There would undoubtedly be an improvement of the complaints investigation procedure if each of the points mentioned above were to be dealt with appropriately. However, it is believed that more fundamental changes need to be made to ensure effective enforcement, as discussed in the conclusion to this article.

V. Access to information

On 8 February 1990, on the initiative of the then Commissioner, Carlo Ripa di Meana, the Commission issued a Press Release on the first Commission report on the monitoring of the application of Community environmental law.[34] It constituted one page of simplistic, generalized text, and three tables: one on types of infringement; one on Article 169 procedures 'decided' 31 December 1989 (apparently including cases where the decision had been made but the relevant letter had not yet been sent); and one showing a breakdown of procedures by Member State and sector. Seven months later, the Commission published its seventh annual report to the European Parliament on the monitoring of the application of Community law, including in it discursive and statistical information about environmental enforcement.

The annual reports contain many pages of information about environmental law. Their usefulness is, however, limited. Some idea of these limitations can be gained from a brief examination of the last five published:

— the seventh report, for 1989, where the environment warrants just over a page of text;
— the eighth report, where the environment section contains two and half pages of text and two tables, and there is a sixty-five page annex untitled in the index and not referred to in the environment section, on the application by Member States of environmental directives;
— the ninth report, in which there is a thirteen page section on the environment, and a thirty-nine page annex on the monitoring of the application of environmental directives;
— the tenth report, in which there is a forty-five page environment chapter, and no environmental annex; and
— the eleventh report, for 1993, in which the environment section is fifteen pages long and there is again no separate environmental annex.[35]

The introductions to the Reports are, for the most part, general. While setting the scene, they may contain points which illuminate the

[34] Commission Press Release P-5, 1990.
[35] COM(90) 288 final, COM(91) 321 final, COM(92) 136 final, COM(93) 320 final, and COM(94) 500 final.

374   *Rhiannon Williams*

complaint investigation procedures. For example, in all the Reports the introduction makes clear the relative importance in the Commission's control function of complaints (not limited to environmental matters) made by private individuals, and those detected by the Commission itself. Most also comment upon the importance of the European Parliament in bringing infringement cases to the attention of the Commission. The introduction to the Tenth Report suggests reasons for the huge increase in complaints regarding the environment that year. In the introduction to the Ninth Report, mention is also made of a new procedure whereby when a number of complaints relate to the same subject, they are grouped together in one infringement file (an important fact to bear in mind when attempting to compare figures cited in past Reports).

The introduction to the Eighth Report explains that the Report has been restructured. This sets a trend which continues with regard to environmental information throughout the Reports here under consideration. This is of concern, as in many cases the restructuring renders it difficult, if not impossible, to compare like with like from year to year. Such capacity, enabling the spotting of trends and developments, should be one of the main reasons for the publication of an annual report. With any such report, from time to time amendments in structure and information provided may have to be made, but these should be kept to the practical minimum, and should be explained. Not only has that not in general been the case with the five reports under consideration, but the general level of detailed information provided is diminishing, and examination of the five reports together with other sources of information reveals disturbing discrepancies and apparent errors.

The tables and annexes which appear at the back of the reports have changed frequently in structure and content, which makes collation and comparison of information difficult. The author was also struck by a debate recorded in Hansard[36] where the Prime Minister said:

The Commission's 169 Letter of 22 March 1990 alleged infraction of directive 85/337/EEC in connection with a proposed waste disposal installation at Outlands Head quarry, Derbyshire. Following the United Kingdom's reply of 21 May 1990, the Commission sent a reasoned opinion about that case on 28 February 1991, to which the United kingdom replied on 30 April 1991.

In the Eighth Annual Report (for 1990), in Annex B on Infringement of Directives, the only comment made with regard to the United Kingdom is that it has notified national implementing measures for Directive 85/337/EEC.[37] No Article 169 Letter is referred to, although an Article 169 Letter and a Reasoned Opinion sent to other Member States are mentioned. Again, in the same annex in the Ninth Report (for 1991), no

---

[36] 27 Nov 1991, 521.
[37] Eighth Annual Report, 213.

Enforcement of Environmental Law   375

mention is made of the Reasoned Opinion to which the Prime Minister referred.[38]

It therefore appears that there was an omission in this regard from the Reports. As the Government does not routinely broadcast to Parliament its receipt of communications regarding infringement proceedings, it is impossible to know whether such an apparent omission is commonplace, but it is particularly worrying that, assuming that Mr Major was not totally mistaken, the apparent omission should have manifested itself two years running with regard to different stages in the same case. Greater transparency with regard to individual cases should help to prevent such instances recurring without correction or explanation.

The content of the reports is sufficient for the casual reader, but provides little of interest for those whose concern is in the detailed issues of interpretation of Community environmental law or its application and enforcement. In the environment sections and reports there are usually just a few lines on each of the few Directives mentioned. The information tantalizes. In particular, there is scanty, if any, mention of specific points of law which are at issue between the Member States and the Commission with regard to the interpretation of the Directives mentioned. There is little reference to individual Member States and information about their compliance, and the Directives and Regulations discussed are not all those treated in DG XI, just those which the Commission has decided to mention in the non-statistical parts of each Report. The criteria for their inclusion, or for the exclusion of the others are not stated.

Not only does the presentation of the information differ from year to year, but the amount of information given appears to have risen to a peak in the Ninth Annual Report, since when it has steadily fallen. As the recipient of the annual reports, and in a variety of other ways, the European Parliament is of prime importance in accessing information concerning the application of Community environmental law.

The answers to written and oral questions posed by MEPs[39] are published in the Official Journal. MEPs can also make less formal overtures by 'phone or letter. There is no documented rule on the point, but it seems that in general MEPs are entitled to the same information about a given complaint file as the complainant would be, together with a little bit more, informally, at the discretion of the official dealing with the file. The matter is not touched upon in the code of conduct governing relations between the Commission and the European Parliament which was agreed in March 1995. Members of the European Parliament may also, in public hearings, question representatives of the Commission about the progress of investigations into alleged infringements which are the subject of petitions to the Parliament.

---

[38] Ninth Annual Report, 176.
[39] Under Art 140 EC Treaty.

As has been seen above, the information available to complainants as such is minimal. However, for just over a year now, a Commission Decision has enabled a certain measure of greater access to information held by the Commission. There is a Declaration on the Right of Access to Information annexed to the final act of the Treaty on European Union. It provides that:

The Conference considers that transparency of the decision-making process strengthens the democratic nature of the institutions and the public's confidence in the administration. The Conference accordingly recommends that the Commission submit to the Council no later than 1993 a report on measures designed to improve public access to the information available to the institutions.

That first sentence is admirable in scope and aim. However, exactly which decision-making process(es) the authors had in mind is not clear. Further, the 'information available to the institutions' is curious wording, open to wide or narrow interpretation. The use of 'accordingly' would lead the optimist to assume that only the wider interpretation would suffice. Even if that argument were to prevail, the declaration is only a declaration. It only 'recommends' that a 'report' on such measures be submitted. It is not made clear whether the report is to be on measures already in place by 1993, and, by dint of the nature and wording of the declaration, there is no requirement or undertaking that such a report must be produced, let alone that any such measures must or will ever be introduced. Combined with the uncertainty of what is meant by 'the information available to the institutions', this is a rather poor sop to the democratic ideal to which it aspires.

The Declaration was cited in the preamble to the Commission's Decision of 8 February 1994, on public access to Commission documents.[40] The Decision provides as a general principle in its annex that,

The public will have the widest possible access to documents held by the Commission and the Council.

'Document' means any written text, whatever its medium, which contains existing data and is held by the Commission or the Council.

It took effect from 15 February 1994, and has an annex in which the code of conduct on public access to Commission documents is set out.

Article 1 of the Decision, which took effect from 15 February 1994, explains that there is a code of conduct on public access to Commission documents set out in the Annex. Article 2 contains measures effected 'to ensure that effect is given to the code ...'. These provide that:

— applications must be made in writing to the relevant office;
— specified persons 'or an official acting on their behalf' must reply in writing within one month informing the applicant whether the

---

[40] Decision 94/90/ECSC, EC, Euratom.

application is to be granted or whether there is an intention to refuse access, and, if the latter, informing the applicant that he has one month to apply for a review of that intention;

— the President may decide upon applications for review in agreement with the relevant Member of the Commission, or he may delegate this responsibility to the Secretary-General;

— failure to reply within one month of an application being made constitutes a refusal, as does a failure to reply within one month of an application for review being made;

— reasonable fees only may be charged for information provided; and

— documents may be consulted on Commission premises. The third and final Article provides that the decision is to take effect from 15 February 1994.

The Code itself comprises the preamble and general principle mentioned above, and sections on:

— the processing of initial applications (for the most part reincorporated in Article 2 of the Decision);

— the processing of confirmatory applications (or appeals against notification of intention to advise the decisions to refuse—again for the most part reincorporated in Article 2, but the Code also contains mention of the possible means of redress should an applicant wish to challenge a refusal on review to provide certain information, and specifies that details of such means of redress must be given in the letter notifying the applicant of the refusal on review);

— exceptions;

— implementation and review.

Implementation happened more or less on target, and a review of the Code will take place after two years of its operation. The really interesting part of the Code is its list of exceptions to the general principle. It provides that:

The institutions will refuse access to any document where disclosure could undermine:

— the protection of the public interest (public security), international relations, monetary stability, court proceedings, inspections and investigations), (sic)

— the protection of the individual and of privacy,

— the protection of commercial and industrial secrecy,

— the protection of the Community's financial interests,

— the protection of confidentiality as requested by the natural or legal persons that supplied the information or as required by the legislation of the Member State that supplied the information.

They may also refuse access in order to protect the institution's interest in the confidentiality of its proceedings.

378   *Rhiannon Williams*

Depending on their interpretation, the first five indents seem fair enough. The last sentence, however, is of concern. The Commission's interest in the confidentiality of its proceedings could justify the refusal of information which, if released, might legitimately hinder the Commission in the performance of its duties. However, this exception could also be used in cases where the Commission might be concerned about adverse public reaction to the fairness or transparency of its practices. As the exception currently stands, such a stance could arguably be justified.

It is therefore submitted that the exception should be qualified, for example by reference to criteria such as the degree of hindrance potentially caused the Commission in the execution of its duties, to be balanced against the importance and legitimacy of public interest in the matter, (though the need to assess degrees usually creates interpretational difficulties). In an attempt to test the waters of this new openness, in which there is no need to prove any legal interest, the author wrote three letters to the Commission in February and March 1995 requesting information in accordance with the Decision. On the whole, the results were pleasantly surprising, though they brought home the comparative uselessness of statistics without knowledge of the specific instances which went to make them up.

One letter was sent to the Secretariat-General, requesting information on the infringement procedure. This produced the biggest surprise: the release, as mentioned above, of that part of the 'Manuel des procedures operationnelles' or manual of operational procedures concerning complaints. The manual is produced only in French, and for years both it and its contents have been confidential under the Commission's internal rules of procedure. Indeed, the copy received from the Commission, dated September 1994, states on the cover 'document for internal use only'.[41]

The reply to the letter to the Secretariat-General did not include the Commission's 'Guide for all staff on operating the policy on improved access to documents,' which had been requested. As a result of an application for review by the author, it was duly provided. However, the making of the application for review highlighted one potential problem which arises with regard to applications for review of requests for information which were addressed in the first place to the Secretary General. The reply to such an application for review of a notified or implicit intention to refuse access could be made by the President in agreement with the relevant Member of the Commission. However, he could delegate that authority to the Secretary-General. This appears to mean that an application for information addressed in the first place to the Secretary-General, and any resulting application for review, might both be assessed by the same person or team within the Secretariat-General. In the application for review of April 1995, therefore, the author specifically

---

[41] A request was therefore made for the entire document, which was despatched, and is now being read with interest.

Enforcement of Environmental Law 379

requested that, in order to enable consideration of whether it is in accordance with the basic principles of natural justice that the Secretary-General alone should review an intention to refuse access addressed in the first place to another person in the Secretariat-General, it be explained where the author of the reply to the original request is situated in the structure of the Secretariat-General, in particular whether his letters have to receive the Secretary General's approval before they can leave the Commission, and to what extent he is accountable to the Secretary General. This point was ignored in the reply to the letter in which it was contained.

It is arguable that in cases where an initial request for information under the Decision was made to the Secretariat-General, the reply to any application for review of a notified or implicit intention to refuse access should be made by the President in agreement with the relevant Member of the Commission, and that it would be contrary to natural justice for the relevant authority to be exercised by the Secretary General.

The other two letters requesting information under the Decision were sent to DG XI. One concerned information on the administrative and structural history of DG XI. In the replies to it and to the author's appeal against the initial non-provision of certain information, the Commission was most helpful. The second letter requested information about the implementation of Decision 94/90 itself. The amount of information made available exceeded the author's request, and most of the information supplied would almost certainly not have been made available before the Decision came into force. It included a copy of a report evaluating the 260 requests under Decision 94/90 received up to 22 March 1995 by the Commission.

With regard to requests made to DG XI, by 6 April 1995, thirty-five had been registered, and sixteen 'positive replies' sent out, (one, if not both of the author's requests included). It would be interesting to know whether other recipients of 'positive' replies also believe that they initially received some, but not all of the information requested and so lodged an application for review in this regard.

It is encouraging to see that of the DG XI refusals, half were made on the grounds that the information had already been published. And it will be interesting to see whether any of the refused requests for review are appealed to the Court of Justice under Article 173 of the EC Treaty, and, if so, to what extent and on what grounds the Court will find that access should be provided. Similarly, a complaint could be made to the European Parliament ombudsman, under Article 138c of the EC Treaty. Such cases may well involve access to papers concerning environmental law and cases, since so far the environment has provoked 13.2 per cent of the requests for information received by the Commission, second only to those in the competition sector.

From the figures to date, at both DG XI and Commission level, the chances of success on application for review are slim (and slimmer in the

DG than in the Commission as a whole, though as yet the figures are still too low to be able to perceive real trends). It is notable that the most frequently used exception at Commission level, and the second highest at DG XI level, is the confidentiality of internal deliberation.

According to Commission officials, the meaning of 'document ... held by' in the General Principle part of the Annex has already come into question. According to the Secretariat General, it apparently refers only to documents of which Commission is the author. It will be interesting to see whether this interpretation will be challenged, as it would appear to be unduly restrictively interpreting the phrase 'held by'.

There is also apparently an interesting example currently being considered by the Commission, in which a Spanish tribunal has requested information on a complaint file. As it concerns a national legal system, it is the responsibility of the Legal Service to respond to the request. It may be that the Commission will pass over the documents to which it is the author, and refer the tribunal to the national authorities for the rest. If the application is granted to any extent, it may open the way for courts throughout the Community to have access in appropriate circumstances to the complaint files.

Another case throwing more light on the Commission's interpretation of the Decision arose when a request was made for a study of which the Commission was the nominal author because DG XI had financed its production. After some dispute within the DG, the study (on the transfer of waste) was apparently released.

Of most relevance in the context of this article, however, is the Commission's continuing refusal to publish correspondence relating to complaint files, Article 169 Letters, Reasoned Opinions, and references to the European Court. For example, of those who replied to the relevant questions in the questionnaires, with one exception, none were satisfied with the information regarding their complaints to which they were entitled with regard to the formal stages in the processing of the complaints (eg. when decisions are taken, the content of those decisions, and when letters are sent), and none were satisfied with the information to which they were entitled regarding the legal points which the Commission believes to be pertinent to each complaint (eg. the content of informal letters of inquiry to Member States, Article 169 Letters, etc.). For all, however, the most important point was the latter. There was common concern that the provision to them of 'if anything, only a sketchy summary of what passes between the Commission and the Member State'[42] militated against their ability to provide information in rebuttal of claims made by the Member State—information to which Commission officials would not always have access. The Royal Society for the Protection of Birds commented, 'We have unsuccessfully used the

---

[42] In the words of the RSPB.

Enforcement of Environmental Law 381

new formal procedures for challenging non-disclosure of documents [Decision 94/90], and are concerned that this militates against the ethos of open informed decision-making, access to justice and access to environmental information.' All believed that they should have access to correspondence relating to complaints.

The World Wide Fund for Nature (UK) commented that they currently have 'a case against the EC regarding access to Commission documents relating to a decision'. This has arisen out of *An Taisce—The National Trust for Ireland and WWF* v *Commission*.[43] The applicants applied for annulment of a Commission decision of 7 October 1992 not to suspend or withdraw the allocation of Community structural funds for financing the interpretative centre for visitors at Mullaghmore ('the Burren'). The Court of First Instance found that the Commission had not taken any decision not to suspend or reduce Community financing for the centre, so the application was dismissed as inadmissible. The applicants then wrote to DGs XVI and XI requesting access to their respective files (grant of structural funds by DG XVI and complaint file in DG XI) in order to attempt to establish that there had been a decision. Intentions to refuse access were notified in respect of both, so an application for review was made to the Secretariat-General. This also was refused. On 19 April 1995, an application[44] was made to the Court of First Instance, appealing the refusals. The grounds on which the refusals were based were the institution's interest in the confidentiality of its proceedings, and the protection of the public interest, because release of the complaint file (which has been closed since October 1992) could adversely affect the Commission's future investigations. The Secretariat-General apparently argued that the infringement investigation procedure required a climate of mutual confidence between the Member States and the Commission, and that this would be destroyed if any complaint file were to be released. The particularities of the case were not considered. The WWF (UK) is arguing that the contested decision is contrary to Decision 94/90, and that it violates Article 190 EC Treaty because the reasoning is insufficient. The World Wide Fund for Nature (UK)

is of the opinion that [the exceptions to the general principle set out in the Code of Conduct of the Council and the Commission on Access to Council and Commission documents] must, as all exceptions in Community law, be interpreted strictly and in the light of the general rule from which they constitute an exception. Under no circumstances may the application of the exception clauses contained in the Code of Conduct lead to the objective which the code of conduct aims to achieve being jeopardized or its realisation made impossible ... the Commission must, in order to invoke the exception clause, deal with the particularities of the case and with the contents of the documents

[43] Case T-461/93 [1994] ECR-II 733 now being appealed as Case C-325/94 P.
[44] Case C-105/95 *World Wide Fund for Nature (UK)* v *Commission* seeking the annulment of the Commission's decision confirming its refusal to grant access to the relevant documents.

382 *Rhiannon Williams*

to which access is required. It must show that disclosure of the documents would adversely affect the interest which is intended to be protected by the exception clause in question. Further, the Commission must balance the protection of these interests against the objectives of the Community policy on access to Community documents.[45]

Those objectives are cited as including the transparency of the decision-making process, and the strengthening of the democratic nature of the institutions. This will probably be the first case against the Commission under the Decision to be heard before the Court of First Instance.[46] It may set useful guiding principles in the interpretation of the Directive, eg. that, given the nature of the measure and its aims, its exceptions must be narrowly interpreted, or an indication of the factors which must be taken into account in reaching a balanced decision, or a statement that each case must be individually considered. The extent to which the Court decides that the Commission's discretion in the application of the exceptions is bound may be limited to pre-169 material, but perhaps something of wider significance will be formulated. It will also be interesting to see whether reasoning similar to that in *Zwartfeld*[47] will be applied to these differing circumstances—that the Commission must provide the Court with the information required to allow it to decide whether the refusal is justified.

The fundamental question is why any of the documentation on complaint files should not be made public. Article 169 contains no presumption of confidentiality with regard to infringement procedures. Although the Commission is acting on behalf of the Community, and not on behalf of the complainants, there would appear to be much sense in the argument that the current secrecy of the procedure is based on an inappropriate premise of international law—that the dispute is one between the Commission and the Member State, and the individual has no right to be informed of its details. As commented by Ludwig Krämer:

The administrative practice of the Commission shows clearly the derivation of the procedural law provisions of Article 169 *et seq.* from the classic rules of public international law, which relate solely to relations between states or international organisations. Community law by contrast assigns a totally different status to individuals from that under international law. Community legal acts are binding on the Member States and, unlike treaties under international law, do not require prior ratification by the legislatures of the individual States. The constitutional and human rights of the individual are part of the Community legal order and therefore do not have to be conferred on him

---

[45] Background notes on Case C-105/95, see n 44 supra, issued by Schön, Nolte, Finkelnburg & Clemm, Rechtsanwälte, Brussels.
[46] The first such case against the Council, Case T-194/94 *J. Carvel and Guardian Newspapers* v *Council*, concerning access to documents relating to the taking of a Council decision, was heard on 5 July 1995.
[47] Case C-2/88 [1990] ECR 4405.

Enforcement of Environmental Law   383

first. Furthermore, numerous Community decisions are made with immediate effect on individuals and govern the rights and duties of those concerned. Community directives, which like national laws are of a general nature and binding on everyone subject thereto, can nevertheless have direct effects on individual persons in particular cases. Finally, one of the Community's institutions which participates in its legislative procedures and the formulation of its political will, namely the European Parliament, is elected by the free and direct vote of the citizens of the Community.

All these circumstances argue for an extensive assimilation of the procedural rules of Article 169 to those of ordinary procedural law in the Member States, and thus for the publication of procedural decisions. That also applies in cases where the Commission and a Member State are at odds in the preliminary administrative proceedings under Article 169. Furthermore, the European Court of Justice has made it clear that the subject matter of a case before the Court under Article 169 is already fixed by the Commission's letter of formal notice which instituted the proceedings. Therefore the Commission cannot complain of further breaches of Community law at a later stage in the proceedings, because the Member State concerned would have had no opportunity to take issue with such complaints in the initial proceedings ... But if the default procedure is already formalised to such an extent, almost everything would suggest that the Commission's letter of formal notice to the Member State should also be published. That is especially true in the matter of environmental policies, which were not yet a part of Community policy when the Commission's characteristic administrative practices under Article 169 were being developed.[48]

There would appear to be good reasons not to publish informal letters of inquiry and the replies to them, as this might involve inappropriate publicity at a stage before the Commission had been able to establish its belief in an infringement. Improper or mistaken failure to process a case to Article 169 proceedings could still be effectively challenged if Article 169 Letters were systematically published, and the Commission were obliged to explain to complainants in writing why either the whole or part of their complaint was being closed after informal inquiries had been made. It must also be borne in mind that in many cases, most of the information on complaint files has been provided by the Member State. It is arguable that the more information is released by the Commission, the less a Member State is likely to provide.

There is genuine public interest in the contents of Article 169 Letters and Reasoned Opinions, and it would seem that court proceedings and investigations would, on balance, benefit from their disclosure. In addition, in the Netherlands, where MPs have been granted access to such letters[49] under the *Wet Openbaarheid Van Bestuur* (Law of Openness of Public Administration), the experience would not seem to have led to undesirable consequences from an environmental or legal point of view.

[48] L. Krämer *Focus on European Environmental Law* (Sweet & Maxwell 1992) 236 and 237.
[49] A right arguably available to the public generally, though the point remains moot.

VI. More than just a theoretical problem?

The objections raised above to the structure of the Commission and to the procedure.for investigating formal complaints are based on fundamental principles of constitutional law—the separation of powers, access to information, and accountability. They are largely theoretical. It can be strongly argued that the institutions of the European Union should not only function in accordance with those principles, but should be seen so to function. Thus, a well argued theoretical argument should be sufficient to justify appropriate change.

Nevertheless, it may add weight to such an argument if instances illustrating the criticisms are adduced. This section will examine two examples of apparent political influence in enforcement procedures, and will argue that the structures which allowed them to happen are unacceptable. The two instances of, it is submitted, political abuse of the infringement procedures which will be considered here are the uproar over the Article 169 Letter sent to the United Kingdom Government about the transposition and implementation and transposition of Directive 85/337 on environmental impact assessment, and the repeated postponement of the hearing of the case against the United Kingdom Government concerning the quality of the bathing waters at Blackpool.

On 17 October 1991 the Commission issued a press release announcing that it had that day sent to the United Kingdom authorities a Letter of Formal Notice commencing infringement proceedings in accordance with the provisions of Article 169 of the EC Treaty. The letter, signed by Carlo Ripa di Meana, the Commissioner with special responsibility for the environment, concerned the transposition and implementation in the United Kingdom of Directive 85/337/EEC on the assessment of the effects of certain public and private projects on the environment.

The press release[50] was remarkable for two reasons—the extent to which the legal arguments in an Article 169 Letter were made public, and the political storm which it generated. It was followed by days of speculative and often inaccurate media coverage and public debate. Four points of misunderstanding at least appeared to remain uncorrected in public perception until overtaken by other news.

The first was the issue of national sovereignty. According to *The Independent*, 'the anti-federalists in the Conservative Party highlighted the issue as another example of unwarranted, ill-judged EC tampering with national sovereignty.'[51] There was no question of any encroachment upon national sovereignty. In 1985 the Member States agreed unanimously to issue the impact assessment Directive. In considering the transposition and implementation of the Directive in the United Kingdom, in concluding

---

[50] Commission Press Release IP(91)928.
[51] 19 Oct 1991 4.

Enforcement of Environmental Law 385

that these were not adequate, and in issuing the Article 169 Letter, the Commission was acting in accordance with its powers and complying with the obligations imposed upon it by the Treaty.

The second misunderstanding centred on the Commission's alleged order to stop all works.[52] The sending of the Article 169 Letter (which apparently did not suggest the cessation of any construction work) must not be confused with the sending of the personal letter by Mr Ripa di Meana to Mr Rifkind, then Transport Secretary. According to the press release, Mr Ripa di Meana wrote 'asking' Mr Rifkind 'not to proceed with work on these projects so that the environment will neither be lost nor damaged beyond repair.' If the letter was similarly worded, that was clearly a request, not an order. The meaning may have appeared oblique: was the request to stop all works, or it to stop only those which would result in the loss or damage beyond repair of the environment? Apparently no attempt was made to clarify the position. Certainly if the latter interpretation was correct,[53] this would appear to have been a common-sense step. At that stage of proceedings, the Commission could not have applied to the European Court for interim measures.[54] The idea of attempting to prevent irreversible damage in a case where there is a genuine legal dispute is far from unknown in English law, or among the tenets of common sense. The astonishing thing about the request, if anything, is that it is of a type so rare, when large areas of the European environment are constantly being damaged beyond repair.

The request was not, however, entirely without precedent. Mr Ripa di Meana had earlier made a similar, successful request of the Italian Foreign Minister, Gianni di Michelis, in relation to plans to put Venice forward as a candidate for Expo 2000. For his pains, he had received 'perhaps the most bitter [attack of all my experience] from the Italian Government.'[55] Stanley Clinton-Davis, whilst Commissioner for the Environment, had made another such request of the Spanish authorities in relation to the construction of a road in Santoña. His personal request was unsuccessful, but the Commission won the case in the Court of Justice. These requests had not caused a diplomatic incident such as that following the personal request to Mr Rifkind.

The third misunderstanding stemmed from Douglas Hurd's allegation that the Commission was seeking to 'exert its influence in every nook and

[52] See, for example, *The Guardian* 26 Oct 1991: '...Mr Ripa di Meana wrote to the Transport Secretary, Malcolm Rifkind, last week warning him to stop all construction work, for assessment of the environmental impact. As no work had been started, Mr Rifkind accused the Commissioner of confused thinking.' Or *The Independent* of 22 Oct 1991, which referred to the Commission, '...ordering Britain to stop seven building projects on environmental grounds.'

[53] As understood by, for example, *The Independent*, which referred, on 17 March 1992, to Mr Ripa di Meana's '...request ... that no major work should begin before a legal dispute between the European Commission and the Government is settled.'

[54] Even had the Commission considered the issue and then decided to make such an application for interim relief, it would probably not have been heard by the European Court for many months.

[55] *The Financial Times*, 26 Oct 1991.

cranny of daily life' in telling the United Kingdom where to site its roads. Usually reliable newspapers and magazines took up the clarion call with enthusiasm: for example the *Economist* (recently advertising itself with the slogan 'Truth hurts but the price doesn't') in a leading article condemned a subjective subsidiarity which 'allows the European Commission to extend its diktat into matters that are of no cross-border relevance—such as the route of a motorway across England.[56] The leaked Article 169 Letter did not concern the route of the roads in question, the Commission's concern having, quite properly, been limited to the issue of whether Directive 85/ 337 had been correctly applied during the development consent procedures for those roads.

In that leaked letter, the Commission never argued or implied that it had the power to dictate the route of the motorway, or attempted to influence any choice of site. Indeed, a major weakness of Directive 85/337 is that its requirements are purely procedural—it sets out those procedures which must be followed prior to the grant of consent for the projects specified in the Directive. It is the Commission's duty to ensure that those procedures are, where applicable, observed, and it is in the context of the observation of that duty that the infringement proceedings against the United Kingdom were commenced.

Indeed, Mr David Trippier, the Minister for the Environment and Countryside, admitted during close questioning by Mrs Taylor in the House of Commons that it was correct that the Commissioner was 'not dictating planning decisions but asking Britain about the implementation of the European Community Directive'[57] and that, 'contrary to the Foreign Secretary's Statement, the Commissioner [was] not "dictating" through which field a road should go.'[58] Nevertheless, only twelve days later, the Prime Minister said in a debate on the European Community (Intergovernmental Conferences) that, 'whether a town bypass goes to the east or to the west has nothing whatsoever to do with cross-frontier pollution or competition policy or any other aspect of the single market. Those are issues that should rightly be settled at national level.'[59] This would indicate either that Mr Major still had not been correctly briefed about the matter, or that he was unduly influenced by political considerations in his public references to the case. By 9.00pm the same day, the seed had borne fruit and Mr Ron Leighton, (Member for Newham, North-East) was decrying the way that 'The Community even tells us through which fields we are to put our roads.'[60] Both a genuine legal dispute concerning environmental protection and a debate

---

[56] *The Economist*, 2 Nov 1991, 13.
[57] *Hansard*, 8 Nov 1991, 701.
[58] Ibid.
[59] *Hansard*, 20 Nov 1991, 279, and reproduced in *The Financial Times*, 21 Nov 1991.
[60] *Hansard*, 20 Nov 1991, 348.

Enforcement of Environmental Law 387

on proposed major change to the constitution of the Community by treaty amendment deserved better.

The fourth misunderstanding related to the apparent surprise of the United Kingdom Government at the commencement of proceedings. Mr Major was reported to have described the Commissioner's letter as 'astonishing'[61], and to have claimed 'We had no previous notice of it ... It is on the basis of facts that were not discussed with the UK.'[62] As Mr Ripa di Meana explained during an urgent debate in the European Parliament on environmental impact assessment throughout the Community,[63] there had over the previous seven months, been much contact with the United Kingdom Government about the matter, in the form of correspondence and meetings. He then proceeded to provide an unprecedented amount of detail about those contacts. An informal pre-Article 169 letter had, in accordance with the usual procedures, been sent to the United Kingdom on 24 January 1990. The United Kingdom Permanent Representation in Brussels (UKREP) was warned that infringement proceedings would be opened after 20 March 1991. On 10 June 1991, Mr Ripa di Meana's Cabinet had apparently met with the United Kingdom authorities, and on 30 July 1991 he said that Mr Rifkind had sent the Commission a memorandum about the matter. In early September there had apparently been an exchange of information in a 'long and friendly'[64] telephone call between Messrs di Meana and Rifkind, in which the former said that he agreed that there should be a high level meeting between the administrations. Accordingly, on the 16 October there was a meeting between the United Kingdom and Commission officials. The Article 169 Letter was sent the next day. On 17 October 1991 the Article 169 Letter was faxed to UKREP at 12.27 pm. At 12.44 pm it was then faxed to Mr Rifkind. At 17.03 Mr Ripa di Meana's personal letter was faxed to Mr Rifkind, and at 17.10 it was faxed to UKREP. The Press Release was communicated to the press from 18.00, so it was 'wrong' to say that the press were informed before the United Kingdom Government.

It is striking how much of this public misunderstanding of the basic issues was created by senior members of the Government. As Mrs Ann Taylor, MP for Dewsbury, commented, '... the amount of attention that the issue received ... was not due to the letter—nor, alas, because of interest in the environment. The letter received so much attention because of the way in which Ministers reacted to it.'[65] And it is not surprising that the public was unable to ascertain the truth about these basic points because various drafts of the Article 169 Letter had been leaked, but there was no official publication of it or of the accompanying personal letter.

---

[61] *Hansard*, 8 Nov 1991, 701.
[62] *Hansard*, 8 Nov 1991, 727, and *The Guardian*, 22 Oct 1991.
[63] 25 Oct 1991.
[64] According to Mr Ripa di Meana, *The Independent*, 9 Dec 1991.
[65] *Hansard*, 8 Nov 1991, 700.

388   *Rhiannon Williams*

(Though with regard to the latter, there is no reason why such letters should be systematically publicized. In cases such as that under discussion, where a Commissioner has publicized the sending and some of the content òf such a letter, it would be up to him or her to decide whether it would be appropriate to release the actual letter if it was believed that its contents were being misrepresented, or for any other reason).

Mr Tony Baldry, then the Parliamentary Under-Secretary of State for the Environment, made a most interesting speech on the question of the matters at issue. He claimed that:

> Our dispute with the Commission is not concerned with the legal issue, which I am sure can be resolved. Our dispute is simply a straightforward matter of good manners. Having sent what was a purportedly personal letter to the Secretary of State for Transport, the Commissioner leaked it to the press and to various environmental groups before the Secretary of State knew that it was coming. It is as if I wrote a letter to the hon. Member for Dewsbury and, before telling her to expect it, sent a copy to her local newspaper. I think that she would feel that that was simply bad manners. Our complaint is a simple one about bad manners.
>
> There is an accepted convention that communications between the Commission and Member States are confidential. The Commissioner breached that convention by issuing a press notice when he sent the letter, and by making public the contents of a private letter to the Secretary of State for Transport. That is what the row was about.[66]

This passage is fascinating for two reasons. The first is the mixture of disingenuousness in the conclusion and ingenuousness in the admission of perceived bad manners in the Commissioner's action. (One wonders what the press would have made of it had Messrs Major and Hurd, when questioned about the sending of the letters have replied 'It was very bad manners to publicize their transmission' and left it at that). The second is the reference to the 'accepted convention' of confidentiality of communications between the Commission and the Member States. Convention has played a major part in the unwritten constitution of the United Kingdom, but tends to be of less importance in the written constitutions of the other Community Member States. However, the role of convention is changing, if not being substantially undermined, in the modern British constitution. It might have been most unnerving to perceive what appeared to be a major breach of convention at European level and, addressing one's mind to the question of such conventions, to have realized that they did not have the same constitutional status at European level as in the United Kingdom.

Indeed, the question of whether there are constitutional conventions at Community level, and, if so, what they are, how they arose, their status, and so on, deserves further study. However, several short points may be made. There is an accepted convention that certain communications

[66] *Hansard*, 8 Nov 1991, 751.

Enforcement of Environmental Law 389

between the Commission and Member States are confidential. Article 169 Letters and Reasoned Opinions are considered in this regard above. The convention extends to their contents, but not the fact of their having been sent. Complainants are routinely informed of such transmission. In the circumstances of the impact assessment Article 169 Letter in point, when there had been much leaking and public speculation, it would have been inevitable that one or more of the complainants involved would have publicized the sending of the letter, and it was arguably preferable for the Commission to preempt public confusion about how many Article 169 Letters had been sent and their content than to let the information filter out piecemeal via complainants (or more leaks). Indeed, at a Commission press conference on 31 July 1991, Mr Ripa di Meana had commented that there was 'not yet full steam ahead', but that he was organizing a flow of information with regard to 'each case'. Such a flow has not yet materialized. In any event, it is, and was then, not unusual for the Commission to issue press releases when commencing infringements in cases of particular public interest.

It would therefore not have been a breach of convention for the Commissioner to issue a press notice when he sent the Article 169 Letter. However, because private letters such as that in question are rarely sent, let alone made public, it is possible to argue either that there was a breach of convention here, or that no convention yet existed to be breached. The publication of the sending of the letter did catch the Government on the hop, and for that reason alone at diplomatic level could be deemed to constitute an 'act of bad manners'.

It may be that this issue helped to crystallize some form of constitutional convention at Community level, or indeed, simply greater awareness at Community level of the concept. Unless constitutional rules are laid down in greater detail, constitutional conventions will probably assume progressively greater importance in Community constitutional law.

In order to distinguish between the legal nature and interest of the issues addressed in the Article 169 Letter, and the often emotive packaging of words in which they have tended to come wrapped, it is important to understand the context in which the Article 169 Letter was issued. In this regard, it is interesting to note that the United Kingdom was not the first of the Member States to receive an Article 169 Letter in respect of non-transposition and/or failure correctly to implement Directive 85/337. Indeed, at the time, the Commission had opened Article 169 proceedings against ten Member States, and proceedings were shortly to be opened against an eleventh.[67]

Nevertheless, the news made the headlines, and even the Prime Minister entered into the fray, leading Mr Ripa di Meana, whilst engaged in the urgent debate on the matter in the European Parliament, to announce that

[67] Speech by Mr Ripa di Meana to the European Parliament during the urgent debate on Directive 85/337 on 25 Oct 1991.

390   *Rhiannon Williams*

it was offensive and unjust for Mr Major to levy the accusation of partiality against him, that the reaction of the British Government was unfounded, that the independence of the Commission and the Commissioners was protected by Article 157 of the EC Treaty and that as a Commissioner and an individual he would not allow himself to be intimidated.

The reasons for the furore appear to be multiple. If the Commission was right on certain points of its interpretation of the Directive, the United Kingdom faced the possibilities of either having to abandon or revoke the grants of development consent for the projects mentioned and ensure that impact assessment in accordance with the Directive took place in respect of each project (an expensive exercise) or, if it had proceeded to construct in the interim, and the Commission had brought the cases before the European Court and won, the United Kingdom Government would have had to suffer the political embarrassment of a judgment against it. There was also the considerable public interest in relation to three of the projects in particular, the M3, the M11 Link Road, and the East London River Crossing. But similar public interest had accompanied cases which the Commission had earlier investigated of motorways in other countries (eg. the Via do Infante in Portugal), and governmental reaction in those cases had been more muted than that in the United Kingdom. A contributory factor may be the extensive press speculation over the weeks preceding 17 October including reported leaks of Commission working papers for the Article 169 Letter.[68] The proximity of the issue of the Article 169 Letter to the Maastricht summit in December 1991, and the impending national elections may not have been without their influence on the nature of the ensuing debate, given the need for governments to flex a little political muscle at such times.

More was known about the legal issues addressed in the Article 169 Letter than would normally be the case. As discussed above, in accordance with the internal rules of the Commission, a complainant is informed when an Article 169 Letter has been sent to a Member State following enquiries made into the complaint. However, the complainant is not usually informed of the contents of the letter. In this case, because of the misunderstandings and speculation surrounding the imminent release of the Article 169 Letter (and the possibility of a further leak?), the Commission issued a relatively detailed press release setting out at least some of the issues addressed in the letter.

The matters identified in any detail by the Commission in the press release all relate to the transposition of the Directive—the points at issue in relation to the seven cases of alleged non-implementation were not specified. Of the several points listed in the Press Release concerning the transposition of the Directive, the first was the question of whether the Directive applied to all projects in respect of which development consent

---

[68] For example, *The Observer on Sunday* 19 May 1991, *The Independent* week ending 31 May 1991 and 28 Sept 1991, *The Daily Telegraph* 16 and 27 Sept 1991, and *The Times*, 30 Aug 1991.

was granted after 3 July 1988, as the Commission argued, or whether it applied only to projects in respect of which application for development consent was made after the coming into force of the transposing legislation, as was the case in the United Kingdom statute—the 'pipeline' argument. (The various United Kingdom transposing measures all came into force later than the deadline, at dates varying from 15 July 1988 to years later). Concerns over pipeline cases were not limited to the United Kingdom. In the *Bund Naturschutz* case,[69] a German reference for a preliminary ruling, the European Court of Justice ruled that the relevant Article must be interpreted as

not permitting a Member State which has transposed the directive into national law after 3 July 1988 ... to waive, by a transitional provision, for projects in respect of which the consent procedure was already initiated before the entry into force of the national law transposing the directive, but after 3 July 1988, the obligations concerning the environmental impact assessment required by the directive.[70]

The issue differed from that in the United Kingdom Article 169 Letter in that the disputed United Kingdom cases concerned projects in respect of which the consent procedure was initiated not only before the entry into force of the national law transposing the Directive, but also before 3 July 1988. However, the German referring court had also asked for a judgment on the question of consent procedures initiated before 3 July 1988. This led the United Kingdom Government (together with the Governments of Germany and the Netherlands, and the Commission itself) to submit written observations. The Netherlands Government and the Commission argued that the directive provided that assessment was to be undertaken for all projects not yet approved by the deadline for the Directive's implementation, whereas the German and the United Kingdom Governments' took the view that it could not be interpreted in that way. As the Advocate General commented, 'The case involves a question of principle [legal certainty, protection of legitimate expectations and proportionality] and practical importance [potential delays and costs] which is not very easy to answer.[71]

On the grounds that it 'made sense' to deal with the question of consent procedures initiated before 3 July 1988, the Advocate General did so. He found that:

the Member States were not bound to make the projects covered by the directive which were not approved by 3 July 1988 subject to an environmental impact assessment, but could restrict the obligation to projects for which the consent procedure had not yet been initiated.[72]

---

[69] Case C-396/92 *Bund Naturschutz in Bayern* v *Freistaat Bayern* [1994] ECR I–3717.
[70] Ibid, 3717–8.
[71] Ibid, at 3720.
[72] Ibid, at 3731.

392   *Rhiannon Williams*

The Court of Justice usually follows the Opinion of the Advocate General. In this case, however, it limited itself to considering the facts of the German case, finding that:

regardless whether the directive permits a Member State to introduce transitional rules for consent procedures already initiated and in progress before the deadline of 3 July 1988, the directive in any case precludes the introduction in respect of procedures initiated after that date of rules such as those at issue in the main proceedings by a national law which, in breach of the directive, transposes it belatedly into the domestic legal system.[73]

It is unfortunate that the Court evaded the issue with regard to transitional rules for consent procedures already initiated before 3 July 1988, as it had been specifically posed by the referring court, and all parties had been able to make submissions on the point. Its determination to decide the reference in the light only of the facts of the case was not governed by Article 177 of the EC Treaty, which indicates that it would have been within the Court's jurisdiction to decide the matter. However, the Court's unwillingness to intercede at this point may be a reflection of the legal and practical difficulties surrounding the issue.

From that brief consideration of this one point of law raised in the Article 169 Letter, it appears that, at the very least, publication of the contents of Article 169 Letters would be likely to fuel greater public debate on the interpretation of environmental Directives. Importantly, such publication would enable companies, local and licensing authorities, and others affected by environmental directives to know more about points of interpretation of directives at issue, and so choose whether to 'play safe' in their conduct, take a legal risk, or ask for an Article 177 reference on a point if desired. (Although expensive, the last course is much quicker than allowing Article 169 proceedings to run their course).

The Commission appears to have decided to issue the Press Release[74] revealing the transmission of the Article 169 Letter to the United Kingdom concerning the implementation of Directive 85/337/EEC because of the mass of speculative publicity which had preceded its issue. Because of that and, possibly, the subsequent public disagreements between Mr Ripa di Meana and members of the United Kingdom Government, as well as the nature of the public interest in the projects, further developments in the case were also publicized by means of an eight-page Commission Press Release.[75] This meant that not only was more known about the legal arguments involved in the case than otherwise would have been at the stage of issue of the Article 169 Letter, but more information was later provided about why the Commission decided not to proceed with regard to some of the

---

[73] Ibid, at 3753. (Emphasis added).
[74] Commission Press Release IP(91) 928.
[75] Commission Press Release IP(92) 669.

Enforcement of Environmental Law   393

projects, and why it was proceeding to Reasoned Opinion with regard to two of them as well as with regard to one outstanding point of transposition. Yet another Press Release was issued to explain why the Commission then decided to terminate proceedings with regard to one of the remaining two projects at issue.[76] Finally, the Eleventh Annual Report stated that, '[t]the Reasoned Opinion helped to persuade the UK authorities to abandon the East London River Crossing Project'.[77]

Such reports on individual cases are the exception rather than the norm, yet it is difficult to argue that there is greater legitimate public interest in the details of a case simply because there were press leaks and a high level diplomatic row about it. The public have at least as much interest in knowing the details of cases concerning the quality of the air they breathe, and the water they drink and bathe in, as well as other well publicized localized cases, such as the Wheal Jane overflow of 1992. And the environment would benefit. Yet Press Releases in such cases are rarely forthcoming, and, when they do appear, contain little detail.

To return to the case in hand, namely the implementation in the United Kingdom of Directive 85/337 EEC, the latter Directive gives certain rights of information and participation to the public. Those rights are only effective if the procedures set out in the Directive are followed. It is therefore in the public interest that points of dispute as to the interpretation of the Directive are settled, if necessary by the Court of Justice. And that it why it is important that legal questions such as those discussed above and the others raised in the Article 169 Letter are settled through the procedures agreed upon by the Member States for the resolution of such disputes, and why it is desirable that the waters of such matters are not unnecessarily muddied by deliberate or carelessly disseminated inaccuracy or misunderstanding, or by those who are simply out to score political points.

Reports such as the following appeared immediately after the issue of the Article 169 Letter:

John Major has accused the European Commission of wilfully jeopardising hopes of agreement on a new political and monetary union treaty by ordering Britain to stop seven building projects on environmental grounds.

In an angry letter delivered yesterday to the Commission President, Jacques Delors, the Prime Minister spelled out his annoyance and served notice that he would now be less likely to support the treaty, due for signature by EC leaders at the Maastricht summit in December.

This is overt linkage of the political with the legal processes of the Commission. Here, a misrepresentation of a matter where the central issue is the interpretation of the law, has the effect that a Member State

---

[76] Commission Press Release IP(92) 1127.

[77] Eleventh Annual Report by the Commission to the European Parliament on the monitoring of the application of Community law, COM (94) 500 final, 75, para 1.7.

394   *Rhiannon Williams*

announces that it may jeopardize a major political conference. The message is very clear—that the Commission should think twice about such legal proceedings (or, at the very least, their publicity) if it wants the United Kingdom to co-operate politically. As Mr Win Griffiths, the MP for Bridgend put it:

My hon. Friend the Member for Cardiff, West (Mr Morgan) and a number of other hon. Members referred to environmental impact assessments and the way in which the Government seem to be trying to traduce the whole legal process and divert it into an attack on the Commissioner for the Environment, for political purposes connected with the Maastricht Summit.[78]

It is outrageous in a democratic system of government that such manipulation should be allowed to be threatened, carry any weight, or even seem feasible.

Another example of such linkage occurred the next year, but in reverse: political factors appeared to influence the conduct of a legal case. The case brought by the Commission against the United Kingdom concerned the compliance of the quality of the water at Blackpool, Southport, and Formby beaches with Directive 76/160.[79]

The hearing was to be in March 1992.[80] However, it was postponed until 1 July, allegedly

until after the election, at the request of the Government ... A spokesman for the Department of the Environment said the postponement was to give both sides time to prepare their cases. But a spokesman for Carlo Ripa di Meana, the EC Environment Commissioner, said the British Government had asked for the delay.[81]

It was then reported that there had been a second deferral of the hearing

after John Major and Jacques Delors, President of the European Commission, agreed on a postponement ... Lawyers in the European Commission's environment department were startled to learn of the adjournment. There was speculation that a deal had been done to avoid embarrassing Britain.[82]

1 July 1992 was the day Britain assumed the EC Presidency. It was reported that the hearing could not be rearranged to take place before October at the earliest, and that proved to be the case.

It appears, therefore, that one, if not both, of the deferrals were made on political grounds. Suspension on the ground of impending elections so as not to compromise the Government is a justification of arguable validity. The hearing was likely to take up half a day at most, and it was only a hearing, not the giving of a judgment. The adverse publicity which it might

---

[78] *Hansard*, 8 Nov 1991, 745.
[79] Case C-56/90 *Commission v United Kingdom* [1993] ECR I-4109.
[80] *The Independent*, 9 Dec 1991, and 22 Jan 1992.
[81] *The Independent*, 11 Mar 1992.
[82] *The Independent*, 30 June 1992.

Enforcement of Environmental Law 395

have generated would have been minimal (unless, as with the impact assessment Article 169 Letter discussed above, the Government had chosen to make a great deal out of it). In addition, any adverse publicity which would have been generated would arguably have benefitted the opposition, so a postponement on the grounds of impending general elections so as not to damage the Government would appear to discriminate against the opposition parties.

There would appear to be at least two ways to avoid allegations of political influence over the running of cases. One would be to ensure that only legal, and never political considerations are taken into account in arranging the postponement of a hearing, or in publicizing the sending of an Article 169 Letter or a Reasoned Opinion. This would require some sort of separation of the functions of the Commission. The other would be to lay down guidelines whereby no case would be heard or publicized proceedings commenced within a certain period before an election in the Member State in question, or on the day that that Member State assumes the Presidency, or during or in the run up to an intergovernmental conference, or on other similar (and specified) grounds. But the problem with such an approach would be that it could lead to paralysis of the Commission's enforcement function. In Germany there are sixteen *Länder* and a Federal Government, and last year there were twenty-two elections. Local elections may have national impact too. It would be impossible to know where to draw the line.

It is unacceptable, given the delays inherent in the bringing of cases before the Court of Justice, for repeated last minute postponements to be possible in circumstances such as the above, where it had been known for years that the United Kingdom would assume the Presidency on 1 July. The original postponement could have been to early July, rather than three months later. Repeated postponements are in the interests neither of impartial enforcement, nor of environmental protection. As a general rule, the later an environmental case is settled or gets to court, the more pollution or damage occurs, and the longer it is before clean-up begins or the challenged practice ceases.

For these reasons, and the scope for argument as well as procrastination, which the second proposed policy would entail, it is submitted that the only change acceptable from the point of view of a democratic constitution, is that of the total separation of the administrative and law enforcement functions of the Commission. Such a change would also potentially promote greater environmental protection via law enforcement.

In June 1992 Mr Ripa di Meana resigned from the Commission, six months before the end of his four-year term. It was reported that:

'Officials in London and Brussels hinted broadly yesterday that Jacques Delors, the Commission President, gave a nudge to both Mr Ripa di Meana and Vasso

396   *Rhiannon Williams*

Papandreou, the social affairs Commissioner, who is also leaving the Commission. Both have been involved in bitter rows with national capitals, especially London, over their crusading style. Mr Delors is known to be concerned that perceptions of an interfering Commission will hamper ratification of the Maastricht treaty on European Union in Britain.[83]

Whether or not this was so, it is an indictment of the system that it should have been perceived and widely believed to be true that a Commissioner who was committed to law enforcement and openness in that quest should forfeit his job because of the impact of that commitment on political processes.

The underlying message, to Commissioners keen to keep their jobs, is that commencing infringement proceedings is a dangerous matter, that they would do well to cover themselves politically, and to keep proceedings as quiet as possible, and that the power to decide whether or not to commence such proceedings is a useful bargaining pawn in political negotiations. In such circumstances, Article 157 of the EEC Treaty is inadequate to ensure the independence of the Commission. Greater constitutional safeguards need to be put into place.

Finally, there have been too many recent cases of arguable failure by the national courts correctly to apply Community environmental law, for example in *R v Poole BC, ex parte Beebee*,[84] *Kincardine and Deeside DC v Forestry Commissioners*,[85] *Wychavon DC v Secretary of State for the Environment and Velcourt Ltd*[86] and *R v Swale BC and Medway Ports Authority ex parte RSPB*,[87] to name but a few. It might be of assistance to the parties and judges in such cases to know when infringement proceedings on relevant points are on-going, and the arguments being put forward (or which have been put forward if not the matter was resolved before application was made to the European Court of Justice) in such proceedings. At the very least it might encourage greater awareness of the issues and possibly the making of Article 177 references where appropriate.

Other examples of recent cases where it might have been most illuminating, and possibly time, money and environment saving, for all the parties involved to have known the Commission's stance on the issues included *R v Secretary of State for the Environment ex parte RSPB*,[88] as heard before the High Court, the Court of Appeal and the House of Lords, before an Article 177 Reference was finally made, and *R v Secretary of State for the Environment, ex parte Friends of the Earth*,[89] as ruled upon by

---

[83] *The Independent*, 30 June 1992.
[84] [1991] 2 PLR 27. See analysis by J.D.C. Harte in 2 *JEL* 293 (1991).
[85] [1992] SLT 1180. See R. Williams (1991) *CLJ* 383.
[86] [1994] COD 205; *The Times* 7 Jan 1994; as commented upon by Professor Richard Macrory in the *ENDS Report*, 228 (Jan 1994).
[87] [1991] 1 PLR 6; see analysis by Malcolm Grant in 1 *JEL* 135 (1991).
[88] (HL) *The Independent* 10 Feb 1995.
[89] (CA) *The Times* 8 June 1995.

Mr Justice Schiemann on 29 March 1994, and by the Court of Appeal in June 1995.

VII. Possible Remedies

'He that will not apply new remedies must expect new evils; for time is the greatest innovator.'[90]

Whilst it might be possible for approaches to be made to the European Court or the ombudsman, when appointed, with regard to some of the matters of concern raised above, many of them would not easily lend themselves to such action. In any event, it would be far more satisfactory to deal with the problem at source, by introducing appropriate safeguards into the system.

Many of the points considered in this article could be ameliorated to some extent by making adjustments to the administrative practices of the Commission, or taking other appropriate steps, for example by publishing more detailed rules of procedure, speeding up procedures, and providing more staff to deal with complaints. There also needs to be far greater public access to information, from the fact that certain decisions have been taken, and when and why, to the contents of Article 169 Letters and Reasoned Opinions, from the internal administrative rules of procedure relevant to enabling complainants to present complaints in the most effective way, to reasons for the closure of files.

However, the fundamental problem of the absence of formal separation of powers in the Commission would remain. At the very least there should be some form of oversight of performance of the Commission's law-enforcement functions. Parliamentary scrutiny together with greater publication of information might be one way to move forward.

Ken Collins, MEP the Chairman of the European Parliament's Environment Committee, favours the institution of a system whereby Article 169 Letters are forwarded to an appointed MEP for scrutiny when they are sent to the Member State involved, on the understanding that the contents of the Article 169 Letters would not be revealed even to other MEPs.[91]

Whilst not a retrograde step, such parliamentary scrutiny would do little for the wider public interest in environmental enforcement. It would also be difficult for any parliamentary concerns about the conduct of infringement proceedings to force action from a Member State if all correspondence on the subject had to take place in private.

Instead, it is submitted that a far more radical approach is needed in order to ensure the proper application of Community environmental law

[90] Sir Francis Bacon, *Essays: Of Great Place.*
[91] As explained to the author during an interview on 30 March 1995.

398   *Rhiannon Williams*

in a way which is independent, and seen to be independent: the formal
division of the Commission's enforcement and political functions.

The subject cannot be dealt with in detail here, but there are various
possibilities—the setting up of a separate Community law enforcement
bureau as a new, independent body, or, with regard to Community
environmental law alone, the use of the European Environmental Agency
as a combined information gathering and distribution centre and
enforcement unit, with appropriate safeguards to ensure even-handed
and rigorous application of the law. One draw-back to the latter
suggestion might be the extent of the Agency's need to co-operate with
Member States in data collection and analysis.[92]

A body charged with enforcement, with enough staff to do the job
properly, and equipped with environmental (and possibly other) inspectors
with appropriate powers (akin to those of the competition officials who
have powers of search and seizure), would enable those charged with the
enforcement of Community environmental (and possibly other areas of)
law, to take more initiatives and to assume a much less reactive role.[93] In
short, to be more effective.

In the Seventh Annual Report it is stated that:

> Most of the complaints concern inadequate application of existing law. Although
> often it is not difficult to establish the facts, the number of cases is increasing
> where an on-the-spot visit, an analysis by an independent laboratory or
> measurement of the pollution would be useful. On-the-spot visits must be limited
> to exceptional cases, because there are not enough staff and the Commission does
> not have mobile measuring stations to enable it to measure the pollution of the
> environment or analyze the samples.[94]

In addition to inadequate resources, the Commission has no authority to
carry out on-site testing, unless Member States permit such activity. The
theme is taken up again in the Eighth Report, and was echoed in some of
the responses to the author's questionnaire. Greenpeace International, for
example, commenting that, "... the Commission's attempts to undertake
thorough investigations are frustrated by their lack of powers to carry out
on-site investigations".

An investigation force could relatively easily be incorporated within a
body such as one of those suggested above, provided that appropriate
funds and political will could be generated: and therein lies the rub. As
reported by the House of Lords Select Committee on the European
Communities' Ninth Report on the implementation and enforcement of
environmental legislation:

---

[92] See Macrory, 29 *CML Rev* at 363 (1992).
[93] Ibid.
[94] Seventh Annual Report by the Commission to the European Parliament on the monitoring of the
application of Community law, COM (90) 288 final, 25.

Enforcement of Environmental Law 399

Lord Clinton-Davis favoured 'a small but efficient environmental inspectorate capable of, where necessary, undertaking dawn raids to ensure that incriminating evidence is not destroyed' ... When we met the Commissioner in Brussels he indicated his own personal preference for such a form of inspectorate, though he reported that opposition within the Commission and the Council meant that it was not a politically realistic option.[95]

Such opposition is also likely to be met with regard to the suggestion to divide the Commission. However, only if radical steps such as those suggested above are introduced can the Community begin to hope that it may deserve public confidence in its environmental-law enforcement function.

---

[95] HL Paper 53-I, 21, para 46.

[12]

LITIGATING COMMUNITY ENVIRONMENTAL LAW — THOUGHTS ON THE DIRECT EFFECT DOCTRINE†

Derrick Wyatt QC*

1. European Environmental Legislation Prey to Drafting Defects

I cannot resist noting at the outset that I do not regard the adoption of European environmental legislation as being *per se* a positive contribution to environmental protection in the United Kingdom. It is at least as likely as national legislation to be the product of ill considered objectives, and more likely than national legislation to be poorly drafted. This latter feature results from the fact that the European legislative process contains more of an element of negotiation than does the national legislative process. The compromises inherent in this process consign to the judicial process the resolution of issues which in an ideal world would have been resolved by the legislator and expounded with precision by the draftsman. Thus it falls to the European Court of Justice to give a definitive meaning to a text which secured adoption by virtue of its opaqueness or ambiguity. The Court is assisted in its endeavour by arguments which are often disordered and abstract and lacking in exposition of the practical environmental concerns which inspired the legislative process.

2. European Legislation Substitutes Standard setting for the Discretion of the Regulator

All this *may* be so in a particular case. And because this may be so it may seem something of a paradox to claim for European environmental law that if it has a saving grace it is that in the United Kingdom it has largely substituted the fixed points of legally enforceable standards for the general discretion of regulators. If the good old days before European environmental law were the days when statute required drinking water to be 'wholesome', the advent of European environmental law meant that 'wholesome' water meant water complying with specific mandatory standards as regards e.g. nitrates, lead and pesticides. The enforceability of European environ-

† A revised version of a paper given to a conference at Imperial College, London on 27 June 1997.
* Fellow of St Edmund Hall and Professor of Law, University of Oxford.

mental law before courts in the United Kingdom has encouraged individuals in the belief that in certain respects they have a right to a clean environment, and in certain respects they are right.

This development is of course linked to important developments in public law in the United Kingdom. The principle of English law that public authorities may be called upon to perform their public duties (principally through recourse to the prerogative order of mandamus) is a long established principle. What is a relatively new principle is that the range of interested parties who have standing to raise these matters before the courts, and to seek remedies such as mandamus, includes both individuals who might be adversely affected by a failure to enforce the law, and bodies such as Greenpeace and Friends of the Earth, who are recognized as being representatives of members of the public who might be so affected. If a more liberal approach to the law of standing made it more feasible to call to account those public authorities charged with the enforcement of environmental law, European environmental law (for the most part through the medium of directives) provided the environmental standards which transformed challenges to governmental handling of the environment from debates about the reasonableness of the exercise of discretion to more hard edged arguments about compliance with defined procedures, or achievement of defined quality standards.

3. Europeanization through selective Verbatim Incorporation

It is possible to identify, in a general way, two phases in the adaptation of environmental law in the United Kingdom to the requirements of European law. The early phase was characterized by a tendency towards regarding EEC Directives as helpful if eccentric recommendations to be gently eased into the United Kingdom scheme of things, ideally by government circular rather than by legislation, and ideally without cost. Initial implementation of the directives on quality standards for drinking water and bathing water follow this pattern. That phase now appears to be past. The current situation is one in which environmental law in the United Kingdom has become significantly Europeanized, not only because Directives have been transposed into national law (in contrast to being made the subject of government circulars), but because they have been transposed in such a way that the key provisions of the Directives in question have been incorporated into United Kingdom statutory provisions, or into statutory instruments. This technique minimizes the possibility of national judges interpreting statutory implementing measures in a way which differs from the underlying directive. It amounts in a very real sense to the *Europeanization* of United Kingdom environmental law. I offer as important examples bathing and drinking water quality standards, waste management, and the protection of habitats.

4. Water Quality Standards, Waste Management and Habitats

The Directive on Drinking Water Quality (Directive 80/778/EEC) specifies mandatory quality standards for drinking water as regards certain substances, including lead, nitrates and pesticides. Section 68(1)(a) of the Water Industry Act 1991 requires water companies to supply only water which is 'wholesome' at the time of supply, where the water is intended for human consumption. 'Wholesomeness' is defined in regulation 3 and Schedule 2 of the Water Supply (Water Quality) Regulations 1989.[1] The parameters established by those provisions incorporate those required by the Directive (and in some cases lay down more stringent provisions). The obligation laid down by the 1991 Act to supply wholesome water is an absolute one. It is not a defence for a water company to show that it has done everything practicable or possible to supply wholesome water. Furthermore, pursuant to s 37 of the Act, it is the duty of the water company to maintain supplies of water sufficient to ensure that the water company is able to meet all its obligations under part III of the Act, including the obligation under s 68 to supply water which is wholesome. Under the United Kingdom rules, there is thus a legal obligation on water companies to supply water which complies with the standards of the directive.

The Directive on Bathing Water Quality (Directive 76/160/EEC) defines the waters to which it applies. These waters are inter alia those in which bathing is not prohibited and is customarily practised by a large number of bathers. For these waters the directive specifies mandatory quality standards as regards in particular faecal coliforms. The requirements of this Directive are implemented inter alia by the Bathing Waters (Classification) Regulations 1991.[2] Bathing waters are defined in the Regulation by reference to the definition provision in the directive. The Regulations specify monitoring and quality standards for such waters, and these standards are set out in the schedules to the Regulations. The schedules set out virtually verbatim the relevant monitoring and quality standards specified in the directive. The Regulations also impose a duty on the Secretary of State to exercise his statutory powers to apply the relevant monitoring and quality standards to relevant territorial waters, coastal waters and inland waters which are bathing water within the meaning of the Directive. This method of implementation reduces the risk of inadequate implementation by incorporating the Directive's definition of bathing waters, and the Directive's statement of monitoring and quality standards, into the law of England and Wales.

The Waste Framework Directive (Directive 75/442/EEC as amended by Directive 91/156/EEC) provides for the supervision of the collection transport disposal and recovery of waste. Waste is defined in the directive, and Annexes give examples of waste substances, and of disposal and recovery operations as they occur in practice. Implementation of the Directive in the United Kingdom (apart from Northern Ireland) is ensured principally through the Waste Management Licensing Regulations 1994.[3] These Regulations introduce into UK environmental law the concept of 'Directive waste', which is defined by reference to the definition in the Directive and to the potentially waste substances referred to in Annex 1 of the Directive, which is reproduced as Part II of Schedule 4 of the Regulations. The concepts of 'disposal' and 'recovery' are defined by reference to Schedule 4 of the Regulations, which reproduces verbatim Annexes IIA and IIB of the Directive. Once again, key definitions are incorporated into the corpus of UK environmental law in a way which reduces the risk of inadequate or incorrect implementation and ensures that administrators, legal advisers, enforcement bodies, and courts and tribunals address important environ-

[1] SI 1989 1147.
[2] SI 1991 1597.
[3] SI 1994 1056.

mental concepts from the perspective of a single text, rather than from the perspective of different texts which purport to have the same aim and effect, but which may be represented as having different effects in practice.

The Habitats Directive (Directive 92/43/EEC) aims to secure the designation of special areas of conservation in order to create a coherent European ecological network according to a specified timetable. All areas designated under Directive 79/409/EEC on the conservation of wild birds, are to be incorporated into this framework. The Directive contemplates an exercise resulting in a list of sites of Community importance being adopted by the Commission in accordance with the procedure specified in the Directive. The list is to be based on national lists to be transmitted to the Commission. The criteria for the drawing up of national lists are as set out in Annex III (stage I) and in addition 'relevant scientific information'. Once a site of Community importance has been adopted, the Member State shall designate it as a special area of conservation as soon as possible and within six years at most. Implementation is secured by the Conservation (Natural Habitats) Regulations 1994.[4] The Regulations state that they make provision for the purpose of implementing the Habitats Directive in Great Britain. Relevant ministers are required to exercise their functions under the enactment's relating to nature conservation so as to achieve the requirements of the Habitats Directive. Regulation 7 requires the Secretary of State, 'on the basis of the criteria set out in Annex III (stage I) to the Habitats Directive and relevant scientific information' to propose a list of sites. Regulation 8 provides that once a site of Community importance in Great Britain has been adopted 'in accordance with the procedure laid down in paragraph 2 of Article 4 of the Habitats Directive, the Secretary of State shall designate that site as a special area of conservation as soon as possible and within six years at most.' The Regulations in other respects follow the pattern of laying down a framework in national law which incorporates important definitions and requirements verbatim from the directive.

5. The Virtues of Selective Verbatim Incorporation

The above process of transposition by means of selective incorporation of European definitions and requirements is sometimes unhelpfully described as 'copy-out'. I say 'unhelpfully' because the term may seem to imply a passive process of implementation, in which the legislator simply 'tops and tails' a directive, without any serious examination of the substantive and procedural requirements of the directive and without appropriate clarification of general provisions contained in the directive. I do not think that this could be a fair description of the examples of selective incorporation to which I have referred above. Recourse to selective incorporation avoids difficulties arising over possible discrepancies between the requirements of a directive, and the requirements of national rules purporting to implement the directive. The implementation of the waste framework directive is a good example. The definition of 'waste' has caused problems in a number of Member States, and a number of judgments have been given or are pending on the scope of this concept in the directive. It was clearly necessary to adopt a definition of 'waste' in national implementing rules which would

---

[4] SI 1994 2716.

stand the test of time and of any future judgments of the European Court on the scope of that concept as used in the directive. It seems self-evident that use of the Directive definition is appropriate in such circumstances. Similar considerations apply in the other contexts mentioned.

6. Europeanization through Interpretation of National Law in light of Environmental Directives

If selective incorporation of the texts of environmental directives within the framework of national implementing rules is one important reason for the Europeanization of UK environmental law, it is not the only reason. Another reason is the development of a principle of interpretation whereby national courts are obliged to interpret national rules, as far as possible, so as to be consistent with relevant EC Directives. The position was recently confirmed by the European Court in its judgment in Case C-168/96 *Criminal Proceedings against Luciano Arcaro* [1996] ECR I-4705. The national proceedings concerned a prosecution for infringement of national rules purporting to implement Directive 76/464/EEC on pollution caused by certain dangerous substances discharged into the aquatic environment and Council Directive 83/513/EEC on limit values and quality objectives for cadmium discharges. The Court stated that:

... the Member States' obligation, arising under a directive, to achieve the result envisaged by the directive and their duty, under Article 5 of the Treaty, to take all appropriate measures, whether general or particular, to ensure fulfilment of that obligation, are binding on all the authorities of Member States including, for matters within their jurisdiction, the courts. It follows that, in applying national law, the national court called upon to interpret a directive is required to do so, as far as possible, in the light of the wording and purpose of the directive in order to achieve the result pursued by the directive and thereby comply with the third paragraph of Article 189 of the Treaty ...

The Court added an important caveat:

However, that obligation of the national court to refer to the content of the directive when interpreting the relevant rules of its own national law reaches a limit where such an interpretation leads to the imposition on an individual of an obligation laid down by a directive which has not been transposed or, more especially, where it has the effect or determining or aggravating, on the basis of the directive and in the absence of a law enacted for its implementation, the liability in criminal law of persons who act in contravention of that directive's provisions ...

Taking full account of the limits of the above principle, the principle in practice leads, in the United Kingdom, to a concordant interpretation of national laws which implement a directive with the terms of that directive as interpreted by the European Court of Justice. This is likely to be the case even if at first sight there appears to be some divergence between the directive, as interpreted by the European Court, and the text of the national rules. An example may be given from the field of sex discrimination. The House of Lords has shown itself willing to accommodate the text of the Sex Discrimination Act 1975 to the requirements of the equal treatment Directive (Directive 76/207/EEC), as interpreted by the European Court, despite an apparently considerable textual difficulty in so doing (*Webb v EMO Air Cargo (UK) Ltd (No 2)*

[1995] 4 All ER 577; the Court of Appeal had taken the view that to interpret the 1975 Act as it was ultimately interpreted would give it a distorted meaning, [1992] 2 All ER 43 at 57f, 61a, and 64h).

7. The Combined Effect of Selective Verbatim Incorporation and Consistent Interpretation Facilitates the Justiciability of EC Environmental Directives before UK Courts

The use of selective verbatim incorporation, combined with application of the principle that national rules implementing directives are to be interpreted as far as possible so as to give force and effect to such directive, facilitates litigation which has the aim of testing the compatibility of national environmental regulation with relevant EC directives. An example is to be found in the application for judicial review by Friends of the Earth and Andrew Lees/Christine Orengo of the decisions of the Secretary of State to accept (as a measure of enforcement under the Water Industry Act 1991) certain undertakings from Thames Water and Anglian Water Services Limited in respect of compliance with the pesticides parameter as regards water supplied by those water companies.[5] The applicants argued that the Secretary of State was under an obligation, as a matter of Community law, to make enforcement orders against those companies. All the principles and rules of Community law relied upon by the applicants were considered by the High Court and the Court of Appeal, either inasmuch as those rules and principles were reflected in the terms of verbatim incorporation (e.g. of the water standards) or inasmuch as it was accepted that the terms of UK legislation were in any event to be construed and applied so as to give effect to Community law as interpreted by relevant judgments of the European Court. It was accepted by the Secretary of State that in certain respects there was a breach by the United Kingdom of its primary obligation to ensure that the Directive's water quality standards had been achieved in the United Kingdom by the date specified in the Directive, and it was accepted that the duty of the Secretary of State pursuant to the statutory regime of the Water Industry Act was the same as the duty laid down in European Community law to achieve performance of the secondary obligation to rectify breach of the primary obligation as soon as possible. The principal issue in the proceedings became the factual question whether the acceptance of the undertakings in issue amounted to taking the speediest possible steps to secure performance of this obligation. The actions were dismissed by the High Court and the Court of Appeal on the merits of the Community law arguments raised.[6]

8. The Direct Effect of EC Environmental Directives

8.1. The question of direct effect arises if a directive has not been properly implemented and national rules cannot be construed so as to achieve the purposes of the directive

If it appears that a directive has not been properly implemented in the United Kingdom, the question arises whether relevant provisions of the directive give rise to rights

[5] *R v Secretary of State for the Environment ex parte Friends of the Earth* [1996] 1 CMLR 117, CA.
[6] See M. Purdue, 'The Possible Will Take a Long While', *JEL* (1995) 7(1) at 9–28.

in individuals which national courts are bound to safeguard, as against public bodies which exercise the authority of the State. An example is to be found in the application of Twyford Parish Council, pursuant to Schedule 2 of the Highways Act 1980, challenging a road scheme involving widening of the M3 motorway, made by the Secretary of State for Transport, which was alleged to be invalid because no environmental impact assessment had taken place pursuant to the requirements of Directive 85/337/EEC (*Twyford Parish Council v Secretary of State for the Environment* [1992] 1 CMLR 276).[7] This latter Directive provides for an environmental impact assessment to he carried out of certain projects before consent for such projects is given. This latter Directive was made on 27 June 1985 and was notified to Member States on 3 July 1985. Member States were obliged by Article 12 to take the measures necessary to comply with it within three years of notification, i.e. by 3 July 1988. On 14 July 1988, the Secretary of State for Transport made the Highways (Assessment of Environmental Effects) Regulations 1988.[8] These came into force on 21 July 1988. The Regulations amended the Highways Act 1980 by adding section 105A. The effect of this new section was that where the Secretary of State was considering the construction of a new highway he must, before he published the details of the project, determine whether or not it fell within the scope of the directive and whether or not it ought to be assessed. If it was to be assessed, then the assessment procedure would take place before consent was given. Section 105A(7) provided that the section did not apply to a draft order or scheme published before 21 July 1998. The road scheme in issue was published before 3 July 1988 (the date by which the Directive must have been implemented), and consent was given to it after that date. The Secretary of State considered that the Directive required assessments of those projects whose consent *procedure* post dated the implementation of the Directive. Twyford Parish Council argued that the Directive required an environmental impact assessment to be carried out on projects *consented* after 3 July 1988, even if the consent procedure took place before that date. In their view, the Directive applied to projects 'in the pipeline'. Since the United Kingdom implementing rules only applied to projects where the consent procedure was initiated after 21 July 1988, Twyford Paris Council could not pursue their claim in the High Court on the basis of national law. It was necessary to rely upon and argue the direct effect of relevant provisions of the directive. Their claim failed for a number of reasons, including the following: the Directive did not on its true construction apply to a 'pipeline project', and there was no authority for the view that if the terms of a directive, which should have been implemented but had not, were breached, an individual who has not thereby suffered could enforce it against the defaulting State. On the first point McCullough J was right.[9]

8.2. Direct effect against a public authority may have indirect adverse effect for individuals

It is to be noted that if a challenge such as that in issue in *Twyford* succeeds, the consequence of securing a remedy against the competent public authority is likely to be to bring about consequences for private developers and/or contractors. This

[7] See R. Macrory, 'Environmental Assessment and EC Law', *JEL* (1992) 4(2) at 273–88.
[8] SI 1988 1241.
[9] See Case C-431/92 *Commission v Germany* [1995] ECR 1-21-89, paras 28–33 of judgment.

consequence does not appear to be inconsistent with the principle that the direct effect of directives may only be invoked against public authorities which may be regarded as emanations of the State. Thus an individual may rely upon the provisions of a public procurement directive against a public authority, although the consequence will be to affect the position of other individuals who are party to the tendering process.[10]

8.3. Clarity and precision of a provision of a directive for the purposes of direct effect cannot be considered from the point of view of the provision considered in isolation

The direct effect of particular provisions of environmental directives cannot be assumed. The question is in principle whether the provision is sufficiently clear and precise to admit of implementation by a national court. But in practice the question may be more complicated than this, since a provision of a directive may be as clear and precise as one tends to find in directives, but not really apt for judicial application as a free standing source of rights and obligations. An interesting example is to be found in Article 4 of the Waste Framework Directive (text prior to amendment by Directive 91/156/EEC):

Member States shall take the necessary measures to ensure that waste is disposed of without endangering human health and without harming the environment, and in particular:
—without risk to water, air, soil and plants and animals.
—without causing a nuisance through noise or odours.
—without adversely affecting the countryside or places of special interest.

In Case C-236/92 *Comitato di Coordinamento per la Defesa della Cava and Others v Regione Lombardia and Others* [1994] ECR I-483, the Regional Administrative Court in Lombardy, Italy, asked the Court of Justice, inter alia,

Does Community environmental law, in particular Article 4 of Council Directive 75/442/EEC of 15 July 1975 on waste, grant to individuals 'subjective rights' ('diritti soggettivi') which the national court is required to protect?

The Court of Justice stated:

The Court has consistently held . . . that wherever the provisions of a directive appear, as far as their subject matter is concerned, to be unconditional and sufficiently precise, those provisions may be relied upon by an individual against the State where the State fails to implement the directive in national law by the end of the period prescribed or where it fails to implement the directive correctly.
    A Community provision is unconditional where it is not subject, in its implementation or effects, to the taking of any measure either by the institutions of the Community or by the Member States . . .
    Moreover, a provision is sufficiently precise to be relied upon by an individual and applied by the court where the obligation which it imposes is set out in unequivocal terms . . .
    The provision in question does not display the above characteristics.
    Considered in its context, Article 4 of the directive, which essentially repeats the terms of the third recital in the preamble, indicates a programme to be followed and sets out the objectives which the Member States must observe in their performance of the more specific

[10] See Case 103/88 *Fratelli Costanzo v Commune di Milano* [1989] ECR 1839.

obligations imposed on them by Articles 5 to 11 of the directive concerning planning, supervision and monitoring of waste-disposal operations . . .

Thus, the provision at issue must be regarded as defining the framework for the action to be taken by the Member States regarding the treatment of waste and not as requiring, in itself, the adoption of specific measures or of a particular method of waste disposal. It is therefore neither unconditional nor sufficiently precise and thus is not capable of conferring rights on which individuals may rely as against the State.

In the view of the present writer the Court is right.[11] The provision is not unconditional and sufficiently precise in the sense that it is designed to take effect in conjunction with other provisions of the directive and cannot be relied upon *in itself as* a source of rights and obligations. The point is worth making, since there is nothing inherently non-justiciable in the wording of Article 4; indeed the text is incorporated verbatim into Schedule 4 of the Waste Management Regulations 1994. Paragraph 2(1) of the Regulations states:

Subject to the following provisions of this paragraph, the competent authorities shall discharge their specified functions, insofar as they relate to the recovery or disposal of waste, *with the relevant objectives* (emphasis added).

Paragraph 4(1) of the Schedule defines the relevant objectives in relevant part as follows:

For the purposes of this Schedule, the following objectives are relevant objectives in relation to the disposal or recovery of waste
(a) ensuring that waste is recovered or disposed of without endangering human health and without using processes or methods which could harm the environment and in particular without:
 (i) risk to water, air, soil, plants or animals; or
 (ii) causing nuisance through noise or odours; or
 (iii) adversely affecting the countryside or places of special interest; . . .

It is to be noted that paragraph 4(1) sets out verbatim much the text of Article 4 of the Directive. It is clearly justiciable in that it could fall to be applied by a court in e.g. proceedings for judicial review. It is equally clear from the context of the national implementation that it could not be applied as a free standing source of rights and obligations.

The Court took a bolder, and in the view of the present writer, less defensible position on direct effect in the context of Directive 85/337/EEC on environmental impact assessments. Article 2(1) of the Directive provides:

Member States shall adopt all measures necessary to ensure that, before consent is given, projects likely to have significant effects on the environment by virtue *inter alia*, of their nature, size or location are made subject to an assessment with regard to their effects. These projects are defined in Article 4,

Article 4(2) provides:

Projects of the classes listed in annex II shall be made subject to an assessment in accordance with Articles 5 to 10, where Member States consider that their characteristics so require.

[11] See also J. Holder, 'A Dead-end for Direct Effect', *JEL* (1996) 8(2) at 313–35.

18   DERRICK WYATT

In Case C-72/95 *Aannemersbedrijf P.K. Kraaijeveld BV and Others v Gedeputeerde Staten van Zuid-Holland* [1996] ECR I-5403,[12] the Nederlandse Raad van State asked the European Court inter alia whether the obligation in Article 2(1) and 4(2) could be relied upon by an individual before a national court. The Court of Justice held, that the fact that Member States have a discretion under Article 2(1) and 4(2) does not preclude judicial review of the question whether the national authorities have exceeded their discretion (para 59 of Judgment). This of course is unexceptionable in principle. The Court went on say:

> If that discretion has been exceeded and consequently the national provisions must be set aside in that respect, it is for the authorities of the Member State, according to their respective powers, to take all the general or particular measures necessary to ensure that projects are examined in order to determine whether they are likely to have significant effects on the environment and, if so, to ensure that they are subject to an impact assessment.[13]

This conclusion is questionable. While in principle the failure of a public authority to comply with an essential procedural requirement in arriving at a decision may have the consequence of invalidating that decision, the difficulty in this context is that the procedural requirement in question involves a complex administrative process which is not specified in the directive and which leaves a wide discretion to the national authorities (this is particularly true as regards consultation of the public pursuant to Article 6 of the Directive). If the holding is to be justified, it must surely be on the basis that the direct effect of the provisions in question arise in circumstances where national rules make provision for the conduct of an environmental impact assessment but have excluded that procedure, or failed to make applicable that procedure, in a case covered by the directive. That does appear to have been the situation in the Netherlands, since the report of the above mentioned case refers to Netherlands legislation transposing the Directive. But if a Member State had taken no steps to implement the Directive, it is difficult to see how the provisions on consultation could have direct effect, since they involve policy choices on the mechanism of consultation and the definition of the 'public' for the purposes of Article 6. Nor could it make sense to require national courts to invalidate decisions taken without benefit of an environmental impact assessment in circumstances where national courts and administrative authorities lacked the means to carry out an assessment in the absence of national legal rules laying down the procedures for such an assessment. The view that the direct effect or not of a provision of a directive may turn on the state of national law in the Member State in question as well as on the terms of the directive itself is not novel; Directive 76/207 on Equal Treatment is not directly effective as regards any particular remedy, but it may be directly effective if national rules provide for a damages remedy but impose a limit on the amount of damages which can be awarded which prevents the remedy being an effective one.[14]

---

[12] See C. Boch, 'A Breach in the Dyke', *JEL* (1997) 9(1) at 119–38.
[13] Para 61 of Judgment.
[14] See Case C-271/90 *Marshall (No 2)* [1993] 4 All ER 586.

8.4. Direct effect of directives may be invoked against public bodies exercising State authority—but only where the directive has not been properly transposed into national law

The case law of the Court of Justice limits the direct effect of directives to vertical direct effect, that is to say, directives may be invoked against the State, or emanations of the State. The notion of the State has been construed widely. In Case C-188/89 *Foster v British Gas* [1990] ECR I-3313 at p 3348, at para 20, the Court stated:

. . . a body, whatever its legal form, which has been made responsible, pursuant to a measure adopted by the state, for providing a public service under the control of the state and which has for that purpose special powers beyond those which result from the normal rules applicable in relations between individuals is included in any event among the bodies against which the provisions of a directive capable of having direct effect may be relied upon.

This statement inevitably raises the question whether bodies such as water undertakers are to be regarded as bodies against which the provision of a directive are capable of having direct effect may be relied upon. However, in the field of environmental regulation even an affirmative answer *in principle* would not necessarily have the consequence that any particular directive could be invoked against such a body. To take water undertakers as a hypothetical example, and assuming for the sake, of argument that they do fall within the *Foster* formula, would it necessarily follow that they could be called upon directly to comply with Directive 80/778 on the quality of drinking water? For example, could a damages action be mounted against a water company for failing to supply to a consumer with water complying with the standards specified in the directive? A preliminary and perhaps formidable objection to such an action would be to the effect that the direct effect of a directive only arises in circumstances where it has not been transposed into national law, or has not been correctly transposed into national law.[15] In the case of Directive 80/778, national implementing rules do transpose the directive, and provide enforcement mechanisms in the way of statutory enforcement orders and binding undertakings, which may require water companies to take specific and detailed steps to rectify any shortcomings in the quality of the water they supply. There are other interesting issues which might be raised by the question of such a hypothetical damages action, but they fall outside the remit of the present paper. For the sake of completeness, a consumer who suffered ill-health as the result of drinking contaminated water might bring proceedings under Part I of the Consumer Protection Act 1987, which implements Council Directive 85/374/EEC in the United Kingdom.

[15] See Case 270/81 *Felicitas* [1982] ECR 2771.

[13]

DENMARK'S COMPLIANCE WITH EUROPEAN COMMUNITY ENVIRONMENTAL LAW

Peter Pagh*

For many years Denmark has had a strong reputation for complying with European Community environmental law, and the main concern within Denmark has been whether Community Law has prevented higher standards. No cases have been brought against Denmark before the European Court for failure to implement. A close examination reveals this to be a misleading picture. Simply comparing standards on a scale of 'strictness' fails to reflect the complexities of environmental law. Examination of a number of key selected areas of environmental law, including drinking water, wildlife conservation ,freshwater fish, waste incineration, environmental assessment, and air pollution, demonstrate that Denmark has frequently failed to implement EC law correctly, both in formal terms and as a matter of practice. Danish difficulties can be in part explained by substantive differences in structure and traditional approaches between national and EC law. But the absence of enforcement action by the European Commission suggests rather more insidious factors at play.

1. Introduction

Amongst environmentalists Denmark is known for its good environmental law reputation. In both Denmark and other Member States of the Community the impression is that Denmark is complying with EU minimum standards on environmental protection and has even higher ideals. However, over the last two decades public debate in Denmark on EU environmental law has been the other way round: to what extent does EU law prevent Denmark from having a high-level of protection?

The special internal market derogation clause in Treaty Article 100a(4), and its successor in Article 95(40–5), of the Amsterdam Treaty was partly the result of the Danish position during negotiations. The derogation clause and its interpretation were a major public debate issue prior to the Danish referenda of 1986, 1992, 1993 and 1998. Not until the 1998 referendum was substantial attention given to Danish Environment Protection Agency research which showed that new EU standards on environmental protection were often higher, or at least the same as, equivalent Danish standards.

* Associate Professor, Faculty of Law, University of Copenhagen.

302   PETER PAGH

This attitude towards EU and Danish environmental law interrelationship has been indirectly supported by the absence of cases brought before the European Court of Justice (ECJ). Until now, only in one case has a Danish court referred a preliminary question on the interpretation of EU environmental law to the ECJ under Article 177 [now Art 234]—and this, at the time of writing, is still pleading.[1] There have been no cases brought under Article 169 where it had been asserted that Denmark was failing to comply with the EU minimum standards on water, air and soil pollution, waste, or fauna and flora protection. No cases have been reported by the ECJ on Danish violation under Directives: EIA (85/337), Birds (79/409), Drinking Water (80/778), or those on air pollution. The few environmental cases before the ECJ concerning Danish implementation were mainly related to alleged conflicts of Danish environmental legislation and free trade provisions of the Treaty, the *Danish Bottle* case being the best known example.[2] In my opinion the prevailing view of Danish implementation of EU environmental law is confusing and also misleading from both a theoretical and practical legal point of view.

2. Theoretical Objections

The *theoretical* objections are based on two observations: (1) it is misleading to measure environmental protection on a one-dimensional scale; (2) it is not possible to judge what are incomparable entities such as EU and Danish environmental law on a one-dimensional scale.

2.1 The strictness approach

Applying the criteria of 'high/low level of protection' or 'more/less strict protection' reflects something of a one-dimensional approach towards what is a complex issue—the law on environmental protection and improvement. A 'strict' approach to one type of emission or one recipient might adversely affect other types of emission or recipients. There is more than one legitimate interest in the environment (what is strict to one interest might be weak for another) and there are no simple answers to what is good and what is bad. Environmental law protection cannot and should not be squeezed into a one-dimensional scale. The law is not numbers, but reflects the balancing of various interests—and it is not a fairytale.

By applying a one-dimensional scale to such complexities, one could ignore the legitimate interests of other adversely affected parties—or more likely the indirect implications on other elements of the environment. To take one example, Denmark has banned nuclear powerplants. Danish energy production is mainly based on oil, gas and coal; the latter in particular has caused substantial export of sulphur dioxide emissions to Sweden, damaging lakes and forests. Furthermore, Denmark imports nuclear generated electricity and the Swedish powerplant *Barsebäk* is situated only 20 kilometres from Copenhagen.

---

[1] C-209/98, *Contractors Association, Waste Section v City Council of Copenhagen* (whether recovery of building material waste is subject to the principle of self-sufficiency).
[2] *Commission v Denmark*, C-302/86 [1988] ECR 4607.

The 'stricter' or 'higher' approach ignores the complex impact on different environmental elements. What is stricter protection for one environmental medium may have the opposite effect on another. This is reflected by the IPPC Directive (96/61): 'Controlling emissions into the air, water or soil separately may encourage the shifting of pollution between the various environmental media rather than protecting the environment as a whole.'[3] As a concept, 'strictness' is simply inadequate in dealing with the complexity of environmental impacts.

Nor does the 'strict' approach deal adequately with the question of substitution. When certain activities are prohibited they may be substituted by others whose impacts are less clear, or more hazardous in the long-run—or the activities could be relocated to other jurisdictions, which are less prepared to ensure precaution and safety. The 'strict' approach does not take the NIMBY (not in my back yard) syndrome into account. So-called stricter measures such as bans or extreme standards can be used to export environmental problems, with the Danish ban on nuclear powerplants providing one example. The relocation of tanning industries from west to East Europe, and third world countries with lower standards, illustrates how a strict approach can lead to overall increased environmental degradation.[4]

Even from an economic efficiency perspective the strict approach is questionable. The US experience on sulphur dioxide emissions from combustion powerplants illustrates the weakness of the 'best' standards for preventing such emissions. Billions of US dollars were spent on cleaning technology, although lower emissions could have been obtained by substituting West Virginian high-sulphur coal.[5]

The measuring of environmental protection according to a scale of strictness does not provide an adequate basis for choosing policy instruments, nor is it adequate to judge and compare different legislation on environmental protection.

2.2 Incomparable entities

EU and Danish environmental law are not readily comparable. The lack of structural congruence in legislation and institutional systems implies that there will be differences in legal implications between different Member States. The legal tradition in Denmark adds an important dimension to this lack of congruence. Danish environmental law has no tradition of legally binding standards, other than where EU law has been implemented. Under the Danish Environmental Protection Act and other

---

[3] IPPC Directive 96/61, 7. Consideration of the preamble.

[4] In the United States there are several cases on the siting of waste disposal facilities, where federal courts granted permission for such facilities despite local objections. Goldberg J reasoned in *Rollins Environmental Services Inc v Parish of St James* [775 F 2d 627 (5th Circuit 1985)] on the placement of a PCB disposal facility: 'No one wants a toxic waste disposal facility "in his own back yard"—and for good reason. The uncontrolled chemical emissions that have occurred elsewhere this year lend sober perspective to the sanguine assurances of scientists that such mishaps will not—indeed, cannot—occur. [...] Precisely because of such concern, Congress enacted in the Toxic Substances Control Act a broad national program of measures to prevent and guard against uncontrolled and hazardous emission of substances such as PCBs. If every locality were able to dodge responsibility for and participation in this program through artfully designated ordinances, the national goal of safe, environmentally sound toxic waste disposal would surely be frustrated. And for all we know, the electrical transformers of the Romeville Elementary School may present at this very moment far greater danger of uncontrolled and disastrous PCB emissions than the Rollings facility.'

[5] D.P. Mcgrory, 'Air Pollution Legislation in United States and the Community', *European Environmental Law Review*, (1990) p 298.

environmental legislation the competence to set standards is decentralised to local councils (municipalities and counties)—supported by guidelines from the Danish Environmental Protection Agency, together with access by way of administrative appeal to national agencies and boards. With few exceptions, local councils are also granted the discretion to decide when and how to enforce environmental legislation.[6] In contrast, EU directives and regulations on environmental protection attempt to establish common rules, on the assumption that environmental protection is too important to leave to the goodwill and discretion of Member States. The typical directive, therefore, expresses a standard for emission or environmental quality, and provides exhaustively any reasons and procedures for exceptions. In areas such as drinking water, environmental quality standards on air and water, waste incineration, and nature conservation, this lack of structural congruence creates problems for implementation in Denmark, and the specific analysis below indicates strongly that problems have led to the violation of various directives.

Another Danish tradition is that decisions on major or small infrastructure projects (such as highways and railways) are made by means of a Parliamentary Act. Together with constitutional concerns (interference in legislative process) this was a key reason for Denmark opposing the draft EIA Directive between 1980 and 1985. Finally, a compromise was made by the Council of Ministers, which provided a derogation in the case of 'projects the details of which are adopted by a specific act of national legislation'.[7] However, when six years later Parliament adopted an act concerning the construction of a bridge to Sweden, it was doubtful whether the Act complied with the requirements of the derogation clause, and it was also disputed whether the permit to build the bridge met the EIA procedure requirements, as is shown below (3.5).

A rather peculiar Danish phenomenon is the way in which local councils are engaged in waste, drinking water, and waste water tasks. Under the Environmental Protection Act the local councils (municipalities) are responsible for the collection, disposal and, in part, for recovery of waste. The charges for the collection and handling of waste are determined by the same councils leaving the waste producer without any access to administrative appeal. The councils are also granted legislative power on waste, implying that each of the 275 Danish municipalities have their own regulations for different types of waste. At the same time, the local Council has the power to enforce their own legislation. Very similar regimes are established in the fields of waste and drinking water. This concentration of executive and legislative powers in the same body, which to some extent is granted an exclusive economic position, seems to be beyond the scope of the derogation clause in the Article 90(2) (new Article 86) of the Treaty. Furthermore, the incentive to improve environmental protection in accordance with EU environmental law is

---

[6] The paradox caused by the decentralised approach was recently illuminated, when wild boar were discovered in a Danish forest. The response from the Ministry of Environment was that the wild boar must be exterminated in the interests of Danish pig-farming. However, it is a common understanding in Denmark that the poor people in Bangladesh are under an obligation to improve living conditions for the dangerous Bengal Tiger (*Felis tigris*).

[7] Directive 85/337, Article 1(5).

at the very least questionable. The many disputes on compliance with EU law on waste are for this reason hardly surprising.

3. Concrete objections

The assumption that Denmark complied with EU environmental law meant that very little attention was paid by local public authorities or even green organisations to the content of EU environmental law. EU environmental law was (and still is to some extent) expected to be a matter for the government and its agencies to deal with. This attitude can be seen in a 1996 textbook on environmental law. Knowledge of EU environmental law is for this reason rather limited among lawyers in general and administrators at local level, and even the Danish EPA has ignored the implication of EU environmental law in several cases.

Based on almost a decade of comprehensive studies, it is my assertion that Denmark, in certain respects, breaches important parts of EU environmental legislation—and that there were even more breaches in the past. The following sections provide concrete examples of wrongful implementation in a number of selected policy areas, both in formal terms and practice. The examples give an impression of the problems,[8] and the findings in some cases only confirms what is already known: the European Commission can be subjected to political pressure. What is more surprising is how the Danish government has succeeded in continuing to maintain its good reputation.

3.1 The Drinking Water Directive

According to the ECJ ruling, quality standards for drinking water under the Drinking Water Directive (80/778) are legally binding. Exceptions are only permitted where provided for the in the Directive,[9] and these provisions provide three justifications for derogations: geological or meteorological reasons (Article 9); emergencies (Article 10); and exceptional circumstances for geographically defined population groups (Article 20).

Implementation of the Directive in Denmark was at first by means of a Circular which did not comply with the requirements for correct implementation. Only in August 1988—six years after the date for implementation expired—were the quality standards of the Directive implemented into law.[10] If one compares the quality standards there is no doubt that Denmark is complying with the Directive, but when it

---

[8] The fact that the analysis is limited to these few areas does not indicate that the rest are in order. For example, the provision on notification of concerned citizens on civil emergency plans under the Seveso Directive (82/501, now 96/82) has not been implemented into a formal right citizens which are able to claim as required by the ECJ in C-190/90 ([1992] ECR I-3265). The distinction between waste for disposal and for recovery as defined in the Waste Directive (75/442, amended 91/156) was at first not implemented—and the implementation in 1997 is questionable when compared with the ECJ ruling in *Chemische Afvalstoffen Düsseldorp* (C-203/96). The licence requirement for waste recovery plants in the Waste Directive (Article 10) has not been fully transposed into Danish law. The ban of any direct release to the groundwater of hazardous substances listed in Annex I to the Groundwater Directive 80/68 was only implemented in Denmark after criticism from the Commission.

[9] *Commission v Germany*, C-237/90 [1992] ECR I-5973. See comments by J. Holder and S. Elworthy, *Common Market Law Review* (1994) p 123.

[10] Statutory Order 515, 1988.

comes to the derogations, there are at least five instances where Danish law does not reflect the provisions of the Directive:

(a) The derogation for geological or meteorological causes in the Statutory Order does not require, as does the Directive, that the drinking water must not constitute a public health hazard; only consultation of the Public Health Officer is required. Research results are contained in one of the counties' report on observations of 'blue children' caused by contamination of drinking water with nitrates.

(b) Article 9 of the Directive requires notification of the Commission when the permitted exceedence of the limit values relates to a daily water supply of at least 1,000 m³ or a population of at least 5,000. Neither the Statutory Order nor the guidelines on drinking water quality from the Danish EPA [No 3, 1990] include information on this threshold for notification and there have been no case of notification of the Commission based on this derogation clause. According to the Danish EPA this is because the EPA exercises control. However, it is possible to find cases where approval was granted to exceed the limit values for nitrates for a drinking water supply company abstracting 350,000 m³ pr year.[11]

(c) For a lengthy period the phrase 'situations arising from the nature and structure of the ground' in Article 9(1)(a) was interpreted by the Danish EPA and the supervisory authorities as covering contamination of drinking water by nitrates, although this is often caused by farming activities. In several cases the limit values for nitrates have been substantially exceeded over a long period of time. However, after the ECJ ruling in the case against UK,[12] the EPA has changed their interpretation and does not consider contamination by nitrates is covered by the derogation in Article 9.

(d) The Statutory Order does not provide a derogation equivalent to Article 10 of the Directive. According to Danish administrative law this implies—from a strictly legal point of view—that the supervisory authority does not have the competence to approve exemptions from the binding limit values because of manmade contamination of the soil and groundwater or other causes covered by Article 10. However, according to the Danish EPA guiding scheme for measures against unsatisfactory water quality from common water supply plants such an option exists.[13]

(e) The judgment of the ECJ in *Pretura unificata di Torino*[14] presupposes that the competent authority is obliged to intervene in cases where quality standards are breached, unless all four conditions in Article 10 are met.[15] Article 10

---

[11] For example, *Kirsten Nielsen v Hundested Municipality* concerning damages on higher limit values of permangana (Lower Court, 28.10.92, settled after appeal) no notification of the Commission was reported. In another case exemption from the limit values for nitrates was approved by the Danish EPA until 1 January 1994 (Decision by the Danish EPA of 2.4.93 (j nr M 232–0008).

[12] *Commission v UK*, C-337/89 [1992] ECR I-6103. See L. Krämer, *Casebook* (1993) p 251.

[13] EPA Guidelines, No 3 (1990) p 39.

[14] C-228/87 [1988] ECR 5099. The narrow interpretation of derogation is supported by the ECJ ruling in *Commission v Belgium*, C-42/89 [1990-I] 282. Se L. Krämer, *Casebook* (1993) p 237, 246f.

[15] (1) The exceeding concentration of substances must be caused by *emergencies*, meaning urgent situations in which the competent authorities are required to cope suddenly with difficulties in the supply of water intended for human consumption; (2) exceeding the maximum permitted concentration may be allowed only for a limited time period, corresponding to the time normally necessary to restore the quality of the water; (3) the excess

also requires additional notification to the Commission, but according to the judgment in C 228/87, this procedural requirement does not affect the obligation of the national authority to intervene. As indicated under the theoretical objections, the Danish scheme on enforcement is rather different. If the drinking water does not comply with the quality standards, the municipality under subsection 19(1) of the Statutory Order is granted the discretion to order the drinking water supply company to stop operations temporarily or permanently—or to order other precautionary measures—or do nothing. The same discretion is granted even in case of immediate danger by contamination of the drinking water. If the water is harmful to health, the municipality is obliged to make a decision, but it is within the discretion of the local Council to decide whether to do nothing or order a cessation of operations or require precautionary measures [subsection 19(2)]. The provisions reflect the opposition from municipalities against legally binding quality standards and their threat to the principle of decentralised powers concerning drinking water supply: it is for the local Councils to decide what measures to take against drinking water supply companies—which often owned by the same Councils. Infringements of the quality standards are not subject to administrative or criminal penalties,[16] and violation of the quality standards under section 4 without approval is subject not to penalties but to administrative sanctions within the discretion of the local Council. This leaves the recipient of the drinking water with only one legal remedy—the court system. Whether this legal remedy for citizens complies with the ECJ ruling in *Peterbroeck*[17] (no unreasonable difficulty of enforcement) is at least questionable. The lack of criminal sanctions for breach of drinking water quality standards compared to the criminal sanctions of other offences in the Statutory Order indicates discrimination between national and EC law, and it is doubtful whether this is in accordance with the jurisprudence of the ECJ.[18]

3.2 Protection of wild birds and habitats

According to Article 3 of the Birds Directive (79/409), Member States are required to preserve, maintain and/or re-establish habitats for all wild birds. This general obligation is supplemented by Article 4 that requires all Member States to classify the most suitable territories in number and size as special protected areas (SPAs) for the conservation of wild and migratory birds listed in Annex I. As stressed by the ECJ in the *Lappel Banks* case, the designation and definition of the boundaries of SPAs must be based on ornithological criteria, and Member States are not authorised

concentration may under any circumstances not constitute an unacceptable risk to public health; and (4) there must be no possibility of maintaining the supply of water for human consumption in any other way.

[16] According to section 33 of the Statutory Order penalties are limited to the following four types of failure: [a] failure to monitor as required under section 7–15; [b] failure to retain records on monitoring under section 18(1); [c] failure to notify the municipality, when monitoring shows the quality standards are breached; [d] failure to comply with administrative orders under section 19.

[17] C-312/93 [1995] ECR I-4599, premise 12.

[18] For example, *Hansen & Son*, C-326/88 [1990] ECR I-2911.

308   PETER PAGH

to take economic considerations into account in the designation of SPA.[19] Moreover, it follows from the ECJ judgment of 19 May 1998 that Member States are required to designate all sites, which due to ornithological criteria, appear to be the most suitable for the conservation of the species in question—and Member States cannot avoid this obligation by adopting other special conservation methods.[20]

If a Member State ignores this obligation to designate SPAs, it follows from the *Marimas de Santona* case that the undesignated area must be treated in all respects as though it had been designated.[21] Following the interpretation of the ECJ in *Leybucht Dykes* that Article 4(4) of the Birds Directive prevented the intervention in a SPA for economic and recreational requirements,[22] to the Council of Ministers amended this provision under the Habitats Directive (92/43). According to Article 7 of Directive 92/43, interference in SPA is governed by the procedure for direct or indirect intervention under the Habitats Directive, Article 6(2–4). The content of this procedure is illustrated on the Figure 1. While the procedure under Article 6(2)–(4) of the

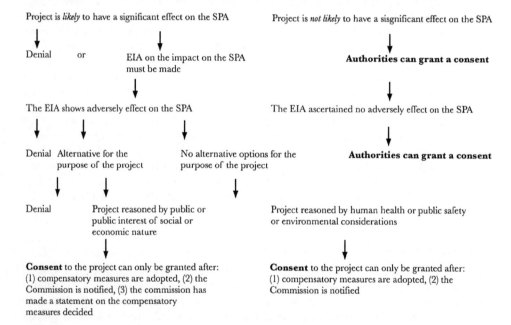

Figure 1. Projects/Plan Procedures in or nearby Habitats/Special Protected Bird areas (SPA)[23]

---

[19] *Regina v Secretary of State for the Environment*, C-44/95 [1996] ECR I-3805. See J.D.C. Harte, JEL (1997) p 139, 168f.

[20] *Commission v The Netherlands*, C-3/96 [1998] ECR I-3031.

[21] *Commission v Spain*, C-355/90 [1993] ECR I-4221. See W.P.J. Wils, 'The Birds Directive 15 Years Later', JEL (1997) p 219, 233f.

[22] *Commission v Germany*, C-57/89 [1991] ECR I-883.

[23] The scope of this procedure depends on the definition of 'plans' or 'projects'. Neither of the two words are defined in the Habitat Directive, but must presumably cover all activities subject to a prior permission by a public authority—and might even include mandatory announcement. It is not necessary that the project or plan is placed in the SPA. Also projects and plans outside the SPA are subject to the procedure if they are likely to have a significant impact on the SPA, unless the project or the plan is part of the management of the SPA. The phrase 'likely' does not require certainty. It is enough that an impact is possible. Because of the

Habitats Directive is rather precise, the scope of the application of the procedure to SPAs under the Birds Directive could be questioned in the case of migratory birds. According to Article 7 of the Habitats Directive, Article 6(2)–(4) replaces any obligation under the first sentence of Article 4(4) of the Birds Directive: 'in respect of areas classified pursuant to Article 4(1) or similar recognised under Article 4(2) thereof'. This strongly indicates that the whole procedure under Article 6(2)–(4) is mandatory for migratory birds. However, it is the Danish position that in the case of migratory birds the procedures for interference in an SPA do not include the last part of Article 6(4) on interference for economic and social reasons, as this part of the provision covers only 'a site [. . .] hosts a priority natural habitat type and/or a priority species'. In my view, a habitat for migratory birds designated as SPA must be classified as 'a priority natural habitat type and/or a priority species'.

The very strong protection of habitats for endangered birds (Annex I), and migratory birds, should have been implemented by April 1981, but Denmark and other Member States did not implement in time. In 1983 a preliminary designation of SPAs in Denmark was sent to the Commission covering almost identical areas that were covered under the Ramsar Convention. The preliminary designation was rather impressive covering around 6% of the land and territorial sea of Denmark. However, the designation was not legally binding and only provided guidance for planning decisions by local councils. In 1985 the Commission informed Denmark that this preliminary designation was not a satisfactory implementation of the Directive. The Danish response was to assure the Commission that final designation would be made but at the same time insisting that only minor, rather than substantial, changes to the designation would be accepted. However, no final designation under the Birds Directive was adopted in the years that followed. In a number of cases, the Danish Nature Appeal Board permitted construction projects and other interventions in certain SPAs for economic and recreational reasons. These decisions were justified by the Ramsar Convention, Article 2(4), which grants the State power to derogate from the protection of waterfowl habitats. As to the complaint from the Commission, nothing happened except an exchange of opinions.

In 1991 the Danish Ornithological Society brought fresh attention to SPAs under the Birds Directive after the Danish and Swedish governments agreed on the construction of the Öresunds bridge, and in the same year, the project was approved by a Parliamentary act. The bridge project would affect two major bird areas: its construction would be close to Saltholm Island [SPA 110], one of the most important areas for waterfowls in the north of Europe; and the project on the Danish side included a highway crossing of another large SPA at west Amager [SPA 111]. Objections were made by the Danish Ornithological Society and other green associations. However, the Danish Nature Appeal Board upheld the decision on the west Amager highway reasoning that the option of a highway was decided by Parliament in 1976 and that the it was in accordance with the physical planning decision. Complaints

reference in the preamble to the Treaty, Article 130r and the codification of the precautionary principle the scope is presumably to every project and plan where a significant impact cannot be excluded. This mandatory procedure does not only cover endangered birds in Annex I, but also migratory species. On the scope see also, A. Nollkaemper, 'Habitat Protection in European Community Law: Evolving Conceptions of a Balance of Interests', JEL (1997) p 272; W.P.J. Wils, 'The Birds Directive 15 Years Later: A Survey of the Case Law and Comparison with the Habitats Directive', JEL (1994) p 219, 230f.

were also made to the Commission. In the first opening letter to Denmark submitted a few days before Parliament adopted the 1991 Act, the Commission held that the project was in breach of the Birds Directive. This assertion was repeated four months later, following adoption of the Act, but after further negotiations where the Danish government promised to take compensatory measures, and probably for political reasons, the Commission decided not to bring Denmark before the ECJ.[24]

Green organisations and lawyers were unconvinced by the press release. The Danish Ornithological Society decided to initiate legal proceedings on the Birds Directive, and a civil law suit against the Ministry of Traffic was submitted to the Eastern High Court.[25] But the case was dismissed by the High Court in 1994, partly because the allegation was not judicial (i.e. not sufficiently precise), and partly because it was held to be a political rather than a judicial question as to whether the Danish government was obliged to prevent interference in the SPAs on Saltholm Island and west Amager.

Finally, in 1994 the designation of SPA was made legally binding by a Statutory Order.[26] Despite this, it is still possible to identify several cases of interference in SPAs where the authorities were not acting in accordance with the procedural rules laid down in the Habitats Directive. In 1995 a shipping company was granted a temporary consent to route a high-speed ferry through an SPA on Samsö [No 31], because it was not proved that the ferry would substantially affect the birds and their habitat. In 1997 the Copenhagen Airport Company Limited was granted a licence by the county (and upheld by the EPA) under the Danish Environmental Protection Act to enlarge the small Tune Airport with a ten-fold increase of large aircraft take-offs and landings. The airport is situated two kilometres from two SPAs [103 and 104]. After a complaint to the Commission, the Danish EPA acknowledged that they had forgotten to take into account the Habitats Directive.

For the first decade, after the time-limit for implementing the Bird Directive had expired, Denmark clearly did not comply with requirements on protection of SPAs under the Directive—both in formal law and practice. Following the complaints caused by the Öresund bridge project, implementation improved. The designation of SPA was made legally binding, and the very strict procedure for intervention in SPAs which includes the requirement for an Environmental Impact Assessment for possible substantial interference in the habitat area is now accepted both by the Danish Nature Appeal Board, the Danish Environmental Appeal Board and the Danish EPA (provided it does not escape their attention as in the *Tune Airport* case). However, even recent cases indicate that licences are granted to projects potentially affecting SPA habitats, in part for economic reasons. The special procedure under Article 6(4) of the Habitats Directive for such licences has not yet been employed in a single case in Denmark.

---

[24] That the decision on withdrawing the case against Denmark was highly influenced by political considerations is supported by the fact that the Commission informed the public by a press release (11.11.92). The Commission justified the decision not to take action before the ECJ on two grounds: (1) the Danish government had promised to take compensatory measures and restore habitats in other areas of Denmark; (2) Denmark had designated a relatively higher proportion of its territory than any other Member State.

[25] Greenpeace took simultaneously the question on the EIA Directive before the Eastern High Court (see 3.5).

[26] No 407, 1994.

3.3 Freshwater Fish Directive standards

The principles underlying SPA designation are to some extent reflected in the designation of freshwater areas covered by Directive 78/659 on the quality of freshwaters needing protection or improvement in order to support fish life. It follows from ECJ case law that Member States are obliged to designate freshwater areas, which are then subject to the quality standards contained in the Directive.[27] But in contrast to the Birds Directive, Member States are left with a high-degree of discretion as to which areas to nominate.[28]

From a formal perspective the designation of water areas under this Directive has not proved a problem in Denmark which allocated a major proportion of Danish rivers and lakes (21,000 kilometres). However, there have been problems both in law and in practice. In practice, according to the former head of the legal department of the Danish EPA, most of the designated waters are not able to comply with the quality standards.[29] From a legal perspective, because under Danish law the quality standards for waters are not legally binding, but represent a standard with which local Councils must strive to comply. This is contrary to the jurisprudence by the ECJ, which has stressed that the designation of water areas covered by the Directive must be legally binding.[30]

The legal implications of designated water areas under the Directive are not absolutely certain. According to Article 4(1) of Directive 78/659, 'Member States shall, initially within a two year period following the notification of this Directive, designate salmonid waters and cyprinid waters'. According to Article 5, 'Member States shall establish programmes in order to reduce pollution and to ensure that designated waters conform within five years following designation in accordance with Article 4 to both the values set by the Member States in accordance with Article 3 and the comments contained in columns (g) and (i) of Annex I'. The ECJ case law strongly indicates that this must be interpreted as meaning no derogations from quality standards, except where these can be based on provisions of the Directive.[31]

There are two exceptions from the main rule. Article 9 grants Member States the discretion to enact stricter standard and under Article 4(2) Member States may subsequently make additional designations. The question is whether Member States are also granted any powers to annul a designated water area, or to relax the quality standards. Under Article 4(3) Member States 'may revise the designation of certain waters owing to factors unforeseen at the time of designation, taking into account the principle set out in Article 8'. When new problems occur, this provision authorises Member States to annul a designated area and to change the standards. The bottom line is Article 8, which states: 'Implementation of the measures taken pursuant to this Directive may on no account lead, either directly or indirectly, to increased pollu-

---

[27] *Commission v Italy*, C-322/86 [1988] ECR 3995, and for not complying with the decision by the court: C-291/93 [1994] I-859.

[28] This assumption is based on the ECJ ruling in a case against Italy on the Shellfish Water Directive (79/923), which in structure and principle is almost identical with Directive 78/659. See, *Commission v Italy*, C-225/96 [1997] ECR I-6887.

[29] M. Moe, *Environmental Administration in Denmark* (1995) p 153.

[30] *Commission v Germany*, C-298/95 [1996] ECR I-6747.

[31] For example, *Commission v UK (Blackpool)* C-56/90 [1993] ECR I-4109.

tion of fresh water.' This last provision indicates that the economic implications of discharge requirements from large-scale industries do not constitute a legal cause for derogation.

The obligation to ensure the quality standards of the Directive 78/659 was raised by the Danish Anglers Association in a major case on the consent to release water from a large powerplant (Fyns-værket). It was unquestionable that the consent granted by the county would mean that the quality standards of the Directive were substantially breached. However, the Danish EPA ignored this objection and upheld the consent, without any comments on the quality standards of the Directive. The case was then brought before the Environmental Protection Appeal Board which in contrast found that the quality standards were legally binding. But this ruling faced the Appeal Board with another problem. If the consent was denied, the practical consequence would be to close the powerplant although it had previously been granted a preliminary consent by the Danish EPA. This preliminary consent was criticised as illegal by the Danish Ombudsman, the Appeal Board however held that the preliminary consent had the effect of res judicata. If another pipeline for the release of heated water was demanded, an investment of approximately US$100 million was needed. In its decision the Appeal Board chose something of a compromise: the powerplant was only granted a temporary consent until June 2000 after which the plant must either comply with the quality standards of the Directive, or the standards in the receiving waters must be relaxed. As to this last option (impairment of the standards), the Appeal Board found this might be possible under the Directive, leaving some doubt on the issue.

3.4 Waste incineration Directives

In 1989 the EU adopted two Directives on the prevention and reduction of air pollution from municipal waste incineration plants: Directive 89/369 (new plants) and Directive 89/429 (old plants). The emission standards and other technical requirements were implemented within the time-limits in Denmark by Statutory Order (No 10, 1991) under the Environmental Protection Act.

The problem is that both Directives include an enforcement clause requiring mandatory measures where emission limits are exceeded.[32] Under Article 8(2) there is an exception for 'technically unavoidable stoppages of the purification devices', when the competent authority is required to lay down the maximum permissible period for exceeding the limit values, although the discretion of the authority is rather constrained.[33] While EU law in general leaves sanctions to the national legal systems,

---

[32] Article 8(1), Directive 89/369: 'Should the measurements taken show that the limit values laid down in this Directive have been exceeded, the competent authority shall be informed is soon as possible. *It shall ensure that the plant concerned does not continue to operate while failing to comply with emission standards and shall take the necessary measures to ensure it is modified or no longer operated.*' Article 7(1) of Directive 89/429 includes a similarly worded clause.

[33] The last part of Article 8(2) stresses: 'Under no circumstances may the plant continue to operate more than eight hours uninterrupted; moreover, the cumulative duration over a year of operation in such conditions shall be less than 96 hours. The dust content of the discharges shall under no circumstances exceed 600 mg/nm3 during the periods referred to in the preceding subparagraph and all the other conditions, in particular the combustion conditions, shall be complied with.'

this is not always the case, and the enforcement clauses concerning waste incineration plants leave the competent authority with very limited discretion. The authority is not entitled to permit a waste incineration plant to continue if the emission standards are exceeded, it is obliged to stop operations unless the breach can be justified under the derogations in Article 8(2).

However, the enforcement clause has not been implemented into Danish law. Under sections 68 and 69 of the Environmental Protection Act it is for local councils to decide how to respond to an offence under the Act—and no exception has been adopted in the case of waste incinerators. Moreover, even though major breaches of the limit values for waste incineration have been reported from a number of plants in one of the counties (Aarhus), neither the county nor the Danish EPA have taken enforcement action. Despite not being implemented into Danish legislation, the health interests of neighbours could justify the Directive's provisions being held to have direct effect: both the provisions on enforcement and emission standards are precise and unconditional, the bodies responsible for enforcement are emanations of the state, and the time-limit for implementation has expired for both Directives.

3.5 Environmental Impact Assessment (EIA)

In June 1980 the Commission presented a draft directive on Environmental Impact Assessment (EIA). From the commencement of negotiations, the Danish position was negative.[34] The government had five major objections: (1) the EIA Directive would presuppose Community competence on questions of physical planning; (2) the EIA Directive would limit the competence of Denmark to make agreements on environmental procedures with third countries; (3) the EIA Directive would interfere in the legislative power of Parliament, when adopting infrastructure projects by parliamentary act; (4) the Commission should not be given the discretion to decide whether Annex II projects are subject to a compulsory EIA; and (5) Denmark could not accept detailed Community rules on the participation of the public in the decision-making process.

During the ensuing negotiations, certain concessions were given by the Commission and other Member States, and although the Danish position remained rather negative, pressure on the country grew. At the Council of Ministers' meeting on 6 December 1984, the Commission announced that the Danish obstruction to the adoption of the Directive might be in conflict with Article 5 of the Treaty. In Denmark, several memoranda were produced by the government on the legal implications of the latest version of the draft Directive,[35] and in March 1985 the Parliamentary

[34] The positions of different Member States during the negotiation period of draft directives are normally kept secret and not known by the public. Under the Danish constitutional case on the Maastricht Treaty (UfR 1998 800) the Danish Supreme Court ordered the government to give the applicants access to a number of instructions and reports during the negotiation process on certain environmental directives, including the draft EIA Directive. The information on the Danish position towards the different draft directives during the negotiation is based on these documents (the author of this article worked as consultant for the applicants' lawyers).

[35] They concluded: (a) that the new drafting ensured the limitation of EU competence on physical planing; (b) that a declaration to the Directive on the limitation of EU competence in respect of third countries would accommodate the Danish objection on this matter; (c) that an exception clause on projects adopted by the legislature would satisfy the constitutional objections; and (d) that the final draft ensured it was left to Member States to determine whether Annex II projects should be subject to EIA.

Committee gave up the Danish resistance and accepted the final draft. The EIA Directive was adopted one week later as Directive 85/374. Considering the high attention given by Parliament and government to the draft Directive, and the three year time-limit provided for implementation, one would have expected Denmark to implement the Directive in time, and correctly—that did not happen.

When the time for implementation expired in July 1988, the scope of the Danish EIA implementation was limited to transport projects on the territorial seas, and even this implementation did not (and still does not) comply with Directive requirements.[36] In 1989 legislation amending the Physical Planning Act was adopted. This implementation was also defective in two ways: (1) for Annex II projects (the major part), no screening procedure for EIA was required; (2) the implementation covered only land territory and not territorial seas, with the result that major projects such as offshore oil installations were not covered by any EIA procedure. The Danish implementation was criticised by the Commission and in 1994 a screening procedure on Annex II project was adopted.[37] In 1995 the EIA requirement was implemented for offshore projects[38] and finally, in December 1996, EIA was also required on extraction of minerals at sea.[39]

It was not only the formal implementation of the EIA Directive which was defective. The derogation clause on projects adopted in detail by Parliament (Article 1(5)) created further problems. While the Danish Parliamentary Committee in 1985 expected that all Parliamentary Acts were excluded from the scope of the EIA Directive, the formulation and content of the clause indicate a narrower exception. This was the cause for major objections from green organisations when Parliament adopted the 1991 Act on the trans-Danish–Swedish Öresund bridge.[40] A few days before the Act was adopted Denmark received a letter of opinion from the Commission questioning whether the project was complying with the EIA and the Birds Directives. The government responded that the Act was excluded under the derogation clause in Article 1(5) arguing that although the Act itself was not dealing with the project 'in detail', the comments to the Act presented before Parliament under Danish law, and containing details of the project, were in fact legally binding.

In 1993 Greenpeace brought a case before the Eastern High Court claiming that the Act did not comply with the requirements in Article 1(5).[41] After the Eastern High Court recognised that Greenpeace had standing in the case,[42] on 8 July 1994 the Minister of Transport used his discretionary powers under the Bridge Act and

---

[36] The Minister of Transport issued Statutory Order No 379, 1998 on territorial sea transport projects. According to Statutory Order §4 the EIA procedure is not mandatory. It is for the minister to decide when an EIA must be submitted, what the EIA must include and whether a public hearing is necessary. This Statutory Order is still in force.

[37] Statutory Order No 847, 1994 supplemented by guidelines on criteria for screening (Guideline No 182, 1994).

[38] Act 310, 1995.

[39] Act 212, 1995, and Statutory Order No 1165, 1996.

[40] Act 590, 1991.

[41] The case involved certain principle questions concerning the scope of the EIA requirements and is therefore referred to in some detail. The author of this article was one of the legal advisers to Greenpeace before and during the court pleadings, and although the analysis aims to be as objective as possible, this must be taken into consideration.

[42] The position of the High Court on the standing issue was almost similar to the British *Thorp* case. See M. Purdue, 'A Harpoon for Greenpeace? Judicial Review of the Regulation of Radioactive Substances', JEL (1994) pp 297, 339.

issued a consent to the project in relation to the application submitted by the developer on 28 June. The response from Greenpeace was to call for an interim cessation of the project while the case was pleaded before the court. The Danish Civil Procedural Code does not provide for such a legal remedy where the executive power of the state is concerned,[43] and Greenpeace therefore based their arguments on the ECJ ruling in *Factortame*.[44] This claim was dismissed by the High Court, and subsequently appealed to the Supreme Court.[45] The Supreme Court accepted in the ruling that decisions of authorities breaching EU environmental law are subject to interim measures under the same conditions as used by the ECJ under the Treaty, Articles 185 and 186. But Greenpeace was less successful on the merits of the case. The Supreme Court refused to rule on whether the Öresund Bridge Act complied with the derogation clause in Article 1(5).[46] Instead, the Court unanimously found that the consent granted by the Minister of Transport on 8 July 1994 was in accordance with the EIA Directive. The reasoning was that public hearings had taken place in 1993, though this ignored the fact that these hearings were on a preliminary project which were substantially changed when the developer a year later submitted the application for the consent. This preliminary ruling shows how difficult it is to explain to Danish judges how the concept of EIA is totally different from the concept of physical planning under the Danish Planning Act.

The case then returned to the High Court on the merits, but even then the position had changed. At the time when the Supreme Court was ruling on the interim measures, the developer submitted an application to the Minister of Environment for a licence under the Raw Materials Act for extraction from the seabed. There was a surprising lack of knowledge on waterflow impact into the Baltic Sea, which was the key area of dispute, and when the July 1994 consent was given this part of the project did not even exist. Since Denmark at that time had no requirement for an EIA procedure or screening under the Raw Materials Act, no EIA was submitted by the developer. However, in October 1995 the Minister of Environment gave the developer the licence to extract. The response by Greenpeace once again was to ask for interim measures or at least to bring the question on the interpretation of the EIA Directive before the ECJ under the Treaty, Article 177. But again, all requests were denied by the High Court in January 1996. In the final ruling by the High Court in November 1996[47] the same court once again upheld that the consent given by the Minister in July 1994—consent within the meaning of the EIA Directive—relying more on the prejudice of the previous Supreme Court ruling than on the substantial changes in the merits after the ruling. The judgment was unsuccessfully appealed before the Supreme Court, which on 2 December 1998, held that the project was exempted under Article 1(5) of the Directive.[48] Despite the interpretation of the Directive the

---

[43] The Danish Civil Procedural Act, §641 excludes interim measures against decisions taken by executive authority.

[44] C-213/89 [1990] ECR I-2433.

[45] U 1995 634.

[46] In an obiter dictum one of the seven judges found it did not because the project was unclear and had substantially changed more than ten times after the Act was adopted.

[47] MAD 1996 984.

[48] The Supreme Court made clear that the legislative adoption procedure must fulfil the assessment requirements of the Directive, but controversially felt that this had happened in this case. See also, U. Kjellerup, 'Legal Problems in Danish EIA—The Oeresund Case', *Journal of Environmental Assessment Policy and Management*, (1999) 1:1, 131–49.

316   PETER PAGH

final ruling strongly differs from that of the higher court; the Supreme Court rejected the presentation of any preliminary question on interpretation of this provision in the Directive before the ECJ.

The EIA Directive has given rise to various other cases. The conflict between public hearing as part of the EIA process and local democracy was expressed by the mayor of one of the counties, when the Nature Protection Appeal Board in 1994 annulled a consent to a powerplant because of an unsatisfactory EIA. The mayor responded that the EIA procedure was not needed, because public participation was ensured by an election every fourth year. The direct effect of the EIA Directive which is at least presupposed by the ECJ ruling in the *Kraajiveld* case[49] was not followed by the Nature Protection Appeal Board until 1997. In a case of consent to a powerplant, the Board declared that the EIA Directive is not an integrated part of Danish law.[50]

3.6 Air pollution

One of the first well-known transboundary pollution problems concerned sulphur dioxide emissions. To prevent or at least minimise this source of pollution the Council as early as 1975 adopted Directive 75/716 on the approximation of the laws of Member States relating to the sulphur content of certain liquid fuels. In one of the first environmental cases before the ECJ, Italy was convicted for not having implemented this Directive in time.[51]

But Italy was not the only Member State which did not implement the Directive. According to Article 2(1) of the Directive: 'Member States shall take all necessary steps to ensure that type A gas oil can be marketed in the community only if its sulphur compound content [...] does not exceed [...] 0.3% by weight from 1 October 1980.' Denmark did not implement this product standard within the time-limits. Because of the cold climate and the ban on nuclear power sulphur dioxides, emissions from Denmark were substantial. Assisted by prevailing west winds, the major damage did not occur in Denmark, but to Swedish forests and lakes. Sweden made claims during the 1980s and the Danish government then established a committee to advise on new legislation. After a draft was submitted to Parliament, legislation was adopted and in 1986 the Community standards on sulphur content were implemented into Danish law.

However, acid rain in Sweden was also caused by other Danish factors. After the second oil crisis in 1979 a substantial proportion of powerplants, pushed by lower taxes on coal than on oil, moved from oil to coal. This shift generated another potential conflict with EU environmental law. According to Article 4(1) of Directive 84/360 on the combating of air pollution from industrial plants, permits require that: 'All appropriate preventive measures against air pollution have been taken, including the application of the best available technology, provided that the application of such measures does not entail excessive costs.' The wording indicates that the best available technology must be balanced against the economic costs of the polluter. Follow-

---

[49] C-72/95 [1996] ECR I-5403. See C. Boch, 'The Enforcement of the Environmental Assessment Directive in the National Courts: A Breach in the Dyke?', JEL (1997) p 119, 133f.

[50] KFE 1994 89.

[51] *Commission v Italy*, C-92/79 [1980] ECR 1115.

ing this requirement, authorities should have required that sulphur dioxide emission from coal must not exceed the level caused by generation of oil-based energy, unless the costs were higher. The paradox was that the guiding values for sulphur dioxide emission based on coal were higher than on oil. The tax policy meant that the powerplant saved money despite increasing their emissions, and this benefit for powerplants was upheld in several cases by the Environmental Appeal Board.[52]

Another example of defective implementation in air pollution concerns Directive 82/884 on a limit value for lead in the air. The ECJ held: 'It should be pointed out that the obligation imposed on the Member States to prescribe limit values not to be exceeded within specified periods and in specified circumstances [...] is imposed "in order to help protect human beings against the effects of lead in the environment" [...]. It implies, that whenever the exceeding of the limit values could endanger human health, the persons concerned must be in a position to rely on mandatory rules in order to be able to assert their rights. Furthermore, the fixing of limit values in a provision whose binding nature is undeniable is also necessary in order that all those whose activities are liable to give rise to nuisances may ascertain precisely the obligations to which they are subject.'[53] Although it is clear that limit values must be formally implemented by means of law, Denmark has not done so.

4. Conclusions

If one is familiar with both EU and Danish environmental law, it is not an impossible task to identify a number of breaches in the way that Denmark has implemented its Community obligations, both in formal terms and in actual practice. The fact that a Member State, which is known as friendly towards strong environmental protection, is unable to comply with EU law, leads to certain conclusions as well as giving rise to a number of questions.

The general deficit between EU environmental law and implementation in national law is well-known,[54] and a similar deficit in Denmark is unremarkable in this respect. Given that all other Member States have been faced with legal actions before the European Court for failure to implement or for wrongful implementation of EU environmental law, what might come as a surprise is that not even *one* of the considerable Danish breaches in the past has been brought to court.

The ignorance of the Danish public is caused in part by political factors: for almost two decades the political left-wing and the greens in Denmark regarded EU and EU environmental law as the target rather than an ally in their attempts to ensure greater environmental protection. But this ignorance is not only a cause, it is also an effect. To some degree the public ignorance is a consequence of the passivity of the European Commission. Without knowing their internal discussions, it is of course difficult to explain their inaction, but it is possible to identify some factors which explain the Danish record.

---

[52] For example, KFE 1986 248, and KFE 1989 394.
[53] *Commission v Germany*, C-59/89 [1991] ECR-I, p 2607.
[54] L. Krämer, *EC Treaty and Environmental Law* (1998) p 199; L. Krämer, 'Deficits in Application of EC Environmental Law and its Causes', *Focus on European Environmental Law* (1997) p 1.

318   PETER PAGH

The cause of the substantial Danish deficit is not only the Danish self-confidence. Major contributing factors are *structural problems*: lack of congruence in institutional systems, legislative technicalities, administrative procedures and legal traditions seem to create many more obstacles for implementation than it might be first assumed. This is illustrated by the EIA Directive experiences. Another cause for the Danish deficit is *substantial different approaches towards environmental protection law* in at least five respects:

— *Flexibility as against binding rules*: Danish environmental legislation is in the nature of framework laws, granting authorities wide discretion both to set and enforce environmental standards; in contrast, EU environmental legislation (and particularly earlier legislation) is based on legally binding standards;

— *A decentralised approach as against uniform standards*: Danish environmental legislation is based on a decentralised structure, leaving municipalities and counties the power to set standards and to decide how to enforce standards; the EU approach is common, uniform, or minimum standards;

— *Public responsibilities contra public and private interests*: In Denmark environmental protection is generally considered a matter of public interest (on the assumption that the environment must be protected against the citizens) rather than a question of individual rights. From the Danish perspective improved environmental protection therefore requires more discretion to public authorities. In contrast, the ECJ has in various cases stressed that EU environmental law also creates rights for individuals.[55] The different approaches explain why Denmark did not find it necessary to implement Directive 82/884 on lead in the air;

— *Balancing of economic interests towards ecological interests on protection of habitats*: As an overall rule, Danish environmental legislation is based on the discretion for authorities to assess economic and environmental benefits. In contrast, EU environmental quality standards are legally binding and the ECJ has precluded economic interests in the designation of bird habitats (SPAs). Projects substantially affecting SPA are subject to a distinct and comprehensive procedure.

— *Public owned facilities and the potential abuse of power*: The municipalities have substantial economic interests in major tasks in the environmental field (e.g. waste treatment, waste water treatment, drinking water supply, energy supply). When these local institutions are involved at the same time in the permit scheme and enforcement of environmental law, the abuse of power cannot be excluded.

These factors are not the only reasons for the Danish deficit. In part they also explain why there are so few cases in the national courts. However, the lack of cases before the ECJ might also be explained by at least four *cover-up factors*:

---

[55] Public health: *Commission v Germany*, C-131/88 [1991] ECR-I, p 825 (Directive 80/68 on groundwater); *Commission v Germany*, C-361/88 [1991] ECR-I, p 2567 (Directive 80/779 on sulphur dioxide concentration in air); *Commission v Germany*, C-298/95 [1996] ECR-I, p 6747 (Directive 78/659 on fishwater quality and Directive 79/923 on shellfish water). Participation in decision-making: *Krajiveld*, C-72/95 [1996] ECR I-5403; Access to environmental information: *Mecklenburg v Pinneberg*, C-321/96 [1998] ECR-I.

DENMARK AND EC ENVIRONMENTAL LAW 319

— Denmark usually has notified the Commission in time on national implementation of environmental directives: it is rare that Denmark has a delay,
and where this is the case, Denmark seems to be adept at convincing the
Commission that the implementation will soon be in order;
— Danish information to the Commission on implementation often refers to
comprehensive national legislation, and it is difficult to identify precisely how
implementation has been carried out—and therefore even more difficult to
discover incorrect implementation;
— The language: in the past it was usually only Danes, who were able to compare EU and Danish legislation—but this might be changed by the Finish
and Swedish Commission personnel;
— Legislative difficulties: Danish environmental legislation as well as that of
the EU is comprehensive, complex, sometimes inconsistent, and in part,
piecemeal with various technical references.

All this indicates that EU environmental law from an environmental perspective is
better than its reputation in Denmark, but it also shows weaknesses in the transition
process. A high-level of environmental standards does not necessarily secure a high-
level of protection. Moreover, the examples above indicate strongly that environmental protection and nature conservation are too important to be left solely in the
hands of only public authorities. Whether some of these problems can be solved by
the new Aarhus Convention on Access to Information, Public Participation in
Decision-Making and Access to Justice in Environmental Matters are beyond the
scope of this article. In any event, the lack of structural congruence in the enforcement mechanism calls for more attention in this field.

Part III
Improving Environmental Standards in Europe

[14]

CHEMICAL PLANT SAFETY REGULATION: THE EUROPEAN EXAMPLE

Arline M. Sheehan

On June 24, 1982, the European Community (EC) adopted a "Directive on the Major Accident-Hazards of Certain Industrial Activities," more commonly known as the Seveso Directive.[1] The Directive has two goals: to prevent major accidents caused by industrial activities, and to limit the effects of such accidents on workers, adjacent populations, and the environment.[2] It requires industrial facilities handling dangerous substances to identify existing major hazards, to take measures to mitigate their effects, and to supply workers with the information, training, and equipment needed to ensure their safety.[3] Facilities handling particularly dangerous substances face more exacting requirements.[4] They must notify authorities, for example, of the substances handled at the plant, the plant layout, and points where major accidents could occur.[5] Further, they must inform neighboring communities of appropriate measures to adopt in the event of an accident.[6]

In contrast to this prevention-oriented approach of the European Directive, U.S. federal legislation in this area is largely response-oriented, calling for after-the-fact remedial efforts rather than comprehensive preventive measures. Where preventive measures are required they are inadequate, because they sanction the mere disclosure rather than the abatement of risk and fail to include public disclosure provisions.[7] State regulation of the chemical industry similarly is flawed by its reliance on risk disclosure rather than prevention. In addition, disparate regulation by the states not only

---

1. 5 O.J. Eur. Comm. (No. L 230) 1 (1982). A directive is a statutory instrument, binding on Member States of the EC, which sets forth general principles that must be observed. The means of implementing the principles are left to the discretion of the individual national authorities. Moman, *Safety and Health Legislation in the European Communities — An Employer's Guide*, 3 Toxic Substances J. 133–34 (1981).

2. Spokesman's Group for the Commission of the European Communities, Press Release No. 82 (July 25, 1979) [hereinafter cited as Spokesman's Press Release].

3. 5 O.J. Eur. Comm. (No. L 230), art. 4 (1982).

4. *Id.*, art. 5.

5. *Id.*

6. *Id.*

7. *See infra* notes 23–40 and accompanying text.

LAW & POLICY IN INTERNATIONAL BUSINESS

frustrates companies with plants located throughout the United States, but generally is ineffective because it is overbroad and not rigorously enforced.[8]

This Note will examine the role that the U.S. government should play both in preventing major accidents at chemical plants [9] and in ensuring that communities are informed beforehand of appropriate responses to accidents that do occur. The Note first will discuss the hazards which insufficient information and planning pose to public health and the environment. Then, it will describe the problems attendant to the current U.S. approach to regulating chemical plant safety. Drawing from an analysis of the strengths and weaknesses of the European Directive, the Note next will propose changes to existing U.S. legislation. The Note will conclude that U.S. regulation should follow a prevention-oriented approach, and that the states should have primary responsibility for ensuring chemical plant safety.

BACKGROUND

Chemical Plant Hazards

The incidence of major industrial accidents and ensuing deaths is increasing exponentially throughout the world.[10] In the mid-1970s, several catastrophic incidents in Europe aroused public concern about chemical plant safety.[11] An accident in Seveso, Italy, finally

---

8. *See infra* notes 44–55 and accompanying text.

9. Risks posed by industrial activities can be divided into two categories: routine and exceptional. Routine risks occur during normal operating conditions, as typified by the steady release of small quantities of toxic chemicals into the workplace. Exceptional risks result from abnormal operating conditions — accidents — and include, for example, fires, explosions, and massive spills. This Note addresses the second category of risks as they pertain to the chemical industry.

10. Carson and Mumford, *An Analysis of Incidents Involving Major Hazards in the Chemical Industry*, 3 J. HAZARDOUS MATERIALS 149 (1979). This upward trend closely tracks the increased handling of hydrocarbons. Marshall, *Assessment of Hazard and Risk,* in HAZARDOUS MATERIALS SPILLS HANDBOOK 5-1, 5-20 (1982).

11. Spokesman's Press Release, *supra* note 2, at 2. The incidents arousing public concern included: Flixborough, United Kingdom. (In 1974, a reaction system failed, releasing cyclohexane, which exploded and caused a fire. The fire killed twenty-eight persons, seriously injured eighty-nine, and caused $100 million damage. *Id.*) Beek, The Netherlands. (In 1975, a pipe carrying propylene ruptured, causing an explosion that killed four-

PLANT SAFETY REGULATION

prompted the EC to enact a directive on major accident hazards known as the "Seveso Directive."[12] The incident occurred at a trichlorophenol plant on July 10, 1976, where an uncontrolled reaction caused an increase in pressure that ruptured a valve.[13] Because the plant had no vapor recovery system, the escaping fumes were vented to the open air.[14] The resultant cloud was laden with dioxins including TCDD, one of the deadliest substances known to man.[15]

The sequence of events following the release has become a classic example of how not to respond to a chemical emergency, as illustrated by the following:

– Plant management waited fourteen days before informing Italian authorities that there were dioxins in the cloud;

– City officials took twenty-three days to evacuate the most contaminated areas of Seveso;

– The superhighway bisecting the town remained open, thus allowing thousands of cars and trucks to spread dioxins throughout Europe; and,

– Clean-up crews frequented neighboring towns while wearing contaminated protective suits.[16]

As a result of the accident, 81,000 domestic animals either died or were put to sleep, hundreds of people were hospitalized, and many orchards and crops were contaminated.[17]

In the United States, inadequate preparedness also has caused significant health and environmental injury. For example, in 1974

---

teen persons, seriously injured 104 more, and resulted in $40 million damage. *Id.*) Manfredonia, Italy. (In 1976, a tower used to scrub gases produced by the synthesis of ammonia released ten tons of arsenic; many persons suffered from exposure and several square miles were contaminated. *Id.*)

12. 1980–81 Eur. Parl. Doc. (No. 220) 14 (1980).

13. Graham, *How are We Fixed for Toxic Clouds?*, 79 Audobon 137, 138 (1977). Dioxins were inadvertently formed in the course of reacting 1,2,4,5-tetrachlorobenzene with sodium hydroxide in the presence of glycol at elevated temperatures. The glycol polymerized, with a consequent rise in temperature, thus permitting the formation of 2,3,7,8-tetrachlorodibenzo-p-dioxin (TCDD). Marshall, *Assessment of Hazard and Risk,* in Hazardous Materials Spills Handbook, 5-1, 5-15 (1982).

14. Graham, *supra* note 13, at 137–38.

15. *Id.*; see also Harnik, *The Lessons of Seveso,* 64 Sierra 77 (1979).

16. Harnik, *supra* note 15, at 77.

17. *Id.* Hundreds of people experienced dizziness, nausea, diarrhea, impaired vision, liver damage, endocrine malfunctioning, and diminished sexual drive, and several women spontaneously aborted or gave birth to deformed babies. *Id.*; see also Graham, *supra* note 13, at 138.

LAW & POLICY IN INTERNATIONAL BUSINESS

in Chicago, a leak from a storage tank containing silicone tetrachloride produced a thick fog "with a strong gaseous odor and eye-burning and breath-taking effects" that hovered over the city for several days.[18] Unaware of the substance's identity, the response team exacerbated the problem by applying a series of inappropriate measures to stop the leak.[19] Further, because local officials waited several hours before evacuating the area and underestimated the distance that the cloud ultimately would travel, over 300 persons were hospitalized.[20]

The Seveso and Chicago incidents vividly illustrate that when communities are not forewarned of the hazardous characteristics of chemicals released during an accident, unnecessary risks are posed to response teams, to the public, and to the environment. Response teams are jeopardized by their inability to select necessary precautions against exposure,[21] the public is endangered by government indecision over the necessity and required length of evacuation, and the environment may be harmed by chemicals or procedures that would not be used if the characteristics of the released chemicals were known.[22]

CURRENT U.S. REGULATION

Current U.S. laws have serious defects at both the federal and state level. Federal authority for regulating chemical plants is compartmentalized among government agencies so that there is no clear assignment of responsibility for establishing programs to protect

---

18. Graham, *supra* note 13, at 140.

19. Fireman poured water on the leak, thereby converting the hydrogen chloride to hydrochloric acid mist, which caused most of the caustic burns, inflamed throats, and other ailments among the residents. Another crew tried to stop the leak by encasing it in concrete. The gases, however, seeped through the concrete, and the response team then had no way of getting back to the original leak. *Id.*

20. *Id.*

21. Comments of John Ford on the Pennsylvania Right-to-Know bill, *reprinted in* 1 HAZARD COMMUNICATION EXCHANGE 12 (Sept. 15, 1983).

22. For example, applying water to fires involving pesticides that are stable in water often harms the environment to a far greater extent than if foam was used or the fire allowed to simply burn out. In Jacksonville, Florida, in 1979, millions of gallons of water used to extinguish a fire involving the pesticide Dursban posed an environmental threat when it flowed into a nearby creek. 13 FDA CONS. 27 (1979); *see* Diefenbach, *Pesticide Fires,* in HAZARDOUS MATERIALS SPILLS HANDBOOK, 11-2, 11-8 (1982).

PLANT SAFETY REGULATION

communities surrounding chemical plants. State regulation of chemical plants is flawed because the states have followed the federal approach of relying on risk-disclosure rather than risk-prevention in regulating chemical plants. In addition, disparate regulation by the states threatens to disrupt interstate commerce by subjecting chemical plants to different and potentially conflicting regulations.

Federal Agency Responsibility

Responsibility for regulating chemical plant hazards is shared by the Occupational Safety and Health Administration (OSHA) and the Environmental Protection Agency (EPA). OSHA is responsible for regulating worker safety, and primarily is concerned with preventing hazards that endanger plant personnel.[23] EPA has a broader mandate: to protect both the public health and the environment.[24] Often, however, EPA defers to OSHA where activities threatening both the public health and worker safety occur within factory gates.[25] EPA generally exercises its authority only by responding to chemical plant emergencies, not by preventing them.[26] Both agencies fail to adequately protect communities adjacent to chemical plants because neither requires plant operators to prevent major accidents nor to develop contingency plans to minimize the dangers to communities from accidents that do occur.[27]

---

23. OSHA, a division of the Department of Labor, has primary responsibility for carrying out the duties of the Secretary of Labor under the Occupational Safety and Health Act of 1970, 29 U.S.C. §§ 651–78 (1982). The Act provides for the promulgation of regulations governing health and safety conditions in the workplace. *Id.* § 655.

24. EPA's broad authority to control activities that threaten the public health and the environment is described in President Nixon's Reorganization Plan which established the EPA. Reorganization Plan No. 3 of 1970, 5 U.S.C.A. § 8501 app. 1 (West Supp. 1968–83).

25. A recent attempt by the executive branch to ensure that EPA does not regulate activites also subject to OSHA's authority is the issuance by the Office of Management and Budget (OMB) of a "white paper" that is highly critical of several of EPA's rules for premanufacture review awaiting approval by the budget office. The March, 1984 paper recommended that outside reviewers study the degree to which EPA needs to develop occupational standards to supplement OSHA's standards. Chem Reg. Rept. (BNA) 8 (Apr. 27, 1984).

26. *See infra* notes 35–40 and accompanying text.

27. *See infra* notes 31–40 and accompanying text.

LAW & POLICY IN INTERNATIONAL BUSINESS

Worker Safety

Until recently, federal regulations provided employees with only piecemeal information on hazards in the workplace.[28] On November 25, 1983, OSHA promulgated Hazard Communication Rules, requiring that workers be given comprehensive information on each hazardous substance to which they may be exposed under normal operating conditions or in a foreseeable emergency.[29] The rules apply to manufacturers that produce, process, or use chemicals.[30]

The thrust of the regulations, however, is merely on disclosure of risks and present measures to abate them.[31] The rules neither establish an affirmative duty for employers to take preventive measures nor require OSHA to evaluate the adequacy of existing safety measures.[32] Furthermore, because OSHA's mandate is limited to worker protection, the regulations do not require

---

28. The Occupational Safety and Health Act requires warnings to employees only about the hazards of substances for which OSHA sets an exposure standard. *See* Occupational Safety and Health Act of 1970, § (6)(b)(7), codified at 29 U.S.C. § 651 (1982). Recently, under the National Labor Relations Act, the National Labor Relations Board established the right of employee representatives to receive information about health risks because such information is believed necessary for effective collective bargaining. Note, *Occupational Health Risks and the Worker's Right to Know*, 90 YALE L.J. 1792, 1805-06 (1981).

29. Hazard Communication Rule, 48 Fed. Reg. 53340 (1983) (to be codified at 29 C.F.R. § 1910.1200) [hereinafter referred to as OSHA Hazard Communication Rule]. In general, employers are required to provide workers with a Material Data Safety Sheet (MDSS) or the equivalent, for each toxic or hazardous substance used, manufactured or produced in the workplace. The MDSS must specify the name of the substance, the level at which exposure to the substance is considered hazardous, the acute or chronic effects of exposure, and appropriate emergency treatment procedures. Employers also are required to conduct education and training programs in the safe use and handling of toxic substances. *Id.* Foreseeable emergencies include spills and process upsets. *Id.* § (c). It is unclear whether foreseeable emergencies include incidents involving byproducts, as occured at Seveso, Italy. Telephone interview with Jennifer Silk, Office of Special Standards, OSHA (Oct. 10, 1983) [hereinafter cited as Silk Interview].

30. OSHA Hazard Communication Rule, *supra* note 29, § (b). Presumably, because the rule applies only to manufacturers and importers it does not cover facilities that only store hazardous substances. *Id.*

31. *Id.* §§ (d)-(h).

32. Requiring disclosure, however, might provide adequate incentives for most employers to increase efforts to reduce risk in order to avoid paying "risk premiums" to workers.

PLANT SAFETY REGULATION

disclosure to neighboring communities of the risk-related information given to employees.[33] In fact, a chemical's identity need not be revealed even to workers if it is a trade secret.[34]

Public Health and the Environment

There are several response-oriented programs to mitigate the effects of chemical accidents on the surrounding community.[35] Few, however, incorporate preventive measures. Of those that do, the most sweeping is the Spill Prevention Control and Countermeasure Plan (SPCC), authorized under section 311 of the Federal Water Pollution Control Act.[36] Administered by EPA, this statute requires facilities storing oil above a threshold quantity to prepare a plan to prevent spills, to describe the flow-route in the event of a spill, and to devise clean-up procedures.[37] The plan must be certified by a registered professional engineer,[38] but ordinarily is not reviewed by EPA.[39] Even the SPCC program, however, is quite limited; it applies only to oil storage facilities that pose a threat to navigable

---

33. Silk Interview, *supra* note 29.

34. OSHA Hazard Communication Rule, *supra* note 29, § (i). However, trade secrets and chemical identities must be disclosed to health professionals administering occupational health services to employees. *Id.* § (i)(2). In addition, although a chemical's identity need not be disclosed to employees, the properties and effects of the chemical must be revealed. *Id.* § (i)(1)(ii).

35. *See e.g.*, Federal Water Pollution Control Act of 1972, § 311, 42 U.S.C. § 1251 (1982)(controls releases of oil into navigable waters); Comprehensive Environmental Response, Compensation, and Liability Act of 1980, § 104, 42 U.S.C. § 9601 (1982)(commonly known as Superfund; controls releases of materials into the environment that endanger public health or welfare); Safe Drinking Water Act, § 1431, 42 U.S.C. § 300f (1982)(controls releases of contaminants into public water systems); Disaster Relief Act, 42 U.S.C. § 5145 (1982)(authorizes the President to provide assistance to save lives and protect property and public health and safety in emergencies and major disasters).

36. Federal Water Pollution Control Act of 1972, § 311, 42 U.S.C. § 1251 (1982). The other major federal environmental program requiring preventive measures administers the premanufacturing notification regulations under section 5 of the Toxic Substances Control Act, 15 U.S.C. § 2604 (1982). It, however, addresses hazards posed by products only after they leave the plant. *Id.*

37. Thompson, *Intergovernmental Maritime Consultative Organization,* in HAZARDOUS MATERIALS SPILLS HANDBOOK, 1–2, 1–10 (1982).

38. 40 C.F.R. § 112.3 (1983).

39. *Id.* § 112.4. If the facility discharges more than 1,000 U.S. gallons of oil in a single spill event, or discharged oil in harmful quantities within a twelve month period, it then must submit its plan to the Administrator for review. *Id.* § 112.4.

LAW & POLICY IN INTERNATIONAL BUSINESS

waters.[40] Chemical plants storing hazardous materials other than oil, or endangering either air or ground water, are under no federal obligation to prepare a contingency plan.

State and Local Legislation

Because OSHA repeatedly delayed the promulgation of its Hazard Communication Rules and EPA has failed to institute preventive measures to protect communities near chemical plants, many states and localities have enacted laws to fill the gap.[41] Approximately twelve states and six local governments have some type of regulation related to the hazards of chemical substances.[42] About thirteen other states and three other local governments have introduced legislation to achieve the same.[43]

Worker Right-to-Know

Statutes requiring employers to inform workers of the risks of chemicals in the workplace commonly are referred to as "Worker Right-to-Know" (RTK) laws.[44] In general, they require that employees be provided with the same type of information prescribed under OSHA's Hazard Communication Rules.[45] Section 667(d) of the Occupational Health and Safety Act, however, expressly prohibits states from asserting jurisdiction over any occupational safety and health issue with respect to which a federal safety or health standard is in effect.[46] Thus, state RTK statutes enacted solely to

---

40. EPA issued a proposed rule five years ago to control hazardous materials in addition to oil, but never finalized it. 43 Fed. Reg. 39276–90 (1978).

41. OSHA issued a proposed rule on chemical hazard identification on January 28, 1977, 42 Fed. Reg. 5372 (1977), but withdrew it on February 12, 1981, 46 Fed. Reg. 12,214 (1981). A revised proposed rule was not promulgated until March 19, 1982, 47 Fed. Reg. 12,092 (1982), which was finalized on November 25, 1983. Preamble to the OSHA Hazard Communication Rule, 48 Fed. Reg. 53280 (1983).

42. *Id.* at 53284.

43. *Id.*

44. 1 HAZARDOUS COMMUNICATION EXCHANGE 1 (Sept. 15, 1983).

45. OSHA Hazard Communication Rule, *supra* note 29; *see also* Position Paper of the American Petroleum Institute, Communication of Hazards Relating to Workplace Exposure to Chemical Substances and Physical Agents 1 (Aug. 6, 1982).

46. Occupational Safety and Health Act of 1970, 29 U.S.C. §§ 651–78 (1982). States desiring to adopt occupational safety and health standards that preempt federal standards must do so pursuant to a federally approved state plan. *Id.* § 667(b). Because the motivating factor for OSHA's promulgation of federal standards was to decrease disparity

PLANT SAFETY REGULATION

protect worker safety probably will be subject to OSHA's preemptive authority.[47]

Community Right-to-Know

A few state and local laws require that employers inform not only their workers, but also surrounding communities of the risks posed by their facilities.[48] These statutes, known as "Community RTK" laws, are designed to ensure that local response teams know the identity and location of hazardous substances within the community. When an accident occurs, a team can then make a quick and informed judgment and select appropriate action to protect the public from exposure.[49] Because many of the Community RTK laws were adopted as part of local fire codes, they may withstand preemption by OSHA's new rules because they address more than worker safety.[50]

Effect of Disparate State and Local Laws

Local and state Worker and Community RTK statutes differ markedly in terms of the industries and substances covered,[51] the

---

among existing state laws, however, it is unlikely that OSHA will approve state plans with regulations significantly different from those of OSHA. *See, e.g,* HAZARDOUS COMMUNICATION EXCHANGE, *supra* note 44, at 20–21; OCCUPATIONAL HEALTH AND SAFETY LETTER 1 (Nov. 22, 1983); Job Safety and Health Report 203 (Dec. 27, 1983).

47. 1 HAZARDOUS COMMUNICATION EXCHANGE, *supra* note 44, at 20–21. When deciding the preemption issue, it is unclear whether a federal court will allow nonconflicting portions of a state law to stand, or instead hold that federal regulation is exclusive and strike down all state laws, at least where not adopted pursuant to a federally-approved OSHA plan. NEW ENGLAND LEGAL FOUNDATION, MASSACHUSETTS RIGHT TO KNOW HANDBOOK 235 (1983).

48. By September, 1983, New Jersey, Cincinnati, and Philadelphia had enacted public RTK legislation. HAZARDOUS COMMUNICATIONS EXCHANGE, *supra* note 44, at 1, 9, 19, 21; MASSACHUSETTS RIGHT TO KNOW HANDBOOK, *supra* note 47, at 238–44.

49. *See, e.g.,* Preamble to Cincinnati RTK Ordinance, CINCINNATI, OR. 210 ch. 1247, Toxic and Hazardous Substances — Right to Know (1982) [hereinafter cited as Cincinnati RTK Ordinance]; HAZARDOUS COMMUNICATION EXCHANGE, *supra* note 44, at 12 (statement by John J. Ford).

50. HAZARDOUS COMMUNICATION EXCHANGE, *supra* note 44, at 21.

51. For example, Pennsylvania's proposed rule applies to all industries, *id.* at 9, while OSHA's new rule applies only to manufacturers in SIC Codes 21–39, OSHA Hazard Communication Rule, *supra* note 29, § (b). Cincinnati's and Connecticut's rules apply to approximately 400 substances on OSHA's list of toxic and hazardous substances in 29 C.F.R. 1910

LAW & POLICY IN INTERNATIONAL BUSINESS

quantity of substance at the plant triggering regulation,[52] the type of information requiring disclosure or afforded confidential treatment,[53] the parties to whom the information can be disclosed,[54] and the amount of oversight exercised by local authorities.[55] The proliferation of these laws increasingly frustrates chemical manufacturers and suppliers doing business in many states because they must tailor integral plant operations to comply with the requirements peculiar to each individual state or municipality.[56]

THE SEVESO DIRECTIVE

The Seveso Directive was designed to correct two problems with European regulation of chemical plants. First, requirements to prevent major accidents were inadequate in Europe because regulatory responsibility was compartmentalized among worker safety and environmental agencies.[57] And second, disparate regulation by

---

(1983) (Subpart Z list). Schecter, *Right-to-Know: The New Surge in Local Legislation, in* OC-CUPATIONAL HEALTH AND SAFETY 52–53 (Sept. 1982). Pennsylvania's proposed rule, on the other hand, applies to the over 50,000 substances in the National Institute for Occupational Safety and Health (NIOSH) Registry Of Toxic Effects of Chemical Substances (RTECS), HAZARDOUS COMMUNICATION EXCHANGE, *supra* note 44, at 7. The major provisions of eleven state's RTK statutes are summarized and compared in the MASSACHUSSETTS RIGHT-TO-KNOW HANDBOOK, *supra* note 47, at 237–47.

52. Cincinnati's rule applies to toxic or hazardous substances handled in quantities greater than one gallon, Cincinnati RTK Ordinance, *supra* note 49, § 1247–05(A)(5), while OSHA's rule leaves the threshold quantity determination to the discretion of the individual facility, OSHA Hazard Communication Rule, *supra* note 29, § (d)(3)(ii).

53. Most laws require that, among other things, the name of each chemical be disclosed, but differ as to the ease with which this information can be protected as a trade secret. Cincinnati, for example, does not accord trade secret status to carcinogens, whereas OSHA does. *Compare* Cincinnati RTK Ordinance, *supra* note 49, § 1247–29, *with* OSHA Hazard Communication Rule, *supra* note 29, § (h)(i).

54. Cincinnati provides for disclosure to the public, except where the information is protected as a trade secret and the chemical is not carcinogenic. Cincinnati RTK Ordinance, *supra* note 49, § 1247–01. Florida's proposed rule provides that information be given only to firefighters and the police. HAZARDOUS COMMUNICATION EXCHANGE, *supra* note 44, at 4.

55. Connecticut has no oversight provision. Schecter, *supra* note 51, at 56. Cincinatti requires the fire department to inspect facilities to ensure compliance (estimated cost: $80,000 per year). *Id.* at 52.

56. Preamble to the OSHA Hazard Communication Rule, 48 Fed. Reg. 53,284 (1983).

57. 1 O.J. EUR. COMM. (No. C 212) 3 (1979).

> The existing control and prevention machinery with regard to certain types of pollution and nuisance due to human activities is compartmentalized between

PLANT SAFETY REGULATION

individual Member States impaired the functioning of the common market by creating unequal competitive conditions.[58]

Features of the Directive

The Directive prescribes a rigorous level of safety for chemical plants: "Every industrial activity which involves, or may involve, dangerous substances and which, in the event of a major accident, may have serious consequences for man and the environment, must take *all* measures necessary to prevent such accidents and to limit the consequences thereof."[59]

The Directive creates a two-tiered regulatory framework based on the nature and quantity of dangerous substances handled and the type of activity conducted at a given plant.[60] Industrial facilities handling dangerous substances above a certain quantity must make available to local authorities — presumably upon request — a record identifying potential major hazards at the plant and safety measures

---

several administrative authorities. Focusing mainly on pollution control or the protection of workers in the normal operating conditions of industrial activities, legislation is more often than not incomplete as regards the risks of major accidents.

Id.

58. 2 O.J. Eur. Comm. (No. L 230) 2 (1982). "[D]isparity between provisions already applicable or being prepared in the various Member States on measures to prevent major accidents and limit their consequences for man and the environment may create unequal conditions of competition and hence directly affect the functioning of the common market." *Id.*

59. 5 O.J. (No. L 230) 3, art. 3 (1982) (emphasis added). The prescription of this level of protection was not inadvertent. Draft comments submitted by the Economic and Social Committee (ESC) on the proposed directive expressed concern about the stringency of article 3's performance standard, and suggested it be reworded to require preventive measures only where "technically and humanly feasible." European Economic Community, Economic and Social Committee, Report of the Section for Social Questions on the Proposal for a Council Directive on the Major Accidents of Certain Industrial Activities 16 Doc. Com. (79) 384 (Mar. 20, 1980) [herinafter cited as Unofficial Report of the ESC]. The official version of the ESC's comments on the proposal, however, did not contain the suggested language. 21 O.J. Eur. Comm. (No. C 182) 28 (1980).

60. 5 O.J. Eur. Comm. (No. L 230) 3, art. 3 (1982). There are two categories of substances: dangerous and particularly dangerous. The former are defined by a set of characteristics (e.g., toxicity, reactivity) described in Annex IV. The latter are specified in either of two ways: by a list (Annex III) or by a set of physical properties (Annex II). There are also two categories of activities: storage and other. For each chemical, facilities conducting only storage must handle larger quantities to be subject to the same requirements applicable to production or processing facilities. *Id.*, Annex II.

taken to mitigate their effects, and supply workers with the information, training, and equipment needed to ensure their safety.[61] In addition to the above requirements, for particularly dangerous substances, the facility must submit a detailed notification form describing the substances handled at the plant, plant layout, and points where major accidents could occur. Local authorities must ensure that adjacent populations are informed of safety measures at the plant and procedures to follow in the event of an accident.[62] The Directive also requires that Member States establish administrative agencies to evaluate notification forms, ensure that external emergency plans are prepared, and inspect facilities for compliance with the Directive.[63]

Beneficial Aspects of the Directive

The European Directive reflects a sensible compromise between the competing considerations of public safety and administrative realities by targeting government oversight to activities posing the greatest threat. For example, the notification procedure allows a permanent dialogue among the various interested parties,[64] but applies only to facilities handling particularly dangerous substances. This avoids overwhelming local authorities with an unmanageable surfeit of paperwork.[65] Similarly the requirement to disseminate information to nearby populations on plant safety measures and appropriate community response applies only to the higher-tier of dangerous substances.[66] Unfortunately, the administrative resources needed to assess plant measures and devise external emergency procedures precludes extensive plant-community dialogue for every facility.

Although no permanent dialogue is established between local

---

61. *Id.*, art. 4.

62. *Id.*, art. 5. New or modified facilities cannot begin operations until they have complied with the notification procedure. *Id.*, arts. 5, 9.

63. *Id.*, art. 7. The Directive also requires Member States to inform other states of facilities posing a transboundary threat, *id.*, art. 8; to institute a reporting procedure to collect information when accidents occur, *id.*, art. 10; and to protect confidential information submitted in the notification forms, *id.*, art. 13.

64. 24 O.J. EUR. COMM. (No. C 212) 15–16 (1979).

65. *Id.* at 15.

66. In the proposal, the provision also applied to facilities handling the lower-tier of dangerous substances. *Compare* Article 4 in the draft version, 24 O.J. EUR. COMM. (No. C 212) (1979), *with* the final version, 5 O.J. EUR. COMM. (No. L 230) (1982).

PLANT SAFETY REGULATION

authorities and facilities handling the lower-tier of dangerous substances, the Directive nonetheless will increase safety at these plants for two reasons. First, the performance standard — requiring that all measures be taken to prevent accidents — applies to these facilities.[67] Second, the requirement that a written record be kept of safety measures tends to induce plant operators who have not done so to ponder safety problems.[68]

Problems of Implementation

Despite the strengths of the European Directive, two problems have surfaced in EC nations trying to implement it.[69] First, the Directive's pristine performance standard requires that all necessary measures be taken to prevent accidents.[70] Since absolute safety is impossible, officials administering the program probably are prescribing levels of protection based on what they believe is realistic.[71] In all cases, the requisite level of risk prevention is above zero, but how much above is unknown. Thus, administering officials either in the same or different countries might impose different standards on firms in the same industry, thereby affecting a firm's competitive position.[72]

Second, although data submitted in the notification forms may not be disclosed "for any purpose other than that for which it was requested,"[73] the European Council of Chemical Manufacturer's Federations (CEFIC) nevertheless is fearful that different Member States will accord varying degrees of security to confidential business information.[74] Further, CEFIC is worried that the public

---

67. 5 O.J. Eur. Comm. (No. L 230) 3, art. 3 (1982).

68. Unofficial Report of the ESC, *supra* note 59, at 16–17.

69. Member States must take measures necessary to comply with the Directive by January 8, 1984. 5 O.J. Eur. Comm. (No. L 230), art. 20 (1982).

70. *Id.*, art. 3.

71. The German statute implementing the Directive actually changed the performance standard from all measures to "prevent," to all measures to "reasonably exclude" risks from accidents. Int'l Env't Rep. (BNA) 100, 101 (Mar. 10, 1982).

72. Germany plans to develop a standard set of criteria for evaluating the safety analyses required under article 5 of the Directive. *Id.* at 101. Standardized evaluation allows comparisons among different plants, and should lead to a more uniform level of prescribed risk prevention.

73. 5 O.J. Eur. Comm. (No. L 230) 5, art. 13 (1982).

74. Int'l Env't Rep. (BNA) 480 (Nov. 10, 1982).

disclosure requirements[75] may result in either the announcement of information in a manner likely to generate panic, or a breach of confidentiality by "overzealous authorities."[76] Thus, compliance with the Directive may be incomplete until industry is given greater assurance that its sensitive business information will be afforded confidential treatment.

Proposed Changes To U.S. Law

The Seveso Directive differs in three important respects from U.S. programs for regulating chemical plant hazards. First, rather than rely on risk-disclosure or remedial-measures to control major accident hazards, European law requires risk-prevention. Second, instead of having each Member State develop its own framework for regulating chemical hazards, a uniform approach has been adopted by the EC. And third, the regulatory framework reflected in the Seveso Directive does not attempt to address all hazards posed by all chemical plants, but rather provides a mechanism for administering officials to target their finite resources to those facilities posing the greatest risk. U.S. lawmakers should consider restructuring U.S. programs accordingly.

Establishment of Preventive Measures

The European Directive establishes an affirmative duty on chemical plants to take preventive measures to abate risk.[77] Further, facilities handling particularly hazardous chemicals must inform adjacent communities of plant safety measures and appropriate community response procedures.[78] Prevention and preparedness is efficient; it is simpler to avoid trouble than to repair it.[79] Major accidents generally are foreseeable.[80] By requiring that measures be taken in relation to the dangerous nature and quantity of substances involved, the likelihood of major accidents in the United States, and the damage resulting from accidents that occur, can be appreciably

---

75. 5 O.J. Eur. Comm. (No. L 230) 3, art. 5 (1982).
76. Int'l Env't Rep. (BNA) 480 (Nov. 10, 1982).
77. *See supra* note 59 and accompanying text.
78. *See supra* note 68 and accompanying text.
79. Thompson, *supra* note 37, at 1–10.
80. Carson and Mumford, 3 J. Hazardous Materials at 164.

PLANT SAFETY REGULATION

reduced.[81]

Federalization of U.S. Programs

The European Directive also facilitates commerce by eliminating the previous disparity of major accident regulation among EC Member States. A centralized U.S. program similarly could reduce the disruptive effect of inconsistent and potentially conflicting state RTK laws.[82] Differences in U.S. state law probably reflect inadequate resources to investigate the problem, rather than disagreement over the type of information needed. The degree of risk of a major accident depends on the toxic and physical properties of the substances in question, their quantity, the type of technological process used, and the location of the industrial activity.[83] State and local governments generally are unable to weigh the importance of each of these four factors when devising regulatory programs.[84] Consequently, most RTK statutes focus only on the first factor, tending to include long lists of substances subject to regulation.[85] This broad coverage may impose an impossible burden on communities struggling to contend with the sheer mass of forms submitted or made available as required by the statutes.[86] As a result, some communities are unable to enforce their statutes.[87]

The federal government is better equipped to analyze the myriad toxicological, engineering, and economic data relevant to such regulation. Its ability to evaluate factors other than the characteristics of the chemicals themselves may reduce the number of substances ultimately requiring regulation. If the federal government were to identify situations posing particularly high risks, then a tiered regulatory approach could be developed, similar to the one

---

81. Spokesman's Press Release, *supra* note 2, at 1.

82. *See supra* note 56 and accompanying text.

83. 24 O.J. EUR. COMM. (No. C 212) 12 (1979).

84. Simply compiling the toxicological, engineering, economic, and demographic data needed to conduct such an analysis would be an enormous undertaking.

85. *See supra* note 51.

86. This is what caused the EC to take a two-tiered approach in their directive. *See supra* notes 64–66 and accompanying text. Even if states had the resources to conduct the analyses, it is more efficient for the federal government to perform the analyses, rather than have them conducted fifty times by the states.

87. *See, e.g.,* New York's RTK statute, which applies to over 50,000 substances and is not enforced. Preamble to OSHA Hazard Communication Rule, 48 Fed. Reg. 53,284 (1983).

LAW & POLICY IN INTERNATIONAL BUSINESS

used in the Seveso Directive.

Adoption of Realistic Performance Standards

The European Directive provides not only a template for restructuring U.S. law, but also forewarns of pitfalls to avoid. For example, instead of prescribing that *all* measures be taken to prevent major accidents, U.S. legislators should select a realistic performance standard. In addition, criteria should be developed so that administering officials uniformly can evaluate safety measures to assess compliance with the standard.[88] Ideally, the selection of the performance standard should be based on a cost-benefit analysis of the different equipment or process changes — for example, best available or practicable technology — needed to achieve various levels of "acceptable" risk.

Requisite Level of Analysis

To determine the adequacy of existing safety measures, plant operators must assess the risks of the various components of their facilities. The European Directive does not address this issue. There are several types of risk analyses; they vary in precision and expense.[89] The types of hazards for which analyses can be conducted also differ.[90] To reduce uncertainty regarding the chemical industry's obligations under the regulations, legislators should specify a requisite level of analysis. Again, the selection should be based on the differential costs and benefits of evaluating risk with alterna-

---

88. Failure to provide such criteria has caused problems for officials trying to administer the German chemical plant safety statute. Germany plans to develop a standard set of criteria for evaluating safety analyses. *See supra* note 72.

89. *See generally* Cox, *Improving Risk Assessment Methods for Process Plants*, 6 J. HAZARDOUS MATERIALS 249 (1982) (examines the current state of the art in risk assessment of chemical process plants); AMERICAN INSTITUTE OF CHEMICAL ENGINEERS, FIRE AND EXPLOSION INDEX HAZARD CLASSIFICATION GUIDE (1980) (presents the "checklist" method of conducting risk assessments); RIJNMOND PUBLIC AUTHORITY, RISK ANALYSIS OF SIX POTENTIALLY HAZARDOUS INDUSTRIAL PROJECTS IN THE RIJNMOND AREA, A PILOT STUDY (1982) (applies a more detailed version of the "checklist" method to assess the risks from six industrial installations in Rijnmond, the Netherlands).

90. For example, under the German statute the safety analysis must take into account not only accidents within the plant, but also dangers from outside the plant, such as earthquakes and airplane crashes, and interventions by third parties, such as terrorists. INT'L ENV'T REP. (BNA) 101 (Mar. 10, 1982).

PLANT SAFETY REGULATION

tive methods.[91]

Protection of Trade Secrets

Finally, U.S. legislators should specify the balance to be struck between the interest of safety and that of protecting trade secrets. The European Directive contains no special treatment of trade secrets.[92] U.S. RTK laws generally address this issue, but they differ in the scope of confidentiality granted to business information and in the persons given access to it.[93] The size of the audience probably affects industry's enthusiasm in accepting RTK programs. Before deciding on the level of protection to afford confidential information, legislators should be apprised of the trade-offs between restricted access to narrowly defined trade secrets and wide circulation of broadly protected confidential information.

IMPLEMENTING CHANGES IN U.S. LAWS

A concerted effort to revise U.S. chemical plant safety regulation could take one of two forms: the federal government could either administer the new program itself, or supply states with analyses so they can improve their programs.

EPA has authority under the Toxic Substances Control Act (TSCA) to promulgate regulations similar to those called for under the European Directive.[94] A lengthier but more effective approach than using the authorities under TSCA, however, would be for

---

91. If costs were found to be too high for individual firms, another option would be for the government to conduct generic analyses for classes of facilities and to prescribe measures to abate their risks.

92. 5 O.J. EUR. COMM. (No. L 230) 5 (1982). Article 13 states that information supplied to the government cannot be disclosed "for any purpose other than that for which it was requested." *Id.* It is unclear whether this would allow government officials charged with developing external emergency procedures to rely on or disclose confidential information needed to perform the task.

93. *See supra* note 29.

94. Toxic Substances Control Act, 15 U.S.C. § 2601 (1982). TSCA is referred to as the "gap-filling" environmental law because its purpose is to regulate chemical substances in any application not specifically covered by other regulatory authorities. Statement of Don R. Clay, Acting Asst. Admin., Off. of Pesticide and Toxic Substances Before the Subcomm. on Science, Research and Technology and the Subcomm. on Investigations and Oversight of the House Comm. on Science and Technology 7 (June 22, 1983).

LAW & POLICY IN INTERNATIONAL BUSINESS

Congress to enact new legislation. This would be preferable for two reasons.

First, OSHA already has entered the field with its recent regulation on hazard communication.[95] A dual effort by OSHA and the EPA to regulate the risks of chemical plants would be duplicative in terms of training federal employees to oversee the program. It also would be disruptive if the two agencies required disclosure of different information.[96] Second, enacting new legislation would give Congress an opportunity to provide explicit guidance to the executive branch on such matters as the performance standard to use in evaluating safety programs, the type of risk analysis to require of plant operators, and the deference to afford confidential business information.[97]

Federal Guidance Approach

Federally-sponsored guidance, however, may be all that is needed to resolve existing problems with current state statutes. If inadequate evaluative resources is the reason for the states' failure to prescribe different requirements for facilities posing different risks, then providing a means for ranking facilities may be sufficient incentive for states to redesign their programs. Because the information would be provided from a single source, it probably would have the added benefit of decreasing the disparity among state laws.[98]

The federal guidance approach is preferable to federal regulation for at least two reasons. First, because local response teams are the first to arrive, and often are the only government officials at chemical plant accidents, it is more appropriate for local than federal personnel to develop or critique external emergency plans.[99] Second, once provided with a means to rank facilities, local and state officials will be in a better position than federal authorities to estimate

---

95. *See supra* note 29 and accompanying text.

96. OSHA's mandate is to protect worker safety; EPA's is to protect the public. *See supra* notes 23–24. The type of information needed to comply with the two mandates may differ. For example, workers need to know both the acute and chronic hazards of chemicals in the workplace; the public, on the other hand, is more generally concerned about acute risks from major accidents.

97. *See supra* notes 88–93 and accompanying text.

98. *See supra* notes 51–55 and accompanying text.

99. Quarantelli, *Initial Findings From A Study Of Socio-Behavioral Preparations and Planning for Acute Chemical Hazard Disasters,* 3 J. HAZARDOUS MATERIALS 86 (Feb. 1979).

PLANT SAFETY REGULATION

the resources needed to oversee hazardous activities in their communities. This in turn could lead to a more reasonable structuring of regulatory programs than at the federal level, because regulations could be applied to different classes of facilities based on the state's knowledge of funding available to administer the program, as well as the relative hazards of the facilities in the state.

CONCLUSION

The recent proliferation of U.S. state laws related to chemical plant hazards demonstrates general dissatisfaction with the federal government's failure to prescribe *preventive* measures to control the *public* risk posed by chemical plant accidents. In trying to correct this problem by enacting RTK statutes, the states have adopted a flawed approach. First, by focusing on risk-disclosure rather than risk-abatement, the states have provided little incentive for plant operators to mitigate existing hazards. Second, by failing to tier their programs so that particularly hazardous activities receive greater scrutiny, and by subjecting to regulation more chemical plants than they have resources to oversee, the states inadvertently have encouraged noncompliance because of the low threat of enforcement. Further, there is the inherent problem when regulating at the state level of creating barriers to interstate commerce by subjecting companies that do business in several states to different and potentially conflicting regulations.

The Seveso Directive reflects the collective judgment of the EC Member States that preventive measures should be required to protect the public — as well as workers — from major chemical accidents. Recognizing, however, that there are limits on the administrative and fiscal resources that its members can devote to addressing this problem, the EC has developed a regulatory framework that calls for the prevention of chemical plant hazards in a manner that does not overwhelm the ability of its members to implement and enforce the program. Because the framework was agreed to by all Member States, the previous European problem of disparate regulation and the resultant obstruction of interstate commerce has been corrected.

As in Europe, U.S. experts should confer in order to develop a realistic framework for the states to promulgate regulations that protect the public from chemical plant accidents. One means for bringing such experts together is for the Congress to establish and fund a

LAW & POLICY IN INTERNATIONAL BUSINESS

short-lived Commission to recomend a regulatory framework along the lines of the Seveso Directive. Because OSHA and the EPA have acquired substantial expertise on the relative hazards of chemical substances and industrial processes, these agencies should be instructed to assist the Commission in designing the framework. In addition, state and local officials with significant expertise in inspecting chemical plants and responding to emergencies also should participate, as well as representatives from the chemical industry. It is hoped that the Commission's recommendations would provide the impetus for states to revise their programs so that chemical plant safety regulations are not only consistent throughout the United States, but are structured so that facilities posing the greatest threat to the public receive a sufficient amount of government oversight.

Arline M. Sheehan

[15]

Environmental Assessment—The EC Directive

By Nigel Haigh*

Five years between formal proposal and publication of a Directive is long enough but not unknown in the European Community (EC). Given the opposition from many quarters in several countries it is remarkable that Directive 85/337[1] on "the assessment of the effects of certain public and private projects on the environment" was ever agreed at all. The Member States now have until July 3, 1988 to adapt their legislation or administrative procedures to achieve the ends set out.

The Directive is regarded by the EC Commission as an embodiment of the preventative approach to environmental protection; an approach enumerated as the first of 11 principles of EC environmental policy in the first EC Action Programme on the Environment of 1973.[2] In Britain, as I argued in an earlier article,[3] the Directive is more likely to be seen as the first major influence from abroad on British town and country planning and the first incursion by the EC into this field.

Although the Directive is likely to be applied formally to rather few projects, many of which are likely to be the subject of public inquiries, it may nevertheless have a larger influence as its procedures come to be adopted as a matter of course by industry, developers, and planning authorities even where its provisions are not obligatory and even where no public inquiry takes place.

The essential elements of the Directive can be stated quite simply:

— an assessment is to be made of the effects of certain development projects on the environment before development consent is given;

— the developer, as a contribution to this assessment, is to supply, and make public, certain information;

— the public, and those authorities with specific environmental responsibilities likely to be concerned, are to be consulted in advance and their views considered;

— the content of the decision taken by the "competent authority" and any conditions attached to it must be made public.

* Director of the London Office, Institute for European Environmental Policy, 3 Endsleigh Street, London WC1H 0DD.
[1] Official Journal of the EC, L175, 5.7.85.
[2] Official Journal of the EC, C112, 20.12.73.
[3] Haigh, N., *The EEC Directive on Environmental Assessment of Development Projects* [1983] J.P.L. 577–640.

An important point to note is that the "assessment" is not the responsibility of the developer and nor is it necessarily to be embodied in a single document. This is only one respect in which the Directive differs from the source that inspired it: the "environmental impact statement" required in the United States under the National Environment Policy Act (N.E.P.A.) 1969.[3] Although the Directive nowhere says so in as many words, the "assessment" is a procedure involving the provision and publication of information on the part of the developer, the collecting of information from the public and others, and culminating in a mental process on the part of the "competent authority" in arriving at its decision to grant or withhold consent for development. This emerges most clearly from the preamble which says that "whereas this assessment must be conducted on the basis of appropriate information supplied by the developer, which may be supplemented by the authorities and by the people who may be concerned by the project in question . . ."

If the "assessment" is a procedure then it will not consist of an easily publishable document, although an account of the procedure with its conclusions can always be published. In this respect the Directive differs from the draft Directive proposed by the Commission in 1980[4] which would have required two published assessments of environmental effects. One would have been required of the developer as part of the information he supplied with his application, and the other would have been made by the competent authority in reaching its decision. Although the Directive now nowhere says that the "assessment" must be published, it does say that it must identify, describe and assess certain factors in an appropriate manner. If the public is to be satisfied that this has been done it would help if an account of the assessment procedure were to be published. In Britain the report of the inspector who holds a public inquiry effectively already does this, but there is no requirement for such a published report in the case of an ordinary planning application. In the absence of a published assessment there will be the danger that the developer's published document containing the information that he is bound to supply will come to be known as the "assessment." Strictly this is incorrect and may yet cause confusion.

The Directive has in effect been subtly modified in the process of negotiation so that it now accords very closely with existing British development control procedures. In Britain the developer already has to supply certain information; the public already has the chance to comment; the planning authority already goes through a mental process in arriving at a decision which involves considering the information supplied by the developer and others; and when the decision is taken it is published although the reasons for it do not have to be given unless the application is refused. When an application is "called in" and subjected to a public inquiry the main procedures of the Directive are also already followed. It is really only in the type and quantity of the information that will have to be provided, and the range of environmental effects that will have to be considered, that the Directive will introduce anything new to Britain.

These novel provisions are not insignificant since in effect they will bring within the development control procedure considerations of pollution matters that have hitherto often been considered separately by other authorities. In this respect British development control when applied to industrial plants will be brought closer to plant authorisation procedures that exist in several other European countries.

[4] Official Journal of the EC, C169, 9.7.80.

6   Environmental Assessment—The EC Directive

The Directive is also bound, in the long term, to create pressure for environmental assessments for projects that currently do not require planning permission or some other form of authorisation, and the Commission has already announced its intention of extending the principles of environmental assessment to programmes and policies in addition to projects.

The Directive is exceptional in defining the term "competent authority" which appears frequently in EC Directives. The definition says that "the competent authority or authorities shall be that or those which the Member States designate as responsible for performing the duties arising from this Directive." This is the usually accepted meaning, the point being that the authority may differ for different obligations in the Directive and from project to project. In Britain the authority will often be the planning authority, but where a project is subject to special legislation, *e.g.* a power station or trunk road, it may be the Secretary of State. Similarly where a project is "called in" and becomes the subject of a public inquiry, the authority will at that point become the Secretary of State, or indeed the inspector, in those cases where the inspector has powers to take the decision himself.

Below is a fuller summary of the Directive:

1. General Provisions

Projects listed in an Annex I, *i.e.* those that the Directive regards as being likely to have significant effects on the environment by virtue, *inter alia*, of their nature, size or location are to be made subject to an assessment of their effects before consent is given. Other projects, listed in an Annex II, may be subject to an assessment at the discretion of the Member States.

The effects on the following four factors are to be identified, described and assessed, as appropriate:

1. human beings, fauna and flora;
2. soil, water, air, climate and the landscape;
3. the interaction between 1 and 2;
4. material assets and the cultural heritage.

Information supplied by the developer (see 4 below) and gathered as a result of consultations (see 5 below) must be taken into consideration in the development consent procedure. The public is to be informed of the content of the decision and any conditions attached to it, but the authority need not inform the public of the reasons for the decision unless required to by national legislation.

2. Exemptions

In exceptional cases a project may be exempted from the provisions of the Directive. In that event the Member State must make public its reasons and must consider whether another form of assessment would be appropriate and whether the public should be informed of the information collected. The Member State must also inform the Commission which must immediately inform the other Member States.

Projects whose details are adopted by a specific act of national legislation are exempt from all provisions of the Directive, as are projects serving national defence purposes.

3. Projects Subject to Assessment

Projects which *must* be made subject to an environmental impact assessment, unless exempted, fall under nine headings in Annex I. In summary they are:

1. Oil refineries;
2. Large thermal power stations and nuclear power stations and reactors;
3. Installations for storage or disposal of radioactive waste;
4. Iron and steel works;
5. Installations for extracting and processing asbestos;
6. Integrated chemical installations;
7. Construction of motorways, express roads, railway lines and airports;
8. Trading ports and inland waterways;
9. Installations for incineration, treatment or land fill of hazardous waste.

Member States *may*, at their own discretion, make the projects in Annex II subject to an assessment in accordance with the Directive. They may specify certain types of project as being subject to an assessment and may establish criteria or thresholds for deciding when an assessment is necessary. Annex II lists classes of project under 12 headings. Under each heading the class is described in some detail so that the headings below only give a broad indication of the projects for which an assessment may be required:

1. Agriculture;
2. Extractive industry;
3. Energy industry;
4. Processing of metals;
5. Manufacture of glass;
6. Chemical industry;
7. Food industry;
8. Textile, leather, wood and paper industries;
9. Rubber industry;
10. Infrastructure projects;
11. Other projects;
12. Modifications to projects included in Annex I.

4. Information to be Supplied by the Developer

The developer is to supply at least the following information:

1. A description of the project with information on its site, design and size;
2. Measures intended to avoid, reduce or remedy significant adverse effects;
3. The data required to identify and assess the main environmental effects;
4. A non-technical summary of 1, 2 and 3.

An Annex III gives a fuller specification of the information that the developer must supply amplifying these four points. Any authorities with relevant information in their possession are to make it available to the developer. The developer is to supply the Annex III information only in as much as the Member State considers it relevant to a given stage of the consent procedure; to the particular project; to the environmental

8 Environmental Assessment—The EC Directive

features likely to be affected; and that it is reasonable having regard to current knowledge. This specification is set out under seven headings and includes:

1. Production processes, quantity of materials used, expected residues and emissions;
2. Where appropriate, an outline of main alternatives studied by the developer and reasons for his choice;
3. A description of the aspects of the environment likely to be affected including population, fauna, flora, soil, water, air, climatic factors, architectural and archaeological heritage and landscape;
4. A description of the likely significant effects on the environment, and of the forecasting methods used to assess these effects;
5. An indication of any difficulties encountered in compiling the required information.

5. Public Consultations

The arrangements for public consultation are to be decided upon by the Member State but any request for development consent, and the information supplied by the developer, must be made public. The public concerned must also be given the opportunity to express an opinion before the project is initiated.

Authorities with specific environmental responsibilities likely to be concerned by a project must also be given an opportunity to express their opinion. The detailed arrangements for this are again a matter for the Member State.

Where a project is likely to have effects in another Member State, the developer's information is to be forwarded to that Member State and should serve as a basis for any consultations between the two Member States.

*   *   *

One of the British Government's major reservations about the draft Directive was the avenues that it might open for litigation and hence delay. The Commission's proposal for a Directive published in 1980 would have required the competent authority to publish its assessment of the environmental effects of a project and the Government was concerned that if it had to make Regulations requiring applicants for planning permission to submit certain specified information with their applications and requiring the authority to publish an assessment, the door would be opened to members of the public to engage, not in a productive discussion of the merits of the information, but in a discussion of form. The Government feared that opponents would be provided with the opportunity to seize on some procedural failure as a ground for challenging a planning decision in the Courts, perhaps even to the extent of a reference to the European Court of Justice. These possibilities have now been reduced if not eliminated. Much of the information to be supplied by the developer is to be supplied "inasmuch as the Member States consider that the information is relevant to a given stage of the consent procedure" and the detailed arrangements for public consultation are to be determined by the Member States. Thus whatever national legislation or regulations eventually implement the Directive a large measure of discretion can be left.

Until November 1983 Britain put itself in the position of being the leading opponent of the proposed Directive and the House of Commons effectively prevented the Government from agreeing to any significant changes to the existing British system by adopting a resolution that welcomed "the Government's policy of encouraging environmental assessment within the general principles of the existing law."[5] The British objections related not just to the points discussed above but also to the difficulty of defining projects that would be subject to the terms of the Directive. When this objection had been overcome by shortening Annex I and providing for a flexible procedure for exemptions, a Danish objection then continued to delay agreement. The Danish Parliament (the *Folketing*) objected in principle to having to submit development projects to the procedures of the Directive when they were being authorised by an Act of Parliament on the grounds that this infringed upon their sovereignty. The Danish Government refused to make any concession on this point in deference to the views of the *Folketing* so that any project "the details of which are adopted by a specific Act of national legislation" have been made exempt.

The delay over the Danish objection (which was the only point outstanding for many months) enabled the Department of the Environment to begin considering how to implement the Directive even before it was agreed. In 1984 they established a working party with members drawn from industry, local government, the planning profession, environmental groups and other government departments to consider how best to implement the Directive for those projects subject to planning control under the Planning Acts. Some of the projects of Annex I, *e.g.* power stations and highways are approved under separate legislation and are being considered by other government departments. In April 1986 the Department of the Environment issued a consultation paper based on the discussions in the working group. The consultation paper sought comments by July 1986 on a draft advisory booklet which is to be published by the Department setting out the procedures to be followed by both developers and authorities, and also on proposed statutory provisions. The Department is now considering the comments received on the consultation paper and plans to issue the statutory provisions, a circular and the advisory booklet probably in 1987. The statutory provisions are likely to be in the form of Regulations made under the provisions of section 2(2) of the European Communities Act 1972, rather than new primary legislation. That Act enables Regulations to be made to fulfil any EC obligations.[6]

The number of projects likely to fall under Annex I in any one year are few, perhaps as few as five, and considerable interest has focused on Annex II which embraces a much wider range of projects some of which, particularly agricultural projects, have not required any kind of authorisation in Britain. The consultation document said that:

> "the extension of the assessment requirement to Annex II projects is left to the discretion of Member States. In general, the Government does not foresee that it will be necessary to make the carrying out of formal assessments mandatory in such cases . . . It is therefore proposed that in relation to projects falling outside Annex

[5] House of Commons Official Report, First Standing Committee on European Community Documents, June 9, 1981, H.M.S.O.

[6] In a written answer to a Parliamentary Question on November 3, 1986, the Parliamentary Under Secretary of State (Mr. Tracey), reiterated the Government's intention to make full use of existing powers and procedures under planning legislation to implement the requirements of the directive, whilst recognising that a few new legislative provisions would be required. According to him, the Government was still considering the responses made to the consultation paper issued in April 1985 ([1986] J.P.L. 403), and it was too early to say when the necessary orders under the European Communities Act 1972 were likely to be made.

10 Environmental Assessment—The EC Directive

I the appropriate Secretary of State should have the power to direct that an assessment should be carried out in any particular case . . ."

At an earlier stage the Government was not proposing to take any powers to require assessments for projects falling outside Annex I. Not all are satisfied with the proposal that powers should exist just on a case by case basis, and the suggestion has been made that the Secretary of State ought to be able to require assessments also for certain classes of projects or for those fulfilling certain criteria. This would be closer to the, admittedly optional, wording of the Directive. Until the circular and draft Regulations emerge it will not be known whether the Government has been persuaded.

An outline of the statutory provisions that the Government is proposing is contained in an appendix to the Department's consultation paper. It proposes powers to direct that an assessment is or is not required for a particular development, and powers to exempt a particular development. Obligations will be placed on a developer to provide "an assessment" with his planning application where relevant. (This use of the word "assessment" to cover the "information" required of the developer by the Directive gives official reinforcement to the confusion referred to above). Obligations also will be placed on the planning authority to notify statutory consultees and to place the "assessment" with the planning application on Part I of the planning register. In considering the planning application the authority will be required to have regard to the information contained in the "assessment" and to any comments made by the statutory consultees. The decision, including any conditions imposed, will have to be placed on Part II of the planning register. It remains to be seen to what extent these conditions will cover such matters as consents to discharge to water and air and to what extent these matters will continue to be dealt with separately under separate legislation. It must be remembered that one of the intentions behind the Directive is to consider together, in one decision making process, all environmental effects. There is no suggestion that the Government is taking the opportunity of the Directive to integrate all consent giving procedures into one single procedure.

*   *   *   *   *

Council Directive of June 27, 1985 on the assessment of the effects of certain public and private projects on the environment (85/337/EEC)

The Council of the European Communities

Having regard to the Treaty establishing the European Economic Community, and in particular Articles 100 and 235 thereof,

Having regard to the proposal from the Commission.[7]

Having regard to the opinion of the European Parliament.[8]

Having regard to the opinion of the Economic and Social Committee.[9]

Whereas the 1973[10] and 1977[11] action programmes of the European Communities on the environment, as well as the 1983[12] action programme, the main outlines of which have

---

[7] O.J. No. C169, 9.7.1980, p.14.
[8] O.J. No. C66, 15.3.1982, p.89.
[9] O.J. No. C185, 27.7.1981, p.8.
[10] O.J. No. C112, 20.12.1973, p.1.
[11] O.J. No. C139, 13.6.1977, p.1.
[12] O.J. No. C46, 17.2.1983, p.1.

been approved by the Council of the European Communities and the representatives of the Governments of the Member States, stress that the best environmental policy consists in preventing the creation of pollution or nuisances at source, rather than subsequently trying to counteract their effects; whereas they affirm the need to take effects on the environment into account at the earliest possible stage in all the technical planning and decision-making processes; whereas to that end, they provide for the implementation of procedures to evaluate such effects.

Whereas the disparities between the laws in force in the various Member States with regard to the assessment of the environmental effects of public and private projects may create unfavourable competitive conditions and thereby directly affect the functioning of the common market; whereas, therefore, it is necessary to approximate national laws in this field pursuant to Article 100 of the Treaty.

Whereas, in addition, it is necessary to achieve one of the Community's objectives in the sphere of the protection of the environment and the quality of life.

Whereas, since the Treaty has not provided the powers required for this end, recourse should be had to Article 235 of the Treaty.

Whereas general principles for the assessment of environmental effects should be introduced with a view to supplementing and coordinating development consent procedures governing public and private projects likely to have a major effect on the environment.

Whereas development consent for public and private projects which are likely to have significant effects on the environment should be granted only after prior assessment of the likely significant environmental effects of these projects has been carried out; whereas this assessment must be conducted on the basis of the appropriate information supplied by the developer, which may be supplemented by the authorities and by the people who may be concerned by the project in question.

Whereas the principles of the assessment of environmental effects should be harmonised, in particular with reference to the projects which should be subject to assessment, the main obligations of the developers and the content of the assessment.

Whereas projects belonging to certain types have significant effects on the environment and these projects must as a rule be subject to systematic assessment.

Whereas projects of other types may not have significant effects on the environment in every case and whereas these projects should be assessed where the Member States consider that their characteristics so require.

Whereas, for projects which are subject to assessment, a certain minimal amount of information must be supplied, concerning the project and its effects.

Whereas the effects of a project on the environment must be assessed in order to take account of concerns to protect human health, to contribute by means of a better environment to the quality of life, to ensure maintenance of the diversity of species and to maintain the reproductive capacity of the ecosystem as a basic resource for life.

Whereas, however, this Directive should not be applied to projects the details of which are adopted by a specific act of national legislation, since the objectives of this Directive, including that of supplying information, are achieved through the legislative process.

12 Environmental Assessment—The EC Directive

Whereas, furthermore, it may be appropriate in exceptional cases to exempt a specific project from the assessment procedures laid down by this Directive, subject to appropriate information being supplied to the Commission;

Has adopted this Directive:

Article 1

1. This Directive shall apply to the assessment of the environmental effects of those public and private projects which are likely to have significant effects on the environment.

2. For the purposes of this Directive:
"project" means:

— the execution of construction works or of other installations or schemes,
— other interventions in the natural surroundings and landscape including those involving the extraction of mineral resources;

"developer" means:

the applicant for authorisation for a private project or the public authority which initiates a project;

"development consent" means:

the decision of the competent authority or authorities which entitles the developer to proceed with the project.

3. The competent authority or authorities shall be that or those which the Member States designate as responsible for performing the duties arising from this Directive.

4. Projects serving national defence purposes are not covered by this Directive.

5. This Directive shall not apply to projects the details of which are adopted by a specific act of national legislation, since the objectives of this Directive, including that of supplying information, are achieved through the legislative process.

Article 2

1. Member States shall adopt all measures necessary to ensure that, before consent is given, projects likely to have significant effects on the environment by virtue *inter alia*, of their nature, size or location are made subject to an assessment with regard to their effects.

These projects are defined in Article 4.

2. The environmental impact assessment may be integrated into the existing procedures for consent to projects in the Member States, or, failing this, into other procedures or into procedures to be established to comply with the aims of this Directive.

3. Member States may, in exceptional cases, exempt a specific project in whole or in part from the provisions laid down in this Directive.

In this event, the Member States shall:

(a) consider whether another form of assessment would be appropriate and whether the information thus collected should be made available to the public;

(b) make available to the public concerned the information relating to the exemption and the reasons for granting it;

(c) inform the Commission, prior to granting consent, of the reasons justifying the exemption granted, and provide it with the information made available, where appropriate, to their own nationals.

The Commission shall immediately forward the documents received to the other Member States.

The Commission shall report annually to the Council on the application of this paragraph.

Article 3

The environmental impact assessment will identify, describe and assess in an appropriate manner, in the light of each individual case and in accordance with the Articles 4 to 11, the direct and indirect effects of a project on the following factors:

— human beings, fauna and flora,
— soil, water, air, climate and the landscape,
— the interaction between the factors mentioned in the first and second indents,
— material assets and the cultural heritage.

Article 4

1. Subject to Article 2(3), projects of the classes listed in Annex I shall be made subject to an assessment in accordance with Articles 5 to 10.

2. Projects of the classes listed in Annex II shall be made subject to an assessment, in accordance with Articles 5 to 10, where Member States consider that their characteristics so require.

To this end Member States may *inter alia* specify certain types of projects as being subject to an assessment or may establish the criteria and/or thresholds necessary to determine which of the projects of the classes listed in Annex II are to be subject to an assessment in accordance with Articles 5 to 10.

Article 5

1. In the case of projects which, pursuant to Article 4, must be subjected to an environmental impact assessment in accordance with Articles 5 to 10, Member States shall adopt the necessary measures to ensure that the developer supplies in an appropriate form the information specified in Annex III inasmuch as:

(a) the Member States consider that the information is relevant to a given stage of the consent procedure and to the specific characteristics of a particular project or type of project and of the environmental features likely to be affected;

(b) the Member States consider that a developer may reasonably be required to compile this information having regard *inter alia* to current knowledge and methods of assessment.

2. The information to be provided by the developer in accordance with paragraph 1 shall include at least:

14 Environmental Assessment—The EC Directive

- a description of the project comprising information on the site, design and size of the project,
- a description of the measures envisaged in order to avoid, reduce and, if possible, remedy significant adverse effects,
- the data required to identify and assess the main effects which the project is likely to have on the environment,
- a non-technical summary of the information mentioned in indents 1 to 3.

3. Where they consider it necessary, Member States shall ensure that any authorities with relevant information in their possession make this information available to the developer.

Article 6

1. Member States shall take the measures necessary to ensure that the authorities likely to be concerned by the project by reason of their specific environmental responsibilities are given an opportunity to express their opinion on the request for development consent. Member States shall designate the authorities to be consulted for this purpose in general terms or in each case when the request for consent is made. The information gathered pursuant to Article 5 shall be forwarded to these authorities. Detailed arrangements for consultation shall be laid down by the Member States.

2. Member States shall ensure that:

- any request for development consent and any information gathered pursuant to Article 5 are made available to the public,
- the public concerned is given the opportunity to express an opinion before the project is initiated.

3. The detailed arrangements for such information and consultation shall be determined by the Member States, which may in particular, depending on the particular characteristics of the projects or sites concerned:

- determine the public concerned,
- specify the places where the information can be consulted,
- specify the way in which the public may be informed, for example by bill-posting within a certain radius, publication in local newspapers, organisation of exhibitions with plans, drawings, tables, graphs, models,
- determine the manner in which the public is to be consulted, for example, by written submissions, by public enquiry,
- fix appropriate time limits for the various stages of the procedure in order to ensure that a decision is taken within a reasonable period.

Article 7

Where a Member State is aware that a project is likely to have significant effects on the environment in another Member State or where a Member State likely to be significantly affected so requests, the Member State in whose territory the project is intended to be carried out shall forward the information gathered pursuant to Article 5 to the other Member State at the same time as it makes it available to its own nationals. Such information shall serve as a basis for any consultations necessary in the framework of the bilateral relations between two Member States on a reciprocal and equivalent basis.

Article 8

Information gathered pursuant to Articles 5, 6 and 7 must be taken into consideration in the development consent procedure.

Article 9

When a decision has been taken, the competent authority or authorities shall inform the public concerned of:

— the content of the decision and any conditions attached thereto,
— the reasons and considerations on which the decision is based where the Member States' legislation so provides.

The detailed arrangements for such information shall be determined by the Member States.

If another Member State has been informed pursuant to Article 7, it will also be informed of the decision in question.

Article 10

The provisions of this Directive shall not affect the obligation on the competent authorities to respect the limitations imposed by national regulations and administrative provisions and accepted legal practices with regard to industrial and commercial secrecy and the safeguarding of the public interest.

Where Article 7 applies, the transmission of information to another Member State and the reception of information by another Member State shall be subject to the limitations in force in the Member State in which the project is proposed.

Article 11

1. The Member States and the Commission shall exchange information on the experience gained in applying this Directive.

2. In particular, Member States shall inform the Commission of any criteria and/or thresholds adopted for the selection of the projects in question, in accordance with Article 4(2), or of the types of projects concerned which, pursuant to Article 4(2), are subject to assessment in accordance with Articles 5 to 10.

3. Five years after notification of this Directive, the Commission shall send the European Parliament and the Council a report on its application and effectiveness. The report shall be based on the aforementioned exchange of information.

4. On the basis of this exchange of information, the Commission shall submit to the Council additional proposals, should this be necessary, with a view to this Directive's being applied in a sufficiently coordinated manner.

16 Environmental Assessment—The EC Directive

Article 12

1. Member States shall take the measures necessary to comply with this Directive within three years of its notification.[13]

2. Member States shall communicate to the Commission the texts of the provisions of national law which they adopt in the field covered by this Directive.

Article 13

The provisions of this Directive shall not affect the right of Member States to lay down stricter rules regarding scope and procedure when assessing environmental effects.

Article 14

This Directive is addressed to the Member States.

Done at Luxembourg, June 27, 1985.

For the Council
The President
A. BIONDI

ANNEX I

Projects Subject to Article 4(1)

1. Crude-oil refineries (excluding undertakings manufacturing only lubricants from crude oil) and installations for the gasification and liquefaction of 500 tonnes or more of coal or bituminous shale per day.

2. Thermal power stations and other combustion installations with a heat output of 300 megawatts or more and nuclear power stations and other nuclear reactors (except research installations for the production and conversion of fissionable and fertile materials, whose maximum power does not exceed 1 kilowatt continuous thermal load).

3. Installations solely designed for the permanent storage or final disposal of radioactive waste.

4. Integrated works for the initial melting of cast-iron and steel.

5. Installations for the extraction of asbestos and for the processing and transformation of asbestos and products containing asbestos: for asbestos-cement products, with an annual production of more than 20,000 tonnes of finished products, for friction material, with an annual production of more than 50 tonnes of finished products, and for other uses of asbestos, utilisation of more than 200 tonnes per year.

6. Integrated chemical installations.

[13] This Directive was notified to the Member States on July 3. 1985.

7. Construction of motorways, express roads[14] and lines for long-distance railway traffic and of airports[15] with a basic runway length of 2,100 m or more.

8. Trading ports and also inland waterways and ports for inland-waterway traffic which permit the passage of vessels of over 1,350 tonnes.

9. Waste-disposal installations for the incineration, chemical treatment or land fill of toxic and dangerous wastes.

ANNEX II

Projects Subject to Article 4(2)

1. Agriculture

(a) Projects for the restructuring of rural land holdings.
(b) Projects for the use of uncultivated land or semi-natural areas for intensive agricultural purposes.
(c) Water-management projects for agriculture.
(d) Initial afforestation where this may lead to adverse ecological changes and land reclamation for the purposes of conversion to another type of land use.
(e) Poultry-rearing installations.
(f) Pig-rearing installations.
(g) Salmon breeding.
(h) Reclamation of land from the sea.

2. Extractive industry

(a) Extraction of peat.
(b) Deep drillings with the exception of drillings for investigating the stability of the soil and in particular:
— geothermal drilling,
— drilling for the storage of nuclear waste material,
— drilling for water supplies.
(c) Extraction of minerals other than metalliferous and energy-producing minerals, such as marble, sand, gravel, shale, salt, phosphates and potash.
(d) Extraction of coal and lignite by underground mining.
(e) Extraction of coal and lignite by open-cast mining.
(f) Extraction of petroleum.
(g) Extraction of natural gas.
(h) Extraction of ores.
(i) Extraction of bituminous shale.
(j) Extraction of minerals other than metalliferous and energy-producing minerals by open-cast mining.
(k) Surface industrial installations for the extraction of coal, petroleum, natural gas and ores, as well as bituminous shale.

---

[14] For the purposes of the Directive, "express road" means a road which complies with the definition in the European Agreement on main international traffic arteries of November 15, 1975.
[15] For the purposes of this Directive, "airport" means airports which comply with the definition in the 1944 Chicago Convention setting up the International Civil Aviation Organization (Annex 14).

18   Environmental Assessment—The EC Directive

(*l*) Coke ovens (dry coal distillation).
(*m*) Installations for the manufacture of cement.

3. Energy industry

(*a*) Industrial installations for the production of electricity, steam and hot water (unless included in Annex I).
(*b*) Industrial installations for carrying gas, steam and hot water; transmission of electrical energy by overhead cables.
(*c*) Surface storage of natural gas.
(*d*) Underground storage of combustible gases.
(*e*) Surface storage of fossil fuels.
(*f*) Industrial briquetting of coal and lignite.
(*g*) Installations for the production or enrichment of nuclear fuels.
(*h*) Installations for the reprocessing of irradiated nuclear fuels.
(*i*) Installations for the collection and processing of radioactive waste (unless included in Annex I).
(*j*) Installations for hydroelectric energy production.

4. Processing of metals

(*a*) Iron and steelworks, including foundries, forges, drawing plants and rolling mills (unless included in Annex I).
(*b*) Installations for the production, including smelting, refining, drawing and rolling, of non-ferrous metals, excluding precious metals.
(*c*) Pressing, drawing and stamping of large castings.
(*d*) Surface treatment and coating of metals.
(*e*) Boilermaking, manufacture of reservoirs, tanks and other sheet-metal containers.
(*f*) Manufacture and assembly of motor vehicles and manufacture of motor-vehicle engines.
(*g*) Shipyards.
(*h*) Installations for the construction and repair of aircraft.
(*i*) Manufacture of railway equipment.
(*j*) Swaging by explosives.
(*k*) Installations for the roasting and sintering of metallic ores.

5. Manufacture of glass

6. Chemical industry

(*a*) Treatment of intermediate products and production of chemicals (unless included in Annex I).
(*b*) Production of pesticides and pharmaceutical products, paint and varnishes, elastomers and peroxides.
(*c*) Storage facilities for petroleum, petrochemical and chemical products.

7. Food industry

(*a*) Manufacture of vegetable and animal oils and fats.
(*b*) Packing and canning of animal and vegetable products.

(c) Manufacture of dairy products.
(d) Brewing and malting.
(e) Confectionery and syrup manufacture.
(f) Installations for the slaughter of animals.
(g) Industrial starch manufacturing installations.
(h) Fish-meal and fish-oil factories.
(i) Sugar factories.

8. Textile, leather, wood and paper industries

(a) Wool scouring, degreasing and bleaching factories.
(b) Manufacture of fibre board, particle board and plywood.
(c) Manufacture of pulp, paper and board.
(d) Fibre-dyeing factories.
(e) Cellulose-processing and production installations.
(f) Tannery and leather-dressing factories.

9. Rubber industry

Manufacture and treatment of elastomer-based products.

10. Infrastructure projects

(a) Industrial-estate development projects.
(b) Urban-development projects.
(c) Ski-lifts and cable-cars.
(d) Construction of roads, harbours, including fishing harbours, and airfields (projects not listed in Annex I).
(e) Canalization and flood-relief works.
(f) Dams and other installations designed to hold water or store it on a long-term basis.
(g) Tramways, elevated and underground railways, suspended lines or similar lines of a particular type, used exclusively or mainly for passenger transport.
(h) Oil and gas pipeline installations.
(i) Installation of long-distance aqueducts.
(j) Yacht marinas.

11. Other projects

(a) Holiday villages, hotel complexes.
(b) Permanent racing and test tracks for cars and motor cycles.
(c) Installations for the disposal of industrial and domestic waste (unless included in Annex I).
(d) Waste water treatment plants.
(e) Sludge-deposition sites.
(f) Storage of scrap iron.
(g) Test benches for engines, turbines or reactors.
(h) Manufacture of artificial mineral fibres.
(i) Manufacture, packing, loading or placing in cartridges of gunpowder and explosives.
(j) Knackers' yards.

20   Environmental Assessment—The EC Directive

12. **Modifications to development projects included in Annex I and projects in Annex I undertaken exclusively or mainly for the development and testing of new methods or products and not used for more than one year.**

ANNEX III

Information Referred to in Article 5(1)

1. Description of the project, including in particular:

   — a description of the physical characteristics of the whole project and the land-use requirements during the construction and operational phases,
   — a description of the main characteristics of the production processes, for instance, nature and quantity of the materials used,
   — an estimate, by type and quantity, of expected residues and emissions (water, air and soil pollution, noise, vibration, light, heat, radiation, etc.) resulting from the operation of the proposed project.

2. Where appropriate, an outline of the main alternatives studied by the developer and an indication of the main reasons for his choice, taking into account the environmental effects.

3. A description of the aspects of the environment likely to be significantly affected by the proposed project, including, in particular, population, fauna, flora, soil, water, air, climatic factors, material assets, including the architectural and archaeological heritage, landscape and the inter-relationship between the above factors.

4. A description[16] of the likely significant effects of the proposed project on the environment resulting from:

   — the existence of the project,
   — the use of natural resources,
   — the emission of pollutants, the creation of nuisances and the elimination of waste;

   and the description by the developer of the forecasting methods used to assess the effects on the environment.

5. A description of the measures envisaged to prevent, reduce and where possible offset any significant adverse effects on the environment.

6. A non-technical summary of the information provided under the above headings.

7. An indication of any difficulties (technical deficiencies or lack of know-how) encountered by the developer in compiling the required information.

---

[16] This description should cover the direct effects and any indirect, secondary, cumulative, short, medium and long-term, permanent and temporary, positive and negative effects of the project.

[16]

Waste Policy and European Community Law: Does the EEC Treaty Provide a Suitable Framework for Regulating Waste?

*Jan H. Jans**

INTRODUCTION

European Economic Community (EEC) law on waste disposal is a complex field. Three sources of the complexity stand out: directives, treaty provisions, and case law.

First, there are many directives[1] concerning waste, waste disposal, and waste transportation. The most important of these directives are:

— the Directive on Waste (Directive 75/442,[2] as amended by Directive 91/156[3]), containing general rules which, among other things, mandate that Member States take steps to ensure proper disposal,[4] develop waste disposal plans,[5] and create permit programs;[6]

— the Directive on Toxic and Dangerous Waste (Directive 78/319),[7] containing general rules which mandate that Member States take steps to ensure proper disposal,[8] develop waste disposal plans,[9] and create permit programs;[10]

* Professor of European Environmental Law, Centre for Environmental Law, University of Amsterdam; Ph.D. 1987, State University of Groningen, Netherlands; Advisor to Commissie voor de milieu-effectrapportage [Commission on Environmental Impact Assessment] and to Centrale raad voor de milieunygëine [Central Council on Environmental Hygiene].

1. Directives are statements of EEC policy, which Member States are allowed to implement in ways appropriate to that particular national system. They are binding only "as to the result to be achieved." TREATY ESTABLISHING THE EUROPEAN ECONOMIC COMMUNITY [EEC TREATY] art. 189.

2. Council Directive 75/442, 1975 O.J. (L 194) 39.

3. Council Directive 91/156, 1991 O.J. (L 78) 32.

4. Council Directive 75/442, *supra* note 2, art. 4.

5. *Id.* art. 7.

6. *Id.* art. 9.

7. Council Directive 78/319, 1978 O.J. (L 84) 43. This Directive will be replaced on Dec. 12, 1993 by Council Directive 91/689, 1991 O.J. (L 377) 20.

8. Council Directive 91/689, art. 2, 1991 O.J. (L 377) 20.

9. *Id.* art. 6.

10. *Id.* art. 2.

— the Directive on the Disposal of Waste Oils (Directive 75/439,[11] as amended by Directive 87/101[12]), requiring Member States to ensure the safe collection and disposal of waste oil and to maximize its recycling,[13] and prohibiting certain discharges;[14] and

— the Directive on the Supervision and Control Within the European Community of the Transfrontier Shipment of Hazardous Waste (Directive 84/631,[15] as amended by Directive 86/279[16]), requiring notification of shipments,[17] mandating acknowledgements,[18] and allowing for objections and conditions.[19]

Second, general rules of the EEC Treaty are relevant in Member States' development of waste policies. In particular, the articles concerning the free movement of goods in the community (articles 30, 34, and 36)[20] and the articles on services (articles 59-65)[21] are important.

Third, the European Court of Justice[22] (the Court) has provided substantial new case law on the transportation of waste.[23] The case law of the Court is particularly relevant because the Court has the final word in interpreting the law as it stands; in practice, therefore, case law has great precedential value.

EEC directives, the EEC Treaty, and EEC case law make the understanding of all of the legal aspects of EEC waste law a difficult task.

---

11. Council Directive 75/439, 1975 O.J. (L 194) 23.
12. Council Directive 87/101, 1987 O.J. (L 42) 43.
13. *Id.* art. 3.
14. *Id.* art. 4.
15. Council Directive 84/631, 1984 O.J. (L 326) 31 (to be replaced by Council Regulation 259/93, 1993 O.J. (L 30) 1 (implementing Basel Convention)).
16. Council Directive 86/279, 1986 O.J. (L 181) 13.
17. *Id.* art. 3.
18. *Id.*
19. *Id.* art. 4.
20. Article 30 prohibits quantitative restrictions on imports and all measures having equivalent effects. Article 34 prohibits quantitative restrictions on exports, and all measures having equivalent effects. Article 36 allows for restrictions on trade if they are necessary for human health or the protection of animals and plants. EEC TREATY arts. 30, 34, 36.
21. The articles on services require, for instance, that foreign waste disposal companies have non-discriminatory access to the national waste disposal market. *See id.* art. 65.
22. The Court was established by the Treaty of Paris. TREATY ESTABLISHING THE EUROPEAN COAL AND STEEL COMMUNITY, art. 32, [ECSC TREATY]. The Court is composed of 13 justices, one from each of the Member States, plus a rotating thirteenth justice. *Id.* It is solidly based on the civil law tradition and also serves as a lawmaker.
23. The most important cases are: Case 21/79, Commission v. Italy, 1980 E.C.R. 1, 2 C.M.L.R. 613 (1980); Case 172/82, Syndicat National des Fabricants Raffineurs v. Inter-Huiles, 1983 E.C.R. 555, 3 C.M.L.R. 485 (1983); Case 240/83, Procureur de la Republique v. ADBHU, 1985 E.C.R. 531; Case 239/85, Commission v. Belgium, 1986 E.C.R. 645, 1 C.M.L.R. 248 (1988); Case 372-374/85, Ministère Public v. Traen, 1987 E.C.R. 2141, 3 C.M.L.R. 511 (1987); Case 302/86, Commission v. Denmark, 1988 E.C.R. 4607, 1 C.M.L.R. 619 (1989) [Danish Bottle Case]; Case 380/87, Base v. Comune di Cinicello Balsamo, 1989 E.C.R. 2491, 1 C.M.L.R. 313 (1991); Joined Cases 206/88 & 207/88m, Criminal Proceedings against Vessoso & Zanetti, 1990 E.C.R. 1461.

However, I will not attempt to discuss all the detail of this interesting field of law. Instead, this piece focuses on the following central question: does the EEC Treaty provide an adequate and suitable framework for regulating waste disposal and developing waste prevention policies? In particular, I will discuss some of the consequences of considering, in terms of the EEC Treaty, waste as a "good."[24]

I

IS WASTE A "GOOD"?

Recently, in *Commission v. Belgium*, the Court was faced with the critical question of whether waste is to be regarded as a "good" in the context of the EEC Treaty.[25] Despite arguments that the Court should distinguish between recyclable and non-recyclable waste, the Court held that all waste had to be treated as a "good." The court reasoned that, from a practical point of view ("du point de vue pratique"), serious difficulties would arise, especially with respect to border control, if such a distinction were made.[26] Such a distinction would also be based on uncertain characteristics—which, because of technical developments and the profitability of re-used waste, could be changed in time. Because of these factors, the Court found that all waste should be treated as a "good" under Article 30 of the EEC Treaty.[27]

II

APPLICATION OF EEC LAW TO GOODS

If waste is to be regarded as a "good"—as *Commission v. Belgium* appears to hold—several consequences will follow. Basically, regulation of waste transportation is subject to the same free trade restrictions as other goods.

First of all, the articles in the EEC Treaty become applicable. Article 30 prohibits quantitative restrictions on imports and all measures having equivalent effect between the Member States.[28] Article 34 prohib-

---

24. In this article, I refer to the terms "good" and "product" interchangeably. This convention is commonly observed by other scholars and lawyers.

25. Case C-2/90, Commission v. Belgium, (July 9, 1992), *available in* LEXIS, INTNAT library, CJCS file. A summary of this case is available in Common Mkt. Rep. (CCH) ¶ 96,591 (Oct. 1992). There were also some earlier rulings by the Court which, in a more implicit manner, made it clear that waste falls under the normal rules of the free movement of goods within the EEC. *See, e.g., Inter-Huiles*, 1983 E.C.R. 555; *ADBHU*, 1985 E.C.R. 531.

26. Case C-2/90, Commission v. Belgium, opinion ¶ 27.

27. *Id.* at 15-16. *Cf.* PETER VON WILMOWSKY, ABFALLWIRTSCHAFT IM BINNENMARKT: EUROPÄISCHE PROBLEME UND AMERIKANISCHE ERFAHRUNGEN 161-63 (1990) (arguing that waste is distinguishable from goods, and that waste disposal falls under the rules concerning services as opposed to the rules concerning free movement of goods); Peter von Wilmowsky, *Abfall ud reier Warenverkehr: Bestandsaufnahme nach dem EuGH-Urteil zum Wallonischen Einfuhrverbot*, 1992 EUROPARECHT 414, 416.

28. EEC TREATY, art. 28.

its quantitative restrictions on exports and all measures having equivalent effect.[29]

According to the ruling in the *Dassonville* case, article 30 covers all trading rules enacted by Member States that are capable of hindering, directly or indirectly, actually or potentially, intra-community trade.[30] For the environmental sector, this includes import bans, import licensing systems, packaging and labelling obligations, user restrictions, and duties to notify.

We also must note that these rules on the free movement of goods are not only directed to national authorities, but also to the Commission and the Council. Unlike the United States, where the federal government may burden interstate commerce,[31] the Council is bound by the provisions of articles 30, 34, and 36 of the Treaty—although experts are unsure whether these rules apply to the EEC institutions in exactly the same strict manner as they apply to the Member States.[32] EEC policy and regulations, therefore, must meet, in principle, the requirements of those Treaty provisions.

A ruling on this important issue was made in the *Inter-Huiles* case.[33] In that case, the Court held that article 34's prohibition includes (1) all national measures whose specific object or effect is to restrict patterns of exports and (2) the establishment of differing treatment between the domestic trade of a Member State and its export trade so as to provide a special advantage for domestic products.[34] The Court also held that provisions of EEC directives which create these effects are similarly contrary to article 34.[35] EEC policies are thus restricted to the scope granted to the EEC institutions.

III
ENVIRONMENTAL JUSTIFICATIONS FOR LIMITS TO FREE TRADE

However, restrictions on trade can be justified if they are necessary for "the protection of health and life of humans, animals or plants"[36] or if they are necessary for the protection of the environment.[37] In deter-

---

29. *Id.* art. 34.

30. Case 8/74, Precureur du Roi v. Dassonville, 1974 E.C.R. 851, 852, 2 C.M.L.R. 436, 444 (1974). For a discussion of the *Dassonville* case and EEC articles 30-36, see LAURENCE W. GORMLEY, PROHIBITING RESTRICTION ON TRADE WITHIN THE EEC (1985); PETER OLIVER, FREE MOVEMENT OF GOODS IN THE EEC (2d ed. 1988).

31. U.S. CONST. art. I, § 8, cl. 3.

32. *See* WILMOWSKY, *supra* note 27 (suggesting that the rules on the free movement of goods apply to Community institutions as well as Member States).

33. *Inter-Huiles*, 1983 E.C.R. 555.

34. *Id.* at 566.

35. *Id.*

36. EEC TREATY art. 36.

37. This environmental protection exception derives from the *Danish Bottle Case*, 1988 E.C.R. 4607.

mining the extent of these justifications, the Court has generally used two limiting principles: proportionality and non-discrimination.

A. Commission v. Belgium

Commission v. Belgium[38] is the most recent major case in this area. It has also set the stage by holding that waste is a "good."[39] For these reasons, it is important to take note of the Court's reasoning.

The Court was confronted with the Regional Executive of Wallonia's[40] prohibition of the deposit in Wallonia of waste originating in other Member States.[41] The Commission[42] viewed Wallonia's action as incompatible with EEC law. The Court, in rendering its decision, did find the absolute restriction on hazardous waste trade to be incompatible with the system established by Directive 84/631, but the Court found the non-hazardous restriction—in the absence of any specific provision concerning the transportation of non-hazardous waste in Directive 75/442— to be justified, under article 30, because of the special character of waste.[43]

In analyzing Wallonia's prohibition, the Court first examined the measures in light of Directives 75/442 and 84/631.[44]

With respect to Directive 75/442, the Court pointed out that neither the general framework of that Directive, nor any of its provisions, specifically covered waste trade between Member States. Nor did the Directive impose a prohibition on adopting measures such as those introduced by Wallonia. Therefore, there was no breach of Directive 75/442.[45]

Concerning Directive 84/631, the Court initially noted that the Directive introduced a system under which national authorities could raise objections to the transportation of hazardous waste and thus prohibit a specific transfrontier shipment.[46] Thus, the Court held, the system im-

---

38. Case C-2/90, Commission v. Belgium.

39. *Id.* at 15-16.

40. Wallonia is one of three autonomous provinces in Belgium. Wallonia covers the southeast portion of the country and is French speaking. 1 EUROPA PUBLICATIONS, THE EUROPA WORLD YEAR BOOK 1992, at 482-84 (1992).

In European law, the federal or central government (i.e., Belgium) is liable for breaches of European law caused by the local or regional authorities (i.e., Wallonia). *See, e.g.,* Joined Cases C-227-230/85, Commission v. Belgium, 1988 E.C.R. 1, 2 C.M.L.R. 797 (1989) (internal governmental difficulties not an adequate justification for Belgium's failure to implement environmental directives).

41. Case C-2/90, Commission v. Belgium.

42. The Commission's most important function is to draft all legislation. It also prosecutes all violations of EEC law, negotiates for the EEC, and administers the EEC's budget. 1 EUROPA PUBLICATIONS, *supra* note 40, at 146.

43. Case C-2/90, Commission v. Belgium, opinion ¶¶ 20, 35.

44. *Id.* For a discussion of the directives, see *supra* text accompanying notes 2-6, 15-19.

45. Case C-2/90, Commission v. Belgium, opinion ¶ 14.

46. *Id.* It is important to note that Directive 84/631 only allows this prohibition in order to prevent problems related to environmental protection and public health and safety. Council

plicitly did not allow Member States to *completely* prohibit such movements. Because the Belgian regulation imposed an absolute prohibition on the importation of hazardous waste into Wallonia, it did not comply with Directive 84/631.[47]

Next, on the issue of transportation of non-hazardous waste—which is not covered by directive 84/631—the Court examined the Wallonia legislation in light of articles 30 and 36 of the EEC Treaty. The Court decided that waste, recyclable or not, had to be treated as a product, the free movement of which, pursuant to article 30 of the Treaty, could not in principle be restricted.[48]

However, the Court also found that waste was a product with a special character: the simple accumulation of waste, even before it constituted a danger to health, represented a danger to the environment. The Court found this danger especially present in view of the limited capacity of each region or area to accommodate the storage of vast quantities of waste. Because of this special character, the Court found compelling Wallonia's argument that mandatory requirements of environmental protection justified the disputed measures.[49]

The Commission argued in response that these mandatory requirements for environmental protection and health and safety could not be relied on to allow Wallonia's restrictions. The Commission insisted that the measures at issue discriminated against waste coming from other Member States, though that waste was no more harmful than that produced in Wallonia.[50] The same line of reasoning was developed by Advocate General Jacobs in his opinion.[51] In the Advocate General's view, there was "plain" discrimination between foreign and Belgian waste and therefore the ruling of the Court in the *Danish Bottle Case*[52] could not serve as precedent.

The Court, however, took a surprisingly new approach. The Court found it necessary to take into account the specific nature of the waste in determining whether the barrier in question was discriminatory.[53] The proximity principle of the EEC Treaty[54]—which states that environmen-

---

Directive 84/631, art. 4, 1984 O.J. (L 326) 31, 33, 34.

47. Case C-2/90, Commission v. Belgium, opinion ¶¶ 20-21.

48. *Id.* opinion ¶ 27.

49. *Id.* opinion ¶ 32.

50. *Id.* opinion ¶ 33.

51. The Advocate General is a special lawyer who acts as a permanent amicus curiae for the EEC, and analyzes and evaluates all cases before the Court. There are six Advocates General appointed for six year terms. EEC TREATY arts. 166-67.

52. *Danish Bottle Case*, 1988 E.C.R. 4607.

53. Case C-2/90, Commission v. Belgium, opinion ¶ 34.

54. "Action by the Community relating to the environment shall be based on the principles that preventative action should be taken, *that environmental damage should as a priority be rectified at source*, and that the polluter should pay. Environmental protection requirements shall be a component of the Community's other policies." EEC TREATY art. 130R(2)

tal damage should as a priority be rectified at its source—implied that it was incumbent on each region, community, or other local authority to take the measures appropriate to ensure the proper reception, treatment, and disposal of its own waste. Such waste, therefore, had to be disposed of as close as possible to the place of its production in order to minimize its transportation.[55]

The Court held that the proximity principle was consistent with the principles set out in the Basel Convention on the Control of Transboundary Movements of Hazardous Waste and Disposal,[56] a convention to which the EEC was a signatory.[57] The Court came to the following conclusion: in view of the differences between waste produced in one place and that produced in another, and in view of the waste's connection with the place where it was produced, the Belgian measures could not be considered discriminatory.[58]

B. Proportionality

In relying on environmental justifications for interferences with trade, Member States must first observe the "principle of proportionality": the aim of protecting the environment, or the health and life of humans, animals, and plants, must be achieved by the means least restrictive of intra-Community trade.[59] The Court always examines whether the contested rules are really necessary to achieve the rules' objectives. In *Commission v. Belgium*, however, the Court did not examine whether Wallonia's import bans met the requirements of this prin-

---

(as amended 1987) (emphasis added).

55. Case C-2/90, Commission v. Belgium. If the nearest waste disposal installation is in another country, there can be a tension between the "self sufficiency principle" and the "proximity principle"—with respect to both exports and imports. *See* Directive 75/442, *supra* note 2, art. 5 (delegating authority for planning, organization, authorization, and supervision of waste disposal operations).

56. Case C-2/90, Commission v. Belgium, opinion ¶ 35. Basel Convention on the Control of Transboundary Movements of Hazardous Waste, March 22, 1989, 28 I.L.M. 649 (1989) [hereinafter Basel Convention]. For a comparison of the Basel Convention directives with the EC directives, see Stephen B. Straske II, *The United Nations Basel Convention on the Control of Transboundary Movements of Hazardous Wastes and Their Disposal*, 3 GEO. INT'L ENVTL. L. REV. 183 (1990).

57. The EEC has not yet ratified this convention, partly because Directive 84/631 must be amended so that it is consistent with the Convention. There is a certain amount of consensus on the changes that need to occur in Directive 84/631 and that ratification of the Convention should follow that amendment. *See supra* note 15.

58. Case C-2/90, Commission v. Belgium, opinion ¶ 36.

59. *See, e.g., ADBHU*, 1985 E.C.R. at 549 (finding that the directive providing means by which Member States may dispose of waste oil does not restrict trade in violation of Community law principles); *Danish Bottle Case*, 1988 E.C.R. at 4629 (Danish legislation requiring use of returnable containers was more restrictive of imports than necessary). The principle of proportionality can be traced back to Case 7/68, Commission v. Italian Republic, 1968 E.C.R. 423, 430.

ciple. This seems like a remarkable omission, bringing into doubt the Court's reasoning.

C. *Non-Discrimination*

Another important element to be observed by Member States relying on environmental justifications is the rule of non-discrimination: measures protecting the environment must be applicable to both domestic and imported products, without distinction. Article 36 of the EEC Treaty states this in somewhat different language, leaving the Member States some room for differentiation: Restrictions on trade "shall . . . not constitute a means of arbitrary discrimination or disguised restriction on trade between Member States."[60] However, in the Wallonia case, the Court seemed to limit the significance of this principle, holding that waste has a special character and that legislation can discriminate between domestic and foreign waste.[61]

IV
PROXIMITY

Perhaps the primary guiding value in European waste disposal policy is the "proximity principle."[62] It is now official EEC policy that waste should be disposed of at the nearest appropriate installation. According to the new article 5 of the framework Directive 75/442, Member States are obliged

> to establish an integrated and adequate network of disposal installations, taking account of the best available technology not involving excessive costs. The network must enable the Community as a whole to become self-sufficient in waste disposal and the Member States to move towards that aim individually, taking into account geographical circumstances or the need for specialized installations for certain types of waste. The network must also enable waste to be disposed of in one of the nearest appropriate installations, by means of the most appropriate methods and technologies in order to ensure a high level of protection for the environment and public health.[63]

The problem with the proximity principle is that the nearest installation will generally be in the same country as where the waste is produced. It is more or less a disguised "self-sufficiency principle." However, the nearest waste disposal facility may not operate under the soundest environmental conditions. The proximity principle would then contradict the proportionality requirements, as well as the ethos of environmental protection and the general rules in the EEC Treaty concerning

---

60. EEC TREATY art. 36.
61. Case C-2/90, Commission v. Belgium, opinion ¶¶ 34-36.
62. *Id.*
63. *See* Council Directive 91/156, art. 5, 1991 O.J. (L 78) 34.

the free movement of goods.[64] This seems to be the flaw in the Court's reasoning in the Wallonia case.

The Basel Convention on the import and export of dangerous waste also mandates that states should dispose of their waste in their own country.[65] It states that there should be no free movement of waste, unless there are environmental reasons to decide otherwise. Although this apparently contradicts the EEC Treaty, which states that there should be free movement of goods, including waste, unless there is an environmental reason to restrict trade,[66] the Court does not view the two treaties as contradictory.[67]

V

PROFITABILITY JUSTIFICATIONS

One of the reasons for Member States to prohibit the export of waste is to ensure that their own national waste disposal installations can operate profitably. There is always the danger that, as a result of the export of large quantities of waste, the capacity of national disposal installations will be greater than the demand for waste disposal. This can result in underutilized national waste disposal capacity, inflated prices of waste disposal, and the creation of even more waste exports. To avoid this, some Member States want to restrict the export of waste, improving the supply for their own national disposal installations.

A fine example of this can be found in the *Inter-Huiles* case.[68] According to French law, all waste oil must be delivered to officially authorized waste oil collectors.[69] By implication, this legislation prohibited the export of waste oils to foreign countries, including other Member States, because they were not authorized. The French Government argued that the disputed legislation satisfied an economic requirement, since only the collection of all waste oils sufficiently ensured the profitability of approved waste oil undertakings.[70] The Court rejected this argument. It found that the waste oil directive required Member States to grant indemnities to such undertakings—financed according to the "polluter pays" principle—instead of establishing export restrictions.[71]

A similar decision can be found in the *Nertsvoederfabrick* case.[72] A Dutch law required poultry offal to be delivered only to licensed render-

64. EEC TREATY art. 30.
65. Basel Convention, *supra* note 56, art. 4, sec. 2(d), 28 I.L.M. at 662.
66. EEC TREATY art. 130.
67. Case C-2/90, Commission v. Belgium, opinion ¶ 36.
68. *Inter-Huiles*, 1983 E.C.R. 555.
69. *Id.* at 564.
70. *Id.* at 566.
71. *Id.*
72. Case 118/86, Openbar Ministrie v. Nertsvoederfabrick, 1987 E.C.R. 3883.

ing plants.[73] This law implied a prohibition of exports as well. The Netherlands government argued that the law was essential to maintain the overall effectiveness of the Dutch system.[74] With respect to the export restrictions only, the Court held that these were not necessary and therefore incompatible with article 34 of the EEC Treaty.[75]

On the other hand, Directive 84/631 on the import and export of hazardous waste states that Member States may raise objections to the export of waste on the grounds that the shipment of waste adversely affects the implementation of their waste disposal plans.[76]

In conclusion, it is still uncertain to what extent EEC law allows Member States to restrict the export of waste to ensure the profitability of their national waste disposal installations. This is so because there is a conflict between case law and the directives. The Court, in the *Inter-Huiles* case and the *Nertsvoederfabrick* case, suggests that these restrictions are not allowed, but the new framework directive on waste[77] and the import/export directive[78] seem to point in the opposite direction.

VI
EXTRATERRITORIAL PROTECTION JUSTIFICATIONS

Another legal problem not yet fully resolved in EEC law is the question of extraterritorial environmental responsibilities for the export of waste. Can a Member State refuse to export waste on the grounds that the manner of waste disposal in the import state does not comply with the standards of the export state? The Basel Convention explicitly warrants this sort of regulation.[79]

With respect to waste oils, this question was decided in the *Inter-Huiles* case. The French Government refused to allow the export of waste oil in part because it feared environmental damage in Belgium. The Court, however, rejected this argument. The Court reasoned as follows: "Clearly, the environment is protected just as effectively when the

---

73. *Id.* at 3884 (citing Netherlands Destructiewet (law on the destruction of cattle carcasses and animal offal) of 21 Feb. 1957, Stb. 1975/84).
74. *Id.* at 3889.
75. *Id.* at 3909. The Court did not make any rulings with regard to imports.
76. Council Directive 84/631, *supra* note 15, art. 4, § 6.
77. Council Directive 75/442, *supra* note 2.
78. Council Directive 84/631, *supra* note 15.
79. Each party shall require that hazardous wastes or other wastes, to be exported, are managed in an environmentally sound manner in the State of import or elsewhere. Technical guidelines for the environmentally sound management of wastes subject to this Convention shall be decided by the Parties at their first meeting.
Basel Convention, *supra* note 56, art. 4(8), 28 I.L.M. at 663.
In the Netherlands, for example, no export of hazardous waste is allowed where the standards of the recipient state do not meet Dutch standards. *Decision of the "Voorzitter van de Afdeling Geschillen van de Raad van State" (Chairman of the Public Disputes Division of the Council of State)* 23 March 1989, SOCIALL ECONOMISCHE WETGEVING 36-40 (1989).

oils are sold to an authorized disposal or regenerating undertaking of another Member State as when they are disposed of in the Member State of origin."[80] Because the directive on waste oils harmonized national laws,[81] there was no real necessity for extraterritorial action. Additionally, the directive on import and export does not allow the exporting state to intervene on behalf of the environment of the importing state. The import state exclusively is empowered to assess the environmental consequences within its jurisdiction.[82]

The Court, however, did not decide to what extent a Member State may restrict the export of waste oils to states outside the EEC, where the directive on waste oils is not applicable. In this regard, the exporting state has the responsibility to see that no export takes place unless it has ensured that the importing state has the technical capacity to dispose of the waste properly, so there is reduced danger to human health or the environment.[83] Within the framework of the Lome Convention[84] (which applies to the former colonies of the Member States) the responsibility goes even further. Article 39 of the Lome Convention *prohibits* the export of hazardous and nuclear waste to those states.[85]

CONCLUSION

The cornerstone of the EEC Treaty is the free movement of goods, including environmentally dangerous or hazardous goods. According to the EEC Treaty, restrictions on trade may be allowed if they are necessary to protect the environment. However, these trade restrictions may not go beyond those proportionally necessary. They may not discriminate between domestic and foreign waste. Also, as emphasized in *Commission v. Belgium*,[86] the proximity principle—and to some extent the self-sufficiency principle—require that waste be disposed of locally.

Some uncertainty remains, however. Legal uncertainty exists with respect to whether export restrictions for waste are allowed to ensure the profitability of national waste disposal installations. And another question still in doubt is whether extraterritorial responsibility for preventing environmental damage can restrict the trade of waste.

At the beginning of this paper, I asked if the EEC Treaty provides a suitable framework for an environmentally sound waste disposal policy. *Commission v. Belgium* has given me some hope for the use of environmental justifications, and for the use of the proximity and self-sufficiency

---

80. *Inter-Huiles*, 1983 E.C.R. at 566.
81. Council Directive 75/439, *supra* note 11, art. 17.
82. *See* Council Directive 84/631, *supra* note 15, art. 4.
83. *Id.*
84. Fourth ACP-EEC Convention of Lome, Dec. 15, 1989, 29 I.L.M. 783.
85. *Id.* art. 39, 29 I.L.M. at 819.
86. Case C-2/90, Commission v. Belgium, at 17.

principles, to develop a sound waste disposal policy. The decision also makes clear that the Basel Convention is not problematic. Aside from profitability and extraterritorial concerns, which may in some cases be actually quite important, it does seem that the EEC has developed, with the aid of the Court, a suitable framework for waste disposal policy.

[17]

THE BIRDS DIRECTIVE 15 YEARS LATER: A SURVEY OF THE CASE LAW AND A COMPARISON WITH THE HABITATS DIRECTIVE

*Wouter P. J. Wils**

1. Introduction

1.1 Legislative history

Council Directive 79/409/EEC of 2 April 1979 on the conservation of wild birds[1] (hereafter: 'the Birds directive') constituted one of the very first Community measures concerning the protection of nature.[2] The 1973 Community Programme of action on the environment had announced 'study with a view to possible harmonization of national regulations on the protection of animal species and migratory birds in particular', as well as proposals by the Commission 'where appropriate' before 31 December 1974.[3] On 20 December 1974 the Commission issued a recommendation[4] in which it presented the conclusions of a study it had commissioned, and recommended the Member States, if they had not already done so, to accede to the 1950 Paris Convention on Birds and the 1971 Ramsar Convention on Wetlands.[5] The recommendation did not contain, however, any hint to specific Community legislation. In the meantime a

---

* Law Clerk at the EC Court of Justice. The author thanks Jonathan Robinson for his stimulating comments. All views expressed in this article are entirely personal to the author. The article was completed on 20 January 1994.
   [1] OJ 1979 No L 103/1.
   [2] For a historical overview of EC nature protection policy, see L. Krämer, 'The Interdependency of Community and Member State Activity on Nature Protection Within the European Community', *Ecology Law Quarterly*, 1993, 25, at 28–41.
   [3] Declaration of the Council of the European Communities and of the Representatives of the Governments of the Member States meeting in the Council of 22 November 1973 on the Programme of action of the European Communities on the environment, OJ 1973 No C 112/1, at 40. Two years earlier, the Commission had declared that, for the time being, the protection of (migratory) birds did not figure among its priorities for action in the area of the environment: Answer (12 November 1971) to Written question No 285/71 by Mr Glesener to the Commission, OJ 1971 No C 119/3; compare Answer (10 April 1973) to Written question No 620/72 by Mr Jahn to the Commission, OJ 1973 No C 39/12–13.
   [4] Commission Recommendation 75/66/EEC of 20 December 1974 to Member States concerning the protection of birds and their habitats, OJ 1975 No L 21/24.
   [5] International convention for the protection of birds, signed at Paris, on 18 October 1950, 638 UNTS 185; Convention on wetlands of international importance especially as waterfowl habitat, adopted on 3 February 1971 at the International conference on the conservation of wetlands and waterfowl held at Ramsar, Iran, 996 UNTS 245.

group of leading members of national and international organizations for the protection of animals had presented a petition 'on the need to save the migratory birds' to the European Parliament, Commission and Council. This led the Parliament to adopt a resolution on 21 February 1975 urging the Commission and the Council 'to propose and adopt in the near future practical measures for the protection of migratory birds'.[6] On 20 December 1976 the Commission submitted a first proposal to the Council for a directive on bird conservation,[7] which it modified eight months later to take into account some amendments by the Parliament.[8] It thereafter took the Council 20 months to adopt, with many modifications, the final Birds directive.[9]

1.2. Later modifications and related Community acts

Since its initial adoption in 1979, the Birds directive has undergone a few adaptations and amendments. Some were mere technical adaptations related to the enlargement of the Community.[10] Others widen or narrow the scope of application of certain provisions of the Birds directive, by adding or removing bird species listed in the annexes. In 1985 the number of species listed in Annex I, for which Article 4 of the Birds directive requires special conservation measures concerning their habits, was almost doubled.[11] This list was further lengthened in 1991.[12] In the same year, the Commission proposed to the Council a number of changes to Annex II, which lists the birds which may be hunted according to Article 7 of the Birds directive, in particular the addition of five species not hitherto listed.[13] The only admendment to the wording of the Birds directive itself (as opposed to its annexes) came through Council Directive 92/43/EEC of 21 May 1992 on the conservation of natural habitats and of wild fauna

---

[6] Resolution of 21 February 1975 on Petition No 8/74: 'Save the migratory birds', OJ 1975 No C 60/51, at nr. 11. It would seem that this resolution, as well as a number of questions by MEPs, played an important role in the genesis of the Birds directive. For a general discussion of the role of the Parliament in EC environmental policy, see H. ARP, 'The European Parliament in European Community Environmental Policy', *European University Institute Working Papers EPU* No. 92/13.

[7] Proposal for a Council Directive on bird conservation, OJ 1977 No C 24/3.

[8] Modifications of a proposal for a Council Directive on bird conservation, OJ 1977 No C 201/2.

[9] It may be interesting to note that, although some of the modifications adopted by the Council could be regarded as weakening the protective regime installed by the directive (in particular by weakening the supervisionary role of the Commission; nn63 and 123), several other rather tended to strengthen the protection of wild birds (nn53, 102, 106 and 128).

[10] Council directive 81/854/EEC of 19 October 1981 adapting, consequent upon the accession of Greece, Directive 79/409/EEC on the conservation of wild birds, OJ 1981 No L 319/3 (translation into Greek of the names of the bird species and in the annexes to the Birds directive; indication in Annex II/2 which of the listed species may be hunted in Greece); Council directive of 8 April 1986 adapting, consequent upon the accession of Spain and Portugal, Directive 79/409/EEC on the conservation of wild birds, OJ 1986 No L 100/22 (Spanish and Portugese translations of the names in the annexes); Article 5 of Council directive 90/656/EEC on the transitional measures applicable in Germany with regard to certain Community provisions relating to the protection of the environment, OJ 1990 No L 353/59 (partial delay up to 31 December 1992 of the application of Articles 3 and 4 of the Birds directive for the territory of the former German Democratic Republic).

[11] Commission directive 85/411/EEC of 25 July 1985 amending Council Directive 79/409/EEC on the conservation of wild birds, OJ 1985 No L 233/33; see n59.

[12] Commission directive 91/244/C of 6 March 1991 amending Council Directive 79/409/EEC on the conservation of wild birds, OJ 1991 No L 115/41. This Commission directive also carried out the amendment of Annex III (listing bird species for which marketing may be allowed) called for in Article 6 (4) of the Birds directive; see n104.

[13] Proposal for a Council Directive amending Annex II to Directive 79/409/EEC on the conservation of wild birds, OJ 1992 No C 255/5. The Commission later amended its proposal: OJ 1992 No C 260/9. See n106.

and flora[14] (hereafter: 'the Habitats directive'), which replaces Article 4 (4) of the Birds directive, concerning the measures to be taken with regard to special protection areas.[15]

Among the Community acts which are substantially related to the Birds directive, the Habitats directive just mentioned is probably the most important. Although differing in many details, it very much appears as a broadening of the Birds directive, from just birds and their habitats to the full range of wild fauna and flora and natural habitats.[16]

The Community is also a party to four international conventions which contain provisions on protection of wildlife species and habitats and which overlap in part with the Birds directive and/or the Habitats directive[17]: the 1979 Bern Convention on the conservation of European wildlife and natural habitats,[18] the 1979 Bonn Convention on the conservation of migratory species of wild animals,[19] the 1982 Geneva Protocol concerning Mediterranean specially protected areas to the 1976 Barcelona Convention on the protection of the Mediterranean Sea against pollution,[20] and the 1992 Rio Convention on biological diversity.[21] Finally, reference should be made to the 1973 Washington Convention on international trade in endangered species of wild fauna and flora (CITES). Although the Community is not a party to this convention, it adopted a regulation to implement it.[22] In 1991 the Commission submitted a proposal to the Council to replace the latter by a new regulation on wildlife trade, which is expressly presented as supplementing the Birds and Habitats directives.[23]

1.3. Plan of the Birds directive and of this article

The Birds directive contains two groups of provisions, concerning respectively the protection of habitats of wild birds (Articles 3 and 4) and the direct protection of wild

---

[14] OJ 1992 No L 206/7.

[15] See n81.

[16] The difference should not be overestimated, however: as birds occupy a relatively high place in the ecological pyramid, their protection ensures the conservation of a relatively important number of animal and plant species; N. De Sadeleer, 'La directive 92/43/CEE concernant la conservation des habitats naturels ainsi que de la faune et de la flore sauvages: Vers la reconnaissance d'un patrimoine naturel de la Communauté européenne', *Revue du Marché Commun*, 1993, 24, at 25. Moreover, to the extent that the Birds directive contains stricter provisions than the Habitats directive (see nn80 and 87), the former will continue to be of disproportionate practical relevance.

[17] The Community as such is not a party to the 1950 Paris Convention on Birds and the 1971 Ramsar Convention on Wetlands (n5); as to the latter convention, see Answer given by Mr Ripa di Meana on behalf of the Commission (20 September 1990) to Written Question No 1779/90 by Mr Paul Staes, OJ 1991 No C 90/19-20 and Answer given by Mr Van Miert on behalf of the Commission (28 September 1992) to Written Question No 701/92 by Mr Juan de la Cámara Martínez, OJ 1992 No C 317/24.

[18] Council Decision 82/72/EEC of 3 December 1981 concerning the conclusion of the Convention on the conservation of European wildlife and natural habitats, OJ 1982 No L 38/1 (Convention text at 3).

[19] Council Decision 82/461/EEC of 24 June 1982 on the conclusion of the Convention on the conservation of migratory species of wild animals, OJ 1982 No L 210/10 (Convention text at 11).

[20] Council Decision 84/132/EEC of 1 March 1984 on the conclusion of the Protocol concerning Mediterranean specially protected areas, OJ 1984 No L 68/36 (Protocol text at 38).

[21] Council Decision 93/626/EEC of 25 October 1993 on the conclusion of the Convention on biological diversity, OJ 1993 No L 309/1 (Convention text at 3).

[22] Council Regulation (EEC) No 3626/82 of 3 December 1982 on the implementation in the Community of the Convention on international trade in endangered species of wild fauna and flora, OJ 1982 No L 384/1 (Convention text at 7).

[23] Proposal for a Council regulation laying down provisions with regard to possession of and trade in specimens of species of wild fauna and flora, OJ 1992 No C 26/1.

bird species (Articles 5 to 9).[24] I will hereafter systematically discuss these two parts, in the light of the case law of the Court of Justice,[25] judgments of national courts,[26] and comments in the literature.[27] Following the order of the directive, I start with a discussion of the legal basis, scope of application and general principles of the directive (first recital and Articles 1 and 2), and finish with a discussion of some of the final provisions of the directive (Articles 10 to 19). At various points comparisons will be made with parallel provisions in the Habitats directive, so as to find out to what extent the case law on the Birds directive may be relevant for the interpretation of the Habitats directive as well.[28]

Finally, particular attention will be given to the question of direct effect of the provisions of the Birds directive.[29] According to Article 189, third paragraph, of the EC Treaty, directives are 'binding, as to the result to be achieved, upon each Member State to which it is addressed, but shall leave to the national authorities the choice of form and methods'. This may give the impression that individual citizens, companies or environmental protection groups necessarily have to rely on the national implementation of the directive. Under the doctrine of direct effect, however, they are allowed to invoke the provisions of the directive itself against any public authority. For a provision to have direct effect, a number of criteria have to be satisfied: 'According to a consistent line of decisions of the Court, a provision produces direct effect in relations between the Member States and their subjects only if it is clear and unconditional

---

[24] The same two elements (species protection and habitats protection) can be found in the Habitats directive.

[25] So far the Court has rendered 15 judgments (and one order on interim measures) in cases concerning the Birds directive: Judgments of 8 July 1987 in Case 247/85 *Commission/Belgium* [1987] ECR 3057 (comments N. De Sadeleer, *Aménagement-Environnement*, 1988, 26), in Case 262/85 *Commission/Italy* [1987] ECR 3094, Judgment of 17 September 1987 in Case 412/85 *Commission/Germany* [1987] ECR 3514, Judgment of 13 October 1987 in Case 236/85 *Commission/Netherlands* [1987] ECR 4005, Judgment of 27 April 1988 in Case 252/85 *Commission/France* [1988] ECR 2261 (comments J. Untermaier, *Revue juridique de l'environnement*, 1988, 460), Order of the President of the Court of 16 August 1989 in Case 57/89 R *Commission/Germany* [1989] ECR 2849, Judgment of 15 March 1990 in Case C-339/87 *Commission/Netherlands* [1990] ECR I-878, Judgment of 23 May 1990 in Case C-169/89 *Gourmetterie Van den Burg* [1990] ECR I-2160 (comments J. H. Jans, *Jurisprudentie Milieurecht*, 1992, 571 and E. H. Pijnacker Hordijk, *S.E.W.*, 1991, 261), Judgment of 3 July 1990 in Case C-288/88 *Commission/Germany* [1990] ECR I-2722, Judgments of 17 January 1991 in Case C-157/89 *Commission/Italy* [1991] ECR I-83 (comments G. Stansfield, *Rivista italiana di diritto pubblico comunitario*, 1992, 221), in Case C-334/89 *Commission/Italy* [1991] ECR I-102 (comments N. De Sadeleer, *Aménagement-Environnement*, 1991, 91), Judgment of 28 February 1991 in Case C-57/89 *Commission/Germany* [1991] ECR I-924 (comments D. Baldock, *Journal of Environmental Law*, 1992. 142, J. Bouckaert, *Aménagement Environnement*, 1992, 81, N. De Sadeleer, *Revue juridique de l'environnement*, 1992, 356 and E. Vallejo Lobete, *Gaceta Jurídica de la CEE*, 1991, B-66, 17), Judgment of 6 February 1992 in Case C-75/91 *Commission/Netherlands* [1992] ECR I-553, Judgment of 23 March 1993 in Case C-345/92 *Commission/Germany* [1993] ECR I-1115, Judgment of 2 August 1993 in Case C-355/90 *Commission/Spain* [1993] ECR I-4221, Judgment of 19 January 1994 in Case C-435/92 *Association pour la Protection des Animaux Sauvages* [1994] ECR I-67. No other piece of EC environmental legislation has given rise to as many cases before the Court of Justice.

[26] I am aware of some 50 judgments of national courts, over half of them French, the others Belgian, Dutch and Italian.

[27] Apart from the comments to judgments (n25), only a few published articles specifically deal with the Birds directive: T. Joris and M. Pallemaerts, 'EG-Vogelrichtlijn: wordt de uitzondering de regel?', *Tijdschrift voor Bestuurswetenschappen en Publiekrecht*, 1988, 449; K. Riechenberg, 'La directiva sobre la proteccion de las aves salvajes: Un hito en la politica comunitaria del medio ambiente', *Revista de instituciones europeas*, 1990, 369. Discussion of aspects of the Birds directive can also be found in several contributions on EC environmental law in general or on the Habitats directive.

[28] A more detailed discussion of the latter directive can be found in W. Wils, 'La protection des habitats naturels en droit communautaire', to be published in *Cahiers de Droit Européen*, 1994.

[29] For a systematic discussion of the application of the direct effect doctrine in the field of EC environmental law, see L. Krämer, 'The implementation of Community environmental directives within Member States: Some implications of the direct effect doctrine, *Journal of Environmental Law*, 1991, 39.

and not contingent on any discretionary implementing measure'.[30] The Court of Justice gives a broad interpretation of these conditions, which have recently been restated by Advocate-General Van Gerven as follows: 'provided and in so far as a provision of Community law is sufficiently operational in itself to be applied by a court, it has direct effect. The clarity, precision, unconditional nature, completeness or perfection of the rule and its lack of dependence on discretionary implementing measures are in that respect merely aspects of one and the same characteristic feature which that rule must exhibit, namely it must be capable of being applied by a court to a specific case'.[31]

2. Legal basis, scope of application and general principles

2.1. Legal basis

According to its preamble, the Birds directive was adopted on the basis of Article 235 of the (then) EEC Treaty.[32] The original EEC Treaty, as still unmodified in 1979, did not contain any provision specifically attributing to the Community the power to act in the area of environmental policy.[33] Article 235 allows for unanimous action by the Council 'if action by the Community should prove necessary to attain, in the course of the operation of the common market, one of the objectives of the Community and this Treaty has not provided the necessary powers'. The sixth recital of the Birds directive recalls these conditions, declaring that the conservation of wild species 'is necessary to attain, within the operation of the common market, the Community's objectives regarding the improvement of living conditions, a harmonious development of economic activities throughout the Community and a continuous and balanced expansion', thereby refering to three of the objectives listed in Article 2 of the Treaty.[34] Some further explanation can be found in the third recital which states that the wild birds to which the directive applies 'are mainly migratory species', that 'such species constitute a common heritage', and that 'effective bird protection is typically a transfrontier environment problem entailing common responsibilities'.

The Court of Justice has never explicitly been asked to rule on the validity of the Birds directive's legal basis. There can be little doubt, however, how its judgment would go. In a 1985 decision the Court declared that environmental protection 'is one of the Community's essential objectives',[35] thereby implicitly sanctioning the use of

---

[30] Judgment of 15 January 1986 in Case 44/84 *Hurd* [1986] ECR 47, at paragraph 47.

[31] Opinion of Advocate-General Van Gerven of 27 October 1993 in Case C-128/92 *Banks* (not yet published in ECR), at nr. 27, citing i.a. Judgments of 19 November 1991 in Joined Cases C-6/90 and C-9/90 *Francovich and Bonifaci* [1991] ECR I-5357 and of 2 August 1993 in Case C-271/91 *Marshall* (not yet published in ECR).

[32] The Commission's first proposal (n7) would have based the directive on both Article 100 (concerning the approximation of laws directly affecting the common market) and Article 235. The Parliament proposed to add Article 43 (on the common agricultural policy) as a third basis (Resolution embodying the opinion of the European Parliament on the proposal for a Directive on bird conservation, OJ 1977 No C 163/28, nr2). In its second proposal (n8), the Commission dropped Article 100 and added Article 43.

[33] The word 'environment' was not even mentioned; A. Haagsma, 'The European Community's environmental policy: a case-study in federalism', *Fordham International Law Journal*, 1989, 311, at 315.

[34] In the fourth recital to the 1973 Programme on the environment (n3), it had already been stated that the pursuit of the second and the third of these three objectives 'cannot now be imagined in the absence of (. . .) an improvement in (. . .) the protection of the environment'.

[35] Judgment of 7 February 1985 in Case 240/83 *ADBHU* [1985] ECR 538, at paragraph 13, confirmed in Judgment of 20 September 1988 in Case 302/86 *Commission/Denmark* [1988] ECR 4627, at paragraph 8; compare interpretation by A. Haagsma, n33, at 324–6.

Article 235 for environmental legislation. Furthermore, in its first judgments concerning the Birds directive, the Court repeated that 'the directive is based on the consideration that effective bird protection, and in particular protection of migratory species, is typically a transfrontier environment problem entailing common responsibilities for the Member States (third recital in the preamble)', and went on to stress the particular importance of a faithful transposition of the directive into national law 'in a case such as this in which the management of the common heritage is entrusted to the Member States in their respective territories'.[36] It would seem that the Court thus endorsed the view expressed in the directive's preamble as to the necessity of Community action.

An explicit ruling on the validity of the Birds directive has been rendered by France's highest administrative court. In a 1990 judgment the Conseil d'Etat held that 'it follows clearly from the provisions of the Treaty establishing the European Economic Community that the said directive, taken according to the rules layed down in Article 235 to attain one of the objectives of the Community, has been adopted competently by the Council of the Communities'.[37]

Since its amendment by the Single European Act,[38] the EEC Treaty contained a title dealing specifically with the environment. Article 130s now provides a specific legal basis for environmental legislation. The Habitats directive was adopted on this basis, and the latest Commission proposal for an amendment to the Birds directive[39] is based on it as well. Article 130r (4) introduced a new hurdle, however, by limiting Community action to the extent to which the environmental objectives 'can be attained better at Community level than at the level of the individual Member States'. The Maastricht Treaty on European Union[40] replaced the latter provision by the much-commented Article 3b of the EC Treaty, stating that 'the Community shall take action, in accordance with the principle of subsidiarity, only if and in so far as the objectives of the proposed action cannot be sufficiently achieved by the Member States and can therefore, by reason of the scale or effects of the proposed action, be better achieved by the Community'. It would not seem excessively difficult to make a convincing case for the protection of birds, and of nature more generally, to pass the subsidiarity test.[41] It may be relevant to observe that the protection of birds, other wildlife and natural habitats has been the object of a substantial number of international conventions for several decades now,[42] and is covered by federal law in the USA as well.[43] Anyway, one should not expect the Court of Justice to strike down legislation which has hitherto

---

[36] Judgments 247/85 and 262/85, n25, at paragraphs 6 and 9.

[37] Judgment of 25 May 1990 in Cases 94359–94936, *Ministre délégué chargé de l'environnement et Fédération Rhône-Alpes de protection de la nature/Fédération départementale des chasseurs de l'Isère et autres*, [1990] Receuil des décisions de Conseil d'Etat 133 (my translation). The Conseil d'Etat thereby judged it superfluous to refer the question to the Court of Justice, as was asked by the hunting federation which had raised the issue.

[38] OJ 1987 No L 169; see A. Haagsma, supra n33, 334–53.

[39] 13.

[40] OJ 1992 No C 224; see D. Wilkinson, 'Maastricht and the environment: the implications for the EC's environmental policy of the Treaty on European Union', *Journal of Environmental Law*, 1992, 221.

[41] Compare N. De Sadeleer, n16, at 26–7, L. J. Brinkhorst, 'Subsidiarity and EC Environmental Policy', *European Environmental Law Review*, 1993, 8, at 21, and W. Wils, 'Subsidiarity and EC environmental policy: Taking people's concerns seriously', *Journal of Environmental Law*, 1994, 85.

[42] An overview can be found in A. Kiss and D. Shelton, *International Environmental Law*, New York, Transnational, 1991, at pages 239–305; see also nn17 to 22.

[43] See i.a. 1918 Migratory Bird Treaty Act (16 USCA §§703–11), 1964 Wilderness Act (16 USCA §1131) and 1973 Endangered Species Act (16 USCA §§1531–43).

always been adopted unanimously by the Council,[44] and which benefits from strong support in the European Parliament and among the general public.[45]

2.2. Scope of application (Article 1)

According to its Article 1(1), first sentence, the Birds directive 'relates to the conservation of all species of naturally occurring birds in the wild state in the European territory of the Member States to which the Treaty applies'.[46] Three elements could be singled out.

First, the Birds directive only concerns wild birds naturally occurring *in the European territory of the Member States.*[47] This geographical restriction is not self-evident, as the EC Treaty does not limit Community action to the Community environment.[48] It implies, for instance, that the directive cannot be relied upon to prohibit the marketing of a dead bird imported from a third country,[49] or the hunting of wild birds in an overseas territory of a Member State.[50] On the other hand, the directive applies to the European territory of the Member States *as a whole*, in line with the notion of 'common heritage' (third recital in the preamble). The Court of Justice therefore condemned Belgium for limiting its national legislation implementing the Birds directive to the species of birds living in the wild state in the Benelux countries, and France for restricting its implementation to the protection of its 'national biological heritage'.[51]

Secondly, the Birds directive only applies to bird species *naturally occurring* in the wild state in the Community's European territory. Article 11 of the directive provides that Member States shall see that any introduction of other species of birds does not prejudice the local flora and fauna.

Apart from the restrictions just discussed, 'the general system of protection which the directive seeks to establish applies to *all* bird species, (. . .), even if such species are rare'.[52]

2.3. General principles (Article 2)

Article 2 of the Birds directive reads as follows: 'Member States shall take the requisite measures to maintain the population of the species referred to in Article 1 at a level

[44] Since the Maastricht Treaty on European Union, environmental legislation can be adopted by the Council in principle by qualified majority voting; Article 130s (2), however, contains a 'land use' exception; compare D. Wilkinson, n40, at 228.

[45] 'It is probably true to say, that, of all the aspects of environmental policy, nothing excites so much public interest and concern as the need to protect nature and habitat, landscape, fauna and flora, from the threat of further degradation or depletion' (Council Resolution of 19 October 1987, OJ 1987 No C 328/1, at 29).

[46] Article 1 (1), second sentence, and (2) state that the directive contains rules on protection, management, control and exploitation, and that it applies to birds, eggs, nests and habitats. These limbs do not seem to have any importance other than as an expression of the legislative intent of ensuring a comprehensive bird protection.

[47] Moreover, Article 1 (3) excludes Greenland. As of 1 January 1985, the EC Treaty anyway ceased to apply to Greenland; Treaty of 13 March 1984 amending, with regard to Greenland, the Treaties establishing the European Communities, OJ 1985 No L 29/1.

[48] L. Krämer, 'Community Environmental Law — Towards a Systematic Approach', *Yearbook of European Law*, 1991, 151, at 153.

[49] Cour de Cassation (France), Judgment of 17 June 1985 in Case 84–90547 *ARPON e.a. contre Allamel* [1985] Bulletin des arrêts de la Cour de Cassation — Chambre criminelle 595; summary in *Cahiers de droit européen*, 1989, 483; the case concerned birds imported from Spain, a third country at the time.

[50] Conseil d'Etat (France), Judgment of 24 February 1989 in Case 94330 *Rassemblement des Opposants à la Chasse/ Ministre de l'Environnement* (unpublished); the case concerned the hunting of turtle doves in Guadeloupe.

[51] Judgment 247/85, n25, at paragraphs 18–23 and Judgment 252/85, at paragraphs 13–16.

[52] Judgment 247/85, n25, at paragraph 52 (concerning in particular chromatic aberrations).

which corresponds in particular to ecological, scientific and cultural requirements, while taking account of economic and recreational requirements, or to adapt the population of these species to that level'.[53] It thus imposes a general obligation upon the Member States and describes the general philosophy of the directive.

As Article 2 instructs Member States to take the requisite measures to maintain or bring bird populations to a level which corresponds with the requirements mentioned, the question arises how it relates to the more specific obligations laid down in the subsequent articles of the directive, and more in particular whether a violation of the directive could be based on Article 2 standing on its own. I would argue that this possibility cannot be excluded. The wording of the article is not less conclusive than that of the rest of the directive, nor does it contain any reference to the subsequent more specific provisions to the fulfillment of which the general obligation of Article 2 would be limited. On the other hand, to the extent that other articles in the directive contain specific and detailed rules on certain issues, one would assume the Community legislator to have intended that those specific rules exhaustively define what measures are 'requisite' in the sense of Article 2. The obligation laid down in Article 2 would thus merely be subsidiary.

Apart from imposing a general obligation on Member States, Article 2 appears to describe the general philosophy underlying the Birds directive. The protection of wild birds is conceived as serving ecological, scientific as well as cultural requirements, and these are clearly weighted more heavily than economic and recreational requirements. Indeed, the former determine the objective to be achieved through the directive (primary requirements), whereas the latter are merely to be taken account of (secondary requirements).[54]

In its very first judgments on the Birds directive, the Court held that, 'although Article 2 does not constitue an autonomous derogation from the general system of protection, it none the less shows that the directive takes into consideration, on the one hand, the necessity for effective protection of birds and, on the other hand, other requirements'.[55] The judgments concerned infringement actions brought by the Commission under Article 169 of the EC Treaty against Belgium and Italy, because their national legislation contained exceptions on the prohibitions in Articles 5, 6 and 7, going beyond the derogations allowed by Article 9 of the directive.[56] Belgium and Italy argued that these exceptions were compatible with the Birds directive, as they responded in particular to economic and recreational requirements, which they argued were recognized by Article 2. The Court clearly rejected this defence, and stuck to a

---

[53] The Commission proposal (n7) would only have required measures to maintain populations at (not to adapt them to) 'a level compatible with ecological, economic, recreational and scientific requirements'. The Parliament advised to add 'or restore it to a level' (n32, at p. 30), but the Commission did not change its initial proposal (n8). The final formulation adopted by the Council is very similar to Article 2 of the 1979 Bonn Convention on the conservation of migratory species of wild animals (n19). The cultural importance of birdlife had already been stressed in the advice of the Commission on cultural and youth affairs of the European Parliament on the 1974 petition 'Save the migratory birds' (n6); EP Doc. 449/74, at 22-7.

[54] Given the legislative history (n53), it is beyond doubt that the Council has consciously intended this differentiation.

[55] Judgments 247/85 and 262/85, n25, at paragraph 8; the court lists 'the requirements of public health and safety, the economy, ecology, science, farming and recreation', following the order of Article 9 of the directive, which the Court was interpreting in these two judgments. As ecology and science are among the primary requirements listed in Article 2, the 'on the one hand' 'on the other hand' should not be read as parallelling the primary/secondary requirements distinction.

[56] See n115.

rather strict interpretation of Article 9. Later judgments appear to confirm that Article 2 merely 'shows' the general philosophy of the directive, but does not function as a general principle restricting the scope of other articles, and should not be used to give restrictive interpretations of articles which are sufficiently clear on their own.[57] Only exceptionally, Article 2 may be relevant in interpreting some of the vaguest or most general terms in the Directive.[58]

Article 2 (2) of the Habitats directive states that measures taken pursuant to that directive 'shall be designed to maintain or restore, at favourable conservation status, natural habitats and species of wild fauna and flora of Community interest'. Article 2 (3) adds that they 'shall take account of economic, social and cultural requirements and regional and local characteristics'. As these provisions confirm the precedence of environmental over economic and other considerations even more clearly than Article 2 of the Birds directive, the Court's case law on the latter, limiting the possibility to invoke non-environmental excuses, appears relevant for the Habitats directive as well.

3. Habitats protection (Articles 3 and 4)

3.1. Overview

Article 3 of the Birds directive instructs Member States to 'take the requisite measures to preserve, maintain or re-establish a sufficient diversity and area of habitats for all the species of birds' to which the directive applies. Article 4 (1) states that 'the species mentioned in Annex I shall be the subject of special conservation measures concerning their habitat' (first paragraph) and that 'member States shall classify in particular the most suitable territories in number and size as special protection areas for the conservation of these species' (fourth paragraph).[59] According to Article 4 (2), 'Member States shall take similar measures for regularly occurring migratory species not listed in Annex I'. Article 4 (4) contains obligations as to the avoidance of pollution, deterioration and avoidance of habitats. I will successively discuss the designation of special protection areas (hereafter: 'SPAs'), obligations concerning SPAs, and obligations concerning other or all habitats.

A preliminary question concerns the relationship between the obligations on habitat protection laid down in Articles 3 and 4 and the general aim of the directive, which is the conservation of wild birds (Article 1): are Articles 3 and 4 only binding to the extent that their observance is shown to affect the preservation of the birds to which they apply, or do they contain autonomous obligations to preserve habitats? In a 1993 judgment, the Court of Justice unambiguously chose the latter interpretation: 'Articles

---

[57] As to the interpretation of Article 4 (4): Judgment 57/89, n25, at paragraph 22 ('the interests referred to in Article 2 of the directive, namely economic and recreational requirements, do not enter into consideration'); the Court thus rejected the views of Advocate-General Van Gerven, who would have allowed for some balancing of interests to take place (Opinion of 5 December 1990 in Case C-57/89 *Commission/Germany* [1991] ECR 903, at nr. 39); the Court broadened its holding to the whole of Article 4, thus also 4 (1) and (2), in Judgment 355/90, paragraphs 16–19. As to the interpretation of Article 7 (4): Judgment C-435/92, paragraphs 19 and 20.

[58] The Court has done this only once, concerning the term 'small numbers' in Article 9 (1)(c); n25; Advocate-General Van Gerven used Article 2 to give content to 'sufficient' in Article 3 (1), which explicitly refers to Article 2; n100.

[59] In 1979 the original Annex I listed 74 species; it was lengthened to 144 species in 1985 (n11) and to 175 species in 1991 (n12); no species has ever been removed from the list; the currently valid Annex I is to be found at OJ 1991 No L 115/42.

3 and 4 of the directive require Member States to conserve, maintain and re-establish the habitats as such by reason of their ecological value. It follows moreover from the ninth recital to the directive that the preservation, maintenance or restoration of a sufficient diversity and area of habitats is essential for the conservation of all species of birds. The obligations on Member States under Articles 3 and 4 of the directive accordingly apply before a reduction in the number of birds is observed or a risk of the disappearance of a protected species arises'.[60]

3.2. Designation of SPAs (Article 4 (1) and (2))

The designation of SPAs constitutes one of the most crucial and most contentious issues in the application of the Birds directive. Article 4 (1), fourth subparagraph, states: 'Member States shall classify in particular the most suitable territories in number and size as special protection areas for the conservation of (the species mentioned in Annex I), taking into account their protection requirements (in the European territory of the Member States)'. Paragraph (2) adds: 'Member States shall take similar measures for regularly occurring migratory species not listed in Annex I, bearing in mind their need for protection (. . .). To this end, Member States shall pay particular attention to the protection of wetlands and particularly to wetlands of international importance'. It can be considered as settled that the 'similar measures' refered to in the latter provision include the obligation to designate SPAs in accordance with Article 4 (1), fourth subparagraph.[61] The term 'wetlands of international importance' is understood to refer to the 1971 Ramsar Convention on Wetlands.[62]

The provisions just cited leave it to each Member State to designate SPAs in its own territory. In the Commission's original proposal,[63] the Member States would have had to consult the Commission. The Council did not retain this, but instead added Article 4 (3), which stipulates that Member States shall send the Commission all relevant information so that it may take coordinating initiatives to ensure Community-wide coherence. This provision was made somewhat more specific in a resolution adopted together with the Birds directive, in which the Council also took 'note of the Commission's intention of submitting appropriate proposals regarding the criteria for the determination, selection, organization and methods of administration of the special protection areas'.[64] The Commission has never submitted formal proposals to the Council. Informally, however, it has developed some criteria for the selection of areas to be designated as SPAs.[65]

---

[60] Judgment C-355/90, n25, paragraph 15 (my translation from the French version).

[61] The point was made explicitly by Advocate-General Van Gerven in his Opinion in Case C-57/89 *Commission/Germany* [1991] ECR 903, at nr 27, repeated in his Opinion of 9 June 1993 in Case C-355/90 *Commission/Spain* (not yet reported), at n8, and apparently accepted by the Court which discussed Article 4 (1) and (2) jointly (Judgment C-355/90, n25, paragraphs 24–32).

[62] nn5 and 17; Opinion of AG Van Gerven in C-57/89, n61, nr 27; it remains unclear, however, why the Community legislator has then not explicitly refered to the Convention, although it had been advised to do so (Opinion of the Economic and Social Committee on the proposal for a Council Directive on bird conservation. OJ 1977 No C 152/3, at nr 2.3.).

[63] n7.

[64] Council Resolution of 2 April 1979 concerning Directive 79/409/EEC on the conservation of wild birds, OJ 1979 No C 103/6.

[65] 'The Commission together with the Member States has developed a method which is an objective means of evaluating the endangered status of different bird species thoughout the Community and determining the proportion of each bird population that should be within SPAs in each region (Joint answer to Written Questions Nos 1710/92 and 131/93 given by Mr Paleokrassas on behalf of the Commission (27 May 1993), OJ 1993 No C 258/7, at 8). Although it is laudable that the Commission, in accordance with Article 155 of the Treaty, assists

A crucial point in the interpretation of Article 4 (1) and (2) concerns the degree of discretion which the Member States have in the choice of the areas to be designated. The recent case law of the Court of Justice indicates that this discretion is rather limited, if at all existent.[66] In Case C-355/90 the Court condemned Spain for having failed to classify the Marismas de Santoña, a coastal area in Cantabria, as SPA. As to the Member States' discretion in general, the Court held that 'although it is true that the Member States have some discretion in the choice of the special protection areas, nevertheless the designation of these areas responds to certain ornithological criteria, detemined by the directive, such as the presence of birds listed in annex I, on the one hand, and the qualification of a habitat as wetland, on the other hand'.[67] As to the case at hand, the Court based its condemnation (only) on the following observations: 'it is an established fact that the Marismas de Santoña constitute one of the most important ecosystems on the Iberian peninsula for numerous aquatic birds. Indeed, the marshes are used by numerous birds as hibernation or stopover place during their migrations from the european countries to the southern regions of Africa and the Iberian peninsula itself. Among the birds present in this area, are various endangered species, notably the spoonbill, which feeds itself and rests in the Marismas de Santoña during its migration. Furthemore, it follows from the file and the debates before the Court that the area concerned receives on a regular basis 19 species listed in annex I of the directive as well as at least 14 migratory species'.[68]

This judgment allows the following conclusions to be drawn. First, Article 4 (1) and (2) refer to objective, ornithologic criteria which, if ṣatisfied in a particular case, oblige the Member State to designate the area concerned as SPA. Among these criteria are the presence of birds listed in Annex I or other migratory birds, and the qualification as wetland. Second, the fact that the area concerned constitutes one of the most important habitats for a number of endangered species of birds, or arguably even for only one such species, is sufficient for the criteria to be satisfied.[69] Third, the Court's condemnation of Spain for not having classified the Marismas de Santoña as SPA,

---

the Member States in interpreting and applying the directive, it should be kept in mind that it has no power to limit the obligations which the directive imposes upon the Member States, and which could be enforced via the national courts and the Court of Justice. Finally, if a national court applying Article 4 (1) or (2) were to ask so, the Commission may be obliged under Article 5 of the Treaty to provide it whith the relevant information it holds; compare Order of 13 July 1990 in Case C-2/88 *Zwartveld* [1990] ECR I–3365.

[66] Before the judgment C-355/90, the issue was unclear. In Case 334/89(n25) the Court had condemned Italy for not having adopted or notified any special protection measure consequent upon the extension of Annex I in 1985 (nn11 and 59), which suggested at most a limited discretion. In his Opinion in Case C-57/89 (n61, at nr28), AG Van Gerven had advocated a restricted but still fairly substantial discretion, allowing i.a. Article 2 to be taken into account. In the light of the Court's judgment in Case C-355/90, this view should be considered as rejected.

[67] Judgment C-355/90, n25, paragraph 26 (my translation of 's'il est vrai que les Etats membres jouissent d'une certaine marge d'appréciation en ce qui concerne le choix des zones de protection spéciale, il n'en demeure pas moins que le classement de ces zones obéit à certains critères ornithologiques, déterminés par la directive, tels que la présence d'oiseaux énumérés à l'annexe I, d'une part, et la qualification d'un habitat comme zone humide, d'autre part').

[68] Paragraph 27 (my translation)

[69] To draw this conclusion, one should read paragraph 27 of the judgment in the light of the facts of the case, as described more extensively in the Report for the hearing and the Opinion of the Advocate-General (n61). One then finds that practically all the evidence submitted by the Commission to argue its case against Spain only concerned the spoonbill (Opinion, nr 9). Furthermore, the qualification of the spoonbill as an endangered species does not appear to be based on any substantial evidence beyond the fact that it is listed in Annex I; the only other elements before the Court were that its western European population consists of 1100 couples (of which 600 migrate via northern Spain) and that the Commission failed to establish a reduction of the numbers over the last years (Opinion, nrs 9 and 24, n25).

demonstrates that Article 4 (1) and (2) are sufficiently clear and unconditional on their own to be applied by a court to a specific case, and thus produce direct effect. Indeed, the Court held that Article 4 (1) and (2) contain objective, ornithologic criteria, and applied itself these criteria to the particular case at hand, at the request of the Commission. If the Court of Justice can do this, a national court could do the same, at the request of a private party.

The judgment in Case C-355/90 also provides important indications on other points concerning the designation of SPAs. It made clear that the choice of the precise geographical delimitation of a SPA also responds to objective, ornithological criteria, capable of being applied by a court,[70] and that the classification of an area as SPA cannot consist of a mere declaration but implies some regulatory framework detailing the protective regime.[71] It was also settled that a Member State could not justify its failure to classify one area as SPA by its record of having classified other SPAs which are of importance to other birds,[72] and that Article 4 does not allow for any delay or gradual implementation, but must be applied since the entry into force of the Birds directive.[73] Finally, the Court clearly denied the possiblity to invoke the economic interests mentioned in Article 2 as a justification for failing to comply with Article 4 (1) and (2) or as a general principle limiting their scope: 'it follows from (the judgment of the Court in Case C-57/89) that the Member States, in implementing the directive, are not entitled arbitrarily to rely on reasons for derogation based on other interests. Concerning more in particular Article 4 of the directive, the Court has made it clear in the judgment referred to, that those reasons, to be admitted, must correspond to a general interest which is superior to the general interest represented by the ecological objective of the directive. In particular, the interests referred to in Article 2 of the directive, namely economic and recreational requirements, do not enter into consideration'.[74]

Articles 3 to 11 of the Habitats directive contain provisions on a 'coherent European ecological network of special areas of conservation' to be set up under the name 'Nature 2,000'. It is to be composed of sites hosting the natural habitat types listed in Annex I and habitats of the species listed in Annex II to the Habitats directive. The procedure for designating these special areas of conservation is radically different from the designation of SPAs under the Birds directive. Whereas the latter is the obligation of each Member State in its territory, the Habitats directive installs a Community procedure. As a first step, each Member State shall propose a list of sites, on the basis of the objective criteria mentioned in Article 4 (1) of the Habitats direct-

---

[70] Paragraphs 28 and 29.

[71] Paragraphs 28, 30 and 31; the Court considered this to be a requirement laid down in Article 4 (1) and (2), independent thus of Article 4 (4); this point may be of relevance as the Habitats directive replaces the latter but not the former provision; nn80 and 81.

[72] The issue was addressed in detail by the Advocate-General in his Opinion, nr. 15, third subparagraph. The Court appears to have rejected Spain's defense together with its broader defense that the obligations in Articles 3 and 4 of the directive had to be implemented only gradually and not immediately (Judgment, paragraphs 10–12). Moreover, the conclusion directly follows from the Court's assertion that Article 4 (1) and (2) contain objective, ornithological criteria.

[73] Judgment, paragraphs 10–12.

[74] Paragraphs 18 and 19 (my translation); see n57 as to Judgment C-57/89; the paragraphs cited here widen the holding of the latter judgment, which only concerned (aspects of) Article 4 (4), to the whole of Article 4. The place of the cited paragraphs in the plan of Judgment C-355/90 (especially in comparison with the place of the corresponding nr 25 in the Opinion of the Advocate-General) indicates that this widening was not unintentional.

ive.[75] If the Commission finds that a national list fails to mention a site which it considers essential, it can initiate a bilateral consultation procedure and ultimately submit a proposal to the Council which has to decide unanimously.[76] In a second stage, a list of sites of Community importance will be adopted by the Community.[77] Only thereafter shall the Member States concerned designate those sites as special areas of conservation 'as soon as possible and within six years at most'.

According to Article 3 (1), second subparagraph, of the Habitats directive, 'the Natura 2,000 network shall include the special protection areas classified by the Member States pursuant to Directive 79/409/EEC'. The rules according to which SPAs are to be designated under the Birds directive, however, are not changed by the Habitats directive.[78] Indeed, Article 4 (1) and (2) of the former directive are in no way altered or restricted by the latter. This point may be of significant practical relevance, as many sites throughout the Community which should be classified according to Article 4(1) and (2) of the Birds directive (as interpreted by the Court in Case C-355/90), have not yet been classified, while they may also host natural habitat types or animal species listed in the annexes to the Habitats directive. The existence of the Habitats directive, with its admittedly less demanding rules, does not dispense Member States from their obligation to classify these sites as SPAs under the Birds directive.[79] The rules laid down in the Habitats directive do not alter the interpretation of Article 4(1) and (2) of the Birds directive, as discussed above.[80]

3.3. The protective regime applicable to SPAs (Article 4(4) first sentence)

In its original version, Article 4(4), first sentence, of the Birds directive stated that, in respect of SPAs, 'Member States shall take appropriate steps to avoid pollution or deterioration of habitats or any disturbances affecting the birds, in so far as these would be significant having regard to the objectives of this Article'. Article 7 of the Habitats directive replaces the obligations arising under this sentence by the obligations arising under Article 6(2), (3) and (4) of the Habitats directive,[81] 'as from the

---

[75] This list has to be transmitted to the Commission within three years of the notification of the Habitats directive, i.e. by 10 June 1995.

[76] Article 5(3) states that the Council, 'acting unanimously, shall take a decision within three months of the date of referral'. The question arises what happens if the Council does not reach a unanimous decision in tir The practical importance of this issue is somewhat limited by Article 5(4) which provides that Article 6(2) — but apparently not the rest of Article 6 — applies pending the Council decision.

[77] The Commission will first establish a draft list of sites drawn from the national lists. A committee of national representatives then delivers a (majority) opinion. The Commission then either adopts the list in accordance with the opinion, or, if it disagrees with the opinion or no opinion has been delivered, submits a proposal to the Council. The Council has three months to act by qualified majority; otherwise the Commission decides (Articles 4(2) and 21 of the Habitats directive).

[78] On the other hand, the Habitats directive does change the protective regime applicable to the SPAs, because it replaces Article 4(4), first sentence, of the Birds directive; n81.

[79] As Article 4(1) and (2) of the Birds directive have not been amended or replaced, they remain in full, binding force; Member States do thus not have any freedom to opt for the rules of the Habitats directive instead; contra N. De Sadeleer, n16, at 29.

[80] If a site satisfies the ornithological criteria of Article 4(1) and (2) of the Birds directive, its non-classification could thus not be justified, for instance, by the fact that the Member State concerned already contributed more than proportionally to Nature 2000 (Article 3(2) of the Habitats directive); nor is there room for 'flexibility' as meant in Article 4(2), second subparagraph, of the Habitats directive; the lengthy Community procedure laid down in Articles 4 and 5 of the latter directive applies neither; see W. Wils, n28.

[81] Article 6(1) of the Habitats directive which concerns the regulatory framework and planning measures for special areas of conservation, is not declared to apply to SPAs classified under the Birds directive. It would seem, however, that similar requirements have been read into Article 4(1) and (2) by the Court of Justice; n71.

date of implementation of (the Habitats directive) or the date of classification or recognition by a Member State under (the Birds directive), where the latter date is later'.[82]

According to Article 6(2) of the Habitats directive, 'Member States shall take appropriate steps to avoid, in the special areas of conservation, the deterioriation of natural habitats and the habitats of species as well as disturbance of the species for which the areas have been designated, in so far as such disturbance could be significant in relation to the objectives of this Directive'. The wording of this provision differs in some respects from the the wording of Article 4(4), first sentence, of the Birds directive. First, it only mentions the 'deterioration' of habitats instead of their 'pollution or deterioration'. This difference appears rather a matter of form than of substance: pollution is arguably a form of deterioration. Secondly, and more important, the condition of significance clearly only applies to disturbances, not to deteriorations of habitats. On the contrary, Article 4(4), first sentence, has been interpreted by the Court as applying only to *significant* (pollution or) deterioration of habitats.[83] The new provision of the Habitats directive is thus stricter as to the obligations it imposes on Member States with regard to the avoidance of the deterioration of protected habitats, in that it covers all forms of deterioration, not only those which could be significant in relation to the objectives of the directive.[84]

Article 6(3) of the Habitats directive provides that 'any plan or project not directly connected with or necessary to the management of the site but likely to have a significant effect thereon (. . .), shall be subject to appropriate assessment of its implications for the site (. . .)'. Moreover, 'the competent authorities shall agree to the plan or project only after having ascertained that it will not adversely affect the integrity of the site concerned, and, if appropriate, after having obtained the opinion of the general public'. This provision forms a useful addition to the previous rules under Article 4(4) of the Birds directive.[85]

Article 6(4), first subparagraph, of the Habitats directive reads as follows: 'If, in spite of a negative assessment of the implications for the site and in the absence of

---

[82] According to Article 23 of the Habitats directive, it has to be implemented by 10 June 1994. In my understanding, the term 'date of implementation' in Article 7 here cited, does not refer to this date, but to the date of actual implementation by each Member State. In those Member States which failed to implement the Habitats directive by 10 June 1994, the question then arises whether Article 4(4), first sentence, of the Birds directive continues to apply or whether, by application of the doctrine of direct effect, Article 6(2), (3) and (4) apply anyway. In sofar as the latter provisions are more protective for the wild birds concerned, the second possibility seems the correct one. On the basis of Article 14 of the Birds directive and Article 130t of the EC Treaty, the first seems to be the right one in sofar as the application of Article 4(4), first sentence, of the Birds directive leads to stricter protection.

[83] Explicitly by Advocate-General Van Gerven in his Opinion in Case C-57/89, n61, at nr 33 and his Opinion in Case C-355/90, n61, at nrs 23 and 24; implicitly but surely by the Court in Judgment C-355/90, n25, at paragraphs 46 and 52, where it establishes the significant nature of the deterioration at hand.

[84] The phrase 'significant in relation to the objectives of *this* Directive' (my italicization) in Article 6 (2) of the Habitats directive sounds somewhat strange when this provision is applied to SPAs classified under the Birds directive. Article 4 (4), first sentence, of the Birds directive referred to the objectives of that article only. Arguably all this does not matter much, as the objectives referred to are basically the same; see text accompanying 46 and 53 and following n58.

[85] The provision falls short, however, of the Commission's proposal to amend Article 4 of Council Directive 85/337/EEC of 27 June 1985 on the assessment of the effects of certain public and private projects on the environment, to require an environmental impact assessment in accordance with Articles 5 and 10 of that directive for all projects located in or likely to affect special areas of conservation (Commission proposal, OJ 1988 No C 247/3, proposed Article 11). This would have assured the applicability of the procedural guarantees laid down in Directive 85/337/EEC; N. De Sadeleer, 16, n35.

alternative solutions, a plan or project must nevertheless be carried out for imperative reasons of overriding public interest, including those of a social or economic nature, the Member State shall take all compensatory measures necessary to ensure that the overall coherence of Nature 2000 is protected (. . .)'. The second subparagraph continues: 'Where the site concerned hosts a priority natural habitat type and/or a priority species, the only considerations which may be raised are those relating to human health or public safety, to beneficial consequences of primary importance for the environment or, further to an opinion from the Commission, to other imperative reasons of overriding public interest'.[86]

For a proper understanding, this paragraph should be read in the light of the case law of the Court of Justice on Article 4(4), first sentence, of the Birds directive, especially of its Judgment of 28 February 1991 in Case C-57/89 *Commission/Germany*, which appears to have influenced the Council when adopting the Habitats directive.[87] This case concerned the reinforcement of a dyke in the Leybucht, an area in northern Germany which is part of a SPA. The project led to a reduction of the size of the SPA, apart from temporary disturbances caused by the works. The Court held that (significant) pollution, deterioration or disturbances in the sense of Article 4(4), first sentence, of the Birds directive 'can be justified only on exceptional grounds. Those grounds must correspond to a general interest which is superior to the general interest represented by the ecological objective of the directive. In that context the interests referred to in Article 2 of the directive, namely economic and recreational requirements, do not enter into consideration'.[88] In the case at hand, the Commission did not dispute that the reinforcement of the dyke was necessary for the protection of the people living behind the dyke, and that this was the only reason for the initiation of the project.[89] The Court accepted this as a sufficiently serious reason.[90] It was established, however, that the determination of the precise new line of the dyke had been influenced by considerations relating not only to coastal protection but also by the concern to ensure access for fishing vessels to a nearby harbour. Although such an economic interest could not have justified the project in the first place, the Court accepted its secondary role in determining part of the new line of the dyke, because 'that part of the project (had) at the same time specific positive consequences for the habitat of birds', which, according to the Court's judgment, amounted to 'offsetting ecological benefits'.[91]

---

[86] According to Article 1 (d) and (h), priority natural habitat types and priority species are those natural habitat types or species which are indicated by an asterisk in Annex I respectively Annex II to the Habitats directive.

[87] Compare D. Babcock, *Journal of Environmental Law*, 1992, 142, at 144.

[88] Judgment C-57/89, 25, at paragraphs 21 and 22. The judgment did not discuss (significant) pollution, deterioration and disturbances in general, but spoke in particular of reductions of the size of SPAs. In his Opinion in Case C-355/90, n61, at nr 26, Advocate-General Van Gerven argued that the principles of Judgment C-57/89 applied more broadly to the whole of Article 4 (4), first sentence. The Court appears to have adopted this view in its subsequent judgment, as it applied the principles of Judgment C-57/89 to a number of facts most of which did not, or not primarily, involve reductions of the size of the SPA.

[89] Opinion of the Advocate-General, at nr 37.

[90] Judgment, paragraph 23.

[91] Judgment, paragraphs 24–26; more details about the offsetting benefits can be found in the Opinion of the Advocate-General, at nrs 20 and 41: the completion of the project would permit the closure of two channels crossing the SPA, which until then had been regularly dredged, causing disruption and dredged material to be dumped; another nearby dyke would be opened, allowing an additional area to become tidal; the pits from which clay was taken to strengthen the dyke would not be filled in, but would be declared a protection area.

Returning to Article 6(4) of the Habitats directive, it appears clearly that the phrase 'including those of a social or economic nature' reverses the Court's position as to the possibility of such reasons to justify a project which deteriorates a protected habitat.[92] A number of restrictive conditions apply, however: First, the reasons which justify the project must be 'of overriding public interest', which does not seem to be different from what the Court called 'a general interest which is superior to the general interest represented by the ecological objective of the directive'. Whereas Article 6(4) of the Habitats directive thus reverses the Court's *a priori* rejection of the possibility that economic interests might amount to this level, it nevertheless keeps in place a arguably demanding test. Second, the reasons invoked must be 'imperative', and alternative solutions have to be absent. The deterioration or disturbance must thus be limited to the strictly necessary. Third, if a priority natural habitat type or priority species is at stake, the Commission must be consulted.[93] Fourth, the obligation to take compensatory measures is generalized.

Some final remarks should be added to the discussion of Article 4 (4), first sentence, of the Birds directive and the provisions of the Habitats directive which have replaced it. These provisions apply not only to sites which have been classified as SPAs, but also to sites which should have been classified according to the criteria of Article 4 (1) and (2) of the Birds directive, but which the Member State failed to classify so far.[94] As to SPAs classified (or to be classified) under the Birds directive, each Member State is solely responsible on its territory for executing the obligations arising under Article 6 (2) of the Habitats directive, and thus also for financing the necessary measures. This follows from the Court's judgment in Case C-355/90. One of the infringements of Article 4 (4) of the Birds directive for which the Court condemned Spain in this case, consisted in Spain's failure to stop the release of non-purified waste water from neighbouring communes into the marshes of Santoña, which should have been protected as SPA. Spain based its defense on the very substantial cost of constructing installations to treat the waste water, and the refusal by the EC to take up the bill under the structural funds. This did not prevent the Court from condemning Spain.[95] As Article 6 (2) of the Habitats directive charges the Member States with taking appropriate steps to avoid deterioration or disturbance, in the same wording as Article 4 (4), first sentence, of the Birds directive, this judgment remains valid.[96] Finally, the

---

[92] The Court repeated its refusal to accept such grounds as primary justification in Judgment C-355/90, n25, at paragraphs 37 and 45 (concerning the amelioration of road access to a seaside resort and industrial zone, respectively the economic and social importance of the fish farming industry).

[93] The wordings used (in the various languages) does not allow the interpretation that the opinion of the Commission is binding. A negative opinion, however, could provide evidence which may be used before a national court or the Court of Justice to stop the project (possibly as an interim measure) or establish an infringement of the directive.

[94] Judgment C-355/90, n25, paragraphs 20–22. Article 4 (5) and 5 (4) of the Habitats directive apply the same principle to the procedure of designating special areas of conservation under the Habitats directive. As discussed above, this procedure does not affect Article 4 (1) and (2) of the Birds directive, which continue to be fully applicable. The Court's holding in Case C-355/90 thus remains of importance as well.

[95] The Court thus apparently adopted the view explained in more detail by Advocate-General Van Gerven in his Opinion, n61, at nr 54, who pointed out that the wording of Article 4 (4) of the Birds directive undeniably charges the Member States with taking the necessary measures.

[96] Article 8 (5) of the Habitats directive allows Member States, under certain conditions, to postpone measures for which Community financing was asked but not obtained, but it appears from the rest of Article 8 that this provision concerns demands for Community financing linked to the procedure for designating special areas of conservation under Articles 4 and 5 of the Habitats directive. As explained above, Article 4 (1) and (2) of the Birds directive continue to control the designation of SPAs for bird habitats. As Article 7 of the Habitats directive

provisions of Article 6 (2), (3) and (4) of the Habitats directive are directly applicable. The Court's judgments in Cases C-57/89 and C-355/90 demonstrate that Article 4 (4), first sentence, was sufficiently clear and unconditional to be applied by a Court in a particular case.[97] The new provisions of the Habitats directive are not different in this respect.

3.4. Other obligations concerning bird habitats

Article 3 (1) of the Birds directive states that 'in the light of the requirements referred to in Article 2, Member States shall take the requisite measures to preserve, maintain or re-establish a sufficient diversity and area of habitats for all species of birds' to which the directive applies.[98] Almost no case law exists on the interpretation of this provision. In Case C-355/90 the Commission had based its complaints on both Article 3 and Article 4. The Court, however, did not go into the arguments based on the former: it repeated that Article 3 applies to all species of wild birds, whereas Article 4 only applies to those listed in Annex I and to other species of migratory birds. As it was established that the former two categories of birds were represented on the site which the case at hand concerned, 'it is sufficient to examine the Commission's objections from the point of view of Article 4 of the directive'.[99] This statement should probably be interpreted as meaning that in the particular case there was no reason to go into Article 3, as the Commission could base all its grounds on Article 4 so as to obtain a condemnation of Spain under Article 169 of the EC Treaty. It should thus not be read as implying that Article 3 does not apply to SPAs or, more generally, to birds listed in Annex I or migratory birds.[100]

Article 4 (4), second sentence, states that 'Member States shall also strive to avoid pollution or deterioration of habitats' *outside* SPAs. It has been pointed out that this provision leaves too large a discretion to Member States to be directly applicable.[101] On the other hand, direct application of Article 3 should not be excluded.

4. Species protection (Articles 5 to 9)

4.1. General system of protection (Article 5)

Article 5 of the Birds directive instructs Member States to 'take the requisite measures to establish a general system of protection for all species of birds' to which the directive

does not declare Article 8 (5) applicable to SPAs either, it follows that the Habitats directive does not change the preexisting law on this issue concerning SPAs; see W. Wils, n28.

[97] See also L. Krämer, n29, 46. As the Order of the President of the Court in Case C-57/89, n25, exemplifies, these provisions could also be used to obtain an injunction to prevent the execution of a project which violates them. In this case the action for an injunction was dismissed, but only because the Commission's demand was not deemed urgent anymore: the Commission had waited a long time before it lodged the application for interim measures; in the mean time the project had been largely completed, and the Commission failed to provide evidence that an injunction at such a late stage could still have any impact; see paragraphs 16–22 of the order.

[98] Article 3 (2) lists four types of actions which should be included 'primarily': creation of protected ares, upkeep and management in accordance with the ecological needs of habitats, re-establishment of destroyed biotopes and creation of biotopes.

[99] Judgment C-355/90, n25, paragraph 23 (my translation).

[100] Had the Court meant this, it would have had to be more explicit, as Advocate-General Van Gerven had argued that the two articles do not exclude each other mutually; Opinion in Case C-355/90, n61, nr 57. Under nrs 58 and 59, the Advocate-General had also provided some elements towards the interpretation of Article 3.

[101] L. Krämer, n29, at 46.

applies, 'prohibiting in particular': (a) killing or capture, (b) destruction of nests and eggs, (c) egg collection, (d) significant disturbance and (e) keeping birds of species the hunting and capture of which is forbidden.[102] The Court of Justice has been quite strict in requiring a full transposition of these prohibitions into national law: 'in order to secure the full implementation of directives in law and in fact, Member States must establish a specific legal framework in the area in question'; 'the fact that a number of activities incompatible with the prohibitions contained in the directive are unknown in a particular Member State cannot justify the absence of appropriate legal provisions'.[103]

4.2. Marketing (Article 6)

Article 6(1) of the Birds directive requires the Member States to prohibit, for all the bird species to which the directive applies, 'the sale, transport for sale, keeping for sale and the offering for sale of live or dead birds and of any readily recognazible parts or derivatives of such birds'. Paragraph (2), however, excepts the birds listed in Annex III/1 and paragraph (3) allows Member States (after having consulted the Commission) to make further exceptions for the birds listed in Annex III/2, always 'provided that the birds have been legally killed or captured or otherwise legally acquired'.[104] As paragraph (3) only allows Member States to make exceptions, without requiring them, one could clearly not rely on the Birds directive to escape punishment under national legislation prohibiting the marketing of birds listed in Annex III/2.[105]

4.3. Hunting (Article 7)

Article 7(1), first sentence, of the Birds directive states that 'the species listed in Annex II may be hunted under national legislation'. Paragraphs (2) and (3) distinguish between the species which may be hunted in all the Member States, which are listed in Annex II/1, and those listed in Annex II/2, which may be hunted only in the

---

[102] The Commission's original proposal, n7, only contained a (less comprehensively worded) prohibition of (a), (b) and (c). The prohibitions (a), (b) and (d) only cover 'deliberate' actions. Article 12 of the Habitats directive, which requires the establishment of a similar system of strict protection for other animal species than birds, also explicitly requires monitoring and possibly further measures with regard to *incidental* capture and killing (paragraph 4). One could argue that this obligation also exists under Article 5 of the Birds directive, as it demands 'the requisite measures' for 'a general system of protection', and is not limited to the five prohibitions to be assured 'in particular'.

[103] Judgment 339/87, n25, at paragraph 25. In another case the Court condemned France because its legislation only provided for the protection of nests and eggs during the close season, whereas 'the prohibitions set out in Article 5 (b) and (c) of the Directive must apply without any limitation in time' (Judgment 252/85, n25, at paragraph 9), and also because its legislation prohibited the capture, the removal, the use and the offering for sale of the purchase of protected species, but not their keeping, as required by Article 5 (e) (paragraphs 17–19).

[104] Annex III/1, which has never been modified, lists 7 bird species. Annex III/2 initially listed 10 bird species. Article 6 (4) instructed the Commission to carry out studies concerning 9 other species listed in a further Annex III/3 with a view to a decision on their entry in Annex III/2. Commission Directive 91/244/EEC, n12, added 7 of these 9 species to Annex III/2 and removed Annex III/3. The currently valid Annexes II are thus to be found in OJ 1991 No L 115/54.

[105] Cour de Cassation (France), Judgment of 14 June 1988 in Case *Guilbert/Ministère public* [1988] Bulletin des arrêts de la Cour de Cassation—Chambre criminelle 719. See also Article 14 of the Birds directive.

Member States in respect of which they are indicated.[106] For all other bird species, hunting must be prohibited according to Article 5.[107] Derogations are only possible under Article 9 of the directive.[108]

Article 7(1), second sentence, and (4), first sentence, require Member States to ensure that the hunting 'does not jeopardize conservation efforts' and 'complies with the principles of wise use and ecologically balanced control'. The second and third sentences of Article 7(4) instruct Member States to see 'in particular that the species (. . .) are not hunted during the rearing season nor during the various stages of reproduction. In the case of migratory species, they shall see in particular that the (they) are not hunted during their period of reproduction or during their return to their rearing grounds'.

In two recent judgments[109] the Court of Justice interpreted the latter sentences as requiring that the opening and closing dates for the hunting of birds 'must be fixed in accordance with a method which guarantees complete protection' during the rearing, reproduction and migration periods. 'Methods whose object or effect is to allow a certain percentage of the birds of a species to escape such protection do not comply with that provision'.[110]

4.4. Hunting methods (Article 8)

According to Article 8 (1) of the Birds directive, 'Member States shall prohibit the use of all means, arrangements and methods used for the large-scale or non-selective capture or killing of birds or capable of causing the local disappearance of a species, in particular the use of those listed in Annex IV (a)'. Article 8 (2) instructs Member States to 'prohibit any hunting from the modes of transport and under the conditions mentioned in Annex IV (b)'.[111] The Court of Justice held that 'in view of the principle of legal certainty the relevant prohibitions must be reproduced in mandatory legal provisions'. 'The fact that a practice incompatible with the directive is not carried on

---

[106] Anexes II/1 and II/2 list 24 respectively 48 bird species. Council Directive 81/854/EEC, n10, amended Annex II/2 by indicating which species may be hunted in Greece, without adding any species to the list. The currently valid Annexes II are thus to be found in OJ 1981 No L 319/8. In 1991 the Commission submitted a proposal, n13, to add 5 species to Annex II/2 and to indicate which species may be hunted in Spain and Portugal. The five species concerned (jay, magpie, jackdaw, rook and carrion/hooded crow), regarded as 'pest birds' in several Member States, would have been allowed to be shot according to the Commission's original proposal for the Birds directive (n7), which was modified in this respect by the Council. They had since been the object of many derogations under Article 9 of the directive. In 1992 the Commission modified its proposal (n13) to adopt an amendment proposed by the Parliament, to omit three birds from Annex II/2 only with regard to Italy, because of the risk of confusion with another endangered bird.

[107] The Court of Justice condemned Belgium for creating 'a legally ambiguous situation by not excluding the possibility that species other than those listed in Annex II to the Directive may be hunted'; Judgment 247/85, n25, at paragraph 16. Those other species were classified as 'game' under Belgian law, but could not be hunted in the absence of a decision of the competent authorities laying down each year the hunting season for each species.

[108] Judgment 262/85, n25, paragraphs 12 and 13.

[109] Judgments C-157/89 and C-435/92, n25.

[110] Judgment C-435/92, paragraph 13 (my translation from the French version). The Court thus rejected the French practice to close the hunting season for birds of passage and waterfowl when 'migration can be regarded as significant', meaning when 10% of the birds are involved.

[111] Annex IV lists five groups of means, including snares, artificial light sources, explosives, nets, traps and automatic weapons. Annex IV (b) lists aircraft, motor vehicles and (certain) boats. Both annexes have never been modified; they are to be found in OJ 1979 No L 103/18.

does not release the Member State in question from its obligation (. . .).'[112] It should be noted that the list in Annex IV (a) is not exhaustive, and that means, arrangements or methods which serve another purpose than catching birds, may nevertheless fall under Article 8 (1) if 'capable of causing the local disappearnce' of a wild bird species.[113]

4.5. Derogations (Article 9)

Article 9 authorizes Member States to derogate from the provisions of Articles 5, 6, 7 and 8.[114] 'However, this possibility is subject to three conditions: first, the Member State must restrict the derogation to cases in which there is no other satisfactory solution; secondly, the derogation must be based on at least one of the reasons listed exhaustively in Article 9 (1) (a), (b) and (c); thirdly, the derogation must comply with the precise formal conditions set out in Article 9 (2), which are intended to limit derogations to what is strictly necessary and to enable the Commission to supervise them. Although Article 9 therefore authorizes wide derogations from the general system of protection, it must be applied appropriatly in order to deal with precise requirements and specific situations.'[115]

The reasons for which derogations may be granted, do not include agricultural, forestry or fishing purposes in general,[116] nor historical or cultural traditions.[117] Article 2 of the directive cannot be used to add reasons not listed in Article 9.[118] Among the reasons listed, the most difficult to interpret is the one mentioned under Article 9 (1) (c), namely 'to permit, under strictly supervised conditions and on a selective basis, the capture, keeping or other judicial use of certain birds in small numbers'. It has been held that 'the criterion of small quantities is not an absolute criterion but rather refers to the maintenance of the level of the total population and to the reproductive situation of the species concerned',[119] and that the limitation to small quantities applies

[112] Judgment 339/87, n25, at paragraph 22.

[113] The Belgian Conseil d'Etat may thus have jumped too quickly to its conclusion when it held that traps used to catch rabbits do not fall under Article 8 (1), stating that the provision should not be interpreted as prohibiting 'the use of any device which serves other purposes than the capture of birds, but may nevertheless turn out accidentally damaging to these'; Judgment of 20 February 1991 in Case 36.467 *LBPO/Région Wallonne*. Receuil des Arrêts du Conseil d'Etat, 1991, 36.467 (my translation). Annex IV (a) mentions 'traps', not 'bird traps'.

[114] The Community legislator did not follow the recommendation of the Economic and Social Committee (n62, at 5) to exclude certain provisions, in particular part of Article 8, such as the prohibition on snares, from the possibility offered by Article 9. Of course, certain provisions may in practice never be derogated from, in sofar as the conditions imposed by Article 9 cannot be met; see n121.

[115] Judgments 247/85 and 262/85, n25, paragraphs 7. These conditions have been interpreted and applied in a number of cases by the Court of Justice (Judgments 247/85, 262/85, 412/85, 236/85, 252/87 and 339/87; n25) and by national courts.

[116] Judgment 412/85, n25, paragraphs 8 and 19; Article 9 (1) (a) does list, however, the 'prevent(ion of) serious damage to crops, livestock, forests, fisheries and water'; as to the requirement of seriousness, see Judgment 247/85, paragraphs 56 to 58 and Judgment 236/85, paragraphs 8 and 9.

[117] Judgment 236/85, n25, paragraphs 20 to 23.

[118] n55.

[119] Judgment 252/85, n25, at paragraph 28; the Court considered this as being 'apparent from Article 2, in conjunction with the 11th recital of the preambule to the Directive'. The case concerned the capture of thrushes and skylarks in certain French departments. France's acquittal has been considered surprising, as the numbers of birds captured annually probably amounted to several hunderd thousands; see Untermaier, n25, at 469. The explanation can be found in paragraph 30 of the judgment, which mentions that the Commission had not contested France's argument that a 'very small percentage' of the bird population was concerned. In proceedings brought under Article 169 of the EC Treaty, the burden of proof lies entirely on the Commission's side. If the Commission decides not to press its case, the Court has no other choice than to declare the case unfounded. But

for each species seperately.[120] Finally, it would seem that, because of its condition of selectivity, Article 9 (1) (c) could not justify a derogation from Article 8 (1).[121]

Article 9 does not make the granting of derogations subject to any public procedure.[122] Article 9 (3) only requires Member States to send a yearly report to the Commission on the application of the article.[123]

4.6. Direct effect

The provisions laid down in Articles 5, 6, 7, 8 and 9 of the Birds directive are all directly applicable. The prohibitions on marketing (Article 6), hunting of birds not listed in Annex II (Articles 5 and 7), hunting during the rearing season (Article 7 (4)), non-selective hunting methods (Article 8), as well as the other prohibitions in Article 5, are all clear and unambiguous, and sufficiently operational in themselves to be applied by a court.[124] This conclusion is not altered by the fact that Article 9 allows Member States to make derogations. As discussed above, the latter provision imposes a number of conditions which aim to limit derogations to the strictly necessary. These conditions are directly applicable as well.[125] All derogations which fail to satisfy Article 9 should be put aside, leaving the general prohibitions of Articles 5 to 8 fully applicable.[126]

5. Final provisions

Articles 10 to 19 of the Birds directive contain a number of final provisions. I only discuss here Articles 14 and 13, which concern stricter national protection measures,

it would thus be wrong to interpret Judgment 252/85 as implying that hundreds of thousands of birds can be 'small numbers' in the sense of Article 9 (1) (c).

[120] Conseil d'Etat (Belgium), Judgment of 9 December 1988 in Case 31.573 *LBPO/Région Wallonne*, Receuil des Arrêts du Conseil d'Etat, 1988, 31.573, refering to the Opinion of Advocate-General da Cruz Vilaça in Case 252/85 [1988] ECR 2254, at nr 44.

[121] As to snares in particular, this reasoning was applied by the French Conseil d'Etat in its judgment of 26 October 1990 in Case 91.974 *ROC/Ministre de l'Environnement*, summarily reported in *Gazette du Palais*, 1991, No 142, p. 33.

[122] Conseil d'Etat (Belgium), Judgment 36.467, n1 13. Of course, national law may impose publicity; moreover, under Article 3 of Council Directive 90/313/EEC on the freedom of access to information on the environment (OJ 1990 No L 158/56), national authorities should make available information regarding derogations under Article 9 of the Birds directive to any natural or legal person at his request and without his having to prove an interest.

[123] When adopting the Birds directive, the Council rejected the proposals which would have given a role to the Commission in approving derogations under Article 9 ex ante; see Commission's first and second proposal and Parliament's opinion, nn7, 8 and 32.

[124] In the same sense: L. Krämer, nn29, 45–6.

[125] This appears from the several judgments (n115) in which the Court of Justice applied the criteria of Article 9 to various derogations.

[126] The direct effect of Articles 5 to 9 has been recognized for several years now by the highest administrative courts of France, the Netherlands and Belgium: see i.a. Conseil d'Etat (France), Judgment of 7 December 1984 in Case 41.971 *Fédération française des sociétés de protection de la nature/Ministre de l'Environnement* [1984] Receuil des décisions du Conseil d'Etat 410; Afdeling Rechtspraak Raad van State (Netherlands), Judgment of 6 March 1986 in Case A-1.0511 (1982), *Milieu en Recht*, 1987, 16; Conseil d'Etat (Belgium), Judgment of 9 December 1988 in Case 31.573 *LBPO/Etat belge*, Receuil des Arrêts du Conseil d'Etat, 1988, 31.573. In 1991 the highest Italian administrative court denied direct effect to the Birds directive: Consiglio di Stato, Judgment of 27 February 1991 in Case 100 *WWF/Regione Marche* [1991] Il Consiglio di Stato I-281; critical comments to this judgment, which appears clearly erroneous, were made by R. Caranta and by C. Di Paolo, *Rivista italiana di diritto pubblico comunitario*, 1992, 508 and 524.

and Article 18, which provides a basis for a few remarks on the implementation and enforcement of the directive.[127]

5.1. Stricter protection under national law (Articles 14 and 13)

Article 14 reads as follows: 'Member States may introduce stricter protective measures than those provided for under this Directive'.[128] In a 1990 judgment, the Court of Justice undertook to 'define the scope of the powers conferred on the Member States' by this article. Having pointed out that the Birds directive grants special protection to migratory birds and to bird species listed in Annex I to the directive, the Court held that 'the Member States are authorized, pursuant to Article 14 of the directive, to introduce stricter measures to ensure that the aforesaid species are protected even more effectively. With regard to the other bird species covered by (the Birds directive), the Member States (. . .) are not authorized to adopt stricter measures than those provided for under the directive, except as regards species occurring within their territory'. The Court thus excluded from Article 14 measures by Member States which enhance the protection of species not occurring in their own territory, and which are moreover neither migratory nor listed in Annex I to the directive. In the case at hand, the Netherlands could thus not prohibit the marketing on its territory of a red grouse (a species not occuring in the Netherlands) which had been lawfully killed in the United Kingdom, in accordance with the combined provisions of Article 6 (2) and (3) and Annex III/1 of the Birds directive.[129]

  According to Article 13 of the Birds directive, 'application of the measures pursuant to this Directive may not lead to deterioration in the present situation as regards the conservation of species of birds' to which the directive applies. The 'present' situation should arguably be read as the situation on 2 April 1979, the day on which the Council adopted the Birds directive.[130] In a case before the Belgian Conseil d'Etat, a bird protection group invoked this provision to ask for the annulment of a decree of the Walloon government which would allow the yearly capture of 12 birds of a certain group of species by each capturer, whereas legislation predating the Birds directive only allowed for 10 birds per capturer. The Belgian court rejected this argument,

---

[127] Article 10 concerns research on bird protection; Article 11 has been mentioned in the discussion of Article 1 above; Article 12 concerns reporting between the Member States and the Commission on the implementation of the directive.

[128] Article 14 (and Article 13) did not figure in the Commission's proposals for the Birds directive; nn7 and 8. The Habitats directive does not contain a similar provision, but, as it was adopted under Article 130s of the EC Treaty, Article 130t applies: 'The protective measures adopted in common pursuant to Article 130s shall not prevent any Member State from maintaining or introducing more stringent protective measures compatible with this Treaty'.

[129] Judgment of 23 May 1990 in Case C-169/89, n25; the judgment has been strongly critisized by several commentators: see Jans en Pijnacker Hordijk, n25, and L. Krämer, 'Environmental protection and Article 30 EEC Treaty', *Common Market Law Review*, 1993, 111, at 119–20. It seems strange indeed that the Court could read any restriction into Article 14 in spite of its general, unrestricted wording. The Advocate-General had advised the Court to condemn the Dutch marketing ban, but on a different ground: he recognized the unrestricted scope of Article 14 of the Birds directive, but thought the marketing ban incompatible with the EC Treaty's provisions on free movement of goods, which bind the Community legislator; Opinion of 20 March 1990 in Case C-169/89 *Gourmetterie Van den Burgh* [1990] ECR I-2151. Although one may disagree with the result he thus reached, the Advocate-General's approach seems logically more conherent than the Court's.

[130] One could also argue for 6 April 1979, the day on which the directive was notified to the Member States. Anyway, Article 13 does not depend on any implementation measures to which the two years deadline of Article 18 applies.

stating that Article 13 should be read in the light of the general objectives of Article 2 of the directive, and that the increase in the number of birds which might be captured did not establish a 'deterioration' as meant in Article 13.[131] This interpretation might be questioned: Article 13 does not speak of 'significant' deterioration only (compare significant deterioration or disturbance in Articles 4 (4) and 5 (d), but appears to forbid any deterioration in the situation—which I interpret to mean the *legal* situation—regards the conservation of wild birds. It should thus be sufficient pointing out any change in the law to the detriment of bird conservation to establish a violation of Article 13.[132] If on the contrary proof were required of a detrimental effect on the factual conservation status as described in Article 2—which is to be achieved anyway by all the other provisions of the directive—Article 13 would not serve any practical purpose in the directive.

5.2. Implementation and enforcement

Article 18 of the Birds directive instructs the Member States to 'bring into force the laws, regulations and administrative provisions necessary to comply with this Directive within two years of its notification'. As the directive was notified on 6 April 1979, the relevant date is 6 April 1981. From that day on, the provisions of the directive must have been tranposed into national law, and must be complied with in practice.[133] Ever since, the actual implementation and enforcement of the provisions of the Birds directive has been problematic.[134] The Commission has brought before the Court of Justice 15 actions under Article 169 of the EC Treaty against various Member States for failure to comply with the directive.[135] It has been handling many more Article 169 infringement proceedings which have not, or not yet, reached the Court.[136] Members of the European Parliament have asked more than 500 questions to the Commission

---

[131] Judgment of 9 December 1988, n126; the decree was annulled, however, on another ground, namely because the maximum number of birds to be captured was not determined for each species seperately (but only among a group of species) which did not allow the court to check the fulfillment of the 'small numbers' condition in Article 9 (1) (c) of the directive.

[132] Article 13 could then be applied directly to discard the new legislation or administrative practice.

[133] The later amendments to the directive (nn10 to 12) each have their own implementation date. Greece also had to comply from 6 April 1981 on, and Spain and Portugal from the date of their entry into the Community (1 January 1986), in the absence of any special provisions in the respective Accession Acts; see Judgment C-355/90, n25, paragraph 11.

[134] Many areas of EC law suffer from defective implementation and enforcement. Environmental law appears to raise more than average problems in this respect; see R. Macrory, 'The enforcement of Community environmental law: some critical issues', Common Market Law Review, 1992, 347. The following figures, which exceed by far the corresponding figures for all other environmental directives, suggest that the Birds directive is singularly problematic.

[135] Two of these, both against Ireland, were withdrawn by the Commission (Cases 240/85 and C-155/90); with the exception of Case C-57/89 (nn25 and 87 to 91), the other cases led to the condemnation of the Member States concerned (n25: twelve judgments other than C-57/89 and other than C-169/89 and C-435/92, which were rendered on requests for a preliminary ruling). Two of these condemnations (C-675/91 and C-345/92) were for failure to comply with an earlier condemnation by the Court.

[136] The Commission's 1992 Tenth annual report to the European Parliament on Commission monitoring of the application of Community law (OJ 1993 No C 233/1) mentions problems with the implementation of the Birds directive in all twelve Member States. In the case of Denmark, the only problem concerned the failure to notify the implementing measures for the 1991 amendments to the birds directive (n12). It appears that Denmark is the only Member State where the Birds directive is otherwise systematically complied with. In its Second report on the application of Directive No 79/409/EEC on the conservation of wild birds, COM(93) 572 final, the Commission mentioned at p. 113 that, as to SPA classification in particular, 'only Denmark and Belgium have almost fully complied with their obligations'.

concerning the Birds directive, in most instances to denounce infringements in their respective Member States.[137] In a few Member States (France, Belgium and the Netherlands), national courts have been playing an important role in enforcing the Birds directive, at least its provisions concerning the direct protection of species (Articles 5 to 9).[138] It would seem to me that the enforcement of the Birds directive at national level could and should become more widespread. As was shown throughout the preceding discussion, most of the provisions of the directive have direct effect, and could thus be relied upon by individuals or environmental protection groups against public authorities before national courts.[139]

---

[137] The number of such questions has dramatically increased since 1990, up to over 100 questions a year. The Commission stated in its Tenth annual report (n136, at 43) that most of the cases of infringement of the Birds directive which it detects, are based on questions or petitions from the Parliament. Others are based on complaints by private individuals and environmental protection groups. See also Parliament's Resolution of 13 October 1988 on the implementation of the directive on the conservation of wild birds, OJ 1988 No C 290/137.

[138] See i.a. the judgments mentioned in nn37, 113, 120, 121 and 126. Only twice a request for a preliminary ruling was made to the Court of Justice: see Cases C-169/89 and C-435/92, n25.

[139] In some Member States, especially the United Kingdom, high legal costs may constitute an obstacle to the enforcement of the Birds directive through the national courts. France, Belgium and the Netherlands are all countries in which legal costs are sufficiently low as to allow environmental protection groups to engage in litigation against public authorities. This adds another dimension to the debate on the even-handedness of the current sytem for the enforcement of EC environmental law, questioning in particular the UK's claim to be among the Member States where enforcement is more effective; see i.a. speech by UK environment secretary Michael Howard at the Environment for Europe Minister's Conference, Lucerne, 28–30 April 1993, reported by *The Financial Times*, 1–2 May 1993.

[18]

Environmental Planning and Spatial Planning from a European Community Perspective

European Parliament, in a resolution of 15 December 1983 on a "European Scheme for Spatial Planning".

Against this background, the further purpose of this article is to analyse:

(i) the policy declarations of the institutions of the European Community in the field of spatial planning;

Prof. Dr. Kurt Deketelaere
Institute for Environmental Law, K.U.
Leuven, Arthur Andersen, Brussels

This article is published in two parts; the first appeared in the October issue of European Environmental Law Review; the concluding part appears below.

III: Spatial Planning: Observations from a European Community Perspective

A. Introduction

Spatial planning policy, at various levels, has been the subject of much interest in recent years. A few examples:

(i) in 1996, the Flemish Parliament adopted a decree concerning spatial planning;

(ii) in 1996, the Ministers for Spatial Planning of the Netherlands, Luxembourg and the three Belgian regions proposed the concept of the second[48] Benelux Structure Sketch[49, 50]

(iii) in 1994, the European Commission presented the document *Europe 2000+, Cooperation for European territorial development.*[51, 52]

So, not only the Flemish Region and the Benelux are thinking about their policy concerning spatial planning, but apparently also the European Community.[53] On this latter policy level, it can clearly be noticed that interest in spatial planning is steadily growing:[54] in 1992, the concept of "town and country planning" was explicitly introduced into Article 130S(2) ToM; in 1993, explicit, though modest, attention was paid to "spatial planning" in the Fifth European EAP;[55] in 1994, the above-mentioned policy document *Europe 2000+, Cooperation for European territorial development, was drafted;*[56] in the progress report drafted in 1995,[57] ample attention was given by the European Commission to "spatial planning"; in 1996, for the first time a directive was adopted in which an Article explicitly deals with "land-use planning", namely Article 12, "Land-use planning", of Directive 96/82/EC of the Council of 9 December 1996 on the control of major-accident hazards involving dangerous substances,[58] the so-called new[59] Seveso Directive; in 1997, a proposal for a directive "on the assessment of the effects of certain plans and programmes on the environment" was adopted, which primarily refers to specific town and country planning plans and programmes.[60]

These initiatives of the European Community concerning spatial planning will be further analysed hereafter. However, curiously enough, the first ideas[61] concerning Europe and spatial planning had already been formulated in 1983 by the

---

[48.] In October 1986, the first Benelux Global Structure Sketch concerning spatial planning was published.

[49.] *Space for cooperation – Second Benelux Structure Sketch – Concept May 1996*, Benelux, Brussels, 1996, 185p.

[50.] D'HONDT, F., "Concept Tweede Benelux Structuurschets", *Ruimtelijke Planning*, 1996, nr. 27, 5; D'HONDT, F., "Ruimte voor grensoverschrijdende samenwerking – Een ruimtelijke structuurschets voor de lage landen", *De Europese Gemeente*, 1997–6, 18–21; ZONNEVELD, W. en D'HONDT, F., "Ruimtelijke ordening in de Benelux", in D'HONDT, F. en ZONNEVELD, W. (eds.), *Europese ruimtelijke ordening – Impressies en visies vanuit Vlaanderen en Nederland*, Vlaamse Federatie voor Planologie (VFP)/Nederlands Instituut voor Ruimtelijke Ordening en Huisvesting (NIROV), Gent/Den Haag, 1994, 103–116.

[51.] X., *Europe 2000+, Cooperation for European territorial development*, European Commission, Brussels/ Luxembourg, 1994, 247.

[52.] DEKETELAERE, K., "De Europese Gemeenschap en de ruimtelijke ordening", *Nieuwsbrief Ruimtelijke Ordening en Stedebouw*, 1994, nr. 1, 33–35; DEKETELAERE, K., "Communautaire initiatieven op het gebied van de ruimtelijke ordening: "Europa 2000+", *Nieuwsbrief Ruimtelijke Ordening en Stedebouw*, 1995, nr. 2, 11–12.

[53.] MARTIN, D., "Europese ruimtelijke ordening: inzicht en uitzicht", in D'HONDT, F. en ZONNEVELD, W. (eds.), *Europese ruimtelijke ordening – Impressies en visies vanuit Vlaanderen en Nederland*, Vlaamse Federatie voor Planologie (VFP)/Nederlands Instituut voor Ruimtelijke Ordening en Huisvesting (NIROV), Gent/Den Haag, 1994, 15–27; WILLIAMS, R.H., *European spatial policy and planning*, London, Paul Chapman Publishing, 1996, 283.

[54.] DE LANGE, C., "Europese Ruimtelijke Ordening", *De Europese Gemeente*, 1996, nr. 3, 19–22; DE LANGE, C., "Europese Regiostudies", *De Europese Gemeente*, 1996, nr. 5, 21–24; D'HONDT, F. en ZONNEVELD, W. (eds.), *Europese ruimtelijke ordening – Impressies en visies vanuit Vlaanderen en Nederland*, Vlaamse Federatie voor Planologie (VFP)/Nederlands Instituut voor Ruimtelijke Ordening en Huisvesting (NIROV), Gent/Den Haag, 1994, 162; KORMOSS, I.B.F., "Een terugblik op Europa en ruimtelijke planning", in D'HONDT, F. en ZONNEVELD, W. (eds.), *Europese ruimtelijke ordening – Impressies en visies vanuit Vlaanderen en Nederland*, Vlaamse Federatie voor Planologie (VFP)/Nederlands Instituut voor Ruimtelijke Ordening en Huisvesting (NIROV), Gent/Den Haag, 1994, 33–41; PASCALLON, P., "La politique communautaire d'aménagement du territoire: du Traité de Rome à l'Acte Unique", *Revue du Marché Commun*, 1990, 514–519.

[55.] OJ 17.5.93 C 138/70.

[56.] WILLIAMS, R.H., European spatial policy and planning, London, Paul Chapman Publishing, 1996, 218–228.

[57.] COM(95) 624 final Brussels, 10 January 1996, 107–110.

[58.] OJ 14.1.97 L 10.

[59.] According to Article 23 of Directive 96/82/EC, the so-called old SEVESO directive – Directive 82/501/EEC of the Council of 24 June 1982 on the major-accident hazards of certain industrial activities (OJ 5.8.82 L 230 (as modified)), will be withdrawn two years after the coming into force of Directive 96/82/EC.

[60.] OJ 25.4.97 C 129.

[61.] WILLIAMS, R.H., *European spatial policy and planning*, London, Paul Chapman Publishing, 1996, 65–90.

308 European Environmental Law Review November 1997

Environmental and Spatial Planning

(ii) the possibilities for primary community legislation with a view to adopting measures in the field of spatial planning;

(iii) which measures of secondary Community legislation already contain provisions in the field of spatial planning (and their consequences);

(iv) the future perspectives for a European policy concerning spatial planning.

Finally by way of introduction, something must be said about the term "spatial planning" itself. Although Article 130S(2) ToM refers to "town and country planning" and "land use",[62] it is preferable to use what Williams calls the "Euroenglish" expression, "spatial planning". Williams states correctly:[63]

> "Town planning is a generic term in British English ... but translates as "urbanisme" (French) or "Städtebau" (German), both of which have much narrower urban planning or urban design meanings. The American generic term equivalent to the British town planning is "city planning". The Euroenglish word, as used here, is "spatial planning", a term not used on a day-to-day basis in domestic UK practice although its use and recognition as a Euroenglish term is increasing. It is a valid translation of "aménagement du territoire" (French) or "Raumplanung" (German). "Raumordnung" used in the treaty, pedantically could be taken to mean something different but in practice is recognised by German professionals as being coterminous with "Raumplanung". The Dutch have similar words, although some Dutch professionals claim to recognise a distinction between the Dutch equivalents of the German words, i.e. "ruimtelijke planning" and "ruimtelijke ordening".

Although in this article the terms "spatial planning" and "spatial policy" are used systematically, the terms "land use" and "town and country planning" will be used when they are mentioned as such in official Community documents or Treaty articles. As a consequence, and again following Williams,[64] a broad definition of the scope of spatial policy and planning will be taken in this article:

> "The word spatial is used to express a focus on the location and distribution of activity within the territory or space of Europe. Spatial policy includes any policy designed to influence locational and land use decisions, or the distribution of activities, at any spatial scale from that of local land use planning to the regional, national and supranational scales."

B. Policy Declarations of the European Community Institutions on Spatial Planning

(i) General

Since the beginning of the eighties, different institutions of the European Community (European Commission, European Parliament, Economic and Social Committee, Committee of the Regions) have formulated different points of view with regard to a European spatial planning policy. For example: Resolution of the European Parliament of 15 December 1983 concerning "a European Scheme for spatial planning",[65] Resolution of the European Parliament of 26 October 1990 concerning "a coordinated policy of spatial planning";[66] Communication of the European Commission

the future spatial planning of the Community";[67] Communication of the European Commission (September 1994) concerning "Europe 2000+, Cooperation for European territorial development".[68]

These four documents contain an explicit plea for the development of a European policy vision and a European policy framework concerning spatial planning, in order to:

(i) counter excessive population concentrations,

(ii) maintain and protect the environment, landscapes and cultures in Europe, and

(iii) evaluate infrastructure projects on European, national and local levels, but with respect for the subsidiarity principle.

Since these documents have already been extensively discussed and analysed in the literature on spatial planning,[69] the immediate focus hereafter will be the question of what the European Community is intending to do in the coming years in the field of spatial planning.

(ii) Progress Report

General

An answer (albeit from an environmental point of view) to the above-mentioned policy question can be found in the *Progress Report from the Commission on the Implementation of the European Community Programme of Policy and Action in Relation to the Environment and Sustainable Development – 'Towards Sustainability'*.[70] As already mentioned, this Progress Report evaluates the implementation of the Fifth EAP[71] in the period 1992–1995. The Progress Report does not in fact evaluate spatial planning, but rather gives a further elaboration of the ideas of the Community on this point: while the Fifth EAP dealt only in a modest way with "sectoral planning and spatial planning",[72] the Progress Report discusses spatial planning on both Community and national levels (cf. subsidiarity), from the perspective of "sustainable development".

---

62. What is the difference?

63. WILLIAMS, R.H., *European spatial policy and planning*, London, Paul Chapman Publishing, 1996, 58–59.

64. WILLIAMS, R.H., *European spatial policy and planning*, London, Paul Chapman Publishing, 1996, 7.

65. OJ 16.1.84 C 10/115–117.

66. OJ 26.11.90 C 295/652–657.

67. COM(91)0452; reaction of the European Parliament: Resolution A3-0253/92, OJ 2.11.92 C 248; reaction of the Economic and Social Committee: advice 91/C 339/18, OJ 31.12.91 C 339; advice 92/C 287/03, OJ 4.11.92 C 287.

68. COM(94) 0354 – C4-0216/95; reaction of the European Parliament: advice A4-0147/95, OJ 17.7.95 C 183; reaction of the Economic and Social Committee: advice 95/C 133/03, OJ 31.5.95 C 133; reaction of the Committee of the Regions: advice 96/C 100/16, OJ 2.4.96 C 100.

69. D'HONDT, F. en ZONNEVELD, W. (eds.), *Europese ruimtelijke ordening – Impressies en visies vanuit Vlaanderen en Nederland*, Vlaamse Federatie voor Planologie (VFP)/Nederlands Instituut voor Ruimtelijke Ordening en Huisvesting (NIROV), Gent/Den Haag, 1994, 162p.; WILLIAMS, R.H., *European spatial policy and planning*, London, Paul Chapman Publishing, 1996, 283.

70. COM(95) 624 final, Brussels, 10 January 1996, 107–110.

71. OJ 17.5.93 C 138.

72. OJ 17.5.93 C 138.

Environmental and Spatial Planning

Goals

In the Progress Report, four goals are formulated for the future concerning spatial planning:[73]

(i)   agreement on a directive on environmental impact assessment for plans and programmes;

(ii) further development of the "Europe 2000+" and "European Spatial Development Perspective (ESDP)" initiatives as the basis for creating consensus among policy-makers on the main principles to guide the future spatial development of Europe in a sustainable way;

(iii) definition of methodologies and tools to develop the potential of spatial planning for environmental integration;

(iv) analysis of the links between environmental instruments and spatial planning and the definition of strategic environmental frameworks in particular sectors to support sustainable spatial planning.

As regards goal (i), a call for environmental impact assessment for plans and programmes[74] had already been formulated in the Fifth EAP:[75]

"Within the Community, land-use and structural planning generally follows an identifiable sequence starting with national or regional economic plans and ending with local physical development and environmental protection plans. The sequence has two principal components – the upstream policies or plans including control principles and statements of intent, and the downstream programmes and projects which form the basis of action. Given the goal of achieving sustainable development it seems only logical, if not essential, to apply an assessment of the environmental implications of all relevant policies, plans and programmes. The integration of environmental assessment within the macro-planning process would not only enhance the protection of the environment and encourage optimisation of resource management but would also help to reduce those disparities in the international and interregional competition for new developments projects which at present arise from disparities in assessment practices in the Member States."

Meanwhile, the European Commission has already taken initiatives in this field. In the Official Journal of 25 April 1997, a proposal for a directive "on the assessment of the effects of certain plans and programmes on the environment" was published. European Commissioner Ritt Bjerregaard said the following with regard to the proposal:[76]

"Perhaps the key requirement is for an environmental 'statement' to be prepared prior to the adoption of plans or programmes, giving information on the contents of the land development plan or programme; the environmental characteristics of any area likely to be significantly affected by the plan or programme; any existing environmental problem; the environmental protection objectives established at international, Community and Member States' level; the likely 'significant' environmental effects of implementing the plans; any alternative ways of achieving the objectives of the plan; and measures envisaged to prevent, reduce, and where possible offset any significant adverse effects of implementing the plan".

As concerns goal (ii), it is the intention of the European Commission to pursue further the goals embedded in the

communication "Europe 2000+". For clarity, the content of this voluminous document can be summarised as follows.

Section A[77] examines the main trends affecting European territory. It begins by describing changes in the territorial distribution of population over recent years and goes on to consider divergences between the mobility of population and changes in employment. The next part examines the role of international investment in regional development. Trans-European networks of telecommunications, transport and energy are then considered in terms of their spatial implications. Finally, two major environmental issues, the protection of open spaces and water resources, have been selected to illustrate the importance of transnational cooperation.

Section B[78] considers major developments in urban, rural and border areas. Attention is drawn to the renewed growth of large cities in most parts of Europe, with increased problems of social exclusion and spatial segregation as well as those of the environment and transport, and to the growing fragility of small and medium-sized towns which necessitates specific policy action. So far as rural areas are concerned, the focus is on the diverse trends affecting different types of region and the possible ways of responding to the changing pattern of agricultural activity and the role of towns in local development. The section ends with an examination of the internal and external border areas of the Union, for which cooperation on spatial planning organisation is of special relevance.

Section C[79] is concerned with spatial planning systems in Member States and attempts a first examination of the diverse planning instruments and policies in force in each country. It looks, in particular, at the changes which they are undergoing as a result of the increasing European dimension of spatial planning issues. In addition, it includes a preliminary consideration of the regional effects of public sector transfers and taxation, directed in part at redistributing income and resources.

In the annex,[80] a transnational perspective on the European territory is presented, based on a series of studies launched by the Commission during the last three years, analysing the trends and prospects for groups of regions which cut across national boundaries. Eight such groups are identified in the Union itself, one of which is the new Länder which are treated separately because of the special problems they face. Developments in surrounding areas to the North,

---

73. COM(95) 624 final, Brussels, 10 January 1996, 88.

74. See Directive 85/337/EEC of the Council of 27 June 1985 on the assessment of the effects of certain public and private projects on the environment, OJ 5.7.85 L 175.

75. OJ 17.5.93 C 138/70.

76. Europe Environment, nr. 491, 14 January 1997.

77. X., *Europa 2000+, Cooperation for European territorial development*, European Commission, Brussels/ Luxembourg, 1994, 29–92.

78. X., *Europa 2000+, Cooperation for European territorial development*, European Commission, Brussels/ Luxembourg, 1994, 93–136.

79. X., *Europa 2000+, Cooperation for European territorial development*, European Commission, Brussels/ Luxembourg, 1994, 137–166.

80. X., *Europa 2000+, Cooperation for European territorial development*, European Commission, Brussels/ Luxembourg, 1994, 167–245.

310   *European Environmental Law Review   November 1997*

Environmental and Spatial Planning

East and South of the Union are then examined to assess their potential impact on European spatial organisation. Various policy options for avoiding unbalanced spatial development are identified for each regional grouping.

The Progress Report focuses on one of the above-mentioned goals, namely the achievement of a viable territory through sustainable development.[81] It makes the safeguarding of the environment and its biodiversity, as well as wise management of natural resources, a priority for spatial planning in the Member States and a major dimension of relevant Community programmes and policies.

Concerning the "European Spatial Development Perspective (ESDP)",[82] after preparatory work in Strasbourg in March 1995, the Ministers responsible for Spatial Development agreed that a European Spatial Development Perspective should be presented in 1996 (or as soon as possible). This document will adopt the achievement of sustainable and balanced development as a basic principle of the ESDP. The Perspective is a policy-oriented document which has to be seen as a substantial contribution to the effective application of a new development model encompassing the economic, social and environmental dimensions. It identifies wise management and development of the natural and cultural heritage as one of three spheres of activity, along with a more balanced and polycentric urban system, and parity of access to infrastructure and knowledge. This is of key importance for the overall goal of balanced and sustainable organisation of the Community's territory. In that context, it sets as an operational objective the establishment of a European network of open spaces for the preservation of natural resources, including protected areas, to be classified according to their different functions (natural habitats and species habitats, water reserves, recreation, climatic compensation, agriculture and forestry, etc).

Goals (iii) and (iv) are further discussed below, under IV: Secondary Community Law and Spatial Planning.

On spatial planning, the Progress Report concludes as follows:[83]

"The potential of spatial planning as an instrument to achieve sustainable development is much greater than has been exploited so far. There is increasing recognition of the need for a more comprehensive framework addressing, in any given territorial area, the complexity of policies and procedures at the most appropriate level, with a view also to encouraging dialogue between actors. Such a framework could ensure the convergence of policies and measures which have an impact on the territory towards the same fundamental objectives, even complementing or reinforcing each other. The development of a spatial policy approach could provide a solution to conflicts between sectoral policies. But it would need to be flexible and to be complemented by effective tools such as state of the environment reports, environmental indicators, permanent monitoring and systematic environment impact assessment, in particular at the earliest stage of plans and programmes. It would also be necessary to ensure that environmental authorities are both closely and actively involved in the spatial planning process."

C. Primary Community Law and Spatial Planning

Introduction

The formulation of a European policy vision on spatial planning is of course only a first step in the development of such a policy. However, the implementation of this policy vision demands a policy framework within which the envisaged policy can take legal shape. Here arises the central question: what are the competences of the European Community, at this moment, to adopt measures in the field of spatial planning? This question will be dealt with hereafter, on the basis of the articles of the ToM which (can) have a link with the field of spatial planning, and thus, directly or indirectly, can serve as a Treaty basis for European measures on the subject.

Explicit Treaty Provision: Article 130S(2) ToM

Article 130S(2) ToM stipulates:

"By way of derogation from the decision-making procedure provided for in paragraph 1 and without prejudice to Article 100A,[84] the Council, acting unanimously on a proposal from the Commission and after consulting the European Parliament and the Economic and Social Committee, shall adopt:

– provisions primarily of a fiscal nature;
– *measures concerning town and country planning, land use with the exception of waste management and measures of a general nature,*[85] and management of water resources;
– measures significantly affecting a Member State's choice between different energy sources and the general structure of its energy supply."

This provision, stipulating that Community measures concerning spatial planning cannot be approved by a qualified majority of votes, but only by unanimity, is the only disposition of the ToM which explicitly mentions spatial planning (in the sense of town and country planning and land use). But it is this ToM which contains the first explicit reference to spatial planing at this level. Neither the Treaty of Rome (1957) nor the European Single Act (1986) dealt with the topic at all.

However, the second dash of Article 130S(2) ToM is a strange provision. Article 130S ToM deals with the decision-making procedures on European environmental measures and not with environmental competences (including, eventually, competence concerning spatial planning) of the European Community. These competences are embedded

---

[81.] COM(95) 624 final, Brussels, 10 January 1996, 86.
[82.] COM(95) 624 final, Brussels, 10 January 1996, 86.
[83.] COM(95) 624 final, Brussels, 10 January 1996, 87.
[84.] Article 130S(1) of the Treaty of Maastricht stipulates that the Council, acting in accordance with the procedure referred to in Article 189C and after consulting the Economic and Social Committee, shall decide what action is to be taken by the Community in order to achieve the objectives referred to in Article 130R.
[85.] Emphasis added.

European Environmental Law Review November 1997 311

Environmental and Spatial Planning

in Article 130R ToM.[86] But this Article nowhere explicitly states that (the competences concerning) spatial planning are part of the environmental competences of the Community. According to Verhoeve & Co,[87] it is remarkable that after years of silence about the competence for spatial planning, spatial planning measures now emerge as part of the category environmental policy measures, and then not even in the framework of the discussion on the content of environmental policy, but in the decision-making procedures. In his turn, Jans states the following about this:[88]

"But is there then any power at all to pursue an independent town and country planning policy under the title on the environment? This does not follow from the objectives of Article 130R(1). Nor will a comprehensive Community competence in the field of town and country planning be found elsewhere in the Treaty. But if such a power does not fall within the scope of Article 130R, there is no need to except it."

Taking into account the obscurity[89] of the passage "measures concerning town and country planning", I would dare to defend the thesis that the environmental competences, as embedded in Title XVI ToM, extend to the competence of the Community to adopt measures in the field of spatial planning. A first argument for this thesis is not even of a juridical nature: in many countries it is to be observed that the environmental policy and environmental legislation *senso lato* embrace policy and legislation concerning spatial planning, even when the concrete political competences are spread among different ministers. A second step in this argument can be formulated, in that the second dash of Article 130S(2) ToM in fact concerns specific types of environmental measure, which have in common that they cannot be adopted by a qualified majority of votes, but only by unanimity: town and country planning, land use[90] and management of water resources.

This thesis of course leads directly to the following pertinent question of Jans:[91]

"The question which then arises is of course whether it was the intention that any measure which has consequences for the physical layout of the territory of a Member State, and in that sense "concerns" town and country planning, should be taken unanimously. That would mean that any area-related environmental policy would have to be adopted unanimously, whether within the framework of the protection of flora and fauna (wild birds and habitats directives), water quality policy (designation of fishing and swimming areas) or the combating of air pollution (zoning in connection with air quality policy). And what about measures in connection with environmental impact assessment?"

This question must of course be answered in the negative: in my view, it seems defensible that unanimity will be required only when the measure in question primarily deals with aspects of spatial planning, since in such a case Article 130S(2) ToM will be applicable. However, when the measure only indirectly concerns aspects of spatial planning, Article 130S(1) ToM will be applicable, and so only a qualified majority of votes will be needed.

Support for this reasoning can in my view be found in the above-mentioned Directive 96/82/EC of the Council of 9 December 1996 on the control of major-accident hazards involving dangerous substances. This directive was adopted on the basis of Article 130S(1) ToM, although one (long) Article explicitly deals with spatial (in the sense of land use) planning. As a consequence, it is not because there is a spatial planning aspect embedded in a directive that Article

---

[86] Article 130R of the Treaty of Maastricht:
"1. Community policy on the environment shall contribute to pursuit of the following objectives:
  – preserving, protecting and improving the quality of the environment;
  – protecting human health;
  – prudent and rational utilization of natural resources;
  – promoting measures at international level to deal with regional or world-wide environmental problems.
2. Community policy on the environment shall aim at a high level of protection taking into account the diversity of situations in the various regions of the Community. It shall be based on the precautionary principle and on the principles that preventive action should be taken, that environmental damage should as a priority be rectified at source and that the polluter should pay. Environmental protection requirements must be integrated into the definition and implementation of other Community policies.
   In this context, harmonization measures answering these requirements shall include, where appropriate, a safeguard clause allowing Member States to take provisional measures, for non-economic environmental reasons, subject to a Community inspection procedure.
3. In preparing its policy on the environment, the Community shall take account of:
  – available scientific and technical data;
  – environmental conditions in the various regions of the Community;
  – the potential benefits and costs of action or lack of action;
  – the economic and social developments of the Community as a whole and the balanced development of its region.
4. Within their respective spheres of competence, the Community and the Member States shall cooperate with third countries and with the competent international organizations. The arrangements for Community cooperation may be the subject of agreements between the Community and the third parties concerned, which shall be negotiated and concluded in accordance with Article 228.
   The previous subparagraph shall be without prejudice to Member States' competence to negotiate in international bodies and to conclude international agreements."

[87] VERHOEVE, B., TILMANS, R. and BENNETT, G., *EG-Beleid en ruimtelijke ordening*, Instituut voor Europees Milieubeleid, Arnhem, 1993, 6.

[88] JANS, J.H., *European Environmental Law*, Kluwer Law International, The Hague/London/Boston, 1995, 37.

[89] This passage is not clear for VERHOEVE & Co: Seemingly, only environmental measures with a spatial planning component are envisaged; indeed, many spatial planning goals can be realised by environmental measures; if this interpretation is followed, Article 130S(2) does not yet offer a basis for a real spatial planning policy (that is, going further than environment); another possible interpretation is that the Commission regards spatial planning as part of environmental policy; in that case, Article 130S(2) offers more possibilities (VERHOEVE, B., TILMANS, R. and BENNETT, G., *EG-Beleid en ruimtelijke ordening*, Instituut voor Europees Milieubeleid, Arnhem, 1993, 6).

[90] With the exception of waste management and measures of a general nature.

[91] JANS, J.H., *European Environmental Law*, Kluwer Law International, The Hague/London/Boston, 1995, 37–38.

312   *European Environmental Law Review   November 1997*

Environmental and Spatial Planning

130S(2) ToM should be the designated Treaty basis. In my view, a parallel must be drawn with fiscal environmental measures: when an environmental measure is primarily of a fiscal nature, Article 130S(2) ToM (and thus unanimity) applies; when an environmental measure contains only indirectly a fiscal element, than Article 130S(1) ToM (and thus qualified majority) applies. However, in all fairness it must be said that:

(1) Article 130(2) ToM explicitly refers to "provisions *primarily*[92] of a fiscal nature";
(2) the "proposal for a directive on the assessment of the effects of certain plans and programmes on the environment" is also based on Article 130S(1) ToM, although one could have expected[93] that Article 130S(2) ToM would apply here: in my view, the proposal for a directive thus deals more than indirectly with spatial planning. As regards this last point, European Environment Commissioner Bjerregaard was, however, of another opinion:[94]

"... The main objective of the proposal is to ensure that during an administrative procedure and before adopting the final decision, the competent authority examines and takes into consideration the impact that the final decision is likely to have on the environment. So much the statement on the state of the environment prepared by the competent authority than the consultation of the environmental authorities and of the public concerned constitute supports to the decision making. Basically, therefore, it is only the protection of certain environmental interests – by means of the awareness raising of the authorities having a decisional power – which is directly aimed by this proposal. It must also be underlined that this proposal is of a "procedural" nature. This means that it provides for assessment and consultations during the preparatory procedure and the taking into consideration of the results of this assessment and consultations in the final decision, in view of the protection of the environment, without therefore allotting any binding effect to these results in relation to the decision making, the assessment power as well as the final decision remaining entirely within the only competence of the competent authorities. *The possible effects of the measures provided for by the proposal on the land use planning as such can therefore be considered only as indirect.... Within this perspective, it appears that the legal base for the proposal is article 130S paragraph 1 of the Treaty.*"[95]

The importance of the motivation of Commissioner Bjerregaard does not immediately lie in the fact that she is of the opinion that the proposed directive deals only indirectly with spatial planning, although that is also important. Of greater importance is that in her reasoning, she implicitly confirms the above-formulated thesis, namely that when an environmental measure deals only indirectly with spatial planning aspects, it should be based on Article 130S(1) ToM, and not on Article 130S(2) ToM.

On the reason for the call for unanimity for spatial planning measures, Kramer gives the following comment:[96] "The ratio behind this provision is that decisions which affect the utilisation of the ground should not be taken without the agreement of the Member State concerned". This is confirmed[97] by Verhoeve & Co,[98] who state that the demand for unanimity is probably of a political nature: different Member States, especially Spain, were afraid of too much Community interference with spatial planning; as a consequence, in order to secure the influence of the Member States, unanimity is demanded; this means of course that Member States can veto spatial planning measures.

A last question with regard to Article 130S(2) ToM is the exact meaning of measures concerning "land use with the exception of waste management and measures of a general nature".[99] It is obvious that measures concerning land use can also be measures concerning spatial planning. Taking into account their separate enumeration, it seems that the drafters of the ToM saw town and country planning as something different from land use.[100] Jans formulates the following important question for a possible policy concerning spatial planning:[101]

"It is not apparent from the text what is to be understood by 'measures of a general nature'. In the first place it could be asked whether the exception to the requirement

---

[92.] Emphasis added.

[93.] Europe Environment, nr. 491, 14 January 1997: "After one or two hesitations, the Directive has in the end been grounded on Article 130S(1) of the EU Treaty (cooperation procedure, qualified majority decision-making in the Council of Ministers)."

[94.] Europe Environment, nr. 491, 14 January 1997.

[95.] Emphasis added.

[96.] KRAMER, L., "Community environmental law under the Maastricht Treaty on European Union and the fifth environmental action programme", in ABRAHAM, F., DEKETELAERE, K., STUYCK, J. (eds.), *Recent economic and legal developments in European environmental policy*, Leuven Law Series 5, Leuven, Leuven University Press, 1995, 85.

[97.] Although correctly immediately shaded: the explicit mention of spatial planning can of course have just the opposite effect (increasing Community activity in this field) (VERHOEVE, B., TILMANS, R. and BENNETT, G., *EG-Beleid en ruimtelijke ordening*, Instituut voor Europees Milieubeleid, Arnhem, 1993, 7).

[98.] VERHOEVE, B., TILMANS, R. and BENNETT, G., *EG-Beleid en ruimtelijke ordening*, Instituut voor Europees Milieubeleid, Arnhem, 1993, 7.

[99.] JANS, J.H., *European Environmental Law*, Kluwer Law International, The Hague/London/Boston, 1995, 38: "Equally, the rule of unanimous decision-making in respect of land use is ambiguous. Would it, for example, cover an amendment of Directive 86/278 ... concerning the protection of the environment and in particular of the soil, when sewage sludge is used in agriculture? The text in no way makes this clear. However, an exception is made to the requirement of unanimity for waste management and measures of a general nature. In these cases the normal procedure contained in Article 130S(1) applies again. This means that a directive concerning the landfill of waste or other measures designed to protect the soil against environmental hazards caused by waste would in any event fall within the scope of application of Article 130S(1)."

[100.] This is also indicated by VERHOEVE & Co who make the following comparative remark: is the English "land use" the same as the French "affectation du sol" or the German "Bodennutzung" or the Dutch "bodembestemming"? (VERHOEVE, B., TILMANS, R. and BENNETT, G., *EG-Beleid en ruimtelijke ordening*, Instituut voor Europees Milieubeleid, Arnhem, 1993, 6).

[101.] JANS, J.H., *European Environmental Law*, Kluwer Law International, The Hague/London/Boston, 1995, 38.

Environmental and Spatial Planning

of unanimity for 'measures of a general nature' refers only to the category land use, or whether it also applies to measures concerning town and country planning. If the latter were the case, and the text does seem to indicate this, it would mean that general measures regulating town and country planning and land use are not covered by the requirement of unanimity laid down in Article 130S(2). However it is still not clear how this interpretation accords with the remarks made above about area-related environmental policy."

In my view, the passage "with the exception of waste management and measures of a general nature" covers land use measures only. As already pointed out, the second dash of Article 130S(2) ToM must be seen as an enumeration of three categories of environmental measure (a,[102] b[103] and c[104]) for which unanimity of votes is required for adoption. For one of these three categories, namely land use measures, two exceptions (measures concerning waste management and measures of a general nature) are foreseen, which means that these measures can still be adopted on a qualified majority of votes.

Implicit Treaty Provisions: Articles 38, 74, 128, 129B and 130A ToM

In addition to Article 130S(2), second dash, ToM, which explicitly refers to spatial planning, there are a few other articles (concerning different policy areas) in the ToM, the use of which, through concrete policy measures, may also be of importance (whether in the positive sense or the negative sense) for spatial planning in the European Community and the Member States. The following provisions of the ToM may be mentioned. All may have consequences in the field of spatial planning, and some examples are given:

- Article 38 ToM[105] (agricultural measures), e.g. the regulation of fallow land;
- Article 74 ToM[106] (transport measures), e.g. the construction of a railway;
- Article 128 ToM[107] (cultural measures), e.g. the protection of monuments and landscapes;
- Article 129B ToM[108] (measures concerning trans-European networks). For example, of special interest for a possible European spatial planning policy is Article 129C ToM which formulates the possibility for the Community to contribute,[109] by means of the Cohesion Fund,[110] to the financing of specific projects in Member States in the field of transport infrastructure).[111]
- Article 130A ToM[112] (measures concerning economic and social cohesion), e.g. aid from the Structural Funds to regions where countryside development is necessary.

agricultural products must be accompanied by the establishment of a common agricultural policy among the Member States."

[106] "The objectives of this Treaty shall, in matters governed by this Title [transport], be pursued by Member States within the framework of a common transport policy."

[107] "1. The Community shall contribute to the flowering of the cultures of the Member States, while respecting their national and regional diversity and at the same time bringing the common cultural heritage to the fore.

2. Action by the Community shall be aimed at encouraging cooperation between Member States and, if necessary, supporting and supplementing their action in the following areas:
   - improvement of the knowledge and dissemination of the culture and history of the European peoples;
   - conservation and safeguarding of cultural heritage of European significance;
   - non-commercial cultural exchanges;
   - artistic and literary creation, including in the audiovisual sector.

3. The Community and the Member States shall foster cooperation with third countries and the competent international organizations in the sphere of culture, in particular the Council of Europe.

4. The Community shall take cultural aspects into account in its action under other provisions of this Treaty.

5. In order to contribute to the achievement of the objectives referred to in this Article, the Council:
   - acting in accordance with the procedure referred to in Article 189B and after consulting the Committee of the Regions, shall adopt incentive measures, excluding any harmonization of the laws and regulations of the Member States. The Council shall act unanimously throughout the procedures referred to in Article 189B;
   - acting unanimously on a proposal from the Commission, shall adopt recommendations."

[108] "1. To help achieve the objectives referred to in Articles 7A and 130A and to enable citizens of the Union, economic operators and regional and local communities to derive the full benefit from the setting up of an area without internal frontiers, the Community shall contribute to the establishment and development of trans-European networks in the areas of transport, telecommunications and energy infrastructures.

2. Within the framework of a system of open and competitive markets, action by the Community shall aim at promoting the interconnection and interoperability of national networks as well as access to such networks. It shall take account in particular of the need to link island, landlocked and peripheral regions with the central regions of the Community."

[109] See Article 130D (2) ToM: "The Council, acting in accordance with the same procedure, shall before 31 December 1993 set up a Cohesion Fund to provide a financial contribution to projects in the field of environment and trans-European networks in the area of transport infrastructure."

[110] Regulation 1164/94 of the Council of 16 May 1994 establishing a Cohesion Fund, OJ 25.5.94 L 130.

[111] See also: WILLIAMS, R.H., *European spatial policy and planning*, London, Paul Chapman Publishing, 1996, 167–183.

[112] "In order to promote its overall harmonious development; the Community shall develop and pursue its actions in leading to the strengthening of its economic and social cohesion.

In particular, the Community shall aim at reducing the disparities between the level of development of the various regions and the backwardness of the least favo... ed regions, including rural areas."

---

[102] Town and country planning.
[103] Land use.
[104] Management of water resources.
[105] "4. The operation and development of the common market for

314 European Environmental Law Review November 1997

Environmental and Spatial Planning

IV. Secondary Community Law and Spatial Planning

A. General

Secondary community law (the body of regulations, directives and decisions) created in the past decade, of course also has an impact (once again, in either a negative or a positive sense) on spatial planning in the European Community and its Member States. A detailed study on this point has been undertaken by Verhoeve & Co.[113] In this study, the impact on spatial planning of measures in five important policy fields is examined. The five fields are environment,[114, 115] agriculture,[116] regional policy,[117] transport,[118, 119] and tourism.[120]

In respect of "environment", measures on air, water, waste, nature protection, industrial risks, environmental impact assessment, urban environment and coastal protection were analysed. Under the heading "agriculture", measures concerning agriculture in mountain districts and in some problem areas, extensification of agricultural production, the laying fallow of agricultural land and environment friendly agriculture, were analysed. On "regional policy", measures concerning structural funds and regional policy were analysed.

In this way, the study affirms one of the theses of the European Commission as embedded in the Progress Report,[121] namely that spatial planning permeates almost all policies of the European Community: it is a practical integration tool in the drive for economic and social cohesion within the European Community, as well as an important means of integrating the environment within other policy areas alongside economic, financial and legislative instruments. This analysis also paves the way for two of the above-mentioned goals of the Progress Report concerning spatial planning, namely: (iii) definition of methodologies and tools in order to develop the potential of spatial planning for environmental integration; (iv) analysis of the links between environmental instruments and spatial planning and the definition of strategic environmental frameworks, in particular sectors to support sustainable spatial planning.[122]

The link between Community policy instruments and spatial planning has already been further discussed in the Progress Report itself.[123] The European Commission correctly indicates that, although spatial planning and development is not an existing competence of the Community, spatial planning and Community environmental policy interact at all levels of Community policy and interventions. Just like Verhoeve & Co, the Commission indicates the existence of a number of Community instruments which by their nature impinge on how land can be used, or require that a certain type of land use be respected in territorial development (e.g. the directives concerning birds,[124] habitats,[125] nitrates,[126] urban waste water[127] and environmental impact assessment[128]). The European Commission also indicates that the implementation of certain international conventions on nature conservation, such as the Berne Convention on habitats, the Alpine Convention and various conventions designed to reduce transfrontier and marine pollution from land-based sources, have spatial planning implications. This is also true of the establishment of the trans-European networks (TENs) for transport and energy.

They will have land use impact both directly in their implementation, and indirectly from their operations. As part of the TENs process, an initiative in relation to Joint Environment Infrastructure Projects (JEPS) is a strategic response to the need to coordinate spatial planning at Community level in the fields of water resources and waste. The Commission points out that at regional level also, a number of initiatives have been taken or are in the process of finalisation in the fields of urban development (Sustainable Cities, Urban Initiative), management of wetlands and integrated management of coastal zones. These serve to enhance the role of spatial planning for sustainable development in such sensitive areas. The Commission concludes by emphasising that there is increasing awareness at both regional and local levels that reductions in pollutants from area-based sources (air pollution from traffic for example) can be brought about only by coordinated physical planning measures, designed to influence and moderate the impact of the activities causing damage to the environment, economic activity and human health. The same conclusions apply to the prevention of natural risks such as flooding.

[113.] VERHOEVE, B., TILMANS, R. and BENNETT, G., *EG-Beleid en ruimtelijke ordening*, Instituut voor Europees Milieubeleid, Arnhem, 1993, 77.

[114.] VERHOEVE, B., TILMANS, R. and BENNETT, G., *EG-Beleid en ruimtelijke ordening*, Instituut voor Europees Milieubeleid, Arnhem, 1993, 8–53.

[115.] See also: WILLIAMS, R.H., *European spatial policy and planning*, London, Paul Chapman Publishing, 1996, 184–203.

[116.] VERHOEVE, B., TILMANS, R. and BENNETT, G., *EG-Beleid en ruimtelijke ordening*, Instituut voor Europees Milieubeleid, Arnhem, 1993, 54–65.

[117.] VERHOEVE, B., TILMANS, R. and BENNETT, G., *EG-Beleid en ruimtelijke ordening*, Instituut voor Europees Milieubeleid, Arnhem, 1993, 66–72.

[118.] VERHOEVE, B., TILMANS, R. and BENNETT, G., *EG-Beleid en ruimtelijke ordening*, Instituut voor Europees Milieubeleid, Arnhem, 1993, 73–75.

[119.] See also: WILLIAMS, R.H., *European spatial policy and planning*, London, Paul Chapman Publishing, 1996, 167–183.

[120.] VERHOEVE, B., TILMANS, R. and BENNETT, G., *EG-Beleid en ruimtelijke ordening*, Instituut voor Europees Milieubeleid, Arnhem, 1993, 76–77.

[121.] COM(95) 624 final, Brussels, 10 January 1996, 86.

[122.] COM(95) 624 final, Brussels, 10 January 1996, 86.

[123.] COM(95) 624 final, Brussels, 10 January 1996, 86.

[124.] Directive 79/409/EEC of the Council of 2 April 1979 on the conservation of wild birds, OJ 25.4.79 L 103.

[125.] Directive 92/43/EEC of the Council of 21 May 1992 on the conservation of natural habitats and of wild fauna and flora, OJ 22.7.92 L 206.

[126.] Directive 91/676/EEC of the Council of 12 December 1991 concerning the protection of waters against pollution caused by nitrates from agricultural sources, OJ 31.12.91 L 375.

[127.] Directive 91/271/EEC of the Council of 21 May 1991 concerning urban waste water treatment, OJ 30.5.91 L 135.

[128.] Directive 85/337/EEC of the Council of 27 June 1985 on the assessment of the effects of certain public and private projects on the environment, OJ 5.7.85 L 175.

European Environmental Law Review November 1997 315

Environmental and Spatial Planning

B. Directive 96/82/EC on the Control of Major-accident Hazards Involving Dangerous Substances

In the context of secondary Community law and spatial planning, attention must be paid to Directive 96/82/EC of the Council of 9 December 1996 on the control of major-accident hazards involving dangerous substances.[129]

According to Article 1, this directive is aimed at the prevention of major accidents[130] which involve dangerous substances,[131] and the limitation of their consequences for man and the environment, with a view to ensuring high levels of protection throughout the Community in a consistent and effective manner.

Article 12 of the directive contains three major obligations for the Member States concerning land use planning:

(1) Member States shall ensure that the objectives of preventing major accidents and limiting the consequences of such accidents are taken into account in their land use policies and/or other relevant policies; they shall pursue those objectives through controls on:
 a) the siting of new establishments;
 b) modifications to existing establishments;
 c) new developments such as transport links, locations frequented by the public and residential areas in the vicinity of existing establishments, where the siting or developments are such as to increase the risk or consequences of a major accident;

(2) Member States shall ensure that their land use and/or other relevant policies and the procedures for implementing those policies take account of the need, in the long term, to maintain appropriate distances between establishments covered by this directive and residential areas, areas of public use and areas of particular natural sensitivity or interest, and, in the case of existing establishments, of the need for additional technical measures so as not to increase the risks to people;

(3) Member States shall ensure that all competent authorities and planning authorities responsible for decisions in this area set up appropriate consultation procedures to facilitate implementation of the before mentioned policies; the procedures shall be designed to ensure that technical advice on the risks arising from the establishment is available, either on a case-by-case or on a generic basis, when decisions are taken.

It is obvious that these provisions will have an important impact on the domestic legislation of the Member States.

C. Proposal for a Directive on the Assessment of the Effects of Certain Plans and Programmes on the Environment

As already mentioned, in the Official Journal of 25 April 1997, a proposal for a directive "on the assessment of the effects of certain plans and programmes on the environment" was published.

According to Article 1, the objective of this directive is to provide for a high level of protection of the environment by ensuring that an environmental assessment is carried out of certain plans and programmes, and that the results of the assessment are taken into account during the preparation and adoption of such plans and programmes.

According to Article 2 of the directive, "plan" and "programme" refer only to town and country planning plans and programmes:

(1) which are subject to preparation and adoption by a competent authority for adoption by a legislative act, and

(2) which are part of the town and country planning decision-making process for the purpose of establishing the framework for subsequent development consents, and

(3) which contain provisions on the nature, size, location or operating conditions of projects.

They also include modifications of existing plans and programmes. This definition includes town and country planning plans and programmes in sectors such as transport (including transport corridors, port facilities and airports), energy, waste management, water resource management, industry (including extraction of mineral resources), telecommunications and tourism.

According to the same Article, "environmental assessment" means the preparation of an environmental statement, carrying out consultations, and taking into account the environmental statement and the results of the consultations in accordance with Articles 5 to 8 of the directive.

According to Article 5 and the Annex to the directive, the environmental statement must contain the following types of information:

(1) the contents of the plan or programme and its main objectives;

(2) the environmental characteristics of any area likely to be significantly affected by the plan or programme;

(3) any existing environmental problems which are relevant to the plan or programme including, in particular, those relating to any areas of particular environmental importance;

(4) the environmental protection objectives, established at international, Community and Member State level (including objectives established in other plans and programmes in the same hierarchy), which are relevant to the plan or programme and the way these objectives and any other environmental considerations have been taken into account during its preparation;

(5) the likely significant environmental effects of implementing the plan or programme;

(6) any alternative ways of achieving the objectives of the plan or programme which have been considered during its preparation (such as alternative types of development or alternative locations for development) and the reasons for not adopting these alternatives;

---

129. OJ 14.1.97 L 10.

130. This is, according to Article 3 (5), an occurrence such as a major emission, fire, or explosion resulting from uncontrolled developments in the course of the operation of any establishment covered by this directive, and leading to serious danger to human health and/or the environment, immediate or delayed, inside or outside the establishment, and involving one or more dangerous substances.

131. This is, according to Article 3, (4), a substance, mixture or preparation listed in Annex 1, part 1, or fulfilling the criteria laid down in Annex 1, part 2, and present as a raw material, product, by-product, residue or intermediate, including those substances which it is reasonable to suppose may be generated in the event of accident.

316 *European Environmental Law Review November 1997*

Environmental and Spatial Planning

(7) the measures envisaged to prevent, reduce and where possible offset any significant adverse effects on the environment of implementing the plan or programme;

(8) any difficulties (such as technical deficiencies or lack of know-how) encountered in compiling the required information.

It is obvious that, once adopted, this directive will have a great impact on the environmental and spatial planning processes in the Member States.

IV: Suggestions: Policy Visions and Policy Framework

A. General

At the end of this introduction to environmental planning and spatial planning from a European Community perspective, it is opportune to look to the future.[132] This will be limited to spatial planning since the further development of environmental planning, on both macro-level and micro-level, is quite obvious. As regards spatial planning, it is important to visualise an optimal policy vision and an optimal policy framework for future European spatial planning policy.

B. Policy Vision

As regards policy vision, this seems closely linked to the "options for a better territorial organisation", as formulated in the document *Europe 2000+, Cooperation for European territorial development*.[133, 134] As already mentioned, this document includes a strong plea for strengthening cooperation on spatial planning, which is presently characterised by a trend towards greater complexity and diversity.[135] According to the European Commission, three options must be examined in this context: general options, transnational options, and options for cooperation with neighbouring countries of the European Community.

As concerns general options,[136] it is said that the need for competitiveness, for organising the economy based on a new model of sustainable development, and for equity, has obvious territorial implications. In this regard, it is particularly important to take account of returns over the long-term and not just the short-term. The overall strategy defined in the provisions of the Maastricht Treaty and by the European Council following the publication of the White Paper contains a strong spatial planning component in relation to the three following aspects: a more competitive European territory; a viable territory for sustainable development; a territory with greater solidarity, organised more equitably and respecting economic and social cohesion. A spatial planning policy developed at European level must be able to contribute to the realisation of each of these three points.

As concerns the transnational options,[137] it is said that restoring spatial balance entails the implementation of specific transnational measures in four areas: the development of cross-border cooperation, the reduced isolation of peripheral regions, ensuring the balanced development of the urban system, and the preservation of rural areas. These are examined in the annex to *Europe 2000+*, which summarises the results of the transnational studies carried out as part of the Europe 2000+ programme.

On the options for cooperation with neighbouring countries of the European Community,[138] it is said that programmes of cooperation with the countries to the North, East and South of the Union could be envisaged, to foster coherent management of the European region as a whole. These programmes would require agreement between the areas concerned on guidelines for spatial development and would entail specific cooperative actions.

C. Policy Framework

As regards policy framework, the above analysis of the primary Community law in general and Article 130S(1)(2) ToM, has made clear that the legal anchorage of European spatial planning policy must be clarified and consolidated. In all the policy documents which have been mentioned, the different European institutions (European Parliament,[139] Economic and Social Committee,[140] Committee of the Regions[141]) have made clear that the best way to achieve this clarification and consolidation would be to amend the Treaty of Maastricht. Changing the Treaty in the direction of a clearer and more consolidated legal anchorage of European spatial planning policy would bring with it certain novelties and modifications in the institutional field. For example, the European Parliament has pleaded in the past[142] for (1) granting official status to the Council of Ministers competent for spatial planning,[143] (2) granting a

---

[132] See also: WILLIAMS, R.H., *European spatial policy and planning*, London, Paul Chapman Publishing, 1996, 255–265.

[133] X., *Europe 2000+, Cooperation for European territorial development*, European Commission, Brussels/Luxembourg, 1994, 15–23.

[134] See also, closely connected to "Europe 2000+", the recent advice of the Committee of the Regions on the theme "Town and country planning in Europe" (OJ 14.4.97 C 116).

[135] X., *Europe 2000+, Cooperation for European territorial development*, European Commission, Brussels/Luxembourg, 1994, 15: "The result within the Union, in particular, is a mosaic in which areas of modernity and prosperity exist side by side with areas of depression."

[136] X., *Europe 2000+, Cooperation for European territorial development*, European Commission, Brussels/Luxembourg, 1994, 15–19.

[137] X., *Europe 2000+, Cooperation for European territorial development*, European Commission, Brussels/Luxembourg, 1994, 19–21.

[138] X., *Europe 2000+, Cooperation for European territorial development*, European Commission, Brussels/Luxembourg, 1994, 22–23.

[139] OJ 17.7.95 C 183.

[140] OJ 31.5.95 C 133.

[141] OJ 2.4.96 C 100.

[142] OJ 17.7.95 C 183.

[143] Since the first meeting in November 1989, seven informal meetings have already taken place within the framework of the European Community. Since 1993, the meeting has become an informal Council. See: DE LANGE, C., "Europese Ruimtelijke Ordening", *De Europese Gemeente*, 1996, nr. 3, 20; MARTIN, D., "Europese ruimtelijke ordening: inzicht en uitzicht", in D'HONDT, F. en ZONNEVELD, W. (eds.), *Europese ruimtelijke ordening – Impressies en visies vanuit Vlaanderen en Nederland*, Vlaamse Federatie voor Planologie (VFP)/Nederlands Instituut voor Ruimtelijke Ordening en Huisvesting (NIROV), Gent/Den Haag, 1994, 21; X., *Europa 2000+, Samenwerking voor de ruimtelijke ordening van Europa*, Europese Commissie, Brussel/Luxembourg, 1994, 13–15.

European Environmental Law Review November 1997 317

Environmental and Spatial Planning

permanent character to the Committee for Spatial Development[144] and (3) accelerating the creation of the European Spatial Development Perspective. At the same time, of course, the subsidiarity principle[145] should be taken into account, as it is embedded in Article 3B(2) ToM:[146, 147]

"So far as spatial organisation is concerned, the policies carried out will need to conform with the division of responsibilities resulting from the application of the principle of subsidiarity. These policies will primarily be national, regional and local because they flow mainly from the decision-making processes and the choices made in each country. However, the complexity, diversity and growing interdependence of areas in the Community together with the increasing importance of transnational issues mean that policies also need to be undertaken at the European level to influence the development of the territory as a whole. European cooperation is the only way to foster a territorial development which does not lead to excessive disparities between regions and which provides a more equal possibility of establishing the various conditions necessary for improving competitiveness. Several levels of regional cooperation appear to be necessary, the starting point being that centralisation would not be viable and that each participant should take decisions in their own area of responsibility, that are consistent with commonly agreed general guidelines."

Although all these desires were formulated repeatedly during the Intergovernmental Conference preparing the Treaty of Amsterdam, not one of these suggestions was followed. One can only hope for a different outcome in the next revision of the Treaty.

This article may be concluded by posing the following question: should spatial planning legislation as its presently exists in the different Member States of the European Community be harmonised?[148] Various studies ("Compendium of Spatial Planning Systems and Policies"[149] "Ruimtelijke regelgeving in Noord-West-Europa[150]) give a good overview of the spatial planning legislation in the European Community. As Albrechts and Meuris say,[151] it is possible to defend the thesis that harmonisation of national planning legislation is not possible, and even undesirable: not possible because the way in which planning systems function is strongly connected with the structure of the state, and in particular the specific division of competences between the government levels; not desirable because this would mean a loss of an element of identity by every Member State (which would certainly lead to strong reactions by different countries). Much more meaningful and important, it seems, would be the introduction, step by step, of spatial quality standards (comparable with those existing in the environ-

mental policy of the Community) which guarantee the specificity of every Member State.

[144.] In this informal Committee, the different national planning services and/or ministries are represented. See: MARTIN, D., "Europese ruimtelijke ordening: inzicht en uitzicht", in D'HONDT, F. en ZONNEVELD, W. (eds.), *Europese ruimtelijke ordening – Impresses en visies vanuit Vlaanderen en Nederland*, Vlaamse Federatie voor Planologie (VFP)/Nederlands Instituut voor Ruimtelijke Ordening en Huisvesting (NIROV), Gent/Den Haag, 1994, 21.

[145.] WITSEN, J., "Subsidiariteit in het Europa van de regio's", in D'HONDT, F. en ZONNEVELD, W. (eds.), *Europese ruimtelijke ordening – Impresses en visies vanuit Vlaanderen en Nederland*, Vlaamse Federatie voor Planologie (VFP)/Nederlands Instituut voor Ruimtelijke Ordening en Huisvesting (NIROV), Gent/Den Haag, 1994, 65–72.

[146.] "In areas which do not fall within its exclusive competence, the Community shall take action, in accordance with the principle of subsidiarity, only if and in so far as the objectives of the proposed action cannot be sufficiently achieved by the Member States and can therefore, by reason of the scale or effects of the proposed action, be better achieved by the Community".

[147.] X., *Europe 2000+, Cooperation for European territorial development*, European Commission, Brussels/Luxembourg, 1994, 23.

[148.] X., *Europe 2000+, Cooperation for European territorial development*, European Commission, Brussels/Luxembourg, 1994, 139–158.

[149.] ALBRECHTS, L. en MEURIS, F., "Het Compendium en de feitelijke ruimtelijke ordening in Europa", in D'HONDT, F. en ZONNEVELD, W. (eds.), *Europese ruimtelijke ordening – Impresses en visies vanuit Vlaanderen en Nederland*, Vlaamse Federatie voor Ruimtelijke Ordening en Huisvesting (NIROV), Gent/Den Haag, 1994, 97–100; MASTOP, H. en NEEDHAM, B., "Regelgeving en bestuurlijke organisatie", in D'HONDT, F. en ZONNEVELD, W. (eds.), *Europese ruimtelijke ordening – Impresses en visies vanuit Vlaanderen en Nederland*, Vlaamse Federatie voor Planologie (VFP)/ Nederlands Instituut voor Ruimtelijke Ordening en Huisvesting (NIROV), Gent/Den Haag, 1994, 88–89.

[150.] MASTOP, H. en NEEDHAM, B., "Regelgeving en bestuurlijke organisatie", in D'HONDT, F. en ZONNEVELD, W. (eds.), *Europese ruimtelijke ordening – Impresses en visies vanuit Vlaanderen en Nederland*, Vlaamse Federatie voor Planologie (VFP)/ Nederlands Instituut voor Ruimtelijke Ordening en Huisvesting (NIROV), Gent/Den Haag, 1994, 89–90.

[151.] ALBRECHTS, L. en MEURIS, F., "Het Compendium en de feitelijke ruimtelijke ordening in Europa", in D'HONDT, F. en ZONNEVELD, W. (eds.), *Europese ruimtelijke ordening – Impresses en visies vanuit Vlaanderen en Nederland*, Vlaamse Federatie voor Ruimtelijke Ordening en Huisvesting (NIROV), Gent/Den Haag, 1994, 100.

[19]

Thirty Years of EC Environmental Law: Perspectives and Prospectives

Ludwig Krämer*

I. Introduction

Principles of European Community (EC) environmental policy were for the first time formulated in 1971/2,[1] and progressively expanded in the period that followed. During the first fifteen years, EC environmental policy lacked an explicit legal basis in the EC Treaty, but such legal grounding was finally established in 1987, by the Single European Act (SEA),[2] which inserted Articles 130r to 130t EC into the Treaty. These provisions have since been renumbered, and now form Articles 174 to 176 EC. The Treaties of Maastricht[3] and Amsterdam[4] further fine-tuned these environmental provisions, and the Treaty of Nice, which still must be ratified by the fifteen Member States, contains some other—minor—amendments of the environmental chapter in the EC Treaty.

The European Union (EU) does not enjoy the prerogatives of a state; it may act only where it has been expressly so authorized by the Treaty.[5] Any comparison with domestic environmental law in the Member States, or with that the USA is therefore necessarily misleading. In particular, there exists no 'European public opinion', 'European media', or pan-European interest groups pursuing the general interest of the Community.[6] In the area of environmental protection, which is a general interest, the EC's *sui generis* character implies considerable disadvantages. Indeed, 'Community' lawyers hardly exist in the EC. Instead, lawyers still perceive, interpret, and discuss EC environmental law from a national law perspective.

* DG Environment, Commission of the European Communities, Professor of Law, University of Bremen, Germany. Opinions expressed are personal to the author.
[1] The first significant political statement is the Communication from the Commission on a Community environmental policy SEC(71)2616. It was followed by a political agreement among Member States on the guiding principles of a Community environmental policy, which was reached at 15 Sept. 1972. Subsequently, this agreement was inserted into the Declaration of the Council and of the Representatives of the Governments of the Member States on the Programme of Action of the European Communities on the Environment (First Community Environmental Action Programme) [1973] OJ C112/1. In Oct. 1972 the Heads of State and Government, which met in Paris, favoured Community measures on the environment, and asked the Community to elaborate a Community environmental action programme, see Commission, *6th General Report* (Luxembourg: Office for Official Publications, 1972), 8.

[2] [1987] OJ L169/1.   [3] [1992] OJ C191/1.   [4] [1997] OJ C340/1.

[5] Art. 5(1) EC: 'The Community shall act within the limits of the powers conferred upon it by this Treaty and of the objectives assigned to it therein.'

[6] Wording derived from Art. 157(2) EC.

This chapter endeavours to provide a balanced assessment of EC environmental law achievements and disappointments.

Having briefly summarized the historical development of primary EC environmental law (Section II), the role played by the EC institutions in this development will be examined (Section III). Section IV focuses on processes, instruments, and principles of EC environmental law. An analysis of substantive EC environmental law is undertaken in Section IV. Crucial issues of implementation are dealt with in Section VI, which simultaneously paves the way for a discussion of the political results of thirty years of EC environmental law in Section VII. Some conclusions are articulated in Section VIII.

II. Primary EC Environmental Law

The environmental provisions, which were originally inserted in the EC Treaty in 1987, now form Articles 174–6 EC. These provisions establish objectives and principles for EC environmental policy and action, specify decision-making procedures, and allow Member States, after the adoption of Community measures, to maintain or introduce more stringent environmental measures, provided these are compatible with the other provisions of the Treaty, in particular Article 28 EC.

At a more general level, Article 2 EC instructs the Community to promote 'a high level of protection and improvement of the quality of the environment'. Article 3(1) EC provides that EC activities shall include 'a policy in the sphere of the environment', and Article 6 EC continues that 'environmental protection requirements must be integrated into the definition and implementation of the Community policies and activities . . ., in particular with a view to promoting sustainable development'.

The provision of Article 95 EC, found in the chapter on the approximation of laws with a view to establishing an internal market, instructs the Commission to elaborate proposals in the area of the environment that have 'as a base a high level of protection'. After the adoption of a Community measure based on Article 95 EC, Member States may, under certain conditions, maintain or introduce more stringent environmental measures.

Finally, Article 161(2) EC concerns the setting up of a Cohesion Fund with the task to provide financial contributions to projects in the field of the environment. This provision contributes to realizing the objectives of Article 158 EC, which includes the reduction of 'the backwardness of the least favoured regions or islands, including rural areas'.

The structure of the EC Treaty still reflects the preponderance of economic interests, evidenced in particular by the provisions on the internal market, agriculture, competition, and transport. Thus, Article 28 EC contains the principle that (national) barriers to trade which impair the free circulation of goods are prohibited,[7] Article 81 EC stipulates that agreements and concerted practices

---

[7] Art. 28 EC reads: 'Quantitative restrictions on imports and all measures having equivalent effect shall be prohibited between Member States.'

between undertakings are illegal,[8] and Article 87 EC declares that, in principle, state aids are prohibited;[9] Articles 174–6 EC, however, do not contain a prohibition to cause pollution. Rather, these provisions are drafted in a way so as to entrust the protection of the environment to public administration, which may adopt regulatory measures, or provide for incentives to preserve the environment. In contrast to the free-trade provisions, individuals enjoy no participation or enforcement rights.

This has led the Avosetta Group, a recently created group of environmental lawyers in the Community, to suggest that a new provision be inserted into the EC Treaty, which would read:

Subject to imperative reasons of overriding public interests, significantly impairing the environment or human health shall be prohibited.

This provision would hence come to mirror the present Articles 28 and 30 EC, the basic Treaty provisions on the free circulation of goods.

No specific environmental provisions have been inserted into the Treaty establishing the European Coal and Steel Community (ECSC) or the Treaty establishing the European Atomic Energy Community (EURATOM). As regards the EURATOM Treaty in particular, this omission is regrettable, since the policies of this Treaty now hardly take account of the requirement to integrate environmental requirements into nuclear energy policy.

Neither does the Treaty on European Union (TEU) refer to the protection of the environment, except for a marginal reference in its eighth recital,[10] which is striking, because this contrasts with other policies such as the internal market, monetary policy, and the free movement of persons.

When negotiating international Conventions, Protocols, Agreements, or Declarations at international level, the Community, within its sphere of competence, in theory is represented by the Commission, which conducts the negotiations on the basis of a mandate by the Council, and in concertation with a Council working group.[11] In practice, however, Member States are often unwilling to follow these rules, as they do not want to be seen, at international level, as having forfeited their sovereignty. Therefore, they frequently conduct

---

[8] Art. 81(1) EC reads: 'The following shall be prohibitied as incompatible with the common market: all agreements between undertakings, decisions by associations of undertakings and concerted practices which may affect trade between Member States and which have as their object or effect the prevention, restriction or distortion of competition within the common market.'

[9] Art. 91(1) EC reads: 'Save as otherwise provided in this Treaty, any aid granted by a Member State or through State resources in any form whatsoever which distorts or threatens to distort competition by favouring certain undertakings or the production of certain goods shall, insofar as it affects trade between Member States, be incompatible with the common market.'

[10] Treaty on European Union, 8th Recital (Maastricht, 7 Feb. 1992) [1997] OJ C340/145:

Determined to promote economic and social progress for their peoples, taking into account the principle of sustainable development and within the context of the accomplishment of the internal market and of reinforced cohesion and environmental protection, and to implement policies ensuring that advances in economic integration are accompanied by parallel progress in other fields.

[11] See Art. 300 EC.

158   *Ludwig Krämer*

these negotiations themselves, a problem which goes well beyond the environmental aspects of the Treaty. The idea of progressively transferring national sovereignty to the Community in practice still meets objections from diplomats and foreign policy administrations.

However, the insertion of environmental provisions into the EC Treaty appears to have been successful. The broad formulation of environmental objectives and principles, the integration requirement of Article 6 EC, and the different provisions which formulate the relationship between Member States and the Community give a sufficient legal basis for a coherent and progressive environmental policy at Community level. The question whether the Community has adequately made use of these opportunities, which is a question of policy, rather than law, nevertheless needs to be addressed.

III. Community Institutions

A. THE COMMISSION

Over the past thirty years, the Commission changed its environmental bureaucracy only slightly. In 1973 it set up an Environment and Consumer Protection Service, conceived as a horizontal Service placed under one of the Commission's Vice-Presidents which should, in a way similar to the Legal Service, influence policies of all other departments. However, this initiative met the resistance of existing administrative departments, and was therefore soon abandoned.

When Greece acceded to the Community in 1981, the Service was transformed into a Directorate-General. Following the accession of Spain and Portugal, environmental and consumer protection matters were separated in 1989, and two independent Directorate-Generals were formed. At present, the environmental department counts approximately 500 officials, roughly 10 per cent of which are on secondment from national administrations for a maximum period of three years. However, other EC policies such as industry, internal market, energy, regional, agriculture, transport, research, consumer protection, and the legal service, also have to deal with environmental questions, so that the total number of Commission officials working in the area of the environment is considerably higher.

The Commission instituted a Consultative Forum on the Environment and Sustainable Development,[12] and a Scientific Committee for Toxicity, Ecotoxicity and Environment.[13] Both bodies only play a limited role in the decision-making process at Community level. Furthermore, the Commission is supported by the European Environmental Agency, which was set up by the

---

[12] Commission Decision 97/150/EC on the Setting-Up of a European Consultative Forum on the Environment and Sustainable Development [1997] OJ L58/48; the Forum was set up in 1993.
[13] Commission Decision 97/579/EC Setting-Up Scientific Committees in the Field of Consumer Health and Food Safety [1997] OJ L237/18; this Scientific Committee was first set up in 1978

Council,[14] and has the task to collect, process, and distribute information on the environment. The approximately seventy officials of the Agency are too few in number to allow the Agency to assume additional functions, such as relating to monitoring and control. In any event, Member States do not wish to see the Agency develop in this direction. Instead, they set up an informal, more or less intergovernmental network, IMPEL (European Network on the Implementation and Enforcement of Environmental Law), to discuss and promote implementation of Community environmental legislation. Although IMPEL closely cooperates with the Commission, its influence on the latter and on the implementation of Community environmental law remains fairly limited.

Attempts in the early 1980s to set up an environmental fund failed, which find its expression in the present Article 175(4) EC, stipulating that, in general, 'the Member States shall finance . . . the environment policy'. Apart from the Cohesion Fund,[15] the Commission administers a financial instrument, LIFE,[16] which is equipped with about 100 million euros per year, and cofinances pilot and demonstration projects for clean technologies, and nature protection projects.

B. THE COUNCIL OF MINISTERS

The Council of Ministers (the Council) meets as Environment Council four times per year. In addition, there are two informal Council meetings which discuss more basic problems, and which do not take decisions. This frequency is high compared to other policy areas, which allows, at least in theory, for a close alignment of policy and legal approaches among Member States' governments.

Until 1993, the Council decided unanimously on environmental matters. For environmental issues adopted under Article 100a EC (now Article 95 EC) concerning the establishment of the internal market, majority voting was introduced in 1987. This dichotomy gave rise to frequent discussions as to whether Article 175 EC or Article 95 EC was the appropriate legal basis for environmental measures.[17] In 1993 the TEU introduced majority decisions for the majority of environmental measures adopted under Article 175 EC. This amendment, in conjunction with the Treaty of Amsterdam, largely eliminated any procedural differences between both provisions, thus removing many

---

[14] Council Reg. (EEC) No. 1210/90 on the Establishment of the European Environment Agency and the European Environment Information and Observation Network [1990] OJ L120/1. The Agency started to work only in 1994.

[15] The Cohesion Fund was set up by Council Reg. (EC) 1164/94 Establishing a Cohesion Fund [1994] OJ I.130/1; see Council Reg. (EC) 1265/99 Amending Annex II to Reg. No. 1164/94 [1999] OJ L161/62.

[16] European Parliament and Council Reg. (EC) 1655/2000 Concerning the Financial Instrument for the Environment (LIFE) [2000] OJ L192/1. The Fund and its predecessors have existed since 1991.

[17] See Cases C–300/89, *Commission v. Council* [1991] ECR I–2867; C–155/91, *Commission v. Council* [1993] ECR I–939; C–187/93, *European Parliament v. Council* [1994] ECR I–2857.

grounds for litigation. De facto, however, the Council on environmental matters frequently continues to decide unanimously.

Decisions of the Council are prepared by working groups, composed of the environmental *attachés* of Member States' representations with the Community, whom officials from Member States' ministerial departments assist. The Council Presidency, which also chairs the working groups, determines which Commission proposals are discussed in the working groups, and subsequently submitted for a decision by the Council.

Between 1973 and 2000, the Council adopted, in part together with the European Parliament, some 150 environmental directives and regulations, as well as decisions to adhere to international environmental agreements. A similar number of amendments was adopted, in part also by the Commission by virtue of the Comitlogy procedure pursuant to Article 145 EC. The exact number of measures adopted depends on the method of calculation. It is not easy to define what constitutes an environmental measure. For example, it is debatable whether this should include emission standards for cars or airplanes, provisions on chemicals or pesticides, and measures to combat mad cow disease. Similarly, amendments of existing directives may sometimes be of minor technical significance, but in other cases may have considerable political and legal implications.

C. THE EUROPEAN PARLIAMENT

The European Parliament (EP), directly elected since 1979, saw its role in the decision-making procedure progressively strengthened. While, originally, it was only to be consulted, it is now partner in the co-decision procedure in almost all environmental decisions. The consultation process only continues to apply in the cases specified in Article 175(2) EC, where the Council decides by unanimity, in the agricultural sector (Article 37(2) EC), and for basic decisions in the transport sector (Article 71(2) EC).

The opinions and positions of the EP in the past were strongly influenced by its progressive Environmental Committee, and it normally called for stronger environmental measures than proposed by the Commission or the Council. Since 1999, the EP, for the first time since 1979, has a conservative majority, and a shift may take place in this regard, although it is too early to categorically confirm this tendency.

The EP once used the prerogative granted to it by Article 192 EC, and formally requested the Commission to submit a proposal for a Directive on Environmental Liability. However, the Commission was of the opinion that its right of initiative for new proposals could not be affected by such a request, and refused. The practical significance of this prerogative therefore remains uncertain.

Strikingly, environmental petitions addressed to the EP pursuant to Article 194 EC, are not administered or monitored by Parliament itself. Rather, the EP asks the Commission to investigate the matter. This might well be the only example of an elected parliament renouncing the use of the instrument of petitions, as a means of autonomous control of any incriminating behaviour.

Parliament also sporadically organizes hearings on environmental matters, but this occurs in a form which all too clearly shows the absence of a European public opinion.

D. THE ECONOMIC AND SOCIAL COMMITTEE AND THE COMMITTEE OF THE REGIONS

The Economic and Social Committee, and the Committee of the Regions, set up by Articles 257 EC and 263 EC, have advisory tasks, and play a limited role in environmental matters. Their opinions are rarely echoed in the Council or the EP. The Economic and Social Committee regularly supports Commission proposals, while the Committee of the Regions, set up only in 1993, still seems to struggle to adopt a cohesive position as regards environmental questions.

E. THE EUROPEAN COURT OF JUSTICE

The European Court of Justice (ECJ) and the Court of First Instance (CFI) have delivered judgments in over 200 environmental cases.[18] These judgments often enhance the legal status of the environment, in particular the integration of environmental requirements into other policy areas. For instance, the ECJ ruled that Community environmental directives are binding legal instruments, rather than voluntary guidelines lacking binding force. During the first years of environmental policy, this clearly had been different.

ECJ procedures in environmental matters, on average, take approximately twenty months. However, for infringement procedures under Article 226 EC, the duration of the prejudicial phase should also be taken into account. Consequently, at present the overall average duration of litigation in environmental matters pursuant to Article 226 EC, exceeds five years (68 months).[19]

A penalty payment, first introduced in 1993 after an amendment of Article 228 EC, was only once applied, in a case against Greece for not having taken necessary measures to comply with an earlier ECJ judgment of 1992.[20] This new provision clearly has a deterrent effect, in the sense that Member States will seek to comply with earlier judgments in order to avoid a second ECJ judgment and a penalty payment. The problem of Article 228 EC lies elsewhere, however. Between the formal opening of infringement proceedings and the second judgment pursuant to Article 228 EC, more than nine years usually pass,[21] a time-span which makes this sanction relatively ineffective.

In summary, it may be concluded that all EC institutions by now have adapted to the requirements of the policy area 'environment'. Yet problems for

[18] Once more, this number depends on the exact definition of 'environmental case'.

[19] For details, see L. Krämer, 'Die Rechtsprechung der EG-Gerichte zum Umweltschutz 1998 und 1999' (2000) 24 *Europäische Grundrechte Zeitschrift*, 265.

[20] Case C–387/97, *Commission v. Greece* [2000] ECR I–5047.

[21] In Case C–387/97, n. 20 above, this period exceeded eleven years (134 months).

individuals to enforce a right to a clean and healthy environment continue to exist. There also remains a gap in the effectiveness of enforcement and monitoring mechanisms for EC environmental law. Finally, reliable Community-wide data and statistics on the environment, which are necessary in order for decisions to be based on sound knowledge and *ex post* impact assessment, are still largely lacking.

IV. The Framework of EC Environmental Law

A. LEGAL PRINCIPLES

The EC Treaty contains a number of guiding principles which concern action in the field of the environment. The EC Treaty contains the precautionary principle, the principle of prevention, the principle that environmental damage should be rectified at source, the polluter-pays principle (all in Article 174 EC), and the principle that environmental requirements must be integrated into other Community policies (Article 6 EC). The legal status of these principles, however, remains ambiguous. Although, as early as in 1975, the Council adopted a Recommendation on the polluter-pays principle,[22] and the Commission issued a Communication on the precautionary principle,[23] these merely raised questions on the political relevance of the principles, rather than clarifying their substantive scope. The ECJ justified a Belgian import ban on hazardous waste in 1992, *inter alia*, with reference to the principle that environmental damage should be rectified at source.[24] In 1998 the ECJ declared that the Community export ban for British beef was justified, *inter alia*, by virtue of preventive considerations laid down in Article 174 EC, in conjunction with the integration principle.[25]

It should be noted that the ECJ has consistently held that provisions of Community law could not be interpreted in such a way 'as to give rise to results which are incompatible with the general principles of Community law, and in

---

[22] Council Rec. 75/436/Euratom, ECSC, EEC regarding Cost Allocation and Action by Public Authorities on Environmental Matters [1975] OJ L194/1.

[23] Communication from the Commission on the Precautionary Principle, COM(2000)1, 2 Feb. 2000.

[24] Case C–2/90, *Commission* v. *Belgium* [1992] ECR I–4431, para. 34: 'The principle that environmental damage should as a priority be rectified at source—a principle laid down by Article 130r(2) EEC for action by the Community relating to the environment—means that it is for each region, commune or other local entitiy to take appropriate measures to receive, process and dispose of its own waste.'

[25] Case C–180/96, *United Kingdom* v. *Commission* [1998] ECR I–2265, paras 99–100: Where there is uncertainty as to the existence or extent of risks to human health, the institutions may take protective measures without having to wait until the reality and seriousness of those risks become fully apparent. That approach is borne out by Article 130r(1) of the EEC Treaty, according to which Community policy on the environment is to pursue the objective, *inter alia*, of protecting human health. Article 130r(2) provides that that policy is to be based in particular on the principles that preventive action should be taken and that environmental protection requirements must be integrated into the definition and implementation of other Community policies.

particular with fundamental rights'.[26] It does not seem likely that the ECJ would ever consider the principles of Article 174 EC 'general principles of Community law' in this sense. The environmental principles are not 'general principles of Community law', but rather 'specific principles', which may help support a specific decision or interpretation, but which lack the legal force to justify any decision on their own.[27] They serve as *leitmotifs*, or guidelines for action in environmental matters. This does not rule out that they may progressively acquire a more precise meaning, and develop into proper principles of law.

The political nature of these principles may be demonstrated by the integration principle of Article 6 EC, which refers to 'policies and activities', rather than to individual measures taken in pursuance of such policies. The principle requires the 'greening' of Community policies, by taking into consideration environmental objectives, principles, and concerns. This, however, does not imply that each individual regulation, directive, or decision, which is taken in the context of such policies, must fully respect the objectives and principles of Article 174 EC. Taken to its logical conclusion, such a requirement would mean that numerous measures would have to be declared illegal.

B. LEGAL INSTRUMENTS

i. Environmental Programmes

Environmental policy is unique in that it is the only Community policy sector which, from its inception and throughout its existence, has been based on environmental action programmes. In the absence of an explicit legal competence for environmental action in the EC Treaty in the early 1970s, these programmes were designed to articulate the objectives, principles, and priorities of Community environmental action. Adopted by the Commission, the Council and the Representatives of Member States meeting in Council subsequently approved the general principles of these programmes in the form of a political Resolution, but not the programme as such.[28] Between 1973 and 1993, five such action programmes were adopted at Community level.

With the Maastricht Treaty of 1993, Article 175(3) EC was inserted in the EC Treaty, which provides that 'general action programmes' were to be adopted jointly by the EP and the Council. Community action programmes thereby

---

[26] Joined Cases 97/87, 98/87, and 99/87, *Dow Chemical Ibérica, SA, and others* v. *Commission* [1989] ECR I-3165, para. 9; see also Case C-22/94, *The Irish Farmers Association and others* v. *Minister for Agriculture, Food and Forestry, Ireland and Attorney General* [1997] ECR I-1809, para. 27.

[27] If Community measures in the area of transport or agricultural policy were to be assessed under the principles that environmental damage should be prevented, that the polluter should pay, or that damage should be rectified as source: not many measures would survive such a test.

[28] See e.g. the Resolution of the Council and the Representatives of the Governments of the Member States on a Community Programme of Policy and Action in relation to the Environment and Sustainable Development (5th Environment Action Programme) [1993] OJ C138/1: 'The Council and the Representatives of Member States meeting in Council] approve the general approach and strategy of the programme "Towards sustainability" presented by the Commission.'

acquired a more legal character. At the same time, the EP, by virtue of the co-decision procedure of Article 251 EC, for the first time may co-decide on specific actions to be undertaken within the life-span of these action programmes. While, in theory, the Commission remains free to ignore a request for a proposal on a specific directive by the EP and the Council formulated in the decision that adopts an action programme, in practice the pressure to take heed of such a request will be considerable. This is also because the EP and the Council are the budgetary authorities for the Commission, and also possess other means to exercise political pressure on the Commission.

The response of the institutions to the new legal status of action programmes was almost immediate: when the fifth environmental action programme was revised in 1998, the Council, supported by the Commission, fixed objectives and principles, but avoided specific actions.[29] The Commission proposal for a decision to approve the sixth environmental action programme for the years 2001 to 2010 also very carefully avoids any wording which could be interpreted as a commitment, and refers to 'priority areas for action', rather than actions.[30] The political struggle for power between the EP and the Council is decisive in respect of the follow-up of action programmes. This is evidenced by the fact that, in the past, the Commission frequently has not undertaken the actions promised in a programme. Conversely, legislation has been adopted which had not previously been anticipated in an action programme.

ii. Regulations

According to Article 249 EC, numerous different legal instruments are available for Community action: regulations, directives, decisions, recommendations, and opinions. Environmental law does not reflect much creativity in the use of these instruments, however. Recourse to regulations is essentially limited to either monitoring, control, or other forms of administration,[31] or to transposition of obligations flowing from an international environmental convention.[32] Environmental regulations mostly do not exhaustively regulate a specific subject matter at Community level. Rather, they contain substantive

---

[29] European Parliament and Council Dec. 2179/98/EC on the Review of the European Community Programme of Policy and Action in relation to the Environment and Sustainable Development 'Towards Sustainability' [1998] OJ L275/1.

[30] Communication from the Commission to the Council, the European Parliament, the Economic and Social Committee, and the Committee of the Regions on the Sixth Environment Action Programme of the European Community 'Environment 2010: Our Future, Our Choice'— The Sixth Environment Action Programme and Proposal for a Decision of the European Parliament and of the Council Laying Down the Community Environment Action Programme 2001–2010, COM(2001)31, 24 Jan. 2001.

[31] Examples are Council Reg. (EEC) No. 880/92 on a Community Eco-Label Award Scheme [1992] OJ L99/1; Council Reg. (EEC) No. 1836/93 Allowing Voluntary Participation by Companies in the Industrial Sector in a Community Eco-Management and Audit System [1993] OJ L168/1.

[32] Examples are Council Reg. (EEC) No. 259/93 on the Supervision and Control of Shipments of Waste within, into and out of the European Community [1993] OJ L30/1; Council Reg. (EC) No. 338/97 on the Protection of Species of Wild Fauna and Flora by Regulating Trade therein [1997] OJ L61/1.

provisions requiring Member States to take action, leaving issues of enforcement to Member States.

iii. Directives

As regards environmental directives, they are frequently less precise than internal market or agricultural directives. This is partly due to the fact that most directives were based on Article 175 EC, which allows Member States, by virtue of Article 176 EC, to maintain or introduce more stringent environmental measures. In effect, Article 176 EC has spurned legislation reflecting standards lower than those envisaged by Article 176 EC. Member States desiring to introduce or maintain more stringent standards were entitled to do so on the basis of that provision. At the same time, the provision has influenced the content of directives. While Community directives on motor vehicles (i.e. internal market regulation) consist of countless pages, outlining in detail the composition of products, test methods, control mechanisms, etc.,[33] such degree of detail has been avoided in the case of environmental directives. More recently, environmental directives have even failed to fix methods and frequencies of analyses, and other measurement requirements.

Since about a decade, environmental directives, apart from lacking measurement provisions, have more generally developed into framework measures preferring quality standards over emission limits, and increasingly resorted to clean-up or management plans, leaving the final responsibility for their implementation to Member States. This tendency to resort to looser and less precise regulatory techniques is a direct product of a political, largely Anglo-Saxon driven demand for environmental deregulation.

With Directive 94/62/EC on Packaging and Packaging Waste,[34] the Community for the first time applied the so-called 'new approach' in the field environmental legislation. Directive 94/62/EC fixed general requirements for the safety and environmental aspects of packaging. The details were to be elaborated in the shape of technical standards under the authority of the European Committee for Standardization (CEN). Industry largely elaborating these standards itself, the added environmental value of the new approach, in this case, was not visible.

Another important feature of many environmental directives is that, since they address administrations their provisions are not directly applicable. This may lead to considerable application problems at a later stage. At the same time, directives on air quality standards are drafted in such a way that they are hardly enforceable against recalcitrant Member States. Meanwhile, the drafting of directives was made more onerous by virtue of the Anglo-Saxon requirement of prior cost–benefit analyses and risk assessments, because any generally accepted criteria for such assessments as yet are lacking.

---

[33] European Parliament and Council Dir. 97/24/EC on Certain Components and Characteristics of Two- or Three-Wheel Motor Vehicles [1997] OJ L226/1 has a length of 454 pages in the *Official Journal*.

[34] European Parliament and Council Dir. 94/62/EC on Packaging and Packaging Waste [1994] OJ L365/10.

Directives which introduce economic and financial levies, or similar constraints or incentives, have not yet been developed. Some waste directives contain general provisions in this regard, by allowing Member States to introduce
economic instruments (a power they had in any event) but without obliging
them to do so. A proposal for a directive on the introduction of an environmental tax on fossil fuels, made in 1992,[35] did not garner the unanimous agreement in the Council necessary under Articles 93 and 175(2) EC. Since then, no
further attempts have been undertaken in the sphere of economic instruments.

iv. Recommendations

Because they are not binding, the Community has not frequently resorted to
environmental recommendations. The experience with the Council of Europe
and OECD, which have adopted numerous (non-binding) measures without
much visible effect, has probably influenced this practice. Similarly, the few
Community environmental recommendations that were adopted have had an
almost negligible effect.[36]

v. New Instruments[37]

In the early 1990s environmental agreements were considered a contempor-
ary form of standard setting which, in concertation with economic operators,
would allow the realization of environmental objectives quicker and more
effectively than 'command- and control-measures', such as legislation.[38] A
Commission Communication of 1996 set out the conditions for environmental agreements at Community level.[39] This has not resulted in increased
use of such agreements, however. The only significant agreement is the unilateral commitment of car manufacturers to reduce CO_2 emissions of new cars,
from 2008 onwards, to 140 grammes CO_2 per kilometre. The Commission
tacitly agreed to abstain from legislating on CO_2 emissions from cars, as long
as this commitment is honoured.[40] This agreement shows that its main attraction for industry is that it pre-empts binding legislation, rather than any environmental considerations.[41] Constitutionally, the question how agreements

---

[35] [1992] OJ C196/1; amended by COM(95)172, 10 May 1995.

[36] See e.g. Council Rec. 75/436/Euratom, ECSC, EEC (n. 22 above); Council Rec. 79/3/EEC regarding Methods of Evaluating the Cost of Pollution Control to Industry [1979] OJ L5/28; Council Rec.
81/972/EEC concerning the Re-Use of Waste Paper and the Use of Recycled Paper [1981] OJ L355/56.

[37] See generally on this question, J. Golub (ed.), *New Instruments for Environmental Policy in
the EU* (London/New York: Routledge, 1998), where these questions are mainly discussed from a
policy perspective.

[38] See Fifth Environment Action Programme, n. 28 above.

[39] Communication from the Commission to the Council and the European Parliament on
Environmental Agreements, COM(96)561, 27 Nov. 1996.

[40] For details, see L. Krämer, *EC Environmental Law* (London: Sweet & Maxwell, 2000), 214 ff.

[41] Thus, the agreement does not provide for the overall reduction of CO_2 emissions from cars;
its environmental effects are thus likely to be at least in part outweighed by increased numbers of
cars. Furthermore, it is questionable whether car production should really limit itself to this one
measure or whether other measures—concerning raw materials, construction plants, etc.—are
also necessary to combat the generation of greenhouse gases. Similarly, it may be asked whether
the production of cars in the Community that are to be exported outside the Community should
not also have reduced CO_2 emissions.

can be concluded at Community level which preserve the institutional participatory rights of the EP, the Council, the Economic and Social Committee, and the Committee of the Regions, has not yet been resolved. It is also unclear how such agreements are to be applied, monitored and enforced in non-oligopolistic markets. Although Directive 2000/53/EC for the first time stipulates that some of its environmental provisions may be implemented by agreements at Member State level,[42] the legal aspects of environmental agreements at Community level remain ambiguous. Such agreements seem geared more towards deregulation, than to the protection of the environment.[43]

Another species of new instruments, tradable pollution permits, have not yet been developed at Community level. Pursuant to the Kyoto Protocol to the Convention on Climate Change, which was internationally agreed in 1998, the Community will have to develop such tradable permits for greenhouse gas emissions, and for that purpose issued a Green Paper in 2000.[44] Beyond climate issues, such instruments do not appear to be planned.

C. CITIZENS' INVOLVEMENT

i. Institutional Questions

Environmental organizations are hardly represented in the Community institutions.[45] The Commission has not provided for a consultative committee of environmental organizations or any other form ensuring their institutional representation. Consequently, the influence of vested interest groups on Community environmental policy and law is considerably bigger than that of environmental interest groups. Neither is there any institutional representation of environmental organizations in the European industrial standardization organizations CEN and CENELEC (European Committee for Electrotechnical Standardization). The formal argument is that environmental organizations are free to participate in standardization work. However, since travel and other costs are borne by participants themselves, this system is not necessarily equitable.[46]

Hearings of interested groups are hardly ever organized by the Commission, never by the Council and, as noted, sporadically by the EP. The fact that discussions are therefore often essentially unstructured works to the disadvantage of environmental groups.

---

[42] European Parliament and Council Dir. 2000/53/EC on End-of-Life Vehicles [2000] OJ L269/34.

[43] See on Community and Member States' environmental agreements, J. Verschuuren, 'EC Environmental Law and Self-Regulation in the Member States: In Search of a Legislative Framework' (2000) 1 *Yearbook of European Environmental Law*, 103 ff. Verschuuren discusses the issue from a Dutch perspective.

[44] Commission, Green Paper on Greenhouse Gas Emissions Trading within the European Union, COM(2000)87, 8 Mar. 2000.

[45] See generally on this question, P. Newell and W. Grant, 'Environmental NGOs and EU Environmental Law' (2000) 1 *Yearbook of European Environmental Law*, 225 ff.

[46] For the same reason as the statement 'The access to the Ritz Hotel in Paris is open for everybody' is not constructive.

168   *Ludwig Krämer*

No Community measures exist which require institutional representation of environmental interest groups or individual citizens in the Member States, since this question is left entirely to Member States.

ii. Legal Issues

A Directive of 1990 grants everybody a right of access to environmental information held by public authorities in Member States.[47] Until recently, a similar right of access to environmental information held by Community institutions had been lacking. However, the Council and the Commission also have adopted measures to provide for access to documents, and Article 255 EC now articulates a right of access to documents for any person residing in the Community, and furthermore provides that before 1 May 2001 specific rules are elaborated on this right.[48]

As regards participation in public decision-making, Directive 85/337/EEC on the Assessment of the Effects of Certain Public and Private Projects on the Environment grants the 'public concerned' a right to express its opinion in environment impact assessment procedures relating to certain public or private projects.[49] A proposal for a directive, which would grant similar rights in respect of environmental plans or programmes, is under discussion at present. Participation rights for measures emanating from Community institutions, in particular the Commission, do not exist, however.

No general legislation has yet been adopted on access to national courts. Directive 90/313/EEC, mentioned above, provides for access to national courts where access to environmental information has been refused. Community provisions grant a right to apply to European courts when the right of access to documents has been refused.[50]

Access to information, participation in public decision-making, and access to the courts in future might be further regulated, as a UN Convention on these matters was opened for signature in 1998 in Aarhus, and signed by the Community.

As regards information on the state of the environment and of the relevant law, the Commission published several reports which, overall, were not always informative. The European Environmental Agency now has the statutory duty to publish a report on the state of the environment every five years.[51] Thus far, two such reports have been published.[52] In addition, numerous environmental

---

[47] Council Dir. 90/313/EEC on the Freedom of Access to Information on the Environment [1990] OJ L158/58.

[48] Council Dec. 93/731/EC on Public Access to Council Documents [1993] OJ L340/43; Commission Dec. 94/90/EC on Public Access to Commission Documents [1994] OJ L46/58. Latest developments are published on the Internet at: http://www.europa.eu.int/comm/secretariat_general/sgc/acc_doc/en/index.htm#2.

[49] Council Dir. 85/337/EEC on the Assessment of the Effects of Certain Public and Private Projects on the Environment [1985] OJ L175/40.

[50] European Parliament and Council Reg. (EC) No. 1049/2001 regarding public access to European Parliament, Council and Commission documents [2001] OJ L145/43.

[51] Article 2(VI) of Council Reg. (EEC) No. 1210/90, n. 14 above; amended by Council Reg. (EC) No. 933/1999 [1999] OJ L117/1.

[52] See European Environment Agency, *Environment in the European Union at the Turn of the Century* (Luxembourg: Office for Official Publications, 1999).

directives and regulations require regular Commission reports regarding their implementation. In reality, however, such reports were produced very unsystematically. An attempt to rationalize and standardize such implementation reports had only limited success.[53] It must be noted that, significantly, these implementation reports are based on data provided by Member States, rather than some independent EU agency.

V. Sectoral Perspectives

A. HORIZONTAL QUESTIONS

i. Products

The Community has yet to develop a 'green' product policy.[54] Despite the requirement of the EC Treaty that products circulating in the internal market must reflect high environmental standards, free trade considerations often have prevailed.[55]

In particular, the Commission in the past has concentrated on tackling national product-related measures aiming at the protection of the environment but which contained, in its view, a protectionist element. This position in turn was based on the assumption that any national product-related environmental measure constituted a threat to the free circulation of goods. The ECJ has corrected the most obvious excesses in this regard.[56]

EC environmental product regulation has been elaborated in a piecemeal fashion.[57] Some random examples may serve to illustrate this. No attempt has been made to introduce a 'substitution principle' into Community law, requiring the replacement of known harmful substances, whenever less harmful alternatives exist. The use of pesticides and pesticide residues, fertilizers and similar products in agriculture was largely left unregulated from an environmental perspective.[58] As regards cars, although the introduction of the catalytic converter for all *new* cars became mandatory as of 1 January 1993, no measures were introduced for cars already on the market, so that, *de facto*, cars may be equipped with a catalytic converter as late as around 2006. Similarly,

---

[53] Council Dir. 91/692/EEC Standardizing and Rationalizing Reports on the Implementation of Certain Directives Relating to the Environment [1991] OJ L377/48.

[54] See also H. Temmink, 'From Danish Bottles to Danish Bees: The Dynamics of Free Movement of Goods and Environmental Protection—a Case Law Analysis' (2000) 1 *Yearbook of European Environmental Law*, 61 ff.

[55] See the remarks under Sect. II above.

[56] Cases C–302/86, *Commission* v. *Denmark* [1988] ECR I–4607; C–473/98, *Kemikalieinspektionen* v. *Toolex Alpha AB* [2000] ECR I–5681.

[57] See in particular, Council Dir. 76/769/EEC on Restrictions on the Marketing and Use of Certain Dangerous Substances and Preparations [1976] OJ L262/201, which has been amended about twenty times in an unsystematic way, resulting in numerous derogations, exceptions, transitional periods, etc.

[58] Council Dir. 91/414/EEC concerning the Placing of Plant Protection Products on the Market [1991] OJ L230/1 was adopted after fifteen years of discussion. It provides for uniform standards for the authorization of pesticides, which are still being elaborated.

when asbestos was finally banned from the Community market in 1999, following sixteen years of discussion and a ban at national level in nine Member States,[59] no measure was taken as regards asbestos already on the market. When PCB/PCT products were banned from the Community market in 1985, discussion shifted to the removal of the existing PCB/PCT. After ten years of discussions, Member States were finally granted until 2010 to remove them.[60]

In respect of products containing genetically modified organisms, the Community first adopted legislation in 1990. However, it soon appeared that this directive could not be enforced in view of consumer objections to biotechnology echoed in a number of Member States. In the first half of 2001, much more stringent Community legislation was drafted, aiming to overcome popular objections against this new technology.[61]

As already noted, harmonization of fiscal and financial product-related provisions has not yet occurred, as this requires unanimity in the Council. In this respect, Member States therefore enjoy considerable discretion to adopt legislation, and the Commission constantly seeks to narrow down national autonomy in this field.[62]

As regards exports, it has been decided not to prohibit or restrict the export of products which themselves are prohibited or their use restricted within the Community. Instead, it adopted the international trade principle to allow the export of dangerous chemicals subject to 'prior informed consent' (PIC). Pursuant to this principle, the importing third country must be informed of any risks and the internal Community restrictions. The importing country shall then decide if and what form of import restrictions it wishes to establish.[63] Beyond the chemical sector, no export provisions exist, with the notable exception of the waste sector, which will be examined elsewhere in this chapter.

ii. Production Processes

EC law contains no provision which, by way of a general principle, obliges installations to have a permit and respect certain emission limits. Rather, legislation applies to certain specific as well as large installations. For example, Directive 76/464/EEC requires permits for installations which discharge certain dangerous substances into water,[64] and Directive 84/360/EEC similarly

---

[59] The Commission did not take action against these Member States. However, prior to 1998, it did not propose to extend such a ban to the whole of the Community.

[60] Council Dir. 96/59/EC on the Disposal of Polychlorinated Biphenyls and Polychlorinated Terphenyls (PCB/PCT) [1996] OJ L243/31.

[61] European Parliament and Council Dir. 2001/18/EC on the Deliberate Release Into the Environment of Genetically Modified Organisms and Repealing Council Dir. 90/220/EEC [2001] OJ L106/1.

[62] See also Communication from the Commission to the European Parliament and the Council: Single Market and Environment, COM(99)263, 8 June 1999.

[63] Council Reg. (EEC) No. 2455/92 concerning the Export and Import of Certain Dangerous Chemicals [1992] OJ L251/13.

[64] Council Dir. 76/464/EEC on Pollution Caused by Certain Dangerous Substances Discharged into the Aquatic Environment of the Community [1976] OJ L129/23.

Thirty Years of EC Environmental Law 171

requires prior authorization for industrial installations which discharge certain pollutants into the air.[65]

In the early 1990s, without any prior public debate, it was decided not to adopt harmonized standards for production processes. The basic approach of the Community is now contained in Directive 96/61/EC,[66] the elaboration of which has been influenced considerably by United Kingdom experience. The Directive applies to certain types of installations enumerated in an Annex, which thereby must obtain a permit laying down emission limits which 'shall be based on the best available techniques' (BAT). The notion of BAT includes economic considerations, and the permit has also to take into consideration the specific local conditions of the installation. This approach in practice means that for identical installations, different emission standards may apply, impacting on the competitiveness of the installation, and also on the environmental performance of the products which are produced. Although guidance documents elaborated for different types of installations should mitigate these effects, it is noteworthy that these Best Available Techniques Reference Notes (BREFs) are elaborated with the very active participation of industry. Neither are these documents binding on competent authorities.

Originally, it was anticipated that the scope of Directive 96/61/EC would extend to smaller installations. This approach appears later to have been abandoned, however. Exceptionally, the Community opts to adopt uniform emission limit values at Community level. Such limit values were fixed for large combustion installations,[67] and for waste incinerators.[68]

For installations, very few monitoring requirements exist. The auditing system set up by Regulation (EC) No. 1836/93 allows for the voluntary participation of industries.[69] Installations which process dangerous substances fall within the field of application of Directive 96/82/EC,[70] and waste incinerators[71] must regularly be inspected by the competent national authorities.

No provisions exist, however, concerning the export of production installations to third countries.

---

[65] Council Dir. 84/360/EEC on the Combating of Air Pollution from Industrial Plants [1984] OJ L188/20.

[66] Council Dir. 96/61/EC concerning Integrated Pollution Prevention and Control [1996] OJ L257/26.

[67] Council Dir. 88/609/EEC on the Limitation of Emissions of Certain Pollutants into the Air from Large Combustion Plants [1988] OJ L336/1. This Directive is presently being revised.

[68] European Parliament and Council Dir. 2000/73/EC on the Incineration of Waste [2000] OJ L332/91. This Directive will progressively substitute earlier directives on the incineration of waste: Council Dir. 89/369/EEC on the Prevention of Air Pollution from New Municipal Waste Incineration Plants [1989] OJ L163/32; Council Dir. 89/429/EEC on the Reduction of Air Pollution From Existing Waste-Incineration-Plants [1989] OJ L203/50; Council Dir. 94/67/EC on the Incineration of Hazardous Waste [1994] OJ L365/34.

[69] Council Reg. (EEC) No. 1836/93, n. 31 above.

[70] Art. 18 of Council Dir. 96/82/EC on the Control of Major-Accident Hazards Involving Dangerous Substances [1997] OJ L10/13.

[71] Council Dir. 75/442/EEC on Waste [1975] OJ L194/39; as amended by Council Dir. 91/156/EEC [1991] OJ L78/32 (Art. 13).

iii. *Other Measures*

Rather than a single Community-wide environmental label, specific labels have been developed for organic food, dangerous chemicals, energy, water and noise of household appliances, genetically modified products, and the separate collection of waste, in addition to a general eco-label.[72] Participation in this eco-label scheme is voluntary, and the label coexists with national eco-labels. The number of products on the Community market which carry the EC eco-label remains relatively small.

More than twenty years of efforts to introduce Community provisions on civil liability for damage caused to the environment thus far have not produced a final outcome. The Commission elaborated a proposal for liability for damage caused by waste,[73] which was not discussed in the Council, as well as a Greenbook,[74] and a White Paper on Environmental Liability.[75] Furthermore, a Directive on Liability for Defective Products applies to defective products, including waste.[76]

No Community provisions are in force regarding criminal sanctions for environmental impairment. For years, it was believed that the EC enjoyed no competence in this field of criminal law, but this assessment has recently changed. A recent proposal for the first time requests Member States to fix criminal sanctions where national law transposing Community environmental law has been breached.[77]

B. WATER LAW

Community water legislation has not evolved out of a clear concept. Based on the aforementioned framework Directive 76/464/EEC, emission limits for discharges in water were fixed for seventeen dangerous substances, which had been selected on the basis of their toxicity, persistence, and bioaccumulation. However, confronted with UK objections against the emission limits approach, the Community also fixed quality objectives in parallel. Comparative studies were to be carried out in order to decide which approach should be retained as a definite Community solution.

This approach was abruptly overhauled in the first half of the 1990s, when the Commission shifted towards quality objectives and framework provisions. These ideas were provisionally given shape in the Water Framework Directive

---

[72] Council Reg. (EEC) No. 880/92, n. 31 above; amended by European Parliament and Council Reg. (EC) No. 1980/2000 on a Revised Community Eco-Label Award Scheme [2000] OJ L237/1.

[73] [1989] OJ C251/3.

[74] Communication from the Commission to the Council and Parliament and the Economic and Social Committee: Green Paper on Remedying Environmental Damage [1993] OJ C149/2.

[75] Commission: White Paper on Environmental Liability, COM(2000)66, 9 Feb. 2000. See also Betlem and Brans elsewhere in this volume.

[76] Council Dir. 85/374/EEC on the Approximation of the Laws, Regulations and Administrative Provisions of the Member States concerning Liability for Defective Products [1985] OJ L210/29.

[77] See COM(2001)139, 13 Mar. 2001; [2001] OJ C180E/238.

in 2000,[78] which is progressively to be put into operation over the next fifteen years.

As regards earlier measures in this area, the Community traditionally has focused on elaborating quality objectives, which were fixed for surface water, bathing water, fresh fish, and shellfish water. Directive 76/160/EEC on the Quality of Bathing Water[79] enjoyed considerable public attention because of its impact on tourism. The Directive led to considerable investment in combating coastal discharges. Other directives were more difficult to monitor for the Commission, undermining their ultimate efficiency.

Yet, Directive 80/778/EEC on Drinking Water,[80] an 'end-of-the-pipe' directive, fixed maximum concentrations for pollutants in drinking water and required considerable investment for clean-up measures for surface and groundwater, in particular in respect of parameters for heavy metals, pesticides, nitrates, and other chemicals. Attempts from the agricultural and chemical sectors to relax these standards essentially failed.[81]

Directive 91/271/EEC required Member States, for urban agglomerations with more than 5,000 inhabitants, to provide canalization and waste-water treatment installations,[82] which once more necessitated considerable investments in all Member States. Finally, Directive 91/676/EEC intends to protect water against nitrates from agricultural sources.[83] For that purpose, the number of livestock per hectare must be limited in vulnerable zones, which has a considerable impact on agricultural practice, and the implementation of this directive therefore causes controversy in all Member States.

The Community deals with questions of marine pollution mainly by way of regional conventions. These are ratified by some Member States, and the Community also adheres to them. Likewise, the clean-up of international rivers such as the Rhine, Elbe, Danube, and Oder takes place through the cooperation between Member States and third states, rather than autonomous Community activities. Questions of quantitative management of water resources were left practically untouched by the Community.

C. AIR POLLUTION

The Community has approached air pollution issues rather more systematically than water pollution, partly in response to the widespread phenomenon

---

[78] European Parliament and Council Dir. 2000/60/EC Establishing a Framework for Community Action in the Field of Water Policy [2000] OJ L327/1.

[79] Council Dir. 76/160/EEC concerning the Quality of Bathing Water [1976] OJ L31/1.

[80] Council Dir. 80/778/EEC relating to the Quality of Water Intended for Human Consumption [1980] OJ L229/11.

[81] Council Dir. 98/83/EC on the Quality of Water Intended for Human Consumption [1998] OJ L330/32.

[82] Council Dir. 91/271/EEC concerning Urban Waste-Water Treatment [1991] OJ L135/40; this is the only environmental directive, which requires the construction of installations by Member States.

[83] Council Dir. 91/676/EEC concerning the Protection of Waters against Pollution Caused by Nitrates from Agricultural Sources [1991] OJ L375/1.

of *Waldsterben* in continental Europe. Early progress to tackle pollution by installations systematically[84] gradually slowed down, and were eventually substituted by the Integrated Pollution Prevention and Control (IPPC) approach for bigger installations. For the most common air pollutants, the quality objective approach was pursued, although the quality objectives were hardly monitored or enforced.[85] Later quality directives were drafted in a way which makes them almost unenforceable, and in any event are not yet fully operational.[86]

As regards atmospheric emissions from transport, the Commission, with the support of the Council and the EP, negotiated an 'auto oil programme' with the car and the mineral oil industries, which led to the fixing of emission standards for motor vehicles, and product standards for different types of fuels.[87] To what extent this agreement constitutes the environmental optimum and incites technological improvement remains to be seen. Similarly, the car industry entered into an environmental agreement on CO_2 reductions with the Commission.[88]

The Community transposed the provisions of the Montreal Protocol on Substances that Deplete the Ozone Layer into Community law, took the lead in international discussions, and adopted EC-wide legislation which, in several aspects, went beyond international commitments.[89]

Community discussions as regards climate change issues started in the late 1980s. However, this led only to few specific measures regarding the reduction of greenhouse gases. Plans for a directive to reduce CO_2-emissions from cars were replaced by an agreement with the car industry.[90] Modest energy conservation measures were adopted in 1993, and supported by measures allowing financial incentives.[91] A monitoring mechanism for greenhouse gases was set

---

[84] Council Dir. 84/360/EEC (n. 65 above), Council Dir. 88/609/EEC (n. 67 above), Council Dir. 89/369/EEC (n. 68 above).

[85] Council Dir. 80/779/EEC on Air Quality Limit Values and Guide Values for Sulphur Dioxide and Suspended Particulates [1980] OJ L229/30; Council Dir. 82/884/EEC on a Limit Value for Lead in the Air [1982] OJ L378/15; Council Dir. 85/203/EEC on Air Quality Standards for Nitrogen Dioxide [1985] OJ L87/1.

[86] Council Dir. 96/62/EC on Ambient Air Quality Assessment and Management [1996] OJ L296/55; Council Dir. 1999/30/EC relating to Limit Values for Sulphur Dioxide, Nitrogen Dioxide and Oxides of Nitrogen, Particulate Matter and Lead in Ambient Air [1999] OJ L163/41.

[87] Council Dir. 1999/32/EC relating to a Reduction in the Sulphur Content of Certain Liquid Fuels and Amending Dir. 93/2/EEC [1999] OJ L121/13.

[88] Further discussed elsewhere in this chapter.

[89] Council Dec. 88/540/EEC concerning the Conclusion of the Vienna Convention for the Protection of the Ozone Layer and the Montreal Protocol on Substances that Deplete the Ozone Layer [1988] OJ L297/8; Council Reg. (EC) No. 3093/94 on Substances that Deplete the Ozone Layer [1994] OJ L333/1. This last Regulation is now replaced by European Parliament and Council Reg. (EC) No. 2037/2000 on Substances that Deplete the Ozone Layer [2000] OJ L244/1.

[90] Further discussed elsewhere in this chapter.

[91] Council Dir. 93/76/EEC to Limit Carbon Dioxide Emissions by Improving Energy Efficiency (SAVE) [1993] OJ L237/28; Council Dec. 96/737/EC concerning a Multiannual Programme for the Promotion of Energy Efficiency in the Community [1996] OJ L335/50; Council Dec. 98/352/EC concerning a Multiannual Programme for the Promotion of Renewable Energy Sources in the Community (Altener II) [1998] OJ L159/53.

Thirty Years of EC Environmental Law 175

up,[92] but the proposal for a tax on fossil fuels could not be adopted.[93] At international level, the Community succeeded to speak with a single voice at the Kyoto meeting, where a Protocol on the reduction of greenhouse gases was agreed, and the reduction for the Community was fixed at 8 per cent. As a follow-up after the Kyoto meeting, Member States agreed in Council, without a corresponding Commission proposal, the relative percentages of reductions for each Member State. This state of affairs perfectly illustrates the tension between Community and national environmental policy.[94]

D. NOISE

Community noise legislation did not primarily aim to address environmental problems, but stems from internal market considerations. Noise emission standards apply to new products (mainly to means of transport such as cars, motorcycles, aircraft, and trucks), and construction equipment, and were based on their technical feasibility. No standards for products already on the market, and no noise quality standards, for instance in respect of airports, schools, or hospitals, were fixed. A new, more environmentally oriented approach was initiated by the Commission in 1999 and 2000, the impact of which needs to be awaited.

E. NATURE PROTECTION

The Community imposed a legal requirement for Member States to designate habitats for fauna and flora species and other habitats.[95] Implementation of this requirement, however, has proved problematic. Other conservation measures for birds, endangered fauna and flora species also exist.[96] In an effort to include wild animal welfare into the Community's sphere of competence, and due to public pressure in certain Member States, measures to protect baby seals,[97] whales,[98] and animals caught in leghold traps[99] were also adopted. Although not a member of the International Convention on Trade in Endangered Species (CITES), the Community adopted provisions to transpose,

---

[92] Council Dec. 93/389/EEC for a Monitoring Mechanism of Community CO_2 and Other Greenhouse Gas Emissions [1993] OJ L167/31; amended by Council Dec. 1999/296/EC [1999] OJ L117/35.

[93] Further discussed elsewhere in this chapter.   [94] See Krämer, n. 40 above, 225.

[95] Art. 4 of Council Dir. 79/409/EEC on the Conservation of Wild Birds [1979] OJ L103/1; Council Dir. 92/43/EEC on the Conservation of Natural Habitats and of Wild Fauna and Flora [1992] OJ L206/7.

[96] Ibid.

[97] Council Dir. 83/129/EEC concerning the Importation into Member States of Skins of Certain Seal Pups and Products Derived therefrom [1983] OJ L91/30.

[98] Council Reg. (EEC) No. 348/81 on Common Rules for Imports of Whales or Other Cetacean Products [1981] OJ L39/1.

[99] Council Reg. (EEC) No. 3254/91 Prohibiting the Use of Leghold Traps in the Community and the Introduction into the Community of Pelts and Manufactured Goods of Certain Wild Animal Species Originating in Countries which catch them by means of Leghold Traps or Trapping Methods which do not Meet International Humane Trapping Standards [1991] OJ L308/1.

176   *Ludwig Krämer*

in toto, the requirements of the Convention, and occasionally went considerably beyond these requirements.[100]

International efforts to preserve biodiversity were supported by the Community, which did not, however, take specific measures of its own for that purpose.

F. WASTE MANAGEMENT

Community waste legislation was adopted from the mid-1970s onwards. The EC adopted three types of legislation: horizontal provisions on waste,[101] provisions on hazardous waste,[102] and a regime on the shipment of waste.[103] As for horizontal provisions, Community-wide definitions of 'waste', a general permit requirement and basic substantive requirements for the handling of waste, and Member State waste management plans are now in place. As regards shipment of waste, the Community, following OECD developments, differentiated between shipments for waste recovery, and shipments for waste disposal. While shipments for recovery are controlled according to the hazardousness of waste, Member States are allowed to prohibit shipments for waste disposal altogether. Also, the shipment of hazardous waste to non-OECD countries has been prohibited.[104]

A separate set of rules concerns waste incinerators,[105] landfill installations,[106] and port reception facilities,[107] for which stringent minimum requirements are fixed. Another distinct set of rules concerns deals with individual waste streams such as waste oils,[108] sewage sludge,[109] batteries,[110] packaging waste,[111] and end-of-life vehicles.[112]

The elaboration and implementation of waste legislation was and continues to be marked by tensions between the Community and Member States regarding their respective responsibilities. While disputes over the legal basis for waste legislation have by now been resolved in favour of the application of Article 175 EC, controversies continue in particular as regards the scope for Member States to adopt more specific waste legislation, mainly in those areas where the Community provisions are not sufficiently precise.

---

[100] Council Reg. (EC) No. 338/97, n. 32 above.
[101] Council Dir. 75/442/EEC, as amended by Council Dir. 91/156/EEC; n. 71 above.
[102] Council Dir. 91/689/EEC on Hazardous Waste [1991] OJ L377/20.
[103] Council Reg. (EEC) No. 259/93, n. 32 above.
[104] Council Reg. (EC) No. 120/97 Amending Reg. (EEC) No. 259/93 [1997] OJ L22/14.
[105] See the references cited in n. 68 above.
[106] Council Dir. 1999/31/EC on the Landfill of Waste [1999] OJ L182/1.
[107] European Parliament and Council Dir. 2000/59/EC on Port Reception Facilities for Ship-Generated Waste and Cargo Residues [2000] OJ L332/81.
[108] Council Dir. 75/439/EEC on the Disposal of Waste Oils [1975] OJ L194/23.
[109] Council Dir. 86/278/EEC on the Protection of the Environment, and in particular of the Soil, when Sewage Sludge is Used in Agriculture [1986] OJ L181/6.
[110] Council Dir. 91/157/EEC on Batteries and Accumulators Containing Certain Dangerous Substances [1991] OJ L78/38.
[111] European Parliament and Council Dir. 94/62/EC, n. 34 above.
[112] European Parliament and Council Dir. 2000/53/EC, n. 42 above.

VI. Implementation

Under Article 175(4) EC, Member States must implement EC environmental policy, which of course includes the implementation of the measures adopted in pursuance of that policy. Under Article 211 EC, it is the Commission's task to ensure that the measures adopted by the Community institutions are properly applied.

Whereas the Commission, during the first decade of EC environmental law, did not closely monitor the practical application of environmental directives, it has progressively made this a priority from 1985 onwards. Cases of non-application were more systematically pursued, applications to the ECJ more frequently made, individuals actively encouraged to file complaints,[113] and breaches of Community law by Member States systematically made public. This policy increased attention in Member States for the implementation, application, and enforcement of environmental legislation. Progress remained slow, however, also because particular administrations were not used to see their administrative practice challenged by an outside body.[114] At present, at any given moment, the Commission monitors about 1,100 cases of presumed breaches of Community environmental law.

In environmental matters, the Commission does not dispose inspectors to check whether the law is actually applied on the ground. Cooperation by Member States is limited for obvious reasons. Almost the only sources of information for the Commission in respect of specific cases are information from private complainants, and replies to questions by national administrations.

Attempts to locate some enforcement monitoring tasks with the European Environment Agency were resisted by Member States, and at present are no longer pursued. No alternative external body was set up to monitor application of the law. This means that the administration which has to elaborate EC environmental law in close collaboration with Member States simultaneously is to pursue the latter under Article 211 EC, and to take formal legal action against them. Indeed, the infringement procedure under Article 226 EC is the only means available to enforce application of Community environmental law against Member States. The use of financial means to exercise pressure on recalcitrant Member States is not foreseen by EC law, and not really accepted as a possibility by the Commission.

The Commission does not systematically ensure that international environmental conventions to which the Community has adhered and which thereby

---

[113] The number of environmental complaints rose from eight in 1983 to 525 in 1989; see Krämer, n. 40 above, 286 (n. 39). At present, there are about 600 environmental complaints per year.

[114] See, on these developments in particular, Eighth Annual Report to the European Parliament on Community Monitoring of the Application of Community Law (1990) [1991] OJ C338/1 (Annex).

become part of Community law,[115] are applied, since there is no monitoring of such international conventions. The situation is different only in cases where the Community has adopted specific legal provisions to transpose provisions of a convention. It is submitted that this is not only a rather serious breach of the Commission's obligations flowing from Article 211 EC, but also an omission which is highly detrimental to the environment.

Apart from this formal side concerning monitoring, several aspects add to the problem of the application of environmental law. The lack of a 'European' public opinion, has already been mentioned. Equally important is the existence of distinct legal cultures in Member States, developed over centuries. Uniform environmental law which originated from Community institutions therefore produces different effects in these different legal cultures, which also has implications for the effectiveness of subsequent implementation. A Member State such as Portugal which, according to its own estimation, did not possess any environmental legislation prior to its accession in 1986, will inevitably take a different position vis-à-vis implementation of an environmental directive from a Member State such as the Netherlands, which disposes a sophisticated and complete system of national environmental law.

Also, while some Member States appear to regard it a point of principle to transpose, implement, and apply EC environmental law timely and correctly, experience shows that other Member States more systematically transpose environmental law too late, and may not invest much effort in applying EC environmental law at local, regional, or even national level.[116] Such differences are also expressions of the value which Member States attach to the protection of the environment, the degree to which a tradition of an 'open society' exists, the value attached to legal rules, and the degree to which Member States are prepared to limit the power of administrations to disregard environmental provisions.

VII. State of the Environment

The state of the environment provides the ultimate yardstick against which to evaluate the success of the protection of the environment by means of law. In 1999, the European Environment Agency published its report on the state of

---

[115] Art. 300(7) EC: 'Agreements concluded under the conditions set out in this Article shall be binding on the institutions of the Community and on Member States.'

[116] The judgments of the ECJ are rife with examples. For example, in December 2000, the Commission decided to apply a second time to the ECJ, because bathing water in Blackpool (UK) continued to breach the requirements of Council Dir. 76/160/EEC (n. 79 above), despite a first judgment by the ECJ in 1993 (Case C–56/90, *Commission* v. *United Kingdom* [1993] ECR I–4109); in Case C–168/95, *Criminal Proceedings against Luciano Arcaro* [1996] ECR I–4705, the ECJ found that Italy had not transposed the requirement of permits for cadmium discharges from existing industrial installations, about twenty years after the adoption of Council Dir. 76/464/EC (n. 64 above); and by the end of 1996, the ECJ found that Germany had not transposed two water directives from 1978 and 1979 into national law (Case C–298/95, *Commission* v. *Germany* [1996] ECR I–6747).

Thirty Years of EC Environmental Law   179

the European environment,[117] which gave rise to the following assessment of the present situation as shown in Table I.[118]

The chapter which carries this table, and explains the present situation and likely future developments, carries the sober title: 'some progress, but a poor picture overall', and this might well apply more generally to the state of the environment in the EU. The particularly negative evaluation for the natural environment (biodiversity, coastal and marine areas, rural areas, mountain areas, soil degradation) confirms the impression that, despite all our best efforts, nature slowly but progressively withdraws from Western Europe.

The Commission's Sixth Environmental Action Programme observes in this respect:

despite the improvements on some fronts, we continue to face a number of persistent problems. Of particular concern are climate change, the loss of biodiversity and natural habitats, soil loss and degradation, increased waste volumes, the build-up of chemicals in the environment, noise and certain air and water pollutants. We also face a number

Table I: State of the European environment

Environmental issue	Present pressure	Present state and impact
Greenhouse gases and climate change	0	—
Ozone depletion	+	—
Hazardous substances	0	0
Transboundary air pollution	0	0
Water stress	0	0
Soil degradation	—	—
Waste	0	—
Natural and technologcal hazards	0	0
Genetically modified organisms	0	?
Biodiversity	—	0
Human health	0	—
Urban areas	0	0
Coastal and Marine Areas	—	—
Rural areas	—	—
Mountain areas	—	—

[117] European Environment Agency, n. 52 above.
[118] Ibid. 23; the signs mean: +: positive development; 0: some positive development, but insufficient; —: unfavourable development; ?: uncertain.

180   *Ludwig Krämer*

of emerging issues such as pollutants that affect the functioning of our hormone systems. Forecasts suggest that, with current policies and socio-economic trends, many of the pressures that give rise to these problems, such as transport, energy use, tourist activities, land-take for infra-structure, etc. will worsen over the coming decade. [119]

VIII. Conclusion

What, then, has EC law achieved or failed to achieve over the past thirty years? It is obvious that because of the interdependence of EC environmental law and national environmental law, many developments cannot be attributed to one sphere of law or the other. Through cross-fertilization, national developments are sometimes communitarized which, in turn, influence the evolution of law in the Member States. With this proviso, the following observations may be made.

Environmental law has reached constitutional status in the EU. In numerous Member States, there now exist express constitutional provisions pertaining to the constitution which require the protection of the environment. This constitutional development has occurred over the last thirty years, reached the EU in 1987, and continues to influence constitutional developments in Central and Eastern Europe. The positioning of environmental needs at a level equal to human rights or social rights is important. It conveys the message to all stakeholders, including citizens, that the need to protect, preserve, and improve the quality of the environment is of fundamental importance, vital for the state and for society as a whole.

Environmental law in the EU has thus led to the emergence of administrative infrastructures in the Member States. Over the past thirty years, progressively, environmental bureaucracies were set up at Community, state, regional, and local level. Overall, it seems fair to say that environmental administration, policy, and law is most structured, developed, and sophisticated, where economic performance is highest.

Environmental law has now come to regulate all aspects of the environment, from the more classical areas such as water, air, products, noise, nature, and waste, to more intricate areas such as town and country planning, climate change, transport and energy law. Again, the number, substance, and intensity of regulation varies, and the evolution of environmental law, including the 'conquest' of new areas, has not yet come to a halt.

Environmental law has also begun to permeate universities, environmental organizations, lawyers, and courts. While there may exist a general problem in any affluent society to interest the young in anything beyond wealth and leisure, environmental law, human rights law, and legal disciplines linked to modern technology are taken up by young lawyers not merely seeking personal wealth.

---

[119] Sixth Environment Action Programme, n. 30 above, 10.

Thirty Years of EC Environmental Law 181

Environmental law thereby has become a most important tool in the fight against environmental impairment in the EU. Although such impairment continues to exist, public authorities in the EU which now tolerate the impairment of the environment do so at their peril. Enviromental impairment has become socially undesirable behaviour, and environmental law has reached a social status equivalent to human rights law.

European integration was and remains a powerful tool to ensure the spread of environmental laws and know-how well beyond the territorial limits of the EU.

Meanwhile, the enforcement of EC environmental law vis-à-vis Member States remains a task of paramount importance. ECJ judgments against Member States now have become routine, and although often with some delay or even reluctance, Member States normally do comply with these judgments, if only to avoid penalty payments under Article 228 EC. The progress which the EC has achieved with this procedure can only be fully appreciated if it is realized that the USA, Japan, Russia, or any other state are not prepared to accept judgments from foreign courts. It is often argued that the environment knows no frontiers. Yet, when it comes to enforcing (environmental) provisions of international conventions, national sovereignty directly conflicts with the supremacy of the jurisdiction of a foreign court. In this regard, the Community truly is a model for other parts of the world.

Meanwhile, the Community has entrusted the protection of the environment almost exclusively to the administration. It is the administration which takes thousands of administrative decisions on a day-by-day basis, that permit emissions of pollutants into the environment, allows certain substances to be marketed, projects to be realized, or industrial activity to take place. Administrations are also in charge of monitoring application of, and compliance with the law, and may, by taking action or by failing to do so, very substantially affect the environment. In environmental matters, it is often still presumed that the public administration can do no wrong. Administrations serve multiple interests, which are linked to the governing classes, and they are not politically neutral, as the theory of the modern state might suggest. They are inherently conservative, and therefore tend to protect the *status quo*. Since the rise of modern administration, the status quo has felt at liberty to use and abuse the environment.

Similarly, from the start, the EC's administration favoured the free circulation of goods, services, capital, and labour, and only reluctantly and slowly took into consideration environmental imperatives. The Community's administration, which is not particularly accountable or transparent for citizens and environmental groups, often may appear to be little responsive to critique.

Environmental law, of course, is heavily dependent on measurement methods, frequencies of analysis, the location of measurement stations, etc. However, even the contours of principles such as 'sustainable development', 'the polluter shall pay', the 'precautionary principle', or the 'integration requirement' remain so vague that by themselves they do not help solve daily threats to the environment. In particular, these principles must not obscure the technical details related to their implementation. Nobody is opposed to sustainable development or a high level of environmental protection, but when it comes to a ban of cadmium in batteries or lead in the environment, such high principles are all too quickly forgotten. EC environmental law therefore must also remain concerned about details.

Even if Community law is adequately drafted, if the political will is lacking, it becomes extremely difficult to ensure that such legislation is properly applied. Increased recourse to framework legislation will only add to these difficulties. Framework legislation increases inconsistent interpretation and application of such legislation, and thus will contribute to different levels of environmental protection in Member States.

EC environmental legislation should, in the present writer's opinion, over the next years regulate the protection of soil, fix uniform emission standards (air, water, and soil) for the most important industrial installations, ensure the protection of groundwater, provide for serious provisions on energy saving, contain an export ban on nuclear waste to non-OECD countries in the same way as for hazardous waste, and provide for effective rules to promote waste recycling. It should systematically phase out heavy metals and other hazardous substances where less hazardous substitutes are available, provide for an EC-wide ban on night flights, create a public pollution emission register, and apply the provisions of the Aarhus Convention to Community institutions. It must reduce the overall output of greenhouse gases by cars, provide for prices of fuels that reflect environmental costs of exhaust emissions from vehicles, develop a uniform eco-label at Community level, and develop instruments in order to protect nature, biodiversity, and climate more effectively.

Community environmental law cannot be developed without Community environmental lawyers, however. Placing this law into the hands exclusively of administrations or, worse, vested interest groups, could have disastrous effects on the law, as it could become placebo law.

To be sure, Community environmental law is a success story. A considerable amount of Community legislation discussed in this chapter is truly innovative, and has paved the way to progressive legal standards throughout the EU and beyond.

The environment would be much worse off if there had not been a constant flow of EC environmental provisions. The challenge with which our industrialized society is confronted, is whether we can attach even more importance to the environment. Attempts to find legal answers to environmental challenges must therefore continue, in particular at EC level. Without the political will to improve the EU and global environments, not much will be achieved. And without laws on the statute books, all political arguments about the environment will remain greenspeak.

Name Index